Thomas Bird Mosher

Pirate Prince of Publishers

Thomas Bird Mosher at age 49, c. 1901.

Thomas Bird Mosher
Pirate Prince of Publishers

A Comprehensive Bibliography & Source Guide to
The Mosher Books
Reflecting England's National Literature & Design

By Philip R. Bishop

With an Introduction by William E. Fredeman

OAK KNOLL PRESS
AND
THE BRITISH LIBRARY

First Edition

Thomas Bird Mosher—Pirate Prince of Publishers was published by:

Oak Knoll Press, 414 Delaware Street
New Castle, DE 19720
and
The British Library, 96 Euston Road
NW1 2DB, London, U.K.

Copyright © 1998 by Philip R. Bishop

ISBN 1-884718-49-3 Oak Knoll Press
ISBN 0-7123-4602-3 The British Library

Library of Congress Cataloging-in-Publication Data
Bishop, Philip R., 1951-
Thomas Bird Mosher: pirate prince of publishers/Philip R. Bishop.
    p. cm.
"A comprehensive bibliography & source guide to the Mosher books reflecting England's national literature and design."
Includes bibliographical references (p.   ) and index.
ISBN 1-884718-49-3
1. Mosher, Thomas Bird, 1852-1923—Bibliography. 2. Thomas B. Mosher (Firm)—Catalogs. 3. Private press books—United States—Bibliography—Catalogs. 4. Limited editions—United States—Bibliography—Catalogs. 5. Fine books—United States—Bibliography—Catalogs. 6. Aestheticism (Literature)—Bibliography—Catalogs. 7. Literature publishing—United States—History—20th century. 9. English literature—Publishing—United States—History—19th century. 10. English literature—Publishing—United States—History—20th century. 11. Books—Pirated editions—United States—History—19th century. 12. Books—Pirated editions—United States—History—20th century. 13. Catalogs, Publishers'—United States. I. Title.
Z232.M886B57 1998
016.0705'0973—dc21   97047040
                                                              CIP

British Library Cataloging-in-Publication Data available from the British Library

Typography by Dianne Nelson, Shadow Canyon Graphics, Golden, CO
Cover design by Michael Höhne Design
Printed in the United States of America by Braun-Brumfield, Ann Arbor, MI
on 60% and 70# coated white acid-free paper

"Qui pourrais-je imiter pour être original?"

(Who must I copy to be original?)

—François Coppée, *Le Trésor*
Last line of Scene 3, found on the title page of
Edwin Arlington Robinson's *The Torrent and the Night Before*

Dedicated
to the Memory of

KENNETH H. SHANKS
(1911-1989)

*Mosher Books collector,
par excellence, whose collection
now forms the core of the
Mosher Collection in the
Special Collections,
University of Louisville*

CONTENTS

ACKNOWLEDGEMENTS

The following people and institutions deserve much credit for assisting me in the completion of this new bibliography on The Mosher Books. One of them once referred to me as "the anal analyst *ad nauseam* of Mosher." Quips like that helped me to keep a sense of humor amidst all the research and seemingly endless revisions and alterations. With all of them I share in the credit, but of course, to me alone belongs the responsibility for any errors. I hope I have not forgotten to mention anyone who in any way helped. If I have, please pardon the unintentional omission.

SPECIAL NOTE:
The publishers and the author wish to publicly thank
GEORGE T. MCWHORTER
for his generous gift in support of this publication.

To all the people at the following academic institutions whose co-operation helped to make this bibliography possible, I want to give my thanks:

Amherst College: John Lancaster, Curator of Special Collections, Amherst College Library, for his suggestions in helping to track down a Roger de Coverly binding which, unfortunately, was never found.

Arizona State University: Marilyn Wurzberger, Head of Special Collections, for permission to use photographs and quotes from material in the Thomas Bird Mosher papers, and for the use of their extensive collections, photocopying pertinent material, and for her willingness to answer my many questions via e-mail throughout the past several years, all with the added charm that only she can provide; to professor Gene Valentine of the Almond Tree Press for his masterful photography of bindings, his hospitality while I was at ASU, and his continued support of my research on Mosher; and to professor Nicholas Salerno for his cooperation, on-campus hospitality, and for granting permission for the photographs on behalf of the Mosher family.

Bowdoin College: Diane Gutscher, Curator, Special Collections, for the use of their large collection. A special thanks to Susan Ravdin, Assistant, Special Collections, for making the initial arrangements and for her continued enthusiasm over this project.

The British Library: David Way, Director of Publishing, for his agreeing to co-publish the book. And thanks to Christopher Fletcher, Curator of Modern Literary Manuscripts, for checking on the library's holdings and for guiding me to the Royal Commission on Historical Manuscripts website. Special thanks are directed to Elizabeth James, Curator of Nineteenth-Century Books, for looking over my manuscript and for providing constructive comments and criticism. Also thanks to the folks who operate the OPAC-97 website for its assistance in locating Mosher books at the library.

Brown University: Jean Rainwater, Co-ordinator of Reader Services at the John Hay Library, for whom I have only praises for her assistance in locating a wonderful Hampstead binding and for accessing other Mosher books in Brown's collections, and for doing so in a most efficient and professional manner.

Bryn Mawr College: James Tannis, Director of Libraries (now retired), for the use of their rare books in Special Collections.

Carnegie Mellon University, Hunt Institute for Botanical Documentation: Charlotte Tancin, Librarian, for personally allowing me to see Mrs. Hunt's bindings on the Mosher books, for making all the arrangements for professional photography, and for "cutting through the red tape" in granting permission to use a photograph of one of Mrs. Hunt's bindings.

Colby College: Nancy S. Reinhardt, Special Collections Librarian at the Miller Library, for assistance in locating some fascinating information, for being a critical reader of one of the last drafts of the manuscript, and for relaying samples of the manuscript to The Houghton Library; thanks too, to Abigail Chandler, Senior Student Advisor, who assisted me while I was on-campus.

Dartmouth College: Philip N. Cronenwett, Chief of Special Collections and Curator of Manuscripts, Dartmouth College Library, for assistance in locating and photocopying important manuscript holdings at Dartmouth. Special thanks to Stanley Brown, Curator of Rare Books, for allowing me to examine, via inter-campus loan, the two *Hobby Horse* volumes, for the information supplied on the Thomas Jones keepsake, and for researching the list of Mosher books at Dartmouth.

Fairleigh Dickinson University: James Fraser of the Florham-Madison Campus Library, for sending the keepsake on Loyd Haberly.

The Grolier Club: Eric Holzenberg, Cataloguer (now Librarian); and Librarian, Martin Antonetti, for their assistance in finding useful material related to bindings and designs, and for the use of their auction sales catalogues.

Harvard University, The Houghton Library: Thomas L. Amos, then Head of Public Services and Curator of the Harry Elkins Widener Memorial Room (now at Western Michigan University); to Susan Halpert, Reference Librarian, who came to my aid on several occasions, and to the many attendants who always saw to the prompt retrieval of material requested. As a researcher there, I also felt like an honored guest which is unusual in today's callous world. Special thanks go to Leslie Morris, Curator of Manuscripts, for her permission to quote from various letters in their extensive collection. Also special thanks to Roger Stoddard, Curator of Rare Books, for his helpful comments on pursuing a publisher, his words of encouragement, and for kindly looking over samplings from the bibliography.

The Huntington Library, San Marino, CA: Kristin Cooper of the Manuscripts Department, for her assistance in getting me the copies of the Mosher letters to W. Irving Way; and to David S. Zeidberg, Director of the Library, for his permission to reproduce quotes from five letters in the principal bibliography.

Johns Hopkins University: Allan Holtzman, for making arrangements for me to use the Eisenhower Library.

Library of Congress: For research into its vast holdings and for hosting its Experimental Search System on the Internet.

Maine Historical Society: William D. Barry, Reference Assistant, and Nicholas Noyes, Director, for their assistance at the Society.

Maine State Library: Bonnie Collins, Coordinator, Collection Services; Elaine Stanley, Reference Librarian; and Chris Boynton, Library Assistant, for their help in locating and using the Mosher collection there.

Millersville University: Leo Shelley for his computer search list help, and to the library in general for having open use of the *NUC* which had to be frequently consulted; special thanks to Suzanne Rohrer for her occasional checks in OCLC which greatly helped pin down locations of material available; and to Robert Coley, University Archivist and Special Collections Librarian, for assisting in the inter-campus loan from Dartmouth.

New York Public Library: Jennifer Lee, Head of Public Service, Miriam Maudelbaum, Rare Book Librarian, and Valerie Wingfield, Manuscript Specialist, for their assistance in locating and photocopying material; and to Nancy Finlay for looking over several unidentified designs, and for pointing out the Mosher book in a Sears & St. John binding pictured in her chapter in *Inspiring Reform...*

Newberry Library, Special Collections: Paul F. Gehl, curator of the Wing Collection, for permission to quote a letter and for his very kind assistance in locating information in the Wing Collection; and to Margaret Kulis, Reference Librarian, for her assistance while I was at the Newberry.

Portland Public Library: Thomas Gaffney, Special Collections Librarian in the Portland Room, for allowing me to closely examine their collection.

Swarthmore College: Edward Fuller, Head of Special Collections at Swarthmore's McCabe Library, for freedom to inspect their Mosher and related press holdings.

Syracuse University: Terrance Keenan, Special Collections Librarian at the Bird Library, for researching and sending all those computer listings, and for personally checking on many items for which I had numerous questions.

Temple University: Thomas Whitehead, Head, Special Collections Department, for the use of their collections, and for hosting the 1992 Mosher exhibit which helped to nurture all of this along.

The Free Library of Philadelphia: Martha Repman, and to Ms. King of the Rare Book Department of The Free Library of Philadelphia for finding those Mosher books in exquisite bindings and allowing me to consult needed reference sources. Also thanks to William Lang, now Head of Rare Books, for making the arrangements for the photography of two of the library's bindings.

University of British Columbia. Christopher Hives, Archivist at the University of British Columbia Library, for checking on a design in The Norman Colbeck Collection, and George Brandak, Curator of Manuscripts with librarian responsibilities over the Norman Colbeck Collection.

University of California-Berkeley, The Bancroft Library: Particular thanks to Anthony Bliss, Curator of Rare Books, for his help in locating the unrecorded vellum version of *Tristram of Lyonesse*, for accessing particular books, for answering numerous other requests I'd fire away at him via e-mail, and for granting permission to reproduce several photographs. Thanks, too, to Richard Ogar, Head of Duplication Services Unit, for expediting all my photographic requests.

University of Cincinnati: Rosemary Franklin, English Literature Bibliographer at the Langsam Library, for assisting me in getting photocopied material from the John Donne book.

University of Delaware: Thanks for the use of material in Special Collections, and general stacks of bibliographic and book arts material.

University of Louisville: George McWhorter, now Curator of the Burroughs Memorial Collection, Rare Books, Ekstrom Library, for sending two nearly impossible-to-find books, and for providing enthusiastic encouragement throughout. It was also George McWhorter's alphabetical "cut and paste" version of the Hatch bibliography which interested me in the "by title" arrangement which was adopted for the new bibliography. Also thanks to Delinda Stephens Buie, Curator of Rare Books in Special Collections for allowing me to examine their entire collection in an organized fashion.

University of Pennsylvania: For use of general stacks and research material, and for the help by Alan Morrison, Fisher Fine Arts Librarian, in assisting me in locating some of George Auriol's designs.

University of San Francisco, the Richard A. Gleeson Library: Benjamin Watson, Rare Books Librarian at the Donohue Rare Book Room, for extraordinary cooperation in the use of the extensive Mosher collection given by Norman Strouse. Also, a very special "thank you" to Ben Watson and the Library Dean, Tyrone Cannon, for underwriting all photography costs of special bindings on Mosher books at the library, and for their permission to use these photos in the bibliography. Their generosity will not only be long remembered, but their assistance appropriately honors the memory of Norman Strouse and Father Monihan, two men for whom the name of Mosher resonated in a very special way.

University of South Florida: Paul Eugene Camp, University Librarian, Special Collections, The Library of the University of South Florida, in appreciation for his sharing a list of the library's holdings, and for photocopying some useful material.

University of Texas at Austin, the Harry Ransom Humanities Research Center Library, for giving me detailed access to their holdings through UTNetCAT.

University of Virginia, The Clifton Waller Barrett Collection: Felicia Johnson and Michael Plunkett, for supplying copies of several letters from Mosher.

Yale University, Sterling Memorial Library. Particularly Tom Schneiter, Head of Circulation Services, and Louis Silverstein, then Curator of the Arts of the Book Collection.

To all the following individuals whose co-operation helped make this bibliography possible, I want to give my thanks:

Cathleen Baker, conservator of art on paper, for her explanation of Japan vellum paper and its components.

Robert Barry, Jr. of C. A. Stonehill Books, Inc., for taking the time to introduce me to the folks at The Sterling Library, and for guiding me to the Mudd Library.

Susann Bishop, my wife, for her ongoing encouragement, help, and proofing of the manuscript, and for her sharing the enjoyment of assembling a major Mosher Books Collection which often helped in checking and double-checking information in the bibliography, but which perpetually overcrowds our living space. We spent many an hour, and miles and miles of driving, just to find some of the Mosher books. I hope you have enjoyed it as much as I have.

Thomas Boss, for general encouragement, and for finding me good and unusual Mosher material over the years. You have been an enthusiastic proponent of 1890's publications (and art nouveau, book design, etc.), and have helped to support all manner of projects relating to this period. You can add this Mosher bibliography to the list as one more that you've had some role in developing.

Joan Broderick, for her outstanding professional photography of bindings from The Bishop Collection, and those taken at The Philadelphia Free Library.

Catherine Brody, for supplying information on the Alcuin Society's *In Praise of the Book*, her general well wishes, and for putting me in contact with some folks up in Canada.

Kim Coventry of Community Relations, and Susan Levy of the Archive Project at R. R. Donnelley in Chicago, for sharing their company's historic documents on bindings.

Donald Dede, for his encouragement over these several years, and for being a reader of the manuscript—many times over (your late-night cigar smoke still permeates past revisions I haven't had the heart to throw away). Also thanks for sending copies of Mosher books that I didn't have, but needed to see, and for keeping your eyes open for Mosher citations wherever and whenever they popped up. You have been a true and steady supporter.

William Fredeman, under whose tutelage and guidance the bibliography has flourished in its advanced stages, for sending several obscure Mosher related articles, for writing the important introduction to this new bibliography, for supplying a certain "gift," and for being one of the first to realize the importance of my work.

Joseph W. P. Frost, cousin to Robert Frost, for his encouragement and for sharing Hatch's own annotated copy of the Hatch *Check List*.

James Gerencser, graduate student and intern at Dickinson College, for his assistance with some last minute research.

Jim and Devon Gray, for the shared use of their apartment while I was researching at the Houghton Library at Harvard.

Tony Haverstick, for the translations of German quotes from Sturm.

Michael Höehne Design for their work on the dust jacket and the eight-page color section.

Cesi Kellinger, bookseller in Chambersburg, PA, for supplying all those books from Mosher's library over the years.

Mark Samuels Lasner, for referrals, information, and willingness to share his thoughts and advice at length.

Eugene LeMire, William Morris bibliographer in Australia, with whom I have had several fruitful communications via overseas mail, fax and e-mail transmissions.

Maggs Bros. Ltd., with special thanks to Ed Maggs and Robert Harding for their help in locating the Sybil Pye binding and for the information on the binder, L. Broca.

Kay McKay, for her reading of the bibliography in its early stages, and who offered kind words of encouragement throughout this venture.

Lori Bishop Murphy, my sister, and her husband, Patrick Murphy, whose home became, "The Inn," and was always open to me on many occasions when I trekked up to New England for research at Yale, Harvard, Bowdoin, Colby, and in New York City. I also want to especially thank Lori for donating her expertise in color separation during the production of the color section of the book. You're recognizably one of the best in the business!

S. A. Neff, Jr., for his introductions to the people at the Hunt Institute, for pointing out the Silvia Renni designed binding, for having me deliver a talk on Mosher to The Pittsburgh Bibliophiles, and for many kind words of encouragement that only a friend knows how to say.

Dianne Nelson, owner of Shadow Canyon Graphics, for her expert work on the book's design and layout, and for her willingness to answer my many questions before she even got the manuscript.

Oak Knoll Books, for photocopying occasional information from their extensive stock of books-on-books. Special thanks to Bob Fleck for sharing that information and, of course, for agreeing to publish this new bibliography. Thanks, too, to Andy Armacost for finding information in a few bibliographies at Oak Knoll, to John von Hoelle, Director of Publishing at Oak Knoll Press for his enthusiasm, backing, and willingness to grant me a small extension so that I could further improve the bibliography. It paid off John.

Francis O'Brien, no longer with us, but instrumental in getting information and directing valuable research material to my attention. Furthermore, thanks to Bevin, his daughter, and Frank Wood, another bookseller in Maine, for supplying relevant material even after Francis' death. I miss Francis and our talks, and only wish he could have seen the outcome for himself.

John William Pye, many thanks for his suggestion to use the François Coppée quote found in Edwin Arlington Robinson's *The Torrent and the Night Before* which so beautifully captures Mosher's publishing plan in a nutshell.

Andrea Reithmayer, book conservator for the University of Rochester, for the useful information she shared on binders Peter Verburg and Ellen Gates Starr.

Allen Scott, a bookseller in Portland, Maine, for his assistance in helping me to locate some material.

Eliot Stanley, President of the Baxter Society and Grolier Club member who is renown for his Rockwell Kent collection, for sharing information on the special copy of Mosher's *The Romance of Tristan and Iseult* for which Kent produced a new title page, and for getting information on the Turner talk to the Baxter Society.

Susan Otis Thompson, for kindly looking over some of the unattributed designs and offering her informed opinions, and for her encouragement.

Trinity Graphics in Cherry Hill, NJ, in particular Tommy Williams and Jack Ryan, in Cherry Hill, NJ for their expertise in photo-imaging and digitizing, and for allowing me to personally work with them, shoulder to shoulder, while we directly digitized the images from the hundreds of books I carted to their establishment.

David Turner and Norma Carlson, for being an important source for Mosher material over the years, for helping to keep the Mosher name alive on Exchange Street, and for seeing the importance of adding unique research material to my collection.

Lynn Veatch of The Veatchs Arts of the Book, for sharing information on Sotheby's practices, and for allowing me to copy some pertinent information on the Caxton Club's exhibitions.

Jean-François Vilain, for being an expert reader many times over, and for offering his editorial guidance and considerable expertise in book design of the period, for the use of his own Mosher collection and references, and for sharing new found information. Frankly, without his co-curatorship of the Temple University exhibition and co-authorship of *Thomas Bird Mosher and the Art of the Book*, and his own passion revolving around printing of this period (as evidenced by his own collection and writings), this Mosher bibliography probably would have never seen the light of day.

Grace Bishop Williard, my mother, who really pitched in and checked the accuracy for all those cross-references in the principal bibliography, and who patiently photocopied countless pages.

Melissa Zane, my daughter, who ardently worked on two graphs and the sample entries page, producing high-quality "service bureau" renderings, and for her photograph on the back flap of the dust jacket.

I also want to thank my Internet service provider, PenTeleData Prolog, for keeping my connection afloat, and a special thanks to RLIN and the Research Libraries Group, Inc. for its massive databases and the use thereof. So much time and energy was saved through the use of these and other electronic databases supplied by scores of institutions. My research could have never reached so far and wide without them, and my e-mail connections to England, Canada, Australia, and all across the USA, were a real boon to the progressive advance of my research.

Mosher once wrote to W. Irving Way that "bibliographies should never be undertaken by save those who, like H. M & Co., make a business of it, or by some one who has money to burn and don't mind burning it!" With that in mind, I personally want to thank all those bibliographers out there, both living and dead, who struggled to provide those works I referenced. I certainly have a new insight and appreciation for the work that you have done, and hope that my own work may be as thoughtfully referenced in the future as your work was by me.

FOREWORD

I embarked on this bibliography and guide in an attempt to comprehend the unique publishing venture of the Portland, Maine publisher, Thomas Bird Mosher, whose works have been a collecting passion of mine since 1985. No claim can be made for Mosher as *the* most significant or influential publisher of the period 1891–1923, but the books issued under his imprint during those years are collectively among the most interesting, in terms of design, content, and the range of books produced during those three decades. His publishing aims and his marketing strategies were startlingly innovative, the more so given that his was essentially a one-man operation. My purpose is not to exaggerate his importance in the history of the American private press movement, but to locate him *accurately* within that context.

A "mere publisher" rather than an original designer or a printer, Mosher had limited impact on book design or the history of printing. His contributions lay in other areas, chief among which was the promotion of English literature to an American public. It is no exaggeration to say that Mosher was an educator, a kind of "literary Johnny Appleseed," disseminating to a mass audience the seeds of literary appreciation and cultural revival through the production of discreet, elegantly formed, and well-produced volumes of poetry and *belles lettres*, at a cost his wide readership could afford. Mosher's mission was demonstrably messianic. His success lay in the discovery of a practical formula that both accomplished his aims and brought him financial success, and his thirty year achievement is quite remarkable. Spurred on by a genuine love of literature, he introduced, by precept and example, two generations of emergingly literate Americans to the best that had been thought and written, especially by mostly British and some American writers from the mid-19th century through the *Fin de Siecle*. During the course of his career he published over 300 separate titles and issued more than 750 volumes; and for twenty years he produced—in 240 monthly numbers—an anthology of literary gems called *The Bibelot,* at a nickel a copy, post included! *The Bibelot* was the cultural equivalent of that greatest of all American desiderata: the five-cent cigar—each replete with a personal introduction by the publisher. Concomitant with his enthusiasm for literature was his commitment to produce accurate texts of the authors he published, and detailed accounts of their publication histories, a concern shared by few of his contemporaries. Withal, he was at the same time a literary (and graphics) pirate who seized on anomalies in the copyright laws to achieve his publication ends. Whose curiosity would not be aroused by such a man? A frustrate lecturer, book collector, a poet manqué, an aspiring bibliographer wearing the mantle of publisher, Mosher was certainly a strange amalgam of the American educator, Mark Hopkins, and an honest T. J. Wise.

These were the underlying factors that led to my initial fascination with Mosher. As I began to collect his books, that fascination fanned my desire to discover as much about him as possible, tracking him through institutional collections, personal letters and documents, writings about him, and correspondence and acquaintance with other collectors such as Norman Strouse, the preeminent collector and authority on Mosher whose book *The Passionate Pirate* (1964) is still the only full-scale biography ever published. Through a series of discoveries relating to his long-term secretary, Flora Lamb, and his part-time publishing assistant, Oliver Sheean, I acquired documents relating to Mosher's publications and to his business affiliates, his dealing with authors and publishers, and his collection of books which were sold at auction in 1948. By the time I joined with Jean François Vilain in mounting the Mosher exhibition at Temple University, and co-compiling the catalogue entitled *Thomas Bird Mosher and the Art of the Book* (1992), I decided that I had also become something of an authority on Mosher. I felt that the mantle had been passed from Norman Strouse (with whom I long corresponded but who, unfortunately, I never personally met) to me; and I determined to prepare as nearly definitive a reference work on Mosher as I was capable of producing. This bibliography is the fruit of my thirteen year association with the man and his work.

At the outset, I confess I was somewhat diffident about undertaking this project in view of Benton L. Hatch's relatively recent pioneering *Check List* of Mosher's publications, which since 1966 has been the standard reference work on the subject. It was, indeed, a formidable piece of research at the time it appeared. Only Norman Strouse, in an abbreviated compilation at the end of his biography, and Keith Huntress in his unpublished University of Illinois dissertation, "Thomas Bird Mosher: A Bibliographical and Literary Study" (1942), had previously attempted to trace Mosher's canon in any detail. Hatch's work certainly proved invaluable in the initial stages of my research, and Mosher devotees will always be in his debt for breaking new ground and laying the foundation for further study. What I wanted to know about Mosher, however, was not answered by Hatch's essentially non-annotated catalogue entries, or if it was, it was not readily accessible. There were too many areas relating to Mosher's books and to his publishing activities and practices about which Hatch was totally silent: the duplication of titles in different series; the identification of Mosher's books that were first editions or first American editions; the origin of the Mosher publisher's devices; a compilation of his books published on vellum; the designers he employed; the identification of both his graphic and literary sources; and the finer points of his reprint editions. Because Hatch did not—perhaps could not—supply the answers to many of my questions about these and other topics, and because I began to uncover titles and editions which he either missed or failed to locate, I became increasingly confident that I had adequate material to mount a completely new bibliography. This compendium, tracing every aspect of Thomas Bird Mosher's publishing activity, aspires to answer all my formally unanswered questions, with what success the reader may judge for him or herself.

The bibliography seeks to identify bibliographically, and to describe fully in terms of content and design, every book and pamphlet (excluding advertising ephemera) for which Mosher was personally responsible. In two other listings I explore the output of Mosher's two successors, Flora Lamb and The Williams Book Store, that perpetuated Mosher's imprint into the 1970's. A series of introductory sections, tabular listings, graphs, illustrations, and appendices, supplement the principal bibliographical entries in ways that Professor Fredeman, in his remarkable introduction which neatly synthesizes Mosher's life and career, describes in sufficient detail to preclude the necessity of my repeating them here.

Thomas Bird Mosher received many accolades over the course of his career. A man of substance, as well as stature, Mosher was recognized during his lifetime with an honorary Master's degree from Bowdoin College, and membership in The Grolier Club. Variously labeled "The Pirate of Portland," a "Benign Pirate," "the Aldus of the 19th Century, " "Aldi Discipulus Americanus," and "A Rare Spirit," Mosher received many tributes from his contemporaries. Bruce Rogers, the finest American book designer of his time, said that he would rather have produced Mosher's work than his own, and Will Ransom, one of the leading authorities on private presses, compared the restraint of Mosher's books to those produced by Cobden-Sanderson. But perhaps the greatest encomium paid to Mosher was made by the collector, A. Edward Newton, who in his book *The Book Collecting Game (1938)* rounded off his discussion of Morris and Mosher with the comment: "There is a little Mosher in all well-printed books, but the best-printed books are all Mosher." Hyperbolic? Perhaps, but it is a fitting epitaph that would have pleased Mosher immensely; and it is an equally appropriate epigraph to launch this new bibliography.

PRB

THOMAS BIRD MOSHER AND
THE LITERATURE OF RAPTURE

A CHAPTER IN THE HISTORY OF AMERICAN PUBLISHING

William E. Fredeman

It is a curious irony of the Arts and Crafts Movement, which in England dates roughly from the building of Red House and the founding of the Firm of Morris, Marshall, Faulkner & Co. in the 1860s, that its latest endeavour, printing, should be its most lasting legacy. Morris & Co. had been in operation for over thirty years, engaged in the manufacture of furniture, carpets, tapestries, wallpapers, stained glass, and other artifacts, when Morris launched his Kelmscott Press. Its first title, *The Story of the Glittering Plain*, issued in April 1891, followed two experiments issued under the imprint of the Chiswick Press, and represented, for Morris, the culmination of a long interest in publishing. Virtually at the inception of *The Earthly Paradise* in 1865, he had planned with Burne-Jones an illustrated edition of that work, the history of which is meticulously traced by Joseph Dunlap in *The Book That Never Was* (1971). That it never was, delayed, perhaps by two decades, the private press movement that burgeoned on both sides of the Atlantic in the last decade of the nineteenth century.

Apologists for William Morris argue strongly for the primacy of his influence, but while Morris & Co. had established a showroom in New York as early as 1881, it was only one of several organs promoting the arts and crafts. In 1882, A. H. Mackmurdo founded the Century Guild and issued, with Selwyn Image and Herbert Horne, an abortive single number of the journal the *Hobby Horse* in 1884, which was revived two years later. In 1884, W. R. Lethaby and Walter Crane started the Art Workers' Guild, and in 1888, C. R. Ashbee founded the Guild and School of Handicraft. Whereas Morris appears to have come to printing, as it were, by the backdoor, extending his overall concern with design to books, some of his contemporaries fostered quite independently the idea of fine printing as an end in itself, removed from those broader social reforms that inspired Morris' multifarious activities. In the *Hobby Horse*, Image and Mackmurdo, who is generally credited with designing the first Art Nouveau book cover and title page—for *Wren's City Churches* (1883)—produced a journal unique among magazines of the day, whose profound formative influence on Mosher will be discussed later. In 1898, Ashbee went on to start the Essex House Press, the last of whose publications in 1909 was *The Private Press: A Study in Idealism*.

The history of private presses is a long one, involving a number of amateurish, sometimes vanity, enterprises, but including, in the century before Kelmscott, to name only a few highlights, several presses that took their names from the estates of their founders, a tradition that still persists. Horace Walpole's Strawberry Hill Press (1757-1789), Sir Egerton Brydges' Lee Priory Press (1813-1823), Sir Alexander Boswell's Auchinleck Press (1815), and the Hon. Ivor Bertie Guest's Canford Manor Press (1867) were all conducted by men of rank and material substance. In contrast, presses such as those established by Charles Daniel (1845-1906) and Gaetano Polidori (1840-1850) were namesake presses, less grandly endowed. During the same period, almost the only significant American private press was the Appledore Press (1867-1895) set up by the expatriate English engraver William James Linton in Hampton, Connecticut, whose output was restricted almost exclusively to limited editions of his own volumes.

Aprés Kelmscott (1891-1898) *le deluge*: in quick succession, a host of English and American private presses was founded, many of them less in direct imitation of Morris' printing than simply manifestations of the new emphasis on book design promulgated by Morris and others associated with the revival of fine printing, the impact of Art Nouveau on book design (particularly illustrations) and the tenets of the Aesthetic Movement, which focused on all aspects of the life beautiful, free from the social theorizing that buttressed the Arts and Crafts Movement. These influences, as Susan Otis Thompson convincingly argues, generated two related, sometimes overlapping, but essentially distinct typographic styles: the classic and the romantic. The two styles subsume, taxonomically, works influenced by either neo-classical or Aesthetic models, on the one hand; and on the other, those imitating the productions of William Morris and the Arts and Crafts Movement. In America, these styles were epitomized by the extremes of the two most popular publishers of the *fin de siècle*—Thomas Bird Mosher of Portland, Maine, and Elbert Hubbard at the Roycroft Press in East Aurora, New York, who began publishing in 1891 and 1896 respectively.

While these two presses were essentially commercial, Mosher and Hubbard were both concerned with the book as artifact, and both issued books in limited editions. Neither publisher achieved the reputation of the finest of the private presses in Great Britain—St. John Hornby's Ashendene Press (1894), Lucien Pissarro's Eragny Press (1894), Charles Ricketts' Vale Press (1896), James Guthrie's Pear Tree Press (1899), T. Cobden-Sanderson's Doves Press (1900), C. R. Ashbee's Essex House Press (1898), or Elizabeth Yeats' Cuala Press (1901); but some of Mosher's best work compares favourably with the productions of the more distinguished American private presses of men like Daniel Berkeley Updike at the Merrymount Press (1893), Clarke Conwell at the Elston Press (1901), and Frederick and Bertie Goudy at the Village Press (1903). However, because Mosher was a publisher and not a printer, no convincing case can be made for his influence on these craftsmen. Bruce Rogers and Will Ransom, two of the most important American book designers, whose earliest work dates from this period, praised Mosher's work. Although he was critical of Mosher's type sizes and his too "dainty bindings," Ransom nevertheless praised his work over Hubbard's on the grounds that Mosher's twin concerns with fine writing and fine printing, involving a typography that was at once "sane and charming," made the writings of "some of the most delightful stylists among modern authors" available to Americans for the first time. And Bruce Rogers, whose first book designs were commissioned by Mosher for his 1895 edition of George Russell's *Homeward Songs by the Way* (B152), and who, fifteen years later, inscribed a copy of his *IV Sonnets / Wordsworth* (1909) to Mosher, as "the Aldus of the xixth century / from an amateur printer" (Strouse 1964: 62) is reported by A. Edward Newton as having told a member of the Grolier Club, "I would rather have done his work than mine" (*This Book-Collecting Game*: 124).

William Morris, Emory Walker, and Charles Ricketts are "authoritatively bracketed," as Ransom says in his *Private Presses and Their Books*, as "the masters of the revival of great printing." Of that triumvirate, Morris is traditionally regarded as the founding father, and Susan Thompson's *American Book Design and William Morris* (1977, rptd. 1996 by Oak Knoll Press) is only the most recent and most extensive examination of Morris' influence on American printing and publishing. Printing historians tend to lump Mosher and Hubbard together as disciples of Morris, and Thompson concludes her parallel discussions of the two American publishers, in unequal chapters on Mosher as "Aesthetic

Pirate" and on Hubbard as "An American William Morris," with the interesting, if somewhat anomalous, observation, that

> ...good taste becomes perhaps less necessary with the distance of time, so that Hubbard's extravagance now looks charming and Mosher's restraint a trifle chilly. The clean, pure silhouettes of the latter's books are, nevertheless, an antidote to all those limp suede bindings of Hubbard's (107).

While it is not part of my purpose to debate either the lasting significance of William Morris or the relative importance and quality of Mosher and Hubbard, it should be noted that, without in any sense denigrating Morris' contribution to the revolution in printing, not all critics toe a common line in assessing his influence. Holbrook Jackson, for example, in a Morris Centenary dinner address to the Double Crown Club in 1934 on "The Typography of William Morris," later collected in *The Printing of Books* (1938), argued that it was the "magnificence of the Kelmscott adventure" that "impressed and influenced printers" (182) rather than the architectonics—"the organic assembly of paper, type, and binding"—or the pursuit of beauty: "bad taste in the arts," Jackson insists, "is invariably the result of beauty-mongering." Nor was Jackson willing to concede any originality to Kelmscott books; Morris, he says, was essentially "a revivalist, and all his work is derivative" (176). Kelmscott books, Jackson concludes, reflecting, as they do, Morris' intense typophilia and his preoccupation with decoration, are "overdressed" and "ask you to look at them rather than to read them." And because "reading is best when you are least conscious of print or paper or binding," Kelmscotts are for him "typographical curiosities" (175)—"models of what a book should *not* be" (185, my emphasis). Jackson's view is admittedly an extreme one, designed to enflame modern-day Morriseans, but it does provide a convenient instrument for discriminating between Hubbard and Mosher.

In his Roycroft manufactures, Fra Elbertus, as he was quaintly known to the Roycrofters, servilely imitated, even parodied, Morris, giving rise to Jackson's observation quoted in Roderick Cave, *The Private Press* (1971, 155), that the Kelmscott Press "found its nemesis in Elbert Hubbard's Roycroft books." Less flamboyant than Hubbard, Mosher responded to the subtler influences that Morris unquestionably exerted on the revival of printing. If readability is the ultimate desideratum in the making of books, Mosher succeeded, as A. Edward Newton notes, where Morris, and even more patently his American shoehorn, Hubbard, failed. Notwithstanding Morris' avowed *Aims in Founding the Kelmscott Press* (1898), to produce books that "would have a definite claim to beauty" and that would be "easy to read" without dazzling the eye or intellect of readers "by eccentricity of form in the letters," Kelmscott books are not, by any objective standard, readable, though they are beautiful. Hubbard's imitations, in the words of Roderick Cave, are merely "horrid": "articrafty in the most vulgar and meretricious sense—poorly printed on rough paper, using ugly types with the nastiest of art nouveau decoration, and bound in the cheap soft suede known appropriately in the trade as "'limp ooze'" (155). In contrast, Mosher—who, paradoxically, receives only two casual references in Cave's monumental study—produced books that are, in their very simplicity, eminently readable.

Mosher's reputation does not rest solely on his artifacts. His books are elegant edifices, appropriate to the authors who inhabit them; but Mosher's claim on a prominent place in the history of American publishing depends equally on a two-pronged philosophy that, first, extended the idea of the total book to include its contents as well as the externals of paper, type, and binding, thereby achieving an organic unity; and, second, sought practical means of printing, marketing, and disseminating inexpensive and tastefully chosen texts to a select audience whom he consciously hoped to educate. This was Mosher's goal, and in working toward it he discovered a middle ground between the exclusivity of Morris' Kelmscott Press books, the prices of which, because Morris eschewed machine technology in everything he produced, precluded their acquisition by the populace he sought to serve, and the tasteless, exploitative hucksterism of Elbert Hubbard.

- ii -

In October 1891, when Thomas Bird Mosher published his reprint of George Meredith's *Modern Love* (B244), a poem whose appeal for him must have been in part the narrative similarities with his own unhappy first marriage, he was nearly forty years of age, and there was seemingly little in his background to prepare him for the new career on which he was embarking. He may well have been, as Christopher Morley wrote, "the potential author of one of the most fascinating autobiographies that were never written" (*Amphora*, 1926, 112), but the disk files on which that story was recorded have long been lost, and it would require a powerful retrieval program to resurrect them. The factual record of Mosher's publishing career has gradually been pieced together over the years by a small coterie of devotees consisting principally of book collectors and bibliophiles, but also including two of Mosher's long-time employees, his secretary, Flora Lamb and his Press assistant, Oliver Sheean. Together, their separately compiled lists of the Mosher Books—(Lamb's dating from about 1928, Sheean's from 1931) and Sheean's twin catalogues of his own collection of Mosher books (c. 1949), and of Mosher's home library (1931/32), augmented by the two Parke-Bernet sales of his library (1948)—provide, along with Mosher's own lists and catalogues, the principal primary sources for establishing both his canon as a publisher and the extent of his collecting. Prior to Bishop's bibliography and source guide, the most important secondary sources were Keith Gibson Huntress' unpublished "Thomas Bird Mosher: A Bibliographical and Literary Study" (University of Illinois, 1941), the sole dissertation on Mosher; Norman Strouse's *The Passionate Pirate* (1964), the only separately published biographical account of Mosher; Hatch's *Check List*, with Ray Nash's prefatory biographical essay; and Jean-François Vilain and Philip Bishop's *Thomas Bird Mosher and the Art of the Book*, a catalogue of an exhibition held at Temple University in 1992.

Most of what is known about Mosher's public and private life derives from Mosher's own writings—his prefaces to *The Bibelot*; his introductions to his printed books, and those charming but, in the main, personally unrevealing essays printed in his annual catalogues and partially collected in the two *Amphora* volumes of 1912 and 1926; and, surprisingly, a "mock-interview" with himself published in the *Boston Globe* by one Anthony J. Philpott, probably a sobriquet adopted by Mosher for the occasion. Additional resources include a handful of impressionistic recollections by friends such as Christopher Morley and Frederick A. Pottle; interviews with his long-time associate, Flora M. Lamb, who survived him, carried on the Mosher Press after his death, and oversaw its sale and transfer to the Williams Book Store of Boston at the end of 1941; occasional correspondence and business papers that survive in the Mosher archives at Harvard, Arizona State University, the University of San Francisco, and other institutional repositories—all conveniently listed by Bishop in Appendix V; and a number of other signed and anonymous fugitive accounts of Mosher and his Press. Collectively, the bibliography of publications on, or mentioning, Thomas Bird Mosher (see Section V) is extensive and impressive.

The known facts of Mosher's life are calendared in Bishop's Chronology. The son of Benjamin Mosher, a sea captain and ship owner, Thomas Bird Mosher was born in Biddeford, Maine on 11 September 1852. He abandoned formal education after completing grammar school in Boston in 1864. He went to sea with his father and family for three years between 1867–70. He returned to Portland in March 1870 and in December secretly married and eloped with Ellen (Ellie) Dresser a few months after his eighteenth birthday. He remarried her, at her family's insistence, in the following year, and in 1872 they lost a son, who died shortly after birth. In 1871, he took a job as clerk in a local firm owned by Ellie's uncle, Dresser, McClellan & Co. dealing in law reports, stationery, and textbooks, where he was first introduced to the rudiments of printing and publishing. In the summer of 1875, he met a young man, Leopold Lobsitz, with whom he shared a literary vacation in Springfield, Massachusetts. Between 1879, the year Leopold died unexpectedly of blood poisoning and Ellie deserted their marriage, and 1883, Mosher's employment was peripatetic: he clerked in bookstores and was engaged in various capacities by printing firms in St. Louis, New York, Boston, and Philadelphia.

In December 1882, shortly after his divorce from Ellie, Mosher, with funds supplied by his father, entered into a junior partnership with his former employer, Ruel T. McLellan, in the firm of McLellan, Mosher and Co. where he gained practical experience in publishing textbooks such as George J. Varney's *A Brief History of Maine* to which he contributed a preface. He lost his father in 1885. When the firm went bankrupt in 1889, Mosher formed the Thomas B. Mosher Company, a wholesale stationery business operating out of 37 Exchange Street. Specializing in the manufacture of lithographs and the publishing of legal books, he advertised himself as "Publisher and Law Bookseller." From the proceeds of the business, which he retained until December 1895, Mosher, at mid-life, launched his career as a publisher of *belles lettres* and books in limited editions, issuing his first volume, Meredith's *Modern Love* in October 1891, just a month after he published a Law Book Catalogue. He remarried in 1892, and by this marriage to Anna M. Littlefield of Sacco, Maine had two sons by 1907, the oldest nicknamed "Bibbs;" the youngest, his namesake, nicknamed "Biblet." He was elected to the Grolier Club in 1895, and in that year started a magazine, *The Bibelot*, which went through twenty volumes; and in 1896, he changed his business address to 45 Exchange Street. He traveled to England in 1901 where he met various authors and publishers; was awarded an Honorary M. A. by Bowdoin College in 1906; suffered a stroke three years later; and died on 31 August 1923. The record has it that at the time of his death he was virtually unknown in his home town of Portland.

But what of Mosher the man, about whom this skeletal survey reveals next to nothing? He is reported to have hidden a gentle disposition beneath a gruff exterior. His anonymity in Portland suggests a private man, but from printed reminiscences he comes through as portly and genial, and, in the right company, garrulous. In appearance, he bore a close resemblance to President Taft, as noted by Simon Nowell-Smith, the *Times Literary Supplement* reviewer of Hatch's bibliography. Principally, though, he was bookish: an erudite, serious, and sensitive collector, who read his books and who was willing to discuss them with a few kindred spirits, some of whom, like Frederick Pottle in his reminiscent essay entitled "Aldi Discipulus Americanus," published a few months after Mosher's death, have left behind nostalgic accounts of happy encounters with Mosher in the comfort of his office-library on Exchange Street or in his home, Woodfords, both of which were dominated by book-lined walls. He was a poet manqué who published verses in ephemeral journals and newspapers using the sobriquet Richard Merrill, and he had a passion for literature, especially the writings of mid-to-late nineteenth century poets and *belles-lettrists*, his area of specialization as a publisher.

Yet even these details are mere gleanings, glimpses offering occasional insights into the man, but they do not present him in the round. Mosher's true biography, his "buried life," is not really documented by the factual record. That is, perhaps, best discoverable in his publications which reflect both his taste and his mission, and in the two equally nebulous personalities, who, apart from his father, appear to have figured most prominently in his life, Jane Sonntag and Leopold Lobsitz, the first of whom exists, literally, in name only; the other died at the age of twenty: both were the dearest friends of Mosher's youth.

Before pursuing these elusive shadows in his life, however, it is necessary to pose a question, already hinted at, which is crucial to any attempt to comprehend Mosher as man and publisher. How, where, and when did Mosher, given his background, acquire the detailed knowledge of literature and the taste and sensibility evident in his choice of the poets and writers he published. In an impressionistic essay entitled "A Golden String," first published in the *Saturday Review of Literature* over seventy years ago, Christopher Morley put the question this way:

> What was there in this hearty sea-bred uncolleged down-easter that made him open so many magic portholes? He had the pure genius of book-fancy; an uneducated man, as uneducated as Chaucer and Lamb and Conrad; and I like to think that when he took Aldus' device for himself there was some memory of the time when an anchor meant more to him than an emblem printed on a title-page. (*Amphora* 2: 110)

And memory does, after all, provide a key. In one of his best essays, "The Books I Shall Not Read Again" (a title lifted with slight modification from a line in Gissing's *The Private Papers of Henry Ryecroft*, which Mosher published in 1914, B313), printed in that "breviary for book-lovers" that he entitled *Amphora* (1912, B2), he recounts the story of his years at sea as an impressionable teenager, most of which were spent poring over the 140 dramatic compositions, commencing with *Comus* contained in the 34 volumes of *Bell's British Theatre*, a gift from "an indulgent father in the winter of 1866-67 when I crossed the Atlantic to meet him in Hamburg and began a voyage which did not end until the late summer months of 1870" (173). These volumes, Mosher confides, which introduced him to a "New World" of writing belonging to "the Old World of the Eighteenth Century"—Bell's reprint of "the most esteemed plays" was published in 1792—"first unlocked to me the treasure-trove of English Literature" (174). Besides the plays themselves, Mosher's imagination was arrested by the provenance of the set, each volume of which "bore the delicately written signature of an unchronicled and shadowy Jane Sonntag" (173). "Now," Mosher reminisced nearly half a century later,

> ...how gladly would I know the history of my set of Old Plays. Who was Jane Sonntag, its original owner, and what chain of circumstances set these volumes to the second-hand shop at Hamburg? Possibly no other form of human art retains that first fine careless rapture—the magic of a forgotten day— still alive to work its will upon me as do these dear, dumpy eighteenmos. My regard for George Farquhar dates from this period: *The Recruiting Officer*, *Sir Harry Wildair*, *The Inconstant*, *The Beaux' Strategem*,—a world of passionate dust, once living, but now gone! The name itself—Jane Sonntag! In reading the tragedy of Gustavus Vasa I found an old-fashioned pin, hand wrought, with welded head, inserted as a placemark when the volume was laid aside for that day's reading, and if ever resumed this little relic would serve as a reminder. Truly, it may belong to a period "when these old plays were new." (174-75)

Echoing Wordsworth on Nature in "Tintern Abbey," Mosher concludes:

> No, I shall never again read books as I once read them in my early seafaring, when all the world was young, when the days were of tropic splendour, and the long evenings were passed with my books in a lonely cabin, dimly lighted by a primitive oil-lamp, while the ship was ploughing through the boundless ocean on its weary course around Cape Horn. These shadows of the past are still very real to me. But fellow-travellers over the same road may be reminded by my musings of familiar stations which they have passed likewise in their life's journey. (174-75)

This is a romantic, if not a sentimental, view of life and art, but it is central to an understanding of the development of Mosher's literary taste. It accounts for the appeal that particular classes of writing had for him and for his philosophical ideals as a publisher, both of which were based, in part at least, on a theory of Palingenesis, compounded from a congeries of sources: the beliefs of the hermetic philosophers, the mystic books of the East, especially *The Bhagavad-Gita*, the *Rubáiyát of Omar Khayyám*, *The Kasîdah of Hajî Abdu el-Yezdî*, the writings of Ruskin, Pater, and Yeats, and the poetry of Whitman, Longfellow, and Tennyson, whose commitment to the principle of "the Passion of the Past" impels so many of his poems. In the evolution of these views, Jane Sonntag served as a kind of extended metaphor, a symbol for the young and impressionable Mosher.

Although Leo Lobsitz is a ghost from Mosher's actual rather than his imaginative life, little is known of him beyond the dates of his birth and death (1 October 1858-17 February 1879) which Mosher records in the *Amphora*, to whose memory the book is dedicated. He is first mentioned simply as "my friend to be," in the foreword Mosher wrote for his 1906 catalogue entitled "In the Bright Lexicon of Youth" (reprinted in *Amphora* [B2], a title adapted from Bulwer-Lytton's *Richelieu*), in which Mosher, reliving a "summer's brief vacation" in Springfield, Massachusetts in 1875, describes his encounter with "a youthful High School graduate" whose brief history is recounted in a footnote (115). At the time of their meeting, Mosher was twenty-three; Leo was six years his junior, and Mosher, though well-versed in dramatic literature, may, under the influence of this precocious high school graduate (as Mosher was not), have first been introduced to poetry as a distinct literary genre. He recounts their reading together "poets new and old," mentioning specifically Browning's *Paracelsus* and *The Ring and the Book* and Whitman's *Leaves of Grass*, and dabbling in Buckle, Lecky, Spencer, Darwin, Huxley, and Mill. Their friendship, it seems—from Mosher's allusion to a "little packet of Leo's letters" that he has been consulting—lasted beyond the period of personal contact, until Leo's untimely death less than four years later while he was attending Harvard Medical School. Sometime after Leo's death, Mosher, who had begun composing autobiographical poetry as early as 1876, wrote a long prose-poem on their relationship. Whether Mosher had an equal impact on Leo is not known, but from the younger man he gained what he calls "a gleam of the Vision Splendid." "Is it not well to speak of these things?" Mosher asks:

> This boy, with his love of the True, the Beautiful, the Good became my friend. Without him I would have suffered irreparable, life-long loss. This friendship still has its beneficial results in reacting upon the good work I hope to achieve. (116)

It is clear from Mosher's account that Leo was for him the aesthetic equivalent of Arthur Henry Hallam for Tennyson: a friend, a mentor, a source of future inspiration. Like Hallam, he was a younger man, who had died before he could deliver on his enormous talent and promise; and Mosher, as Tennyson with Hallam, kept his memory ever green:

Thus I have come to see that the thing of Beauty in art, in letters, in music,–in a word the beauty of an idea,–is given to few to create, while to enjoy it, should be the inalienable birthright of all. Hence I accept Literature for what it seemed in those golden hours to my friend and myself, a guide with whom we could trust ourselves in the dark as with a lamp that the night of ages has never extinguished. What, think you, are all its messages and ministries, if not addressed to this eternal need in the soul of man? They cannot fail us.... How else evolve a deeper and undying music out of an otherwise dead and numb Past...? The revelation of just this truth came to me and my friend over thirty years ago. I wish to transmit it to others who pass along the self-same way. (116-17)

Though Mosher's account of Leo is retrospective, there is a nostalgic immediacy in his understated description of his relationship with Leo that lends it a Platonic poignancy. The similarities between Mosher's admiration for Leo and Tennyson's for Hallam are too striking to be ignored. He does not, it is true, resort to the widow imagery that runs throughout *In Memoriam*; but, reading between the lines, it is pretty clear that Mosher's sense of loss was as intense as the future Laureate's. The situation between the two sets of men was, of course, quite different. Hallam, who was Tennyson's junior by two years, was engaged to Tennyson's sister Emily. A fellow student and member of the Apostles at Cambridge, where he took a degree in 1832, Hallam looked forward to a promising career as a poet when he died unexpectedly in Vienna in 1834 at the age of 23. Mosher was just Hallam's age and married when he and Leo met in 1875. The bond in both cases was literary: Tennyson and Hallam were both poets who had planned to publish a joint volume of poems. Mosher, who had a thorough grounding in drama, branched out into poetry, history, and philosophy under Leo's tutelage. Just as Tennyson would never have written *In Memoriam* had Hallam not died, Mosher, had he not encountered and lost Leo, might never have become a literary publisher. The closeness of their friendship does not necessarily suggest an overt relationship in Wilde's sense of a "love that cannot speak its name," anymore than does Tennyson's for Hallam, but it is symptomatic of the latent sensuality inherent in shared intellectual endeavours. Just as A. S. Byatt could not resist speculating imaginatively on how Emily Tennyson responded to Tennyson's confessional revelations in *In Memoriam*, one cannot resist wondering what Ellie's attitude was to Mosher's friendship with Leo and whether there was any connection between the propinquity of her desertion of her husband in the fall of 1879 and Leo's death earlier in the year. At this distance in time, there are no firm answers to such questions. What can be asserted is that Mosher's meeting with Leo Lobsitz was a pivotal event in his life, and that, as Hallam was for Tennyson, Leo was a shaping force in Mosher's intellectual and aesthetic development.

- iii -

It is safe to assume that between 1875 and 1891, Mosher continued a regimen of reading, broadening his horizons and entrenching his familiarity with the older and modern classics of English Literature. In the Eighties, when he had a readier and more reliable source of income, he began systematically to collect books, as the catalogue of his library compiled in 1887–89 bears witness. Throughout this decade he also developed that keen business sense evident in his later management of the Press. At the same time as he was conducting his business, the idea of sometime becoming a producer, as well as a reader, of books was simmering on the back burner of his aspirations as he slowly formulated his philosophy of publishing. Emile Pons in his *La Jeunesse de Jonathan Swift* points out that Swift began his career with a set of controlling ideas that he never abandoned. So, too, Mosher from the start had firmly formulated views on what he hoped to achieve as a publisher. His introduction to literature had come by way of a thirty-four-volume anthology of the English drama, and he saw his mission as essentially that of an anthologist—a "resurrectionist" his friend William Marion Reedy, editor of the *St. Louis Sunday Mirror*, called him. Mosher would not have taken umbrage: his third "List of Books" issued in 1895 contains this epigram from Emerson:

> We are as much informed of a writer's genius by what he selects as by what he originates. We read the quotation with his eyes, and find a new and fervent sense; as a passage from one of the poets, well recited, borrows new interest from the rendering. As the journals say, "the italics are ours." The profit of books is according to the sensibility of the reader. The profoundest thought or passion sleeps as in a mine, until an equal mind and heart finds and publishes it. (B200)

Summarizing Mosher's achievement in his essay "The Ending of *The Bibelot*" in the Index (B39), Reedy continues:

> The perfect marriage of thought or feeling with expression was what Mosher sought–and found, and gave to us. And to that union he added another element–beautiful, chastely beautiful printing. His idea ...has been to [set] and [lead] people in the way of culture–not the culture that has for object one's superiority over others, but the culture that is inclusive in its effect, the culture that is essentially sympathy with all the living. (189-90)

Reedy was referring specifically to *The Bibelot*, Mosher's little-magazine anthology that Reedy labeled "an encyclopaedia of the literature of rapture," but the editor's own statement of purpose in the first number of that journal in January 1895 is no less applicable to his other publications: "To bring together the posies of other men bound by a thread of one's own choosing." He put it more messianically in "The Vision Splendid," an essay in his 1907 catalogue, reprinted in the *Amphora* (1912):

> To what conclusion would I, therefore, bring you? To the sole viewpoint that I had in mind, the "one thought ever at the fore" in the work I offer: that in it all and transfusing it all should be some of this limitless vision–the Vision Splendid which does not fade away! (67)

A similar message runs consistently throughout the forewords of his catalogues, which, quaintly composed in third person until he abandoned the practice with a flourish in 1905, contain the fullest accounts of his philosophy of publishing.

If Leo Lobsitz was the primary force that shaped Mosher's overall aesthetic philosophy, reinforcing his commitment to literature, the singular force in shaping his literary taste and his conception of the book beautiful was *The Century Guild Hobby Horse*. Mosher's complete set of this remarkable periodical, including the rare "trial" issue of 1884 and the three issues of the New Series, with some duplication, was in the 1948 sale of his library at Parke Bernet (I, 71). Mosher tended to annotate many of his books in the margins, marking passages he wished again to consult with either a "check" or a vertical line. Fortunately, his annotated volumes of the *Hobby Horse*, which were sold as a single lot, survive, though at some point they mysteriously became separated: Volumes I (1886) and V (1890) are in the Baker Special Collections of the Dartmouth College Library, which also houses his 1889 holograph catalogue of his library; Volumes II-IV (1887-89) and VI-VII (1891-92) are in the Bishop Collection. The

Hobby Horse struck an instant chord with Mosher, who discovered in both its literary content and graphic designs a treasure trove; and it may well have been in the pages of the early volumes that he first encountered the Pre-Raphaelite artists Ford Madox Brown, Rossetti and Burne-Jones and the writings of Oscar Wilde, Arthur Symons, Lionel Johnson, Walter Pater, and other writers of the *Fin de Siècle*. Mosher borrowed freely and repeatedly in his own books from the same sources, including the *Hobby Horse*, Morris' Kelmscott Press books, Charles Ricketts' designs for the Vale Press and from books like *Silverpoints*, the Chiswick Press books, and Lucien Pissarro's designs for his Eragny Press, often engaging in what Bishop refers to, in the case of Michael Field's *Long Ago* (B219), as "textual and graphic piracy." But it was the underlying spirit behind the conception of the *Hobby Horse*—the first, really, of the art journals—that most attracted him. He placed his recall "checks" against passages in several works by Herbert P. Horne, Frederick Shields' "Notes" on Rossetti, and Lionel Johnson's review of Kineton Parkes' *The Painter Poets*, and indicated special vertical emphasis beside the following passage from Laurence Binyon's "On Certain Confusions of Modern Life, Especially in Literature," an observation that might have emanated from Mosher's own pen:

> The reading of a great poem, or the hearing of great play, should be like an experience, like life: when we make acquaintance with them first in youth, they move us with a "fine, careless rapture," they enchant us with their beauty and magnificence; but as they grow more familiar, it is the thoughts, the truth, the reality, that fill us and impress us more; and the words take a profounder, often a more pathetic meaning. So it is with the great books of the world; so it is with life. (*Hobby Horse* 5/2 [1890]: 67)

It was this sense of literary "rapture," noted above by Reedy, that particularly appealed to Mosher: not only did it determine the direction of his own reading, it was also his principal criterion in selecting the books he published. In choosing them he followed his own taste, concentrating, as he said in the preface to *The Bibelot*, on "those exotics of Literature that might not immediately find a way to wider reading," re-sowing them in "fields their authors never knew." "It was not the publisher's wish," he wrote in his third catalogue (1895), quoting from the same preface, to exploit the new

> ...forces and ferment of *fin de siècle* writers. Rather has he sought to appeal to a more catholic and saving taste in Literature "that is not of today or yesterday." He would offer the less accessible "things that perish never," showing by his printed work that beautiful typography and inexpensiveness need not lie far apart. (B200)

Rephrasing this sentiment in his "farewell" foreword to the Index volume of *The Bibelot*, Mosher wrote:

> If *The Bibelot* means anything it means definitely an aid to self-culture in Literature and is based upon the underlying spirit of beauty as expressed in the "things that perish never," not only as seen in the classics or well known works of any age or of any writer, but which are discoverable in scarce editions and rescued from sources not generally known.

> The contents of *The Bibelot* possess unity of purpose: it represents what I have personally accepted as specimens of the finer spirit,–what I have individually felt as making the deepest impression upon myself. Only an intimacy with the completed work can establish my claim that in these pages there is that which makes for the widest self-development." (B39: xi-xii)

His "theory of book-making," however, did not extend to providing his readers with a definitive group of books, as he said in his foreword to his 1903 catalogue; and in "The Great Companions" (1909), reprinted in the *Amphora*, he decried the ideas of both the "Best Hundred Books" and the "three or five foot shelf of books" as "crass method[s] of laying hold upon the intellectual treasure-trove of the ages" (B2: 96). Rather, he envisioned something more along the line of Edmund Gosse's concept of an "ideal library"—"a small one where the books are carefully selected and thoughtfully arranged in accordance with one central code of taste"—in this instance, Mosher's own. The 1903 foreword also provides the best synthesis of Mosher's ideals with his business practices, for it was the translation of all his lofty ideals and aims into practical terms that was to become the real test of Mosher's acumen and ultimately the measure of his success: "What then does Mr. Mosher claim for his products as distinct and different," he asks, after comparing his total output of 160 books produced over a dozen years with the annual production of a score of publishers:

> For one thing, this: If Literature is, as some of us believe, finally resolvable into and coextensive with the term Ecstasy, and if the comprehension of Literature is not a mere process of formal logic but rather a return through the heart to the lost garden of the heart, then this collection most decidedly offers aesthetic values not elsewhere discoverable in like combination.

> First and last, the production of these books has been a labour of love, began as an escape from the commercialism which as one grows older tends to obscure and make less realisable the things that are more excellent. Not for mere profit in dollars and cents but from the desire of producing beautiful books at a moderate price—"things of beauty rather than of mere utility"—thereby inducing that personal relationship between craftsman and client without which all doing is labour misapplied—was and is the measure of our intent in reaching out towards that ever-growing republic of booklovers, whose appreciation is alone worth while. (B247: 6)

Abhorring cheap books and determined at the outset not to produce expensive ones, as Pottle noted, Mosher began with understandable apprehensions and predictions of instant failure. He told Anthony J. Philpott in the "mock interview" in the Boston *Globe* in 1897, "I never dreamed, when I started on this venture six years ago, that it would be such a success." Mosher's formula for that success involved seven specific strategies:

1. The adoption of the net price system, postage included, which, by virtually eliminating the middleman, reserved the bulk of the profits to the publisher and insured payment in advance. He had, of course, a network of booksellers and other retail outlets, ranging across the continent from Brentano's in New York City to Paul Elder in San Francisco, and including cities in between such as Boston, Philadelphia, Cincinnati, Memphis, Chicago, and Minneapolis, who either carried his books in stock or served as distributors or agents. As Bishop notes, he "also advertised and took orders from such companies as Bertram Dobell and A. & H. B. Bonner of London" (annotation to B72). To these he offered variable trade discounts. The great majority of the 17,000 customers on his mailing list, however, which included subscribers in the U.S., Great Britain, and the English speaking countries of the then British Empire, dealt directly with the Press (see Bishop's "Marketing Strategy" in Section I).

2. The efficiency and cheapness of the U. S. postal service; prices included postage and books were shipped the same day an order was received. "The

mailing system is now so perfect throughout the Postal Union," he informed his readers in 1901, "that delivery is guaranteed to any part of the world by the publisher."

3. The publication of printed catalogues in lieu of book notices and advertisements in newspapers and magazines. He did advertise, and even sent out a limited number of review copies, but in general he depended on his lists and his network of customers to advertise his books. His views on these matters are discussed fully in his foreword to his 1901 catalogue.

4. The practice, honestly stated from the beginning, of reserving the right to increase prices when a first edition was nearly exhausted or when the work was not to be reissued, as was the case with several of his series. In the case of *The Bibelot*, which in 1895 sold for a nickel, post included, the print-run was 5,000 (4,000 bound up for distribution; the sheets of the remaining 1,000 he held back for eventual binding-up to sell as sets when the journal was completed).

5. The institution of a reprint policy based on demand. Early on, his stated policy was to abjure reprints, and neither of his first two series, the English Reprint Series and the Bibelot Series, was ever reprinted. However, he appears to have come early to the recognition—if it was not, indeed, part of his original intent—that his policy of issuing editions that "should not be so large as to almost necessarily result in depreciated remainders; nor yet so very limited as to render their value a fictitious one" (B200:[6]) had a distinct appeal to collectors. Over the course of his publishing career, the reprint editions almost certainly supported the business.

6. The operation of a non-labour-intensive business. Until 1897, when he employed Flora Lamb as secretary, Mosher ran what was essentially a one-man operation, employing only one or two clerks and stock boys. Owning only his ornaments, Mosher relied on local, inexpensive printers. Most of his books were printed by Smith & Sale, located above his office on 45 Exchange Street, but he also used Brown, Thurston, and the printer, George D. Loring, whose shop was across the hall.

7. The selection of modern titles that did not have copyright protection in America and therefore did not involve the payment of royalties, a practice that explains the paucity of American writers in his canon. It is not true, however, that Mosher paid no royalties or that all his publications were unauthorized, as many of Bishop's entries testify.

In combination, these factors enabled Mosher to keep his prices low and ensured his success, which, contrary to expectations, was almost immediate, although the momentum of the press and the accumulation of a backlog of original and reprint editions took several years to establish. By 1908, he was able to repay the loans he had taken out against his father's estate and elsewhere, although with the death of his mother in 1907, he probably received a reasonable inheritance (see Nash in Hatch: 23). His decision to forego royalties, however, gave rise in his own lifetime to charges of piracy and a series of press controversies that have tended to overshadow the more positive aspects of his life and work.

- iv -

Mosher books, like the Gibson and "Taylor-made" girls of the same era, have a quality that makes them instantly recognizable. In his first book, Meredith's *Modern Love*, Mosher established a standard "look" from which he seldom departed. Viewed from the vantage of the advances made in book design in the last half-century, Mosher's productions admittedly now appear somewhat dated —"fussy, fragile, and precious," as Ray Nash says of them—but, as indicated in the first part of this introduction, in the context of American book production at the beginning of the 1890s, the books emanating from Portland, Maine were regarded as innovative departures in popular printing. Press response in New York, Boston, and Philadelphia was enthusiastic, and contemporary notices were punctuated with calorific hyperboles describing his productions. Adjectives like "fastidious," "perfect," "artistic," "captivating," "elegant," "dainty," and "charming" abound in these early critiques. A writer in the *Philadelphia Public Ledger* of 19 December 1894, observed that Mosher "seems to have solved the problem how to present a choice poem in choice dress at a very small price."

For all his books, Mosher designed a common dress, but the claim of some critics that they are simply monotonous replications is unjustified. His early decision to print titles in different series—he created fourteen separate series in all—insured a wide variety of formats and states. Each of the series, with the exception of the largest, the Miscellaneous, consisting of 98 volumes, and the Reprints of Privately Printed Books, is characterized by a standard format. The Miscellaneous Series, a term equally applicable to the contents and format, was a name Mosher adopted only after he had printed several titles that did not belong to other on-going series. The title is also apt in that the series contains both the largest book Mosher published, *The Kasîdah* (B182), and the smallest in a regular series (outside of the Brocade Series), *George Meredith* (B129), with a disparate range of sizes and formats in between. Three of the series have fully decorated soft covers—the Ideal Series of Little Masterpieces (12), the Golden Text Series (8), and the Venetian Series (7); another, the Lyra Americana Series (6) is bound in patterned Fabriano boards. In the Brocade Series (51), so named because of the brocade designs on their boxed cases, all are printed on Japan vellum. Books in the Vest Pocket Series (25) contain one of four variant printed designs, all by Frederic Goudy, while those in the Lyric Garland Series (26) are uniformly bound with a printed label (in two colours) in the upper right-hand corner. The Reprints from "The Bibelot" Series (12) were plain with printed covers, but all were printed only on Japan vellum. The three titles in the English Reprint Series were issued with printed paper covers over boards and were available in both small and large paper copies, the only ones he ever produced. Books in the Quarto Series (10) were issued in blue boards with white spines and paper spine labels; the Japan vellum copies had Japan vellum wrappers over boards with a printed spine. The binding design and size of the Reprints of Privately Printed Books (13) differ from volume to volume. Books in the Bibelot Series (10) are all bound in flexible Japan Vellum covers, with yapp edges and a printed cover design. The printed cover designs of the fifty titles in the Old World Series vary, but because the books in this series were the most frequently reprinted and are now the most readily available, they tend collectively to be boringly similar, except for the Japan vellum copies, which, in pristine condition, are aesthetically most attractive. A fifteenth series, the "Breviary," intended to accommodate a number of religious texts, was planned but never effected. Four volumes that would have been included in the series—*The Sayings of the Lord Jesus Christ* (B343), *The Sermon on the Mount* (B345), *Circum Praecordia: The Collects of the Catholic Church* (B71), and *Ecclesiastes or the Preacher* (B98)—were published but in the end they only formed a sub-series in the Miscellaneous Series. Perhaps Mosher felt that a Breviary Series might appear a trifle too messianic, even for him.

What all the books share is an internal artistic uniformity. With the exception of three facsimiles, all are printed from hand-set type, distributed after each edition. The least original aspect of Mosher's books, unlike Morris', is their type, almost invariably either old-style Roman or a modified Caslon; the Bibelot Series was set completely in italic type. His pages, however, are neatly composed and characterized by a clean, crisp quality. The books were printed on hand-made paper, usually Van Gelder, made expressly for Mosher in Holland, but he did print a few on Kelmscott, Italian, or other wove papers. As already noted, only two series—the Brocade and Reprints from "The Bibelot"—were published only on Japan vellum, but for most titles in the other series, a limited number of copies were available on Japan vellum. Forty-seven titles in all were printed on Roman or classic vellum, the smallest run consisting of a single copy, for *Cicero. De Amicitia* (B82, printed for Mosher himself), the largest 15, *The Casket of Opals* (B56, one of two books issued *only* in Roman vellum, the other being a *Rubáiyát*, B337), both private printings. None of the vellum copies in the regular series exceeded 10 copies and most were limited to 4-7 copies. To protect the paper and Japan vellum covers or boards, Mosher enclosed his books in parchment or tissue wrappers with a gilt seal and a slip case, on the spine of which the title was usually (but not always) printed.

Additional variety was provided in some series by boxing sets of related volumes either by author or subject, such as the Morris titles in the Brocade Series, or by format, as were some of the volumes in the Bibelot Series. The largest groupings of these "sub-series" are identified in the notes to the Brocade Series in Section I. A set uncharacteristic of most of the boxed sets consisted of the four volumes of Henley in the Lyric Garland series (B99, 165, 218, 323), with a printed label identifying the contents as the "Collected Poems of W. E. Henley." Most of Mosher's books were issued in limited, some in diminishing, editions, generally common to a series, with certifications identifying the number printed either on the verso of the title page or in a colophon. The number of these limited copies issued ranges from the two lowest—the anonymous work, *Verses and a Dream* (B426) and Mosher's own compilation of *The Works of Arthur Symons: A Bibliographical Note* (B441), both privately printed and issued in three and five copies respectively—to the highest, the eleventh Old World edition of Burton's *The Kasîdah* (B181.11), which, with a print-run of 1500, is the largest in the series and probably in Mosher's entire canon. Pater's *The Child in the House* (B62) went through two more editions for a total of 14, the highest number in any of the series.

Most Mosher series carried limitation certificates of between 400 and 950 copies. However, the twelve titles in the Reprints from "The Bibelot" Series were issued only on Japan vellum in editions varying in size, depending on the title, from 25, to 35, to 50 copies, making them the scarcest of all Mosher's productions, except for the vellum copies. Hatch and Strouse both had reservations about the reliability of Mosher's certifications, and there is evidence of occasional confusion on the publisher's part, about either edition numbers or print runs. There are several examples of the former in Bishop: they mainly occur in multiple reprints and probably derive from a misunderstanding between the publisher and the printer (for example, see B10.3-4, 171.2-4, 181.2-3, 334.5-6, 335.2-3). Two examples of the latter involve Burton's *The Kasîdah* in the Old World Series (B181) referred to above: 1) Mosher's appended bibliography (181.5) identifies the number of Japan vellum copies as 50, but the book's printed certification is 100; 2) Again, the stated limitation of 1500 in the 11th edition (B181.11) contradicts the limitation of 925 cited in the bibliography. In both instances, Mosher clearly nodded; however, his certificates of limitation are generally reliable, and there is no suspicion of conscious deception.

- v -

Mosher's choice of authors, both in his published books and in the selections printed in *The Bibelot* reflected, as has already been noted, his personal taste, but his list reveals an extraordinary catholicity. As the "Frequency Checklist" (Appendix IV) shows, his list is dominated by twenty-five writers from the period 1850 to the end of the century who account for roughly 35% of the individual numbers of *The Bibelot* and 60% of his original reprints. That last oxymoron is intentional, for one of Mosher's main distinctions as a publisher is that he made available in North America, often for the first time, editions by British writers published only in England. While many of his favourite writers—Arnold, Morris, Rossetti, and Swinburne—had been published in America years before Mosher began publishing, his printings of other authors constitute the first American editions of their works. Robert Bridges, Ernest Dowson, W. E. Henley, Richard Jefferies, Andrew Lang, Vernon Lee, Fiona Macleod (William Sharp), George Meredith, Walter Pater, Arthur Symons, Francis Thompson, and James ("B.V.") Thomson all first appeared in America in Mosher editions, and most, in a strict if not a legal sense, were piracies. The ultimate rebuttal to the charges against Mosher clearly resides in the number of first editions and first American editions he issued. In all, some 85 Mosher books fall into this class.

Not all Mosher's editions were unauthorized, however; he often made arrangements with authors and publishers to reprint their works, as he did with Fiona Macleod, whose identity Mosher became apprised of much later, George Russell ("A.E."), Bertram Dobell, E. C. Stedman and his publishers (Houghton, Mifflin), and W. B. Yeats. Through these negotiations, Mosher ensured that a number of his books would have primary status. The Mosher edition of George Russell's *Homeward Songs by the Way* (B152) includes twenty poems provided by "A.E." that are not in the Dublin edition, and Michael Field's *Underneath the Bough* (B424) contains a new preface and authorial revisions, giving both volumes first-edition status. His edition of Dowson's *Poems* (B301), antedating John Lane's London edition of 1905 by three years, ranks as the first collected edition. One of the most valuable offerings in Bishop is Appendix II, "Royalties and Payments," which provides the first hard evidence of the prices and royalty percentages Mosher paid for the rights to publish. Unfortunately, the whereabouts of Mosher's account books, which for unexplained reasons were not transferred to the Williams Book Store with the rest of Mosher's stock and his ornament cabinet in 1941, is unknown. The loss of this vital documentation is partially offset by an unpublished 1941 letter from Flora Lamb to Dane Yorke that Bishop prints in this appendix, in which she sends Yorke, who was writing a biography of Mosher (never published), a list of exact prices Mosher paid to a number of British and American authors and publishers. Although invaluable, her list is only fragmentary, and in his annotations Bishop provides supplementary information from Mosher's catalogues, correspondence, and other sources on his publishing arrangements with other authors and publishers not mentioned in Lamb's letter. One such, among dozens, is Arthur Symons' *Lyrical Poems* (B227, 1903), "reprinted with Mr. Symons' permission, from his *Collected Poems* of last year. . . ." In his introduction to Symons' translations of Baudelaire's *Poems in Prose* (B299), Mosher says that it was Symons' "express desire that I should publish his twelve selections from Baudelaire. . . ." As an aside, it should be noted that Arthur Symons, who does not appear as one of Mosher's major authors in Appendix IV, is represented in the Mosher canon by eight complete and three partial numbers of *The Bibelot*, his poems and essays appearing in 13 of the 20 numbers. Mosher also issued five books by Symons, including, besides those already mentioned, an introduction to Browning's *Pompilia* (B307), a collection of his complete poems, *Silhouettes* (B354), which is a first American edition; and Mosher's bibliography (B441, 1912), issued in only 5 copies. As a poet, contributor to *The Savoy*, biographer of Beardsley, and the author of *The Symbolist Movement in England* (1898), Arthur Symons was precisely the kind of writer to whom Mosher was attracted. The attraction appears to have been reciprocated, for not only did he readily consent to Mosher's reprinting his writings, he also presented to Mosher a copy of his first book, *An Introduction to the Study of Browning* (1886), with an inscription that overrides the printed dedication to Meredith: the unsent copy he inscribed for Browning with an unpublished quatrain, presumably at the time of the book's initial appearance. He later reinscribed this volume, with an explanation (unquoted here), "to Thomas B. Mosher, printer of beautiful books" (see B441).

That Mosher was not wholly indifferent to the claims of copyright is clear from a document Bishop quotes requesting from the Library of Congress the copyright status of Michael Fairless' *The Road Mender* (B326) to insure that he could proceed with publication with legal impunity. On at least one occasion, an authorized publication backfired. Eugene Lee-Hamilton's *Mimma Bella* (B243), which originally appeared in the *Fortnightly Review* for November 1907, was printed in America with the permission of the author's widow, who, her husband having died before the work appeared in the journal, corrected the proofs for its first appearance in *The Bibelot* in June 1908. Mosher's reprint of the work in the Miscellaneous Series (No. 45, B243, 1909) forestalled republication by both an American and British publisher and jeopardized her income—or so the widow informed Mosher when imploring him for post-publication "monetary recognition" of her loss on *Mimma Bella* and its companion volume in the Miscellaneous series, *Sonnets of the Wingless Hours* (No. 47, B377), published in the same year.

Many of Mosher's individual editions command attention, but only a handful can here be singled out. Among these, special notice should be given to his three facsimiles, two of which are reproduced by photolithography. Rossetti's *Hand and Soul* (B139, Miscellaneous Series-8, 1899) was advertised as a "facsimile reprint" of Morris' Kelmscott Press edition, but in fact it is only a quasi-facsimile of the Chicago Way & Williams printing in which, though printed in black and red, the type—American Type Founder's Jenson—only resembles Morris' Golden type. Mosher's edition contains three Morris borders against two in the Kelmscott edition. The two borders on the opening spread are identical in both editions; however, whereas in Kelmscott the title page faces the commencement of Rossetti's text, in Mosher it faces his preface. This substitution necessitates the introduction of the third border—of grape, leaf, and vine—that does not appear in the Kelmscott edition, as the surround for the first page of Rossetti's text. Like Arnold's *Empedocles on Etna* (B103, Miscellaneous Series-13, 1900), which employs four variations of Morris' borders, *Hand and Soul* contains what Bishop calls "a hint" of the Vale Press edition, owing to the blue boards and front cover label of the Kelmscott paper copies.

Fitzgerald's *Rubáiyát* was one of Mosher's favourite books, and he reprinted it in no fewer than four series and twice privately printed it. The facsimile (B336), the twelfth volume in the Reprints of Privately Printed Books Series, is of the first edition of 1859. It was printed in 250 copies, 10 on Roman vellum, numbers 1-5 of which contained an original etching by Edwin Edwards, a canceled frontispiece to the third British edition. The book which Mosher called "the most wonderful work of my life" was his typographic facsimile, imitative down to the binding itself, of Whitman's 1855 *Leaves of Grass* (B192, Miscellaneous Series-35, 1919). Whitman was unquestionably Mosher's favourite American poet, and through Whitman's literary executor, Horace Traubel, he acquired most of Whitman's first editions, including *Leaves of Grass*, and a manuscript for his personal library.

Not a facsimile, but one of the most handsome of all Mosher's productions and representative of the kind of book that most appealed to him is *The Garland of Rachel* (B125, Reprints of Privately Printed Books-11, 1902), originally issued in 1881 by the Daniel Press in 36 copies only—18 with variant title-pages for the 18 contributors, the remainder "By Divers Kindly Hands"—and one of the scarcest of all nineteenth-century privately printed books. For his reprint, Mosher wrote a nineteen-page preface outlining his eventually successful search for a copy of the book, and supplied an appendix containing both a history of the volume by Henry R. Plomer and a bibliography by Henry W. Poor, the famous New York City collector.

One of Mosher's most ambitious projects is his third printing of Wilde's poems in *The Poetical Works of Oscar Wilde* (B305, Miscellaneous Series-41, 1908). Cased in blue decorated boards, this thick octavo of 396 pages—the largest book in terms of the number of pages that Mosher issued—the volume contains as its full title indicates, a bibliographical index and six facsimiles of title pages from Wilde's separately printed works. Its importance, however, lay in the additions Mosher made to his copy text, the 1908 London (Methuen) edition. Mosher's edition included corrected texts of all the poems published in his two earlier editions (B304 & 304.1), 20 uncollected poems, and *Poems in Prose*. Regarding the Wilde text as now virtually complete, Mosher called his edition the "Bibliographical Edition," and gloated that it was "the latest and only entire collection of [Wilde's] poetical works." As Bishop shows, however, Mosher was one-upped within a year by the appearance of Methuen's 9th edition containing "two newly recovered poems from Wilde's manuscript copies."

The hubristic conclusion to the above episode illustrates the inherent danger of overconfidence (or pride), a recurring sin in Mosher's introductions. More importantly, however, the building of his edition of Wilde, like the textual collations in his editions of Rossetti's *The Blessed Damozel* (B47), *Ballads & Sonnets* (B16) and *Poems* (B294), also illustrates his preoccupation with bibliographic accuracy and textual collation. Although not a trained scholar, Mosher was greatly interested in textual variants (as opposed to bibliographical points), and he treats them in the prefaces, forewords, and appendices to many of his editions. The collations printed in *The Blessed Damozel*, an edition in which he sought, with only indifferent success, to improve upon Ricketts' Vale Press edition, must have been enormously valuable at the time. Some volumes contain detailed bibliographies, such as the one compiled by Bertram Dobell and J. M. Wheeler in Mosher's second book, James Thompson's *The City of Dreadful Night* (B72, English Reprint Series-2, 1892), or his evolving bibliography in the several editions of the *Rubáiyát* (B334.1-9), culminating in his privately printed *Rubáiyát* bibliography of 1907, which he printed in 25 numbered copies on Japan vellum issued for distribution to his friends (B40).

Modern textual criticism involves far more sophisticated techniques than Mosher employed, or had access to, but his decision to apply these limited techniques to establish accurate texts of *modern* authors was uncommon among publishers of his generation. In this, Mosher was ahead of his time, and because of his concern, many of his editions are elevated well above the status of ordinary reprints. And since they were mainly devoted to the texts of the English authors he was advancing, often introducing them for the first time to an American audience, they have a distinct place in textual history, as the repeated citations made to his editions in the standard bibliographies of these authors cited throughout Bishop's bibliography amply testify. Definitive editions they certainly are not, but they are tributes to the national literature of Victorian England, and Mosher deserves to be credited as the first publisher to attempt to give these writers international recognition.

Among the many distinctive books Mosher published, the black orchid, for me at least, is his reprint of the Pre-Raphaelite magazine, *The Germ*, the pure vellum edition of which is a magnificent specimen of book production. Mosher plundered many other serials—*The Oxford and Cambridge Magazine, Undergraduate Papers, The Dark Blue, The Century Guild Hobby Horse, The Yellow Book*—for literary and graphic materials, publishing, for example, in *The Bibelot* all the fugitive writings by William Morris that he could identify. With admirable perspicacity, he printed the Pre-Raphaelite magazine *The Germ* in toto, replete with photographic reproductions of its covers and illustrations and embellished by the addition of James Ashcroft Noble's essay, "A Pre-Raphaelite Magazine." Edward Calvert's *Ten Spiritual Designs* (B405, 1913), issued in a portfolio, were taken from a scrapbook in Mosher's library, whose provenance suggests that it originally belonged to the engraver. The scrapbook, which contains proofs of eleven Calvert engravings in various media and seventeen woodcuts by Blake, is *sui generis* among Mosher's publications. Not only is it *not* a book in the conventional sense of the term, there is also no prototype publication behind it: it is, in other words a Mosher "original." Though the designs had been published in Calvert's son's biography of his father in 1893, the plates there differ from those in Mosher's portfolio where they are considerably enlarged. In a related volume, *William Blake's XVII Designs to Thornton's Virgil* (B347, 1899), Mosher reproduced the Blake designs from the same scrapbook. Three of the designs appeared in *The Century Guild Hobby Horse* in 1888, but Mosher's was the first complete reprinting of Blake's designs since their initial printing in 1821. He later reprinted them in *The Bibelot* (December 1914). Each Mosher collector or enthusiast will have his own particular favourite among Mosher's productions: reflecting Mosher's own opinion, Norman Strouse refers to the facsimile *Leaves of Grass* as Mosher's "*tour de force.*"

An amusing episode in Mosher's career as a publisher was his accidental reprinting of two of Thomas J. Wise's fabrications in *The Bibelot*, Morris' *Two Sides of the River* (September 1899) and Swinburne's *Dead Love* (June 1901). Both were later reprinted in the Reprints from "The Bibelot" Series: Morris as No. 6 in 1899 (B419), Swinburne as No. 10 in 1901, with "Other Inedited Pieces" (B81). *Dead Love* was condemned as a forgery on three counts of paper, type, and imprint in John Carter and Graham Pollard's *An Enquiry into the Nature of Certain Nineteenth-Century Pamphlets* (London: Constable, 1934). Morris' pamphlet, only suspect in 1934, was indicted as a forgery by Maurice Pariser in 1950 and confirmed in Nicolas Barker and John Collins' recent *Sequel to an Enquiry* (London: Scolar, 1983). Needless to say, neither reprint is mentioned by either H. Buxton Forman or Wise in their respective bibliographies of Morris and Swinburne. Mosher, on the other hand, cites the Wise-Forman pamphlet in both *The Bibelot* and the reprint, obviously unaware that it was a forgery. Wise was too grand to form a collection of books by Mosher, who is represented in the *Ashley Catalogue* by only four of his editions of Swinburne (see Bibliography in Section V). Poetic justice turned the tables on Mosher in 1900, when Mosher was himself pirated by Mr. Cook, the publisher of Burton's *The Kasîdah*, who lifted Mosher's note from his 1896 List of Books and included it in his third edition of Burton's work as his own publisher's note (see B181).

To these noteworthy titles must be added Andrew Lang's *Aucassin and Nicolete* (B10), the second volume in the Old World Series (1895), only because it sparked the first charge against Mosher for piracy, a fact he freely, and from the evidence of his letters, unashamedly admitted. In 1896, Lang drew Mosher into an invidious correspondence that ran sporadically for nearly a year in *The Critic*. In a long letter of defense printed in the number for 11 July 1896, Mosher presented legal, moral, and aesthetic justifications for his actions.

Legally, he had a perfect right to reprint the book since no application had been made to copyright Lang's work (originally published in 1887) in the United States by either the author or the publisher, David Nutt. Mosher was no more culpable than dozens of other American publishers; he did, however, offer to pay Lang a post facto honorarium, which Lang publicly disparaged. Mosher's moral and aesthetic grounds were less convincing, and his argument that he had "faithfully printed an inaccessible book" led Lang to denounce him as a Robin Hood of publishing, a charge parodied in a ballad entitled "The Publishing Privateer" in *The Critic* on 10 October 1896, which concluded:

> Dear Andrew of the brindled mane,
> The Yankee pirate may be rude;
> But anger never yet has slain
> This literary Robin Hood.

Mosher was not only not slain; he was not even chastened: he went on to publish four selections from Lang in *The Bibelot*, another in his 15th catalogue (B251, 1907), a further four books in three series (B11, 14, 80, 146), including a reprint of *Aucassin & Nicolete* in the Vest Pocket series (B15), and to use an essay by Lang as the preface to his 1901 edition of Edgar Allan Poe (B300). According to Strouse, when Mosher met Lang on his trip to England in 1901, he had the effrontery to tell him: "You don't know America. Our little tiff has sold twice as many of your books and mine as all your publications ever did for you (see B10). In 1901, Lang's *Aucassin and Nicolete* had gone through five editions; by 1922 the number had risen to nine! Mosher was right.

Mosher weathered two further exposures of his piratical activities, the first in *The Publishers' Circular* in 1909, when the editor, R. B. Marston, conducted a survey of Mosher's pirated authors for their opinions of his practices. The second occurred in the correspondence section of *The Times* in 1914 in a series of letters initiated by James B. Blackwood, the President of the Publishers' Association of Great Britain and Ireland, whose particular grievance related to the importation of Mosher's books into Britain. But Mosher did not on either occasion enter the lists to defend himself. Surprisingly, one British publisher, Grant Richards, came to Mosher's defense, arguing that the term "pirate" was inaccurately applied to Mosher and urging that the proper course to curtail Mosher's (and other publishers') legal activities, was for the British government to pressure the United States to "enter into a more comprehensive agreement in matters of copyright." Many of Lang's fellow writers objected to what *The Times* called "The Mosher Method," but others, like George Russell, William Sharp's alter ego, Fiona Macleod, and Richard Le Gallienne were all pleased with Mosher's presentation of their works and happy for the American exposure. Macleod's *By Sundown Shores* (B53) was not only sanctioned by the author but bore a dedication to Mosher as the title of the prologue. Even Bridges and Meredith wrote flattering letters to Mosher expressing their gratitude. Le Gallienne wrote a lengthy tribute to Mosher, originally published in *The Forum* in January 1914, which Mosher reprinted no fewer than three times—separately in September 1914, in which he thanks Mitchell Kennerley for permission to reprint it (B408); a month later in his 1914 catalogue *The Mosher Books* (B258) as a substitute for the publisher's usual preface; and again in the Index to *The Bibelot* the following year (B39). Not all the writers Mosher pirated were so charitable, however. In his annotation to *The Sign of the Lion* (B8), Bishop quotes a letter sent by Hilaire Belloc to Duff Cooper accompanying a copy of the London edition of this work, in which he also alludes tangentially to the only other book by Belloc published by Mosher, his translation of Bédier's *The Romance of Tristan and Iseult* (B327):

These little books have a history. They were pirated in America by a Yid called Mosher & sold for a Dollar: me, no money, him, all the money. At last he proposed to treat my Verses in the same fashion, but the worm turned & I told him (being then young & hearty) that if he did I would cross over to America & beat him with a cane. I specified the cane. I said: "A light rattan cane." He replied with a torrent of abuse, but forbore to steal as he had proposed.

As Keith Huntress noted in his 1942 dissertation, Mosher was quite literally caught on the horns of an ethical dilemma: had he not pirated, he could not have been a publisher. Further, in a perverse twist, the notoriety generated by the controversies brought Mosher more publicity than he could possibly have afforded to buy. That a number of his victims felt that the end justified the means does not, in absolute terms, exculpate Mosher, but it does offer an explanation, and perhaps even a justification, for his life's endeavours, aptly expressed in two quotations on which it is suitable to close this section of the introduction. In 1903, Le Gallienne inscribed a copy of his book, *An Old Country House*: "To Thomas Bird Mosher: A Highwayman of Letters who robs us with such grace, that not to be robbed by him would be a disappointment: From a humble victim of his art." Twenty years later, after Mosher's death, Christopher Morley made this metaphorical assessment of Mosher's practices:

> If it be piracy to take home a ragged waif of literature found lonely by the highway, to clothe her in the best you have and find her rich and generous friends–if this be piracy, then let any other publisher who has never loitered a little in the Public Domain cast the first Stone and Kimball. (*Amphora* 2: 113)

Thomas Bird Mosher—publisher of more than 1,000 separate items, pirate, editor, anthologist, bibliographer, author of 236 prefaces to the separate numbers of *The Bibelot* and roughly 220 signed and unsigned prefaces, forewords, introductions, and bibliographical notes to his published books, and of many essays and poems—who introduced Americans to "the literature of rapture" through the writings of the Pre-Raphaelites, the French Symbolists, and the poets of the Celtic Revival, would doubtless have agreed, though he would have phrased it in a more mannered style, reminiscent of Pater.

- vi -

Philip Bishop's *Thomas Bird Mosher: Pirate Prince of Publishers: A Comprehensive Bibliography and Source Guide to the Mosher Books Reflecting England's National Literature & Design* is a signal event in the history of scholarship on American private presses operating during the *Fin de Siècle* and first two decades of this century. His title is a conflation of Norman Strouse's *The Passionate Pirate* (1964), and the phrase used by the firm of William H. Wise to describe Mosher in advertising its reprint of *The Bibelot*: "America's Prince of Publishers." Far more than a simple "checklist"—the title that Benton L. Hatch accurately used to describe his minimally annotated listing of Mosher's books (1966)—Bishop's work is a detailed, encyclopaedic examination of Mosher's canon by a collector and bookseller so thoroughly immersed in his subject's life and productions that he has even named his own bookselling business "Mosher Books."

But Bishop's work is also no "Bookman's Catalogue"—a neutral and intentionally nonpejorative term I invented to reflect more accurately, in contrast to the formulaic prescriptions of descriptive bibliography, the sometimes limp, sentimental annotations and imprecise physical descriptions in Norman Colbeck's invaluable two-volume register of his impressive library of 19th-century poetry and *belles lettres* in the Special Collections of the University of British Columbia (1987). Correspondingly, it also is *not* (nor does it pretend to be) a "Soho"-type bibliography in terms of descriptive thoroughness. However, Bishop's entries contain sufficient detail, especially in combination with the "Series" descriptions that precede the general bibliography and the generous illustrations of title pages and wrappers accompanying the entries, that the reader can easily, with a little imaginative calisthenics, recreate in his mind's eye the formats and dimensions of the books themselves.

The primary purpose of the Bishop bibliography is to establish, firmly and finally, the Mosher canon—a mission the compiler achieves with admirable success in terms of accuracy, comprehensiveness, presentation (layout and arrangement), and ease of access. Its function as a "source guide" is equally valuable and important. Each entry contains, following the title and author, the bibliographic essentials (number of pages, including preliminaries and illustrations, and dimensions in centimeters), the series and number to which it belongs, the Hatch number, the book's edition status within the Mosher canon and, in the right-hand column, the number of copies printed in each format and its publishing status as either a first edition or first American edition. Besides providing full information on the contents of each book, a necessity given Mosher's practice of enhancing his editions with further selections from either the title-author or other writers plus his own commentaries and notes, the annotations to the 445 entries contain *inter alia* substantive information on a variety of related subjects. Among these the most important are: 1) the printed sources for texts and designs Mosher used and the identities of the designers he employed or whose work he copied, together with cross-references to other related books in other series; 2) notes on paper, type, bindings, and format; 3) salient facts about the particular book, such as its appearance in another series, its position at the end of a series, or its inclusion in one of the many sub-series, again cross-referenced to other related entries; 4) clarification of any problematic points affecting certification of the number of copies printed or edition number; 5) identification of variant or unique copies, special bindings, and presentation or endorsed copies, frequently citing present locations; 6) Mosher's business arrangements with authors and other publishers, including royalty payments; 7) relevant quotations from other commentaries; and 8) anecdotal accounts, such as the identification of Violet Neale as "the obvious muse for Dr. Garnett's love notes" (B87) and of Aimee Lenalie as Mosher's first wife, Ellie Dresser, by whom he published two translations of Marcel Schwob and to whom he paid respectively royalties of $90 and $50 (B242, 325). Where applicable, entries conclude with a list of cross-references to the "Bibliography of Thomas Bird Mosher" in Section V. Much of the material contained in the annotations draws on the author's own extensive Mosher library, which not only includes the books Mosher published but also printer's copies, books from his library (many of them annotated), holograph letters, manuscripts and other documents, and allied secondary and reference material.

Beyond the details contained in the taxonomical divisions in each entry, there is a surprising amount of less obvious information embedded throughout the bibliography, the value of which, owing to Bishop's minute collations of every volume listed, may not be immediately recognized by the casual user. For those who naively believe that a reprint is a reprint, and that because the vast majority of Mosher's books are reprints, successive reprintings of the originals must be identical, a close comparison of selected items is most instructive. Of Mosher's 331 separately printed books in the fourteen series, 137 went into one or more reprintings; and for five of these the replication is double-digit. In every instance, except Yeats' *The Land of Heart's Desire* (B186, the Lyric Garland Series-1, 11 editions), there is at least one variation in later reprints. Most, admittedly, are minor, such as the shift in pagination in editions 4-14 in Pater's *A Child in the House* (B62) or the transposition of the limitation page in editions 5-11 in Stevenson's *Father Damien* (B107). The reprints of the two remaining titles, however, contain significant variations. The confusion of edition numbers for Burton's *The Kasîdah* (B181) has already been mentioned; in addition, the notes were expanded in the 3rd and 5th editions, increasing the pagination in the first instance from 99 to 123 pages, in the second by another three pages, largely owing to updates in the bibliography. Curiously, the pagination then decreases, notwithstanding the new material added to the 8th edition, the first to contain both a frontispiece portrait etching of Burton and Swinburne's "Elegy 1869-1891," reprinted from *Astrophel and Other Poems* (1894), which commemorates not the years of Burton's life (1821-1890), but the year their closest friendship began, 1869, when Swinburne joined him in Vichy for a month after his return from Brazil, and his burial in the Catholic cemetery at Mortlake on 15 January 1891, after his wife returned his body from Trieste. It is curious that Mosher chose to reprint the "Elegy," which contains an attack on Isabel Burton, over Swinburne's lines "On the Death of Richard Burton," an oversight he corrected in his 1915 edition of *The Kasîdah* (B183) where he printed both poems plus Swinburne's "To Sir Richard F. Burton."

Continuing the survey of edition variants in *The Kasîdah*: the 10th (B181.10) contains a printed leaf announcing that 20 copies have been bound in Japan vellum for presentation to the Omar Khayyám Club of America, which Bishop speculates are part of the 925 Van Gelder count. The most radical variations, however, occur in the 10 editions of Fitzgerald's *Rubáiyát* (B334, No. 1 in the Old World Series), in part owing to recurring updatings of Mosher's preface and bibliography and of W. Irving Way's biography in subsequent editions. Pagination increases from 124 to xxxiv + 154 in the 9th edition, then drops back to 117 in the 10th edition, from which the bibliography is omitted. Major differences occur in the 7th edition, for which Bishop prints the particulars from Mosher's 1900 Spring Announcement. In the 8th edition, a photographic frontispiece portrait of Fitzgerald is introduced. The 9th, with a revised preface by Mosher, contains what he, in a letter quoted by Bishop, calls "the best all-round, up-to-date edn of Omar I have, or ever will, issue." Bishop identifies the separate printing of the bibliography (B40, Privately Printed Books-10) as an "offprint" from B334.9, but this may be over stressing the consanguinity of the two works. From both a bibliographer's and a collector's standpoint, these distinctions are invaluable as very few Mosher enthusiasts will ever have access to so complete a collection of Mosher's books as Bishop enjoys. The lesson gleaned from Bishop's detailed descriptions of the minutiae of the Mosher books confirms an old bibliographical adage: *Never assume that two books are either identical or complete without collating them.* Bishop's admirably clear demonstration of how truly distinctive many of Mosher's seemingly similar editions are constitutes one of his major achievements in the bibliography.

Perhaps Bishop's most impressive accomplishment, however, is the enormous amount of primary research he has done in identifying the sources of the designs Mosher expropriated from other private presses and earlier printed books. Most of this information appears under "Binding & Embellishment" or, in some entries, under "Design." Since Mosher lifted both text and graphic designs, these sections identify the sources (often more than one) that Mosher raided. His printed sources, some of which have already been mentioned above in the context of *The Century Guild Hobby Horse*, Mosher tends to acknowledge in his prefatory remarks. However, his graphic sources—illustrations, ornaments, head & tail-pieces, typography & layout, rules & borders, initials & dingbats, and printers & publisher's devices—he credits less frequently. Bishop is the first scholar to fully address this important aspect of Mosher's process, which is not only central to the production of his books, but also a sensitive area in the context of his piratical reputation. Bishop's assiduity notwithstanding, the occasional design proved untraceable. One such is the panpiper design that first adorned the title page of Mosher's 1909 catalogue of books (B253). Reused in two other books—once on the front cover of *Masterpieces* (B235, 1912), again on the back cover of *For Those Who Love Music* (B115, 1918)—the panpiper last appeared as the cover design for Mosher's last book: *The Children's Crusade* (B66), which was published in August 1923. Mosher died on the 31st. Although Mosher also bought up the sheets of a commercial edition published in the same year by Maynard & Co., rebound them using the same cover designs as B115, and offered the copies for sale in his catalogue, bringing to five the total number of times the designs was employed, he never divulged its source.

If Mosher had any originality as a publisher, it depended more on his taste than his creativity. His talent, as almost anyone who physically handles his books senses instinctively, lay in his ability to realize the book as a unified aesthetic object. No designer himself, Mosher nevertheless had an exquisite discrimination that enabled him, through the application of criteria akin to Arnold's touchstones, to select the best graphic elements of book designs to embellish his own publications. It has been Bishop's task to track these down, using whatever evidence is available: Mosher's own commentaries as set forth in his books; secondary reference material on book design and on specific designers; intuition; and a collector's and antiquarian bookseller's specialized knowledge of printing and publishing. Without engaging in an entry for entry analysis, it is difficult to indicate the magnitude of Bishop's bibliographical sleuthing. Paraphrasing Dr. Johnson, the catalogue may the coward's last refuge, but it is the only way to suggest the scope of Bishop's contribution. Beginning with general external and internal stylistic resemblances in page layout, borders, and over all design—including typography and paper, such as Kelmscott, on which seven Mosher books are printed (listed in B47)—Bishop identifies several levels of design models, only four of which can be treated here at any length:

1. Cover & title-page designs, and occasional full book copycats from a handful of private presses—Morris/Kelmscott (B103, 139, 187); Pissarro/Eragny (B52, 98, 169, 189, 230), Ricketts/Vale (B56, 175, 302, 319, 411, 439), Ashbee/Essex House (B30 note, 216, 440)—many used more than once.
2. Identified designs, ornaments—head- & tail-pieces, initial letters, &c.— some of them signed, attributed to specific designers. By far the greatest number of identified designs are those by Charlotte and Elizabeth Whittingham and Mary Byfield for the Chiswick Press: too numerous to list, they include criblé head-pieces (B61), Chiswick lead initials (B66), and other ornaments (B180). Among designers frequently used by Mosher, Bishop identifies, among others, T. M. Cleland (B6), E. S. Crawford (B88), E. B. Edwards of the De Vinne Press (B132), Frederic Goudy (B1), Frank R. Rathbun (B107), the designer of Mosher's bookplate (see Appendix VII), and Bruce Rogers (B152; 334.7 is a Rogers incunable discovered by Bishop). The designs for each are cross-listed under a home entry and are also accessible through the index. Besides these designers, Mosher also borrowed the

designs of other artists he admired, such as Dante Gabriel Rossetti, attaching his cover design for Swinburne's *Atalanta in Calydon* to a book for which it was not intended (W. C. Leith's *Sirenica* (B356, Miscellaneous series-74), perhaps because Swinburne's tragedy appeared only in the Old World Series (B9, No. 9, 1897), whose titles appear within a decorative cartouche stamped on the cover. Rossetti's design for Swinburne's *Songs before Sunrise* was properly wedded to Mosher's reprint of the volume (B364). More accurately, it was when it was first used in 1901: on the subsequent occasions it was employed, it appeared on the covers of no fewer than four later reprints of books by W. H. Mallock (B223), W. E. Henley (B323), Marcel Schwob (B325), and E. S. Harden (B402). In a similar way, Beardsley's cover design for Leonard Smithers' edition of Ernest Dowson's *Verses* (1896) was appropriated for one of the two variant designs for Thomas Moore's *By Bendemeer's Stream* (B52; the variant design is taken from the 1903 Eragny Press edition of Ronsard's *Abrégé de l'Art Poétique*) and for Fiona Macleod's *Runes of Woman* (B339), but it is not joined with any of the four books by Dowson that Mosher published (B78, 189, 301, 392).

3. Besides the quasi-facsimiles Mosher did of other press books, notably Kelmscott and Vale, discussed above, it was not uncommon for him to model his covers on specific designs taken from books issued by other publishers. This was a long-standing Mosher practice, which he clearly continued to the end of his career. Two cover designs by Herbert P. Horne, of *Hobby Horse* fame—one for his own small Chiswick Press book of poems, *Diversi Colores* (1891), the other for Selwyn Image's *Poems and Carols*, published by Elkin Matthews and printed by the Chiswick Press in the same year—were shanghaied for Mosher titles (B171, 243). Two sets of Laurence Housman's designs for two books published by John Lane at the Bodley Head adorn the title-page and colophon of James Russell Lowell's *The Present Crisis* (309). George Russell's "The Sword of Light" design for the Dublin edition of his *The Nuts of Knowledge*, published by the Dun Emer Press in 1903, was used as the title-page design of Mosher's second (but new) edition of *Homeward: Songs by the Way* (B153, 1904), but at least the design appeared in a book by the same author, presumably with his permission since he accepted a royalty. Whether he acceded to its being used a second time—in Yeats' *The Land of Heart's Desire* (B187)—is less certain.

4. A number of Mosher's books are illustrated internally with works of art, adding an additional dimension to the external designs and ornaments that appear on the binding. A title-page etching, printed in sepia and three woodcut designs by P. Jacomb Hood, taken from what Mosher calls "the scarce London edition" adorned his first printing of Andrew Lang's *Aucassin & Nicolete* (B10), the book, one might say, that launched a thousand slips! The 1899 edition of John Addington Symonds' *Wine Women and Song* (B439, Privately Printed Books-4) is the more elegant of the two editions of the work Mosher published, largely owing to Ricketts' border design on the wrappers done for a limited Vale press edition of Campion (1896) and the red initial on the first page of text, designed by Lucien Pissarro, the cover design of which is reproduced in colour on two extra leaves in the vellum copies. However, the edition of the same title in the Miscellaneous Series (B440, No. 84) is also a beautifully designed volume. Commencing with a stunning frontispiece portrait of Symonds by the American artist Samuel Richards, the volume also contains the most striking title page of any Mosher book. In this instance, Mosher identifies fully in his foreword the sources for his graphic embellishments. William Strang's engraved borders for the title page and the first page of text and the tail-piece are taken

from the Essex House edition of Erasmus' *The Praise of Folie* (1901); his two full-page woodcuts, *Death and the Dancers* and *Death the Lover*, are reduced reproductions from his *The Doings of Death*, a portfolio of a dozen wood engravings also issued by the Essex House Press in an edition limited to 140 copies (1902). Only two Mosher books boast coloured frontispieces: *The Soul of Man Under Socialism* (B378), which contains a portrait drawing of Oscar Wilde commissioned by Mosher from Thomas Maitland Cleland, who executed a number of other designs for Mosher's books; and *Sylvie: Souvenirs du Valis* (B394), a collotype of an original aquarelle by Andhré des Gachons, which Mosher not only commissioned but also purchased from the artist.

One of the most tantalizing original designs in any Mosher volume is the title-page woodcut for his 20th catalogue (B256 [illustrated], 1912; reused in the 1914 catalogue [B258]), which he apparently commissioned from Elizabeth Alden Curtis, who signed it "e.a.c." in lower-case letters in the right-hand corner. The design, which closely resembles a book-plate (in fact, a proof of one exists in the Arizona State University collection), is clearly allegorical—"autobiographical," as Bishop notes, "with images from Mosher's life and career." The drawing, which is vertical, is divided into two compartments, the top half of which depicts the upper masts of a tall ship in full sail, highlighted, by the adjacent half moon, against a black sky sprinkled with stars. The bottom half appears almost as a still-life: carefully arranged on what appears to be a rock ledge or altar are various nautical items—a ship's log, a pen and holder, a couple of books, perhaps a calendar; on the ground below there is a roll of charts, a compass, and a navigational rule. Embedded in the wall above the ledge is a stone with the engraved motto: "I STEER BY THE STARS;" beneath the words are Mosher's publisher's device and the date, "MDCCCCXII." The whole scene has about it a haunting, nostalgic air that is intensified by the only sign of life in an otherwise inanimate memory picture: a sprig from an nondescript plant, perhaps Forget Me Not or Rue, appropriate to the foreword that follows: "The Books I Shall Not Read Again."

A final design remains to be discussed, not because of its elegance but because it forms a link between the decorations for Mosher's volumes and the twenty-six publisher's devices he used to identify the books emanating from his press, all of which are reproduced actual size in Section I of Bishop's book. All but five of Mosher's devices incorporate some form of the dolphin & anchor devices of Aldus Manutius and William Pickering, conveniently reproduced for purposes of comparison by Bishop, that Mosher adapted for his books and which became his trademark. These were intended to impress on his readers Mosher's succession in a triumvirate of recognizably great printers and publishers—one Italian, one English. Four of the variants are rectangular, two employ Mosher's initials, "T. M." This one (No. 17), a cupid standing with one foot on a ball that is balanced on a bordered circle, containing the inscription "Amoris Speculum," bears no resemblance whatever to his other devices. Adapted from a design in Beeching, Mackail, and Nichols' *Love's Looking Glass* (London: Percival, 1891), where it is identified as having been adapted from the *Hypnerotomachia*, it is used in five of Mosher's books (B52, 69, 87, 129 [illustrated], 339—all in the Miscellaneous Series). Bishop is probably right to identify this design as a publisher's device, but one searches in vain to discover a reason, other than eccentricity, to explain why "Old Moshwig" (as Falconer Madan affectionately called Mosher) should in these books abandon the trademark for which he was best known in publishing circles.

It is impossible in so short a compass to do justice either to the diversity of design and decoration employed in the Mosher books or to the depth of Philip

Bishop's research in identifying them. The above discussion merely scratches the surface of the Mosher-Bishop collaboration, but it does provide an indication of the variety evident in the work of both the publisher and his bibliographer.

The principal bibliography in Section II is supported by a complex apparatus consisting of an introduction and a chronology, four additional tabular, discursive, and illustrative sections, and seven appendices, which bring together a myriad of factual and ancillary documentation designed to place Mosher's publishing activities into the broadest possible perspective. Section I commences with a detailed overview of Mosher's printing and publishing practices, including notes on the types, papers, bindings, processes, and printers used; a breakdown of the total output of the press; and a note on Mosher's marketing strategies with a list of the booksellers and other commercial outlets that served as agents for distributing his books; and concludes with a table and graph tracing the production history of the Press. This is followed by an overview of the fourteen series which commences with a general description and a useful time-line showing the duration of each series throughout the publishing program. These are followed by thorough discussions of each of the categories into which Mosher's publications are grouped: 1) the fourteen series to which all his published books were relegated by him, each providing notes on the series, with an illustration, a breakdown of the number of copies printed, and a listing by author and/or title with the Bishop number; 2) a listing of Private Printings of the Mosher Press; 3) a history of *The Bibelot*, probably the work for which Mosher was, and still is, best known; 4) an overview of Mosher's annual catalogues; 5) a discussion of Mosher Books Printed on vellum, a unique feature of Mosher's publishing venture; and 6) a layout of the Mosher publisher devices.

The official *terminus ad quem* of Bishop's main bibliography coincides with Mosher's death in 1923, but the story of the Mosher Press does not end there: the Mosher Press imprint continued to be used as late as 1974, first in books printed and issued under Flora Lamb's direction; and then, after 1941, in publications emanating from the Williams Book Store in Boston. Both stages in the continuation of the Press are catalogued in the two Checklists in Section III. The first, listing 137 books published between 1924-1941, are given "FL" numbers; the second, listing 14 books published after 1941 are given "WB" numbers. Both lists consist of abbreviated descriptive bibliographical entries, arranged by author. Only a single volume among the "WB" books located by Bishop, who makes no pretext for the completeness of this section, has any inherent interest —*Mirrors of the Fire*, a book of poems and translations by Bernard Grebanier (WB4, 1946)—and that only because it contains a pastiche of designs and printer's devices from earlier Mosher books. Not all the books issued by Flora Lamb, however, can or should be so easily dismissed. Because of her lengthy association with Mosher and her business affiliation with Mrs. Mosher after his death, she was concerned to carry on the tradition of the Press, and continued issuing annual catalogues of *The Mosher Books* through eleven numbers (ending in 1935-36), which contained, in addition to new books published, books remaining from Mosher's stock, including *The Bibelot*, from which she also offered a dozen separately bound copies of popular numbers (FL12). She published fifteen volumes from the several series of previously published Mosher titles in new editions, including a fifth edition of the *Amphora* (B2) in 1926 (FL1). In the same year she edited a second anthology of selections "chosen by the editor of the *Bibelot*" as a memorial tribute to her former employer, who was represented by ten selections (*Amphora 2* [FL2]). Two other books she published confirm her devotion to Mosher: a 4-page reprint of Christopher Morley's *A Golden String* (FL77) and a reprint of Richard Le Gallienne's *An Appreciation* (FL67). Of special interest among the titles in her list is *The Arts*

Anthology, Dartmouth Verse-1925, with an introduction by Robert Frost (FL30, 1925). As Bishop notes in his article on Mosher in the July 1997 number of *Biblio*, Frost, with whom Mosher was friendly, tried unsuccessfully to get him to publish his first book, but Mosher printed only a single poem by the future American Poet Laureate: "Reluctance," in his 1913 catalogue (B257), where he appeared in the company of such distinguished poetasters as Louise Morey Bowman, Frances Chesterton, E. G. Buckeridge, G. H. R. Dabbs, E. L. Darton, and Sara M. B. Piatt. A two-stanza excerpt from the same poem appeared in the complete index volume to *The Bibelot* (B39). Under Flora Lamb's aegis, Frost finally made it into the Mosher canon—alas!, two years too late to be included in Section II of Bishop's bibliography.

The last two sections in the bibliography differ substantially from the first three. Section IV is a lavishly illustrated descriptive account of 84 primary entries, some mentioning multiple titles of Mosher books that have either been bound in luxurious fine bindings or illuminated. The books are arranged alphabetically by binder or illuminator, from the Adams Bindery to Zaehnsdorf; each is fully described, with locations when known; eleven are from Bishop's own collection. The colour photographs of some of these bindings make this one of the most attractive sections of Bishop's study. However, the interest in these bindings extends far beyond the illustrations. Distinguished binders—and many of the great English, American, and European (especially French) binders of this century are represented in Bishop's catalogue—tend to select only books that they regard as meriting their time and talent. As Bishop notes in his introduction to this section, the sheer number of so many designer bindings on Mosher's books gives a special cachet to his works. Besides the items described, Bishop, with characteristic thoroughness, concludes this section on art bindings with a listing of other recorded binders who are known to have executed less elegant, but still "skillful and respectable," bindings for Mosher books.

Section V consists of two parts: the first contains extensive excerpts from early reviews of Mosher books, contemporaneous accounts of and memorial tributes to Mosher and his books, and selections from modern assessments. Many of the shorter pieces are printed in full, including Le Gallienne's *Appreciation*. Not all the commentaries are laudatory: the section includes both attacks and negative assessments of Mosher's work as well as encomia. That Bishop is predisposed in Mosher's favour is self-evident throughout his study; indeed, a dispassionate sympathetic attitude is a *sine qua non* for success in any extended scholarly work. Nevertheless, it is a mark of Bishop's critical perception and his judgment that he is able to sustain a balanced and equitable assessment of Mosher's strengths and weaknesses. The second part of Section V is a remarkably extensive and thorough annotated bibliography of writings on and reference works relating to Mosher and the Mosher Press, with relevant items cross-referenced to the principal bibliography.

All seven appendices are valuable additions to Bishop's work, but the first—a reciprocal two-part conversion table of the item numbers in Bishop and Hatch—is crucial to the usefulness of the bibliography, given that the listings in the two bibliographies are arranged so differently—Hatch, chronologically, Bishop, alphabetically by title. A close comparison of the two tables quickly reveals the strength of Bishop, in terms of completeness, over Hatch. Hatch listed 59 private printings (as opposed to Bishop's 61), seven of which he was unable to locate, and in an appendix, he identified another eight unlocated trade editions. In all, he either missed or discovered too late to be included in his book Mosher's first published catalogue (B4) and 21 reprints. Hatch subsequently located five of the trade editions and 11 of the reprints. His reporting of these items was published posthumously in *Thomas Bird Mosher and the Art of the Book* (cited above), where they were assigned "A" numbers. In all, 22 of the Hatch items in the conversion tables have "A" numbers, six of them newly located by Bishop. Three remaining problematical editions in Hatch's appendix listing of unlocated trade editions are assigned square-bracketed "xx" symbols in Bishop's bibliography, where they are given tentative hypothetical numbers, suggesting that they may not exist (B157, 315.3, 436). These are not included in the conversion tables. In contrast to Hatch, only a single volume in Bishop's bibliography—B167: Jane Annan Bell's *In Memoriam* (Privately Printed-41)—is recorded as "no copy has been located."

The remaining six Appendices provide supporting documentation to other sections of the Bibliography. The second examines Mosher's royalties and other payments made to authors and publishers; the third and fourth provide tabular listings of the duplications of titles in Mosher's publications and of the frequency with which he reprinted his favourite authors; the fifth is a descriptive catalogue of major institutional holdings of Mosheriana. The last two pertain to Mosher the collector: Appendix VI briefly examines the general content of Mosher's library based on Bishop's catalogue (discussed below); the seventh and last is a note on Mosher's bookplate. The bibliography and source guide concludes with a list of illustrations and a comprehensive analytical index.

- vii -

While I am diffident about challenging the opinion of the undisputed authority on Thomas Bird Mosher, no assessment of such an important book as Bishop's would be complete without at least one caveat from the reviewer or, in this case, the introducer, the interlocutor between the bibliographer and his audience. In fairness, however, it is necessary to explain that my stricture pertains to an assessment of the Mosher books that is never actually advanced in the bibliography. In the draft of an article on Mosher intended for *Biblio*, but for which a completely different article was substituted and published there (cited above), Bishop addresses the subject of condition from the collector-dealer's point of view:

> Some people say condition isn't just important, it's *everything*. For the most part I wholeheartedly agree, at least for press books or modern firsts. If you buy a book in fine condition, and keep it that way, the book's value will hold or even increase. Once a marred copy, always a marred copy. And what you buy with flaws, you have to sell with flaws, Besides, the original publisher—and this holds especially true with press books—intended the book to have a certain look. A Mosher Press book with tattered covers was not the way the publisher originally intended the public to see that book. I've gone so far as to say that a Mosher book in fine condition is a pleasure to behold, but there's nothing uglier than a beat up, browned, and sullied copy of one of his books.

I disagree and I suspect Mosher might also. There is, after all, a certain romance about any well-thumbed book that gives it an attraction over and above its physical state. The condition of the 34 volumes of *Bell's British Theatre* that Captain Mosher presented to his son is never revealed, but the pin-marker Mosher found inside one of the volumes captured his imagination equally together with the inscribed name of the former owner, Jane Sonntag. Mosher's books, elegant as they indeed are in a pristine state, were also by design intentionally fragile, and it may be that he expected them to be rebound especially by his more affluent purchasers, not unlike French books that are issued in paper wrappers with the same expectation. By issuing his books in three states, Mosher consciously catered to different classes of readers and collectors. But the larger print-runs of the "ordinary" paper copies with their multiple editions that he offered the public at nominal prices he certainly intended to be read, and even moderate handling of these, particularly if they were passed from reader to reader, were destined, by their very fragility to become "soiled" and "shaken," a point Mosher was too shrewd not to be aware of, though these conventional booksellers' labels tend almost always to apply to the external wrappings of the volumes rather than to the printed text. Besides, it was part of his mission as a publisher that his books should be read. Considering that about 55 of the books Mosher published between 1891 and 1898 will soon be a century old, it is remarkable that so many have survived unread in their original state for collectors to hoard. As a modest collector, I can readily comprehend Bishop's preference, but I must confess that when I encounter those tattered copies he despises, my sympathies go out to all their former readers, and I imagine Mosher somewhere gloating over the success of his venture.

It remains only to note that Bishop has also compiled a draft catalogue of the books in Mosher's library, conflating Mosher's own 1889 catalogue, those by Oliver Sheean and Flora Lamb discussed above, the two 1948 auction catalogues, and other sources. Too lengthy to be published with the bibliography and guide book, the catalogue provides the raw material for much of the documentation in the individual entries. At some point in the future, the publication of the catalogue would form a valuable supplement to the present study.

In sum, Bishop's bibliography and guide book is an ambitious undertaking that answers virtually every question anyone interested in The Mosher Books might be inclined to pose. That these questions were not by and large resolvable using the resources presented in Benton L. Hatch's pioneering *Check List* is the justification for this new study. That the focus of Bishop's bibliography and source book is on the books rather on the man behind them was the motivation for this introduction.

The first five sections of the introduction have been adapted, with considerable revision and elaboration, from a lecture I delivered at a meeting of the Bibliographical Society of Canada in Vancouver on 10 June 1987 and published in the *PBSC*, 26 (1987): 27-64.—WEF

CHRONOLOGY OF MOSHER'S LIFE

1852   Thomas Bird Mosher was born in Biddeford, Maine on September 11 to Captain Benjamin and Mary Elizabeth (Merrill) Mosher. "Thomas" was the name of Mrs. Mosher's brother who died at the age of 16, and "Bird" was the last name of a minister Mrs. Mosher highly respected.

1854   One of Thomas Mosher's sisters, Elizabeth (Lizzie) Sarah, was born on May 24.

1858-1862   Three younger brothers (Charles Samuel, Frank Benjamin, and Willie), would be born to Captain Mosher and his wife, but would die early.

1863   Sails with father on the *DeWitt Clinton* during the spring, running the Confederate blockade with troops and horses from Fort Monroe to New Orleans in support of General Butler. Arrives in New Orleans around June.

Again on the *DeWitt Clinton*, traveled with father and family to Liverpool, England, beginning October 8 and arriving back in Boston on Christmas Day. During this trip to London Thomas's father buys him a copy of *The Pilgrim's Progress*. It was this title, other than stories from Mother Goose, which first left an impression on him.

1864   Certificate of Merit from Boston's Quincey Grammar School. This is the only formal education he will receive. He uses a private tutor for reading, a local Biddeford minister: Rev. John D. Emerson, Pastor of White Church.

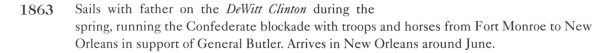

1865   Another sister, Leila, is born on July 5.

1867-1870   Travels with mother shortly after Christmas 1866 to meet with father in Germany. Then from February 22, 1867-March 10, 1870 (3 years and 17 days), Captain Benjamin Mosher takes his family along on a working world tour aboard the clipper ship *Nor'wester*. This voyage takes the Mosher family to England, Europe, South America, the North American West Coast, the Pacific Islands, and four times past Cape Horn. At the beginning of this trip Captain Mosher buys his son a set of *Bell's British Theatre* which opens up a treasure trove of literature to young Tom Mosher.

1870-1871   Mosher's entrance in 1870 into the Phillips Exeter Academy in Andover, MA is aborted. Family tradition has it that he left after only one night's stay.

On December 10 Mosher elopes with hometown girl, Ellen S. Dresser, who lived with her aunt and uncle (Jere Hobson). Later the disgruntled families demand a formal union on July 4, 1871.

Tom leaves his father's home and begins work at the firm of his wife's uncle, at Dresser, McClellan and Co. in Portland, Maine. It is here that Mosher first becomes acquainted with the ins and outs of printing papers, types, supplies and publishing.

1872   According to an entry in Mary Elizabeth Mosher's diary (Mosher's mother) for June 18, 1872, "Ellie Mosher had a son born Albion Ernest." Though clouded in obscurity, some of Mosher's autobiographical poetry and writing suggests that the child was either stillborn or died shortly after birth.

1875   Mosher first meets Leopold Lobsitz who becomes his dearest friend and literary soul-mate.

1879   While attending Harvard Medical School, Mosher's close friend, Leopold Lobsitz, suffers an untimely death from a chest abscess with resulting blood poisoning.

After irreconcilable differences, Ellie Dresser abandons Tom in the fall, goes to live with her aunt in Springfield, MA, and then on to New York City.

1879-1880/81   In the summer of 1879 Tom goes to St. Louis where he clerks in a bookshop. He sees Walt Whitman on the street there. Also works for Hugh R. Hildreth Printing Co. of St. Louis, MO.

This period in Mosher's life is also marked by poetical and prose activity which stretches from 1876 through 1893. He writes autobiographical poems, and completes a lengthy prose-poem on his relationship with Leopold Lobsitz, a prose work called "In Biddeford Town," and even works on a detailed outline of a five-act play, "Sowing the Wind."

1882   Different jobs in various places: working in book-shops and selling printing equipment in New York and then in Philadelphia. He even works in his father's coal office, a job his father took after retiring from seafaring.

The divorce between Tom and Ellie is granted on September 25 and becomes effective in March 1883. A new firm with Mosher as partner is formed, called McClellan, Mosher & Co.

1884   Mosher's old friend and former employer, forty-six year old Aurin Dresser, dies unexpectedly in Boston of catarrhal fever on March 9.

1885   Mosher's father dies.

1886-1888   Some of Mosher's poems are published in the *Traveler's Record* (house organ for Traveler's Insurance Co., Hartford, CT) under the pen name of Richard Merrill, the name of his mother's favorite brother. These include "Ballade of the Seasons" (Sept. 1886), "With an Easter Lily" (April 1887), "Two Houses" (July 1887), and "In Peru" (Dec. 1888). He also publishes a few poems in the local Portland paper.

1888   The first preface (unsigned) ever written by Mosher appears in the second edition of George Varney's *A Brief History of Maine* (Portland: McClellan, Mosher & Co., 1888).

1889   The law book and stationery business under the name of McClellan, Mosher & Co. ends in bankruptcy. Mosher then forms his own Thomas B. Mosher Company (claiming establishment back to 1882 as successor to McLellan, Mosher & Co.), a wholesale stationers' business, manufacturer of lithographs and legal black books, operating out of 37 Exchange Street in Portland, ME. He also publishes the Maine Reports, sells other law books, and he calls himself a "Publisher and Law Bookseller." Mosher's success in this business allows him to begin publishing a few literary books (beginning in 1891) until which time he can start publishing choice literature on a full-time basis.

January 1889 Mosher finishes a comprehensive hand-written list of over 350 books, and sets of books, he has bought for his personal library.

1891   On March 1 Mosher completes a lengthy, unpublished bibliographical study entitled "Old Plays" which evidences his continued interest in drama, an interest which he would cultivate throughout his life. He also continues to write autobiographical poetry like "Apologue of the Young Man and Woman" which also remains unpublished.

Mosher issues a Law Book Catalogue in September.

At age 39, Mosher publishes his first literary book in October, George Meredith's *Modern Love*. Across the ocean, William Morris has brought out his first book in August of the same year.

1892   Marries Anna M. Littlefield of Saco, Maine, on July 2.

Publishes his second book, *The City of Dreadful Night* by James Thomson.

1893   Mosher publishes his third book, and first anthology, *Songs of Adieu: A Little Book of "Finalé and Farewell,"* which is also the first book in the newly christened, The Bibelot Series.

1895   Mosher's success with his own publications (7 books and 2 lists) leads him to believe he can carry on in the publishing business –making fine books. He sells out his stationery and law book business in December and borrows $2,000 from Albro Chase (who first tried to teach him accounting at the old Dresser, McClellan, Co.). Added to this, he borrows the proceeds from his father's insurance to start his publishing career.

Begins his editing and publication of *The Bibelot*.

Elected to the Grolier Club on December 3, 1895. Mosher would also become a member of The Caxton Club and The Dofobs (both of Chicago), and of The Bibliographical Society

(London). He also held memberships in the Author's Club, the Omar Khayyám Club, and the City Club, all of Boston.

An irate Andrew Lang labels Mosher a "pirate" in the British literary periodical, *The Critic,* for reprinting his translation of *Aucassin and Nicolete* without his permission. This is the first of a series of exchanges denouncing Mosher as a literary pirate. Similar British claims would again resurface just before WW I.

1896   Harrison Hume Mosher (nicknamed Bibbs) born to the Moshers on January 8.

Mosher changes his business address to its final location at 45 Exchange Street in Portland, ME.

1897   Flora MacDonald Lamb is hired as a clerk and secretary and becomes an indispensable office assistant and later executive manager, a role she would play throughout Mosher's publishing career and beyond.

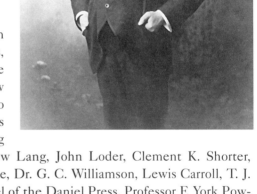

1898   Publishes the first and only American edition of the important Pre-Raphaelite publication, *The Germ.*

1899   Publishes Swinburne's *Laus Veneris-Poems and Ballads.*

1901   Travels with Mrs. Mosher to England from April 27 to June 20, visiting rare book dealers, noted publishers (including John Lane of the Bodley Head, and his former partner but now separate publisher, Elkins Matthews). He also meets with various authors, literary figures and/or their relatives and other notables, among them being: William Michael Rossetti, Andrew Lang, John Loder, Clement K. Shorter, Austin Dobson, Robert Bridges, Edmund Gosse, Dr. G. C. Williamson, Lewis Carroll, T. J. Wise, Mrs. Richard Jefferies, Mrs. Henry Daniel of the Daniel Press, Professor F. York Powell of Oxford, the actress Ellen Terry, and Emilie Grigsby.

1902   Publishes the first absolute facsimile reprint of the FitzGerald's *Rubáiyát of Omar Khayyám* of 1859.

Publishes Rossetti's poetical works.

1904   On February 8, Mosher gives a talk entitled "The Celtic Revival in Some of Its Lyrical Aspects" at the annual supper of the De Burians, a book club in Bangor, ME.

1906   Travels to the West Coast going from Portland to Boston, to New York City, to Washington, to New Orleans, to Los Angeles (in company with Irving Way of Chicago publishing fame), to San Jose (experiences the earthquake at 5:12 a.m.), to Colorado Springs, to Denver, to Omaha, to St. Louis (meets with William Marion Reedy), to Chicago (meets with the Caxton

Club), to Niagara Falls, to Buffalo, to Philadelphia (meets with Horrace Traubel), to New York City, to Boston, to Biddeford, and lastly back to Portland.

Bowdoin College grants Mosher an honorary degree of Master of Arts.

1907 Mosher's mother dies on January 28. Thomas Bird Mosher, Jr. (nicknamed Biblet) is born to the Moshers on March 31.

1908 The family moves to a house on Highland Street, Longfellow Heights, where Mosher installs his ever growing library.

1909-1910 The piracy controversy flares up. An article in the January 1909 *The Publisher's Circular*: "Thomas Bird Mosher, The American Book Pirate–A Warning to English Booksellers" mentions that most Mosher books cannot be legally carried in Great Britain. Mosher replies in March that he was just "Taking what I had a perfect legal right, and... a perfect moral right to use." A June letter follows on "The Method of Mosher" followed by other letters over the next five years. Mosher was also supported by several Englishmen during the controversy, including Clement Shorter in *The Sphere*, 31 Dec. 1910.

During this winter Mosher suffers a debilitating attack of neuritis which leaves his right arm lame. He learns to write all over again with his left hand which explains the radical change in handwritten signatures and notes after this time.

1914 Again the piracy controversy comes to the head with a fiery eruption in the March 7, 1914 *The Times* of London, and in *The Publisher's Circular* by James H. Blackwood, president of the (English) Publishers' Association. Again the support of Clement Shorter in *The Literary Digest* of May 9 says that the outrage is not commensurate with the offense. The English publisher, Grant Richards, also defends Mosher in the March 13 issue of *The Times*.

1915 A fire at Mosher's 45 Exchange Street publishing rooms destroys many books of unknown value, first editions, and a large number of volumes out of print, with the total damage in the thousands.

1919 Mosher produces his *tour de force*, the facsimile reprint of Walt Whitman's *Leaves of Grass* as it first appeared in 1855, complete in detail down to the very binding.

1922 Ellery Sedgwich, editor to the *Atlantic Monthly*, moves to convince Mosher to sell The Mosher Press to the *Atlantic*. The transactions are never completed.

1923   Thomas Bird Mosher dies of arterio-sclerosis at his home on Friday, August 31, at the age of 71 (several days shy of his 72nd birthday). He is buried in the Littlefield family plot of the Laurel Hill Cemetery in Sacco, Maine.

                Upon his death, his assistant, Flora Lamb, destroys the many years of correspondence between Mosher and his first wife who translated, under the name of Aimee Lenalie, two books by Marcel Schwob which were published by Mosher. Mosher's close contact with his first wife throughout his lifetime remains a secret for many years.

                Flora Lamb takes over the reins of the Mosher publishing business.

1924   Mosher's first wife, Ellie Dresser, a. k. a. Aimee Lenalie, dies in Boston on October 5.

1941   The Mosher publishing business and its remaining stock is sold by Mrs. Mosher to the Williams Bookstore in Boston, MA through the agency of Jack Neiburg.

1947   Mosher's second wife dies. This is also the year that Flora MacDonald Lamb, Mosher's long-time executive manager, dies.

1948   The Mosher library is sold at Parke-Bernet Galleries in New York.

Mosher's publishing office in Portland, Maine (c. 1914)

Section I

GENERAL PRINTING AND PUBLISHING FACTS
ABOUT THE MOSHER BOOKS

The following information on the printing types, papers, bindings, and processes used gives the reader a general overview of Mosher's publishing program. There is also information on the range of book sizes, the number of books produced and the basic marketing strategy Mosher employed. More specific details on the various series of books, yearly production, etc., are given in this same section following these general facts.

Processes & Printers

Mosher used the letterpress printing services of three Portland printers:

– Brown, Thurston Company printed the first three books
– Smith & Sale who produced the majority of Mosher's publications, mostly under the care of pressman Frank Mangum
– George D. Loring

For most of his monochrome frontispieces Mosher employed the services of Edward Bierstadt of New York. He sometimes indicated such a plate is an "artotype by Bierstadt," but other times he calls it a "Bierstadt reproduction" or done by "Bierstadt process." This was a photo-mechanical, non-screen printing process used for fine detail reproductions in color or in monochrome. According to Luis Nadeau's *Encyclopedia of Printing, Photographic and Photomechanical Processes* (New Brunswick, Canada: Atelier Luis Nadeau, 1989): "This process was very similar to collotype... A mixture of soluble glass (sodium silicate) and albumen was used as a substrate, thus avoiding the necessity of first exposing a dichromated layer to the light to give a stronger matrix, as in the original Albertype process... The foremost user was probably Edward Bierstadt, of New York, who used it primarily for illustrations of business catalogues."–p.37.

Types Used

Fred Anthoensen is quoted: "If I am not mistaken the majority of his books were set in the Boston series, a modified old style something on the roman order, of good color, and supplied by the Dickinson Type Foundry of Boston. Caslon was also employed for some of the larger books in later years." –Hatch, p.25. Flora Lamb notes: "The types he used were the old-style and Caslon on practically all his books." –April 30, 1933 letter.

Jenson type was used for some cover titles (Brocade Series) and colophons (samples in the Old World Series), and for the text of several books: *George Meredith: A Tribute*, 1919 (Sect. II, B129); *Hand and Soul* (B139); *Empedocles on Etna* (B103) and *In Praise of Omar* (B172). Jenson type is the American Type Foundry's version of William Morris's Golden type. In his catalogues Mosher calls it "golden type."

The Bibelot Series uses "Elzevir Italic Body 8" type font.

Papers Used

Mosher imported finely made Dutch Van Gelder paper from the Netherlands and used it predominantly throughout his publishing career. A few books were printed on Old Stratford white wove paper (e.g., *Leaves of Grass*, B192). At times other papers such as Kelmscott handmade paper from England, and Italian handmade paper were used. In two instances Mosher used Kisogawa handmade paper: the 1919 issue of *George Meredith—A Tribute* (B129); and *In Praise of Omar* published in 1920 (B172). In another instance he employed "toned Van Gelder" paper for four copies of the large paper edition of *The Growth of Love*, 1894 (B137).

English "Dickinson" handmade paper was used for *In Memoriam* (Sect. II, B169), Italian "Tuscany" paper was used for the second privately printed *Masterpieces* (B236), French Arches handmade paper for *The Present Crisis* (B309) privately printed for Edward Woods, Shogun paper for *Songs with Tears* (B372), and Blue Hill Text paper for *The Sources of the Power of Music* (B379). These more unusual papers were also used for privately printed editions, including *The Works of Arthur Symons: A Bibliographical Note* (B441) printed in five copies on Batchellor's imported blue laid paper. Mosher also used a variety of papers to cover the boards of his books' bindings detailed below. Also, some of the printed dust jackets bear the watermark "POST OFFICE BOND."

Like other publishers of the period who wanted to produce a limited run of a publication targeted for the book collector, Mosher also used imported Japan vellum paper for his more limited editions. In an Autumn 1896 announcement insert for the Brocade Series, Mosher indicates these volumes are printed "on *genuine* Imperial Mills Japan vellum." According to Cathleen A. Baker, paper conservator, a cursory examination of this Japan vellum shows it is most likely *mitsumata* in combination with *gampi*, both taken from the inner barks of these shrubs which are distantly related to the mulberry tree. The brocade paper, used to cover the slipcases of the Brocade Series, was imported from Germany. In one instance, the *Amphora* (B2), Mosher used endpapers of Japan shadow paper which was used in Japan for window decoration.

A few Vest Pocket *Rubáiyáts* (B335), printed on blue-gray charcoal paper, may be part of a curious phenomenon which began with Aldus who in 1514 issued the first book in this manner. These may very well have been unannounced rarities for a few choice buyers of Mosher books. This being the very first Vest Pocket *Rubáiyát*, Mosher most likely used the special blue paper format for a few friends, a method employed as substitute for the use of the far more expensive vellum. Another explanation is that they were trial copies or printer's dummies. Such dummies do exist for other Mosher books, but printed on very cheap, off-white paper, so this explanation is less likely.

The papers for the cover bindings of books were imported French charcoal papers, 18th century-style patterned Italian papers (Venetian Series), a paper called Onyx vellum (see *Autumn Leaves from Maple Cottage*, B12), and Brittany paper wraps (*In Memoriam*, B167). Mosher also employed white paper back strips (B442), and colored Fabriano paper for the binding boards (B239 as an example).

The boards of the privately printed *The Sources of the Power of Music* (B379) are covered with Ancona blue paper. What Mosher called Mexican vellum onyx wrappers was used on *The Holy Jumpers* (B151). The uncharacteristic but quite effective use of a bright red Toyogami paper was used on all Mosher editions of *The Present Crisis* (B309-10).

Bindings

According to numerous references in the Mosher correspondence, the books were all folded, sewn, and bound by hand. The text block and the binding covers were kept separate until copies were needed to fill orders. Mosher mostly used folded wrappers of Japan vellum over boards, stiff Japan vellum boards, or French charcoal paper covered boards.

An early reference was made to the binder of Mosher's first book, *Modern Love* (1891). Local Portland, Maine newspapers cited Mr. Almus D. Butler as the Portland binder who provided both the small and large paper copies with a binding of Japan vellum wrappers folded over boards with spine's title/date printed in black and the title/author (and foreword author's name) printed in red and black. This binding became a characteristic style for Mosher's books, and it may be that Butler bound books for Mosher throughout the history of the press. Regardless of who did the later binding for Mosher, Butler's original style and mechanical construction would be replicated many times up to 1923.

A distinguishing feature of many of the bindings on The Mosher Books (particularly in the Old World Series and The Bibelot Series) is their use of yapp edges. These are overlapping edges or flaps extending from the boards and covering the fore-edges of the book, or in some cases two or all three of the exposed edges of the book.

By and large, Mosher did not publish books in fine leather bindings except for the special issue of *The Bibelot*. He did have some Old World and Vest Pocket books (and an occasional Miscellaneous Series book) bound in flexible leather with gilt decoration on the spine, with additional gilt decorations on the front covers of the Old World copies. Additionally, some Vest Pocket volumes were bound in green cloth, and *The Bibelot* also appeared in blue Hollistan Buckram cloth.

In some instances Mosher also printed 4-10 copies of his books on "pure vellum," calf or sheep skin, either Roman vellum imported from Italy, or American vellum. Some of these copies were bound in Classic vellum (e.g., see *Memories of President Lincoln*, B239), and sometimes in green colored vellum. In a letter to Emilie Grigsby on April 26, 1900, Mosher notes: "The green vellum is seldom, if ever, seen here. I got this from the same people [J. and J. Leighton in London] who made it for Morris" (letter at the University of San Francisco). See "Papers Used" above for papers employed for bindings.

Number of Books Produced

A total of 730 books were printed from 1891-1923. This figure includes all first Mosher editions, their reprints, and privately printed books. If one includes the 53 other publications (the yearly issues of *The Bibelot*, the 2 index volumes to the same, and the 31 annual catalogues), the total number of publications reaches 783.

Of these 730 books, 331 were first appearances of titles (or in a eight instances, newly formulated editions) within the regular series. Following first title appearances, there were 338 reprints, some titles extending from 8 to 13 additional editions. Another 61 books were privately printed, i.e., commissioned by private customers for their own distribution, or printed by Mosher for private circulation.

A total publication count is here provided for the reader in a simple listing:

331	first Mosher book editions
338	reprints of the Mosher books
61	privately printed books
31	annual catalogues
20	separate volumes of *The Bibelot*
2	index volumes for *The Bibelot*

783 total publications*

*Note: Some may be inclined to count the 240 issues of *The Bibelot* instead of the 20 volumes, in which case the count becomes 1,003

The number of copies produced, as found on the limitation page, are generally accurate. There is one major exception, that being the number of vellum copies of The Quarto Series, *Tristram of Lyonesse*. Here Mosher had two sets of four vellum copies printed.

On some occasions there may have been an extra number of regular paper (usually Van Gelder paper) copies printed. Mosher would often provide an original text source to the printer along with numerous editorial notes. He also listed the number of copies he wanted printed. On occasions the limitation instructions call for additional regular paper copies above and beyond the printed limitation in the book, or recorded in Mosher's catalogues. Most likely this was a standard overage needed to replace damaged or misbound copies. Examples of these printer instructions are found in Mosher's edited copies in the Bishop Collection.

Marketing Strategy

Though Mosher relied heavily on direct catalogue sales, he also used a number of retail outlets to carry his books. There are a variety of seasonal announcements, flyers sent with orders, ads in Mosher's own publication, *The Bibelot,* and in publications such as *L'Eroica, Spenzia, Book News Monthly, The Caxton, The Bookman, The Literary Collector, The Biblio,* Chicago's *The Dial, Publisher's Weekly, The Book Buyer, The Literary World, Nation, The Critic, Poet Lore, The Goose Quill, The Living Age,* Reedy's *Mirror,* and early issues of Elbert Hubbard's *The Philistine.*

Mosher maintained a mailing list of about 17,000 customers in the United States, England, and other nations with English-speaking populations, e.g., India and Australia. These customers could order The Mosher Books directly from the publisher. In addition there were retail outlets, distributors, and agents for The Mosher Books. In a May 28, 1894 letter at Arizona State University, Mosher offers discounts of 20% post-paid to the trade; and 25% on 25 assorted copies. In 1913 Mosher had to inform his agents that he had to lower the quantity discount to 20% on all orders with express prepaid, and in a Nov. 1, 1913 letter to Irving Way, he mentions that he could do "very little better" if the order was for $1,000 rather than $50. The following are some of the retail outlets for The Mosher Books as gleaned from various letters in several collections:

Some of the Retail Outlets Mosher Used

The U. P. James Book Store, Cincinnati, OH
Brentano's, New York City
Store of David B. Luyster, 79 Nassau Street, New York City
Bergdorf-Goodman in New York City
Mrs. Horace Traubel, Philadelphia, PA (distributed Mosher books to Charles Sessler, Inc. and Leary's Bookstore)
Laurence Gomme's Little Bookshop Around the Corner, New York City
William Doxey, San Francisco, CA
Elder & Shepard, later Paul Elder Co., San Francisco, CA
W. Irving Way, Los Angeles, CA
The White House (department store), San Francisco, CA
A. C. McClurg and Co., Chicago, IL
Woodworth's Bookstore, Chicago, IL
Marshall, Field & Co., Chicago, IL
Grant's of Utica, NY
Fowler Brothers in Boston, MA
Mansford Co., Memphis, TN
Edmund D. Brooks, Minneapolis, MN
Kaufman's The Big Store, Pittsburgh, PA

Firsts & Onlys, &c.
A Survey of the Mosher Canon
(Jointly compiled by William E. Fredeman and Philip R. Bishop)

FIRSTS

First published book: Meredith's *Modern Love*, 1891 (B244).

First published series: English Reprint Series (3 vols., 1891-94; series named retroactively).

First series in progress to be named by Mosher: Bibelot Series (10 vols., 1893-97).

First book printed in America using the same paper used at the Kelmscott Press: *Hand and Soul*, 1899 (B139).

First issued catalogue: *List of Books, Season of 1893-94* (B198).

First number of *The Bibelot* issued: January 1895 (B18).

First privately printed work: Mosher's sonnet *Inscription for a Fireplace*, [1892] (B173).

First catalogue to list Privately Printed Editions: *The Mosher Books*, 1914 (B258).

First published facsimile: *Rubáiyát*, 1902 (B336).

First anthology compiled by Mosher: *Songs of Adieu*, 1893 (B366).

First (of two) books with a watercolor frontispiece: *Sylvie*, 1896 (B394).

First appearance of the device with stylized dolphins holding an open book: *The Child in the House*, [September] 1895 (B62).

First year any anchor & dolphin device appears on a publication: 1902.

First appearance of Mosher's full name on a title page: *Pearl* (Privately Printed-11), 1908 (B286)

First use of Mosher's full name on a regular series book: Burns' *The Jolly Beggars...* (Miscellaneous-70), 1914 (B180).

Onlys (Books)

Only book with a Boston imprint: Field's *Little Willie* (Privately Printed-9), 1904 (B216).

Only Mosher publication lacking an imprint: Mosher's sonnet *Inscription for a Fireplace*, [1892] (B173).

Only co-published book in regular series: facsimile of Whitman's *Leaves of Grass* (with William F. Gable of Altoona, PA), 1919 (B192).

Only two books published solely in an edition printed on vellum: *The Casket of Opals* (Privately Printed-5) 1900 (B-56); and the *Rubáiyát* (Privately Printed-3) 1899 (B337).

Only book for which there are two distinct states of the vellum copies: Swinburne's *Tristram of Lyonesse and Other Poems* (Quarto-10), 1904 (B416). There were four copies of the entire text, and four containing only the title poem, "Tristram of Lyonesse."

Only book printed at the Press that was dedicated to Mosher: Fiona Macleod, *By Sundown Shores*, (Brocade-36), 1902 (B53).

Only multi-volume work for which Mosher published only the first volume: *Fragments*. Vol. I by Cavé (Privately Printed-21), [c. 1912] (B117).

Only book for which a special limited number of copies were given a "privately printed" imprint of ten copies for England: Burton's *The Kasîdah* (Miscellaneous-30), 1905 (B182).

Only book for which a special limited number of copies were given a specific London imprint of twenty-five copies: *The Germ* (Reprints of Privately Printed Books-3), 1898 (B132) of which 25 copies were printed on Japan vellum for the Guild of Women-Binders.

Onlys (Series)

Only series printed entirely in Italic type: Bibelot Series.

Only series paginated in Roman numerals: Bibelot Series.

Only series issued in large as well as small paper copies: English Reprint Series (3 vols.), 1891-93.

Only two series printed exclusively on Japan vellum: Brocade Series and Reprints from "The Bibelot."

Only four series for which copies on vellum were printed: Quarto Series, Lyric Garland Series, Reprints of Privately Printed Books, and the Miscellaneous Series.

Only four series in which "sub-series" appear: Brocade Series, Vest Pocket Series; the Ideal Series of Little Masterpieces, and the Miscellaneous Series.

Only series projected that never materialized: the "Breviary," intended to consist of books on religious themes; the scheme survived only in a 4-volume sub-series (see note to B343).

Only series to span roughly Mosher's publishing career: Miscellaneous (1895-1923).

Onlys (Miscellaneous Instances)

Only instance of Mosher being pirated: Mosher's descriptive note on Burton's *The Kasîdah*. (Old World Series-5), 1896, was lifted and printed as his own by Cook in his edition of 1900 (see B181 note).

Only example of bowdlerization in the Mosher canon: *The Poems of Master François Villon of Paris*, trans. by John Payne (1900), which excluded 119 "Omitted Lines" considered too risqué for Mosher's edition. These lines were separately reprinted in Van Gelder paper, Japan vellum, and on vellum by H. W. Bryant of Portland and were sold with Mosher's knowledge (B302).

Only volume of the Quarto Series with a colophon: Pater's *Marius the Epicurean* (Quarto-7), 1900 (B231).

Only instance in which a cover design (Chiswick Press) was accidentally printed upside down: Frederick Brush's *Songs of the Susquehanna* (Privately Printed-52), 1920 (B371). See also B207 for a design printed upside down in the text.

Only instance where Mosher planned to act as official distributor of a book he expected to reprint, but died before permission was cleared (the book was later reprinted by Flora Lamb): Thomas E. Jones' *Sonnets of the Cross* (4th ed), FL52, 1927 (see B431.1).

Only instance in which a major writer's corrected copy of an unauthorized Mosher printing (the first in book form) was used as the printer's copy for the authorized edition: Swinburne's *A Year's Letters* (Privately Printed Books-9), 1901, was published in London & NY in 1901 as *Love's Cross-currents–A Year's Letters* (B442).

OTHER FACTS ABOUT MOSHER PRESS BOOKS

Largest book produced (dimensions): Burton's *The Kasîdah* (32.5 x 25.5cm), 1905 (B-182).

Smallest book produced in a regular series other than the Brocade Series (dimensions): J. M. Barrie, *George Meredith* (14.3 x 9.9 cm), 1911 (B129), but the smallest overall is any Brocade Series book (13.5 x 9 cm.).

Longest book produced (pagination): *Poetical Works of Oscar Wilde* (xxxiii+396pp.), 1908 (B305).

Shortest publications produced (pagination): Mosher's sonnet *Inscription for a Fireplace*, 4 pp. (single sheet folded) [1892] (B173); also, *An Appreciation* by Jessie Rittenhouse, 4 pp. (single sheet folded) 1917 (B445). Both were privately printed.

Most expensive book (exclusive of vellum copies): Burton's *The Kasîdah* ($10), 1905 (B182).

Least expensive Mosher publication: individual numbers of *The Bibelot* (240 numbers @ 5 cents each), 1895-1914 (B18-39).

Book with largest print-run: Fitzgerald's *Rubáiyát* (Vest Pocket Series-1), 1900 (B335 to 335.3); 15,000 copies were said to have been sold from June 1899-March 1900.

Books with the shortest print-runs:
1) Privately Printed Editions: *Verses and a Dream* (Privately Printed-55), 1922 (B426). Three copies were printed.
2) Book printed on vellum: Cicero, *De Amicitia* (Privately Printed-26), 1901 (B82). Only one copy was printed for Mosher.
3) Regular series: Reprints from "The Bibelot," Nos. 1-6, and 8, printed from 1897-1900 (B83, 109, 133, 135, 149, 400, 419). Only 25 copies were printed.

Book issued in the greatest number of editions: Pater's *A Child in the House* (Brocade Series), 1895 -1908 (B62 to B-62.13); there were fourteen editions.

Book with highest *stated* limitation: Burton's *The Kasîdah*. 11th ed. (Old World Series-5), 1920 (B-181.11); the limitation reads 1500 copies.

Number of Mosher's titles issued in vellum: 47.

Book printed on pure vellum with the largest print-run: George Parsons' *The Casket of Opals* (Privately Printed-5), 1900 (B56); fifteen copies were printed.

Series with greatest number of titles: Miscellaneous (98).

Series with fewest number of titles: English Reprint (3).

LASTS

Last book published in Mosher's lifetime: Marcel Schwob's *The Children's Crusade* (Miscellaneous Series-98), August 1923 (B66); Mosher died on 31 August 1923.

MOSHER PUBLISHING DATA

A THIRTY-THREE-YEAR OVERVIEW

YEAR	New Editions	Reprints	Private Printings	Total
1891	1	–	–	1
1892	1	–	1	2
1893	2	–	–	2
1894	3	–	–	3
1895	6	2	–	8
1896	8	7	–	15
1897	14	11	–	25
1898	16	22	1	39
1899	20	14	2	36
1900	23	20	1	44
1901	17	10	1	28
1902	21	12	1	34
1903	19	18	1	38
1904	17	16	1	34
1905	17	17	–	34
1906	16	20	–	36
1907	13	28	1	42
1908	14	19	1	34
1909	16	23	1	40
1910	14	11	–	25
1911	14	10	1	25
1912	11	18	8	37
1913	9	12	7	28
1914	5	8	6	19
1915	7	5	4	16
1916	6	11	2	19
1917	5	5	6	16
1918	3	–	–	3
1919	4	5	4	13
1920	5	5	4	14
1921	1	1	1	3
1922	1	7	4	12
1923	2	1	2	5
Sub Total	331	338	61	730
The Bibelot *	annual vols. 20			20
The Bibelot *	index vols. 2			2
Catalogues *	31			31
TOTAL	384	338	61	783

* The yearly volumes of *The Bibelot*, its indices, and the catalogues are not included in the following graph.

The following graph is derived from the publishing data given on the previous page, and visually illustrates the growth and eventual decline of Mosher's publishing efforts over a thirty-three year period. During the first four years (1891-1894) he continued working at his stationary and law book business while printing a few "trial balloons." By 1896, however, his publishing efforts began to expand enough to warrant full-time attention to publishing. This is also the year he started his literary periodical, *The Bibelot*.

As can be readily seen on the graph below, the years from 1895 to 1898 were ones of rapid increase. Mosher was establishing a respectable American sales base for his publications, and he was also rapidly gaining British attention by bringing out such works as *The Germ* (1898) and Swinburne's *Laus Veneris* (1899). The peak year for the Mosher books comes in 1900 when he introduced twenty-three new editions, and twenty reprints of his own previous editions. The noticeable 1901 drop in publications was due to Mosher's trip to England from April to June. The Mosher operation was small enough to show the effects of his absence for those three months.

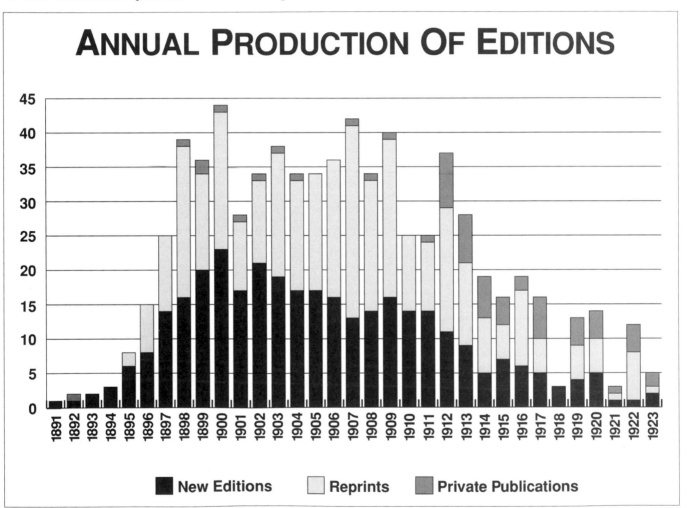

ANNUAL PRODUCTION OF EDITIONS

■ New Editions   □ Reprints   ■ Private Publications

From 1902-1909 there is a concentration of publications averaging about 36 publications a year, with 1907 being the year to come closest to the previous yearly all-time high in 1900. Then in 1910 disaster struck. Mosher suffered a debilitating stroke from which he was never to recover fully. The effects of that stroke carried over to 1911 as well, and by 1912 it seemed as though he might be able to return to his output of the past, but health would not permit this brief resurgence to last. Additionally, part of that short-lived increase was due to the printing of eight privately printed books, the largest number he would ever bring out in any single year.

In looking at the graph from 1912 to 1923, one sees a general decrease in the number of books produced. During 1915 a fire destroyed part of the personal office library and an appreciable amount of stock at Mosher's Exchange Street office. In the following year, mostly reprints of the Mosher books were brought out (11) and only a few new "first editions" were issued (6). The years 1918-23 are mostly ones during which Mosher's poor health, and the increasing effects of old age, diminished the publication program to a mere shadow of its former days of glory.

THE MOSHER SERIES

A SHORT TITLE LISTING, INCLUDING PRIVATE PRINTINGS

The idea of producing books and grouping them around a common theme was not a new idea in the 19th century. William Pickering had his "Diamond Classics" and "The Aldine Poets." George Bell and Sons continued in this vein and also produced an Aldine poets series. By the time Mosher began publishing in 1891, he was already familiar with how some publishers grouped their wares into various series. Some of Mosher's earliest reading and collecting included books published in London by Henry Bohn, whose imprints were grouped into series like "Bohn's British Classics," "Bohn's Ecclesiastical Library," "Bohn's Illustrated Library," and at least ten others. He was also familiar with the German Tauchnitz editions organized into various series like "La France Classique," and the "Collection of British Authors." Macmillan had its "Golden Treasury Series," Humphrey's his "Quarto Series," John Lane had the "Keynotes Series" and Elkin Mathews his "Shilling Garland Series" and "The Vigo Cabinet Series," just to name a few. So for Mosher, selling books by creating several series seemed both the natural and expedient thing to do.

Mosher divided his books into fourteen different series (see following chronologically arranged graph). He advertised these series in various promotional pieces such as advertising flyers, seasonal lists, in *The Bibelot*, and in advertisements which appeared in numerous magazines; however, the most important source of information for the various series of Mosher's books was his annual catalogues. Here Mosher would list a series name like the Old Word Series and then list the titles under that series in chronological order of their first appearance. The number assigned to each title became the number within the series, for example, Rossetti's translation of *The New Life of Dante* was the third Old World Series book to be produced. Both the Hatch *Check List*, and the present bibliography on Mosher's books, include the ordinal number assigned the book in Mosher's catalogues. Using the above example, *The New Life of Dante* is catalogued as Old Word Series-3. One should note that a series name does not appear in the actual physical books, with two exceptions: the Old World and The Bibelot Series, and the books do not contain any notice of their ordinal number within a series. That information is added by the bibliographer, based upon the catalogues and surviving lists compiled by members of Mosher's firm.

There are a few important considerations to keep in mind when using this section. Mosher sometimes switched a title from one series to another. This changed the ordinal number of all the titles in that series and, of course, introduced an addition to the series it was assigned. Utmost care has been given to accurately complete the final list of titles in each series up to 1923, the last year of book production under Mosher's direction.

Two series pose particular problems. The Quarto Series was numbered quite differently by Mosher, and as a result, the titles were not in chronological order. This bibliography restores the chronological order, but still makes reference to the last catalogue numbers Mosher assigned to them (in brackets). The other series which presented problems is the largest of the fourteen, the Miscellaneous Series. After his 1915 book catalogue, Mosher discontinued numbering the books within various series. The Sheean and Lamb typescripts continued the numbering, and Hatch's *Check List* used these to assign the later Miscellaneous Series numbers.

The problem that occurs in Hatch is that "newly formulated" post-1915 editions of earlier titles were not given newly assigned numbers as had been done for books prior to 1915. Mosher's practice was well established throughout the catalogues. *Homeward: Songs By the Way* (Miscellaneous-23) was assigned a different number from its predecessor, *Homeward Songs By the Way* (Miscellaneous-1); *The Kasîdah* of 1915 (Miscellaneous-75) was assigned a different number from *The Kasîdah* of 1905 (Miscellaneous Series-30); the *Father Damien* of 1905 (Miscellaneous Series-29) was assigned a different number from the *Father Damien* of 1897 (Miscellaneous Series-3); and the *Memories of President Lincoln* of 1912 (Miscellaneous Series-59) was assigned a different number from that of the *Memories of President Lincoln* of 1904 (Miscellaneous-26). In keeping with Mosher's practice, the present bibliography used the same approach with the two different formats of *In Praise of Omar* (Miscellaneous Series-4 & 94), *George Meredith–A Tribute* (Miscellaneous Series-52 & 90), and *Ten O'Clock* (Miscellaneous Series-80 & 93). Additionally, similar adjustments were made involving two other series: *The Poems of Master François Villon of Paris* (Reprints of Privately Printed Books-6 & 13), and *Immensee* (Brocade Series-31 & 51). The renumbering from Miscellaneous Series-80 onward (and likewise with the Reprints of Privately Printed Books and the Brocade Series) preserves the established practice, and readers of the Hatch *Check-List* will note the discrepancies, now corrected.

Please Note: There is no particular order to the sequence of the series presented on the following pages. Their placement was a matter of expediency in order to make them fit as well as possible onto one page. Also: the numbers in parentheses, following each book title, refer to the citation number in the bibliography.

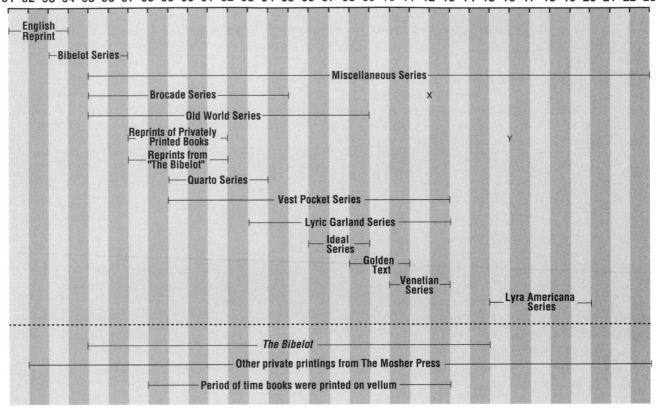

**CHRONOLOGICAL GRAPH OF THE MOSHER SERIES
1891-1923**

X= 1912 edition of *Immensee: An Idyll* (B163), which was a much later addition to the Brocade Series.
Y= 1916 edition of *The Poems of Master François Villon* (B303), which was a much later addition to the Reprints of Privately Printed Books.

The above graph shows the longevity of each of the fourteen regular series and, for comparison, the overlap with the privately printed books, the longevity of *The Bibelot*, and the period during which forty-seven books were printed on vellum.

THE FOURTEEN REGULAR SERIES:

THE BROCADE SERIES

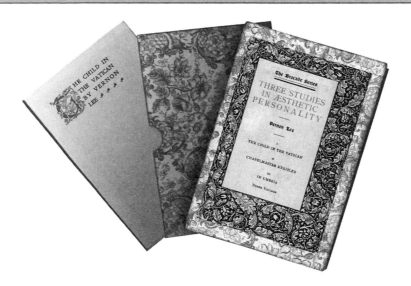

- 50 titles for 51 books from 1895-1905 (and 1912). • Size: 13.5 x 9 cm. • Type: 8-point old-style Roman.
- Content: Romances, tales, prose-fantasies, idylls, studies. • Price: 75¢ each.
- 425 copies on Imperial Mills Japan vellum. Bound in flexible Japan vellum covers and housed in a slipcase covered with a brocade design paper, hence the name of the series "brocade." This paper was imported by Mosher from Germany, and was described by one early reviewer as "of a beautiful texture, pearly white covered with dainty bouquets of flowers in Dresden colors." The caduceus on the back cover (designed by Bruce Rogers) was first used on *Homeward Songs by the Way* in 1895. The slipcases received a different paper treatment in later editions. Customers could order sets, organized by author or topic, which were then further housed in a cabinet-style box covered with matching brocade paper. A Mosher order form lists these sets as: Three Idyls of Childhood–Brown (3 vols.), Idyls of Field and Hedgerow–Jefferies (5 vols.), Studies in Aesthetic Personality–Lee (3 vols.), Old French Romances–Morris (4 vols.), Old English Romances–Morris (4 vols.), Imaginary Portraits–Pater (6 vols.), Five Tales and a Study–Stevenson (5 vols.), The De Guerins and the Centaur–Arnold (3 vols.), Studies and Stories–Fiona Macleod (3 vols.), Prose Selections–Oscar Wilde (5 vols.) and A House of Pomegranates–Wilde (3 vols.).

LIST OF TITLES IN CHRONOLOGICAL ORDER OF PUBLICATION

1. The Child in the House (62)	1895	18. Marjorie Fleming (233)	1899	35. Nature and Eternity (269)	1902
2. The Pageant of Summer (282)	1896	19. Rab and His Friends (318)	1900	36. By Sundown Shores (53)	1902
3. The Story of Amis and Amile (384)	1896	20. A Lodging for the Night... (217)	1900	37. Maurice de Guérin (237)	1903
4. The Story of Cupid & Psyche (385)	1897	21. Bits of Oak Bark (45)	1900	38. Eugénie de Guérin (105)	1903
5. The Story Without An End (391)	1897	22. The Hollow Land: A Tale (150)	1900	39. Some Great Churches... (359)	1903
6. The Centaur & the Bacchante (59)	1897	23. The Sire de MalÈtroit's Door (355)	1900	40. Thrawn Janet: Markheim (409)	1903
7. A Prince of Court Painters (312)	1898	24. The Child in the Vatican (64)	1900	41. Legend of Madame Krasinska (194)	1903
8. Denys L'Auxerrois (89)	1898	25. Saint Guido (340)	1901	42. The Dead Leman (80)	1903
9. Sebastian Van Storck (344)	1898	26. Chapelmeister Kreisler (60)	1901	43. Tale of the Four White Swans (398)	1904
10. Duke Carl of Rosenmold (96)	1898	27. The Portrait of Mr W. H. (308)	1901	44. The Happy Prince... (142)	1904
11. Tale of King Florus... (397)	1898	28. François Villon, Student, Poet (118)	1901	45. Young King & the Star-Child (443)	1904
12. Quattrocentisteria... (315)	1898	29. In Umbria (176)	1901	46. Ulad of the Dreams (420)	1904
13. Tale of King Coustans... (396)	1899	30. A Lady of Sorrow (185)	1901	47. The Fisherman and His Soul (112)	1905
14. The History of Over Sea (148)	1899	31. Immensee (162)	1902	48. The Birthday of the Infanta (44)	1905
15. Emerald Uthwart (102)	1899	32. Gertha's Lovers: A Tale (134)	1902	49. Legend of St Julian, Hospitaler (195)	1905
16. Hours of Spring... (157)	1899	33. Golden Wings (136)	1902	50. The Children's Crusade (65)	1905
17. Will o' the Mill (436)	1899	34. Story of the Unknown Church (390)	1902	51. Immensee: An Idyll (163)	1912

THE ENGLISH REPRINT SERIES

- 3 titles from 1891-1894.
- Size: Small paper copies, 21 x 13 cm.
    Large paper copies, 25.5 x 20.5 cm.
- Type: 10-point old-style.
- Content: Long poetic sequences.
- Price: small paper, $2; large paper, $7.50
    (Japan vellum price was never advertised).
- 400 numbered small paper copies on Van Gelder paper; 40 numbered large paper copies on Van Gelder; 10 numbered large paper copies on Japan vellum and signed by the publisher. All copies are bound in printed Japan vellum wrappers over boards by the Portland binder, Almus D. Butler.
- These were the only books of which Mosher ever produced large paper copies.

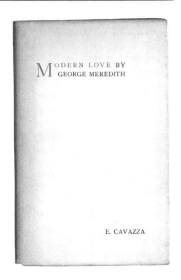

LIST OF TITLES IN CHRONOLOGICAL ORDER OF PUBLICATION

1. Modern Love (244) 1891	2. The City of Dreadful Night (72) 1892	3. The Growth of Love (137) 1894

THE GOLDEN TEXT SERIES

- 8 titles from 1908-1911.
- Size: 14.5 x 14 cm.
- Type: 12-point old-style Roman.
- Content: Single poem. • Price: regular in wrappers, 50¢ each; in marbled boards, 60¢; printed on Japan vellum, $1.
- 925 on Van Gelder paper with printed wrappers of various solid colors over boards; 200 copies of which are bound in marbled paper boards; 100 copies on Japan vellum in decorated Japan vellum wrappers over boards.
- The front cover design, used throughout the series, employs a border of intertwining vines and violet flowers framing the title, author and publisher's device. The design, by Charles Ricketts, is adapted from the Vale Press, 1896 edition of *Fifty Songs by Thomas Campion*. Also, a large red decorative initial is used on each ruled title page

LIST OF TITLES IN CHRONOLOGICAL ORDER OF PUBLICATION

1. The Hound of Heaven (154) 1908	4. Ode...Morning Christ's Nativity (272) 1909	7. Snow Bound... (358) 1911
2. Intimations of Immortality (175) 1908	5. Love in the Valley (221) 1910	8. Threnody and Other Poems (411) 1911
3. Rabbi Ben Ezra (319) 1909	6. Thyrsis and the Scholar-Gipsy (412) 1910	

THE IDEAL SERIES OF LITTLE MASTERPIECES

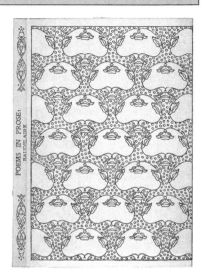

- 12 titles, 1906-1909. Number of copies printed unknown.
- Size: 14 x 9.5 cm. Type: 10 point old-style Roman within a Chiswick format. • Content: Prose poems.
- Price: regular, 50¢ each; Japan vellum, $1.
- Van Gelder copies are bound in wrappers over boards with "all-over" poppy design in gold on green background; Japan vellum copies with Japan vellum wrappers over boards using the same design in gold. The design is by Constance Karslake of the Guild of Women-Binders. The original design first appeared on a specially bound copy of Maurice de *Guérin's The Centaur and the Bacchante*, trans. by T. S. Moore (London: The Vale Press, 1899); see Anstruther, G. Elliot. *The Bindings of To-morrow A Record of the Work of the Guild of Women-Binders and of the Hampstead Bindery* (London: Printed for the Guild of Women-Binders, 1902, entry 6). The designs were copyrighted in England.
- Boxed sets were also available, e.g. "Prose Poems of Fiona Macleod" (3 vols.), or a set of the complete series.

LIST OF TITLES IN CHRONOLOGICAL ORDER OF PUBLICATION

1. The Sweet Miracle (393)	1906	5. Our Lady's Tumbler (280)	1906	9. Ann: A Memory (4)	1908
2. Poems in Prose [Wilde] (298)	1906	6. An Idyl of First Love (161)	1906	10. Three Legends of Christ Child (410)	1908
3. Hand and Soul (140)	1906	7. The Distant Country (90)	1907	11. Poems in Prose [Baudelaire] (299)	1909
4. The Wayfarer (433)	1906	8. Dream of Provence (93)	1907	12. Little Book for O'Mahony's... (208)	1909

THE QUARTO SERIES

- 10 titles from 1899-1904. • Size: 23 x 18.5 cm. • Type: 10 and 12 point old-style Roman.
- Content: Prose and poetry from the English Aesthetic School and its successors. • Price: Van Gelder, $5 for each volume; Japan vellum, $20 for each volume.
- Two distinct formats modeled on the Chiswick-Whittingham books: (1) the prose volumes with rules around each page, original head- & tail-pieces, and rubricated initials designed for Mosher by Edward B. Edwards, and (2) the poetry, without rules and with very ample margins.
- 450 copies printed on Van Gelder paper and bound in blue boards with white spines and paper spine labels. Japan vellum copies bound in Japan vellum wraps over boards with the spine label printed directly on the wrapper.

Limitation for special copies:

25 numbered, signed copies on Japan vellum for titles 1-6 and 10.
35 numbered, signed copies on Japan vellum for titles 7-8
15 numbered, signed copies on Japan vellum for title 9.
4 numbered, signed copies on Roman vellum in folded, unbound sheets for all titles.

LIST OF TITLES IN CHRONOLOGICAL ORDER OF PUBLICATION*

1. Laus Veneris [1] (190)	1899	5. Poems & Ballads. 2nd & 3rd [3] (297)	1902	9. Poems & Ballads. 1st Series [2] (296)	1904
2. Marius the Epicurean, Vol. I [7] (231)	1900	6. Poems by D. G. Rossetti [5] (294)	1902	10. Tristram of Lyonesse [10] (416)	1904
3. Marius the Epicurean, Vol. II [8] (232)	1900	7. The Renaissance [9] (321)	1902		
4. Songs before Sunrise [4] (364)	1901	8. Ballads & Sonnets [6] (16)	1903		

* Mosher listed these titles in a different sequence in his catalogue. His numbering of each book is given in brackets [ ] above.

LYRIC GARLAND SERIES

- 26 titles from 1903-1913.
- Size: 17.7 x 11.5 cm. • Type: 10-point Caslon old-style.
- Content: Lyrical poetry. • Price: Regular, 50¢ each; Japan vellum, $1.
- 950 copies on Van Gelder uniformly bound in gray boards with two-color paper labels on the front cover and the spine. Japan vellum copies bound in stiff Japan vellum boards with title printed directly onto the spine and front cover.
- A boxed set (slipcase with label) of Henley's Poetical Works (4 vols.) was also available from this series.

Limitation for special copies, first editions only:
100 printed on Japan vellum for titles 1-19
50 numbered on Japan vellum for titles 20-26.
10 numbered, signed on vellum for titles 1-8
7 numbered, signed on vellum for titles 9 & 10
5 numbered, signed on vellum for titles 11 & 12

LIST OF TITLES IN CHRONOLOGICAL ORDER OF PUBLICATION

1. The Land of Heart's Desire (186)	1903	10. Memories of President Lincoln (240)	1906	19. The Riding to Lithend... (324)	1910
2. In Hospital (165)	1903	11. Cynara: A Little Book of Verse (78)	1907	20. Lyrical Poems [Shelley] (226)	1910
3. Lyrics (227)	1903	12. A Little Book of XXIV Carols (213)	1907	21. Sonnets and Songs [Upson] (373)	1911
4. The Ballad of Reading Gaol (13)	1904	13. Echoes of Life and Death (99)	1908	22. Songs of the Glens of Antrim (369)	1911
5. A Song of Italy (360)	1904	14. Twenty-One Poems (417)	1908	23. Passages from Song Celestial (285)	1911
6. Ballads into English from Villon (17)	1904	15. A Branch of May (50)	1909	24. The Silence of Amor... (353)	1912
7. Little Garland of Celtic Verse (214)	1905	16. Rhymes and Rhythms (323)	1909	25. Lyrical Poems [Lyttleton] (225)	1912
8. Little Garland of Christmas Verse (215)	1905	17. Proverbs in Porcelain... (314)	1909	26. The Pierrot of the Minute... (289)	1913
9. Tares (401)	1906	18. London Voluntaries (218)	1910		

REPRINTS OF PRIVATELY PRINTED BOOKS

- 12 titles for 13 books from 1897-1902 (and 1916). • Size: Varies. • Type: Varies.
- Content: Select English works and translations. • Price: Regular, $1-$5; Japan vellum, $2-$20 (with *The Germ* being the highest priced book on Japan vellum).
- Size: Like the Miscellaneous Series, each title varies in binding design, size and number printed. For details see each individual entry in Section II.

LIST OF TITLES IN CHRONOLOGICAL ORDER OF PUBLICATION

1. Essays from the "Guardian" (104)	1897	5. Under the Microscope (423)	1899	9. A Year's Letters (442)	1901
2. The Heptalogia (147)	1898	6. Poems Master François Villon (302)	1900	10. Fragilia Labilia (116)	1902
3. The Germ: Thoughts Towards... (132)	1898	7. Fancy's Following (106)	1900	11. The Garland of Rachel (125)	1902
4. Wine Women and Song... (439)	1899	8. The Pilgrims of Hope... (290)	1901	12. Rubáiyát of Omar Khayyám (336)	1902
				13. Poems Master François Villon (303)	1916

MISCELLANEOUS SERIES

- 91 titles for 98 books from 1895-1923. • Size: Varies. • Type: Varies. • Content: Varies (seven titles are reprinted in new format).
- Price: Regular copies from 25¢ *(In Praise of Omar)* to $10 (1905 *The Kasîdah*), but the majority in the $1.50-$4 range; Japan vellum copies ranged from $1 *(In Praise of Omar* and the 1897 *Father Damien)* to $20 (1905 *The Kasîdah*), but the majority of the Japan vellum copies are in the $2-$5 range.
- Each title is treated differently, i.e., the size and number of each edition varies. For details on each title see each individual entry in Section II.
- This series includes books ranging in size from Barrie's *George Meredith* (14.5 x 9.5 cm.) to the largest quarto volume, the 1905 *The Kasîdah* (32.5 x 25.5 cm.). Almost every volume came in a printed plain paper dust wrapper and slipcase.

LIST OF TITLES IN CHRONOLOGICAL ORDER OF PUBLICATION

1. Homeward Songs by the Way (152) 1895	33. Rose Leaf and Apple Leaf (330) 1906	66. Andromache A Play... (3) 1913
2. From the Upanishads (122) 1897	34. Circum Praecordia... (71) 1906	67. Billy–True Story of a Canary... (42) 1914
3. Father Damien... (107) 1897	35. De Flagello Myrteo... (87) 1906	68. Billy and Hans... (43) 1914
4. In Praise of Omar (171) 1898	36. A Defence of Poetry (85) 1907	69. Books and the Quiet Life... (49) 1914
5. The Eclogues (100) 1898	37. The Immortal Hour... (164) 1907	70. The Jolly Beggars A Cantata (180) 1914
6. The Georgics–Vol. I (130) 1899	38. Ecclesiastes, or the Preacher (98) 1907	71. The Last Christmas Tree... (189) 1914
7. The Georgics–Vol. II (131) 1899	39. The Hound of Heaven... (155) 1908	72. Runes of Woman (339) 1915
8. Hand and Soul (139) 1899	40. The Time of Roses (413) 1908	73. Studies in Sentiment... (392) 1915
9. XVII Designs to Thornton's... (347) 1899	41. Poetical Works of Oscar Wilde (305) 1908	74. Sirenica (356) 1915
10. Our Lady's Tumbler... (279) 1900	42. A Vision of Love Revealed... (429) 1909	75. The Kasîdah... (183) 1915
11. Primavera... (311) 1900	43. The Land of Heart's Desire (187) 1909	76. At the Sign of the Lion... (8) 1916
12. Child Christopher & Goldilind... (61) 1900	44. Shelley An Essay (349) 1909	77. Magic in Kensington Gardens (230) 1916
13. Empedocles on Etna... (103) 1900	45. Mimma Bella: In Memory of... (243) 1909	78. To-morrow's Road... (414) 1916
14. The Story of David Gray (386) 1900	46. A Wayside Lute (434) 1909	79. A Quiet Road (317) 1916
15. The Blessed Damozel (47) 1901	47. A Vision of Giorgione... (428) 1910	80. "Ten O'Clock" A Lecture (403) 1916
16. Polonius: Collection of Wise... (306) 1901	48. Passages from Spencer (284) 1910	81. Dreams (94) 1917
17. Mimes... (242) 1901	49. Under a Fool's Cap... (422) 1910	82. By Bendemeer's Stream... (52) 1917
18. Poems of Ernest Dowson (301) 1902	50. Plato's Apology of Socrates... (292) 1910	83. Garlands and Wayfarings (126) 1917
19. Edward FitzGerald... (101) 1902	51. Salomé A Tragedy in One Act (341) 1911	84. Wine Women and Song... (440) 1918
20. The Silence of Amor... (352) 1902	52. George Meredith (128) 1911	85. For Those Who Love Music... (115) 1918
21. The Poems of Oscar Wilde (304) 1903	53. Poems [Francis Thompson] (295) 1911	86. The Present Crisis (310) 1918
22. Uncollected Essays (421) 1903	54. Earthwork Out of Tuscany... (97) 1911	87. Leaves of Grass (192) 1919
23. The House of Usna A Drama (160) 1903	55. Chrysanthema Gathered from... (69) 1911	88. Lucretius on Life and Death... (223) 1919
24. Homeward: Songs by the Way (153) 1904	56. Roses of Paestum (331) 1912	89. Theodore Roosevelt A Tribute (407) 1919
25. Intentions (174) 1904	57. The Renaissance Studies in... (322) 1912	90. George Meredith A Tribute (129) 1919
26. Memories of President Lincoln (238) 1904	58. Il Pesceballo: Opera in One... (288) 1912	91. By the Ionian Sea... (54) 1920
27. The Book of Heavenly Death (48) 1905	59. Memories of President Lincoln (239) 1912	92. "R.L.S." An Essay (325) 1920
28. Soul of Man Under Socialism (378) 1905	60. Amphora: A Collection... (2) 1912	93. "Ten O'Clock" A Lecture (404) 1920
29. Father Damien... (108) 1905	61. Songs of Adieu... (367) 1913	94. In Praise of Omar An Address (172) 1920
30. The Kasîdah... (182) 1905	62. The Sermon on the Mount (345) 1913	95. Private Papers of H. Ryecroft (313) 1921
31. Sayings of Lord Jesus Christ (343) 1905	63. The Growth of Love (138) 1913	96. Odes Sonnets & Lyrics [Keats] (274) 1922
32. Lecture on Eng. Renaissance (193) 1905	64. Dreamthorp A Book of Essays (95) 1913	97. A Free Man's Worship (119) 1923
	65. Ten Spiritual Designs... (405) 1913	98. The Children's Crusade (66) 1923

OLD WORLD SERIES

- 50 titles from 1895-1909. • Size: 18 x 10 cm. • Type: 8 point old-style Roman. • Content: Varies from poetry to prose. • Price: Van Gelder copies, $1 each; if bound in "Old-Style Blue Paper Boards" $1.25; copies in flexible leather binding, $1.50; Japan vellum copies, $2.50.
- 925 copies on Van Gelder paper and bound in flexible Japan vellum covers with yapp fore-edges, with tissue wrapper fastened with a gold seal. The customer could elect to have them bound in "old-style" blue paper boards with white paper spine and spine label. Copies were also available in full smooth flexible leather with gilt top page edges (first offered in 1904). The leather bindings have heavy foliated gilt design on the spine and a circular gilt "cloud-waxing crescent moon-star" vignette (originally designed by D. G. Rossetti for Swinburne's *Songs before Sunrise*. London: Ellis, 1871) on the front cover.
- 100 numbered copies on Japan vellum (sometimes this was reduced to only 25 or 50 copies) for at least the first edition, and bound in flexible Japan vellum boards. Not all later editions came with Japan vellum printings. It seems that Japan vellum copies were printed when supplies from a previous edition were low or exhausted.
- Head- and tail-pieces used throughout the series are stylistically very similar to those identified as being by Charles M. Jenckes (see the *Rubáiyát*, B334), and are closely allied in design to those of the Chiswick Press.

LIST OF TITLES IN CHRONOLOGICAL ORDER OF PUBLICATION

Title	Year	Title	Year	Title	Year
1. Rubáiyát of Omar Khayyám (334)	1895	18. The Tale of Chloe... (395)	1899	35. Songs of Innocence... (368)	1904
2. Aucassin and Nicolete (10)	1895	19. My Sister Henrietta (268)	1900	36. The Isle of Dreams (177)	1905
3. The New Life of Dante... (270)	1896	20. Underwoods (425)	1900	37. The Roadmender (326)	1905
4. Ballads & Lyrics of Old France (15)	1896	21. Sesame and Lilies... (346)	1900	38. Astrophel and Stella (7)	1905
5. The Kasîdah... (181)	1896	22. Letters of a Portuguese Nun (196)	1900	39. A House of Pomegranates (159)	1906
6. Sylvie: Souvenirs du Valois (394)	1896	23. The Poems of Edgar Allan Poe (300)	1901	40. A Shropshire Lad (350)	1906
7. Sonnets of Michael Angelo... (376)	1897	24. From the Hills of Dream... (121)	1901	41. Ariadne in Mantua (6)	1906
8. Helen of Troy... (146)	1897	25. Shakespeare's Sonnets (348)	1901	42. The Happy Prince... (143)	1907
9. Atalanta in Calydon A Tragedy (9)	1897	26. In Memoriam (168)	1902	43. Gaston de Latour... (127)	1907
10. Sonnets from the Portuguese (374)	1897	27. Pippa Passes (291)	1902	44. Ballades in Blue China... (14)	1907
11. The House of Life... (158)	1898	28. A Dream of John Ball (92)	1902	45. The Hour of Beauty (156)	1907
12. Modern Love & Other Poems (245)	1898	29. Pompilia (307)	1903	46. Liber Amoris (197)	1908
13. The Story of My Heart... (388)	1898	30. The Divine Adventure (91)	1903	47. Sonnets of the Wingless Hours (377)	1908
14. Underneath the Bough... (424)	1898	31. Deirdrê and The Sons of Usna (88)	1903	48. Pearl An English Vision... (287)	1908
15. The Story of Ida... (387)	1899	32. The City of Dreadful Night... (73)	1903	49. Silhouettes (354)	1909
16. A Child's Garden of Verses (67)	1899	33. The Love Sonnets of Proteus (222)	1904	50. Félise: A Book of Lyrics... (111)	1909
17. Monna Innominata... (246)	1899	34. Romance of Tristan & Iseult (327)	1904		

REPRINTS FROM "THE BIBELOT"

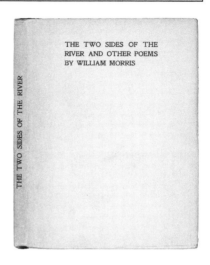

- 12 titles from 1897-1902.
- Size: 15.5 x 11.5 cm. • Type: 8-point old-style Roman.
- Content: Individual titles from the periodical, *The Bibelot.*
- Price: $4 each.
- All these titles were printed only on Japan vellum and bound in Japan vellum wraps over flexible boards. The number of volumes printed varies:

  25 copies on Japan vellum for titles 1-6, & 8.
  35 numbered on Japan vellum for titles 9-11.
  50 numbered on Japan vellum for titles 7 & 12.

LIST OF TITLES IN CHRONOLOGICAL ORDER OF PUBLICATION

1. Father Damien... (109)	1897	5. Gertha's Lovers A Tale (133)	1899	9. The Churches of North France (70)	1901
2. The Hollow Land A Tale (149)	1897	6. The Two Sides of the River... (419)	1899	10. Dead Love and Other Pieces (81)	1901
3. Death of Marlowe A Tragedy (83)	1898	7. A Song to David (361)	1900	11. Story of the Unknown Church (389)	1902
4. Tares: A Book of Verses (400)	1898	8. Golden Wings [&] Svend... (135)	1900	12. William Morris An Address... (435)	1902

THE VENETIAN SERIES

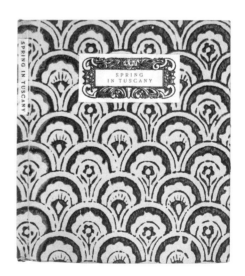

- 7 titles from 1910-1913. • Size: 15 x 12.5 cm.
- Type: 10 point old-style Roman.
- Content: Mostly poetry with Italian themes. • Price: 50¢ each; Japan vellum, $1 each.
- Printed on Van Gelder paper, but the number of copies printed is unknown. Bound in brightly designed Italian handmade paper wrappers, most likely provided through the Japan Paper Company, or allied firm.

  Copies were printed on Japan vellum, but again the number printed is not known. Some copies could be obtained in slipcase with label and decorated in a design used for the Brocade slipcases, or in a cabinet box decorated with one of the Italian papers. Japan vellum copies are bound in Japan vellum wraps over boards with printing of the spine title, and front cover title, directly on the Japan vellum (including the front cover's Renaissance design framing the title printed in red).

LIST OF TITLES IN CHRONOLOGICAL ORDER OF PUBLICATION

1. Siena (351)	1910	4. A Masque of Dead Florentines (234)	1911	7. Songs from an Italian Garden (365)	1913
2. Italy My Italy: IV Lyrics (179)	1910	5. The Sphinx (380)	1911		
3. Dante at Verona (79)	1910	6. Spring in Tuscany... (382)	1912		

LYRA AMERICANA SERIES

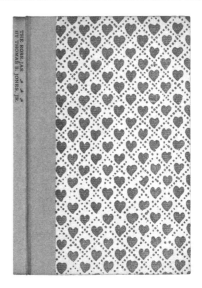

- 6 titles from 1915-1920.
- Size: 18 x 11 cm. • Type: 10 point Caslon old-style.
- Content: American lyrical poetry.
- Price: Regular, $1.50; Japan vellum $3.
- 450 printed on Van Gelder paper, uniformly bound with a colored Fabriano paper spine over patterned Italian handmade paper boards exhibiting a field of hearts and crisscrossing dots; title and author stamped directly on the spine in a darker color; page edges uncut, in slipcase; 25 numbered copies of each first edition on Japan vellum, bound in decorated Japan vellum boards repeating the same design used on the Van Gelder copies, but printed directly on the Japan vellum boards and spine. Title pages and colophons in red and black; Chiswick head- and tail pieces.

LIST OF TITLES IN CHRONOLOGICAL ORDER OF PUBLICATION

1. The Rose-Jar (329)	1915	3. The Flower from the Ashes... (114)	1915	5. The Voice in the Silence (431)	1917
2. A Handful of Lavender (141)	1915	4. Lyrics from a Library (229)	1917	6. A Branch of May: Poems (51)	1920

THE BIBELOT SERIES

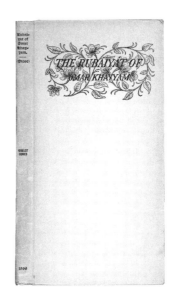

- 10 titles: 1893-1897. • Content: Series of poetical reprints. • Price: Regular, $1; Japan vellum, $2.50.
- Size: 21 x 10 cm. • Type: Elzevir Italic Body 8 typeface. All pages are numbered using Roman numerals.
- 925 on Van Gelder for titles 7-10
  725 copies on Van Gelder for titles 1-6
  25 on Japan vellum for titles 1-4
  50 on Japan vellum for titles 5-6
  100 on Japan vellum for 7-10
- Mosher states in his 1902 catalogue: "The Bibelot Series is modeled on the Aldine format, and like those early books of the great Italian printers, each volume is printed in Italic type throughout. It is the only series of Italic books ever printed in this country..."–p. 41. According to Arthur Stedman in *The Dial* (Dec. 16, 1893), Mosher "got this idea from reading Pollard's *Last Words on the History of the Title-page*;" however, credit must also be given to The Bodley Head book designed by Charles Ricketts, John Gray's *Silverpoints* (1893), the size and format which Mosher most certainly copied.
- "Original cover design[s]" according to Mosher's catalogues, bound in flexible Japan vellum covers.

LIST OF TITLES IN CHRONOLOGICAL ORDER OF PUBLICATION

1. Songs of Adieu: A Little Book... (366)	1893	5. Michael Angelo... His Sonnets (241)	1895	9. Long Ago (219)	1897
2. Old World Lyrics... (275)	1893	6. The Blessed Damozel... (46)	1895	10. An Italian Garden (178)	1897
3. Rubáiyát of Omar Khayyám... (332)	1894	7. Rubáiyát of Omar Khayyám (333)	1896		
4. Félise: A Book of Lyrics... (110)	1894	8. Defence of Guenevere... (84)	1896		

THE VEST POCKET SERIES

- 25 titles from 1899-1913.
- Size: 14.5 x 7 cm. • Type: 8 point old-style Roman. • Content: Poetry and prose. • Price: Regular copy in blue wrappers, 30¢; in limp cloth, 50¢; in flexible leather, 75¢; and printed on Japan vellum, $1.
- Printed on Van Gelder paper bound in printed blue wraps over boards. Copies could also be had in green flexible hemp cloth with gilt on spine and front cover, or in flexible full green leather bindings with the same gilt stamping as the cloth bindings, but with the top pages edges gilt and a gilt caduceus on the back cover, designed by Bruce Rogers. The number of copies printed is unknown; however, the printing must have been high. If we can believe an advertisement in the May 15, 1900 *Goose Quill*, 15,000 copies of the Vest Pocket *Rubáiyát* had been sold to date.
- The Japan vellum copies were bound in printed Japan vellum wraps over boards which were printed with the same designs as the Van Gelder covers. The four cover designs used throughout the series were created by Frederic Goudy, and are different but closely interrelated, and consist of black rectilinear rules interlaced at each corner. The rules enclose intertwining vines printed in red (see Bruckner, 48-49).
- One could order boxed sets of what Mosher called the "Nature Thought Series" (4 vols.) and Stevenson's Essays (4 vols.).

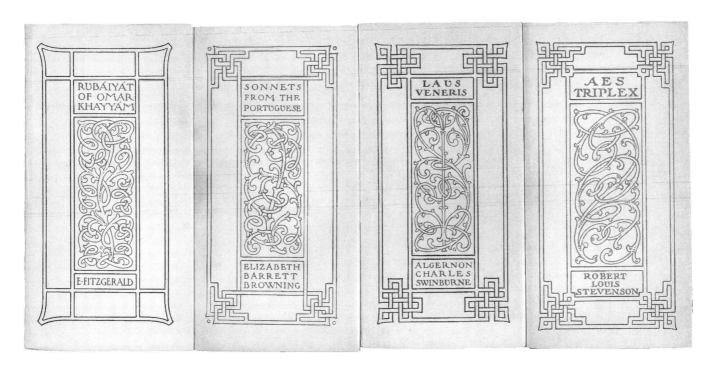

LIST OF TITLES IN CHRONOLOGICAL ORDER OF PUBLICATION

1. Rubáiyát of Omar Khayyám (335)	1899	10. An Apology for Idlers... (5)	1905	19. Lyric Love (224)	1910
2. Sonnets from the Portuguese (375)	1900	11. Little Book Nature Thoughts (212)	1906	20. A Defence of Poetry (86)	1910
3. Laus Veneris (191)	1900	12. Little Book Nature Themes (209)	1906	21. Will o' the Mill (437)	1911
4. Aes Triplex (1)	1902	13. Crabbed Age and Youth (76)	1907	22. Sister Benvenuta... (357)	1911
5. Little Book Nature Thoughts (210)	1903	14. Stars of Thought (383)	1907	23. The Flight of the Princess... (113)	1912
6. Aucassin and Nicolete (11)	1903	15. Little Book Nature Thoughts (211)	1908	24. In Praise of Old Gardens (170)	1912
7. Virginibus Puerisque (427)	1904	16. Toward Humanity (415)	1908	25. From the Upanishads (123)	1913
8. Quattrocentisteria... (316)	1904	17. The Child in the House (63)	1909		
9. The Pageant of Summer (283)	1905	18. The Lost Joy & Other Dreams (220)	1909		

— END OF THE FOURTEEN SERIES —

OTHER MOSHER PUBLICATIONS

In addition to the fourteen series, there were 61 private printings, the little literary periodical *(The Bibelot)*, the annual book catalogues, and books printed on vellum for private distribution.

The private printings of The Mosher Press began in 1892 with Mosher's own poem, "Inscription for a Fireplace" for private distribution. It became Mosher's practice to occasionally print something he only wished to distribute to friends and colleagues, rather than to sell through his catalogues. These special printings include:

Celtic-A Study in Spiritual History (1901)
Concerning a Pilgrimage to the Grave of Edward Fitzgerald (1902)
The Land of Heart's Desire (1903)
A Bibliographical List of the Editions of Fitzgerald's Rubáyát (1907)
Pearl (1908)

Lyrics and Sonnets (1909)
The Works of Arthur Symons (1912)
Thomas Bird Mosher-An Appreciation (1914)
An Appreciation [of Thomas S. Jones] (1917)

In 1898 he began to offer vanity press printing for clients. Anyone wishing to have their book printed (or the book of a friend or loved one) could do so, as long as they could afford it. He began with *Collectors & Collecting* for Edwin Bolles, however, he first announced in his 1914 The Mosher Books catalogue that "in 1912 Mr. Mosher began the issue of limited editions under the imprint of The Mosher Press... Such work stands outside the ordinary commercial bookmaking..." Why he chose 1912 as his starting point is uncertain, since he had clearly printed 13 items before that year. It may be because the "Privately Printed Editions" he offered for sale in the catalogue only began with 1912. Other privately printed editions include: 4, 9, 13-19, 21-25, 27-32, 35-37, 40-43, 47, 49-53, 56, 59, and 61 below.

One exceptional client of Mosher's was the Pittsburgh insurance executive, Edward A. Woods, who lived in Sewickley, PA. He personally selected books to be printed and distributed during the Christmas season from 1913 to 1923 (and even continued to have books privately printed after Mosher's death). Many of these books still contain the special presentation slip from Woods and his wife, and can be located in the chart below: 26, 38, 39, 44, 45, 48, 55, 58, and 60.

Mosher also privately co-published two books on vellum and placed his name, and his partner's name, in the colophon. *The Rubáiyát of Omar Khayyám* (3 below) was co-published by Mosher and Emilie Grigsby. Mosher did the same thing with Gertrude Cowdin in printing *The Casket of Opals* in 1900 (5 below). The financial and other arrangements surrounding the printing and distribution of these books remain unknown.

Lastly, it should be added that some of these titles either previously appeared in the Mosher canon (e.g., 3, 38, 44, 48, & 60), or would become titles in the fourteen series after being privately published (e.g., 24, 35, & 45).

PRIVATE PRINTINGS OF THE MOSHER PRESS

- 61 titles from 1892-1923.
- Size & Printings: Differs from title to title (see individual entries in Section II for details). • Type: Varies.

LIST OF TITLES IN CHRONOLOGICAL ORDER OF PUBLICATION

1. Inscription for a Fireplace (173)	1892	21. Fragments. Volume One (117)	1912	41. In Memoriam [Bell] (167)	1917
2. Collectors & Collecting... (74)	1898	22. Tam O'Shanter–A Tale (399)	1913	42. Masterpieces A Dobbs Book... (236)	1917
3. Rubáiyát of Omar Khayyám (337)	1899	23. A Walled Garden... (432)	1913	43. Sources of the Power of Music (379)	1917
4. In Measured Language (166)	1899	24. The Rose-Jar (328)	1913	44. Our Lady's Tumbler... (281)	1917
5. The Casket of Opals (56)	1900	25. Relation of School and Home (320)	1913	45. The Present Crisis (309)	1917
6. Celtic A Study in Spiritual... (58)	1901	26. De Amicitia (82)	1913	46. An Appreciation [of T. S. Jones] (445)	1917
7. Concerning a Pilgrimage to... (75)	1902	27. Ode to Gertrude... (273)	1913	47. Songs With Tears (372)	1919
8. The Land of Heart's Desire (188)	1903	28. On the Heights... (276)	1913	48. Happy Prince & Other Tales (144)	1919
9. Little Willie (216)	1904	29. Songs of the Susquehanna (370)	1914	49. A Carlyle Calendar... (55)	1919
10. Bibliographical List of Editions (40)	1907	30. Sprays of Shamrock (381)	1914	50. Autumn Leaves from Maple... (12)	1919
11. Pearl (286)	1908	31. Songs & Sonnets [Ballard] (362)	1914	51. The Tender Memories (402)	1920
12. Lyrics and Sonnets [Upson] (228)	1909	32. From the Foothills (120)	1914	52. Songs of Susquehanna (371)	1920
13. Orations and Addresses... (278)	1911	33. Thomas Bird Mosher... (408)	1914	53. Sanctuary: Poems (342)	1920
14. The Norseman A Drama... (271)	1912	34. The King of the Golden River (184)	1914	54. In Memoriam [Tennyson] (169)	1920
15. Masterpieces selected from... (235)	1912	35. The Voice in the Silence (430)	1915	55. The Cricket on the Hearth (77)	1921
16. Songs Before Birth (363)	1912	36. Thé Dansant in the Bowery (406)	1915	56. Verses and a Dream (426)	1922
17. On the Wings of the Mind (277)	1912	37. The Holy Jumpers (151)	1915	57. The Celestial Country (57)	1922
18. Billy (41)	1912	38. Will o' the Mill (438)	1915	58. Young King & Other Tales (444)	1922
19. Gabriel A Pageant of Vigil (124)	1912	39. A Christmas Carol (68)	1916	59. Heart's Ease A Little Book... (145)	1922
20. Works of Arthur Symons... (441)	1912	40. Playing the Tank Towns... (293)	1916	60. Rubáiyát of Omar Khayyám (338)	1923
				61. Twice Told Tales (418)	1923

THE BIBELOT

- 240 monthly issues comprising 20 volumes from 1895-1915.
  Plus 2 indices: 1906 for Vols. 1-12, 1915 for Vols. 1-20. • Size: 15.5 x 11.5 cm.

- Content: Poetry, poem-sequences, one-act plays, single acts from longer dramas, essays, short stories, prose poems, short bibliographies, and introductions (mostly by the editor).

- An original contract found at the University of San Francisco indicates that the standing order to the printer was 5,000 of which 1000 were delivered in sheets for later issue in sets. *The Bibelot's* circulation peaked at about 4,000 in 1907-09, according to an interview Dane Yorke conducted with Mosher's assistant, Flora M. Lamb, on Sept. 22, 1941.

- Each monthly issue was bound in blue printed wraps and contained advertisements which were later taken out for customers who ordered the year's issues bound into one volume, or who ordered a complete set of 21 volumes (including index) bound as described below. The effect of the black printing on the *turchino* (i.e., medium colored) blue wraps is heightened by the additional use of red ink for the periodical's general title, the specific issue's title and author selection, price, and the boxed Florentine lily on the back cover. According to Mosher's notices sent to subscribers (found at Bowdoin College), "the January number is not issued before the 15th of that month. All other numbers are sent out on or about the 25th of each month preceding date of issue."

- The red printer's device on the back cover of each blue wrapper is the Florentine lily of the distinguished Giunta printing family of Venice (but of Florentine origin). A reproduction of this device appears in *The Century Guild Hobby Horse* (1888), Vol. III, between pages 56/57, taken from a Roman missal printed by Lucantonio dc Giunta at Venice, 1509. Mosher had a copy of this volume of the *Hobby Horse* in his library. He also had a copy of Pollard's *Last Words on the History of the Title-page* (London: J. C. Nimmo, 1891) in which the same device appears opposite pp. 25 & 26. The initials "L" and 'A" on either side of the lily were dropped by Mosher, and his replication of the device retains the off-center placement of the lily within its rectangular frame. Much of the detail of the *Hobby Horse* reproduction has been lost; after all, Mosher's is a reproduction of a reproduction.

- Regular sets of *The Bibelot* were bound in blue boards with white spines, or in full blue library buckram. One hundred sets were specially bound in red, green, or brown half crushed levant with gilt tops and uncut edges for $125 a set. One could also order extra tooling and inlays on the spines for $150 a set. Each set came with an index volume containing a personally signed photo-gravure portrait of Mosher, and a numbered certificate on Japan vellum, also signed by Mosher.

- Japan vellum copies of *The Bibelot* were kept to a bare minimum with only 12 copies on Japan vellum for Volumes I-XV (1895-1909), and reduced to only 6 copies from Volume XVI (1910) to Volume XX (1914). The first Index Volume covering Volumes I-XII was limited to 12 copies on Japan vellum, and the complete Index Volume (which became Volume XXI of the full set of *The Bibelot*) was limited to 8 copies on Japan vellum. The Japan vellum copies contain all the contents of the original monthly issues, including the advertisement pages, order blanks, and preview fall listing of The Mosher Books.

- Twelve individual monthly issues were bound in blue boards with cover labels, but this was done as a marketing strategy after Mosher's death, and is discussed in entry FL12 of the "Checklist of The Mosher Press Publications Under Flora MacDonald Lamb & Mrs. Mosher, 1924-1941" (Section III).

- Only 6 illustrations accompanied the whole set, loosely laid in (see Section II, entries 21-24).

- *Note:* Authentic sets of *The Bibelot* should not be confused with the New York reprint done by Wm. H. Wise & Co. in 1925. For further information on this reprint of *The Bibelot*, see the Mosher entry under "Bibliography of Thomas Bird Mosher" in Section V.

- Bibliographic identification for entries in *The Bibelot* include Wright, 161-162; Chielens, 63-65; and Mott IV, 415-426.

THE DEVELOPMENT OF MOSHER'S ANNUAL CATALOGUES

- **31 catalogues** from 1893-1923 were issued both in paper wrappers and in boards with labels, and were generally mailed out in October of each year. According to a letter from Mosher to a Mr. Grover dated Oct. 23, 1905 (University of San Francisco), Mosher maintained a mailing list of about 17,000 customers.

- The catalogues start with Mosher's first *List of Books* in 1893-94 (15.3 x 10.1 cm.). Although Hatch did not include this as a catalogue in his bibliography, Mosher himself called it "the first catalogue I ever issued... In 1891-2 I simply had announcements of the only volumes I had issued up to that date. But in 1893 I began with an 8 page affair which is a very rare thing to turn up" (Mosher to T. N. McKean, Nov. 8, 1918). One of the interesting features of this catalogue is the publisher's device printed in red on the front cover. This device takes the form of a bookseller's hanging sign with fancy wrought iron work around all sides and a small book atop. Interestingly enough, this image is very similar to a Bodley Head logo pictured in advertisements accompanying their books. Mosher also used this image on his earliest stationary. The design is signed "R•". Only two designers with last names beginning with an "R" were known to be working with Mosher at this early date, Bruce Rogers and Frank Rathbun.

- The 1894 *List of Books* was also a rather ephemeral announcement of 16 pages and measuring about 18.5 x 9.5 cm. with light gray printed wraps. A distinctive feature of this catalogue is the first use of the double dolphins holding a book with their tails. Mosher would use this image on his stationary, and on the title pages of the Old World Series, Little Masterpieces Series, Vest Pocket Series, and in some of the books in the Miscellaneous Series.

- The 1895-1901 catalogues are basically uniform in size, roughly 18 x 9 cm. From a cover design perspective, the most notable are the 1897 cover designed by Frank R. Rathbun, the Lucien Pissarro cover of 1898, and the 1899 & 1900 cover designs by Frederic Goudy.

- The 1902-1904 catalogues have a larger trim size following a long and narrow format of about 23 x 12 cm. Beginning with the 1903 catalogue, Mosher changes the title of his catalogues from "A List of Books..." to a distinctive and final name, "The Mosher Books." Graphically speaking, the most interesting cover is that of 1904 with a design by Charles Ricketts of the Vale Press.

- From 1905-1915 Mosher issued catalogues (size of about 24 x 15 cm.) which contain some of his best and most appealing work, both from the literary perspective of Mosher's forewords, and from the angle of graphic design. The most notable covers are the 1906 "Silverpoints" by Charles Ricketts, the 1908 and 1909 covers by Earl Stetson Crawford, and the 1913-15 covers with a border design initially created by Frederic Goudy for the first issues in the Vest Pocket Series.

- Beginning with the 1916 catalogue, the pressure of adverse conditions resulting from the World War and its consequences are quite visible. The 1916 catalogue scales down to 21 x 13 cm., and all subsequent issues from 1917-1923 are in the much reduced format of 21 x 11 cm. These catalogues reuse cover borders created by Frederic Goudy, including the 1917 cover which employs a whole Goudy design and is signed "G". As Mosher stated in the 1917 foreword, "It is with regret that owing to the excessive advance in the price of paper, I am no longer able to send out my unique Catalogues as in former years. Instead, I have preferred to put all possible value into the books I publish."

MOSHER BOOKS PRINTED ON VELLUM

The books listed below were printed on vellum, sometimes referred to as "Roman vellum" (imported from Rome, Italy), English "classic vellum" (calf skin) or its American equivalent. Vellum is the untanned, de-greased and specially treated skin of a calf, kid, or lamb, at times procured from an unborn or still-born animal. The skin is stretched and polished with alum and smoothed with pumice. Throughout the centuries it has been the practice of some printers and publishers to produce a few copies of a book on vellum, especially if the book is of importance, typographically pleasing, or for special presentation. It should be noted that vellum is costly and not the easiest printing medium, but it usually accepts a printer's ink better than most papers do. A thicker gauge vellum was often used for bookbinding. The skin remains unsplit and the skin's pores and vein marks can be seen on the surface.

Mosher had forty-seven of his books printed on vellum, usually from four to ten copies each. With one exception, these copies were not advertised in his catalogues and were reserved for particularly wealthy clients such as William Henry Poor of New York City. The sale price of these volumes was not advertised, but prices discovered on just a few give us some idea. Accompanying a November 19, 1901 letter from William Henry Poor to Mosher (Houghton Library), a note lists several vellum books and the price paid by Poor. Each of the Quarto Series volumes cost $150; the copy of *Intentions*, $75; the smaller Lyric Garland Series books went for $15 each; and *Father Damien* for $25. Besides the Quarto Series, one of the most expensive vellum productions known is the 1905 *The Kasîdah* which is listed at $100. The only vellum book Mosher ever publicly listed was in his 1902 catalogue (p. 36), the facsimile edition of the *Rubáiyát* tersely described as: 10 COPIES ON PURE VELLUM (ALL SUBSCRIBED).

It should be noted that Mosher printed a limited number of *éditions de luxe* on Japan vellum. Japan vellum is not vellum at all, but a paper hand-made in Japan from the fibers of a shrub distantly related to the Mulberry tree. It is somewhat stiff like vellum, hence the name.

After 1913 Mosher discontinued the practice of printing a few copies of his books on vellum. The price of vellum had become prohibitive, its availability lessened (especially during the war years), and the pool of primary customers for this material was diminishing. Mosher's publishing program was also beginning to slow down. Nevertheless, it is still a remarkable achievement that forty-seven of his books, from 1898-1913, were printed on vellum. Few other American publishers or printers even approached this record. The Grolier Club, a bastion for the well-to-do collector in America, only published thirty-one titles on vellum between 1884-1923 (see *The Grolier Club, 1884-1984. Its Library, Exhibitions, and Publications*. NY: The Grolier Club, 1984), and most of these were 2-3 copies per title. Mosher's chief rivals in vellum printing were the British private presses: Kelmscott, Ashendene, Doves, and Essex House.

* * * * * * * *

The following information was garnered from seven sources: (1) the Hatch bibliography, (2) the Sheean typescript, (3) the Lamb typescript, (4) the sale catalogue of the *Library of the Late Thomas Bird Mosher and Examples of His Own Publications – Many printed on Vellum*. Part One. New York: Parke-Bernet Galleries, Inc., May 10 &11, 1948, (5) the sale catalogues of *The Library of Henry W. Poor of New York City*. New York: The Anderson Auction Company, 1908-1909, (6) The Harry Elkins Widener catalogue, and (7) the examination of actual copies. Following each title is the cross reference to the entry number in the Section II bibliography.

—1898—

1. *The Germ*. 1898. (Reprints of Privately Printed Books) 8vo. 4 copies on Roman vellum bound in vellum wrappers, with proof, on vellum, of the cover design used on the wrapper, signed by Mosher. In a March 21, 1898 letter to Emilie Grigsby of New York (University of San Francisco), Mosher mentions this "will be the first book ever so done in Maine, and quite likely the only one." (B132)

2. *In Praise of Omar*. 1898. (Miscellaneous Series) Square 16mo. 4 copies on American vellum, in sheets laid in a vellum wrapper with title printed on front. (B171)

—1899—

3. *Rubáiyát of Omar Khayyám.* 1899. (Privately Printed) 4to. 10 copies on Classic vellum, printed by Thomas B. Mosher and Emilie Grigsby. Full flexible vellum binding with silk ties, signed by Mosher. (B337)

4. *Laus Veneris.* 1899. (Quarto Series) 4to. 4 copies on Roman vellum, signed by Mosher. Bound in full flexible vellum with silk ties. (B190)

5. *Wine Women and Song.* 1899. (Reprints from Privately Printed Books) Small 4to. 4 copies on Roman vellum, signed by Mosher. Full flexible vellum cover with ties; with proofs on vellum of the cover design used on the wrapper. (B439)

—1900—

6. *The Poems of Master François Villon.* 1900. (Reprints of Privately Printed Books) Small 4to. 4 copies on Roman vellum, signed by Mosher. Bound in full flexible vellum with ties. Copies may have a loosely inserted "Omitted Lines." Technically speaking, the latter is not a Mosher production, though Mosher may have had something to do with it. For further information, see the discussion under the entry in the bibliography. (B302)

7. *Fancy's Following.* 1900. (Reprints of Privately Printed Books) 8vo. 4 copies on American vellum, signed by Mosher. Bound in flexible vellum with grey silk ties; gilt title and date on spine. Vellum cover and spine decorations bound in at rear. Boxed. (B106)

8. *The Casket of Opals.* 1900. (Privately Printed) 8vo. 15 copies on Roman vellum. Printed by Thomas B. Mosher and Gertrude Cowdin. Copies were bound in flexible vellum with brown silk ties and title in gilt on the spine, in board case. (B56)

9. *Our Lady's Tumbler.* 1900 (Miscellaneous Series) 8vo. 4 copies on American vellum, signed by Mosher. Bound in Classic vellum with grey ties; title gilt stamped on spine. Vellum proof of the cover design used on the wrapper bound in the back. (B279)

10. *Primavera: Poems by Four Authors.* 1900. (Miscellaneous Series) 8vo. 4 copies on Classic vellum, signed by Mosher (thick gauge vellum pages). Bound in full green flexible vellum made by the same firm that supplied William Morris; green silk ties. Title gilt stamped on spine. Vellum printed cover and spine design placed at back. (B311)

11. *The Story of David Gray.* 1900. (Miscellaneous Series) Small 4to. 4 copies on Roman vellum, signed by Mosher. Bound in flexible vellum with silk ties. At the end of volume there is a proof on vellum of the cover and backstrip designs for the volume as issued in wrappers. (B386)

12. *Marius the Epicurean.* Volume I. 1900. (Quarto Series) 4to. 4 copies on Roman vellum, signed by Mosher. Loose folded sheets, as issued, uncut, partly unopened, in board case. (B231)

13. *Marius the Epicurean.* Volume II. 1900. (Quarto Series) 4to. 4 copies on Roman vellum, signed by Mosher. Loose folded sheets, as issued, uncut, partly unopened, in board case. (B232)

—1901—

14. *Polonius.* 1901. (Miscellaneous Series) Small 4to. 4 copies on Roman vellum, signed by Mosher. Issued in folded sheets, unbound. (B306)

15. *Mimes.* 1901. (Miscellaneous Series) Crown 8vo. 6 copies on Roman vellum, signed by Mosher. Vellum wrappers over boards with original color-printed design on front cover and spine. In printed dust wrapper and board slip-case. (B242)

16. *Songs before Sunrise.* 1901. (Quarto Series) 4to. 4 copies on Roman vellum, signed by Mosher. Loose folded sheets, as issued, uncut, unopened, in board case. (B364)

17. *The Pilgrims of Hope.* 1901. (Reprints from Privately Printed Books) 4to. 4 copies on Roman vellum, signed by Mosher. Loose folded sheets, as issued, uncut, unopened, unbound. (B290)

18. *The Blessed Damozel.* 1901. (Miscellaneous Series) Square 16mo. 10 copies on Roman vellum, signed by Mosher. Vellum wrappers over boards with silk ties, uncut, partly unopened. (B47)

—1902—

19. *Rubáiyát of Omar Khayyám.* 1902. (Reprints of Privately Printed Books) 4to. 10 copies on Roman vellum, signed by Mosher. Copies 1-5 have the facsimile frontispiece and an additional, original etching on India paper (of which only 25 proofs were printed) of the frontispiece by Edwin Edwards. Copies 6-10 have only the facsimile frontispiece by Edwards. Bound in full flexible vellum with green silk ties. Spine is gilt stamped with the title running lengthwise at the top and date "1859" in Roman numerals along the lower part of the spine. (B336)

20. *Poems and Ballads.* 2nd and 3rd Series. 1902. (Quarto Series) 4to. 4 copies on Roman vellum, signed by Mosher. Loose folded sheets, as issued, unbound. (B297)

21. *Fragilia Labilia.* 1902. (Reprints of Privately Printed Books) 8vo. 5 copies on Roman vellum, signed by Mosher. Loose folded sheets, as issued, unbound. (B116)

22. *Poems by Dante Gabriel Rossetti.* 1902. (Quarto Series) 4to. 4 copies on Roman vellum, signed by Mosher. Loose folded sheets. as issued, unbound. (B294)

23. *The Poems of Ernest Dowson.* 1902 (Miscellaneous Series) Small 4to. 4 copies on Roman vellum in folded sheets, as issued, unbound. (B301)

24. *The Renaissance: Studies in Art and Poetry.* 1902. (Quarto Series) 4 copies on Roman vellum, signed by Mosher. Loose folded sheets, as issued, unbound. (B321)

—1903—

25. *Ballads & Sonnets.* 1903. (Quarto Series) 4to. 4 copies on Roman vellum, signed by Mosher. Loose folded sheets, as issued, unbound. (B16)

26. *The Poems of Oscar Wilde.* 1903. (Miscellaneous Series) Small 4to. 6 copies on Roman vellum, signed by Mosher. Loose folded sheets, as issued, unbound. (B304)

27. *The Land of Heart's Desire.* 1903. (Lyric Garland Series) Fcap 8vo. 10 copies on Roman vellum, signed by Mosher. Some bound in full flexible vellum, some in folded sheets, boxed. (B186)

28. *Lyrics.* 1903. (Lyric Garland Series) Fcap 8vo. 10 copies on Roman vellum, signed by Mosher. Bound in full flexible vellum. (B227)

29. *In Hospital.* 1903. (Lyric Garland Series) Fcap 8vo. 10 copies on Roman vellum, signed by Mosher. Bound in full flexible vellum. (B165)

—1904—

30. *Intentions.* 1904. (Miscellaneous Series) Small 4to. 6 copies on Roman vellum, signed by Mosher. Loose folded sheets, as issued, unbound. (B174)

31. *Ballad of Reading Gaol.* 1904. (Lyric Garland Series) Fcap 8vo. 10 copies on Roman vellum, signed by Mosher. Bound in full flexible vellum. (B13)

32. *Tristram of Lyonesse.* 1904. (Quarto Series) 4to. Two sets of 4 copies (i.e., 8 copies in all) on Roman vellum, signed by Mosher. Four were in loose folded sheets, as issued, unbound, and four were bound in flexible vellum with silk ties. The Lamb typescript includes the following entry: "Tristram (only) 4, 4to, flexible vellum silk ties, Roman vellum" and includes these additional four copies in a frequency chart as a second quarto printing for the year. This strongly suggests that four additional copies (limited to just the title poem) were printed on Roman vellum and bound in vellum. The printers copy of the source text also notes: "4 skin [and] 4 of Tristan only skin." Indeed, two copies on pure vellum have been located, both of which bear the same limitation number, No. 4 (Bancroft Library and Bishop Collection). The pagination for the Bancroft copy is *viii* preliminary leaves, 193 pp.; the Bishop copy is [*xii*], 389 pp. With the addition of the "Tristram (only)" copies, the vellum count for this book is brought to 8 copies: 4 of the complete volume, and 4 with just the Tristram poem. Some bibliographers may be inclined, as Flora Lamb was, to count this as another quarto book on vellum, which would bring the total count of books Mosher published on vellum to 48. (B416)

33. *Ballads Done Into English from the French of François Villon.* 1904. (Lyric Garland Series) Fcap 8vo. 10 copies on Roman vellum, signed by Mosher. Bound in full flexible vellum. (B17)

34. *A Song of Italy.* 1904. (Lyric Garland Series) Fcap 8vo. 10 copies on Roman vellum, signed by Mosher. Bound in full flexible vellum. (B360)

—1905—

35. *The Book of Heavenly Death.* 1905. (Miscellaneous Series) Small 4to. 5 copies on Roman vellum, signed by Mosher. Bound in full flexible vellum with silk ties, uncut, partly unopened. (B48)

36. *A Little Garland of Celtic Verse.* 1905. (Lyric Garland Series) Fcap 8vo. 10 copies on Roman vellum, signed by Mosher. Copies bound in full flexible vellum, and unbound, in sheets, as published, uncut, partly unopened, in board case. (B214)

37. *A Little Garland of Christmas Verse.* 1905 (Lyric Garland Series) Fcap 8vo. 10 copies on Roman vellum, signed by Mosher. Copies bound in full flexible vellum, and unbound, in sheets, as published, uncut, partly unopened, in board case. (B215)

38. *The Kasîdah.* 1905. (Miscellaneous Series) Royal 4to. 5 copies on Roman vellum, signed by Mosher. Issued in sheets, and also available in full flexible vellum with gold stamping and silk ties. The Norman Strouse copy at The Bancroft Library, in a modern commissioned binding by Roger Powell, was originally in unbound sheets. (B182)

39. *Father Damien.* 1905. (Miscellaneous Series) 4to. 4 copies on Roman vellum, signed by Mosher. Bound in full flexible vellum with silk ties. The Harry Elkins Widener catalogue, entry 116, describes this as bound in "white vellum paper [sic] wrappers, uncut and unopened, with the original blue ties." Examination of this copy shows it to be bound in flexible vellum with grey ties, title in gilt running along spine. The limitation number is altered to look like copy #1. (B108)

—1906—

40. *Tares.* 1906. (Lyric Garland Series) Fcap 8vo. 7 copies on Roman vellum, signed by Mosher. Copies bound in full flexible vellum, and unbound, in sheets, as published, uncut, partly unopened, in board case. (B401)

41. *Memories of President Lincoln and Other Lyrics of the War.* 1906. (Lyric Garland Series) Fcap 8vo. 7 copies on Roman vellum, signed by Mosher. In sheets, uncut and unopened, as issued, in board case. Some copies were bound in full flexible vellum. On one copy Mosher wrote "This copy has portrait of W.W. on vellum & facsimile of his h.w. [handwriting] inserted. T.B.M. The only copy with these additions, the two having been made for Bk. of IU.S. (the 5 on vellum), & this one left over of the h.w. facsimile. Of the portrait 10 only were done by E. Bierstadt on vellum. Jan. 10, 1907." (B240)

42. *Rose Leaf and Apple Leaf.* 1906. (Miscellaneous Series) 8vo. 5 copies on Roman vellum, signed by Mosher. In sheets as issued, uncut, partly unopened, in board case. Some copies bound in full flexible vellum. Note: The Wm. H. Poor catalogue (Part V, #834) lists this as 7 copies on vellum, but all other sources, including Sheean and Lamb, list 5 copies on vellum. (B330)

<h3 style="text-align:center">—1907—</h3>

43. *A Little Book of XXIV Carols.* 1907. (Lyric Garland Series) Fcap 8vo. 5 copies on Roman vellum, signed by Mosher. In sheets as issued, uncut, partly unopened, in board case. Some copies bound in full flexible vellum. (B213)

44. *Cynara.* 1907. (Lyric Garland Series) Fcap 8vo. 5 copies on Roman vellum, signed by Mosher. In sheets as issued, uncut, unopened, in board case. Some copies bound in full flexible vellum. (B78)

<h3 style="text-align:center">—1912—</h3>

45. *Memories of President Lincoln.* 1912. (Miscellaneous Series) 10 copies on Roman vellum, signed by Mosher. Bound in classic vellum with gold stamping. Mrs. Mosher's own copy, now at Arizona State University, is bound in the full flexible vellum with ties. (B239)

<h3 style="text-align:center">—1913—</h3>

46. *Songs of Adieu.* 1913. (Miscellaneous Series) Narrow 8vo. 5 copies on Roman vellum. Bound in classic vellum covered boards, uncut with green silk ties, in board case. (B367)

47. *De Amicitia.* 1913. (Privately Printed) Small 4to. 1 copy printed for Mr. Mosher on pure vellum and bound in "binder's vellum" with silk ties. (B82)

THE MOSHER PUBLISHER'S DEVICES

The famous American book designer, Bruce Rogers, twice made reference to Mosher as "the Aldus of the XIX Century," although that claim would need to be qualified, for certainly the firm of William Pickering (and his son, Basil Montagu Pickering), held that place of honor for most of the 1800's. Perhaps Mosher could be dubbed an American Aldus, or the Aldus of the American *fin-de-siècle* and into the 20th century. It should be noted that Mosher was not the first American publisher to use the anchor and dolphins. At least two Boston firms preceded him, e.g., we find the anchor and dolphin on *The Poetical Works of John Milton.* (Boston: Hilliard, Gray, and Company, 1841) and on *Poems by David Gray.* (Boston: Roberts Brothers, 1865). But it was Mosher who would make something distinctive of the motif in his publications, sometimes using one dolphin around an anchor, sometimes two, and other times using just the anchor or just the dolphins.

Mosher paid homage to other early printers as well. His little periodical, *The Bibelot*, bore the Florentine lily of the Giunta printing family, the cupid on a ball device adopted from the *Hypnerotomachia Poliphili* first printed by Aldus in 1499, and the cross and orb device of Nicolaus Jenson, another famous 15th Century printer of Venice. Almost all of Mosher's devices are derived from these famous printing sources.

On the following pages appear printer's and publisher's devices for comparison. Presented first are some of the earlier devices once used by Aldus Manutius (1450-1515), the famous early Venetian scholar/printer (and by his sons), and by William Pickering (1796-1854), the London bookseller and publisher who, in collaboration with the Chiswick Press, styled himself as the "Aldi Discipulus Anglus", i.e., the English disciple of Aldus. The predominant device used by Pickering was based upon that of Aldus, the anchor and dolphin motif. Obviously, Mosher saw himself in this lineage of printers and publishers who sought to disseminate fine writing in inexpensive format to the masses.

SAMPLE PRINTER'S DEVICES OF ALDUS MANUTIUS

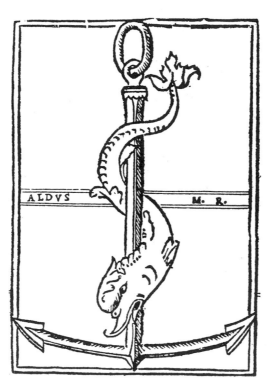

SAMPLE PUBLISHER'S DEVICES OF WILLIAM PICKERING

PUBLISHER'S DEVICES EMPLOYED IN THE MOSHER BOOKS (70% ACTUAL SIZE)

(1) Title pages of the Ideal Series, the Brocade Series, and small Miscellaneous Series books. (2) Old World Series title pages, title pages on the Reprints from "The Bibelot" Series, and used in several Miscellaneous Series books. (3) From the Miscellaneous Series *Wayside Lute, Garlands & Wayfarings*; on back of the 1918 catalogue, et. al. (4) Title page of the Quarto Series *Poems & Ballads*, and *Tristram of Lyonesse* by Swinburne. (5) From *Leaves of Grass* and the large Miscellaneous Series' *Memories of President Lincoln*. (6) This large device appears on the 1915 *The Kasîdah*. (7) Appears in Emerson's *Threnody* of the Golden Text Series, and many Miscellaneous Series books. It also appears, sans initials, on *Dreamthorp*. (8) Smaller version is used throughout the Lyric Garland Series. (9) This device only appears in the 1905 *The Kasîdah* from the Miscellaneous Series, and on the back of the 1914 catalogue. (10) Used at the back of *Ten Spiritual Designs* of 1913, and at the end of the 1911 catalogue. (11) From *Ecclesiastes*, and the Venetian Series, front cover of *The Celestial Country*, et.al. A framed version appears on the 1901 Miscellaneous Series, *The Blessed Damozel*. (12) From *Billy & Hans*, the *Odes & Sonnets of Keats*, and the *Amphora* of 1912, et.al. (13) From the title page of *The Rose-Jar*, 1913. (14) The Florentine lily device found on the back cover wrapper of *The Bibelot*.

(OPPOSITE PAGE): (15) *In Memoriam* privately printed in 1920; first appeared in *Runes of Woman* and on back of 1915 catalogue, then on many later catalogues. (16) Back of 1920 catalogue. (17) From the title page of *Chrysanthema*, 1911. (18) Back of the 1919 and inside 1905 catalogues (designed by Rathbun who did a similar bookplate design). (19) *George Meredith* by Barry, *The Sermon on the Mount*, et.al. (20) Front cover of Golden Text Series. (21) Covers of some catalogues and inside the 1906 catalogue. (22) Walter Pater titles from the Quarto Series. (23) Back cover of 1916 catalogue. (24) Title page and colophon of *A Vision of Giorgione*. (25) On the front of the 1903 catalogue. (26) Title page of 1897 catalogue, and on the back of 1921 catalogue.

PUBLISHER'S DEVICES EMPLOYED IN THE MOSHER BOOKS (ACTUAL SIZE)

(15)

(16)

(17)

(18)

(19)

(20)

(21)

(25)

(22)

(23)

(24)

(26)

Section II

SAMPLE ENTRIES WITH NOTES

(See Further Notes for Additional Details)

Book's title as appears
on the title page

Pages & book size
(if size is not listed, see
Section I for standard size)

Author or translator

Edition size & paper used

Significance of book in
addition to Mosher's edition.
(see Further Notes)

Entry
number

Hatch number

Which Mosher edition
(see Further Notes)

Name of Series

160. **THE HOUSE OF USNA A DRAMA** by Fiona Macleod. 1903.
xxxii, 76, [1] pp.   21 x 12.5 cm.
Miscellaneous Series-23   H 250.   Only edition.

450 on Van Gelder; 50 numbered copies on
Japan vellum, signed by the publisher.
First edition.

Content: The work and the foreword are both by Fiona Macleod. According to Mrs. Sharp,
" 'the House of Usna' was performed at the Fifth Meeting of the [Stage] Society at the Globe
Theatre April 29th, 1900... The drama itself was printed three months later in *The National
Review*, and eventually published in book form in America by Mr. T. B. Mosher, in 1903."

Comment: Fiona Macleod was a pseudonym used by William Sharp who also published
works under his real name.

Binding & Embellishment: Both the Van Gelder and the Japan vellum copies are bound in
green printed Japan vellum wraps over boards. Renaissance border on cover signed "CW"
for Charlotte Whittingham, designer for the Chiswick Press of London. Warren shows the
actual Chiswick border design; however, Mosher interchanges the top and bottom portions.
The circular Celtic device in the center of the front cover is from the front cover of the
first English edition of *From the Hills of Dream* published in Edinburgh by Patrick Geddes
in 1896.

The cover design is very similar to *The Silence of Amor* (352).

Reference: Sharp, pp. 317-18; Boss XV 157; Quinn 8652 (indicates First American
Edition); DeVinne 1113; Jenkinson II, 946; Warren, p. 253.

Special notes on the book
• Contents of book, sources
• Comments
• Binding information, designs, format

References consulted
(see end of Section V)

Sample page or design from book
(see List of Illustrations for details)

Cross reference to
another entry

Line showing break
from one series to
another series

Order of appearance
within a series (see Section I
for whole series overview)

Progression of Mosher's
edition within a series

10.9 **AUCASSIN & NICOLETE** done into English by Andrew Lang.
1922.
Old World Series.   H 693.   Ninth edition.

925 on Van Gelder. No Japan vellum
copies were printed.

——————— *Same Title, Change of Series* ———————

11. ANDREW LANG **AUCASSIN & NICOLETE**. [October] 1903.
Vest Pocket Series-6   H 258.   First edition.

Limitation unknown for both Van Gelder
and Japan vellum copies.

Content: Publisher's note opposite the title page mentions this work "was first re-
issued in America in the *Old World Series* in 1895." This statement is also
given in Mosher's 1903 catalogue.

Reference: Vilain 35.

11.1 ANDREW LANG **AUCASSIN & NICOLETE**. [December] 1905.
Vest Pocket Series.   H 346.   Second edition.

FURTHER NOTES AND EXPLANATIONS
IN USING THIS BIBLIOGRAPHY

- Entries are in alphabetical order by book title, in bold italic. Where the author's name appears first on the title page (but is not part of the title itself), the name will appear first in the entry, in plain type. *Example:* RICHARD JEFFERIES *THE PAGEANT OF SUMMER*... Doing so preserves the flow of information as it is found printed on the title page.

- After each printing of a book the type was distributed, so subsequent printings of the same title are *separate editions* and not re-issues using plates of the previous edition. Examination of Mosher's later editions show a variety of typographic differences that would not appear if the later editions were printed from the same plates.

- Pagination is presented in simplified form for each entry. *Example: xvii,* 145, [1] pp. Page counts include unnumbered pages, but final blank pages are not included in the count. The preliminary leaves are given in lowercase Roman numerals, and the main text is given in Arabic numerals. The last bracketed number usually stands for a printed leaf reserved for the colophon or the name of the printer. The aim is not to give a detailed and exhaustive pagination of each and every page, but to show the general number of pages. If a more thorough pagination is needed, see Hatch's *Check List.* If there are discrepancies between Hatch and the present bibliography, they will be mentioned in the annotations accompanying the entry.

- A separator line within a column of like titles is used to show the change in series. *Example:* The first two entries for *HAND AND SOUL* (139, 139.1) are from the Miscellaneous Series, whereas the third entry with this title (140) is from the Ideal Series of Little Masterpieces, so a line separates 140 from 139.1 & 139. Lines are not placed between different editions *within* the same series.

- Notes in the right column provide information on the number of copies printed, on the paper used, and whether the book is signed by the publisher. It will also be stated if a book's appearance is a significant edition, i.e., known to be a first edition, a first American edition, or a first separately printed edition (meaning it previously appeared as part of a collected edition, but now makes its appearance for the first time on its own).

  Note: For the purposes of this bibliography, a pirated edition preceding an authorized edition is still a first, albeit unauthorized, edition. The "significant edition" is not to be confused with the statement of edition directly under the entry. That edition note refers to the edition sequence within Mosher's publications only.

  The first appearance of a title in a different series is abbreviated as "First thus." A first appearance of a newly revised edition *within* a series will be marked as "New Edition/Same Series."

  The right column is also reserved for an illustration: a design, title page, or binding (reduced in size). The text to the left often makes it clear which design is being shown, and many of the designs are taken from the front cover, but see the "List of Illustrations" if additional clarification is needed.

- The left-hand column includes a variety of information such as actual content, sources for texts if such were identified or otherwise recognized, comments on the content, designs used and their sources, comparative details between Mosher's edition and some other edition, and the binding used on the regular, Japan vellum and vellum copies.

  The left-hand column is also used to reference other bibliographies or publications in which the book is catalogued or discussed. *Example:* Madan 20. To find the full title and annotated comments on the work cited, refer to Madan in the Bibliography of Thomas Bird Mosher in Section V at the end of the present bibliography. *Note:* When a number follows directly after the source name, as in the above example, then the reference is to entry #20 in Madan. If page location is used, it is clearly identified as p. 77, or pp. 56-58.

- The order in which a title appeared within a given series follows directly after the name of the series, e.g., Miscellaneous Series-24. This same order is found in the series charts in Section I.

- Each entry in the bibliography references a "Hatch" number. Hatch refers to the earlier 1966 Mosher bibliography, *A Check-list of the Publication of Thomas Bird Mosher.* The new Mosher bibliography includes entries that were not published in this 1966 bibliography. Some of these new entries were later identified in the Hatch "Addenda & Corrigenda" which was published in Vilain and Bishop's *Thomas Bird Mosher and the Art of the Book* (1992). New Hatch locations, e.g., Hatch 301A, are assigned to fit in between the original Hatch entries 301 and 302. The present bibliography continues this practice, and the position Hatch would have most likely assigned a new entry has been followed.

* * * * * *

GLOSSARY OF TERMS AND ABBREVIATIONS USED

The following list gives some terms, used throughout the bibliography, with which readers might not be familiar.

---

a.e.g.— All [page] edges gilt, i.e., gold runs across all the page edges, most evident when the book is closed giving the appearance of three solid sides of gold (top, fore-edge, and bottom). If only the top edges are gold, then the term t.e.g. is used.

A.L.S. — Autographed letter signed.

albertype — According to *Glaister's Glossary of the Book,* this is "a planograpic, photo-mechanical, non-screen printing process suitable for fine detail reproductions in monochrome or colour. Printing is done from a glass plate prepared by printing a negative on a gelatin film containing dichromate." The practical application of this printing method was perfected by Joseph Albert of Munich during 1867-71, hence the name albertype. The more frequently used name is collotype.

Bierstadt process — Also called artotype or the Bierstadt Artotype System, this was a photo-mechanical, non-screen printing process used for fine detail reproductions in color or in monochrome. According to Nadeau's *Encyclopedia of Printing, Photo-graphic and Photomechanical Processes* (New Brunswick, Canada: Atelier, 1989): "This process was very similar to collotype... A mixture of soluble glass (sodium silicate) and albumen was used as a substrate, thus avoiding the necessity of first exposing a dichromated layer to the light to give a stronger matrix, as in the original Albertype process... The foremost user was probably Edward Bierstadt, of New York, who used it primarily for illustrations of business catalogues."—p. 37. Many of the portrait and other frontispieces for the Mosher books were printed using this process.

criblé initial — A decorative lead initial with an overall background of small dots behind the letter. Head- or tail-pieces, and even borders, can employ this same background.

dingbat — A printer's typographical ornament used to call attention to an opening sentence, or to mark a break between two sentences or paragraphs. These often take the shape of a leaf or some other small yet noticeable form.

drop-cap — A drop-cap or "drop initial" is an initial capital letter, e.g., at the beginning of a book's title or at the start of a chapter, which is larger than the other type used. It extends from the top of the first line of text and drops downward, i.e., extends down two or more lines of text.

head-piece — This is a type-ornament used at the head of a chapter or at the beginning of a section of a book. A small scene or vignette may also serve this purpose.

introuvable — Literally meaning not capable of being found, Mosher often used this term to mean a book or writing deliberately kept by its author or publisher to a very limited edition or small printing (usually in England) so that it was nearly impossible for any member of the American public to find a copy. If a copy could be found, the price would be prohibitive due to its scarcity.

Japan vellum boards — The use of Japan vellum paper as a binding paper over stiff, substantial boards.

Japan vellum wraps — The use of Japan vellum paper as a paper loosely fitted and folded around flexible boards.

NUC — The National Union Catalogue.

RLIN — Research Libraries Information Network.

tail-piece — A type-ornament used at the end of a chapter or of a section of a book. A small scene or vignette may also serve this purpose.

t.e.g. — Top [page] edges gilt (see a.e.g.)

yapp board edges — These are overlapping edges or flaps which cover either the fore-edges of a book, or in some cases all the page edges of a book. Technically the former is "yapp style" and the latter "yapp edges," but generally speaking, Mosher referred to all of these as yapp edges. The bindings in the Old World Series have flaps or yapp edges over their fore-edges, while the bindings in The English Reprint Series are examples having yapp edges over the top and the fore-edges.

Alphabetical List (By Title)

of

The Mosher Books

Published from
1891–1923

A

1.   ROBERT LOUIS STEVENSON. *AES TRIPLEX AND OTHER ESSAYS.*
[March] 1902.   *xiv*, 78 pp. (for all editions)
Vest Pocket Series-4   H 227.   First edition.

Limitation unknown for both Van Gelder and Japan vellum copies.

Content: The unsigned foreword is by the publisher. In addition to "Aes Triplex," the two other major essays included are Stevenson's "Ordered South" and "Walking Tours." Also included are Austin Dobson's "In Memoriam," Stevenson's own "Epitaph," two excerpts from Stevenson's *A Christmas Sermon*, and the lyric by W. E. Henley which appeared at the end of that work in the original edition.

Aes Triplex was first printed by Mosher in his October 1901 issue of *The Bibelot* (24).

Comment: This volume is part of Mosher's Vest Pocket Series publication of twelve essays collectively known as *Virginibus Puerisque and Other Papers,* which first appeared in 1881 (London, C. Kegan Paul & Co.). See entries 5, 76, and 427 for the other Vest Pocket titles containing essays from this collective work which forms a sub-series in the Vest Pocket Series.

Design: According to Bruckner, the cover design is one of the first four done for this series by Frederic Goudy (see 191, 335, and 375 for the others) and subsequently used sporadically throughout the series. For other Goudy designs see entries 67, 121, 204, 205, 216, 246, 257, 258, 259, 261, 268, 270, 348, 387, 395, and 425.

Reference: Beinecke I, 92 & 93; Prideaux, p. 15; Vilain 34 (plate 42, p. 96); Bruckner, p. 48; Gerstley 12 J-K.

1.1   ROBERT LOUIS STEVENSON. *AES TRIPLEX AND OTHER ESSAYS.*
[November] 1903.
Vest Pocket Series.   H 280.   Second edition.

1.2   ROBERT LOUIS STEVENSON. *AES TRIPLEX AND OTHER ESSAYS.*
[November] 1907.
Vest Pocket Series.   H 424.   Third edition.

2.   *AMPHORA: A COLLECTION OF PROSE AND VERSE* Chosen
by the Editor of The Bibelot. [October] 1912.   18 x 11 cm.
xvi, 190, [1] pp. (last page 190 is misnumbered as 192; corrected in other editions]
Miscellaneous Series-60   H 560.   First edition.

925 on Van Gelder; 50 numbered copies on Japan vellum; (4 other copies?). Same number of Van Gelder copies for later editions except for the 3rd edition (2.3), and no more on Japan vellum except where noted.

Content: The foreword is signed by the publisher. Selections from the following authors and poets appear in this anthology:

Russell Alexander	John M. Falkner	Richard Le Gallienne	Sir Arthur Quiller-Couch
William Archer	Michael Field	A. Lenalie (translator)	Walter Raleigh
Matthew Arnold	Théophile Gautier	Amy Levy	Wilfrid L. Randell
Henry H. Bashford	Elizabeth Gibson	George H. Lewes	Lizette W. Reese
E. F. Benson	Wilfrid Wilson Gibson	James Russell Lowell	Ernest Renan
Laurence Binyon	George Gissing	E. V. Lucas	Wallace Rice
William Blake	Edmund Gosse	St. John Lucas	A. Mary F. obinson
George Borrow	Reuben A. Guild	Lucy Lyttelton	Robert Ross
Gordon Bottomley	Philip G. Hamerton	F. W. MacDonald	John Runcie
F. W. Bourdillon	Thomas Hardy	Arthur Machen	John Ruskin
Rupert Brooke	Frederick Harrison	J. W. Mackail	William Sharp
Richard M. Bucke	William Hazlitt	Fiona Macleod	A. Forbes Sieveking
John Burroughs	Ella Heath	Maurice Maeterlinck	Robert L. Stevenson
Alfred J. Butler	William E. Henley	Stéphane Mallarmé	A. C. Swinburne
I. C—	Robert Herrick	John Masefield	Arthur Symons
L. A. C—	Katherine Tynan Hinkson	William Matthews	Rachael Annand Taylor
Thomas Carlyle	W. G. Hole	Justin H. McCarthy	Viola Taylor
R. T. Chandler	Thomas Hood	Dora G. McChesney	Edith M. Thomas
T. J. Cobden-Sanderson	Father Gerard Hopkins	John Stuart Mill	Henry D. Thoreau
Mary Colborne-Veel	Herbert P. Horne	T. Sturge Moore	John Todhunter
Mary E. Coleridge	A. E. Housman	John Morley	Horace Traubel
Samuel T. Coleridge	Leigh Hunt	Sir Lewis Morris	Arthur Upson
Frances Cornford	Robert G. Ingersoll	Thomas B. Mosher	Rosamund M. Watson
W. L. Courtney	William James	E. Nesbit (Mrs. Bland)	Theodore Watts-Dunton
John Davidson	Francis Jammes	Henry Newbolt	J. A. McNeill Whistler
Richard De Bury	Richard Jefferies	Cardinal Newman	Walt Whitman
Austin Dobson	Lionel Johnson	Alfred Noyes	Oscar Wilde
James Douglas	Andrew Lang	Georgina B. Paget	James J. G. Wilkinson
George Du Maurier	W. E. H. Lecky	Thomas W. Parsons	Iolo A. Williams
George Eliot	Gerald S. Lee	Stephen Phillips	Dorothy Wordsworth
Havelock Ellis	Vernon Lee (V. Paget)	Eden Phillpotts	William Butler Yeats
Ralph W. Emerson			

Comment: In the original Certificate of Copyright Registration (Nov 1, 1912, No. 327646), Thomas Bird Mosher is listed as editor (University of San Francisco).

Oliver Sheean recorded a copy of the *Amphora* in Mosher's home library (bookcase P, shelf 8) without a date, and as being one of four copies only. No copy has ever been recorded in the Lamb or the Sheean typescripts. The Sheean manuscript record of Mosher's home library (Bishop Collection) provides the only reference to this special limited edition.

There is a second *Amphora* which was posthumously published in 1926 (see FL2), and which may be considered a companion volume to this first *Amphora*. It includes several tributes to Mosher, and ten selections from Mosher's catalogue introductions and poetry.

For Mosher's first anthology, and other anthologies assembled by him, see 366.

Binding & Embellishment: Van Gelder copies bound in old style blue "ribbed" boards (raised bands) with white label on the spine; Japan vellum copies in Japan vellum wraps over boards with label information printed directly on the spine. Title page in red and black; Chiswick ornaments and red initial letters. Wheeler notes a fellow member of the Zamorano Club (book club of Los Angeles) identified the inside endpapers as "Japan shadow paper, which is used in Japan for window decorations." The Japan Paper Company identifies this as "Ju-ichi ban" shadow paper.

Reference: Wheeler (H. O.), p. 9; Japan Paper Company (Japanese Shadow Paper).

2.1 *AMPHORA: A COLLECTION OF PROSE AND VERSE* Chosen by the
Editor of The Bibelot. [October] 1913. (Pagination for all editions same as first edition)
Miscellaneous Series.   H 600.   Second edition.

2.2 *AMPHORA: A COLLECTION OF PROSE AND VERSE* Chosenby the
Editor of The Bibelot. [Colophon reads October 1913] 1914.
Miscellaneous Series.   H 617.   Second edition.

Comment: A reprint of 2.1 with change of date on the title page, but no
change of edition date on the verso, or change of colophon date?

2.3 *AMPHORA: A COLLECTION OF PROSE AND VERSE* Chosen by the
Editor of The Bibelot. [September] 1919.
Miscellaneous Series.   H 673.   Third edition.

450 copies on Van Gelder; 25 numbered copies on Japan vellum.

2.4 *AMPHORA: A COLLECTION OF PROSE AND VERSE* Chosen by the
Editor of The Bibelot. [January] 1922.
Miscellaneous Series.   H 698.   Fourth edition.

Comment: A reprint of 2.3 with change of date on the title page, but no
change of edition date on the verso?

Binding: Some copies of this edition are found bound in 3/4 calf with blind-tooled
darts wrapping around the spine. Mosher never had his books bound in this manner, so it appears that these were bound at a later date. In 1926 Mosher's assistant, Flora Lamb, made arrangements with The Monastery Hill Bindery to bind
left over copies of this fourth edition of *Amphora* to match copies of the
Amphora II published in 1926 (see Section III). Both editions were similarly
bound in either red, brown, green or blue leather under Flora Lamb's direction.

---

3. *ANDROMACHE A PLAY IN THREE ACTS* by Gilbert Murray.
[October] 1913. *vi*, 88, [1] pp.   19 x 13.5 cm.
Miscellaneous Series-66   H 590.   Only edition.

450 copies on Van Gelder; 25 numbered copies on Japan vellum. First American edition.

Content: According to Mosher's 1913 catalogue, "we have sought and obtained
permission [from Murray] to reprint this play... The text has some slight revision..." –p. 74. The revision was made from the first London edition published
by W. Heinemann in 1900.

Binding & Embellishment: Van Gelder copies bound in marbled paper with
quarter white spine; title/author in red and black on spine and upper left hand
corner of front cover. Title page in red and black. The Japan vellum copies are
bound in Japan vellum wrappers over boards.

Reference: Arlen 411; Gilbert Murray's letter of permission is at The Houghton
Library (bMS Am 1096).

---

4. *ANN: A MEMORY* By Thomas De Quincey. 1908.   *xi*, 37 pp.
Ideal Series of Little Masterpieces-9   H 440.   Only edition.

Limitation unknown for both Van Gelder and Japan vellum copies.

Content: The foreword is signed by the publisher. Two brief selections from
Victor Hugo appear in the preliminaries. The text of this work was first printed
by Mosher in his November 1903 issue of *The Bibelot* (26).

5. ROBERT LOUIS STEVENSON. *AN APOLOGY FOR IDLERS AND OTHER ESSAYS.* [October] 1905.   102 pp.
    Vest Pocket Series-10   H 329.   First edition.

    Limitation unknown for both Van Gelder and Japan vellum copies.

Content: In addition to "An Apology for Idlers," there are three other Stevenson essays in this book: "Eldorado," "The English Admirals," and "Child's Play."

Comment: This volume is part of Mosher's Vest Pocket Series publication of twelve essays collectively known as *Virginibus Puerisque and Other Papers,* which first appeared in 1881 (London, C. Kegan Paul & Co.). See entries 1, 76, and 427 for the other Vest Pocket titles containing essays from this collective work and forming a sub-series in the Vest Pocket Series.

Reference: Beinecke I, 98; Prideaux, p. 15; Gerstley 12 P.

5.1 ROBERT LOUIS STEVENSON. *AN APOLOGY FOR IDLERS AND OTHER ESSAYS.* [September] 1908.   iv, 96 pp.
     Vest Pocket Series.   H 458.   Second edition.

5.2 ROBERT LOUIS STEVENSON. *AN APOLOGY FOR IDLERS AND OTHER ESSAYS.* [September] 1916.   102 pp.
     Vest Pocket Series.   H 646.   Third edition.

AN APPRECIATION by Jessie B. Rittenhouse (see entry 445).

---

6. *ARIADNE IN MANTUA   A ROMANCE IN FIVE ACTS*
    by Vernon Lee. 1906.   *xiv,* 87, [1] pp.
    Old World Series-41   H 352.   First edition.

    925 on Van Gelder; 50 numbered copies printed on Japan vellum.

Content: The prefatory note is signed by the publisher and designates the reprint's source as the 1903 publication by B. H. Blackwell of Oxford, and Simpkin, Marshall, *et al,* of London.

Mosher also printed the text of this work in his January & February 1906 issues of *The Bibelot* (29).

Comment: Vernon Lee is the pseudonym of Violet Paget.

Design: The cover design bears the "C" monogram of Thomas Maitland Cleland. Other Cleland designs are found in entries 73, 91, 127 (possibly by Crawford), 143 , 156, 159, 177, 197, 242 (title page), 287, 350, 374, and 378.

6.1 *ARIADNE IN MANTUA   A ROMANCE IN FIVE ACTS*
     by Vernon Lee. 1912.   xii, 87, [1] pp.
     Old World Series.   H 571.   Second edition.

---

7. *ASTROPHEL AND STELLA* by Sir Philip Sidney. 1905
    viii, 140, [1] pp.
    Old World Series-38   H 317.   First edition.

    925 on Van Gelder; 50 numbered copies printed on Japan vellum, without the edition note.

Content: The preface is signed by the publisher. The text is based upon Alfred W. Pollard's *Sir Philip Sidney's Astrophel and Stella* (London: David Stott, 1888). An epilogue contains eleven songs selected from the sonnets of the 1597 edition. A poem by Algernon Charles Swinburne appears opposite the title page.

ASTROPHEL AND STELLA (continued)

Mosher first printed selections from this work in his June 1896 issue of *The Bibelot* (19).

Comment: Mosher's edited copy of this book, provided for the printer, is in the Bishop Collection.

Design: The cover design is signed with the unattributed monogram "EC".

---

8.   *AT THE SIGN OF THE LION AND OTHER ESSAYS* from the Books of Hilaire Belloc. [October] 1916.   *x*, 66, [1] pp.   18.5 x 9.5 cm. Miscellaneous Series-76   H 635.   Only edition.

950 copies on Van Gelder, 25 numbered copies on Japan vellum.

Content: Besides the title essay, the other four essays include "The Autumn and the Fall of Leaves," "On Sacramental Things," "On Rest," and "On Coming to an End." The foreword is signed by the publisher, and a selection from Burnell Payne also prefaces the main text.

The last three essays in the book were first printed in the November 1914 issue of *The Bibelot* (37).

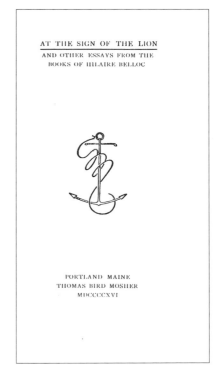

Comment: In 1994 James Fergusson, the London bookseller, listed a copy of this book (in his "More of the Obelus" catalogue) with the bookplate of Duff Cooper, which had an inserted 2 page presentation ALS to Cooper from the author on letterhead from The Reform Club, dated 10 July 1929:

> My dear Duff, I have long wanted to give you my Tristan & Iseult: but when I went to find the little finicky edition in a case, I discovered I had none left... I send you, as next best, the companion volume, The Sign of the Lion. It's 20 odd years since I read it & I don't know what I should think of it now... These little books have a history. They were pirated in America by a Yid called Mosher & sold for a Dollar: me, no money: him, all the money. At last he proposed to treat my Verses in the same fashion, but the worm turned & I told him (being then young & hearty) that if he did I would cross over to America & beat him with a cane. I specified the cane. I said: 'A light rattan cane'. He replied with a torrent of abuse, but forbore to steal as he had proposed.

Binding & Embellishment: Van Gelder copies are found in two variant bindings: (1) in quarter gray spines over decorated paper boards, or (2) the same patterned boards, but with a wider quarter blue spine (extends 3 cm. rather than the 1 cm. of the first variant). Both use a white paper label printed in red and black on the spine. The Japan vellum copies are bound in Japan vellum boards with title/author printed directly on the spine. Chiswick ornaments and some lead initials outlined in red; title page in red and black. This book is stylistically uniform with *Books and the Quiet Life* (49) and *Billy and Hans* (43).

Reference: Quinn 444 & 445.

---

9.   *ATALANTA IN CALYDON   A TRAGEDY* by Algernon Charles Swinburne. 1897.   *xvi*, 99, [1] pp. Old World Series-9   H 40.   First edition.

925 on Van Gelder, 100 numbered copies printed on Japan vellum.

Content: In addition to the work itself, there are several pages of text in Greek. The source text is *Atalanta in Calydon: A Tragedy*. A New Edition (London: Chatto & Windus, n.d. [ca. 1883]). The edited printer's copy is in the Bishop Collection.

Reference: Quinn 9467.

9.1 *ATALANTA IN CALYDON   A TRAGEDY* by Algernon Charles   925 on Van Gelder.
     Swinburne. 1902.   x, 103, [1] pp. (same for remaining editions)
     Old World Series.   H 235.   Second edition.

     Comment: The change in pagination results from the way the preliminary
     pages are organized in this second edition, and resultant renumbering of the
     regular pages of text. A half title was also dropped.

9.2 *ATALANTA IN CALYDON   A TRAGEDY* by Algernon Charles   925 on Van Gelder.
     Swinburne. 1907.
     Old World Series.   H 405.   Third edition.

9.3 *ATALANTA IN CALYDON   A TRAGEDY* by Algernon Charles   925 on Van Gelder.
     Swinburne. 1912.
     Old World Series.   H 569.   Fourth edition.

10. *AUCASSIN & NICOLETE* done into English by Andrew Lang.   925 on Van Gelder; 100 numbered
     1895.   88, [1] pp.; front. (same pagination for second edition)   copies printed on Japan vellum.
     Old World Series-2   H 12.   First edition.   First American edition (see note
                                                                           to 11)

     Content: The publisher's note on the verso of the half-title indicates the pre-
     sent edition is a direct reprint of the David Nutt edition (London, 1887)
     printed at the Chiswick Press. In addition to the main work, Edmund Clarence
     Stedman's translation of a passage in *Aucassin & Nicolete* appears as an
     appendix, taken from George P. Lathrop's *A Masque of Poets* (Boston: Roberts
     Brothers, 1878).

     Comment: It was this pirated edition that caused a long and heated exchange
     between Mosher and the author/translator through *The Critic* and other literary
     periodicals of the day. Mosher delighted in the controversy and the attention it
     attracted for it only increased demand for the Mosher Books. In a personal
     meeting with Lang, Mosher told him "You don't know America. Our little tiff has
     sold twice as many of your books and mine as all your publications ever did for
     you" (Strouse). The book was afterwards pirated by at least five other presses.
     See Van Trump and Ziegler for a concise yet superb overview of the controversy.
     See also William E. Fredeman's *PBSC* article for an illuminating discussion.

     Design: According to the 1895 Mosher catalogue, this volume "reproduces in
     artotype the etched title-page of the scarce London edition, printed in a deli-
     cate Sepia ink on Japan vellum. Three little wood-cut designs [by P. Jacomb
     Hood] are also taken from the original edition."

     Reference: Crichton 42; Van Trump & Ziegler, p. 307; *PBSC*, pp. 42-44; Grigsby
     698, 690 & 691 (Lang-Mosher Controversy); Strouse, p. 25.   *(a)*

10.1 *AUCASSIN & NICOLETE* done into English by Andrew Lang.   925 on Van Gelder; 100 numbered
     1896.   copies on Japan vellum.
     Old World Series.   H 30.   Second edition.

     Comment: This second edition corrects some mistakes that were pointed out
     to Mosher at the beginning of the Mosher/Lang controversy over the printing
     of this title (see *The Critic*, November 23, 1895, p. 355). The typographical
     error on p. 45, line 8 was corrected from "they kin" to "thy kin." Also the
     notes of the first reprint edition mistakenly followed the pagination of the
     original London edition published by David Nutt, an error corrected in this
     edition.   *(b)*

10.2   *AUCASSIN & NICOLETE* done into English by Andrew Lang.
     1897.   *xxiv* [but actually *xxii*], 66, [1] pp.; front. (same pagination through the seventh edition)*
     Old World Series.   H 53.   Third edition.

     925 on Van Gelder; 100 numbered copies on Japan vellum.

     Comment: Though the preliminary pagination ends on p. xxiv, there are only xxii pages from the first half-title up to p. 1 (excluding the frontispiece, since the Mosher books do not include it in their pagination).

     *The Japan vellum printing of this edition still follows the pagination of 10 & 10.1 (i.e., 88, [1] pp.).

     The Japan vellum printing was not noted by Hatch.

10.3   *AUCASSIN & NICOLETE* done into English by Andrew Lang.
     1898.
     Old World Series.   H 83.   Fourth edition.

     925 on Van Gelder. No Japan vellum copies were printed.

10.4   *AUCASSIN & NICOLETE* done into English by Andrew Lang.
     1899.
     Old World Series.   H 126.   Fourth edition.

     925 on Van Gelder. No Japan vellum copies were printed.

     Comment: Either an error in edition note, or a reprint of previous entry with change of date on the title page. Note previous entry 10.3.

10.5   *AUCASSIN & NICOLETE* done into English by Andrew Lang.
     1901.
     Old World Series.   H 200.   Fifth edition.

     925 on Van Gelder; 100 numbered copies on Japan vellum.

     Comment: The 1901 Japan vellum edition states FOURTH EDITION on the verso of the title page, whereas the Van Gelder copy states Fifth Edition, perpetuating the confusion between 10.3 & 10.4 above. Apparently the publisher and printer did not always pay close attention to the edition notice and allowed the same edition note to appear in succeeding editions before rectifying the problem. For record of another such problem, see 171.2.

     Unlike the pagination of the third Japan vellum edition (see comment under 10.2), the pagination of this "fourth" Japan vellum edition now conforms to the page count of the Van Gelder copy (*xxiv*, 66, [1] pp.).

     The Japan vellum printing was not noted by Hatch. A copy is located in the Bishop Collection.

10.6   *AUCASSIN & NICOLETE* done into English by Andrew Lang.
     1903.
     Old World Series.   H 266.   Sixth edition.

     925 on Van Gelder; 100 numbered copies on Japan vellum.

     Comment: The Japan vellum printing was not noted by Hatch.

10.7   *AUCASSIN & NICOLETE* done into English by Andrew Lang.
     1907.
     Old World Series.   H 404.   Seventh edition.

     925 on Van Gelder; 100 numbered copies on Japan vellum.

     Comment: The Japan vellum printing was not noted by Hatch.

10.8   *AUCASSIN & NICOLETE* done into English by Andrew Lang.
     1913.   *xxii*, 66, [1] pp.; front. (same pagination for ninth edition)
     Old World Series.   H 596.   Eighth edition.

     925 on Van Gelder. No Japan vellum copies were printed.

10.9 *AUCASSIN & NICOLETE* done into English by Andrew Lang.
1922.
Old World Series.   H 693.   Ninth edition.

925 on Van Gelder. No Japan vellum copies were printed.

——————— *Same Title, Change of Series* ———————

11. ANDREW LANG *AUCASSIN & NICOLETE*. [October] 1903.
xxvi, 75 pp. (same for all editions)
Vest Pocket Series-6   H 258.   First edition.

Limitation unknown for both Van Gelder and Japan vellum copies.

Content: Publisher's note opposite the title page mentions this work "was first re-issued in America in the *Old World Series* in 1895." This statement is also given in Mosher's 1903 catalogue. Indeed, the closest American edition to appear was that co-published by David Nutt of London, and Way & Williams of Chicago, in 1896.

Reference: Vilain 35.

11.1 ANDREW LANG *AUCASSIN & NICOLETE*. [December] 1905.
Vest Pocket Series.   H 346.   Second edition.

11.2 ANDREW LANG *AUCASSIN & NICOLETE*. [September] 1909.
Vest Pocket Series.   H 499.   Third edition.

12. *AUTUMN LEAVES FROM MAPLE COTTAGE*. The Mosher Press.
1919. *x*, 37 pp.   14 x 9.5 cm.
Privately Printed-50   H 750.   Only edition.

500 copies on Old Stratford paper; 200 copies printed on Van Gelder.

Content: The foreword is unsigned and not attributed. An invocation is signed by George Lawson, and selections from Philippians and the Sanskrit also precede the work. The text includes selections from Phillips Brooks, Samuel Smiles, Hugh Black, Cavé (see 117), Harry E. Fosdick, George L. Perin, Albert C. Grier, Bishop Brent, George Eliot, St. Paul, Angela Morgan, and John Burroughs.

Comment: A note in Hatch, and in a copy in the Bishop Collection, indicates that this anthology was compiled by Mrs. Walter G. Ladd. Gift copies were given to guests who stayed at Maple Cottage. The Lamb typescript questions whether or not it was done "for Dr. Ludwig Kast?"

Binding & Embellishment: Bound in Onyx vellum wrappers picturing an autumnal leaf on the front cover. Title page in red and black; Chiswick ornaments and lead initial letters; all pages ruled in black.

B

13. *THE BALLAD OF READING GAOL* by Oscar Wilde. [March] 1904.
vi, 34, [1] pp. (same pagination for all editions)
Lyric Garland Series-4   H 296.   First edition.

950 on Van Gelder paper for each edition.
First edition only: 100 numbered copies on Japan vellum; 10 numbered copies on Roman vellum signed by the publisher.

Content: Mosher printed a short bibliographic listing on p. [2] suggesting that the text is from the 1898 London edition published by Leonard Smithers, but Smithers also published a second edition in the same year with numerous changes. A textual comparison of the Mosher reprint with these two 1898 editions reveals the source to be the text of the second Smithers edition.

Reference: Mason (*Poems*), p. 86 (VIII); Cowan III, pp. 7 & 8.

13.1 *THE BALLAD OF READING GAOL* by Oscar Wilde. [November] 1905.
Lyric Garland Series.   H 348.   Second edition.

13.2 *THE BALLAD OF READING GAOL* by Oscar Wilde. [November] 1907.
Lyric Garland Series.   H 427.   Third edition.

13.3 *THE BALLAD OF READING GAOL* by Oscar Wilde. [December] 1911.
Lyric Garland Series.   H 553.   Fourth edition.

13.4 *THE BALLAD OF READING GAOL* by Oscar Wilde. [September] 1919.
Lyric Garland Series.   H 674.   Fifth edition.

---

14. *BALLADES IN BLUE CHINA AND OTHER POEMS* by Andrew Lang.
1907.   *viii*, 144, [1] pp.
Old World Series-44   H 390.   Only edition.

925 on Van Gelder: 50 numbered copies printed on Japan vellum.

Content: Contains a prefatory ballad by Frederick Pollock. This book is modeled upon, but not a reprint of, Lang's *Ballades and Verses Vain* which Austin Dobson prepared for the American market (New York: Scribner's, 1884). A poem by Austin Dobson also appears opposite the title page.

Comment: Some copies printed on Van Gelder paper are missing the last leaf found in most copies. The Japan vellum copy at The Houghton Library collates without the preliminary leaves.

---

15. *BALLADS & LYRICS OF OLD FRANCE WITH OTHER POEMS*
by Andrew Lang. 1896.   *xiii*, 124, [1] pp. (same through third edition)
Old World Series-4   H 22.   First Edition.

925 on Van Gelder: 100 numbered copies on Japan vellum.
First American edition.

Content: The text is that of the Longmans, Green & Co. edition (London, 1872) of which Mosher said that it "remains *introuvable*," i.e, cannot be found. This was a condition Mosher repeatedly sought to correct by bringing out his own reprints. The text includes translations of Charles d'Orleans, François Villon, Du Bellay, Remy Belleau, Ronsard, Jacques Tahureau, Passerat, Victor Hugo, Gérard De Nerval, Alfred De Musset, Henri Murger, and various Greek ballads. A publisher's note appears opposite the title page.

Comment: The preliminary pagination is misnumbered. As Hatch notes, the preliminary pages run: 3 *p.l.*, *ix-xiii*, [1]p., 1 *l.*; but there are no pp. *i-ii*. The printer should have noticed that there should have been four preliminary leaves before starting the page numbering on p. *ix*. If one counts all the preliminary pages up to and including the half-title, then one arrives at *xiii* pp.

15.1 *BALLADS & LYRICS OF OLD FRANCE WITH OTHER POEMS*
by Andrew Lang. 1897.
Old World Series.   H 55.   Second Edition.

925 on Van Gelder (see following entry). No copies were printed on Japan vellum.

15.2 *BALLADS & LYRICS OF OLD FRANCE WITH OTHER POEMS*
by Andrew Lang. 1898.
Old World Series.   H 84.   Second Edition.

925 on Van Gelder. No copies were printed on Japan vellum.

Comment: Either an error in edition note, or a reprint of 15.1 with change to date on the title page.

15.3   ***BALLADS & LYRICS OF OLD FRANCE WITH OTHER POEMS***
by Andrew Lang. 1902. *xiv*, 123, [1] pp.
Old World Series.   H 233.   Third edition.

925 on Van Gelder. 100 numbered copies on Japan vellum.

Comment: The pagination is one less page at the end due to a tightening up of the "List of Poets Translated" section at the end.

15.4   ***BALLADS & LYRICS OF OLD FRANCE WITH OTHER POEMS***
by Andrew Lang. 1909.   *xiv*, 123, [1] pp.
Old World Series.   H 481.   Fourth edition.

925 on Van Gelder. No copies were printed on Japan vellum.

Content: There are some changes to this last edition. A foreword by Mosher (with Andrew Lang's quote) is added, and the dedication leaf "To E. M. S." has been omitted. The number of preliminary pages, however, remains constant.

Comment: In a special note of vindication, Mosher writes in the foreword to this edition:

> In 1907 Mr. Lang saw fit to recognize the fact which he has always disputed that our faithful reprint of these Ballads and Lyrics was from a literary point of view at least as justifiable as we had assumed it to be. It only remains to say that our fourth edition follows the original text with the two or three misprints corrected as indicated by Mr. Lang in the brief Preface to his second edition in Longmans' Pocket Library *format*.

16.   ***BALLADS & SONNETS*** By Dante Gabriel Rossetti. 1903.
1 ⟨ *xxxvii*, 335 pp.; port. front. & facsim
Quarto Series-8   H 259.   Only edition.

450 on Van Gelder; 25 numbered & signed on Japan vellum; 4 on Roman vellum, signed by the publisher.

Content: The poem "In Memoriam / Dante Gabriel Rossetti" by A. Mary F. Robinson (pp. *v*-[*vi*]), the unsigned preface by the publisher (pp. *xvii*-[*xx*]), and Walter Pater's 1883 essay "Dante Gabriel Rossetti" (pp. *xxiii*-[*xxxvii*]), all precede the principal text. The text primarily follows the *Ballads and Sonnets* of 1881 (carefully designating those which appeared in the *Poems* of 1870). There are 40 additional poems and translations which were first brought together in *The Collected Works* (London: Ellis & Scrutton, 1886). The notes at the back (pp. 325-[335]) include variants in *The House of Life*, and pertinent notes from William Michael Rossetti's comments found in *The Collected Works* of 1886.

Two facsimiles (illustration opposite p. [103] and a handwriting sample opposite p. 173) were taken from William Sharp's *Dante Gabriel Rossetti: A Record and a Study* (London: Macmillan, 1882), and the portrait frontispiece is an enlarged Bierstadt reproduction of the original 1862 photograph by W. & D. Downey.

Comment: For Mosher this work, together with the Quarto Series *Poems* (294), formed a complete set of Rossetti's poetical works. In his 1903 catalogue he states that "from now on copies of the *Poems* can only be sold in connection with *Ballads and Sonnets*..."

Reference: Fredeman 23.24 (pp. 93-94); Boss XI 131; Ransom 267.

17.   ***BALLADS DONE INTO ENGLISH*** from the French of François Villon.
[October] 1904.   *viii*, 45, [1] pp.
Lyric Garland Series-6   H 298.   First edition.

950 on Van Gelder for each edition. The first edition only: 100 numbered copies on Japan vellum; 10 numbered copies on Roman vellum signed by the publisher.

Content: The translations are by A. C. Swinburne with ten, D. G. Rossetti with three, and John Payne with seven. A poem by Andrew Lang honoring Villon appears opposite the title page. Swinburne's poem "A Ballad of François Villon...Prince of all Ballad Makers" appears before the contents page, and a page of notes on p. [45].

BALLADS DONE INTO ENGLISH *(continued)*

Swinburne's ten translations and "A Ballad of François Villon..." were also printed in *The Bibelot* (22), and five of Payne's translations appeared in *The Bibelot* (18); see also 302. One of Rossetti's translations also appeared in *The Bibelot* (18).

Reference: Peckham, p. 100 (Eng 1904) also includes the 1907, 1913, and 1916 editions in his bibliography; Sturm 212 & 231; Quinn 10541.

17.1 **BALLADS DONE INTO ENGLISH** from the French of François Villon.
[April] 1907. *viii*, 43 pp., [2] ℓ (same pagination for other editions)
Lyric Garland Series.   H 428.   Second edition.

Comment: The text was tightened up a little and the two notes, first integrated with the text in the first edition, are now placed at the back of the book.

17.2 **BALLADS DONE INTO ENGLISH** from the French of François Villon.
[May] 1913.
Lyric Garland Series.   H 605.   Third edition.

Comment: The same edition note is printed on 17.3.

17.3 **BALLADS DONE INTO ENGLISH** from the French of François Villon.
[September] 1916.
Lyric Garland Series.   H 648.   Third edition.

Comment: There is either an error in edition note, or the book is a reprint of 17.2 with just a change of date on the title.

18. **THE BIBELOT   A REPRINT OF POETRY AND PROSE FOR BOOK LOVERS,** chosen in part from scarce editions and sources not generally known...
Vol. I. 1895. *viii*, 352, [1] pp., plus 48 pp. of half-titles and forewords not noted in the pagination. (All paginations are *only* for *bound volumes* of *The Bibelot*)
15.5 x 11.5 cm.
12 monthly issues.   H 15.   First thus.

In addition to the regular copies, 12 were printed on Japan vellum.

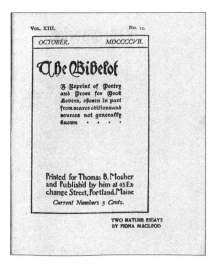

Content:

1. Lyrics from William Blake*
2. Ballades from François Villon translated by John Payne*
3. Mediæval Latin Students' Songs translated by J. A. Symonds*
4. A Discourse of Marcus Aurelius by Walter Pater*
5. Fragments from Sappho translated by H. T. Wharton
6. Sonnets on English Dramatic Poets by Algernon C. Swinburne
7. The Pathos of the Rose in Poetry by John Addington Symonds
8. Lyrics from James Thomson ("B.V.")*
9. Hand and Soul by Dante Gabriel Rossetti*
10. A Book of Airs from Dr. Thomas Campion
11. A Lodging for the Night; A Story of Francis [sic] Villon by R. L. Stevenson*
12. The Fifth Act of The Cenci by Percy Bysshe Shelley

[Note: 1-12 refers to the months within the year]

* Starred entries in the above issues of *The Bibelot* are works found in other series published by Mosher: for (1) see entry 368; for (2) see 17 and 302; for (3) see 439; for (4) see 231 (Chapt. 12); for (8) see 73; for (9) see 139 & 140; for (11) see 217. (*Note:* In some instances throughout *The Bibelot* (entries 18-39) the title of the work referenced in the footnote will differ from the title of the monthly issue.)

THE BIBELOT   A REPRINT (continued)

Comment: There are a few, and now exceedingly rare, copies of *The Bibelot*, Vol. I, No. 1, bound in brown paper wraps. Mosher mentions in a Dec. 8, 1909 letter to Frank H. Chase of Beloit, Wisconsin: "That original brown cover is a rarity. I have but one myself." (Bishop Collection, both the letter and the brown paper copy). In this study, no attempt has been made to locate the source text for each and every entry in *The Bibelot*.

The 240 issues of *The Bibelot* (18-37) constitute a 20 year anthology of Mosher's own making. For Mosher's first anthology, and other anthologies assembled by him, see 366.

Reference: Boss XI 132; Via and Searl, p. 38 for a color photo contrasting *The Bibelot* with a copy of Hubbard's *The Philistine*; Colbeck II, p. 987 (2); Chielens, pp. 63-65.

---

19.   ***THE BIBELOT   A REPRINT OF POETRY AND PROSE FOR BOOK LOVERS***, chosen in part from scarce editions and sources not generally known... Vol. II. 1896.   *iv*, 394, [1] pp.
12 monthly issues.   H 27.   First thus.

In addition to the regular copies, 12 were printed on Japan vellum.

Content:

1. A Flower of Laurium: Translations from Meleager and other Greek lyricists
2. A Maker of Forgotten Tunes by Vernon Lee & A Toccata of Galuppi's by Robert Browning
3. Sentences from The Story of My Heart by Richard Jefferies*
4. Songs of Dead Florentines: Translated-by J. A. Symonds
5. Quattrocentisteria by Maurice Hewlett*
6. Certain Songs & Sonnets from Astrophel and Stella by Sir Philip Sidney*
7. The Sire de Malétroit's Door by R. L. Stevenson*
8. An Idyl of First Love by G. Meredith*
9. Lyrics from Robert Bridges*
10. Joachim Du Bellay: A Renaissance Study by Walter Pater*
11. Epigrams of Art, Life and Nature by William Watson
12. The Death of Darnley: Four Scenes from Bothwell: A Tragedy by A. C. Swinburne

* Starred entries in the above issues of *The Bibelot* are works found in other series published by Mosher: for (3) see entry 388; for (5) see 315 & 316; for (7) see 355; for (8) see 161; for (9) see 137 & 138; for (10) see 321 & 322.

---

20.   ***THE BIBELOT   A REPRINT OF POETRY AND PROSE FOR BOOK LOVERS***, chosen in part from scarce editions and sources not generally known... Vol. III. 1897.   *iv*, 398, [1] pp., including facsim.
12 monthly issues.   H 50.   First thus.

In addition to the regular copies, 12 were printed on Japan vellum.

Content:

1. Three Greek Idyllists: I. Theocritus
2. Three Greek Idyllists: II. & III. Bion and Moschus
3. The Exequy and Other Poems by Henry King, D.D.
4. Selections from Dr. John Donne
5. Letters of Marque: Selections from a suppressed book by Rudyard Kipling
6. Father Damien: An Open Letter by Robert Louis Stevenson*
7. The Hollow Land: A Tale by William Morris. Part I.*
8. The Hollow Land: A Tale by William Morris. Part II.*
9. Sandro Botticelli & Luca della Robbia: Two Renaissance Studies by Walter Pater*
10. The Scholar-Gipsy & Thyrsis, a Monody by Matthew Arnold*
11. Odysseus in Phaeacia by J.W. Mackail
12. .The Death of Marlowe, A Tragedy by Richard Hengist Horne*

THE BIBELOT   A REPRINT (continued)

* Starred entries in the above issues of *The Bibelot* are works found in other series published by Mosher: for (6) see entries 107, 108 & 109; for (7 & 8) see 149 & 150; for (9) see entries 321 & 322; for (10) see 412; for (12) see 83.

21. ***THE BIBELOT   A REPRINT OF POETRY AND PROSE FOR BOOK LOVERS***, chosen in part from scarce editions and sources not generally known...
Vol. IV. 1898.   *iv*, 420, [1] pp., plate
12 monthly issues.   H 79.   First thus.

In addition to the regular copies, 12 were printed on Japan vellum.

Content:

1. Saint Agnes of Intercession by Dante Gabriel Rossetti
2. Lyrics from Paul Verlaine§
3. Browning's "Men and Women": A Review by William Morris
4. The Poetry of Michelangelo by Walter Pater*
5. Tares: A Book of Verses by Rosamund Marriott Watson*
6. The Flight of the Princess by Robert Louis Stevenson*
7. Saint Guido by Richard Jefferies*
8. Wordsworth's Grave, and Lachrymæ Musarum, both by William Watson
9. The School of Giorgione by Walter Pater*
10. Essay on the Newcomes by Sir Edward Burne-Jones
11. Echoes from Theocritus by Edward Cracroft Lefroy
12. Memorial Verses on the Death of Théophile Gautier, and Ave Atque Vale (in memory of Charles Baudelaire), both by A. C. Swinburne*

*Starred entries in the above issues of *The Bibelot* are works found in other series published by Mosher: for (4) see entries 321 & 322; for (5) see 400 & 401; for (6) see 113; for (7) see 340; for (9) see 321 & 322; and for (12) see 297.

Comment: § Includes a "symbolic design" to accompany Verlaine's lyrics, "Sonnet to a Woman" on the fly-leaf (facing p. 57). The design is a woman's profile done by the young French artist, Andhré des Gachons, who also did the frontispiece to *Sylvie* (see 394). Accompanying the illustration is a tissue sheet with a Verlaine poem "A Une Femme" (Sonnet to a Woman) translated by A. Lenalie. See also 242 for the use of this poem.

22. ***THE BIBELOT   A REPRINT OF POETRY AND PROSE FOR BOOK LOVERS***, chosen in part from scarce editions and sources not generally known...
Vol. V. 1899.   *iv*, 402, [1] pp.
12 monthly issues.   H 123.   First thus.

In addition to the regular copies, 12 were printed on Japan vellum.

Content:

1. Gertha's Lovers. Part I by William Morris*
2. Gertha's Lovers. Part II by William Morris*
3. Lyrics from Thomas Lovell Beddoes
4. Orgeas and Miradou: Dream of Provence by Frederick Wedmore*
5. Songs in Absence and Other Poems by Arthur Hugh Clough
6. Demeter and Persephone: Three Translations by Walter Pater
7. Translations from the French of Villon by Algernon Charles Swinburne*
8. Earthwork Out of Tuscany: Two Selections by Maurice Hewlett*
9. The Two Sides of the River and Other Poems by William Morris*
10. Two Appreciations by Walter Pater I. Æsthetic Poetry. II. Dante Gabriel Rossetti
11. Our Lady's Tumbler. Trans. by P. H. Wicksteed*
12. Adonais: An Elegy on the Death of John Keats by Percy Bysshe Shelley

*Starred entries in the above issues of *The Bibelot* are works found in other series published by Mosher: for (1 & 2) see entries 133 & 134; for (4) see 93; for (7) see 18; for (8) see 97; for (9) see 419; for (11) see 279-281.

23.   **THE BIBELOT A REPRINT OF POETRY AND PROSE FOR BOOK**
      LOVERS, chosen in part from scarce editions and sources not generally known...
      Vol. VI. 1900.   *iv*, 428, [1] pp., 2 ports.
      12 monthly issues.   H 159.   First thus.

In addition to the regular copies, 12 were printed on Japan vellum.

Content:

1. The 'Orfeo' of Poliziano: Translated
    by John Addington Symonds
2. Leonardo Da Vinci: A Renaissance
    Study by Walter Pater*§
3. Lyrics by Cosmo Monkhouse
4. Golden Wings: A Tale by Wm Morris*
5. A Song to David by Christopher Smart*
6. In the Shadows: A Poem in Sonnets
    by David Gray
7. The Field-Play by Richard Jefferies
8. A Little Garland of Celtic Verse*
9. Svend and His Brethren: A Tale
    by William Morris*
10. Ernest Dowson: An Essay by
    Arthur Symons*
11. Old Italian Gardens by Vernon Lee*
12. Lyrics From the Hills of Dream
    by Fiona Macleod*

* Starred entries in the above issues of *The Bibelot* are works found in other series published by Mosher: for (2) see entries 321 & 322; for (4) see 135 & 136; for (5) see 361; for (8) see 214; for (9) see 135 & 136; for (10) see 301; for (11) see 170; for (12) see 121.

Comment: § Includes a portrait of Andrea Salaino with a fly-leaf quotation from Pater's essay (facing p. 60), and a portrait of Christopher Smart (facing p. 152).

24.   **THE BIBELOT A REPRINT OF POETRY AND PROSE FOR BOOK**
      LOVERS, chosen in part from scarce editions and sources not generally known...
      Vol. VII. 1901.   *iv*, 419, [1] pp., plate, port.
      12 monthly issues.   H 198.   First thus.

In addition to the regular copies, 12 were printed on Japan vellum.

Content:

1. In Hospital: Rhymes and Rhythms
    by William Ernest Henley*
2. Gérard De Nerval, an essay by
    Arthur Symons
3. The Churches of North France.
    No. I by William Morris*
4. Lyrics from 'Ionica' by William Cory
5. Clifton and a Lad's Love by John
    Addington Symonds
6. Dead Love, and Other Inedited Pieces
    by Algernon Charles Swinburne*
7. A Minor Poet and Lyrics by Amy Levy §
8. A Venetian Painter of the Last Century
    by John Addington Symonds
9. Proverbs in Porcelain by Austin Dobson*
10. Æs Triplex by R. L. Stevenson*
11. Celtic: A Study in Spiritual History
    by Fiona Macleod*
12. In Praise of Thackeray, including:
    - William Makepeace Thackeray by
      Thomas William Parsons
    - In Memoriam by Charles Dickens
    - Thackeray's Death by Dr. John Brown

*Starred entries in the above issues of *The Bibelot* are works found in other series published by Mosher: for (1) see entry 165, for (3) see 70, for (6) see 81, for (9) see 314, for (10) see 1, for (11) see 58.

Comment: §Includes a design by M. J. Lawless, "Dead Love" (facing p. 189), and a portrait of Amy Levy at the beginning of the issue.

25.   **THE BIBELOT A REPRINT OF POETRY AND PROSE FOR BOOK**
      LOVERS, chosen in part from scarce editions and sources not generally known...
      Vol. VIII. 1902.   *iv*, 440, [1] pp.
      12 monthly issues.   H 231.   First thus.

In addition to the regular copies, 12 were printed on Japan vellum.

THE BIBELOT   A REPRINT (continued)

Content:

1. London Voluntaries: [and] Rhymes and
   Rhythms by William Ernest Henley*
2. An Essay on Percy Bysshe Shelley
   by Robert Browning
3. The Story of the Unknown Church:
   Lindenborg Pool by William Morris*
4. Pervigilium Veneris (Latin Text and
   Four Translations)
5. Doris: An Idyl of Arcady by Augustus
   Jessopp, D. D.
6. Sonnets of the Wingless Hours by
   Eugene Lee-Hamilton*
7. A Dream by William Morris
8. In Praise of Old Houses by Vernon Lee
9. William Morris: An Address
   by J. W. Mackail*
10. Rossetti and the Religion of Beauty
    by F. W. H. Myers
11. The New Mysticism by Ernest Rhys
12. Ballads and Lyrics by William
    Makepeace Thackeray

* Starred entries in the above issues of *The Bibelot* are works found in other series published by Mosher: for (1) see entries 218 & 323; for (3) see 389 & 390; for (6) see 377; and for (9) see 435.

---

26. ***THE BIBELOT A REPRINT OF POETRY AND PROSE FOR BOOK LOVERS***, chosen in part from scarce editions and sources not generally known...
    Vol. IX. 1903.   *iv*, 416, [1] pp.
    12 monthly issues.   H 263.   First thus.

    In addition to the regular copies, 12 were printed on Japan vellum.

    Content:

    1. Chrysanthema: Gathered from the
       Greek Anthology by Wm. M. Hardinge*
    2. Chrysanthema, (concluded)*; also A
       Little Cycle of Greek Lyrics translated
       by J. W. Mackail and others
    3. Stéphane Mallarmé by Arthur Symons
    4. Lyrics by Arthur Symons*
    5. A Second Little Garland of Celtic Verse*
    6. The Land of Heart's Desire by W.B.
       Yeats*
    7. Lyrics by Andrew Lang
    8. Popular Songs of Tuscany by
       John Addington Symonds
    9. Virgil in English Verse: An Essay
       by J. W. Mackail
    10. Lyrics by William Ernest Henley*
    11. Ann: A Memory by Thomas De-
        Quincey*
    12. A Christmas Garland*

    * Starred entries in the above issues of *The Bibelot* are works found in other series published by Mosher: for (1 & 2) see entry 69; for (4) see 227; for (5) see 214; for (6) see 186-188; for (10) see 99; for (11) see 4; for (12) see 215.

    Reference: Green, p. 246.

---

27. ***THE BIBELOT A REPRINT OF POETRY AND PROSE FOR BOOK LOVERS***, chosen in part from scarce editions and sources not generally known...
    Vol. X. 1904.   *iv*, 418, [1] pp.
    12 monthly issues.   H 299.   First thus.

    In addition to the regular copies, 12 were printed on Japan vellum.

    Content:

    1. A Masque of Dead Florentines
       Part I by Maurice Hewlett*
    2. A Masque of Dead Florentines
       Part II by Maurice Hewlett*
       and an Extract from Symonds'
       Renaissance in Italy
    3. Poems by Lionel Johnson* with brief
       article by Katherine Tynan-Hinkson
    4. Sea Magic and Running Water by
       Fiona Macleod
    5. Lyrics by Rosamund Marriott Watson
    6. Poems in Prose by Oscar Wilde*
    7. Roses of Paestum by Edward McCurdy*
    8. Memories of President Lincoln by Walt
       Whitman (also selections from Drum Taps
       and Songs of Parting)*
    9. Along the Trail: Lyrics by Richard Hovey
    10. Ballades by William Ernest Henley
    11. I. Percival Stockdale and Baldock Black
        Horse by Edward Fitz-Gerald. II. The Only
        Darter. III. "Master Charley" by Archdeacon
        Groome*
    12. The Strayed Reveller and Other Lyrical
        Poems by Matthew Arnold

THE BIBELOT   A REPRINT (continued)

* Starred entries in the above issues of *The Bibelot* are works found in other series published by Mosher: for (1 & 2) see entry 234; for (3) see 417; for (6) see 298; for (7) see 331; for (8) see 238-240; for (11) see 101.

28.   ***THE BIBELOT   A REPRINT OF POETRY AND PROSE FOR BOOK LOVERS***, chosen in part from scarce editions and sources not generally known...
Vol. XI. 1905.   *iv*, 403, [1] pp.
12 monthly issues.   H 332.   First thus.

In addition to the regular copies, 12 were printed on Japan vellum.

Content:

1. Esther: A Young Man's Tragedy. I-XXVI by Wilfrid Scawen Blunt
2. Esther: A Young Man's Tragedy. XXVII-LIII (concluded)
3. For Those who Love Music, [and] Raffaella, both by Axel Munthe*
4. Four Selections from the Prose and Poetry of George Eliot: I. Proem to Romola, II. Prelude to Middlemarch, III. Brother and Sister, IV. "O May I Join the Choir Invisible"
5. In Scheria and Other Poems by J. W. Mackail

6. To Nancy by Frederick Wedmore
7. Lecture on the English Renaissance, Rose Leaf and Apple Leaf: L'Envoi by Oscar Wilde*
8. Poems in Verse and Prose by Ernest Dowson*
9. Letter to a Gentleman Respecting Pooley's Case by Henry Thomas Buckle
10. Death's Disguises and Other Sonnets by Frank T. Marzials
11. Vision and Memory by Edward McCurdy
12. The Fisher of Men by Fiona Macleod, and The Sweet Miracle by Eça de Queiroz*

* Starred entries in the above issues of *The Bibelot* are works found in other series published by Mosher: for (3) see entry 115; for (7) see 193 & 330; for (8) see 301; for (12, Part II), see 393.

29.   ***THE BIBELOT   A REPRINT OF POETRY AND PROSE FOR BOOK LOVERS***, chosen in part from scarce editions and sources not generally known...
Vol. XII. 1906.   *iv*, 419, [1] pp.
12 monthly issues.   H 366.   First thus.

In addition to the regular copies, 12 were printed on Japan vellum.

Content:

1. Ariadne in Mantua. Acts I, II. Vernon Lee*
2. Ariadne in Mantua. Acts III-V. Vernon Lee*
3. Lyrics by Margaret L. Woods
4. Two Songs of the Springtides: I. Thalassius II. On the Cliffs, by A. C. Swinburne
5. Mediæval Norman Songs by John Addington Symonds
6. Poems by Thomas William Parsons
7. Charles Lamb: An Appreciation by Walter Pater

8. Lyrics: Original and Translated by James Clarence Mangan
9. On Going a Journey by William Hazlitt
10. Giordano Bruno by Walter Pater. Four Sonnets on Bruno by A. C. Swinburne
11. The Last Days of John Addington Symonds by Margaret Symonds
12. Three Selections from Fiona Macleod. I. The Distant Country* II. A Memory of Beauty III. The Wind, the Shadow, and the Soul

*Starred entries in the above issues of *The Bibelot* are works found in other series published by Mosher: for (1 & 2) see entry 6; for (12, Part I) see 90.

Reference: Vilain, p. 105, plate 67 showing the white spine and label of volume in boards.

30.   ***THE BIBELOT   A REPRINT OF POETRY AND PROSE FOR BOOK LOVERS***, chosen in part from scarce editions and sources not generally known...
Vol. XIII. 1907.   *iv*, 424, [1] pp.
12 monthly issues.   H 401.   First thus.

In addition to the regular copies, 12 were printed on Japan vellum.

THE BIBELOT   A REPRINT (continued)

Content:

1. A Defence of Poetry by Percy Bysshe Shelley*
2. A Defence of Poetry (concluded)*
3. The Seven Golden Odes of John Keats*
4. Selections from Walter Savage Landor
5. Lyrics from Thomas Hood
6. A Little Book for John O'Mahony's Friends by Katherine Tynan*
7. Three Letters to Dead Authors by Andrew Lang: I. To Pierre de Ronsard, II. To Theocritus, III. To Q. Horatius Flaccus
8. Modernity in Verse by Arthur Symons
9. A Little Book for Mary Gill's Friends by Katherine Tynan
10. Two Nature Essays by Fiona Macleod I. Where the Forest Murmurs II. Rosa Mystica (and Roses of Autumn)
11. A Note on Omar; Quatrains from Omar Khayyám; and Four Translations from the French, all by York-Powell
12. Sister Benvenuta and the Christ Child: An Eighteenth-Century Legend by Vernon Lee*

* Starred entries in the above issues of *The Bibelot* are works found in other series published by Mosher: for (1 & 2) see entries 85 & 86; for (3) see 274; for (6) see 208; for (12) see 357.

30.01   A very unusual item is a bound copy of K. Tynan's "A Little Book for Mary Gill's Friends" (see the August issue, # 9 above) now in the Bishop Collection. This copy has the Mosher bookplate and is bound in Japan vellum wraps over flexible boards (15.7 x 11.6 cm.) with the title at top of the cover, the author's name at the bottom, and a single flower in the center, all printed with brown ink. The flower (a pink) is C. R. Ashbee's device for the Guild of Handicraft (see Taylor, p. 33). This same flower device was used by Mosher on the last page of *Little Willie* (216). The purpose of this bound issue of *The Bibelot* may have been for presentation to the author and/or close friends, with a copy being kept by Mosher. The "book" does not contain a title page. The companion piece by Tynan, printed three months earlier in *The Bibelot* (Vol. XIII, June) did appear as a separate Mosher book entitled *A Little Book for John O'Mahony's Friends* (208). This practice of binding single issues of *The Bibelot* apparently established the precedent for Flora Lamb to bind select issues of *The Bibelot* for sale, after Mosher's death (see FL12). In an August 11, 1911 letter from Mrs. Katherine Tynan Hinkson to Mosher (The Houghton Library, bMS Am 1096 [656]), she thanks him "for the beautiful little special copy of *Mary Gill*."

31.   ***THE BIBELOT   A REPRINT OF POETRY AND PROSE FOR BOOK LOVERS,*** chosen in part from scarce editions and sources not generally known... Vol. XIV. 1908.   *iv*, 417, [1] pp.

12 monthly issues.   H 444.   First thus.

In addition to the regular copies, 12 were printed on Japan vellum.

Content:

1. The Story of Frithiof the Bold: Translated from the Icelandic by William Morris
2. The Story of Frithiof the Bold (concluded)
3. Seven Poems by Francis Thompson, and A Word on Thompson by Arthur Symons*
4. Obermann: An Essay and Two Poems by Matthew Arnold
5. Three Poets of French Bohemia by Andrew Lang
6. Mimma Bella: In Memory of a Little Life by Eugene Lee-Hamilton*
7. Pearl: Rendered into Modern English Verse by S. Weir Mitchell, M.D.*
8. Songs from An Italian Garden by A. Mary F. Robinson*
9. Simeon Solomon: Notes on His "Vision of Love" and Other Studies by Algernon Charles Swinburne
10. Maeterlinck as a Mystic by Arthur Symons
11. Lyrics by Austin Dobson*
12. Diversi Colores by Herbert P. Horne

THE BIBELOT   A REPRINT (continued)

* Starred entries in the above issues of *The Bibelot* are works found in other series published by Mosher: for (3) see entries 154, 155 & 295; for (6) see 243; for (7) see 286; for (8) see 178 & 365; for (11) see 314.

Reference: Green, p. 248; Vilain, p. 105, plate 66 showing one issue in wraps, and plate 69 showing the spine of a morocco bound volume.

---

32. *THE BIBELOT A REPRINT OF POETRY AND PROSE FOR BOOK LOVERS*, chosen in part from scarce editions and sources not generally known... Vol. XV. 1909.   *iv*, 447, [1] pp.
     12 monthly issues.   H 479.   First thus.

In addition to the regular copies, 12 were printed on Japan vellum.

Content:

1. A Vision of Love Revealed in Sleep by Simeon Solomon*
2. A Vision of Love Revealed in Sleep (concluded), and Review by J. A. Symonds*
3. Lyrics and Sonnets by Arthur Upson*
4. Poems in Prose from Charles Baudelaire: Translated by Arthur Symons*
5. The Fire of Prometheus by Henry W. Nevinson
6. Translations from Heine by James Thomson ("B. V.")
7. Notes on Poems and Reviews by Algernon Charles Swinburne
8. George Meredith: An Appreciation by Oliver Elton, and Margaret's Bridal Eve by George Meredith
9. The Crier by Night: A Play in One Act by Gordon Bottomley
10. The Little Crow of Paradise and Other Fantasies by J. H. Pearce
11. Alexander Smith: An Essay by James Smetham
12. A Little Child's Wreath by Elizabeth Rachel Chapman

* Starred entries in the above issues of *The Bibelot* are works found in other series published by Mosher: for (1 & 2) see entry 429; for (3) see 228; for (4) see 299.

---

33. *THE BIBELOT A REPRINT OF POETRY AND PROSE FOR BOOK LOVERS*, chosen in part from scarce editions and sources not generally known... Vol. XVI. 1910.   *iv*, 468, [1] pp.
     12 monthly issues.   H 518.   First thus.

In addition to the regular copies, a reduced number of 6 copies were printed on Japan vellum. Previous issues were limited to 12 copies for the Japan vellum printing.

Content:

1. The Riding to Lithend: A Play in One Act by Gordon Bottomley*
2. The Riding to Lithend (concluded)* and a review by Lascelles Abercrombie
3. Three Selections from *Vagaries* by Axel Munthe: I. Instead of a Preface II. Toys: from the Paris Horizon. III. To —(on Dogs)*
4. Lyrics by Arthur O'Shaughnessy
5. Under a Fool's Cap by Norman Roe, and XIII Lyrics from Under a Fool's Cap by Daniel Henry Holmes*
6. The Dearest of All by Katharine Tynan Hinkson
7. How to Fail in Literature: A Lecture by Andrew Lang
8. How to Fail in Literature (concluded) Does Ridicule Kill? by Andrew Lang
9. London Streets: A Book of Lyrics by Arthur H. Adams
10. The Two Boyhoods by John Ruskin
11. Lyrics by Seumas O'Sullivan with preface by "A.E."
12. Passages from The Song Celestial: Translated by Sir Edwin Arnold*

* Starred entries in the above issues of *The Bibelot* are works found in other series published by Mosher: for (1 & 2) see entry 324; for (3, part III) see 115; for (5) see 422; and for (12) see 285.

Reference: Green, p. 248.

34. *THE BIBELOT A REPRINT OF POETRY AND PROSE FOR BOOK LOVERS*, chosen in part from scarce editions and sources not generally known...
Vol. XVII. 1911. *iv*, 436, [1] pp.
12 monthly issues. H 544. First thus.

In addition to the regular copies, there were 6 copies printed on Japan vellum.

Content:

1. Lucretius on Life and Death in the Metre of Omar Khayyám by W.H. Mallock*
2. Lucretius on Life and Death (concluded)*
3. Aubrey Beardsley: An Essay with a Preface by Arthur Symons
4. Three Appreciations: I. Aubrey Beardsley II. Simeon Solomon by Robert Ross III. Note on Simeon Solomon by Arthur Symons
5. From the Heart of a Garden by Rosamund Marriott Watson: I. Lyrics II. The Road to Spring
6. Francine's Muff (A Scene from La Vie de Bohême) by Henri Murger.
7. Francine's Muff (concluded)
8. Proud Maisie and Other Lyrics by Sir Walter Scott
9. Selections from Leonardo Da Vinci translated by Edward McCurdy
10. Three Dreams in a Desert by Olive Schreiner: I. Three Dreams in a Desert, II. "I Thought I Stood,"* and III. "The Policy in Favour of Protection—"
11. Il Pesceballo: Opera in One Act by Francis James Child (Eng. text by James Russell Lowell)*
12. Yoshida-Torajiro by Robert Louis Stevenson

* Starred entries in the above issues of *The Bibelot* are works found in other series published by Mosher: for (1 & 2) see entry 223; for (10, Parts I & II) see 94; and for (11) see 288.

35. *THE BIBELOT A REPRINT OF POETRY AND PROSE FOR BOOK LOVERS*, chosen in part from scarce editions and sources not generally known...
Vol. XVIII. 1912. *iv*, 443, [1] pp.
12 monthly issues. H 566. First thus.

In addition to the regular copies, there were 6 copies printed on Japan vellum.

Content:

1. A Prelude to Life by Arthur Symons
2. A Prelude to Life (concluded)*
3. The Dying of Francis Donne: A Study, and Prose Poems by Ernest Dowson*
4. Under an Elm-Tree by William Morris, [and] The Happiest of the Poets by W. B. Yeats
5. Three Selections from Leaves of Grass by Walt Whitman: I. Passage to India, II. Song of the Open Road, and III. Song of the Universal *§
6. Casanova at Dux: An Unpublished Chapter of History by Arthur Symons
7. Two Selections from John Inglesant: I. The Vielle-Player's Story, II. Old Dance Music by J. H. Shorthouse: [and] In a Gondola by Aureolus Paracelsus
8. Three Poems of England's Glory: I. Drake's Drum by Henry Newbolt, II. The Burden of the Armada by Theodore Watts-Dunton, and III. "The Revenge" by Alfred Lord Tennyson, with a note on "The Revenge": A Ballad of the Fleet by J. A. Froude
9. Two Stories by Ernest Dowson: I. The Eyes of Pride, and II. Countess Marie of the Angels*
10. Two Chapters from Marius the Epicurean by Walter Pater: I. Euphuism, and II. Pagan Death*
11. Three Nature Essays by James Douglas: I. A Mood Without a Moral, II. Magic in Kensington Gardens, and III. An Autumnal Idyll*
12. The Thoughts of the Emperor Marcus Aurelius Antoninus by Herbert P. Horne

* Starred entries in the above issues of *The Bibelot* are works found in other series published by Mosher: for (2) bibliography of Symons at conclusion of issue, see 441; (3) see entry 301; for (5) see 192; for (9) see 392; for (10) see 231 & 232; for (11) see 230.

Comment: §A facsimile of Whitman's "Joy, Shipmate, Joy" appears facing p. 137 of the May issue.

36. **THE BIBELOT A REPRINT OF POETRY AND PROSE FOR BOOK
     LOVERS**, chosen in part from scarce editions and sources not generally known...
     Vol. XIX. 1913.   *iv*, 426, [1] pp.
     12 monthly issues.   H 594.   First thus.

     Content:

     1. The Little Schoolmaster Mark: A Spiritual
         Romance by J. H. Shorthouse
     2. The Little Schoolmaster Mark (con-
         cluded), with a review by Vernon Lee
     3. A "Canterbury" Whitman by Richard
         LeGallienne
     4. The Spell of Old Music and Other Essays
         by Henry Noel Brailsford: I. The Spell
         of Old Music, II. On Handel's Largo,
         III. The Sea in Music, and IV. Of Fauns
         and Oboes
     5. Four Translations from Theocritus, and
         Epitaph of Bion by Moschus translated
         by Edmund Clarence Stedman
     6. Mr. Stevenson's Forerunner: An Essay
         by James Ashcroft Noble*

     7. Riders to the Sea: A Play in One
         Act by J. M. Synge
     8. In the Shadow of the Glen: A Play
         in One Act by J. M. Synge
     9. The Poetry of Robert Bridges: An
         Essay by Arthur Symons
     10. Poems of Mary Coleridge: An Essay
         by Robert Bridges
     11. Three Essays by Charles Lamb: I. Old China,
         II. Dream-Children, and III. The Child Angel
     12. The Last Chapter of Hydriotaphia by Sir
         Thomas Browne. Also I. An Appreciation
         by Walter Pater, II. The Epistle Dedicatory
         by Thomas Browne, and III. A Brief Dis-
         course on Urne-Buriall by Thomas Browne

     * Starred entry in the above issues of *The Bibelot* is a work found in another
     series published by Mosher: for (6) see entry 95.

     In addition to the regular copies,
     there were 6 copies printed on
     Japan vellum.

37. **THE BIBELOT A REPRINT OF POETRY AND PROSE FOR BOOK
     LOVERS**, chosen in part from scarce editions and sources not generally known...
     Vol. XX. 1914.   *iv*, 439, [1] pp., incl. illus.
     12 monthly issues.   H 612.   First thus.

     Content:

     1. Belcaro—Three Selections by Vernon
         Lee: I. The Book and Its Title. II. Orpheus
         and Eurydice. III. Postscript or Apology*
     2. Belcaro—Three Selections (concluded)*
     3. Lyrics by Edmund Gosse
     4. Lyndall by Olive Schreiner
     5. The Picture of Dorian Gray: Chapter
         XI by Oscar Wilde
     6. Prelude to Songs before Sunrise [and]
         Prelude to Tristram and Iseult by Algernon
         Charles Swinburne*
     7. Sir Peter Harpdon's End by William Morris

     8. Sir Peter Harpdon's End (concluded).
         A Critical Estimate by John Drinkwater
     9. Consule Planco by Sir James H. Yoxall
     10. Where the Forest Murmurs: Two Nature
         Essays by Fiona Macleod: I. Still Waters,
         and II. The Rainy Hyades
     11. Three Essays by Hilaire Belloc:* I. On
         Sacramental Things, II. On Rest, and
         III. On Coming to an End
     12. XVII Woodcut Designs to Thornton's Virgil
         by William Blake with Introduction by
         Laurence Binyon* and Thenot and Colinet,
         An Eclogue by Ambrose Philips

     * Starred entries in the above issues of *The Bibelot* are works found in other
     series published by Mosher: for (1&2) see 64; for (6) see entries 364 & 416
     respectively; for (11) see 8; for (12) see 347.

     In addition to the regular copies,
     there were 6 copies printed on
     Japan vellum.

38. **THE BIBELOT A REPRINT OF POETRY AND PROSE FOR BOOK
     LOVERS,** chosen in part from scarce editions and sources not generally known...
     General Index Volumes I to XII. 1906.   *viii*, 64 pp.
     The Bibelot Index.   H 367.   First index.

     Content: The note on p. [*v*] is by the publisher. On p. [*viii*] there appears a
     list of the volumes I-XII, along with their dates and pagination. A list of five
     illustrations appears on p. [64]. Previously omitted names of authors, quoted
     on some half-titles, were supplied with the index.

     Comment: This was the first index covering only the first 12 volumes. It was
     issued both in blue wraps, and in "Old Style" boards.

     In addition to the regular printed
     copies, 12 numbered copies were
     printed on Japan vellum.

39. **THE BIBELOT A REPRINT OF POETRY AND PROSE FOR BOOK
     LOVERS,** chosen in part from scarce editions and sources not generally known…
     General Index Volumes I to XX Inclusive (1895-1914)
     Compiled by Milton James Ferguson. 1915.   *xiv*, 191 pp., port. front.
     The Bibelot Index.   H 628.   Second index.

The Japan vellum printing was
limited to 8 numbered copies (not
6 as incorrectly given in Hatch).

Content: Includes "Salve et Vale" by Eleanor Cuyler Patterson, "Thomas Bird
Mosher—An Appreciation" by Richard Le Gallienne*, "The Ending of *The
Bibelot*" by William Marion Reedy, two stanzas from Robert Frost's "Reluctance," and a quote from Novalis. The forward is by Mosher, who also provides
a two-page note on pagination, and a volume-by-volume breakdown of the
contents of *The Bibelot* (following the index).

* Starred entry in the above index of *The Bibelot* is found in another series
published by Mosher: see entries 258 & 408. The complete poem by Robert
Frost also appeared in entry 257.

Comment: This was the final, complete index with an oval portrait frontispiece of Mosher and his signature in facsimile (actual signature in morocco
and Japan vellum copies only).

The 3/4 leather-bound volume contains a limitation certificate signed by
Mosher (see *The Bibelot* in Section I), with numerous blank pages for notes
bound in front and rear.

---

40. **A BIBLIOGRAPHICAL LIST OF THE EDITIONS OF EDWARD
     FITZGERALD'S RUBÁIYÁT OF OMAR KHAYYÁM, 1859-1907.** 1907.
     iv, 33, [1] pp.   21.5 x 13 cm.
     Privately Printed-10   H 712.   Only edition.

25 numbered copies on Japan
vellum.

Content: The note at the beginning is signed by the publisher. In it he
acknowledges the "kindly assistance of Mr. Nathan Haskell Dole, of Boston,
Eben F. Thompson, Esq., of Worcester, Mass., and Mr. H.[Herman] M.
Schroeter of Los Angeles, Cal." There are 10 numbered entries under Authorized English Editions, 10 numbered entries under Other English Editions, 17
numbered entries under English Reprints of 1859 text, and 69 numbered
entries under American Editions. Some entries contain several later editions.
Mosher's own editions are given as entries 9, 10, 32, 34, and 59.

The content, with modifications to the head- and tail-pieces, is an offprint of
the bibliography appearing in the ninth edition of the Old World *Rubáiyát*
(334.9) which also appeared in 1907.

Comment: T. B. Mosher compiled this book for distribution to his friends and,
according to the Sheean Typescript, to members of The Omar Khayyám Club
of America at their annual meeting in 1907. See Vilain for a description of a
printer's dummy for this work which shows it was under consideration as
early as 1903, but not finally completed until 1907 (printer's dummy is in the
Bishop Collection). The original typescript for this bibliography is located at
The Grolier Club in New York City. It is basically a list of the *Rubáiyáts* in
Mosher's own collection, and contains additional notes not present in the
printed work.

Mosher's fame as an "Omarian" was well known. In the introduction for *To
Omar: Spoil of the North Wind* (Chicago: Blue Sky Press, 1901), Edward Martin Moore acknowledges Mosher as an avid collector of publications by and
about Omar Khayyám.

EDWARD FITZGERALD'S RUBÁIYÁT OF OMAR KHAYYÁM (continued)

Binding & Embellishment: Bound in Japan vellum wraps over boards with title along the spine. The title page is ruled in black and printed in red and black. The text-block is the type width of the Old World Series, so there is generous margin space. Chiswick ornamentation.

Reference: Potter 640; Vilain 48 & plate 50 on p. 99.

---

41. ***BILLY*** by Maud Thornhill Porter. 1912.   *vi*, 54, [1] pp.   19.5 x 14 cm.
Privately Printed-18   H 720.   First thus.

Printed for Mrs. E. W. Cohen. 500 copies on Van Gelder; 25 numbered copies on Japan vellum. First edition.

Content: The text first appeared in *The American Magazine* (September 1912) under the title "Billy: An Extraordinary Biography." The inscription before the title text is by Mrs. Caroline Cohen, the person for whom the book was privately printed and the owner of the copyright.

Binding & Embellishment: The Van Gelder copies are bound in green paper boards with white label on the spine. Title page in red and black; Chiswick ornament and red lead initial. The bird illustration on p. [54] is by Reginald Birch.

---

42. ***BILLY THE TRUE STORY OF A CANARY BIRD*** by Maud Thornhill Porter. [March] 1914.   *viii*, 55, [1] pp.   17.5 x 11 cm.
Miscellaneous Series-67   H 607.   First thus.

950 copies on Van Gelder; 25 numbered copies on Japan vellum.

Content: The text is a reprint of the privately printed edition (41) with a foreword added and signed by the publisher. The inscription by Mrs. Caroline Cohen (p.*v*) is maintained, and the copyright remains under her name.

Binding & Embellishment: Van Gelder copies are bound in quarter brown paper over decorative floral "Rizzi" paper boards. The Japan vellum copies are bound in Japan vellum boards. Title page in red and black; Chiswick ornaments; some initial letters in red outline. The bird illustration on p. [55] is by Reginald Birch as in the privately printed edition (41).

---

43. ***BILLY AND HANS MY SQUIRREL FRIENDS A TRUE HISTORY***
by W. J. Stillman. [April] 1914.   *xxii*, 48, [1] pp.   18 x 9.5 cm.
Miscellaneous Series-68   H 608.   Only edition.

950 copies on Van Gelder; 25 numbered copies on Japan vellum.

Content: This story by the American born journalist, William James Stillman, first appeared in the *Century Magazine* (February 1897) and later a revised and enlarged edition was published in the *Life and Light Books* (London, 1907). The latter became the source for Mosher's reprint, published with the permission of the author's wife, Mrs. Marie Stillman. The copyright is held by both The Century Co. and Marie Stillman. The unsigned note on p. [*ii*] is by the publisher.

Binding & Embellishment: Van Gelder copies are bound in quarter dark-green paper over decorated paper boards; white label on the spine. Japan vellum copies are bound in Japan vellum boards. Title page in red and black; Chiswick ornaments; some initial letters in red outline. This book is stylistically uniform with *Books and the Quiet Life* (49), and *At the Sign of the Lion* (8).

44.   *THE BIRTHDAY OF THE INFANTA* by Oscar Wilde. [August] 1905.
      51, [1] pp. (same for both editions)
      Brocade Series-48   H 325.   First edition.

      Content: The text is reprinted from Wilde's *A House of Pomegranates* (London: Osgood & McIlvaine, 1891).

      Comment: This title is part of a sub-series. See note to entry 308.

      Reference: Cowan II, pp. 6-7.

425 on Japan vellum for each edition.

44.1 *THE BIRTHDAY OF THE INFANTA* by Oscar Wilde. [October] 1907.
      Brocade Series.   H 422.   Second edition.

45.   *BITS OF OAK BARK AND MEADOW THOUGHTS* by Richard Jefferies.
      [July] 1900.   56, [1] pp. (same for all editions)
      Brocade Series-21   H 147.   First edition.

      Content: The first work appears on pp. 7-[32], and "Meadow Thoughts" concludes the book from pp. 35-56.

      Comment: This title is part of a sub-series. See note to entry 282.

      Reference: Jenkinson II, 661 references the second edition.

425 on Japan vellum for each edition.

45.1 *BITS OF OAK BARK AND MEADOW THOUGHTS* by Richard Jefferies.
      [December] 1901.
      Brocade Series.   H 207.   Second edition.

45.2 *BITS OF OAK BARK AND MEADOW THOUGHTS* by Richard Jefferies.
      [October] 1907.
      Brocade Series.   H 416.   Third edition.

46.   *THE BLESSED DAMOZEL A BOOK OF LYRICS* Chosen from the works
      of Dante Gabriel Rossetti. 1895   94 pp. (numbered in Roman numerals)
      Bibelot Series-6   H 10.   Only edition.

725 on Van Gelder; 50 numbered copies on Japan vellum.

      Content: This work includes a dozen additional lyrics besides the title lyric which is taken from *The Germ*. There are also three translations from François Villon, three ballads, and eight songs from *The House of Life*. Additionally, the tribute "In Memoriam" by A. Mary F. Robinson appears on p. *vii*, and "For a Venetian Pastoral" by Giorgione appears opposite the title page. Mosher's Autumn List published along with *The Bibelot* for October 1895 indicates that "Through the courtesy of POET-LORE [January 1895] the poem 'Jenny' [pp. 21-32] has some new readings from manuscript sources that now appear for the first time in any edition of the poet's works." These new readings appear at the end of the book under "Notes" (pp. 91-93), followed by a final selection from Rossetti's *The House of Life*, Sonnet 77, which appears on the last page.

      Reference: Grigsby 963.

——————— *Same Title, Change of Series* ———————

47. ***THE BLESSED DAMOZEL*** by Dante Gabriel Rossetti. 1901.
    xiii, 33, [1] pp.; front. (same for all editions)   15 x 13 cm.
    Miscellaneous Series-15   H 184.   First edition.

450 on "Hammer & Anvil" Kelmscott handmade paper; 50 numbered copies on Japan vellum; 10 numbered copies on Roman vellum signed by the publisher.
First complete variorum edition.

Content: The text contains the original version as published in *The Germ* (1850), and variants from *The Oxford and Cambridge Magazine* (1856), *Poems* (1870), and the *Collected Works* (1885). Mosher refers to this variorum edition as his *édition définitive*. A variorum edition was originally suggested by William Sharp, and generally advocated by Swinburne for all of Rossetti's poems, but Mosher's edition was the first to be so assembled. The unsigned preface is by the publisher, the first part of which is a selection from Swinburne's *Essays and Studies* (London: Chatto & Windus, 1875). The photo-gravure portrait of Alexa Wilding used as a frontispiece is after a portrait done by Dante Gabriel Rossetti.

Comment: On p. 58 of the 1901 catalogue, Mosher states that "based on the format of the Vale Press, as our reprint professedly is, it shows conclusively how much more beautiful a book can be made by adhering to well recognized standards of page and margin, than by treating the poem as a mere bit of decorative type-work as in the London edition." Textual differences between the Mosher edition and the Vale Press edition include Mosher's additional 11 page preface, 2 pages of notes, and the addition of variant phrases from other editions, including an alternate 10th stanza.

Binding & Embellishment: The Kelmscott paper copy is bound in charcoal blue boards with white labels printed in red and black on the spine and front cover. The Japan vellum copies are bound in Japan vellum wraps over boards with the label information printed directly on the cover. For other books printed on Kelmscott paper see 66, 103, 106, 116, 139, 311 & 345.

Despite Mosher's assertions, anyone comparing the original London, Hacon & Ricketts edition of 1900 with this edition will be immediately struck by their similarities even though the Mosher edition is larger (15 x 13 cm. as opposed to the small oblong 10 x 13cm.). Mosher's edition uses the same alternating black and red Ricketts initials and text, the same red rules at the two-page openings of the book following the half-titles, and the same red Roman numerals of each stanza. With these similarities noted, there are other differences. Mosher uses a slightly smaller type, keeps all page numbers near the gutter, uses different dingbats (Mosher uses Kelmscott dingbats), and drops the use of catch-words as found in the original London edition. Mosher also employed a frontispiece whereas the London edition does not.

For other books using Vale Press & Charles Ricketts designs, see 56, 103, 132, 139, 154, 175, 221, 248, 250, 254, 272, 302, 319, 358, 366, 411, 412, 439 & 440.

Reference: Vilain, p. 19 (see also Vilain 15 and plate 23 of the opening spread on p. 89); Boss XV 156; Quinn 8196 & 8197; Grigsby 969. Technically relating to the third edition of this title, Fredeman 28.9 refers readers to "the brief article in *Academy*, LXXII, no. 1823 (13 April 1907), 365-366, mentioning 'the benign pirate' T. B. Mosher's edition of the poem with variant readings," p. 114; Japan Paper Company (Kelmscott Hand-made Paper from England); Lowden, p. 15 (references the third edition).

47.1 *THE BLESSED DAMOZEL* by Dante Gabriel Rossetti. 1902.
Miscellaneous Series.   H 237.   Second edition.

450 on Kelmscott paper for this and the third edition; no Japan vellum copies.

47.2 *THE BLESSED DAMOZEL* by Dante Gabriel Rossetti. 1905.
Miscellaneous Series.   H 340.   Third edition.

---

48. *THE BOOK OF HEAVENLY DEATH* by Walt Whitman compiled from *Leaves of Grass* by Horace Traubel. [April] 1905.
xxiii, 103 pp.; portrait front., facsim. (same for both editions)   19 x 14.5 cm.
Miscellaneous Series-27   H 318.   First edition.

500 copies on Van Gelder; 50 numbered copies on Japan vellum; and 5 copies on Roman vellum.
First edition of this anthology.

Content: The source of the material used in this book is the Small, Maynard and Co. authorized edition of *Leaves of Grass* (Boston, 1900). On p. [xvi] Horace Traubel notes that "the idea of this collection was first discussed by me with the late Herbert Small, of Small, Maynard and Company, Boston. I discovered later on that Thomas B. Mosher had independently conceived the same idea. I ought also to acknowledge in this place the editorial advisorship of Anne Montgomerie, Thomas B. Harned and Thomas B. Mosher." The book's preface is by Horace Traubel, and the book's copyright is also under his name. Traubel was a close friend of Whitman's and one of his literary executors. In addition to the table of contents (page numbers referring to the location in the Small, Maynard edition), there is a first-line index (pp. 99-[103]), both of which refer to the entries using Roman numerals.

The 1880 "King Lear" albertype photo of Walt Whitman is used for the frontispiece. According to the 1905 catalogue, this was taken from the "original and heretofore unused photograph of Whitman."

Comment: Walt Whitman had himself assembled 19 poems and entitled them "Whispers of Heavenly Death." These poems were assembled for an edition of *Leaves of Grass* sometime after 1870. This grouping was given by Whitman to Horace Traubel in 1889, and later given by Traubel to Mosher in 1906. So though Traubel edited 128 of Whitman's poems relating to the subject of death, the idea for this assemblage was first Whitman's.

Binding & Embellishment: The Van Gelder copies are bound in charcoal blue boards with a white spine label printed in two colors. The Japan vellum copies are bound in Japan vellum wraps over boards with the label information printed directly on the spine. Renaissance head-bands signed "CW" for Charlotte Whittingham who was a designer for the Chiswick Press of London (see Warren, p. 311 which also pictures the other two head-pieces in the book).

For other Chiswick Press designs used, see 61, 160, 164, 258, 279, 281, 284, 306, 349, 352 & 386. Many other Mosher books, too numerous to enumerate, also used Chiswick designs.

Reference: Myerson C.19.1.a-d; Quinn 11007; Boss XI 134; Warren, p. 311. For further comment, see Schreyer, p. 54.

48.1 *THE BOOK OF HEAVENLY DEATH* by Walt Whitman compiled from *Leaves of Grass* by Horace Traubel. [August] 1907.
Miscellaneous Series.   H 412.   Second edition.

500 copies on Van Gelder only.

49. ***BOOKS AND THE QUIET LIFE*** Being Some Pages from the Private Papers
     of Henry Ryecroft by George Gissing Chosen by W R B. [April] 1914.
     vii, 57, [1] pp. (same for both eds.)   18 x 9.5 cm.
     Miscellaneous Series-69   H 609.   First edition.

950 copies on Van Gelder; 25 numbered copies on Japan vellum.

Content: The foreword is by W. R. Browne, with bibliographical footnotes by
the publisher. According to a May 29, 1936 note from Flora Lamb quoted in
Wheeler, "these passages were compiled by W. R. Browne of the Chicago *Dial*
and presented to Mr. Mosher for publication."

Binding & Embellishment: The Van Gelder copies are bound in quarter dark-
blue paper over decorative patterned boards; white label in two colors on
spine. Japan vellum copies are bound in Japan vellum boards. Title page in red
and black; Chiswick ornaments; some lead initials in red outline. This book is
stylistically uniform with *Billy and Hans* (43) and *At the Sign of the Lion* (8).

Reference: Garland IA & ID (p. 20); Quinn 3379; Wheeler (H.O.), p. 15.

49.1 ***BOOKS AND THE QUIET LIFE*** Being Some Pages from the Private Papers
      of Henry Ryecroft by George Gissing Chosen by W R B. [July] 1922.
      (special copy has inserted leaf)
      Miscellaneous Series.   H 699.   Second edition.

950 on Van Gelder; 50 special copies (see comment under entry).

Comment: Before the half-title of one copy appears this printed limitation note:
"Fifty copies of this edition of Books and the Quiet Life have been prepared for
those friends of John W. Hancock who appreciate beauty in books." It is not
clear whether these copies were included in, or in addition to, the 950 printed
on Van Gelder paper. The Lamb and Sheean typescripts are mute on this.

Binding & Embellishment: The binding changes from that of the first edition
(49). The Van Gelder copies are in blue paper boards with a dark blue, art
nouveau floral design at the top of the front cover (see 275 for an illustration
of this design), and title/author in red and dark blue on the spine and front
cover. The special copy (1 of 50) examined in the Bishop Collection is
designed just like the regular Van Gelder copies, but the boards are of a much
lighter charcoal blue. The format remains the same as 49.

50. ***A BRANCH OF MAY   POEMS*** by Lizette Woodworth Reese.
     1909.   *vi*, 42, [1] pp.
     Lyric Garland Series-15   H 472.   First edition.

950 on Van Gelder; 100 numbered copies on Japan vellum.

A BRANCH OF MAY
POEMS BY LIZETTE
WOODWORTH REESE

PORTLAND MAINE
THOMAS B MOSHER
MDCCCCIX

Content: This edition is a reprint of *A Branch of May* published in Baltimore
by Cushings & Bailey in 1887. Both the Portland and the Baltimore editions
are reprints of the first thirty-three poems of *A Handful of Lavender* (Boston
and New York: Houghton, Mifflin, 1891). See note to entry 141 for more information.

Comment: The copyright was owned by the poet.

This title was omitted in Ransom's *Selective Check List* and is the only trade
title he missed.

Reese received a 10% royalty on all her books sold.

Several publishers sought to imitate Mosher's book designs, especially those of
the Old World Series, the Vest Pocket Series, and the Lyric Garland Series.
One notable example is that of The Norman Remington Co. of Baltimore.
Lizette Woodworth Reese, a Baltimore native, decided to have this local firm

A BRANCH OF MAY POEMS (continued)

reprint some of her poems in 1922. The result was *Spicewood*, a very close imitation of Mosher's Lyric Garland style down to cover design, labels, slip-case, and interior design.

Reference: Correspondence surrounding this publication is located at The Houghton Library (bMS Am 1096); see Vilain, pp. 52-54 for the chapter on "Borrowing from the Pirate;" see the Nov. 17, 1941 letter from Lamb to Yorke for Mosher's payment terms (see Appendix II).

——————— *Same Title, Change of Series* ———————

51. **A BRANCH OF MAY: POEMS** by Lizette Woodworth Reese. With a Foreword   450 numbered copies on Van
     by Jessie B. Rittenhouse. [October] 1920.   *xvi*, 45, [1] pp.   Gelder; 25 numbered copies on
     Lyra Americana Series-6   H 680.   First thus.   Japan vellum.

Content: Contains the same thirty-three poems as first published by Mosher in 1909 (50). A bibliographical note appears on pp. [43-45]. The foreword by Jesse B. Rittenhouse was added to this edition, and did not appear in the first Mosher reprint.

Comment: Last title in the Lyra Americana series. Reese received a 10% royalty.

Binding & Embellishment: The Van Gelder copies are bound in quarter green paper over patterned paper boards. See series in Section I for further details.

Reference: See the Nov. 17, 1941 letter from Lamb to Yorke for Mosher's payment payment terms (see Appendix II).

52. **BY BENDEMEER'S STREAM A BOOK OF XXXII LYRICS** [by]   450 copies on Van Gelder; 25
     Thomas Moore. [October] 1917.   *xiv*, 47, [1] pp.   18.5 x 14.5 cm.   numbered copies on Japan vellum.
     Miscellaneous Series-82   H 654.   Only edition.

Content: The foreword is signed by the publisher. Selections from T. Campbell, E. B. B. (Elizabeth Barrett Browning), and the poem "To Thomas Moore" by Byron, prefix the title text.

Comment: Mosher's 1918 catalogue announces 500 copies on Van Gelder, but the book's colophon states otherwise.

Binding & Embellishment: Two variant bindings for the Van Gelder copies: one with an Eragny Press design from the 1903 edition of Ronsard's *Abrégé de l'Art Poétique*, and one printed in gilt using the Aubrey Beardsley design first used on the cover of Dowson's *Verses* published in London by Leonard Smithers, 1896. Both include a gilt-printed glassine dust wrapper over the green boards. The Japan vellum copies are bound in cream Japan vellum boards with the Beardsley design. See also entry 339 for other details about the same Beardsley design used on another Mosher book cover. Title page in green and black; initial letters are outlined in green.

The "cupid standing on a ball" device on the title page also appears on entries 69, 87, 129 & 339 (see design note to 69 for details).

For other books using Eragny Press & Lucien Pissarro designs, see 94, 98, 129, 169, 189, 192, 203, 207, 230, 338, 345, 405, 407, 418 & 439.

53.   ***BY SUNDOWN SHORES: STUDIES IN SPIRITUAL HISTORY***
by Fiona Macleod. [September] 1902.   94, [1] pp.(same for all eds.)
Brocade Series-36   H 221.   First edition.

Content: This Mosher reprint was authorized by the author, who also titled
the prologue of the book "To My Friend, Thomas B. Mosher (To Whom I Dedi-
cate This Little Book)." "Lynn of Dreams" appears here for the first time in
print. According to the prefatory note, the work "Sheumas"... "has been in
part gathered from the notes to *The Divine Adventure*, and in part augmented
by further reminiscence." The balance of the seven writings collected here are
all from *The Divine Adventure: Iona: And Other Studies in Spiritual History*
(London: Chapman & Hall, 1900).

Comment: Fiona Macleod was a pseudonym used by William Sharp who also
published works under his real name.

This book forms a sub-series along with two others which Mosher called
"Studies and Stories by Fiona Macleod." The other two books in this sub-
series are *The Tale of the Four White Swans* (398) and *Ulad of the Dreams*
(420). These books are grouped together in the Mosher catalogues and were
also sold as sets in cabinet-style boxes.

Mosher paid Macleod $32 outright for the publication of this book in America.

Reference: Quinn 8648; see the Nov. 17, 1941 letter from Lamb to Yorke for
Mosher's payment terms (see Appendix II); Macleod IV, p. 433 & V, pp. 391-92.

53.1   ***BY SUNDOWN SHORES: STUDIES IN SPIRITUAL HISTORY*** by
Fiona Macleod. [February] 1904.
Brocade Series.   H 311.   Second edition.

53.2   ***BY SUNDOWN SHORES: STUDIES IN SPIRITUAL HISTORY*** by
Fiona Macleod. [December] 1907.
Brocade Series.   H 418.   Third edition.

425 on Japan vellum for each
edition.
First separate book edition, and
first appearance of "Lynn of
Dreams."

---

54.   ***BY THE IONIAN SEA NOTES OF A RAMBLE IN SOUTHERN ITALY***
by George Gissing. 1920.   *viii*, 215 pp.   18 x 11 cm.
Miscellaneous Series-91   H 677.   Only edition.

Content: The foreword is by the publisher. Mosher never mentions the source
for his reprint, but records of his personal library show he owned the 1901 first
edition, and the 1905 edition, both published by Chapman & Hall of London.

Comment: A copy of this edition was found by Austryn Wainhouse, director and
publisher of The Marlboro Press, and it formed the textual basis for his own
reprint published in Marlboro, VT in 1991. Wainhouse wrote in his copy of the
Mosher edition: "Come upon in Albany, in the course of a visit to the Dove and
Hudson Bookstore there, this edition of *By the Ionian Sea* provided the basis
(and the inspiration) for the Marlboro Press imprint of 1991. A.W." (Bishop Collection). The credit to Mosher on the back cover states: "*By the Ionian Sea*, originally published in England in 1901, was last brought out in this country [Amer-
ica] in 1920 by Thomas Mosher, whose lovely little edition of what he called this
'beloved book of Italian wandering' is the basis for the present reprint."

Binding & Embellishment: The Van Gelder copies are bound in old style
green ribbed boards (raised bands) with a white spine label in two colors.
Japan vellum copies are in Japan vellum wrappers over boards with label
information printed directly on the spine.

700 on Van Gelder "for sale in
America;" 25 numbered copies on
Japan vellum.

BY THE IONIAN SEA
NOTES OF A RAMBLE IN SOUTH-
ERN ITALY BY GEORGE GISSING

PRINTED FOR THOMAS B MOSHER AND
PUBLISHED BY HIM AT 45 EXCHANGE
STREET PORTLAND MAINE MDCCCCXX

BY THE IONIAN SEA (continued)

The bindings of *Earthwork Out of Tuscany* (97) *Roses of Paestum* (331), *By the Ionian Sea* (54), and *The Renaissance* (322) are uniform in style. In his foreword to *By the Ionian Sea* Mosher identifies these as forming a sub-series. Also, all of these titles carry the limitation statement "Limited to 700 Copies for Sale in America." Chiswick lead initials and head-pieces used throughout.

Reference: Garland IB (p. 20).

C

55. *A CARLYLE CALENDAR   WEEKLY VISITS TO THE SAGE OF CHELSEA*
Compiled by Ellen Crane Woods. 1919.   70 pp.   19 x 11.5 cm.
Privately Printed-49   H 749.   Only edition.

100 (125?) copies printed on Tuscany paper.

Content: The text of the calendar consists of quotes from Thomas Carlyle and monthly calendars for the year 1920.

Comment: Privately printed for Edward A. Woods of Sewickley, PA, the compiler's son. Some copies will have a loosely inserted presentation slip, from Mr. and Mrs. Woods, bearing the family coat of arms and the title of the book.

The Sheean and Lamb typescripts indicate 125 copies, but the colophon in copies examined states 100 copies. Neither typescript mentions anything under Japan vellum copies printed. Perhaps the discrepancy is due to the printing of 25 special copies, or an overrun as was sometimes practiced with these privately printed books (see comment under 309).

Binding & Embellishment: The Italian handmade paper copies are bound in decorated Japan vellum boards. Large red and black Morrisian initial "A" on the front cover. Red Chiswick initials and black head-pieces throughout. The source of the floral design on back cover has not been identified.

56. *THE CASKET OF OPALS* by George Parsons Lathrop. [May] 1900.
[4 leaves], 19 numbered leaves, [1 leaf]   19 x 14 cm.
Privately Printed-5   H 707.   Only edition.

15 copies only on Roman vellum, printed on one side of the page only.

Content: This poem by George Lathrop is divided into 10 stanzas printed on the recto side of each of the 19 leaves of text.

Comment: The limitation reads: 'This book, of which 15 copies and no more are done on pure vellum, was privately printed by THOMAS B. MOSHER and GERTRUDE COWDIN at Portland, Maine, in the month of May, M•D•CCCC, and the type distributed. This is Number " The colophon reads: "HERE ENDS THE CASKET OF OPALS BY GEORGE PARSONS LATHROP ORIGINALLY PUBLISHED IN THE CENTURY MAGAZINE FOR NOVEMBER A D MDCCCLXXXVIII DONE INTO TYPE AND FIFTEEN COPIES PRINTED ON PURE VELLUM BY THOMAS B. MOSHER AND GERTRUDE COWDIN AT PORTLAND MAINE DURING THE MONTH OF MAY A D M•D•CCCC." Gertrude Cheever Cowdin was the wife of John E. Cowdin of New York.

This is one of three collaborations in which Mosher's name is stated along with a partner, on either the colophon or the title page. The other two are the *Leaves of Grass* (192 & 192.1) and the privately printed *Rubáiyát* (337).

Never having seen a copy, Benton Hatch incorrectly listed the title beginning with the article "A." All copies examined begin with the article, "The."

THE CASKET OF OPALS (continued)

Binding & Embellishment: Copies were bound in flexible vellum with brown silk ties, and the title in gilt on the spine.

The first leaf has a full Ricketts designed border of leaves, vines and flowers. This design is adapted from the 1891 Vale Press edition of *Fifty Songs by Thomas Campion*. For other books using Vale Press & Charles Ricketts designs, see entry 47.

Copy #6 at the University of San Francisco is bound in an elaborate binding by Toof & Co. and leaf [1] is printed with the red Chiswick drop cap and a Ricketts border which is illuminated with purple, white, red and yellow violets, leaves of shaded greens, and vines of burnished gold. The "drop cap" is also illuminated in this copy. All copies were not illuminated (e.g., the copy in the Vilain/Wieck Collection).

Reference: Grigsby 696.

---

57.   ***THE CELESTIAL COUNTRY*** From the Rhythm of St. Bernard of Cluny
     Translated by The Rev. John Mason Neale D. D. 1922.
     xiv, 26, [1] pp.   18.5 x 14 cm.
     Privately Printed-57   H 757.   Only edition.

125 printed copies on Van Gelder paper.

Content: The preface is unsigned and its authorship undetermined. The selections are taken from Neale's translation in *The Rhythm of Bernard de Morlaix* of 1858. Selections from T. W. Parsons and Dante precede the preface.

Comment: Printed for Ellen Crane Woods (mother of Edward A. Woods, a Mosher Press patron who had several books privately printed by Mosher).

The Sheean typescript indicates there were 150 copies printed, but the colophon in copies examined indicates 125 copies. The Sheean typescript mentions nothing under Japan vellum copies printed. Perhaps the discrepancy is due to the printing of 25 special copies, or an overrun as was sometimes practiced with these privately printed books (see comment under entry 309).

Binding & Embellishment: Bound in Japan vellum boards with title on the spine and title and publisher's device on the front cover. Title page in red and black; red decorative initials; several head- and tail-pieces are Selwyn Image designs from *The Century Guild Hobby Horse*. Many of these same designs also appear in *XVII Designs to Thornton's Virgil* (347), and in *Theodore Roosevelt* (407). See also *Primavera* (311) for another Selwyn Image design.

---

58.   ***CELTIC A STUDY IN SPIRITUAL HISTORY*** by Fiona Macleod.
     1901.   1 *ℓ, xvii*, 23 pp.   15.5 x 11.5 cm.
     Privately Printed-6   H 708.   Only edition.

50 numbered copies printed on Japan vellum by Thomas B. Mosher for presentation to his friends. First separate edition; first revised edition.

Content: The foreword is by the author, signed F.M., and dated September 1901. An essay entitled "Celtic'" originally appeared in *The Contemporary Review* (May 1900) and a few months later as part of *The Divine Adventure: Iona: And Other Studies in Spiritual History* (London: Chapman & Hall, 1900). It touched off both literary and political debate in Scotland and Ireland. According to Elizabeth Sharp, "William Sharp realised that since his essay had given rise to misapprehension of his aims and ideas, it would be well to further elucidate them... He, therefore, revised and enlarged his essay, and, with an added foreword of explanation, had it published separately in America by Mr. T. B. Mosher; and, finally, he included it in *The Winged Destiny*."

CELTIC A STUDY IN SPIRITUAL HISTORY (continued)

The text of this work was also printed by Mosher in his November 1901 issue of *The Bibelot* (24).

Comment: Fiona Macleod was a pseudonym used by William Sharp who also published works under his real name.

This little volume was a model for yet another privately printed volume, *Concerning a Pilgrimage to the Grave of Edward FitzGerald* (entry 75) which came out a year later in the same binding style and limitation, but enlarged in size. See also the 1901 *Lyrics and Sonnets* by Arthur Upson (228) for a volume uniformly bound to match *Celtic...*

Binding & Embellishment: Bound in flexible Japan vellum boards with yapp edges on the top and fore-edge; title on spine and title/author on front cover with red Chiswick initial. Title page printed in red and black.

Reference: Quinn 8645; Sharp, p. 322; Grigsby 1021; Macleod V, p. 391.

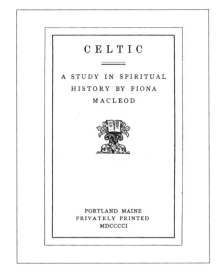

59. *THE CENTAUR AND THE BACCHANTE TWO PROSE POEMS*
done into English from the French of Maurice de Guérin by Lucie Page.
[September] 1897.   46, [1] pp. (same for all eds.)
Brocade Series-6   H 46.   First edition.

425 on Japan vellum for each edition.
First edition of this translation.

Content: Part I of the foreword is by Matthew Arnold; Part II is by the publisher, but consists mostly of quotes from others. Mosher indicates in the foreword to his Brocade Series reprint of *Maurice de Guérin* (237) that these studies (59, 105 & 237) were taken from Matthew Arnold's *Essays in Criticism* (First Series), but he does not cite the exact imprint.

Comment: Title page in brown and black (most other Brocade Series title pages are in red and black). See entries 217, 268 & 394 for other works translated by Lucie Page.

This volume and two others form a sub-series of De Guérin related books, the other two volumes being *Maurice de Guérin* (237) and *Eugénie de Guérin* (105), both essays by Matthew Arnold.

Reference: Quinn 3680 (third edition).

59.1 *THE CENTAUR AND THE BACCHANTE TWO PROSE POEMS*
done into English from the French of Maurice de Guérin by Lucie Page.
[December] 1897.
Brocade Series.   H 62.   Second edition.

59.2 *THE CENTAUR AND THE BACCHANTE TWO PROSE POEMS*
done into English from the French of Maurice de Guérin by Lucie Page.
[August] 1903.
Brocade Series.   H 273.   Third edition.

60. *CHAPELMEISTER KREISLER: A STUDY OF MUSICAL ROMANTICISTS*
by Vernon Lee. [July] 1901.   46, [1] pp. (same for second ed.)
Brocade Series-26   H 188.   First edition.

425 on Japan vellum for each edition.
First edition in separate book form.

Content: The publisher's note opposite the title page indicates this title is reprinted from *Belcaro: Being Essays on Sundry Æsthetical Questions* by

CHAPELMEISTER KREISLER:(continued)

Vernon Lee, London, 1882 (actually London, W. Satchell, [1881]). Mosher printed other selections from this work in *The Bibelot* in January & February 1914 (see 37).

Comment: Vernon Lee is the pseudonym of Violet Paget.

This volume, along with *The Child in the Vatican* (64) and *In Unbria* (176), form a sub-series which Mosher called "Three Studies in Æsthetic Personality by Vernon Lee."

Reference: *DLB* LVII, p. 158; Vilain 28.

60.1 *CHAPELMEISTER KREISLER: A STUDY OF MUSICAL ROMANTICISTS*
by Vernon Lee. [October] 1906.
Brocade Series.   H 375.   Second edition.

61. *CHILD CHRISTOPHER AND GOLDILIND THE FAIR* By William Morris. [November] 1900.   *ix*, 218, [1] pp.   23.5 x 15.5 cm. Miscellaneous Series-12   H 142.   Only edition.

450 on Van Gelder; 50 numbered copies on Japan vellum.
First American ed. (unauthorized).

Content: The book is prefixed by an unsigned bibliographical note from the publisher. The text is from the two-volume Kelmscott printing of 1895, and the exact copy which Mosher used is in the Bishop Collection.

Comparison with the Kelmscott edition reveals that Mosher changed the text from the small two-volume Kelmscott format to that of a larger single volume Chiswick format with old-style rules. Mosher's edition follows the Kelmscott text with the following changes: (1) Mosher followed the errata sheet in Vol. I and corrected p. 18 to read "some four years" rather than "some two years," (2) each ampersand sign is changed to "and," and (3) Mosher continued the use of shoulder notes in the margin. With regard to the shoulder notes, Mosher exchanges two notes in Vol. I of the Kelmscott edition which were inappropriately placed ("Goldilind waxeth very fair" on p. 41 is exchanged with "She makes the best of it" on page 42). Then he places the shoulder note of p. 80 ("They are bound for the Tofts") of the Kelmscott Vol. I, and uses it between "Simon will not fight" and "Of Jack o' the Tofts." Other changes to the shoulder notes include changing "Of Christopher's aspect" (Vol. I, p. 228) to "Of Christopher's aspects"; the entire omission of "Comes in Goldilind" (Vol. II, p. 2); and a moderate revision of Morris' colophon on p. 239.

CHAPTER I. OF THE KING OF OAK-
ENREALM, AND HIS WIFE AND HIS
CHILD

OF old there was a land which was so much a wood-land, that a minstrel thereof said it that a squirrel might go from end to end, and all about, from tree to tree, and never touch the earth: therefore was that land called Oakenrealm.

The lord and king thereof was a stark man, and so great a warrior that in his youth he took no delight in aught else save battle and tourneys. But when he was hard on forty years old, he came across a daughter of a certain lord, whom he had vanquished, and his eyes bewrayed him into longing, so that he gave back to the said lord all the havings he had conquered of him that he might lay the maiden in his kingly bed. So he brought her home with him to Oakenrealm and wedded her.

The King of Oaken-realm takes a wife

Comment: Mosher's catalogue for 1900 indicates this tale: *"has never been reprinted in any other form..."* He further indicates that the model used is one of the "most approved Whittingham editions. Chiswick head- and tail-pieces are used, each page being within old-style rules." He also mentions that it is printed *"in type that is readable,"* a reference to the oft stated criticism that the type employed in Kelmscott books unduly labors the eye. According to Eugene D. LeMire, William Morris bibliographer, "the reason the *Child Christopher...* was not reprinted elsewhere after the Kelmscott Press edition is that Morris guaranteed the subscribers to the K. P. edition that it would not be reprinted in a cheaper form. This was to compensate for the print run being more than doubled (to 600), to

CHILD CHRISTOPHER AND GOLDILIND THE FAIR (continued)

meet the expenses without raising the price for the 2-vols., set at 15s." —April 5, 1995 letter to P. R. Bishop (see May Morris' introduction to *The Collected Works of William Morris* (1936), Vol. 17, pp. xl-xli, for confirmation).

Binding & Embellishment: Van Gelder copies are bound in quarter white paper spine over blue paper boards with white title label printed in two colors on the spine. Japan vellum copies are bound in Japan vellum wraps over boards with print in two colors along the spine *and* on the front cover, unlike the Van Gelder edition.

The attractive reddish-orange criblé initial "O" on p. 3 was used in the *Victoria Book of Common Prayer* and was most likely first engraved by Mary Byfield for its publisher, London's Chiswick Press. The criblé head-pieces used throughout were designed by Charlotte and Elizabeth Whittingham (daughters of the printer) and are all pictured on the same page in Warren. The triangular criblé tail-pieces are designed by Elizabeth Whittingham. For other Chiswick Press designs used, see entry 48.

Reference: *DLB* LVII, p. 195; Walsdorf 78; Thompson, p. 196; Boss VII 26; Quinn 7009 & 7010; Warren, pp. 165, 187, 317; Grigsby 826; DeVinne 1422.

---

62. ***THE CHILD IN THE HOUSE AN IMAGINARY PORTRAIT*** by Walter Pater.
[September] 1895.   45, [1] pp. (same through third ed.)
Brocade Series-1   H 14.   First edition.

425 on Japan vellum for each edition.

Content: The preliminaries include a bibliographical note, the poem "Walter Pater" by Michael Field, and a brief quote from George Eliot.

Colbeck states that "this is a reprint of H. Daniel's 1894 edition." Madan notes "there is a Mosher Reprint of this essay, perhaps not from Daniel's edition, certainly not with his leave."—p. 114.

Comment: In his 1909 catalogue (p. 50) Mosher notes that "in 1895 the first American edition appeared as the initial number of the *Brocade Series*" (Mosher also provided a similar bibliographical note in entry 63); however, the Copeland & Day issuance of this title probably predates Mosher's. According to Wright, Copeland & Day's publication of *The Child in the House* (printed in July) was published "by the early part of September 1895," and he cites two supporting announcements in *The Nation* for September 5 and 18, 1895. Wright determined that the Copeland & Day imprint "is probably the first *public* appearance of *The Child in the House* in book form," a conclusion which, if true, would equally apply to its status as a first American edition. No other evidence has been found showing Mosher published his book before early September, in fact, no advertisement for the book even appears in his 1895 *List of Books* (200) issued in October. Therefore, Mosher's reprint is not assigned the first edition status that he claimed.

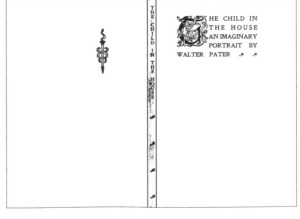

Mosher envisioned this work as one of six "miniatures of romance" by Walter Pater, the whole forming a sub-series of "Imaginary Portraits." The other titles are: *A Prince of Court Painters* (312), *Denys L'Auxerrois* (89), *Sebastian Van Storck* (344), the *Duke Carl of Rosenmold* (96), and *Emerald Uthwart* (102). These works are grouped together in Mosher's catalogues, and were offered as

THE CHILD IN THE HOUSE (continued)

a boxed set. The first four of these titles were taken by Mosher from the book *Imaginary Portraits* (London & New York: Macmillan, 1887). *Emerald Uthwart* appeared in *The New Review* for June & July, 1892, and then as part of *Miscellaneous Studies: a Series of Essays* (New York & London: Macmillan, 1895).

The date on the binding is printed vertically at the bottom of the spine. No other title in the Brocade Series has the date printed on the spine.

Reference: Wright, p. 162 (see also Wright's discussion in Section I, entry "a 27"); Madan 33; Colbeck II, p. 640 (20); Quinn 7587 (9th ed.); Jenkinson II, 844 (13th ed.).

62.1   *THE CHILD IN THE HOUSE   AN IMAGINARY PORTRAIT* by Walter Pater. [November] 1895.

      Brocade Series.   H 18.   Second edition.

62.2   *THE CHILD IN THE HOUSE   AN IMAGINARY PORTRAIT* by Walter Pater. [January] 1896.

      Brocade Series.   H 31   Third edition.

62.3   *THE CHILD IN THE HOUSE   AN IMAGINARY PORTRAIT* by Walter Pater. [September] 1896   46, [1] pp. (same through the fourteenth ed.)

      Brocade Series.   H 32.   Fourth edition.

      Comment: The change in the number of pages in this and subsequent editions is the result of slightly different word spacing. There is also a noticeable difference in thickness. The later editions are thinner than the first few. This difference is due to the use of a thinner Japan vellum paper.

62.4   *THE CHILD IN THE HOUSE   AN IMAGINARY PORTRAIT* by Walter Pater. [December] 1896.

      Brocade Series.   H 33.   Fifth edition.

62.5   *THE CHILD IN THE HOUSE   AN IMAGINARY PORTRAIT* by Walter Pater. [September] 1897.

      Brocade Series.   H 57.   Sixth edition.

62.6   *THE CHILD IN THE HOUSE   AN IMAGINARY PORTRAIT* by Walter Pater. [March] 1898.

      Brocade Series.   H 91.   Seventh edition.

62.7   *THE CHILD IN THE HOUSE   AN IMAGINARY PORTRAIT* by Walter Pater. [December] 1898.

      Brocade Series.   H 92.   Eighth edition.

62.8   *THE CHILD IN THE HOUSE   AN IMAGINARY PORTRAIT* by Walter Pater. [February] 1900.

      Brocade Series.   H 168.   Ninth edition.

62.9   *THE CHILD IN THE HOUSE   AN IMAGINARY PORTRAIT* by Walter Pater. [December] 1900.

      Brocade Series.   H 169.   Tenth edition.

62.10 *THE CHILD IN THE HOUSE AN IMAGINARY PORTRAIT* by Walter Pater.
[January] 1902.
Brocade Series.   H 238.   Eleventh edition.

62.11 *THE CHILD IN THE HOUSE AN IMAGINARY PORTRAIT* by Walter Pater.
[December] 1903.
Brocade Series.   H 271A.   Twelfth edition.

Comment: This edition was listed in the Hatch *Check List* as an unlocated
trade edition, but was later added by Hatch in 1972 (see Vilain).

Reference: Hatch, p. 168; Vilain, p. 64.

62.12 *THE CHILD IN THE HOUSE AN IMAGINARY PORTRAIT* by Walter Pater.
[January] 1906.
Brocade Series.   H 373.   Thirteenth edition.

62.13 *THE CHILD IN THE HOUSE AN IMAGINARY PORTRAIT* by Walter Pater.
[December] 1908.
Brocade Series.   H 452.   Fourteenth edition.

——————— *Same Title, Change of Series* ———————

63.   WALTER PATER *THE CHILD IN THE HOUSE.* 1909.   Limitation unknown for both Van
       xix, 42 pp.   Gelder and Japan vellum copies.
       Vest Pocket Series-17   H 470.   Only edition.

Content: Includes the poem "Walter Pater" by Michael Field. The preface is by
the publisher who includes a brief bibliographical note on the publication of
this title. Mosher's preface consists mostly of quotes from A. C. Benson,
Edmund Gosse, and Arthur Symons.

Reference: Wright, p. 162 (see also I a 27).

64. *THE CHILD IN THE VATICAN* by Vernon Lee. [September] 1900.   425 on Japan vellum for each
     63, [1] pp. (same in all editions)   edition.
     Brocade Series-24   H 150.   First edition.   First edition in separate book form.

Content: The publisher's note opposite the title page indicates this title is
reprinted from *Belcaro: Essays on Sundry Æsthetical Questions by Vernon
Lee.* London, 1882 (actually London: W. Satchell, [1881]). Mosher printed
other selections from this work in *The Bibelot* in January & February 1914.
See also entry 60.

Comment: Vernon Lee is the pseudonym of Violet Paget.

This book forms a sub-series along with two others in what Mosher called
"Three Studies in Æsthetic Personality by Vernon Lee." The other two books
are *Chapelmeister Kreisler* (60) and *In Umbria* (176). These books are
grouped together in the Mosher catalogues and were sold as sets in cabinet
boxes.

Reference: *DLB* LVII, p. 158; Vilain 28 (plate 36, p. 94 shows the book with a
cabinet box of other Brocade Series books).

64.1 *THE CHILD IN THE VATICAN* by Vernon Lee. [August] 1902.
Brocade Series.   H 242.   Second edition.

64.2 *THE CHILD IN THE VATICAN* by Vernon Lee. [January] 1910.
Brocade Series.   H 526.   Third edition.

---

65.   *THE CHILDREN'S CRUSADE* translated from the French of Marcel Schwob
by Henry Copley Greene. [September] 1905.
       xxvi, 27-87, [1] pp. (same in second edition)
Brocade Series-50   H 327.   First edition.

425 on Japan vellum for each edition.

Content: This is a revised translation to Marcel Schwob's *Le Croisade des Enfants*, previously translated by Greene for the 1898 Small, Maynard, and Co. edition. The preface (pp. *vii-[xxvi]*) is also rewritten by Greene for this Mosher edition.

Comment: Generally speaking, this is the last *title* published in this series, but it is not the last *publication* to appear in the Brocade Series. That distinction goes to *Immensee* (163) which was published in 1912 with its title remaining the same as the former editions (B162 & 162.1), but with a wholly new translation (see "comment" under 163).

DLB only notes the 1923 Mosher edition and incorrectly attributes the translation to John Foley.

Green was paid $15.94 outright for his translation.

Reference: *DLB* CXXIII, p. 242; see the Nov. 17, 1941 letter from Lamb to Yorke for Mosher's payment terms (see Appendix II).

65.1   *THE CHILDREN'S CRUSADE* translated from the French of Marcel
Schwob by Henry Copley Greene. [December] 1907.
Brocade Series.   H 423.   Second edition.

——————— *Same Title, Change of Series* ———————

66.   *THE CHILDREN'S CRUSADE* MDCCCCXXIII. [August] 1923.
The colophon reads: "The Children's Crusade Translated from the French of Marcel Schwob by Henry Copley Greene with an Introduction by John L. Foley..."
xvii, 68, [1] pp.   15 x 11 cm.
Miscellaneous Series-98   H 701.   Only edition.

450 copies on Kelmscott "Hammer & Anvil" handmade paper, and 50 numbered copies on Japan vellum.

Content: The text of these eight French tales is that of the revised translation Henry Copley Greene did for the Brocade Series (65), with the omission of Greene's introductory essay on Marcel Schwob, and with a new introduction by John L. Foley taking its place.

Comment: Last title published in this series.

Mosher bought the remainder sheets of the 1898 Small, Maynard edition of *The Children's Crusade* "which he [Maynard] never sold." (Mosher to W. Irving Way, July 7, 1914 letter at The Huntington Library, WY 95). In another letter to Way written over four years later (Dec. 16, 1918; The Huntington Library, WY 152), Mosher added:

> Do you recall the 30 copies I had of the first edition of "The Children's Crusade" printed in a style which will not be easily equalled [sic] now or henceforth? I am just putting these into grey boards with a lovely little decoration. Referring to my catalogue you will see they are $1.50 net. The Japan vellum one in [the] Brocade Series has already been sold since [the] catalogue was issued [see the 1918 catalogue (262), p. 12].

THE CHILDREN'S CRUSADE (continued)

The binding design, front and back, is identical with *For Those Who Love Music* (115); the "lovely little decoration" is described below. A copy of this 1898 Boston edition in Mosher's grey-boards binding is in the Bishop Collection.

Binding & Embellishment: The Kelmscott paper edition is bound in blue paper boards with rounded spine; spine and cover title and design printed in dark blue. Japan vellum copies are bound in Japan vellum boards, again with rounded spine and the same information on the spine and design on the front cover. For other books printed on Kelmscott paper, see entry 47.

The charming cover and title page design consists of a child playing the panpipes against a background of oak leaves. Vilain suggests the designer may be Jean Webber. The panpipes design was also used by Mosher on the back cover of *For Those Who Love Music* (115), on the front cover of *Masterpieces* (235), and on the title page of the 1909 catalogue (253).

The typography of Mosher's title on the cover and the title page (above the panpipe player) is taken from the title page of the edition by Small, Maynard, and Co. (Boston, 1898, printed at the Heintzeman Press). In fact, the whole book follows the same basic internal format of the Small, Maynard edition. Also in keeping with the Small, Maynard format, "The Tale of François Longuejoue, Clerk" is the only one of the eight tales printed in black letter. The volume also uses Chiswick lead initials.

Reference: Vilain, pp. 38-39 for discussion of the design; Japan Paper Company (Kelmscott Hand-made Paper from England).

---

67. *A CHILD'S GARDEN OF VERSES* by Robert Louis Stevenson. 1899.
    x, 88, [1] pp. (same for all three editions)
    Old World Series-16   H 104.   First edition.

925 on Van Gelder; 100 numbered copies on Japan vellum.

Content: In addition to a core of 41 poems under "A Child's Garden of Verses," the volume includes poems grouped under the headings "The Child Alone" (9 poems), "Garden Days" (8 poems), and "Envoys" (6 poems), and the dedicatory poem by Stevenson, "To Alison Cunningham / From Her Boy" (p. [*v*]). Mosher's reprint is enhanced by two poems: one by William Blake opposite the title page, and one by Samuel Taylor Coleridge at the end of the book.

Comment: Based on stylistic evidence and the time period, the design on the front cover is most likely by Frederic Goudy. For other Goudy designs, see entry 1.

Reference: Vilain, p. 84, plate 10; Beinecke I, 204 (2nd edition).

67.1 *A CHILD'S GARDEN OF VERSES* by Robert Louis Stevenson. 1902.
     Old World Series   H 236.   Second edition.

Comment: Page 87 is misnumbered 69.

925 on Van Gelder. No copies were printed on Japan vellum for this and the third edition.

67.2 *A CHILD'S GARDEN OF VERSES* by Robert Louis Stevenson. 1907.
     Old World Series   H 405A.   Third edition.

925 on Van Gelder.

Comment: This edition was not listed in the Hatch *Check List*, but was later added by Hatch in 1972 (see Vilain).

Reference: Vilain, pp. 64-65.

68. DICKENS *A CHRISTMAS CAROL.* [October] 1916.
    viii, 185, [1] pp.   19.5 x 15 cm.
    Privately Printed-39   H 740.   Only edition.

300 copies printed on Van Gelder paper; 25 copies on Japan vellum.

Content: The introduction consists mostly of a quote from John Foster's *Life of Charles Dickens*, abridged and revised by George Gissing (1907). The very brief preface, opposite the title page, is signed C.D. (Charles Dickens).

Comment: Privately printed for Edward A. Woods of Sewickley, PA. Some copies will have a loosely inserted presentation slip, from Mr. and Mrs. Woods, bearing the family coat of arms and the title of the book.

Binding & Embellishment: Of the Van Gelder copies, 275 are bound in Old-style blue charcoal paper boards with slightly raised bands and white spine label. According to the Lamb typescript, 25 of the Van Gelder copies are bound in half-levant. Japan vellum copies bound in Japan vellum boards with label contents printed directly on the spine. Title page in red and black; Chiswick ornaments; lead initial letters in red outline; pages ruled. A copy at Bowdoin College is bound in marbled paper with label on the right hand corner of the front cover.

Reference: Vilain, p. 68.

---

69. *CHRYSANTHEMA GATHERED FROM THE GREEK ANTHOLOGY*
    by William M Hardinge. 1911.   *xiii*, 65, [1] pp.   15 x 8.5 cm.
    Miscellaneous Series-55   H 534.   Only edition.

450 copies on Van Gelder; 25 numbered copies on Japan vellum.
First Edition.

Content: The signed foreword is by the publisher. Preceding the main text are selections from James Russell Lowell, Walter Headlam, and John Addington Symonds. William Hardinge's 1876 Newdigate Prize Poem "Troy" follows the main text. The text used for *The Bibelot's* appearance of this work (Jan. & Feb. 1903 [26]) and later for this book edition, was from *The Nineteenth Century*, Nov. 1878, pp. 869-888. A bibliography appears on pp. 57-65. The typesetter's copy is located at Arizona State University.

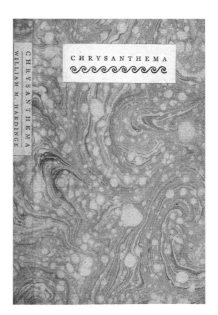

Binding & Embellishment: Van Gelder copies bound in "Rizzi" marbled boards with matching end-papers, and spine and cover labels. Japan vellum copies are bound in Japan vellum printed wrappers over boards. The binding size and style were meant to be uniform with *De Flagello Myrteo* (87).

The publisher's device, a cupid standing on a ball, all above the circular enclosed motto (Amoris Speculum), is a design adapted from Beeching, Mackail and Nichols' *Love's Looking Glass* published by Percival and Co. (London, 1891). There are some differences between the Percival and Mosher designs, but the basic design elements are present. As noted on the verso of the title page of *Love's Looking Glass*, the design "is adapted from the Hypnerotomachia [Poliphili, in fact, from r^2 and x^2 of the 1499 edition]." Mosher had two copies of the Beeching book in his library. This same device was used in entries 52, 87, 129 & 339. Appearing below the title on the front cover is a Minoan sea wave design.

---

70. *THE CHURCHES OF NORTH FRANCE* by William Morris. 1901.
    iv, 47 pp.
    Reprints from "The Bibelot"-9   H 193.   First thus.

35 copies only printed on Japan vellum.
First edition.

Content: This essay first appeared in *The Oxford and Cambridge Magazine* for February 1856. The introduction by J. W. Mackail is from *The Life of*

THE CHURCHES OF NORTH FRANCE (continued)

William Morris (London: Longmans, 1899). The 1901 Mosher Books catalogue mentions: "Besides the title-essay, our reprint contains a shorter article, 'Death the Avenger and Death the Friend' which appears in these 35 copies only." Indeed, this shorter article does not appear in the March 1901 issue of *The Bibelot* (24), and is taken from *The Oxford and Cambridge Magazine* for August 1856.

Mosher further indicates in the 1901 catalogue that "two more issues will then complete this series of first editions in book-form of Morris' contributions to the *Oxford and Cambridge Magazine* –a series that as time goes on will be vainly sought after by collectors of his earliest prose work." –p. 46. These two further contributions are *The Story of the Unknown Church* (389) and *Gertha's Lovers* (133).

Comment: The Quinn catalogue notes: "These scarce little booklets are not the regular Mosher publications, but are separates in book form from the original setting in the *Bibelot*. They constitute the First Editions of these pieces in book form, being mainly Morris' contributions to the *Oxford and Cambridge Magazine*, discerned by Mosher to be writings meriting a more permanent dress than the pages of a magazine..."

See entry 24 for *The Bibelot* appearance. This same work was also reprinted in the Brocade Series (359) along with two essays by Pater. See also comment under entry 109.

Reference: Quinn 6984; Walsdorf 89.

71.   *CIRCUM PRÆCORDIA THE COLLECTS OF THE HOLY CATHOLIC CHURCH* as set forth by The Church of England in Her Book of Common Prayer for Every Sunday in the Year. Together with A Few Poems by Thomas William Parsons. [September] 1906.   *viii*, 82, [1] pp.   19.5 x 12.5 cm. Miscellaneous Series-34   H 354.   Only edition.

450 copies on Van Gelder; 50 numbered copies on Japan vellum.

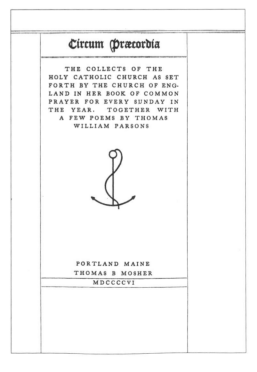

Content: The source for this book was first published and printed by Joseph George Cupples (Boston, 1892), but the copyright was listed under T. W. Parsons. The 1906 Mosher Books catalogue states: "By arrangement with the owner of Dr. Parsons' copyrights Mr. Mosher offers a limited edition of *Circum Præcordia*..." Mosher's copy of the source text (in the Bishop Collection) has Parsons' name in the copyright crossed out and the name Francesca d'Aulby de Gatigny is supplied in ink (the owner of the copyright?).

Comment: Mosher had been planning to create a "Breviary Series," but he never carried through on this formal designation. In his "Daily Reminder, 1906" he wrote:

    "Breviary Series   I Parables, The   II Ecclesiastes   III Circum Paæcordia"

on the page for January 15 (Bishop Collection). Though he never formally grouped them together, he nevertheless published *The Sayings of the Lord Jesus Christ*, 1905 (343), *Circum Præcordia*, 1906 (71), *Ecclesiastes or the Preacher*, 1907 (98), and *The Sermon on the Mount*, 1913 (345).

Binding & Embellishment: The Van Gelder copies are bound with quarter white paper spine over charcoal blue paper boards; white paper tips on corners. Blue label printed in gold on spine, and gold anchor within a box stamped on the front cover. The Japan vellum copies are bound in Japan vellum wraps over boards with gilt stamping directly on the spine and front cover. All pages are ruled in red.

Reference: Vilain, note on p. 72; Adler, p. 53 (entry 193).

72.   *THE CITY OF DREADFUL NIGHT* by James Thomson with an Introduction by E. Cavazza. 1892.   *xxviii*, 123, [1] pp.
English Reprint Series-2   H 2.   First thus.

400 numbered small paper copies on Van Gelder; 40 numbered large paper copies on Van Gelder; 10 numbered copies on Japan vellum, signed by the publisher.
First American edition.

Content: American rights were assigned to Mosher by the British firm of Dobell and Reeves. Two quotes in Italian from Dante and Leopardi appear opposite the opening "Proem." The introduction is by Elisabeth Cavazza (see entry 244 for biographic details). The appendix includes two additional poems, "To Our Ladies of Death" and "Insomnia." A bibliography appears on pp. 99-123.

Comment: Mosher also advertised and took orders for such companies as Bertram Dobell and A. & H. B. Bonner of London, e.g., see the advertisement accompanying *The Bibelot* for November 1898 which includes their cheap edition of that "black pearl of pessimism," *The City of Dreadful Night*. Bertram Dobell also procured many of England's fine press books for Mosher, including the Doves Press Bible, Vale Press and Eragny Press books.

In reference to the appended bibliography, the Quinn catalogue entry mentions: "This is the best Bibliography of Thomson available." The bibliography is by the publishers Bertram Dobell and J. M. Wheeler.

With regard to this book, Theodore DeVinne, America's master printer, wrote on Jan. 12, 1892 to Mosher: "I have to thank you for your kind remembrance in the gift of the 'City of Dreadful Night.' It is a very good bit of book-making." This letter, in the Bishop Collection, was originally kept by Mosher in his office scrapbook labeled *The City of Dreadful Night*. Another letter from DeVinne to Mosher exists in a private collection. The book comes with a printed dust-wrapper.

Reference: *DLB* XXXV, p. 268; Boss VII 142; Vilain 2, and p. 82 (plate 4); Quinn 10236; Grigsby 1202; DeVinne 1424.

——————— *Same Title, Change of Series* ———————

73.   *THE CITY OF DREADFUL NIGHT AND OTHER POEMS*
by James Thomson. 1903.   *x*, 134, [1] pp. (same for all eds.)
Old World Series-32   H 247.   First thus.

925 on Van Gelder; 100 numbered copies on Japan vellum.

Content: A poem by Philip Bourke Marston appears opposite the title page. Brief quotes from Dante and Leopardi are printed on p. 3. A total of 19 poems are in this edition, including all that previously appeared in the English Reprint edition (72).

Comment: The August 1895 issue of *The Bibelot* (18) contained 12 of the poems appearing in this Old World title. The only other poem "Three Lyrics" appeared in *The Bibelot* but was not reprinted here.

Design: The cover design bears the "C" monogram of Thomas Maitland Cleland. For other Cleland designs used, see entry 6.

Reference: Vilain, p. 84, plate 11.

73.1   *THE CITY OF DREADFUL NIGHT AND OTHER POEMS*
by James Thomson. 1909.
Old World Series.   H 487.   Second edition.

925 on Van Gelder. No copies were printed on Japan vellum.

73.2   *THE CITY OF DREADFUL NIGHT AND OTHER POEMS*
by James Thomson. 1922.
Old World Series.   H 694.   Third edition.

925 on Van Gelder. No copies were printed on Japan vellum.

74. *COLLECTORS & COLLECTING AN ESSAY* by Edwin C. Bolles
To Which are Added that the Antidote May Accompany the Bane,
A Few Remarks by a Collector's Wife. Melrose, Massachusetts. 1898.
61 pp.   15.5 x 11 cm.
Privately Printed-2   H 704.   Only edition.

Printed for the author in an edition of 300 numbered copies on linen laid paper, and 20 numbered copies on Japan vellum.

Content: The very brief foreword is by the author, signed E.C.B. The remarks by the collector's wife, Margaret B. Bolles, are entitled "Collegisse Juvat" (i.e., "it is pleasurable to collect").

Comment: The author, Rev. Dr. Edwin C. Bolles, advertised this book for sale in *The Bibelot* for November 1898.

Hatch incorrectly states that 50 copies were printed on Japan vellum.

Binding & Embellishment: Van Gelder copies are bound in charcoal gray paper wrappers. The Japan vellum copies are bound in Japan vellum wraps over flexible boards with title on the spine and title/author on the front cover; floral device in red; title page in red and black. The small floral design on the front cover, appearing also on the title page of *Little Willie* (216), appears in the American Type Founders' *Specimens of Type, ornaments and borders...* (Chicago, 1896) as a Jenson Old-Style page embellishment. It was originally part of a larger Morris border design in the Kelmscott *Tale of Beowulf*, 1895. The noted American printer of Maine, Fred Anthoensen, identified the Dickinson Type Foundry of Boston, a subsidiary of the American Type Founders Company, as one of Mosher's sources.

For other books using Kelmscott Press & William Morris designs, see 103, 139, 187, 216 & 239 (for use of Kelmscott ding-bats, see entries 47 & 345).

Reference: Boss VII 143; American Type Founders, p. 416e, #4284.

---

75. *CONCERNING A PILGRIMAGE TO THE GRAVE OF EDWARD FITZGERALD* by Edward Clodd. 1902.
vi, 14 pp. ; port. front., plate   18.5 x 14.5 cm.
Privately Printed-7   H 709.   Only edition.

50 copies on Japan vellum for presentation to Mosher's friends.

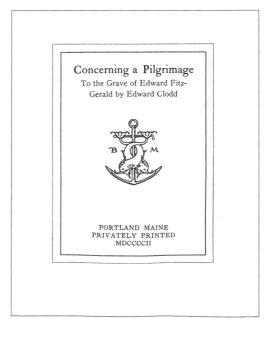

Content: The text for this volume was taken from the 1894 privately printed London edition limited to 50 copies for the members of the Omar Khayyám Club. Preceding the main text is the "Toast to Omar Khayyám" by Theodore Watts-Dunton.

The text is embellished with a frontispiece portrait of FitzGerald, and photo-illustration (facing p. 3) of Boulge Churchyard, FitzGerald's burial place.

Comment: In an April 14, 1908 note from Dole A. Hudson to Edward Clodd (in a copy of *Concerning a Pilgrimage*, inscribed by Mosher for Clodd, November 12, 1902), Mr. Hudson remarks: "Thank you very much for the loan of the charmingly printed brochure [Mosher's *Concerning a Pilgrimage*...]. Mosher may be, and is, a Pirate, but he is an Artist too. And you are a Poet!" (Bishop Collection).

This privately printed volume became a model for what may be looked upon as a sort of sub-series within the Miscellaneous Series. See the note to entry 238 for further information.

CONCERNING A PILGRIMAGE (continued)

Binding & Embellishment: Bound in flexible Japan vellum boards with title on the spine and title/author in upper left corner of front cover; red Chiswick initial; yapp edges on the top and fore-edges. Title page in red and black; Chiswick ornaments; pages ruled.

Reference: Grigsby 220; not in Potter.

---

76. ROBERT LOUIS STEVENSON *CRABBED AGE & YOUTH & OTHER ESSAYS.*
     1907.   *xi*, 115 pp.
     Vest Pocket Series-13   H 395.   Only edition.

Limitation unknown for both Van Gelder and Japan vellum copies.

Content: The signed foreword is by the publisher. The present volume contains "Crabbed Age and Youth," "Some Portraits by Raeburn," "Pan's Pipes," and "A Plea for Gas Lamps." Augmenting the volume is the artistic credo of Robert Louis Stevenson, "The Morality of the Profession of Letters." The poem, "Crabbed Age and Youth..." by Shakespeare appears opposite the title page. The volume contains a bibliographical note on pp. 109-115.

Comment: This volume concludes Mosher's publication in the Vest Pocket Series of twelve essays collectively known as *Virginibus Puerisque and Other Papers*, which first appeared in 1881 (London, C. Kegan Paul & Co.). See entries 1, 5 & 427 for the other Vest Pocket titles containing essays from this collective work, and thereby forming a subseries in the Vest Pocket Series.

Reference: Beinecke I, 99 & 100; Prideaux, p. 15; Gerstley 12 N.

---

77. DICKENS *THE CRICKET ON THE HEARTH.* [October] 1921.
     viii, 194, [1] pp.   18.5 x 14 cm.
     Privately Printed-55   H 755.   Only edition.

300 copies on Van Gelder; 50 copies on Japan vellum.

Content: The introduction is signed by Frederic G. Kitton. This privately printed edition contains all three parts of this classic Christmas tale.

Comment: Privately printed for Edward A. Woods of Sewickley, PA. Some copies will have a loosely inserted presentation slip, from Mr. and Mrs. Woods, bearing the family coat of arms and the title of the book.

Binding & Embellishment: Van Gelder copies bound in blue charcoal paper boards; Japan vellum copies are bound in Japan vellum boards. Title page is printed in black and red; lead initials in red outline; pages are ruled throughout. Chiswick head- and tail-pieces.

---

78. *CYNARA: A LITTLE BOOK OF VERSE* by Ernest Dowson. [October] 1907.
     viii, 37, [1] pp. (same for all three editions)
     Lyric Garland Series-11   H 397.   First edition.

950 copies on Van Gelder for each edition. For the first edition, 100 numbered copies on Japan vellum; and 5 numbered copies on Roman vellum, signed by the publisher.

Content: The foreword is by the publisher. In addition to "Cynara," there are 25 other poems by Dowson. See also note to entry 366.

Reference: Quinn 2689, 7083 & 7084; Cutler & Stiles, p. 38; Cevasco, p. 41.

78.1 *CYNARA: A LITTLE BOOK OF VERSE* by Ernest Dowson. [January] 1915.
     Lyric Garland Series.   H 634.   Second edition.

78.2 *CYNARA: A LITTLE BOOK OF VERSE* by Ernest Dowson. [November] 1916.
     Lyric Garland Series.   H 650.   Third edition.

D

79. ***DANTE AT VERONA*** by Dante Gabriel Rossetti. 1910.
viii, 36, [1] pp.; port. front.
Venetian Series-3   H 517.   Only edition.

Content: The foreword is by the publisher. Two brief selections from *The Divine Comedy* appear on the recto of the half-title, and a comment from William Michael Rossetti appears on p. [34], followed by two pages of notes. The 83-stanza poem, "Dante at Verona," was first published in Rossetti's *Poems* (London: F. S. Ellis, 1870). The frontispiece reproduces D. G. Rossetti's "ideal head" of Dante.

Reference: Quinn 8206.

Limitation unknown for both Van Gelder and Japan vellum copies.

---

80. ***THE DEAD LEMAN (LA MORTE AMOUREUSE)*** translated from the French of Théophile Gautier by Andrew Lang and Paul Sylvester.
[August] 1903.   74, [1] pp. (same for second ed.)
Brocade Series-42   H 256.   First edition.

Content: The publisher's note opposite the title page indicates this work was reprinted from *The Dead Leman and Other Tales from the French*, by Andrew Lang and Paul Sylvester (London: Sonnenschein, 1889). A selection from Swinburne appears on p. [10].

80.1 ***THE DEAD LEMAN (LA MORTE AMOUREUSE)*** translated from the French of Théophile Gautier by Andrew Lang and Paul Sylvester.
[September] 1914.
Brocade Series.   H 618.   Second edition.

425 on Japan vellum for each edition.

---

81. ***DEAD LOVE AND OTHER INEDITED PIECES*** by Algernon Charles Swinburne. 1901.   *iv*, 48 pp. (in some copies, port. front laid in)
Reprints from "The Bibelot"-10   H 194.   Only edition.

Content: The unsigned introduction is by the publisher. Mosher includes Wise's bibliographical entry for the London, 1864 imprint. In addition to "Dead Love" (in *Once A Week*, October 1862), the Mosher reprint also contains material from sources Mosher identifies:

– Stanzas from "Queen Yseult" (taken from "Queen Yseult" Canto i. "Of the birth of Sir Tristram, and how he voyaged into Ireland," printed in the Oxford magazine, *Undergraduate Papers*, No. 1, Dec. 1857).

– "A Letter on Modern Love" (from a letter to the editor of *The Spectator*, June 7, 1862).

– "The Pilgrimage of Pleasure" (from Chapter V in *The Children of the Chapel: A Tale*. Second Edition. London: J. Masters, 1875).

– "Unpublished Verses" (from *Unpublished Verses*, n.p., [1866]).

– "Verses from A Year's Letters" (from chapter XX of "A Year's Letters" in *The Tatler* from Aug. 25-Dec. 29, 1877).

– The text of this work was printed by Mosher in his June 1901 issue of *The Bibelot* (24). The book includes a design by M. J. Lawless entitled "Dead Love" as a frontispiece (also loosely inserted with the issue of *The Bibelot*).

35 copies only printed on Japan vellum.
First appearance of "Queen Yseult" in book form (unauthorized).

DEAD LOVE AND OTHER INEDITED PIECES (continued)

Comment: Livingston notes: "A portion of the first canto [of "Queen Yseult"], however, was printed by Thomas B. Mosher, Portland, Maine, in 1901, and this is really the first time it was collected or reprinted in book form." –p. 7. He further mentions that "... 'A Pilgrimage of Pleasure,' [is] (printed here for the first time with Swinburne's name on the title)..."

First announced by John Carter & Graham Pollard in 1934 (see the Barker & Collins update on their pioneering work), the London 1864 printing of *Dead Love* is one of the H. Buxton Forman-T. J. Wise forgeries. *Unpublished Verses* is yet another. Mosher was not aware that these publications were forgeries.

See also commnet under entry 109 for more information on the 12 imprints in this Reprints from "The Bibelot" Series.

Reference: Livingston, pp. 7, 18 & 31; Barker & Collins, p. 81 for *Dead Love*, and p. 239 for *Unpublished Verses*.

---

82.   CICERO *DE AMICITIA*   Translated with notes by Andrew P Peabody. [October] 1913.   *ix*, 125, [1] pp.   19 x 14 cm. Privately Printed-26   H 727.   Only edition.

450 printed on Van Gelder paper; 50 numbered copies on Japan vellum; 1 copy only printed on Roman vellum.

Content: The foreword to *De Amicitia* (On Friendship) is unsigned but is most likely by the publisher. In the foreword thanks are given to Messrs. Little, Brown & Company of Boston for permission to reprint the Rev. Dr. Peabody's translation of 1884.

Comment: Privately printed for Edward A. Woods of Sewickley, PA. Some copies will have a loosely inserted presentation slip, from Mr. and Mrs. Woods, bearing the family coat of arms and the title of the book.

According to the Sheean and Lamb typescripts, there was printed "... for Mr. Mosher, 1 copy on pure vellum bound in Binders vellum with silk ties."

Binding & Embellishment: Of the Van Gelder copies, 400 are bound in charcoal blue paper boards, and 50 are bound in full leather with gilt decorations on the spine just like the flexible leather bindings on the Old World Series, but without the gilt stamping on the covers. One of these Van Gelder copies in full leather was examined in the private collection of Donald E. Dede of New Hampshire. Japan vellum copies are bound in Japan vellum boards with the label printed directly on the spine.

Title page printed in red and black; Chiswick ornaments; lead initial letters in red outline; all pages ruled.

Reference: Vilain, p. 63 (# 185); Hatch, p. 161.

---

83.   *THE DEATH OF MARLOWE   A TRAGEDY* by Richard Hengist Horne. 1898.   *viii*, 32 pp. Reprints from "The Bibelot"-3   H 75.   Only edition.

25 copies only printed on Japan vellum.

Content: The unsigned preface is by the publisher. Selections from Michael Drayton, A. H. Bullen, and J. A. Symonds accompany the text. The text of this three-scene play was first printed by Mosher in his December 1897 issue of *The Bibelot* (20).

Comment: See entry 109 for further discussion of this series.

84. ***THE DEFENCE OF GUENEVERE A BOOK OF LYRICS*** Chosen from the
works of William Morris. 1896.   93, [1] pp. (numbered in Roman numerals)
Bibelot Series-8   H 20.   Only edition.

925 on Van Gelder; 100 numbered
copies on Japan vellum.

Content: Mosher chose 16 poems from *The Defence of Guenevere and Other
Poems* (1858), 2 poems from *The Life and Death of Jason* (1869), 5 poems
from *The Earthly Paradise* (1868-70), and 4 poems from *Poems by the Way*
(1891). A selection from A. C. Swinburne appears opposite the title page.

Reference: Walsdorf 64; Quinn 6971.

85. ***A DEFENCE OF POETRY*** by Percy Bysshe Shelley. 1907.
xvi, 77 pp.   17.5 x 14 cm.
Miscellaneous Series-36   H 392.   First thus.

50 numbered copies on Japan
vellum only.

Content: The source for this volume is Harry Buxton Forman's *The Prose
Works of Percy Bysshe Shelley* (4 vols., London, 1880). It is largely printed
from the plates of the January & February 1907 issues of *The Bibelot* (30),
with some changes. The signed foreword is by the publisher, and the preface
is by Forman. Selections from Swinburne's "The Centenary of Shelley" and
"Cor Cordium," and two selections from Jowett's translation of *The Dialogues
of Plato,* are also included.

Comment: See note to 238 for information on this volume as one of a sub-
series, uniform in binding style.

Binding & Embellishment: Copies are bound in flexible Japan vellum boards
with yapp top and fore-edges; title printed on the spine and title/author
printed directly on the front cover with lead drop-cap initial in red. Title page
in red and black; head- and tail-pieces are like those from the Old Word
Series, designed by Charles M. Jenckes.

—————— *Same Title, Change of Series* ——————

86. PERCY BYSSHE SHELLEY ***A DEFENCE OF POETRY***. 1910.
xv, 101 pp.
Vest Pocket Series-20   H 509.   First thus.

Limitation unknown for both Van
Gelder and Japan vellum copies.

Content: The text for this reprint was also taken from *The Prose Works of
Percy Bysshe Shelley* edited by Harry Buxton Forman (4 vols., London, 1880).
The foreword is by the publisher. Also included are "Three Fragments on
Beauty" from Richard Garnett's *Relics of Shelley* (London: Moxon, 1862). The
preface and annotations are by Forman. Robert Browning's "Memorabilia,"
Swinburne's "Cor Cordium," and a selection from *The Dialogues of Plato*
(Jowett's translation), accompany the text.

Reference: Vilain 36.

87. ***DE FLAGELLO MYRTEO CCCLX THOUGHTS AND FANCIES OF LOVE***
by Richard Garnett. [November] 1906. *xxiii*, 85, [1] pp.   15.5 x 8.5 cm.
Miscellaneous Series-35   H 355.   Only edition.

925 on Van Gelder; 100 numbered
copies on Japan vellum.
First American edition.

Content: The preface is by Violet Neale (dated October 1906), and a selection
in Latin and a motto in Greek accompany the text. The choice of 360
"thoughts and fancies" corresponds to the 360 degrees of the Zodiac, the circle having both spiritual and symbolic meaning for the author of these love

DE FLAGELLO MYRTEO (continued)

notes. As is made clear in the preface, Violet Neale was the obvious muse for Dr. Garnett's love notes.

This authorized reprint of the third edition (London: Elkin Mathews, June 1906) contains the final revised and enlarged text of *CCCLX Thoughts*, including 40 additional "Thoughts" specially prepared for this American edition by Violet Neale, the owner of the manuscript. The first edition was originally issued anonymously by Elkin Mathews in June 1905.

Comment: In a lovely presentation note to Col. Wentworth Higginson, friend, literary advisor and editor of Emily Dickinson, Mosher wrote on December 22, 1906:

> I trust this copy of Dr. Garnett's little book will not come amiss. It (or as it seems to me) is singularly appropriate both to you and to him, as it serves to show – 'How far the gulf-stream of one's youth may blow into the Arctic regions of our lives'. With all best wishes, Sincerely yours T.B. Mosher" (Bishop Collection)

According to a letter from Violet Neale to Mosher (The Houghton Library, bMS Am 1096), she regretted that Mosher signed her full name to the preface, rather than "V. N." as she had intended.

Mosher paid Elkin Mathews $50 outright for the publication of this book in America.

Binding & Embellishment: The Van Gelder copies are bound in marbled paper boards with matching marbled endpapers, and with Mosher 's double dolphin publisher's device stamped in gold on the front cover. The Japan vellum copies are bound in the customary Japan vellum wraps over boards with the same dolphin device in gold, and with the same layout of gold title on the spine and at the top of the front cover. The book is uniform with *Chrysanthema* (69) in both size and style.

For more information on the "cupid and orb" device used on the title page, see 69. It is also used on 52, 129 & 339.

Reference: Boss VII 144; the original preface by Violet Neale is at The Houghton Library (bMS Am 1096); the edited preface by Symons is also at The Houghton. See the Nov. 17, 1941 letter from Lamb to Yorke for Mosher's payment terms (see Appendix II).

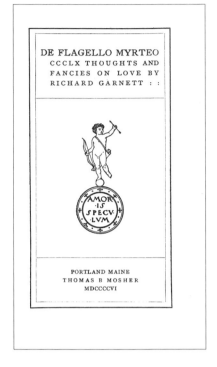

DE FLAGELLO MYRTEO
CCCLX THOUGHTS AND
FANCIES ON LOVE BY
RICHARD GARNETT : :

AMOR
·IS
SPECV
·LVM

PORTLAND MAINE
THOMAS B MOSHER
MDCCCCVI

88. **DEIRDRÉ AND THE SONS OF USNA** by Fiona Macleod. 1903.
xii, 103, [1] pp. (same for second ed.)
Old World Series-31   H 246.   First edition.

Content: Contains the lengthy dedication to Esther Mona. This work first appeared as one of the tales in the *Laughter of Peterkin* (London: Archibald Constable, 1897).

Comment: Fiona Macleod was a pseudonym used by William Sharp who also published works under his real name.

Mosher paid Macleod $100 outright for the publication of this book in America.

Design: The cover is signed with the "C" and crown (on the harp), the monogram of Earl Stetson Crawford. For other Mosher books designed by Crawford, see entries 111, 127 (possibly by Cleland), 206, 242 (cover), 252, 253, 354, 379, 422 & 428.

925 on Van Gelder; 100 numbered copies on Japan vellum.
First separate edition.

DEIRDRÊ

DEIRDRÉ AND THE SONS OF USNA (continued)

Reference: Colbeck II, p. 741 (34); Quinn 8647 & 8650; opening pictured in Thompson, p. 192 (2nd edition); See the Nov. 17, 1941 letter from Lamb to Yorke for Mosher's payment terms (see Appendix II); Macleod I, p. viii, and V, p. 392.

88.1   ***DEIRDRÉ AND THE SONS OF USNA*** by Fiona Macleod. 1909.
   Old World Series.   H 486.   Second edition.

    925 on Van Gelder. No copies were printed on Japan vellum.

   Comment: The Old World Series was basically printed by Smith and Sale in Portland, ME; however, there were exceptions. This second edition of Deirdrê was printed by George D. Loring, also of Portland.

89.   ***DENYS L'AUXERROIS   AN IMAGINARY PORTRAIT*** by Walter Pater.
  [July] 1898.   53, [1] pp. (same for second ed.)
  Brocade Series-8   H 70.   First edition.

    425 on Japan vellum for each edition.
    First separate printing.

   Content: Jenkinson notes this as a "faithful reprint of the first collected edition published in 1887." Publisher's bibliographic note on p. [5].

   See note to entry 62 for this work's inclusion in a sub-series.

   Reference: Wright, p. 162 (see also Wright, Section I , "a 43"); Jenkinson II, 845.

89.1   ***DENYS L'AUXERROIS   AN IMAGINARY PORTRAIT*** by Walter Pater.
  [September] 1898.
  Brocade Series.   H 97.   Second edition.

90.   ***THE DISTANT COUNTRY & OTHER PROSE POEMS*** By Fiona Macleod.
  1907.   *xvi*, 54 pp.
  Ideal Series of Little Masterpieces-7   H 399.   Only edition.

    Limitation unknown for both Van Gelder and Japan vellum copies.

   Content: According to the foreword, the three selections in the book: "The Distant Country," "A Memory of Beauty," and "The Wind, the Shadow, and the Soul" were taken from Macleod's *The Dominion of Dreams* (London: A. Constable, 1899).

   The publisher's foreword mentions how he secured the American publishing rights to Fiona Macleod's writings through "her" publishers (Patrick Geddes and Colleagues) while personally visiting them in 1901 in Edinburgh. Mosher also indicates he met William Sharp only once, and that was while Sharp was in Boston on his last visit to America.

   The text of this work was printed by Mosher as part of the December 1906 issue of *The Bibelot* (29).

   Comment: Fiona Macleod was a pseudonym used by William Sharp who also published works under his real name.

   This volume, along with the *Three Legends of the Christ Child* (410) and *The Wayfarer* (433), formed a sub-series that could be bought together in a cabinet style box.

91. *THE DIVINE ADVENTURE* by Fiona Macleod. 1903.
     vii, 91, [1] pp. (same for all three editions)
     Old World Series-30   H 245.   First edition.

925 on Van Gelder; 100 numbered copies on Japan vellum. First American edition.

Content: *The Divine Adventure* first appeared in *The Fortnightly Review* (1899), and then in book form as *The Divine Adventure: Iona: And Other Studies in Spiritual History* (London: Chapman & Hall, 1900). Mosher does not specify precisely from which source this reprint was taken, but it was certainly with "Miss Macleod's" authorization. Apparently the note at the rear was prepared by the author for the Mosher reprint. The lengthy dedication to Millicent is also by the author.

Comment: Fiona Macleod was a pseudonym used by William Sharp who also published works under his real name.

Mosher paid Macleod $100 outright for the publication of this book in America

Design: The cover design bears the "C" monogram of Thomas Maitland Cleland. For other Cleland designs used, see entry 6.

Reference: Quinn 8647 & 8651; see the Nov. 17, 1941 letter from Lamb to Yorke for Mosher's payment terms (see Appendix II); Macleod IV, p. 433.

91.1 *THE DIVINE ADVENTURE* by Fiona Macleod. 1907.
      Old World Series.   H 408.   Second edition.

925 on Van Gelder. No copies were printed on Japan vellum.

91.2 *THE DIVINE ADVENTURE* by Fiona Macleod. 1915.
      Old World Series.   H 630.   Third edition.

925 on Van Gelder. No copies were printed on Japan vellum.

92. *A DREAM OF JOHN BALL* by William Morris. 1902.
     vi, 143, [1] pp. (same for second ed.)
     Old World Series-28   H 212.   First edition.

925 on Van Gelder; 100 numbered copies printed on Japan vellum.

Content: There are two works in this volume, *A Dream of John Ball*, and *A King's Lesson. A Dream of John Ball* first appeared in *Commonweal II*, (London, November 13, 1886-Jananuary 22, 1887). The short story, *A King's Lesson*, based on the life of Matthias Corvinus, King of Hungary, also appeared in *Commonweal* (September 18, 1886), under the title *An Old Story Retold*. Both works were reprinted together in book form by Reeves & Turner in 1888. There was also a Kelmscott Press reprint in 1892. It is not clear which source Mosher used for his reprint, but a copy of the London, 1888 book did appear in Mosher's library, whereas there is no record of the 1892 Kelmscott imprint in his library.

Reference: Quinn 7026; Walsdorf 99; Lowden, p. 15 (2nd ed.).

92.1 *A DREAM OF JOHN BALL* by William Morris. 1908.
      Old World Series.   H 450.   Second edition.

925 on Van Gelder. No copies were printed on Japan vellum.

93. *DREAM OF PROVENCE (ORGEAS AND MIRADOU)* By Frederick Wedmore. 1907.   *xi*, 41 pp.
     Ideal Series of Little Masterpieces-8   H 400.   Only edition.

Limitation unknown for both Van Gelder and Japan vellum copies.

Content: The foreword is by the publisher. The work was originally entitled *Orgeas and Miradou: Dream of Provence*, but according to Wedmore's bibliographical note on p. *vi*, the title was "transposed, in scrupulous consideration

DREAM OF PROVENCE (continued)

of only English-Speaking folk." In his foreword, Mosher acknowledges that this is a reprint of the 1905 London edition of *Dream of Provence (Orgeas & Miradou)* published by Isbister.

Comment: This work first appeared in *The Bibelot* for April 1899 (22).

---

94.   *DREAMS* by Olive Schreiner. [October] 1917.   *x*, 152, [1] pp.   19 x 14.5 cm. Miscellaneous Series-81   H 653.   Only edition.

450 on Van Gelder; 25 numbered copies on Japan vellum. The 1918 catalogue mentions 500 printed on Van Gelder (an error?)

Content: The text source for this book was *Dreams* (London: T. Fisher Unwin, 1891). To the list of essays that usually comprise this title, Mosher added another section entitled "A Dream of Wild Bees" originally written by Schreiner to a friend, and the section entitled "The Hunter" which Mosher took from the chapter "Waldo's Stranger" in Schreiner's book *The Story of an African Farm* (London: Chapman and Hall, 1887 "New Edition"). Mosher's marked copy of this source is in the Bishop Collection. A brief selection from Swinburne appears opposite the title page.

Two of these selections from Olive Schreiner were previously printed in *The Bibelot* for October 1911 (34).

Binding & Embellishment: The Van Gelder copies are bound in brown boards with title/author printed in black on the spine and front cover. The Japan vellum copies are bound in Japan vellum boards with the Eragny design printed in light-green. The Sheean typescript mentions Japan vellum wraps, but the copy examined in the State Library of Maine is in stiff boards (perhaps some Japan vellum copies are in wraps too). Printed dust cover.

The design at the top edge of the front cover is from the 1903 Eragny edition of Ronsard's *Abrégé de l'Art Poétique...* The decorative red "D" on the title page is yet another design by Lucien Pissarro for the Eragny Press and appears, for example, in Villon's *Autres Poesies* (London: Hacon & Ricketts, 1901). Chiswick head- and tail-pieces are used throughout, and all pages of text are ruled. For other books using Eragny Press & Lucien Pissarro designs, see entry 52.

Reference: Verster 11 (listed as having no date).

---

95.   *DREAMTHORP A BOOK OF ESSAYS* Written in the Country by Alexander Smith. [October] 1913.   *xxxv*, 295, [1] pp.   19 x 14 cm. Miscellaneous Series-64   H 588.   Only edition.

700 copies on Van Gelder; 25 numbered copies on Japan vellum.

Content: The text of this volume was taken from Mitchell Kennerley's 1907 edition; the original marked printer's copy is in the Bishop Collection. The foreword is signed by the publisher. Prefixed to the title work is the essay "Mr. Stevenson's Forerunner" by James Ashcroft Noble, which first appeared in *The Yellow Book* for 1895.

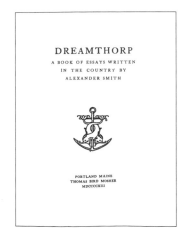

DREAMTHORP
A BOOK OF ESSAYS WRITTEN
IN THE COUNTRY BY
ALEXANDER SMITH

PORTLAND MAINE
THOMAS BIRD MOSHER
MDCCCCXIII

Mosher also printed Noble's essay in the June 1913 issue of *The Bibelot* (36).

Comment: In defending Mosher against attacks of piracy, the British literary critic, Clement Shorter, wrote in the May 9, 1914 issue of *Literary Digest*: "*Dreamthorp* has never been presented in so perfect a form and many English publishers should make Thomas B. Mosher's books a standard for typography and design."

DREAMTHORP A BOOK OF ESSAYS (continued)

Binding & Embellishment: Van Gelder paper copies are bound in dark green "Ancona" paper boards with a cream-colored ribbed spine and white paper label printed in two colors. Japan vellum copies are bound in Japan vellum wraps over boards with the label information printed directly to the wrapper. Title page is printed in red and black.

Reference: MacKay, p. 435; Trovillion, p. 3.

96. *DUKE CARL OF ROSENMOLD AN IMAGINARY PORTRAIT*
by Walter Pater. [August] 1898.   60, [1] pp. (same for second ed.)
Brocade Series-10   H 72.   First edition.

425 on Japan vellum for each edition.

Content: Jenkinson calls this as a "faithful reprint of the first collected edition published in 1887." This work originally appeared in *Macmillan's Magazine* for May 1887 republished as *Imaginary Portraits* (London & New York: Macmillan, 1887). The publisher's bibliographical note appears on p. [5].

Comment: See note to entry 62 for this work's inclusion in a sub-series.

Reference: Wright, p. 162 (see also Wright, Section I , "a 46"); Jenkinson II, 846.

96.1 *DUKE CARL OF ROSENMOLD AN IMAGINARY PORTRAIT*
by Walter Pater. [September] 1898.
Brocade Series.   H 99.   Second edition.

E

97. *EARTHWORK OUT OF TUSCANY BEING IMPRESSIONS AND TRANSLATIONS* of Maurice Hewlett. 1911.   *xiv*, 265 pp.; front.   18 x 11 cm.
Miscellaneous Series-54   H 533.   Only edition.

700 on Van Gelder "for sale in America"; 25 numbered copies on Japan vellum.

Content: The signed foreword is by the publisher. Colbeck notes: "This pirated edition is a reprint of the book of 1895 [published by Dent] with the essay "Boils" ["Of Boils and the Ideal"] added; it also reprints the 3 sonnets for figures of Sandro Botticelli, which appeared in the *Academy* in 1893 and of which this is the first book form appearance. There is a 6 page Bibliographical Foreword by the publisher." The portrait frontispiece is from a painting by Botticelli which appeared in the Dent edition.

Two selections from this work were first printed by Mosher in his August 1899 issue of *The Bibelot* (22).

Comment: Mosher's edition was not the first American; G. P. Putnam's sons co-published an edition with J. M. Dent (London) in 1899.

Binding & Embellishment: The Van Gelder copies are bound in "old style green ribbed boards" (i.e., raised bands) with a white spine label. Japan vellum copies are in Japan vellum wrappers over boards. Title page in red and black; Chiswick ornaments and initial letters.

The bindings of *Earthwork Out of Tuscany* (97), *Roses of Paestum* (331), *By the Ionian Sea* (54), and *The Renaissance* (322) are uniform in style. Also, all of these titles carry the statement "Limited to 700 Copies for Sale in America."

Reference: Colbeck I, p. 373 (36); Quinn 4130.

98. *ECCLESIASTES OR THE PREACHER*. [September] 1907.
viii, 40, [1] pp.   17.5 x 11 cm.
Miscellaneous Series-38   H 394.   Only edition.

500 on Van Gelder; 50 numbered copies on Japan vellum.

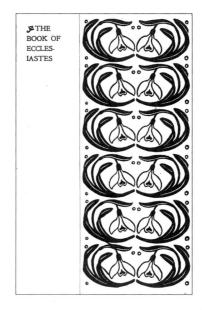

Content: In addition to the title text, there is a brief quote from G. K. Chesterton, and the transcription entitled "A Testimony" written by Christina G. Rossetti.

Comment: For Mosher's plan to include this work in a proposed "Breviary Series," see comment under entry 71.

Binding & Embellishment: The cover design by Lucien Pissarro was taken from the 1896 Eragny Press edition of *The Book of Ruth and The Book of Esther*. The text pages are ruled throughout in red.

For other books using Eragny Press & Lucien Pissarro designs, see entry 52.

The Van Gelder copies are bound in quarter white paper over light green paper boards with title in dark green on the spine and upper left-hand corner of the front cover and the Eragny cover design printed in a dark green. The Japan vellum copies are bound in Japan vellum wraps over boards with the same information and design.

Reference: Vilain, p. 92, plate 31; Boss XV 153.

99. *ECHOES OF LIFE AND DEATH FORTY-SEVEN LYRICS* by William Ernest Henley. [October] 1908.   *vi*, 64, [1] pp. (same for second ed.)
Lyric Garland Series-13   H 438.   First edition.

950 copies on Van Gelder for each edition. For the first edition, 100 numbered copies on Japan vellum.

Content: A two-line selection from Shakespeare appears opposite the title page, and a two-line French selection from *Gil Blas* is on p. [2]. Mosher notes in his 1910 catalogue indicate that these poems were taken from "Henley's poems as revised and arranged by him in his edition of 1898," published by David Nutt.

The first thirteen poems in this book were previously printed by Mosher in the October 1903 issue of *The Bibelot* (26).

99.1 *ECHOES OF LIFE AND DEATH FORTY-SEVEN LYRICS*
by William Ernest Henley. [October] 1916.
Lyric Garland Series.   H 652.   Second edition.

100. VIRGIL *THE ECLOGUES* done into English Prose [by] J W Mackail.
[October] 1898.   *xii*, 96, [2] pp.; front. (same for all eds.)   15.5 x 9 cm.
Miscellaneous Series-5   H 68.   First edition.

450 on Van Gelder; 50 on Japan vellum.

Content: This Mosher reprint is from the Rivingtons edition (London, 1889). A prefatory note, together with the "Arguments," are taken from Sir Charles Synge Christopher Bowen's *Virgil in English Verse* (London: John Murray, 1889).

Comment: Mackail was a British classical scholar and professor of poetry at Oxford, and William Morris' first biographer.

Binding & Embellishment: The binding is the same for both the Van Gelder and the Japan vellum copies: brown printed Japan vellum wraps over boards.

The pastoral cover design of sheep grazing under a tree is framed with rustic stylized branches and is signed by the artist, C.M.J. (Charles M. Jenckes). For

THE ECLOGUES (continued)

other Jenckes designs in the Mosher books, see entries 130, 131, 334, and many of the head- and tail-pieces in The Old World Series.

Ornamental renaissance-style brown border throughout. The frontispiece is an Albertype reproduction of an etching by Samuel Palmer. The book could be ordered in a cabinet box with the same sized and similarly decorated set of Virgil's *Georgics* (130).

Reference: Vilain 12 (Plate 18, p. 87).

100.1 VIRGIL *THE ECLOGUES* done into English Prose [by] J W Mackail. [February] 1899.
Miscellaneous Series.   H 132.   Second edition.

450 on Van Gelder. No copies were printed on Japan vellum.

100.2 VIRGIL *THE ECLOGUES* done into English Prose [by] J W Mackail. [September] 1912.
Miscellaneous Series.   H 572.   Third edition.

450 on Van Gelder. No copies were printed on Japan vellum.

101. *EDWARD FITZGERALD: AN AFTERMATH* by Francis Hindes Groome. With Miscellanies in Verse and Prose. 1902.
xxviii, 156, [1] pp.; 12 plates (incl. port. front.)   18.5 x 14.5 cm.
Miscellaneous Series-19   H 214.   Only edition.

600 on Van Gelder; 60 numbered copies on Japan vellum with an extra set of plates also on Japan vellum (in addition to the regular white paper plates).
First American edition.

Content: The unsigned foreword is by the publisher. Besides Groome's Edward FitzGerald: An Aftermath" (pp. [27]-90) which was taken from *Two Suffolk Friends* (Edinburgh; London: W. Blackwood, 1895, pp. 65-133), there appear 8 of FitzGerald's minor poems (pp. [95]-127), and the following works collected here:

- "Notes on Charles Lamb" taken from *Miscellanies by Edward FitzGerald* (London: Macmillan, 1900).
- Two stories, "The Only Darter" and "Master Charley," by Robert Hindes Groome.
- Edward Clodd's "Pilgrimage" privately printed for members of the Omar Khayyám Club (London, 1894).
- "Proem" by John Hay (from an address given at the Omar Khayyám Club in London, Dec. 8, 1897).
- Tribute to Groome called "The Tarno Rye (Francis Hindes Groome)" by Theodore Watts-Dunton (reprinted from *The Athenaeum*, Feb. 22, 1902).
- A selection signed "The Bird Parliament" appears on p. [*xviii*], and a selection from Tennyson on p. [26].

Twelve photo-illustrations (in two states in the Japan vellum copy), "including a portrait of Fitz-Gerald's mother never reproduced before" (*The Bibelot*, March 1903), and a facsimile of a four-page unpublished letter, accompany the text. According to the foreword (p. *xxiii*) the photos were gathered by John Loder at Mosher's request.

Comment: Robert Hindes Groome was archdeacon of Suffolk, intimate with FitzGerald, and father of Francis Hindes Groome. The archdeacon's two stories were also printed in *The Bibelot* for Nov. 1904 (27). *Two Suffolk Friends* presented the son's sketches of his father and his father's friend, Edward FitzGerald.

In June 4, 1918 letter to Christopher Morley (Special Collections, University of Virginia Library), Mosher indicates he included Edward Clodd's "Pilgrimage"

EDWARD FITZGERALD: AN AFTERMATH (continued)

with the author's permission. See also entry 75 for this same title privately printed.

A few copies have a special portrait plate of FitzGerald, added later, by John Loder. The Quinn catalogue quotes a June 12, 1918 letter from Mosher to John Quinn:

> I have put in the John Loder plate, facing page XXIII, where it belongs... Loder would not allow me to make use of it in the edition that I published and so I never printed any from the plate until now, when I did twenty for those who, like yourself, would be glad to see what he looked like.

The "E. FitzGerald" bookplate which appears on the front pastedown is a facsimile of the only bookplate designed by Thackeray, and the likeness is supposed to be that of a Mrs. Brookfield. According to Edmund Gosse, the plate was done by Thackeray one day in Coram Street in 1842.

A Japan vellum copy at the University of San Francisco is inscribed by Mosher to the publisher Laurens Maynard of the firm Small, Maynard & Co.: "My dear Maynard, I want you to have the Japan vellum copy of a book that I put together myself as the result of a visit to Woodbridge in May 1901. Sincerely yours, Thomas B. Mosher. May 1, 1905" with Maynard's signature on the first blank. Also, a Japan vellum copy is inscribed to Abraham Lincoln's second personal secretary, and later ambassador to England: "To the Hon. John Hay with the highest regards and esteem of the editor. Thomas B. Mosher. Dec 23, 1902" (Bishop Collection). Mosher also published John Hay's *In Praise of Omar* (171); see also 338 for a selection from Hay.

A reprint of Mosher's edition was published by the Books for Libraries Press of Freeport, NY in 1972.

Binding & Embellishment: The Van Gelder copies are bound in charcoal blue paper boards with raised bands and white paper label on the spine. The Japan vellum copies are bound in Japan vellum wraps over boards with the spine label printed directly on the vellum. Pages ruled in black. Chiswick head- and tail-pieces. Mosher saw this as a companion volume to *Polonius* (306).

Reference: Colbeck I, p. 257 (51); Quinn 3016 and 3017; Grigsby 403 & 404.

---

102. *EMERALD UTHWART AN IMAGINARY PORTRAIT* by Walter Pater.
[July] 1899.   *vii*, 84, [1] pp. (same for second ed.)
Brocade Series-15   H 113.   First edition.

425 on Japan vellum for each edition.
First separate American edition.

Comment: The John Quinn catalogue notes this as the "First Separate American Edition." The essay was originally printed in the *New Review* for June and July 1892, and printed in book form for the first time in Pater's *Miscellaneous Studies* (New York & London: Macmillan, 1895).

A publisher's note appears opposite the title page. See note to entry 62 for this work's inclusion in a sub-series.

Reference: Quinn 7586; Wright, 162 (see also Wright, Section I, "a 83"); Jenkinson II, 847 (second edition).

102.1 *EMERALD UTHWART AN IMAGINARY PORTRAIT* by Walter Pater.
[June] 1900.
Brocade series.   H 176.   Second edition.

103. ***EMPEDOCLES ON ETNA A DRAMATIC POEM***. By Matthew Arnold.
[September 19] 1900.   51, [1] pp.   22 x 15 cm.
Miscellaneous Series-13   H 143.   Only edition.

450 on Kelmscott "Hammer & Anvil" handmade paper; 50 on Japan vellum.
First American edition.

Content: Although Mosher does not identify the source for this reprint, it was most likely the Vale Press edition of 1896. A copy was in Mosher's library, and it partially served as the model for Mosher's reprint (see "Binding & Embellishment" below).

Comment: The copy from Flora Lamb's library (assistant to Mosher) was hand-illuminated by Bertha Avery (Vilain-Wieck Collection).

Binding & Embellishment: The Kelmscott paper copies are bound in blue charcoal paper boards with white labels on both the spine and the front cover. The Japan vellum copies are bound in Japan vellum wraps over boards with all label information printed directly on the cover. For other books printed on Kelmscott paper, see entry 47.

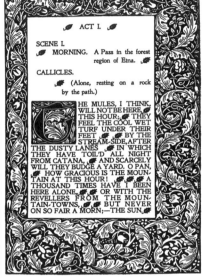

Meant as a tribute to Morris, the paper, borders, red initials, and the Golden type are those of the Kelmscott Press *Poems* of Coleridge. The format, however, still bears noted resemblance to the first edition printed by the Vale Press in 1896. The labels on the spine and front cover are similarly positioned and titled, but Mosher's edition uses Kelmscott rather than Ricketts dingbats. The inner half-title and two pages giving the "Persons and Scene" note are likewise positioned, and THE END at the back is similarly surrounded by four dingbats, again Kelmscott rather than Ricketts in design. The positioning of the lines of text also closely follows the Vale Press edition, but Mosher's large lead initials are red rather than black. A partial Morrisian border and large red initial also appears at the opening of Act II on p. 33. Aside from the opening border, all the Morrisian initials and the border on p. 33 are found listed as Jenson Old-Style initials and page embellishments in the American Type Founders' *Specimens of type...* (Chicago, 1896).

For other books using Kelmscott Press & William Morris designs, see entry 74.
For other books using Vale Press & Charles Ricketts designs, see entry 47.

Reference: *DLB* LVII, 3; Boss XI 135, XV 152; Thompson, p. 195-96 (opening spread pictured on p. 195); Vilain 14 (also plate 22, p. 88 of opening spread); Kaplan 156; American Type Founders, p. 416b, #4263 & 416e, #4285; Trovillion, p. 3; Naylor, p. 148; Japan Paper Company (Kelmscott Hand-made Paper from England); Lowden, p. 15.

104. ***ESSAYS FROM THE "GUARDIAN"*** by Walter Pater. 1897.
xiii, 163, [1] pp.; port. front. (second ed. same)   18.5 x 11.5 cm.
Reprints of Privately Printed Books-1   H 49.   First Edition.

400 on Van Gelder: 50 numbered copies on Japan vellum.
First American edition.

ESSAYS FROM THE "GUARDIAN" *(continued)*

Content: The unsigned bibliographical note (pp. [*v*]-*vii*) is by the publisher. This is a typographic facsimile of the first, privately printed edition by the Chiswick Press in 1896.

Comment: According to the 1897 Mosher catalogue, "Mr. Mosher's reprint, short of absolute photographic reproduction, is in facsimile as far as type, paper and binding can make it. The portrait by [Will] Rothenstein is used as a frontispiece for the first time." The portrait frontispiece was taken by Mosher from his copy of *Oxford Characters* (London: John Lane; New York: R. H. Russell, 1896), a copy of which was in Mosher's library (Bishop Collection). The volume also contains a facsimile of the original title page.

Wright notes that "though of limited issue, it must rank as the first public edition."

Both the first and second editions of this book were printed by "Thurston Print" of Portland, ME.

Binding & Embellishment: The Van Gelder copies are bound in charcoal blue paper boards with a printed white label on the spine; white printed dust jacket. Japan vellum copies are bound in Japan vellum wraps over boards with the label information printed directly on the wraps. The dust jacket on Mosher's copy (Bishop Collection) is printed on charcoal blue paper which matches the boards. Title page printed in red and black; Chiswick lead initials, head- and tail-pieces used throughout.

Reference: Colbeck II, p. 641 (23); *DLB* LVII, p. 217; Quinn 7584 & 7585; Grigsby 895; DeVinne 1502; Wright, p. 111.

104.1 **ESSAYS FROM THE "GUARDIAN"** by Walter Pater. 1898.
  Reprints of Privately Printed Books   H 102.   Second Edition.

      400 copies on Van Gelder.

  Reference: Colbeck II, p. 641 (24); Grigsby 896.

105. **EUGÉNIE DE GUÉRIN** by Matthew Arnold. [July] 1903.
  65, [1] pp.
  Brocade Series-38   H 252.   Only edition.

      425 on Japan vellum.

Content: Mosher indicates in the foreword to his Brocade Series reprint of *Maurice de Guérin* (237) that these studies (59, 105 & 237) were taken from Matthew Arnold's *Essays in Criticism* (First Series), but he does not cite the exact imprint.

Comment: This volume along with two others form a sub-series. See entry 59.

F

106. **FANCY'S FOLLOWING** by Anodos. 1900.
  viii, 57, [1] pp.   19.5 x 11.5 cm.
  Reprints of Privately Printed Books-7   H 154.   Only edition.

      450 on Kelmscott "Hammer & Anvil" handmade paper; 50 numbered copies on Japan vellum; and 4 on American vellum. First American edition.

Content: The unsigned foreword is by the publisher. The text and general format imitate the original 1896 Daniel Press publication.

Comment: Anodos is the pseudonym of Mary Elizabeth Coleridge.

FANCY'S FOLLOWING *(continued)*

Mosher's catalogue of 1900 states this "is the *third* book which Mr. Mosher has printed on genuine hand-made paper, such as William Morris used at his Kelmscott Press." For other books printed on Kelmscott paper, see entry 47.

Binding & Embellishment: The Kelmscott paper copies are bound in charcoal blue printed paper wraps over boards printed in red and green. The Japan vellum copies are bound in Japan vellum wraps over boards with the same green and red design. Title page printed in red, green and black; pages ruled at top.

At least one anomaly has been noted: a Japan vellum copy with blue decorative wraps used for Van Gelder copies, with an additional Japan vellum dust jacket bearing the same decorative design. This is the only known instance of a Mosher book with a *decorated* dust jacket (Bishop Collection).

Thompson mentions that "decoration is used sparingly but sometimes with great effect, as on the cover and title page of *Fancy's Following* by Anodos [Mary Coleridge]. Art Nouveau poppies in red with green stems and leaves are equally striking on the blue wrappers and on the white title page." According to Mosher's Autumn List accompanying *The Bibelot* for October 1900, "the cover design in colors is one of originality and great beauty and is the work of Miss Isadore B. Paine who designed the *Primavera* [311] wrapper last spring." Also see entry 116.

See color illustration on p. 369 (Plate 2).

Reference: Vilain 31 (plates 39 & 41, p. 95); Quinn 7086; Thompson, p. 191; Clark, p. 106 (#136); Grigsby 369 & 370; Naylor, p. 148; Japan Paper Company (Kelmscott Hand-made Paper from England).

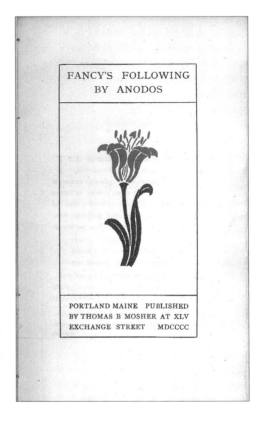

107. **FATHER DAMIEN** An Open Letter to the Reverend Doctor Hyde of Honolulu from Robert Louis Stevenson. 1897.
xvi, 31 pp. ; port. front. (same up to fourth ed.)   15.5 x 8.5 cm.
Miscellaneous Series-3   H 43.   First edition.

450 on Van Gelder; 50 on Japan vellum.

Content: The unsigned foreword is by the publisher. Quotes from H. D. Rawnsley on p. [*viii*] and Robert Browning on p. [*xv*] are also included. The text is from the first published edition (London: Chatto and Windus, 1890). The portrait frontispiece is by Edward Clifford, taken from his book, *Father Damien: A Journey from Cashmere to his home in Hawaii* (London: Macmillan, 1889).

Mosher first printed this text in his June 1897 issue of *The Bibelot* (20).

Binding & Embellishment: Van Gelder and Japan vellum copies are bound in Japan vellum wraps over boards. For larger format of the same book, see 108.

In *all* editions there appears an elaborate red initial "W" beginning the foreword. This signed initial (under the dolphins, an "F" signed with mirror-imaged "R's" on either side) is the work of Frank R. Rathbun of Auburn, NY, who designed Mosher's personal bookplate. Rathbun also designed and signed the red initial "F" (lower right corner) on the front cover and the initial "S" beginning the text on p. 1 (both signed in the lower right corner). For other Rathbun designs see entries 108, 202, 249, 263 & possibly 198.

Reference: *DLB* LVII, p. 295; Beinecke I, 511 &512; Beinecke I, 516 (7th ed.).

(a)

107.1 *FATHER DAMIEN* by Robert Louis Stevenson. 1897.
Miscellaneous Series. H 56. Second edition.

107.2 *FATHER DAMIEN* by Robert Louis Stevenson. 1898.
Miscellaneous Series. H 87. Third edition.

107.3 *FATHER DAMIEN* by Robert Louis Stevenson. 1899.
Miscellaneous Series. H 130. Fourth edition.

107.4 *FATHER DAMIEN* by Robert Louis Stevenson. [December] 1901.
xiv, 31, [1] pp. ; port. front. (same up to eleventh ed.)
Miscellaneous Series. H 203. Fifth edition.

Comment: The limitation page was transferred from the preliminaries to the end of the volume, and remained there for the balance of the editions printed.

107.5 *FATHER DAMIEN* by Robert Louis Stevenson. [November] 1903.
Miscellaneous Series. H 271. Sixth edition.

107.6 *FATHER DAMIEN* by Robert Louis Stevenson. [October] 1905.
Miscellaneous Series. H 338. Seventh edition.

107.7 *FATHER DAMIEN* by Robert Louis Stevenson. [June] 1907.
Miscellaneous Series. H 411. Eighth edition.

107.8 *FATHER DAMIEN* by Robert Louis Stevenson. [June] 1909.
Miscellaneous Series. H 489. Ninth edition.

107.9 *FATHER DAMIEN* by Robert Louis Stevenson. [December] 1911.
Miscellaneous Series. H 549. Tenth edition.

107.10 *FATHER DAMIEN* by Robert Louis Stevenson. [November] 1916.
Miscellaneous Series. H 641. Eleventh edition.

450 on Van Gelder for each edition up to the eleventh edition. No Japan vellum copies printed for this or succeeding editions.

ATHER 🌿 DAMIEN AN OPEN LETTER 🌿 TO THE REVEREND DOCTOR HYDE OF HONOLULU 🌿 🌿 FROM ROBERT LOUIS STEVENSON

(b)

108. *FATHER DAMIEN AN OPEN LETTER* to The Reverend Doctor Hyde of Honolulu from Robert Louis Stevenson. [April] 1905.
viii, 34, [1] pp.; port. front. (same for second ed.) 22 x 17.5 cm.
Miscellaneous Series-29 H 320. New edition/same series.

Content: The text is from the first published edition (London: Chatto and Windus, 1890). In addition to the title text, there are selections from Robert Browning, H. D. Rawnsley, and Archibald Ballantyne. The unsigned foreword is by the publisher. The attending bibliography, pp. [29]-34, is based upon Prideaux's bibliography of Stevenson (London, Frank Hollings, 1903) with Mosher's additions.

Binding & Embellishment: The Van Gelder copies are bound in charcoal blue paper boards with white spine label and front cover label both printed in two colors. The Japan vellum copies are bound in Japan vellum wraps over boards with the label information printed directly to the cover.

Frank R. Rathbun designed the initial on the title page which formerly appeared on the front cover of the smaller format edition (see entry 107). Likewise, Rathbun's large red initial "W" and his large "S" are also retained at the beginning of the foreword. For other Rathbun designs, see entry 107. The

600 on Van Gelder; 50 numbered copies on Japan vellum; 4 copies on Roman vellum, signed by the publisher.

FATHER DAMIEN

FATHER DAMIEN AN OPEN LETTER (continued)

front cover displays a Ricketts-style triangular device of a cross within vines in the upper right-hand corner label. The portrait frontispiece is by Edward Clifford, taken from his book, *Father Damien: A Journey from Cashmere to his home in Hawaii* (London: Macmillan, 1889). Head-pieces are most likely by Edward B. Edwards. For other Edwards designs, see discussion under Design in entry 231.

This new, larger format of 22 x 17.5cm. was called by Mosher a "large type edition" (1905 catalogue, p. 53). Pages are lined, Chiswick-style, in black.

Reference: Boss IX 129; Prideaux, p. 76; Widener 116; Beinecke I, 517 (2nd ed.); Gerstley 44 F.

108.1 ***FATHER DAMIEN AN OPEN LETTER*** to The Reverend Doctor Hyde of Honolulu from Robert Louis Stevenson. [March] 1910.
Miscellaneous Series.   H 523.   Second edition.

600 on Van Gelder. No copies on Japan or Roman vellum.

——————— *Same Title, Change of Series* ———————

109. ***FATHER DAMIEN AN OPEN LETTER*** to The Reverend Doctor Hyde of Honolulu from Robert Louis Stevenson. 1897.
iv, 32 pp.; port. front.
Reprints from "The Bibelot"-1   H 47.   First thus.

25 copies only were printed on Japan vellum.
First American edition.

Content: The unsigned introduction is by the publisher. The book includes selections from Robert Browning and Archibald Ballantyne. According to the bibliography appended to Mosher's 1905 reprint (108), the text is from the first published edition (London: Chatto and Windus, 1890). The portrait frontispiece is by Edward Clifford, taken from his book, *Father Damien: A Journey from Cashmere to his home in Hawaii* (London: Macmillan, 1889).

Comment: In a note to the Stevenson bibliography (see 108 above), Mosher remarks on p. 33: "Only 25 numbered copies of this book were printed on Japan vellum, of which 20 were for sale at $3.00 net. It formed No. 1 of a series of 12 Reprints from "The Bibelot." It was in fact printed from the same forms, only reimposed and with new pagination." As such, this is the first American edition in book form, preceded only by *The Bibelot* publication of June 1897 (20). Mosher also notes in his Autumn List accompanying *The Bibelot* for December 1897: "The 25 copies on Japan vellum were all taken within ten days." Additionally, Mosher gives this edition chronological priority over his "Miscellaneous Series-3" edition (107) of the same year. See Mosher's bibliography in the "Miscellaneous Series-29" *Father Damien* (108), p. 33.

110. ***FÉLISE: A BOOK OF LYRICS*** Chosen from the works of Algernon Charles Swinburne. 1894.   80 pp. (numbered in Roman numerals)
Bibelot Series-4   H 7.   First thus.

725 on Van Gelder; 25 numbered copies on Japan vellum.

Content: This Swinburne anthology, assembled by Mosher, contains 15 poems from *Poems and Ballads* (1866), 2 choruses from *Atalanta in Calydon* (1865), "Cleopatra" from *The Cornhill Magazine* (September 1866), 6 poems from *Poems and Ballads-Second Series* (1878), a poem from *Poems and Ballads-Third Series* (1889), and "Three Songs from the Trilogy of Mary Stuart" and "Adieux à Marie Stuart."

FÉLISE: A BOOK OF LYRICS (continued)

Livingston notes: "This contains 'Cleopatra' collected here for the first time, and never reprinted in England." According to the 1894 List of Books, the poem was reprinted from *Once a Week* (September 1866).

Comment: Williamson recounts how Swinburne himself got hold of a copy:

> I was visiting Lady Jane one day, and showed to her and her daughters a book of Lyrics from Swinburne's Works, that had been published by Mosher, of Portland, U.S.A. It was of course a pirated book, but withal so charmingly printed and bound that it was a pleasure to look at it, and in that light Lady Jane appreciated what she termed a compliment to her gifted son. She asked my permission to show it to him, to which I gladly assented... 'Algernon,' said they, 'has got both your books...' The Mosher book he admired, and the selection from his poems was, he considered, a judicious one..."

For Mosher's first anthology, and other anthologies assembled by him, see 366.

Reference: Vilain, p. 82 (plate 5); Livingston, p. 30; Williamson, pp. 201-03.

——————— *Same Title, Change of Series* ———————

111. ***FÉLISE: A BOOK OF LYRICS*** Chosen from the works of Algernon Charles Swinburne. 1909.　　*vi*, 130, [1] pp.
Old World Series-50　　　　H 464.　　　　First thus.

925 on Van Gelder; 25 numbered copies on Japan vellum.

Content: The Old World *Félise* contains nearly twice the amount of material as the same title previously issued under The Bibelot Series (110). The contents lists 22 poems from *Poems and Ballads* (1866), "Cleopatra" (1866), 8 poems from *Poems and Ballads-Second Series* (1878), a poem from *Poems and Ballads-Third Series* (1889), a poem from *Tristram of Lyonesse* (1882), and "Three Songs from the Trilogy of Mary Stuart."

Comment: As with 110, this Swinburne anthology was collected by Mosher. For Mosher's first anthology, and other anthologies assembled by him, see 366.

Design: The heart-shaped cover design is by Earl Stetson Crawford; his monogram of a "C" with a stylized crown of 3 dots above 2 curved lines appears at the lower right portion of the heart. Last title published in this series. For other Crawford designs used, see entry 88.

This is the last title of the Old World Series.

Reference: Vilain 6 (plate 7 on p. 83).

112. ***THE FISHERMAN AND HIS SOUL*** by Oscar Wilde. [June] 1905.
88, [1] pp. (same for all three editions)
Brocade Series-47　　　　H 324.　　　　First edition.

425 on Japan vellum for each edition.

Content: The publisher's bibliographical note opposite the title page indicates this work was reprinted from Oscar Wilde's *A House of Pomegranates* (London: McIlvaine, 1891). See 159 for the Old World Series *A House of Pomegranates*.

Comment: The note to entry 308 indicates which sub-series this title formed a part.

Reference: Cowan III, pp. 22-23.

112.1 *THE FISHERMAN AND HIS SOUL* by Oscar Wilde. [April] 1907.
Brocade Series.   H 421.   Second edition.

112.2 *THE FISHERMAN AND HIS SOUL* by Oscar Wilde. [February] 1912.
Brocade Series.   H 581.   Third edition.

113. ROBERT LOUIS STEVENSON *THE FLIGHT OF THE PRINCESS AND*   Limitation unknown for the Van
      OTHER PIECES. 1912.   *xiv*, 93, pp.   Gelder and copy; 100 on Japan
      Vest Pocket Series-23   H 561.   Only edition.   vellum.

Content: *The Flight of the Princess* was taken from Stevenson's *Prince Otto*
(London: Chatto & Windus, 1885). The other selections are from Stevenson's
Memories and Portraits (London: Chatto & Windus, 1887): "Old Mortality, An
Old Scotch Gardener," and "A Penny Plain and Two-pence Coloured." The
foreword is by the publisher. Small selections from George Meredith and
Shakespeare are also included in the book.

This text was first printed by Mosher in his June 1898 issue of *The Bibelot* (21).

Comment: Beinecke indicates: "The Japan-paper issue was limited to 100
copies, according to a letter from the Mosher Press."

Reference: Beinecke II, 782-784 (especially p. 407); Prideaux, p. 34; Gerstley,
p. 43 (13).

114. *THE FLOWER FROM THE ASHES AND OTHER VERSE* by Edith M.   450 on Van Gelder; 25 on Japan
      Thomas. [October] 1915.   *vi*, 63, [1] pp.   vellum.
      Lyra Americana Series-3   H 627.   Only edition.   First edition.

Content: Contains 32 poems from periodicals and from three of Edith Thomas'
books (sources are given on p. [*ii*]). A bibliographical note on p. [63] lists 12
other books by Edith Thomas. A lengthy quote from Sir Kenelm Digby's *Discourse Concerning the Vegetation of Plants* appears on p. [2].

Comment: Edith Thomas was from West New Brighton on Staten Island, and
was paid a royalty of 10%.

Binding: The Van Gelder copies are bound in quarter gray paper spine over
gray heart and dot decorated paper boards. See series in Section I for further
details.

Reference: Correspondence and letter of permission between Edith Thomas
and Mosher are at The Houghton Library (bMS Am 1096); see the Nov. 17,
1941 letter from Lamb to Yorke for Mosher's payment terms (see Appendix II).

115. *FOR THOSE WHO LOVE MUSIC AND OTHER VAGARIES* by Axel Munthe.   450 on Italian handmade paper;
      [October] 1918.   *viii*, 53, [1] pp.   16.5 x 12 cm.   25 numbered copies on Japan
      Miscellaneous Series-85   H 664.   Only edition.   vellum.

Content: The foreword is signed by the publisher. Following the title text, the
works entitled "To—" and "Zoology" round out this little volume. Before each
essay is a poem: one untitled by an anonymous author, and the other two
being "The Monkey" and "A Pekinese Puppy, Who Died," both by Nancy
Maude. The introduction to *The Bibelot* for March 1905 indicates these essays
were taken from a collection of fourteen essays by Munthe entitled *Vagaries*
(London: J. Murray, 1898).

FOR THOSE WHO LOVE MUSIC AND OTHER VAGARIES (continued)

The title text of this work was printed by Mosher in his March 1905 issue of *The Bibelot* (28), and the essay "To—" was printed in the March 1910 issue (33).

Comment: Nancy Maude, the author of the two poems, was a friend of Katherine T. Hinkson who probably introduced her to Mosher.

Binding & Embellishment: Van Gelder copies are bound in light green boards with title/author directly printed to the spine and front cover. The Japan vellum copies are similarly decorated but bound in Japan vellum boards.

A design of leaves, branches and flowers appears on the front cover, and the design on the back cover shows a youth perched on an oak limb playing the panpipes.

This same pan-pipes playing youth appears on the front cover of *Masterpieces* (235), the title page of the 1909 catalogue (253), and on the front cover of Mosher's *The Children's Crusade* (66). Title page in red and black; Chiswick ornaments are used throughout; lead capitals in red outline.

For yet another book carrying the same front and back cover designs, see the comment under 65.

For those who love Music
and other Vagaries

Axel Munthe

116. *FRAGILIA LABILIA* by John Addington Symonds. 1902.
vii, 46, [1] pp.   19.5 x 11.5 cm.
Reprints of Privately Printed Books-10   H 224.   Only edition.

450 on Kelmscott "Hammer & Anvil" handmade paper; 50 numbered copies on Japan vellum; 5 Roman vellum, folded, unbound sheets, signed by the publisher. First American edition.

Content: Unsigned foreword is by the publisher. In addition to the thirteen numbered poems, there also appears a poem at the book's end excerpted from *New and Old: A Volume of Verse* (London: Smith, Elder, 1880).

The text and general format are a Daniel Press imitation. Babington notes: "The only accessible issue of the above [1st, Daniel Press, 1884 ed], which I have not seen in the original edition, is one printed by T.B. Mosher in 1902."

Binding & Embellishment: The Kelmscott paper copies are bound in charcoal gray wraps over boards printed in green and orange. Japan vellum copies are bound in Japan vellum wraps over boards printed in the same colors. Title page printed in orange, green and black; pages ruled at top. For other books printed on Kelmscott paper, see entry 47.

The cover design is sufficiently close in style and date to be assigned to the same artist who created the covers of *Fancy's Following* (106) and *Primavera* (311), Isadore B. Paine.

See color illustration on p. 369 (Plate 1).

Reference: *DLB* LVII, p. 321; Boss XV 158; Vilain 32 (plates 40 & 41, p. 95); Babington 35 & 492, and p. 51; *CBEL* III, p. 358; Grigsby 1183-84; Japan Paper Company (Kelmscott Hand-made Paper from England).

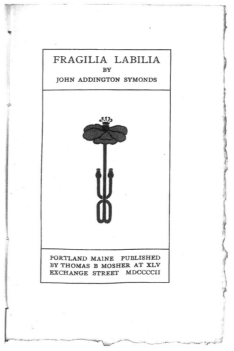

FRAGILIA LABILIA
BY
JOHN ADDINGTON SYMONDS

PORTLAND MAINE   PUBLISHED BY THOMAS B MOSHER AT XLV EXCHANGE STREET MDCCCCII

117. *FRAGMENTS* Volume One by Cavé [pseud]. The Quarterly Book Department.
New York, [ca. 1912].   *ii*, 100 pp.   16.5 x 9.5 cm.
Privately Printed-21   H 722A.   Only edition.

The number of copies is not given.

Content: In the prefatory remarks, Cavé notes that these writings are "Fragments from the Great Books of the Ages, and the Wisdom of all times... the
light of the soul and of its knowledge." (p. 5). The book is divided into three
sections, and contains reflections and meditations on topics like obedience,
ambition, the soul, personality, divine harmony, and various other theosophical tenets.

Comment: Catalogued references to Cavé indicate this is a pseudonym, but
the actual name behind the fictitious one remains unattributed.

On the verso of the title page: "The Mosher Press Portland Maine." The first
volume of a three volume set. Volumes II & III, copyrighted 1916 and 1925
respectively, bear no indication that they were printed by the Mosher Press.
There are slight differences between Mosher's volume and the other two volumes (apparently not printed by The Mosher Press). The most obvious difference is seen in the spines. The Mosher Press edition has a squared off spine
whereas the others are rounded and ruled around the spine's perimeter. The
later two volumes were also published under the auspices of The Theosophical
Society.

This edition was not listed in the Hatch *Check List*, but was later added by
Hatch in 1972 (see Vilain).

See entry 12 for another privately printed volume with Cavé selections.

Binding & Embellishment: White paper over boards with cover and spine
printed in green. The attractive art nouveau cover design is by Birger Elwing
and is present on all 3 volumes. A note on p. [2] indicates "the winged globe
of Egypt, symbol of the radiant and soaring Spirit: above it, that wonderful
sign, the Egyptian symbol of Life, blended of the Cross and the circle of Life
Everlasting."

Reference: Vilain, p. 67.

---

118. *FRANÇOIS VILLON, STUDENT, POET, AND HOUSEBREAKER.*
by Robert Louis Stevenson. [September] 1901.
73, [1] pp. (same for all four editions)
Brocade Series-28   H 190.   First Edition.

425 on Japan vellum for each
edition.

Content: The preface is by Robert Louis Stevenson. According to Sturm:
"Erschien erstmals 1878 als Aufsatz im "Cornhill Magazine", wurde mehrfach
nachgedruckt und auch in die Gesammelten Werke von R.L.St. aufgenommen.
[It appeared first as an essay in *Cornhill Magazine*, was several times thereafter reprinted and also continued in The Collected Works of R.L.S.]" The
Mosher Collection at Arizona State University contains the pages taken from
the *Cornhill Magazine* for August 1877, pp. 215-234, which Mosher used for
the text of this edition.

Comment: This work along with four others appeared in a sub-series. See
entry 436 for details.

Reference: Sturm 198 (p. 93); Gerstley 15 J-K; not in Peckham.

118.1 *FRANÇOIS VILLON, STUDENT, POET, AND HOUSEBREAKER.*
by Robert Louis Stevenson. [October] 1902.
Brocade Series.   H 215A.   Second Edition.

Comment: This edition was listed in the Hatch *Check List* as an unlocated trade edition, but was later added by Hatch in a 1972 unpublished addenda and corregenda to the *Check List* (see Vilain).

Reference: Vilain, p. 64; Hatch, p. 168.

118.2 *FRANÇOIS VILLON, STUDENT, POET, AND HOUSEBREAKER.*
by Robert Louis Stevenson. [April] 1906.
Brocade Series.   H 376.   Third Edition.

118.3 *FRANÇOIS VILLON, STUDENT, POET, AND HOUSEBREAKER.*
by Robert Louis Stevenson. [December] 1911.
Brocade Series.   H 551.   Fourth Edition.

119. *A FREE MAN'S WORSHIP* with a Special Preface by Bertrand Russell.
[August] 1923.   *xvii*, 28, [1] pp.   18 x 10 cm.
Miscellaneous Series-97   H 700.   Only edition.

950 on Van Gelder; 50 numbered copies on Japan vellum.
First edition, and first appearance of the preface.

Content: The introductory note is by the publisher. The preface was written by Bertrand Russell expressly for this edition. Jacob notes that *A Free Man's Worship* was, "reprinted from *Mysticism and Logic* [1918], Chapt. 3. The world of fact is powerful but not good; goodness is a creation of our own conscience. The free man's worship is to abandon the struggle for private happiness and to burn with passion for eternal things." –p. 198. The essay actually first appeared in *The Independent Review*, I, Dec. 1903, pp. 415-24. Rempel notes: "For the publication edited by Thomas Bird Mosher in 1923, Russell wrote a preface, but he made no substantive changes." Correspondence between Russell and Mosher is at The Houghton Library, Harvard, and at the Mills Memorial Library, McMaster University (Canada) which also has the galley proofs according to Blackwell and Ruja. The latter cite this Mosher publication as the "first separate American edition" but no prior separate edition is listed in Blackwell & Ruja, thereby making this the first separate edition in book form, and the first appearance of Russell's preface.

When returning the proofs to Mosher, Russell wrote on 4 July 1923: "There is one very small point as for which I feel slightly undecided. In the first sentence of the Essay I wrote "Mephistophel*i*s", not "Mephistophel*e*s", the allusion being to Marlowe, not to Goethe, as appears by my speaking of "Dr. Faustus'. But apparently no one realizes that Marlowe used the spelling with an *i*, so perhaps it is not worth bothering about... I am grateful to you for bringing out the Essay so beautifully" (The Houghton Library, bMS Am 1096 [1372]). Mosher followed Russell's wishes and the spelling "Mephistophelis" appears in the opening line of *A Free Man's Worship*.

Comment: Examination of The Houghton Library's manuscript material reveals that not only did Russell approve of the publication plans, he also secured permission from Longmans, Green & Co, (publishers of *Mysticism and Logic*) who indicated they would be very willing "that you should fall in with Mr. Mosher's suggestion" (The Houghton Library, bMS Am 1096 [1370]). Russell indicated he very much liked Mosher's production of *Books and the Quiet Life* (see entry 49), and remarked, "it would be a pleasure to have my essay produced so beautifully." Russell asked for, and was paid £5 for his preface and the rights to publish. The cost books indicate that the total payment was $24.26.

A FREE MAN'S WORSHIP (continued)

Binding & Embellishment: Van Gelder copies bound in blue boards with title/author directly printed on the spine and front cover (in red and blue). The front cover design above the title consists of a leafed stem with flowers previously used on the cover of *Michael Angelo Buonarroti His Sonnets* (241). The Japan vellum copies are bound in Japan vellum boards with the same design and lettering. Chiswick ornaments, and lead initials in red outline.

Reference: Jacob 10 on p. 198 (see also Jacob 11); Rempel, pp. 63-64, 507 and 580 (Bibliographical Index); Blackwell & Ruja A 44; see the Nov. 17, 1941 letter from Lamb to Yorke for Mosher's payment terms (see Appendix II).

---

120. ***FROM THE FOOTHILLS*** by Mary Linda Bradley. [July] 1914.
      ix, 87, [1] pp.   17.5 x 11 cm.
      Privately Printed-32   H 733.   Only edition.

300 copies printed on Van Gelder paper.

Content: Contains 56 poems privately printed for the author.

Binding & Embellishment: Bound in gray-green Fabriano boards with title in dark green on the spine and title/author printed in dark green on the front cover. Title page in red and black; Chiswick ornaments and red initial letter. Binding is uniform with the *Songs of the Susquehanna* (370) and *Sprays of Shamrock* (381).

---

121. ***FROM THE HILLS OF DREAM   THRENODIES, SONGS, AND OTHER POEMS*** by Fiona Macleod. 1901.   *xv*, 149, [1] pp. (same for second ed.)
      Old World Series-24   H 182.   First edition.

925 on Van Gelder; 100 numbered copies on Japan vellum.
First American edition.

Content: According to Mosher's note in *The Bibelot* (December 1906), the arrangement to publish this revised and enlarged text was made through Fiona Macleod's Edinburgh publisher, Patrick Geddes, while Mosher was visiting in 1901. In addition to the 92 poems included, a dedication by Macleod to W. B Yeats appears on pp. 83-87.

Mosher's 1901 catalogue notes that: "the re-issue of *From the Hills of Dream* is an authorized one, and contains many additional lyrics, besides having the advantage of the author's careful revision." Additionally, there are a few brief selections from *The Stephanos of Phillippus, Axel, Kalevala*, and from the *Leabhran Mhòr-Gheasadaireachd* ('The Little Book of the Great Enchantment'). Also, unlike the first edition which included the prose work, "The Silence of Amor," at its conclusion, the Mosher imprint drops this work which the author and publisher agreed to print later as a separate book in 1902 (see 352).

William Sharp sent a copy of this book to William Butler Yeats with the explanation that "though it contained new material,... there will be much in it that will be familiar to you... The first 10 poems are those which are in the current October *Fortnightly Review*. But when these are reprinted in a forthcoming volume of new verse... it will also contain some of the 40 'new' poems now included in this American edition..." See also 352.

Some of the text of this volume was printed in the December 1900 issue of *The Bibelot* (23).

Comment: Fiona Macleod was a pseudonym used by William Sharp who also published works under his real name.

Mosher paid $123 for the American copyright.

FROM THE HILLS OF DREAM (continued)

Design: Based upon stylistic evidence and the time period, the design on the front cover is most likely by Frederic Goudy. For other Goudy designs, see entry 1.

Reference: Quinn 8646, 8647 & 8654 (2nd ed.); Sharp, p. 334; Grigsby 1021. See the Nov. 17, 1941 letter from Lamb to Yorke for Mosher's payment terms(see Appendices); Macleod VI, p. 412, and VII, p. 453.

121.1 ***FROM THE HILLS OF DREAM THRENODIES, SONGS, AND OTHER POEMS*** by Fiona Macleod. 1904.
Old World Series.   H 304.   Second edition.

925 on Van Gelder, for each edition, and no copies printed on Japan vellum for this or succeeding editions.

121.2 ***FROM THE HILLS OF DREAM THRENODIES, SONGS, AND OTHER POEMS*** by Fiona Macleod. 1907.   *xv*, 147, [1] pp. (same for remaining eds.)
Old World Series.   H 406.   Third edition.

Comment: The decrease of two pages was due to removing the poem "Nine Desires" from p. 79 (verso blank) and placing it on p. 78 with "Naoi Mainnain."

Some copies have the cover printed in gray rather than the usual brown ink.

121.3 ***FROM THE HILLS OF DREAM THRENODIES, SONGS, AND OTHER POEMS*** by Fiona Macleod. 1910.
Old World Series.   H 522.   Fourth edition.

121.4 ***FROM THE HILLS OF DREAM THRENODIES, SONGS, AND OTHER POEMS*** by Fiona Macleod. 1917.
Old World Series.   H 659A.   Fifth edition.

Comment: This edition was not listed in the Hatch *Check List*, but was later added by Hatch in 1972 (see Vilain).

Reference: Vilain, p. 66.

122. ***FROM THE UPANISHADS*** by Charles Johnston. [March] 1897.
xxii, 60, [1] pp. (same for second ed.)   15.5 X 8.5 cm.
Miscellaneous Series-2   H 42.   First edition.

450 on Van Gelder; 50 numbered copies on Japan vellum.
First American edition.

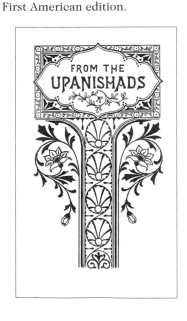

Content: Hume indicates that this is the first American edition reprinted from the Dublin translation. He also notes that the smaller Vest Pocket edition of 1913 (123) contains "excellent translations of Katha, of Prashna, and of Chandogya." Mosher's edition also contains a new foreword by Charles Johnston (highlighting R. W. Emerson), and two additional quotes from Emerson on pp. [*ii*] and [*viii*].

Comment: Ransom notes that an 1896 edition of this translation, with an introduction by George Russell [sic, actually it is *by* Johnston *to* G. W. Russell], was published by Whaley, Dublin, and printed by the Chiswick Press in which "an advertisement inside the back cover indicates that this was a joint publication of Whaley (Dublin), Simpkin Marshall & Co. (London), and T.B. Mosher (Portland); perhaps the last two merely distributed." Examination of the copy of the Whaley imprint not only confirms the Mosher listing, but also reveals advertisements for both the Van Gelder and Japan vellum editions of Mosher's other publication, *Homeward Songs by the Way*. But the question of distributor versus co-publisher still seems unresolved. The following, however, helps to clarify but does not definitively resolve the question.

FROM THE UPANISHADS (continued)

In *The Bibelot* for February 1896, Mosher ran a full-page ad for the Dublin edition without any mention of joint publication, but he mentions he "can supply a limited number of copies of this little book." In his Autumn List of Books accompanying *The Bibelot* for October 1896, Mosher includes this imprint with his own list of The English Reprint Series, and indicates "175 copies only are for sale..." He also lists it along with his other publications in the 1896 catalogue. In an announcement in *The Bibelot*, for April 1897, Mosher states: "The English remainder of FROM THE UPANISHADS, having been rapidly taken up, the first American edition is now in press, and will be ready April 5th. To this new edition Mr. Johnson contributes an interesting and timely note touching Emerson's connexion with Oriental thought." The above suggests that Mosher's role was one of distribution with regard to the English edition.

Binding & Embellishment: The Van Gelder copies are bound in light green paper boards with title and ornamentation in darker green. Japan vellum copies are bound in Japan vellum boards with green title and ornamentation. The unattributed cover design consists of an intricate combination of stylized middle-eastern decorations with stylized western flowers printed in green. In *The Bibelot* for May 1897, Mosher mentions it as an "original cover design." The caduceus, which appears on the back cover, was designed by Bruce Rogers. Perhaps this front cover is also by Rogers? For other Bruce Rogers designs, see entry 152.

Reference: Vilain 10 (plate 16, p. 86); Hume, p. 463; Ransom 117a.

122.1 ***FROM THE UPANISHADS*** by Charles Johnston. [September] 1899.
Miscellaneous Series.   H 129A.   Second edition.

Comment: This edition was not listed in the Hatch *Check List*, but was later added by Hatch in 1972 (see Vilain).

Reference: Vilain, p. 63.

──────── *Same Title, Change of Series* ────────

123. CHARLES JOHNSTON ***FROM THE UPANISHADS***. 1913.   Limitation unknown for both Van
      xxiii, 69, [1] pp.   Gelder and Japan vellum copies.
      Vest Pocket Series-25   H 591.   First thus.

Content: This volume includes several selections from Emerson to embellish the texts taken from the *Katha Upanishad*, the *Prashna Upanishad*, and the *Chandogya Upanishad, VI*, which are the same selections appearing in the Miscellaneous Series version (122).

Comment: Last title published in this series.

Reference: Vilain, p. 96 and plate 42; Hume, p. 463.

G

124. ***GABRIEL A PAGEANT OF VIGIL*** by Isabelle Howe Fiske.   300 copies printed on Van Gelder
      [October] 1912.   *vi*, 56, [1] pp.   19 x 13.5 cm.   paper.
      Privately Printed-19   H 721.   Only edition.

Content: This is a two-part drama, the scene and time of which are "the Mounts of Temptation and of Calvary [where] space and time are measured by infinite realities and not finite conceptions."

GABRIEL A PAGEANT OF VIGIL (continued)

Binding & Embellishment: Bound in gray paper boards; rounded spine with blind-ruled bands; white label. Title page's anchor & dolphin device printed in blue. Errata slip on Japan vellum following the colophon. Pages ruled in black. Hatch listed this as only being in Japan vellum boards (following the Sheean typescript). Copies examined have been in gray paper boards. The Lamb typescript indicates only 50 copies were bound in Japan vellum boards.

Comment: This book was privately printed for Mrs. Isabel Fiske Conant (Isabelle Howe Fiske). See also 363.

---

125. ***THE GARLAND OF RACHEL*** by Divers Kindly Hands. 1902.
xxxi, 64, [1] pp.; including facsim.   21 x 13 cm.
Reprints of Privately Printed Books-11   H 225.   Only edition.

450 on Van Gelder; 50 numbered copies on Japan vellum, signed by the publisher.
First American edition.

Content: The eighteen contributors to *The Garland of Rachael* are: Henry Daniel, Albert Watson, Austin Dobson, Andrew Lang, John Addington Symonds, Robert Bridges, Lewis Carroll, Sir Richard Harington, A. Mary F. Robinson, Edmund Gosse F. W. Bourdillon, W. E. Henley, W. J. Courthope, Frederick Locker-Lampson, T. Humphrey Ward, Ernest Myers, Margaret L. Woods, and C. J. Cruttwell. A reprint of the Daniel Press edition (1881).

The three-part preface is by the publisher. Added to this edition is the poem *Hesperides* by T. Herbert Warren (from an 8 pp. Daniel Press leaflet printed in 1895). There is also an appendix with an overview of the Daniel Press from Henry R. Plomer's article "Some Private Presses of the Nineteenth Century" (*The Library*, September 1900), and the Henry W. Poor checklist of Daniel Press publications (pp. 61-64).

Ransom indicates that this is "a reprint of Daniel Press no. 15 [in Ransom], 'from a unique proof sheet copy.'"

Comment: Falconer Madan points out that the Mosher 1902 "kind of type facsimile" even reproduced the engravings and the Daniel Press mark. He carefully notes Mosher's additions and states: "Mr. Mosher's preface throws considerable light on the literary history of the book, on its preparation, and on the slow recognition of its value (owing to the privacy of the issue)..."

Babington notes that "in view of the extreme rarity of the original [36 copies were printed], this edition is a boon to the collector." Colbeck notes "this is the first reprinting of the book..."

Binding Embellishment: Bound in flexible white Japan vellum boards, the black & red title is printed vertically on the spine, and green silk ties weave through the covers. This binding was used on both the Van Gelder and Japan vellum copies. The head-pieces and the printer's mark by the English artist, Alfred Parsons, were created for the Daniel edition.

Reference: Madan 4; Colbeck I, p. 86 (46) and II (62); Ewelme D.3; Babington 500 (page 218); *CBEL* III, p. 323; Quinn 7085 & 7087; Ransom 292; Dobson, p. 88.

The Garland of Rachel

BY

DIVERS KINDLY HANDS

PORTLAND MAINE
THOMAS B MOSHER
MDCCCCII

126. *GARLANDS AND WAYFARINGS* By William Aspenwall Bradley.
[September] 1917. *viii*, 73, [1] pp. 21.5 x 13 cm.
Miscellaneous Series-83 H 655. Only edition.

450 (Mosher catalogue says 500) on Italian hand-made paper; 25 numbered copies on Japan vellum. First edition.

Content: This book contains thirty-five poems by Bradley, including "Roses of Paestum" which Mosher had included in his 1912 *Roses of Paestum* (331) by McCurdy. Also present is the poem "Jean Moréas" followed by an extensive note on Moréas. Part of the content is from periodicals.

Comment: Bradley was paid a 10% royalty on copies sold.

Binding & Embellishment: Van Gelder copies are bound in charcoal-blue paper boards with an unattributed cover design, and the title/author (in red and blue) on the spine and front cover. The Japan vellum copies are bound in Japan vellum boards with the same design work as the Van Gelder edition. The front cover design appears here in the upright position, but upside down on the cover of *Songs of the Susquehanna* (371). The same design also appears inside the 1912 *Memories of President Lincoln* (239).

GARLANDS AND WAYFARINGS

Reference: See the Nov. 17, 1941 letter from Lamb to Yorke for Mosher's payment terms (see Appendix II).

127. *GASTON DE LATOUR AN UNFINISHED ROMANCE* by Walter Pater.
1907. *xi*, 131, [1] pp.
Old World Series-43 H 389. Only edition.

925 on Van Gelder; 50 numbered copies on Japan vellum.

Content: The introduction is by William Marion Reedy. The source for this reprint is Pater's *Gaston de Latour—An Unfinished Romance* (New York: The Macmillan Company, [Norwood Press] 1901). The copy Mosher edited for the printer, now in the Bishop Collection, contains two more chapters than Mosher printed. Mosher's holograph note at the end of Chapter 5 states: "End of revised copy by Pater."

Design: The cover design bears the "C" monogram of Thomas Maitland Cleland, though the crown in the design itself may be a substitute for a crown over the "C" in which case the design would have to be attributed to Earl Stetson Crawford.

GASTON DE LATOUR

For other Crawford designs used, see entry 88. For other Cleland designs used, see entry 6.

Reference: Wright, p. 163 (Also Wright, Section I, "a 99"); Quinn 7596 & 7597; Court 250.

128. *GEORGE MEREDITH* By J M Barrie. [October] 1911.
viii, 10, [1] pp. (same for second ed.) 14.5 x 9.5 cm.
Miscellaneous Series-52 H 531. First edition.

950 on Van Gelder; 50 on Japan vellum.

Content: The title text was taken from Barrie's article in *The Westminster Gazette* (May 26, 1909). The foreword is signed by the publisher. A selection of poetry from R. Brimley Johnson, and the poem "G.M." by Thomas Hardy, precede the text. The title text was first published as the foreword to Mosher's 1910 catalogue (254), and its popularity with Mosher's readership induced him to reprint it.

GEORGE MEREDITH (continued)

Comment: Cutler mentions that "this is the first American edition... It was first printed by Mosher as a foreword to his annual catalogue in 1910," adding "the original title of this appreciation was *Neither Dorking nor the Abbey* and first appeared in *The Westminster Gazette*, May 26, 1909. It was dated from Box Hill, May 22, which was the day of Meredith's funeral." Cutler is not correct about this edition being the first American. Browne's Bookstore in Chicago published it in 1910 under the title *Neither Dorking nor the Abbey*.

Binding & Embellishment: Both the Van Gelder and the Japan vellum copies are bound in Japan vellum wraps over boards; spine and front cover's title/author in green; front cover is ruled in red. On the back cover appears a red flower with green stem first used on the title page of *Primavera* (311). This design is by Isadore B. Paine (see note to 106). The text pages are ruled in red; title page in red and black.

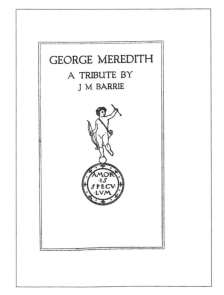

(a)   *(b)*

Reference: Cutler (B.D.) 60, pp. 141-42, 144-45 (Cutler's description mistakenly gives MDCCCIX).

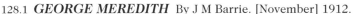

128.1 **GEORGE MEREDITH** By J M Barrie. [November] 1912.
Miscellaneous Series.   H 574.   Second edition.

950 on Van Gelder only for this and the third edition

128.2 **GEORGE MEREDITH** By J M Barrie. [September] 1914.
viii, 11, [1] pp.; port. front.
Miscellaneous Series.   H 615.   Third edition.

Comment: The one page expansion is due to a resetting of the type. A portrait frontispiece is also added.

129. **GEORGE MEREDITH A TRIBUTE** By J M Barrie. 1919.
16 *ℓ*, unnumbered, printed on recto side of each leaf; port. front.   14.3 x 9.9 cm.
Miscellaneous Series-90   H 672.   New edition/same series.

950 copies on Kisogawa handmade paper. No known copies printed on Japan vellum.

Content: The foreword is slightly altered by the publisher, but the selections from R. Brimley Johnson and Thomas Hardy are retained from the previous editions (128-128.2).

Design & Embellishment: In the foreword Mosher indicates: "I reprint it in latest and daintiest format for the fourth time." The color of the cover changes from the Japan vellum beige (entries 128-128.2) to a pale blue-gray, a frontispiece portrait of Meredith is added, the type is larger, the title-page has a new publisher's device, and an Eragny Press decorative initial "A" by Lucian Pissarro is added to the foreword (rather than the Chiswick initial of earlier editions). For other books using Eragny Press & Lucien Pissarro designs, see entry 52.

The pages are printed on the recto side only. Title page in red and black, with the "cupid and ball" device (see entry 69 for details) also used on 52, 69, 87 & 339.

This volume may be considered the fourth edition, but has a *totally new format* which is why it is being assigned as entry 129 rather than 128.3 in the present bibliography.

According to Thompson, this is the only Mosher book printed throughout in Jenson type, but there are several others which extensively use Jenson, including *Hand and Soul* (139), *Empedocles on Etna* (103), and *In Praise of Omar* (172).

GEORGE MEREDITH A TRIBUTE (continued)

Binding: Copies are bound in light gray-blue wraps over boards, with the spine printed in red and the front cover title/author printed in red and ruled in darker gray.

Reference: Thompson, p. 195 (plate 104).

---

130. VIRGIL *THE GEORGICS* done into English Prose [by] J W Mackail.
[September] 1899. [First volume of a two volume set]
xii, 82, [1] pp.; front. (same for second ed.)   15.5 x 9 cm.
Miscellaneous Series-6   H 107.   First edition.

450 copies on Van Gelder; 50 copies on Japan vellum.

Content: The text for this reprint (including 131) is from the Rivingtons edition (London, 1889). The prefatory note is from Mackail's *Latin Literature* (London: J. Murray, 1895), while the "Arguments" prefixed to each book are from the *Works of John Dryden* (Edinburgh: W. Paterson, 1882-93) edited by George Saintsbury.

Comment: John William Mackail was a British classical scholar and professor of poetry at Oxford, and was also William Morris' first biographer.

Binding & Embellishment: The Van Gelder and Japan vellum copies are bound in the same manner, with green print on Japan vellum wraps over boards. The same applies to the second volume of the set. Ornamental borders in green throughout. The frontispieces are Albertype reproductions of etchings by Samuel Palmer. This two volume set was boxed with the similarly designed book of Virgil's *Eclogues* (100) also translated by Mackail.

The pastoral cover design of a plowman is framed with rustic stylized branches. Though the design is not signed, it is evident that it is by Charles M. Jenckes, the same artist who did *The Eclogues*. For other Jenckes designs in the Mosher books, see entry 100, and many of the head- and tail-pieces throughout the Old World Series.

Reference: Vilain 12 (plate 19, p. 87); Crichton 41.

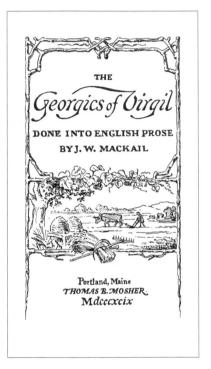

130.1 VIRGIL *THE GEORGICS* done into English Prose [by] J W Mackail.
[December] 1906. [First volume of a two volume set]
Miscellaneous Series.   H 371.   Second edition.

450 copies on Van Gelder only.

---

131. VIRGIL *THE GEORGICS* done into English Prose [by] J W Mackail.
[September] 1899. [Second volume of a two volume set]
vi, 90, [4] pp.; front. (same for second ed.)   15.5 x 9 cm.
Miscellaneous Series-7   H 108.   First edition.

450 copies on Van Gelder; 50 copies on Japan vellum.

Design: The cover design is by Charles M. Jenckes (same as entry 130).

Reference: Vilain 12.

131.1 VIRGIL *THE GEORGICS* done into English Prose [by] J W Mackail.
[December] 1906. [Second volume of a two volume set]
Miscellaneous Series.   H 372.   Second edition.

450 copies on Van Gelder only.

132. *THE GERM: THOUGHTS TOWARDS NATURE IN POETRY, LITERATURE, AND ART. MDCCCL* 1898.
xxxi, 224, [16] pp.; facsims., four illus.   23.5 x 15.5 cm.
Reprints ofPrivately Printed Books-3   H 78.   Only edition.

450 on Van Gelder; 25 numbered copies on Japan vellum; 4 on vellum; 25 numbered copies on Japan vellum for the Guild of Women -Binders, signed by Mosher. First American edition.

Content: The preface, and note on p. [*xiv*], are by the publisher. The introduction is from James Ashcroft Noble's "A Pre-Raphaelite Magazine" as revised in his *The Sonnet in England and Other Essays* (London: Mathews & Lane, 1893) which Mosher heavily annotated in a series of footnotes (the copy of *The Sonnet...,* with Mosher's pencil notes, is in the Bishop Collection). An appendix, with a lengthy quote on "Hand and Soul" (p. [217], from W. M. Rossetti's *Family-Letters*) and on "The Blessed Damozel" (pp. 218-222), is followed by an index of authors, pp. [223]-224, with the original contributors' names fully identified. Following the index are the facsimiles of the wrappers. The book also contains reproductions, in Albertype, of the etchings by Holman Hunt, Ford Madox Brown, James Collinson, and W. H. Deverell.

Ransom indicates that this volume, "contains the four original parts, 1850; second recension of the poems, 1856; final 1870 text; in parallel columns; a history of *The Germ,* and index."

Comment: This is not only the first American Edition *and* the first reprint of this publication, but according to the Grigsby catalogue, and in a 3/21/98 letter from Mosher to Grigsby (University of San Francisco), this is the first book to be printed on vellum in the state of Maine. It is also the first of 47 titles Mosher would eventually print on vellum.

In his *PBSC* article, Professor Fredeman identifies *The Germ* as the "black orchid" of Mosher's many distinctive publications and calls the vellum edition "a magnificent specimen of book production." From his review article of Hosman's edition of *The Germ* (see William Michael Rossetti in Section V, Bibliography), it is also clear that he regards Mosher's edition, with its textual and facsimile embellishments, (e.g., Noble's essay and the wrappers) as a far superior example of book-making than Elliot Stock's typographic "facsimile," printed in parts with an introduction by W. M. Rossetti, for which, ironically, Mosher acted as sole agent for the 250 copies distributed in America. In his introduction, Rossetti explains how Mosher, undeterred by copyright scruples that deferred the English reprint for over a decade, jumped the gun on the English publisher on the very eve of publication: "before Mr. Stock's long-standing scheme could be legally carried into effect, an American publisher, Mr. Mosher, towards the close of 1898, brought out a handsome reprint of 'The Germ' (not in any wise a facsimile), and a few of the copies were placed on sale in London." –pp.27-28. Rossetti further mentions "a very pleasant notice" of the Mosher reprint in the *Irish Figaro* for May 6, 1899.

It has been thought that the 25 copies carrying the Guild of Women-Binders imprint were never actually bound by the Guild; however, two copies have been located: one copy bound in full brown morocco now at Arizona State University, the other recorded in a bookseller's catalogue (see Section IV, Bindings). The publisher information reads: London Guild of Women-Binders 61 Charing Cross Road MDCCC- XCVIII. The limitation page (verso of the half-title) reads: "25 copies only of this book have been printed on Japan vellum, for England. Acquired by the Guild of Women-Binders, 61 Charing Cross

The Germ:
Thoughts towards Nature in Poetry, Literature, and Art.
MDCCCL

Portland, Maine
THOMAS B. MOSHER
MDCCCXCVIII

THE GERM (continued)

Road, London. This is [copy] No. *6. Thomas B. Mosher.*" There is also and example (Copy No. 9) bound by the Hampstead Bindery at the John Hay Library, Brown University.

Binding & Embellishment: Both the Van Gelder and the Japan vellum copies are bound in multi-color printed Japan vellum wraps over boards.

There is one difference between the title pages of a Van Gelder and a Japan vellum copy. The double dolphins of the Japan vellum copy are ensconced within a laurel wreath, whereas in the Van Gelder copy, a somewhat larger set of dolphins appears without any laurels.

According to an inserted printed slip, "the honeysuckle border on the wrapper was designed and cut on the wood by Charles Ricketts, and is taken from *The Poems of Sir John Suckling*, London: The Vale Press, 1896." For other books using Vale Press & Charles Ricketts designs, see entry 47.

The large triangular tail-pieces are designs from London's Chiswick Press and are displayed in Warren, pp. 41, 86, 226, and 340. The somewhat smaller tail-pieces are pictured in Warren, p. 314. Other head-pieces in *The Germ* are given in Warren, pp. 43, 105, 131, and 203.

The unsigned head-piece design on the title-page is possibly by Edward B. Edwards, a process engraver for De Vinne's shop in New York. It's style is identical to the designs found one year later in *A Translation of Giovanni Boccaccio's Life of Dante* (New York: The Grolier Club, 1900). Edwards is credited with the Dante cover design and he may be the designer of the interior designs as well. These designs, in turn, very closely match the title page head-piece of *The Germ*. For other Edwards designs, see discussion under Binding & Embellishment in entry 231.

See color illustration on p. 371 (Plate 11).

Reference: Bloomfield, p. 82; Fredeman 72.2; Colbeck II, p. 692 (1), 696 (38), 697 (43); Vilain 30 & p. 74 (plate 38, p. 94); Ransom 284; Jenkinson 94; Boss XI 136; *CBEL* III, p. 160; Quinn 8185 & 8186; Grigsby 965 & 966; Rossetti, p. 7; *PBSC*, p. 42.; Warren (see above page references).

---

133. *GERTHA'S LOVERS A TALE* by William Morris. 1899.

    vi, 100 pp.

    Reprints from "The Bibelot"-5 H 117.   First thus.

25 copies only printed on Japan vellum.
First edition.

Content: The unsigned preface is by the publisher, and also includes a selection from Morris' *The Earthly Paradise,* and a selection from William Sharp's article in *The Atlantic Monthly* for September 1898. The source of this text is the *Oxford and Cambridge Magazine* for July & August 1856.

The text of this work was first printed by Mosher in his January and February 1899 issues of *The Bibelot* (22).

Comment: The Quinn catalogue notes: "These scarce little booklets are not the regular Mosher publications, but are separates in book form from the original setting in the *Bibelot*. They constitute the First Editions of these pieces in book form, being mainly Morris' contributions to the *Oxford and Cambridge Magazine*, discerned by Mosher to be writings meriting a more permanent dress than the pages of a magazine..." See also comment under entry 109 which describes the printing of this series.

Reference: Quinn 6984; mentioned in Walsdorf 100; Jenkinson II, 799.

———————— *Same Title, Change of Series* ————————

134. ***GERTHA'S LOVERS A TALE*** by William Morris. [June] 1902.
    124, [1] pp. (same for second ed.)
    Brocade Series-32   H 217.   First edition.

    Content: The foreword is by the publisher, and is essentially the same wording of the preface to entry 133, but with some updated footnotes (including the selection from William Sharp as given in 133). For information on the content and source, see notes under 133.

    Comment: This work is one of four which forms a sub-series: see note to entry 150.

    Reference: Walsdorf 100.

425 on Japan vellum for each edition.

134.1 ***GERTHA'S LOVERS A TALE*** by William Morris. [October] 1905.
    Brocade Series.   H 343.   Second edition.

135. ***GOLDEN WINGS** [with] **SVEND AND HIS BRETHREN*** by William Morris.
    1900.   *viii*, 77, pp.
    Reprints from "The Bibelot"-8   H 152.   First thus.

    Content: These tales come from *The Oxford and Cambridge Magazine* for December 1856 and represent some of Morris' earlier writings. The unsigned preface is by the publisher.

    The text of this work was first printed by Mosher in his April and September 1900 issues of *The Bibelot* (23).

    Comment: The Quinn catalogue notes that "these scarce little booklets are not the regular Mosher publications, but are separates in book form from the original setting in the *Bibelot*. They constitute the First Editions of these pieces in book form, being mainly Morris' contributions to the *Oxford and Cambridge Magazine*, discerned by Mosher to be writings meriting a more permanent dress than the pages of a magazine..." See also comment under entry 109 which describes the printing of this series.

    Reference: Quinn 6984; Walsdorf 79; Jenkinson II, 800.

25 copies only printed on Japan vellum.
First edition.

———————— *Same Title, Change of Series* ————————

136. ***GOLDEN WINGS: SVEND AND HIS BRETHREN*** by William Morris.
    [July] 1902.   96, [1] pp. (same for second ed.)
    Brocade Series-33   H 218.   First edition.

    Content: The two-part foreword is by the publisher, the first part of which is essentially the preface from 135, with some alterations. The second part is new. The text for this reprint, as with entry 135, is *The Oxford and Cambridge Magazine* for December 1856.

    Comment: This work is one of four which forms a sub-series (see note to entry 150). The text for this work was printed by Mosher in his April and September 1900 issues of *The Bibelot* (23).

    Reference: Mentioned in Walsdorf 79.

425 on Japan vellum for each edition.

136.1 ***GOLDEN WINGS: SVEND AND HIS BRETHREN*** by William Morris.
[November] 1906.
Brocade Series.   H 378.   Second edition.

---

137. ***THE GROWTH OF LOVE*** By Robert Bridges. 1894. With an introduction by
Lionel Johnson.   *xxxviii*, [84], [2] pp.; facsim.
The English Reprint Series-3   H 5.   First thus.

Content: According to the 1895 Mosher catalogue, "the present reprint is
made direct [from the 1890 Daniel edition], and the half title immediately preceding the Sonnets is that of the actual title-page of this unique volume. The
printer's mark at the end of the volume is also reproduced in *facsimile* from
the Daniel edition." The prefatory "Essay on Bridges" by Lionel Johnson was
taken from *The Century Guild Hobby Horse* of October 1891 (pp. 148-160).
Mosher's annotated copy of the *Hobby Horse* is in the Bishop Collection. A
publisher's note appears opposite the limitation page.

Four sonnets from this book later appeared in *The Bibelot* for Sept.1896 (19).

Comment: Falconer Madan notes this Mosher piracy indicating that the title
and the printer's mark are reproduced in facsimile, and that "the reprinter
seems to know nothing of the 1889 [Daniel] edition of the work, and certainly
had neither the author's nor the printer's leave to reproduce the volume."

In a copy of this edition Mosher has written, after the essay by Lionel Johnson, that "There are 26 pages of this essay, of which some 5 pages - nearly 20%
of the entire article, have been foisted into the first chapter of 'The Art of
Thomas Hardy'." (Bishop Collection).

A facsimile page of the Daniel edition is loosely laid in a copy at the University of
Louisville; large paper copies have this extra leaf bound before the first half-title.

Last title published in this series.

Binding & Embellishment: The Van Gelder copies are bound in printed Japan
vellum wraps over boards. The large paper copies and the Japan vellum copies
are likewise in printed Japan vellum wraps over boards. The book comes in a
printed dust-wrapper. The Daniel edition was printed in Old English Black Letter; Mosher's reprint is in Roman type. The only graphic embellishment is the
Daniel Press printer's mark.

Reference: Madan 20; Boss VII 145, and XIII 145; Grigsby 121 with an ALS by
the author to Mosher. Ewelme A4; *CBEL* III, p. 323; Quinn 960 & 961.

400 numbered small paper copies
on Van Gelder; 40 numbered large
paper copies on Van Gelder; 10
numbered copies on Japan vellum,
signed by the publisher. An additional four copies were lettered A-D
and printed on toned Van Gelder,
in the large paper edition.
First American edition.

——————— *Same Title, Change of Series* ———————

138. ***THE GROWTH OF LOVE*** by Robert Bridges. [Sept.] 1913.
iv, [89], [1] pp.; port. front.   19 x 14 cm.
Miscellaneous Series-63   H 587.   First thus.

Content: The half-title verso indicates this reprint is "from the unique edition... issued by The Daniel Press... (Oxford, 1890)." It contains the same 79
numbered sonnets as the above English Reprints Series edition (137), and the
text was taken directly from an edited copy of the previous reprint. A note
appears on p. [83] and there is an index to first lines on pp. [87-89].

The printer's copy with corrections, now in the Bishop Collection, shows only
minor changes to the title text: the beginning of the second stanza in poem IV

450 on Van Gelder; 25 numbered
copies on Japan vellum.

THE GROWTH OF LOVE (continued)

is indented; the word "labor" in the 2nd line of poem
XXVII is changed to "labour"; the word "whatso'er" in
line five of poem XLIV is changed to "whatsoe'er"; the
month in line seven of poem XLV is capitalized to
"May"; "love's" in the second to last line in XLIX is
changed to "Love's"; and again, the word "love" is
changed to "Love" in the third line of LXXIV. This
Mosher edition, however, lacks the prefatory remarks by
Lionel Johnson, and no longer includes facsimiles of the
Daniel Press title and printer's mark, but contains a
newly added three-page "Index of First Lines."

Comment: The Quinn catalogue, entries 7088 & 7089
indicate there were 100 copies on Japan vellum. This
cataloguing error derives from the note on the verso of
the half-title:

> Faithfully reprinted in Old Style Roman face from the
> unique edition in Fell's Old English Type, (Fcap 4to) issued
> by The Daniel Press, (100 numbered copies) Oxford, 1890.

The pagination of this book differs from that given by
Hatch who records three preliminary leaves. The third
leaf is an inner half-title which Mosher customarily used
to begin his count of the principal text pages following
the preliminaries; therefore, the half-title is used to
begin the count as page [1].

Binding & Embellishment: The Van Gelder edition is bound with "Rizzi" decorated paper boards with a quarter white paper spine; titles appear on both the
spine and upper left-hand corner of the front cover. Portrait frontispiece of
Bridges printed on a Japan vellum leaf. The Japan vellum copies are bound in
Japan vellum wraps over stiff boards, with title/author on spine and on the
upper left hand corner of the front cover. Title page in red and black.

Reference: Quinn 989, 990, 7088 & 7089.

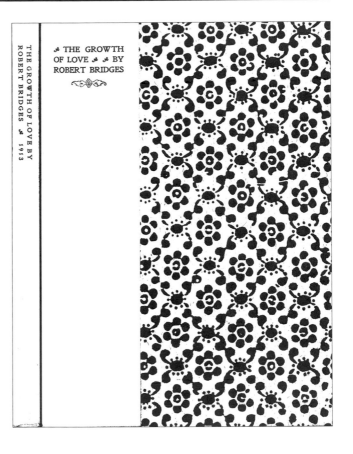

H

139. *HAND AND SOUL.* By Dante Gabriel Rossetti. [November 14] 1899.

    viii, 55, [1] pp. (same for second ed.)   15 x 11 cm.

    Miscellaneous Series-8   H 109.   First edition.

450 on Kelmscott "Hammer &
Anvil" handmade paper: 100
copies on Japan vellum.

Content: This tale was taken from the January 1850 issue of *The Germ*. The
unsigned preface is by the publisher. The quote (in Italian) on p. [*ii*] is by
Bonaggiunta Urbiciani. Mosher first printed this text in the September 1895
issue of *The Bibelot* (18).

Comment: Ransom notes: "This was advertised as a 'facsimile reprint' of the
Kelmscott Press edition, part of which was published in America by Way and
Williams. The 'Golden text' type is evidently the American Type Founders
Jenson, and it is worthy to note that Mr. Mosher 'improved' on the original by
using four borders instead of two." Even W. Irving Way (of Way & Williams)
wanted to know how Mosher was able to get so close a duplicate of the original
Kelmscott book.

HAND AND SOUL (continued)

Mosher's 1899 catalogue notes that "it is believed by Mr. Mosher that this is the first volume printed in America upon absolutely the same paper which Morris used for all his books at the Kelmscott Press." For other Mosher books printed on Kelmscott paper, see entry 47.

Binding & Embellishment: Kelmscott paper copies are bound in charcoal-blue boards with white spine and front cover labels. The Japan vellum copies are bound in Japan vellum wraps over boards with the label information (including red dingbats) printed directly on the cover. There is a hint of the Vale Press' 1899 edition of this title in Mosher's binding. The blue papers used are similar, the size is roughly the same, the front cover labels are positioned in the same location, and the spine label uses the identical leaf dingbats. Even the lettering on the spine is the same, except Mosher reverses the direction so it reads from top to bottom rather than from the bottom up as it does in the Vale edition. For other books using Vale Press & Charles Ricketts designs, see entry 47.

 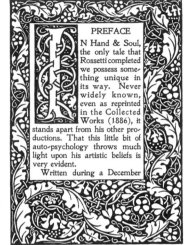

This is a very close rendering of the Kelmscott edition Morris co-published with Way and Williams of Chicago in 1896 (see Vilain, p. 18). The differences are: (a) the use of the red Morrisian initial "I" beginning the preface (and smaller red initials thereafter), (b) a four page Mosher preface, (c) the use of four rather than two borders, and (d) the binding is in old-style blue boards rather than in vellum. The large initial "I" was used again in the new edition of *In Praise of Omar* (172) and appeared in the opening spread of the Kelmscott *The Friendship of Amis and Amile* (1894). Intriguingly, an almost identical "I" appears just three years earlier in the first Roycroft book, *The Song of Songs*, 1896. Both Mosher and Hubbard probably used the initials found in the American Type Founders' *Specimens of type...* (Chicago, 1896) as their source.

For other books using Kelmscott Press & William Morris designs, see entry 74.

Reference: Vilain 13 and p. 87, plate 20 and p. 88, plate 21; Thompson, pp. 195-96 (opening pictured on p. 194); Peterson, pp. 197 & 301; Ransom 121; American Type Founders, p. 413, #4242; Grolier, p. 36; Strouse, p. 65; Japan Paper Company (Kelmscott Hand-made Paper from England); Lowden, P. 14 (2nd ed).

139.1 *HAND AND SOUL*. By Dante Gabriel Rossetti. [October 17] 1900.
        Miscellaneous Series.   H 166.   Second edition.

———————— *Same Title, Change of Series* ————————

140. *HAND AND SOUL*. By Dante Gabriel Rossetti. 1906.   Limitation unknown for both Van
        viii, 53 pp.   Gelder and Japan vellum copies.
        Ideal Seriesof Little Masterpieces-3   H 362.   First thus.

        Content: The preface is by the publisher. For text source, see 139.

141. *A HANDFUL OF LAVENDER* by Lizette Woodworth Reese.
[October] 1915.   *viii*, 57, [1] pp.
Lyra Americana-2   H 626.   First edition.

450 on Van Gelder; 25 on Japan vellum.

Content: The author's note opposite the title page indicates that "this edition of *A Handful of Lavender* is a reprint of the last forty-three lyrics included in the original edition of 1892 [actually Boston & New York: Houghton, Mifflin, 1891]. The first thirty-three poems of that edition were reissued by Mr. Thomas B. Mosher in 1909 under the title of *A Branch of May* [see entry 50]."

A bibliographical note appears on pp. [55-57].

Comment: Reese received a 10% royalty on all her books sold.

Binding: The Van Gelder copies are bound in quarter green paper spine over green heart and dot decorated paper boards. See series in Section I for further details.

Reference: See the Nov. 17, 1941 letter from Lamb to Yorke for Mosher's payment terms (see Appendix II).

141.1 *A HANDFUL OF LAVENDER* by Lizette Woodworth Reese.
[September] 1919.   *viii*, 53, [1] pp.
Lyra Americana.   H 675.   Second edition.

450 on Van Gelder only.

Content: This second edition no longer contains the bibliographical note. Mosher's annotated copy for the printer is located in the Bishop Collection.

Reference: Vilain 47 (plate 49, p. 99).

142. *THE HAPPY PRINCE AND OTHER TALES* by Oscar Wilde.
[June] 1904.   61, [1] pp. (same for all four editions)
Brocade Series-44   H 289.   First edition.

425 on Japan vellum for each edition.

Content: This title also contains the following tales: "The Nightingale and the Rose," and "The Selfish Giant," all from the 1888 London edition published by David Nutt (see also content note under 143).

Comment: This book was part of a sub-series (see 308).

Reference: Cowan II, pp. 33-34, and III, pp.

142.1 *THE HAPPY PRINCE AND OTHER TALES* by Oscar Wilde.
[February] 1906.
Brocade Series.   H 381.   Second edition.

142.2 *THE HAPPY PRINCE AND OTHER TALES* by Oscar Wilde.
[January] 1909.
Brocade Series.   H 495.   Third edition.

142.3 *THE HAPPY PRINCE AND OTHER TALES* by Oscar Wilde.
[November] 1912.
Brocade Series.   H 580.   Fourth edition.

————— *Same Title, Change of Series* —————

143. *THE HAPPY PRINCE AND OTHER TALES* by Oscar Wilde.
1907.   *viii*, 87, [1] pp. (same for second ed.)
Old World Series-42   H 388.   First thus.

925 on Van Gelder; 50 numbered copies on Japan vellum.

THE HAPPY PRINCE AND OTHER TALES (continued)

Content: This book contains the additional four prose fantasies: "The Nightingale and the Rose," "The Selfish Giant," "The Devoted Friend," and "The Remarkable Rocket."

The publisher's note opposite the title page indicates that this reprint was taken from the first edition, London: David Nutt, 1889; however, if dated 1889, then it was the second edition, since the first appeared in 1888. The only early edition recorded in Mosher's library is the second edition of 1889.

Design: The cover design bears the "C" monogram of Thomas Maitland Cleland. For other Cleland designs used, see entry 6.

Reference: Cowan III, pp. 29-30.

143.1   *THE HAPPY PRINCE AND OTHER TALES* by Oscar Wilde.
      1911.
      Old World Series.   H 548.   Second edition.

925 on Van Gelder.

——————— *Same Title, Change of Series* ———————

144.   *THE HAPPY PRINCE AND OTHER TALES* by Oscar Wilde.
     [November] 1919.   *x*, 94, [1] pp.   20.5 x 13 cm.
     Privately Printed-48   H 748.   First thus.

500 on Italian handmade paper; 50 numbered copies on Japan vellum.

Content: The text of this privately printed edition is the same as 143, containing the five pieces from the English edition, and also continuing the same incorrect note on the English edition used as in 143. The only textual addition is the poem "The Happy Prince" by Justin Huntly McCarthy which appear on p. [*vii*].

Comment: Privately printed for Edward A. Woods of Sewickley, PA. Some copies will have a loosely inserted presentation slip, from Mr. and Mrs. Woods, bearing the family coat of arms and the title of the book.

Binding & Embellishment: The regular copies are bound in light blue "Italian" charcoal paper boards with title/author printed in blue and red on the spine and front cover. A Renaissance-style Chiswick design appears on the front cover. The Japan vellum copies are bound in Japan vellum boards with the same cover design. Title page and colophon in red and black; Chiswick ornaments and red initial letters; text pages ruled in black.

145.   *HEART'S EASE A LITTLE BOOK OF GLAD TIDINGS* chosen for her children by their Mother Mary Stillman. 1922.
     iv, 46, [1] pp.   18.5 x 14 cm.
     Privately Printed-59   H 759.   Only edition.

500 copies printed on Van Gelder paper.

Content: This is basically a daily calendar of Bible verses. Quotes from William Blake and Robert Bridges appear at the beginning and the end, respectively. On each inner title is the name of one of Mrs. Stillman's three children, and the letters of each child's name appear in red in the margin along with a verse the first letter of which corresponds to that letter in the child's name.

Comment: Privately printed for Mrs. Chauncey C. Stillman.

Binding & Embellishment: Bound in decorated flexible Japan vellum wrappers, or in charcoal blue boards. Ruled in red throughout.

HEART'S EASE (continued)

The floral, art nouveau design on the front cover is by George Auriol, and is from p. *i* of *Le Premier Livre des cachets, marques et monogrammes dessinés par George Auriol* (Paris: Librairie Centrale des Beaux-Arts, 1901). A copy of this book, and its sequel, was in the Mosher library. For other Auriol designs, see 274 & 407.

146. *HELEN OF TROY HER LIFE AND TRANSLATION* done into Rhyme from the Greek Books by Andrew Lang. 1897. 152 pp. (same for other eds.)
Old World Series-8   H 39.   First edition.

925 on Van Gelder; 100 numbered copies on Japan vellum.

Content: According to the 1897 Mosher catalogue, "the Old World edition has the merit of being the first American edition without abridgment. For some reason... the previous re-issue omitted Mr. Lang's essay... , dealing with the myth of Helen, –an omission now remedied." The publisher's note appears opposite the title page and indicates that this reprint is from the 1883 second edition (London, G. Bell).

Reference: Boss XI 137; Quinn 5445 (2nd edition).

146.1 *HELEN OF TROY HER LIFE AND TRANSLATION* done into Rhyme from the Greek Books by Andrew Lang. 1903.
Old World Series.   H 269.   Second edition.

925 on Van Gelder. No copies on Japan vellum are known to exist (same for third edition).

146.2 *HELEN OF TROY HER LIFE AND TRANSLATION* done into Rhyme from the Greek Books by Andrew Lang. 1910.
Old World Series.   H 520.   Third edition.

147. *THE HEPTALOGIA* by Algernon Charles Swinburne. 1898.
97, [1] pp.; incl. facsim.   22 x 17.5 cm.
Reprints of Privately Printed Books-2   H 77.   Only edition.

450 on Van Gelder; 50 numbered copies on Japan vellum.
First American edition.

Content: The main text is taken from the Chatto & Windus edition of *The Heptalogia* (London, 1880). It contains Swinburne's original seven parodies of Alfred Tennyson; Robert Browning; Walt Whitman; Coventry Patmore; Robert, Lord Lytton (Owen Meredith); D. G. Rossetti; and A. C. Swinburne. Ransom notes that "Mosher added 'Disgust: a Dramatic Monologue,' reprinted for the first time from *The Fortnightly Review*, December 1st, 1881" which appears on pp. 93-[97]. The reprint also contains a facsimile of the original 1880 Chatto & Windus title page, and an unsigned, two-page bibliographical preface by Mosher.

T. J. Wise mentions that "... in 1898 it was published (with Disgust: a Dramatic Monologue added) by Thomas B. Mosher, of Portland, Maine, in a handsome but unauthorized volume of 97 pages, limited to 450 copies."

Binding & Embellishment: Van Gelder copies are bound in charcoal blue paper boards with printed white spine label; printed dust jacket. Japan vellum copies are bound in Japan vellum wraps with the label information printed directly on the wrapper. The title page is printed in red and black. Aside from the facsimile title page, the book employs no other design embellishments.

Reference: Boss XI 184; Livingston, p. 30; *CBEL* III, p. 318; Quinn 9452; Wise I, p. 304; Ransom 283; Jenkinson II, 975; Grigsby 1123.

148. *THE HISTORY OF OVER SEA* done out of the Ancient French into English
      by William Morris. [June] 1899.   67, [1] pp. (same all eds.)
      Brocade Series-14   H 112.   First edition.

425 on Japan vellum for each
edition.
First American edition.

Content: Publisher's note opposite the title page. The source was most likely
Old French Romances edited by Joseph Jacobs (London: George Allen, 1896),
which is the source for other Morris titles and the name of his sub-series, "Old
French Romances." A copy of the Kelmscott Press edition of *The Tale of the
Emperor Coustans* (Hammersmith, 1894) which includes "The History of
Over Sea," was also in Mosher's personal library.

Comment: This title formed part of a sub-series (see note to 396).

Reference: Walsdorf 75. Jenkinson II, 802.

148.1 *THE HISTORY OF OVER SEA* done out of the Ancient French into Eng-
       lish by William Morris. [July] 1900.
       Brocade Series.   H 175.   Second edition.

148.2 *THE HISTORY OF OVER SEA* done out of the Ancient French into Eng-
       lish by William Morris. [November] 1909.
       Brocade Series.   H 493.   Third edition.

149. *THE HOLLOW LAND A TALE* by William Morris. 1897.
      viii, 82 pp.
      Reprints from "The Bibelot"-2   H 48.   First thus.

25 copies only printed on Japan
vellum.
First edition.

Content: This work was taken from the *Oxford and Cambridge Magazine*
(September & October 1856). The unsigned preface is by the publisher. It
includes an original poem by Francis Sherman, and a bibliographic note on
the *Oxford and Cambridge Magazine* of 1856.

Mosher first printed this text in his July and August 1897 issues of *The Bibelot*
(20).

Comment: Forman notes: "Mr. Mosher of Portland, Maine, has made a sort of
piratical first edition which it seems necessary to catalogue—namely *The Hollow Land*. I do not refer to the mere transfer of that early story of Morris' from
The Oxford and Cambridge Magazine to *The Bibelot*...for besides reprinting
the tale in his magazine, Mr. Mosher has issued it in the form of an independent book,—a form which it now takes for the first time... The head-lines
("THE HOLLOW LAND") are of the hideous lop-sided kind now unhappily
becoming fashionable... It is a treasurable little book enough..."

The Quinn catalogue notes: "These scarce little booklets are not the regular
Mosher publications, but are separates in book form from the original setting
in the *Bibelot*. They constitute the First Editions of these pieces in book form,
being mainly Morris' contributions to the *Oxford and Cambridge Magazine*,
discerned by Mosher to be writings meriting a more permanent dress than the
pages of a magazine..." Also see Mosher's remarks under "Comment" in entry
109.

As a side note, in 1903 Longmans (printed by the Chiswick Press) published
all of William Morris' contributions to *The Oxford and Cambridge Magazine*.

Reference: Quinn 6984; mentioned in Walsdorf 80; Forman, pp. 193-194.

———————— *Same Title, Change of Series* ————————

150. **THE HOLLOW LAND A TALE** by William Morris. [August] 1900.
    97, [1] pp. (same for all three eds.)
    Brocade Series-22   H 148.   First edition.

425 on Japan vellum for each edition.

Content: The unsigned foreword is by the publisher, and is essentially the preface of 149. The poem from Francis Sherman is retained, but the bibliographic note is dropped. The source for this reprint is the *Oxford and Cambridge Magazine* (September & October 1856).

Comment: This work is one of four which Mosher grouped together in a subseries called, "Old English Romances by William Morris." The other works included in this sub-series are: *Gertha's Lovers* (134), *Golden Wings: Svend and His Brethren* (136), and *The Story of the Unknown Church and Other Tales* (390).

Reference: Walsdorf 80; Jenkinson II, 803.

150.1 **THE HOLLOW LAND A TALE** by William Morris. [January] 1903.
    Brocade Series.   H 277.   Second edition.

150.2 **THE HOLLOW LAND A TALE** by William Morris. [December] 1908.
    Brocade Series.   H 454.   Third edition.

151. **THE HOLY JUMPERS** By M. T. Space. [October] 1915.
    2 *p. l*, 3-7 numb. *l*, 2 *l*   14 x 9.5 cm.
    Privately Printed-37   H 738.   Only edition.

300 copies printed on Van Gelder.

Content: This is a six-page anecdote.

Comment: M.T. Space is the pseudonym of George W. Elkins of Philadelphia, the person for whom the book was privately printed.

Binding & Embellishment: Bound in Mexican vellum onyx wrappers, ruled in blue. Chiswick initials; pages are ruled in blue on both sides, but text is printed on the recto side only.

152. **HOMEWARD SONGS BY THE WAY** [by] A.E. [George Russell].
    [March] 1895.   87, [1] pp.   15 x 11.5 cm.
    Miscellaneous Series-1   H 13.   First edition.

925 on Van Gelder; 50 on Japan vellum.
First American edition of the author's first book.

Content: According to the 1895 Mosher catalogue, "the American edition contains fifteen poems not in the Dublin issue that are now printed for the first time by special arrangement with the author... The right is reserved by the author to issue through Mr. Mosher a second edition [see entry 153], should such be called for." There are a total of 67 poems, plus a prefatory poem by Russell.

Comment: Denson thought that the "first American edition was pirated, with added poems," but was mistaken. The text was taken from Whaley's second edition (Dublin, 1895), with the permission and the cooperation of both the author and the publisher. In fact, Whaley's 1896 edition of *From the Upanishads* advertises the "considerably enlarged" American edition of *Homeward: Songs by the Way* on the inside of its back wrapper, and promotes Mosher as the American distributor.

Mosher neglected to place a colon after the word "Homeward" on the title page, an omission he corrected in his subsequent edition (153).

Mosher paid an outright, undisclosed amount for the publication of this book in America.

Binding & Embellishment: The binding is of flexible Japan vellum with title/author and design in brown on the front cover, and title/author/date in brown on the spine. Yapp board edges. The binding is the same for both the Van Gelder and the Japan vellum editions.

This is the first book with designs by Bruce Rogers, acknowledged in a colophon and with signed designs: two vignettes on the front and back covers, two fleurons, and the head-pieces (two are signed "BR"). Roger's trademark, the caduceus, appears on the back cover. Press releases to *The Dial* (March 16, 1895) and *The Indianapolis News* (March 27, 1895) further indicate Bruce Rogers was responsible for head- *and* tail-pieces which would therefore include the designs on pages *ix*, *xi* and *xii* as well. According to *The Purdue Alumnus*, "while at Purdue he sometimes signed drawings with a Caduceus and he used this symbol in the Mosher volume of 1895, for the last time." Some of the original Bruce Rogers drawings are in the Printing and Graphic Arts Collection at The Houghton Library. Warde notes that "while still in college he had lettered one or two title-pages for Thomas B. Mosher, and in 1895 the name 'Bruce Rogers' appears for the first time in a colophon, as designer of a few insignificant decorations for one of Mr. Mosher's publications—A.E.'s *Homeward Songs by the Way*." For other Bruce Rogers designs, see entries 122, 207, 334 & 334.7.

Blumenthal mentions that "the first book with the name Bruce Rogers in the colophon was *Homeward Songs by the Way* by A. E. (George Russell), with a few decorations by Rogers..." Likewise, Norman Strouse notes in The Free Library catalogue: "The first book for which Bruce Rogers drew designs for an Eastern publisher."

Reference: Denson 2E & 2 F; *DLB* XIX, p. 9; Warde 3; Thompson, pp. 196-97; Bowles, pp. [6, 11]; Vilain 9 (plates 13-15, p. 85 show the original designs); Free Library 140; Quinn 8314 & 8315 (incorrectly cited as the Second American edition); Warde, p. 9; Blumenthal, p. 5; Grolier, p. 36; *PBSC*, p. 41; Purdue, p. 22; Grigsby 982; no copy of either Mosher edition (152 or 153) is recorded in Colbeck.

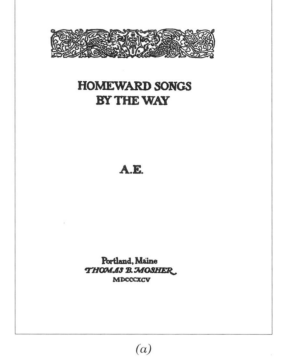

(a)

(b)

---

153. *HOMEWARD: SONGS BY THE WAY* [by] A.E. [George Russell].
[March] 1904.   *xi*, 75, [1] pp.   18.5 x 14.5 cm.
Miscellaneous Series-24   H 285.   New edition/same series.

450 on Van Gelder; 25 numbered copies on Japan vellum.

Content: In a Nov. 26, 1903 letter to Mosher (The Houghton Library, bMS Am 1096 [1378]), Russell made several corrections to six poems in the first Mosher edition (152): "Desire," "Natural Magic," "On a Hill-Top," "Awakening," "A Vision of Beauty," and "Symbolism." He also suggested to Mosher that he might replace Magic with a new enclosed poem, "The Winds of Angus." Mosher declined and "Magic" remained.

Comment: Larger in format size than the previous edition (152).

Russell was paid a royalty of 10% on sales of the Van Gelder copies only. There were no royalties paid for the 25 Japan vellum copies.

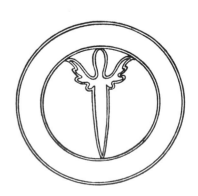

HOMEWARD: SONGS BY THE WAY (continued)

Binding & Embellishment: The Van Gelder copies are bound in green Fabriano boards with a two-color printed white label on the spine. The Japan vellum copies are bound in Japan vellum wraps with the label information printed directly on the spine. Title page and colophon printed in red and black; decorative headpieces and one tail-piece.

The design on the title page, and the colophon, is "The Sword of Light" device designed by George Russell for his *The Nuts of Knowledge* (Dublin: Dun Emer Press, 1903). See entry 187 for another book employing "The Sword of Light" device.

Reference: Denson 2G & 2H; Boss XI 171; Quinn 8322; see the Nov. 17, 1941 letter from Lamb to Yorke letter for Mosher's payment terms (see Section IV).

---

154. ***THE HOUND OF HEAVEN*** by Francis Thompson. [March] 1908.
    x, 12, [1] pp. (same for all eds. except the fifth)
    Golden Text Series-1   H 442.   First edition.

925 on Van Gelder; 100 on Japan vellum.
First separate American edition.

Content: The foreword is by the publisher. Selections from *Psalms* and James Douglas, and a brief selection from Emerson, precede the main text.

Comment: First classified by Mosher in 1908 and 1909 under the *Miscellaneous Series*, it was reclassified in 1910 under the *Golden Text Series* (for another reclassification see 175). Mosher also printed "The Hound of Heaven" and six other poems of Thompson's in the March 1908 issue of *The Bibelot* (31).

According to Connolly, the first edition of the first separate printing was the London: Burns & Oates, 1908 edition. No American edition of the separate appearance of this poem has been found to precede this Mosher reprint.

Special Note: The following disjointed sequence of Van Gelder and Japan vellum editions from entry 154.2-154.4 is perplexing, but the confusion arises from the edition assignments by Mosher. Patient charting of the Van Gelder and Japan vellum editions confirms that all are accounted for. With 154.5 the correct sequence is restored.

Reference: Vilain, p. 98, plate 47 (references the 2nd edition); Beckson B49; Connolly, p. 62.

154.1 ***THE HOUND OF HEAVEN*** by Francis Thompson. [December] 1908.
    Golden Text Series.   H 462.   Second edition.

925 on Van Gelder; 100 copies on Japan vellum.

154.2 ***THE HOUND OF HEAVEN*** by Francis Thompson. 1909.
    Golden Text Series.   H 503.   Third edition on Japan vellum.

100 copies on Japan vellum; no Van Gelder copy of this 1909 stated third edition.

Comment: The third edition Van Gelder copies are dated 1911 (see 154.3). A Japan vellum copy at Portland Public Library does not have an edition note, but is dated 1909.

154.3 ***THE HOUND OF HEAVEN*** by Francis Thompson. [December] 1911.
    Golden Text Series.   H 555.
    Third edition on Van Gelder paper.   Fourth edition on Japan vellum.

925 copies on Van Gelder paper and stated as third edition; 100 copies printed on Japan vellum bear the same 1911 imprint date but are marked as Fourth edition.

Comment: Hatch's original entry in his 1966 bibliography suggests there are both a fourth edition Van Gelder copy and a fourth edition Japan vellum copy; however, he corrected this error in his 1972 update (see Vilain).

Reference: Vilain, pp. 65 & 66.

154.4 **THE HOUND OF HEAVEN** by Francis Thompson. [February] 1914.
Golden Text Series.   H 620A.   Fourth edition on Van Gelder paper.

925 copies printed on Van Gelder paper.

Comment: This edition was not listed in the Hatch *Check List*, but was later added by Hatch in a 1972 unpublished "addenda and corrigenda" to the Mosher *Check List* (see Vilain).

Reference: Vilain, p. 66; Quinn 10203 indicates a copy with the limitation of 200 copies on Japan vellum.

154.5 **THE HOUND OF HEAVEN** by Francis Thompson. [October] 1917.
x, 16, [1] pp.
Golden Text Series.   H 661.   Fifth edition.

925 on Van Gelder; 100 copies on Japan vellum.

Comment: The increase in the number of pages in this fifth edition is due to a reduction in the number of lines per page from 20 to 16, and the division of the poem into six numbered sections.

The original limitation questions in the Hatch *Check List* were later corrected by Hatch in a 1972 "addenda and corrigenda" to the Mosher *Check List* (see Vilain).

Reference: Vilain, p. 66.

—————— *Same Title, Change of Series* ——————

155. **THE HOUND OF HEAVEN AND OTHER POEMS** by Francis Thompson.
1908.   *xxiv*, 36 pp.   17.5 x 14 cm.
Miscellaneous Series-39   H 433.   First thus.

50 numbered and signed copies on Japan vellum; 5 numbered press-proof copies on Japan vellum, all signed by Mosher.

Content: The other poems included are "To the Dead Cardinal of Westminster," "Dream-Tryst," "To My Godchild, Daisy," and "The Poppy, and Cecil Rhodes." Mosher also included before the seven main poems of the volume: "A Word on Francis Thompson" by Arthur Symons on pp. *xix-xxiii* (from *The Saturday Review* for November 23, 1907), a eulogy by James Douglas, a short selection from George Meredith, and Thompson's envoy to his *New Poems* (London: Archibald Constable, 1897).

The five-part foreword to this book is remarkably similar to the typesetting and text appearing in *The Bibelot* for March 1908 (31), except for an added footnote, some design embellishments, and slightly different page breaks. Likewise, the same seven poems appear in *The Bibelot*.

Comment: Press-proof copies, also on Japan vellum, are inscribed on the limitation page, e.g., "*Five Press Proof copies were taken. This is No. __. T B Mosher.*"

For information on this volume being one of six Miscellaneous Series books forming a "sub-series" of uniform style, see 238.

Binding & Embellishment: The press-proof copies are bound in blue paper wraps over cardboard with a spine label and a label on the front cover including a Chiswick drop cap. The Japan vellum copies are bound in flexible Japan vellum boards with yapp top and fore-edges; title printed on the spine and title/author printed directly on the front cover with lead drop-cap initial in red.

Reference: Connolly, p. 62.

156. *THE HOUR OF BEAUTY SONGS AND POEMS* by Fiona Macleod.
1907.   *xiii*, 111, [1] pp.
Old World Series-45   H 391.   Only edition.

925 on Van Gelder: 50 numbered copies on Japan vellum.
First American edition.

Content: As mentioned in Mosher's 1907 catalogue, this book was "published under copyright arrangements with Mrs. Sharp, the poet's widow, and contains all that exists of uncollected verse by the author..."

Three very short selections from Emerson, and Robert Bridges, and a "Sahara Song" appear on p. *vii*; a line quote from Swinburne appears on p. [*x*]. The 54 poems are preceded by a selection from Macleod on p. [2], and are followed by a three-page note taken from *Where the Forest Murmurs* (London: Published at the offices of *Country Life* by George Newnes, 1906).

Comment: Fiona Macleod was a pseudonym used by William Sharp who also published works under his real name.

William Heinemann published the "posthumous English edition" (London, 1907) entitled *From the Hills of Dream: Threnodies, Songs and Later Poems.* A note by Elizabeth A. Sharp mentions that "the Later Poems (1901-1905) are, in the present volume, grouped together in the section The Hour of Beauty, under which title they are published in the United States [by Mosher]."—p. 203

Mosher paid Macleod $50 for the publication of this book in America.

Design: The cover design bears the "C" monogram of Thomas Maitland Cleland.

For other Cleland designs used, see entry 6.

Reference: Colbeck II, p. 742 (36); Quinn 8647; see the Nov. 17, 1941 letter from Lamb to Yorke for Mosher's payment terms (see Appendix II); Macleod VII, pp. 453-454, and VII, p. 453.

---

157. *HOURS OF SPRING AND WILD FLOWERS* by Richard Jefferies.
[August] 1899.   76, [1] pp. (same through fourth ed.)
Brocade Series-16   H 114.   First edition.

425 on Japan vellum for each edition.

Content: The "Hours of Spring" formed a small part of Jefferies' posthumous book, *Field and Hedgerow: being the Last Essays of Richard Jefferies, collected by his Widow* (London: Longmans, Green and Co., 1889). A copy of this book was in Mosher's library.

Comment: This title is part of a sub-series. See note to entry 282.

Reference: Jenkinson II, 662 (third edition).

[xx]. *HOURS OF SPRING AND WILD FLOWERS* by Richard Jefferies.
Brocade Series.   Second edition.

Comment: This edition was listed in the Hatch *Check List* as an unlocated trade edition. If published at all, it was between August 1899 and March 1900. If ever found, this will be numbered 157.01 in this bibliography.

Reference: Hatch, p. 167.

157.1 *HOURS OF SPRING AND WILD FLOWERS* by Richard Jefferies.
[March] 1900.
Brocade Series.   H 177.   Third edition.

Comment: The edition note on this imprint is third edition, but this may be an error and it might actually be the second edition as noted above under [xx].

157.2 *HOURS OF SPRING AND WILD FLOWERS* by Richard Jefferies.
[December] 1903.
Brocade Series.   H 274.   Third edition.

Comment: Either an error in edition note, or a reprint of the previous entry with a change of date on the title page.

157.3 *HOURS OF SPRING AND WILD FLOWERS* by Richard Jefferies.
[December] 1910.   77 pp.
Brocade Series.   H 524A   Fourth edition.

Comment: This fourth edition is new to Mosher bibliographies. A copy was examined, courtesy of Donald E. Dede, who brought it to my attention.

---

158. *THE HOUSE OF LIFE A SONNET-SEQUENCE* by Dante Gabriel
Rossetti. 1898.   *xv*, 104, [1] pp. (same for second ed.)
Old World Series-11   H 63.   First edition.

925 on Van Gelder: 100 numbered copies on Japan vellum.

Content: The poem "Dante Gabriel Rossetti" by Theodore Watts-Dunton appears opposite the title page. Mosher's 1898 catalogue indicates the text is a reprint of "the entire text, as it originally existed in the mind of Rossetti, consisting of 102 sonnets" prior to revisions and one omission.

The source for Mosher's reprint was most likely the Copeland & Day edition of 1894, the first edition to restore the sonnet "Nuptial Sleep" to the sequence; however, he may have used earlier editions in tandem with the Copeland & Day imprint. The sonnet was first published in *Poems* (F. S. Ellis, 1870) as part of "Sonnets and Songs," but Rossetti dropped it from the completed sequence in 1881, largely due to Robert Buchanan's attack on the poem in *The Fleshly School of Poetry* (1872). In the *Collected Works* (Ellis & Scrutton, 1886) William Michael Rossetti respected his brother's wishes and omitted "Nuptial Sleep" (only restoring it in his 1904 edition of his brother's poems). Copeland & Day included the original songs from the 1870 version in *The House of Life*, restricting the sequence to the sonnets, and added, in parentheses following the title of Sonnet 7, "Nuptial Sleep (Placatâ Venere)," the original title of the poem which Rossetti never used in any published edition. Similarly, Mosher printed only the sonnets, but his use of the parenthetical title tends to confirm that he followed the Copeland & Day text, or at least consulted it for the inclusion of "Nuptial Sleep." Mosher recorded a copy of Rossetti's *Poems* (Boston, 1870) in his library by 1889. He also owned a copy of the Copeland & Day imprint, and the 1881 London imprint, among others.

158.1 *THE HOUSE OF LIFE A SONNET-SEQUENCE* by Dante Gabriel Rossetti.
1903.
Old World Series.   H 270.   Second edition.

925 on Van Gelder. No Japan vellum copies.

Comment: In this and the third edition, Mosher drops the parenthetical title, "(Placatâ Venere)," after Sonnet VII, "Nuptial Sleep."

158.2 *THE HOUSE OF LIFE A SONNET-SEQUENCE* by Dante Gabriel Rossetti.
1908.   *xv*, 109, [1] pp.
Old World Series.   H 447.   Third edition.

925 on Van Gelder. No Japan vellum copies.

Comment: The increase in pages is due to the addition of a "Notes" section at the end of the book. The notes are the new readings (variants) given by Rossetti in his 1881 edition of the *Ballads and Sonnets*.

159. *A HOUSE OF POMEGRANATES* by Oscar Wilde. 1906.
     iv, 158, [1] pp. (same for all three eds.)
     Old World Series-39   H 350.   First edition.

925 on Van Gelder; 50 numbered copies on Japan vellum.

Content: A publisher's note opposite the title page indicates that this reprint was taken from the first edition (London: McIlvaine, 1891). The book's four tales: "The Young King," "The Birthday of the Infanta," "The Fisherman and His Soul," and "The Star-Child" also appear separately in Mosher's Brocade Series.

Design: The cover design bears the "C" monogram of Thomas Maitland Cleland. For other Cleland designs used, see entry 6.

Reference: Quinn 11164; Cowan III, pp. 32-33 (2nd ed.), and IV, p. 44.

159.1 *A HOUSE OF POMEGRANATES* by Oscar Wilde. 1908.
      Old World Series.   H 451.   Second edition.

925 on Van Gelder.

159.2 *A HOUSE OF POMEGRANATES* by Oscar Wilde. 1913.
      Old World Series.   H 598.   Third edition.

925 on Van Gelder; 25 numbered copies on Japan vellum.

Comment: This Japan vellum state was unknown to Hatch. There is a copy in the Bishop Collection, and *NUC* records a copy at U.C.L.A.

160. *THE HOUSE OF USNA A DRAMA* by Fiona Macleod. 1903.
     xxxii, 76, [1] pp.   21 x 12.5 cm.
     Miscellaneous Series-23   H 250.   Only edition.

450 on Van Gelder; 50 numbered copies on Japan vellum, signed by the publisher.
First edition.

Content: According to Mrs. Sharp," 'the House of Usna' was performed at the Fifth Meeting of the [Stage] Society at the Globe Theatre April 29th, 1900... The drama itself was printed three months later in *The National Review*, and eventually published in book form in America by Mr. T. B. Mosher, in 1903." The foreword is also by Fiona Macleod.

Comment: Fiona Macleod was a pseudonym used by William Sharp who also published works under his real name.

Mosher paid Macleod (Sharp) $50 for the publication of this book in America.

Binding & Embellishment: Both the Van Gelder and the Japan vellum copies are bound in green printed Japan vellum wraps over boards. Renaissance border on the cover is signed "CW" for Charlotte Whittingham, designer for the Chiswick Press of London. Warren shows the actual Chiswick border design; however, Mosher interchanges the top and bottom portions. For other Chiswick Press designs used, see entry 48. Title page and contents printed in red and black; Chiswick initials.

The circular Celtic device in the center of the front cover is from the front cover of the first English edition of *From the Hills of Dream* published in Edinburgh by Patrick Geddes in 1896.

The cover design is very similar to *The Silence of Amor* (352).

Reference: Sharp, pp. 317-18; Boss XV 157; Quinn 8652 (indicates First American Edition); DeVinne 1113; Jenkinson II, 946; see the Nov. 17, 1941 letter from Lamb to Yorke for Mosher's payment terms (see Appendix II); Macleod I, p. xi, and V, p. 392, and VII, p. 454; Warren, p. 253.

I

161. *AN IDYL OF FIRST LOVE* By George Meredith. 1906.
x, 51 pp.
Ideal Series ofLittle Masterpieces-6   H 365.   Only edition.

Content: The foreword is by the publisher. A selection from *George Meredith; Some Characteristics* by Richard Le Gallienne prefaces the text. *An Idyl of First Love* is actually a selection from Meredith's novel, *The Ordeal of Richard Feverel*, which first appeared in 1859.

Mosher first printed this text in his August 1896 issue of *The Bibelot* (19), and the Ideal Series reprint is basically a new type setting of the former appearance in *The Bibelot*.

Reference: Crichton 44; Grigsby 803.

Limitation unknown for both Van Gelder and Japan vellum copies.

162. *IMMENSEE*: Translated from the German of Theodor Storm
by Irma Ann Heath. [May] 1902.   90, [1] pp. (same for second ed.)
Brocade Series-31   H 216.   First edition.

Content: The copyright notice on the verso of the title page is in the translator's name, and the introduction is also by Irma Ann Heath.

Comment: A February 6, 1902 contract at the Gleeson Library, University of San Francisco, gives some insight into Mosher's publishing arrangements. The translator, living in Grand Rapids, Michigan, received 10% of all copies sold, plus 10 free copies, and kept the copyright under her name.

Reference: Morgan 9185 & 9186.

425 on Japan vellum for each edition.
First edition of this translation.

162.1 *IMMENSEE*: Translated from the German of Theodor Storm by Irma Ann Heath. [June] 1905.
Brocade Series.   H 342.   Second edition.

163. *IMMENSEE: AN IDYLL* Translated from the German of Theodor Storm.
[October] 1912.   x, 84, [1] pp.
Brocade Series-51   H 578.   New edition/same series.

Content: The Heath translation of the previous two Mosher editions is replaced by an anonymous translation which appeared in the periodical, *The Dark Blue* (London: Sampson Low, Son, and Marston, July 1872 issue, pp. 565-93). No translator's name is given in the table of contents, nor with the text in *The Dark Blue*.

Comment: With the appearance of this new translation, this edition of *Immensee* has to be classified as the 51st publication in the Brocade Series, and technically speaking, becomes the last *publication* of the series. *The Children's Crusade* (B65), however, may still be regarded as the last *title* appearing in the Brocade Series.

425 on Japan vellum as with previous Brocade Series editions.

164. *THE IMMORTAL HOUR A DRAMA IN TWO ACTS* by Fiona Macleod.
[September] 1907.   *xi*, 47, [1] pp.   22.5 x 17.5 cm.
Miscellaneous Series-37   H 393.   Only edition.

500 copies on Van Gelder hand-made paper and 50 numbered copies on Japan vellum.
First edition.

THE IMMORTAL HOUR (continued)

Content: The "Forenote" is by Fiona Macleod. Mosher mentions in his 1907 catalogue that the first appearance of this play in print was "published in *The Fortnightly Review* for November, 1900. *The Immortal Hour* was a much shorter dramatic poem which had long been marked for alteration by its author. The final form of the play as it now stands was arranged by the late William Sharp only a few weeks before his death. It may therefore be said to represent his latest literary utterance..." –p. 61

Comment: Fiona Macleod is a pseudonym used by William Sharp who also published works under his real name.

The first British edition was brought out by T. N. Foulis in 1908.

Binding & Embellishment: The Van Gelder copies are bound in charcoal blue boards with white labels on the spine and front cover both printed in two colors. The Japan vellum copies are bound in flexible Japan vellum boards with the same spine and front cover information printed directly on the cover. Title page and colophon printed in red and black; text pages ruled throughout.

The front cover's triangular decoration and the criblé head-piece used on the title page are both Chiswick in origin, designed by Charlotte Whittingham and engraved by Mary Byfield. For other Chiswick Press designs used, see entry 48.

Reference: Colbeck II, 742 (38); Sharp, 318; Quinn 8663; Warren. pp. 187 & 314; Macleod I, p. xi, and VII, p. 455.

THE IMMORTAL HOUR

---

165. ***IN HOSPITAL: RHYMES AND RHYTHMS*** by William Ernest Henley.
[October] 1903.   *vi*, 40, [1] pp. (same for all three eds.)
Lyric Garland Series-2   H 261.   First edition.

950 on Van Gelder paper for each edition. For first edition, 100 on Japan vellum; and 10 on Roman vellum signed by the publisher.

Content: Mosher notes in his 1910 catalogue that these poems were taken from "Henley's poems as revised and arranged by him in his edition of 1898 [London: David Nutt]."

This work was printed by Mosher in his January 1901 issue of *The Bibelot* (24).

Comment: Mosher first listed this book in 1902 under the Miscellaneous Series; however, in 1903, *The Lyric Garland Series* was created and the title was transferred to it (see the 1903 Mosher Books catalogue).

Reference: Boss IX 130; Quinn 4043.

165.1 ***IN HOSPITAL*** by William Ernest Henley.
[October] 1908.
Lyric Garland Series.   H 460.   Second edition.

Comment: In this second edition the sub-title was omitted.

165.2 ***IN HOSPITAL: RHYMES AND RHYTHMS*** by William Ernest Henley.
[August] 1921.
Lyric Garland Series.   H 690.   Third edition.

550 copies on Van Gelder.

Binding: Bound in green Fabriano boards rather than the usual gray boards.

166. **IN MEASURED LANGUAGE** by Ephraim Chamberlain Cummings
1825-1897.   1899.   *xv*, 67 pp.   18.5 x 14 cm.
Privately Printed-4   H 706.   Only edition.

Number of copies printed on Van Gelder is not indicated. No Japan vellum copies.

Content: There are 43 poems including the preliminary "Inscription" and "Rhymes to Order," followed by the sections "Ad Sodales" (5 poems), "Seasons and Friends" (23 poems), "In Memoriam" (10 poems) and "Translations" (2 poems).

Comment: Printed for Mrs. Ephraim Cummings on Van Gelder paper only. Both the Lamb and Sheean typescripts indicate no Japan vellum copies were printed. Also, no limitation statement appears either in the book or the typescripts.

A copy is located at Brown University.

Binding: Japan vellum boards with yapp edges. Cover is printed in brown with title (using drop-caps) and author's initials. There are no other graphic or typographical embellishments.

---

167. **IN MEMORIAM** (JANE ANNAN BELL). [1917]
20 pp.
Privately Printed-41   H 742.   Only edition.

300 copies on Italian handmade paper; 3 copies on Japan vellum.

Comment: The Sheean and Lamb typescripts describe *In Memoriam* as having 20 pages, post octavo, printed for Arthur W. Sewall of Philadelphia. Hatch never saw a copy. No copy has been located.

Binding & Embellishment: Bound in purple Brittany paper wraps sewn with black silk. Three copies on Japan vellum are bound in Japan vellum wrappers. Since no copy has been located, there is no comment about embellishments.

---

168. **IN MEMORIAM** by Alfred Lord Tennyson. 1902.   *iv*, 165, [1] pp.
Old World Series-26   H 210.   First thus.

925 on Van Gelder; 100 numbered copies on Japan vellum.

Content: Mosher does not give the precise source for these 132 poems which begin with "IN MEMORIAM A. H. H. — OBIT MDCCCXXXIII."

——————— *Same Title, Change of Series* ———————

169. **IN MEMORIAM** by Alfred Lord Tennyson. [November] 1920.
iv, 124, [1] pp.   21.5 x 14 cm.
Privately Printed-54   H 754.   First thus.

500 copies on English (Dickinson) handmade paper; 50 on Japan vellum.

Content: Contains the prefatory dedication "In Memoriam A. H. H." and the 131 numbered parts.

Comment: Privately printed for Edward A. Woods of Sewickley, PA. Some copies will have a loosely inserted presentation slip, from Mr. and Mrs. Woods, bearing the family coat of arms and the title of the book.

IN MEMORIAM (continued)

Binding & Embellishment: Bound in blue charcoal paper boards with title/author on spine and front cover. The dark-blue design just above the cover's title is from the 1903 Eragny Press edition of Ronsard's *Abrégé de l'Art Poétique*. The Japan vellum copies are bound in Japan vellum boards with the same printing on the cover (for other books using Eragny Press & Lucien Pissarro designs, see entry 52). Title page and colophon are printed in red and black. A large red initial "I" appearing on p. 5 is the same decorative initial as that employed in *The Kasîdah* of 1905 (182) and 1915 (183).

Note: See note on the title-page's anchor and dolphin publisher's device under entry 339.

---

170. VERNON LEE AND OTHERS *IN PRAISE OF OLD GARDENS*.
     1912.   *xii*, 100 pp.
     Vest Pocket Series-24   H 562.   Only edition.

Limitation unknown for both Van Gelder and Japan vellum copies.

Content: The five works included are A. C. Swinburne's "A Forsaken Garden," Mrs. E. V. Boyle's "The Praise of Gardens," Vernon Lee's "Old Italian Gardens," Rosamund Marriott Watson's "The Road to Spring," and John Brown, M.D.'s "Queen Mary's Child-Garden." The foreword is by the publisher. Listed at the conclusion are eight garden references for suggested further reading. Poems by W. E. Henley, A. C. Swinburne, A. Forbes Sieveking, A. Mary F. Robinson, Rosamund Marriott Watson, and a quote from Richard Le Gallienne also accompany the text. This anthology was assembled by Mosher.

The text of "Old Italian Gardens" was previously printed by Mosher in the November 1900 issue of *The Bibelot* (23). For other Mosher anthologies, see 366.

Comment: Vernon Lee is the pseudonym of Violet Paget.

---

171. *IN PRAISE OF OMAR AN ADDRESS* before the Omar Khayyám Club By The Hon. John Hay. 1898.
     vi, 13 pp. (same for all eds. through the fifth)   15 x 12 cm.
     Miscellaneous Series-4   H 67.   First edition.

925 on Van Gelder; 50 numbered copies on Japan vellum (but see comment); 4 on American vellum.

Content: Selections from Thomas Bailey Aldrich, Justin Huntly McCarthy, and the poem "Omar Khayyám to A.L." by Rosamund Marriott Watson accompany this address given by Hay at a dinner of the Omar Khayyám Club in London on December 8, 1897.

In the 1899 catalogue, Mosher quotes a personal letter from John Hay dated April 24, 1898 (now at the University of San Francisco):

> My Dear Sir: –I thank you most cordially for your kind gift of the *Rubaiyat* and your exquisite setting of my modest little speech. As you ask me for corrections, there is one letter on the 4th page wrong; "before the latter" ought to be "before the letter." On the 8th page I said "frowning" not "pouring," but I don't know but that the types were wiser than I was... I congratulate you on the artistic successes you have made in all your publications, and certainly hope they have not been too expensive for you. Yours sincerely, John Hay.

John Hay, an ardent Omarian, was personal secretary to Abraham Lincoln, and was later made the U.S. Ambassador to England. Curiously enough, Mosher corrected the 4th page in editions after the second, but never changed the 8th page; and with the new edition of 1920 (entry 172), all reverted back to the original uncorrected wording.

(a)

IN PRAISE OF OMAR AN ADDRESS (continued)

Comment: Mosher notes in an advertisement accompanying *The Bibelot* for June 1898, "the first edition having been sold within thirty days from date of issue, the second edition is now ready." The Colbeck copy was inscribed by Mosher to the English publisher, Bertram Dobell, April 9, 1898.

The Mosher catalogue for 1898 indicates 100 copies on Japan vellum; likewise, the Sheean typescript indicates 100 copies on Japan vellum. Copies Hatch and I examined have a limitation of 50. Loosely laid in some copies is an advertising flyer also indicating "50 copies, Japan vellum." The apparent contradiction may be explained in that the first edition quickly sold out, and another 50 copies on Japan vellum were printed for the second edition (see 171.1). Mosher's catalogue may just have been referring to the combined printing over a short period of time.

The first American edition of this address is The Critic's leaflet no. 2: *The Hon. John Hay on FitzGerald's Rubáiyát of Omar Khayyám* (New York: The Critic Co., 1898). Mosher must have been aware of this leaflet, for he states in his 1898 catalogue that his edition "is now for the first time produced in a *format* ensuring its preservation." He may have been alluding to the scant treatment by The Critic.

Binding & Embellishment: Van Gelder copies are bound in charcoal-blue wraps over boards while the Japan vellum copies are bound in Japan vellum wraps over boards, all with the same cover and spine lettering and the cover's red decoration. Title page and p. 1 printed in red and black.

The cover design was originally created by Herbert P. Horne for the title page of *Diversi Colores* (London: Chiswick, 1891). The same floral design was used on the back wrapper of the 1923 Mosher Books catalogue (entry 267). For designs by Horne used elsewhere, see 243, 363 & 413.

Reference: Potter 601; Colbeck I, p. 256 (42); Boss XI 141; *BAL* 7781-C (also see note to A); Grigsby 529; Vilain 11.(second edition).

(b)

171.1 **IN PRAISE OF OMAR AN ADDRESS** before the Omar Khayyám Club By The Hon. John Hay. 1898.
Miscellaneous Series.   H 88.   Second edition.

925 copies on Van Gelder: 50 numbered copies on Japan vellum.

Comment: See comment above for a brief discussion on the limitation of the Japan vellum copies.

Mosher's proof copy, with his note "Copy for 3d. ed." and with corrections in his hand, is at Arizona State University.

171.2 **IN PRAISE OF OMAR AN ADDRESS** before the Omar Khayyám Club By The Hon. John Hay. 1898.
Miscellaneous Series.   H 89.   Third edition on Japan vellum.

100 copies only on Japan vellum (see comment for entries up to 171.7).

Comment: Apparently the demand for Japan vellum copies of this little reprint was strong enough to necessitate printing a third Japan vellum edition even before a third edition on Van Gelder paper (171.4). Why another "third edition" on Van Gelder was printed (171.5) is not known, but at times Mosher and his printer seemed to loose track of which edition they were producing (e.g., see comment to 10.5).

171.3 ***IN PRAISE OF OMAR AN ADDRESS*** before the Omar Khayyám Club By The Hon. John Hay. 1898.
Miscellaneous Series.   H 90.   Fourth edition on Japan vellum.

100 copies only on Japan vellum.

171.4 ***IN PRAISE OF OMAR AN ADDRESS*** before the Omar Khayyám Club By The Hon. John Hay. 1899.
Miscellaneous Series.   H 131.   Third edition on Van Gelder.

925 copies only on Van Gelder (same through fourth edition).

171.5 ***IN PRAISE OF OMAR AN ADDRESS*** before the Omar Khayyám Club By The Hon. John Hay. 1900.
Miscellaneous Series.   H 165.   Third edition.

Comment: Error in edition note? Reprint of previous entry with new date on title page?

171.6 ***IN PRAISE OF OMAR AN ADDRESS*** before the Omar Khayyám Club By The Hon. John Hay. 1905.
Miscellaneous Series.   H 339.   Fourth edition.

171.7 ***IN PRAISE OF OMAR AN ADDRESS*** before the Omar Khayyám Club By The Hon. John Hay. 1913.
Miscellaneous Series.   H 600A.   Fifth edition.

450 copies on Van Gelder.

Comment: A copy of this 1913 edition is new to Mosher bibliography, and has been assigned a Hatch location. Copies are located in Special Collections at the Library of the University of South Florida, and in the Special Collections at the Green Library, Stanford University.

172. ***IN PRAISE OF OMAR AN ADDRESS*** before the Omar Khayyám Club By The Hon. John Hay. 1920.
20 l. printed on recto only; port. front.   14.5 x 10.5 cm.
Miscellaneous Series-94   H 683.   New edition/same series.

Published in an edition of 950 copies printed on Kisogawa paper (printed on one side of paper only). There were no Japan vellum copies printed.

Comment: Stylistically, this edition differs enough from the previous formats to warrant its cataloguing as a new edition in the Miscellaneous Series. The Mosher catalogues list it as a "new edition in larger type and new format."

Binding & Embellishment: The binding of this new edition is a gray and white Japanese paper over boards giving a cloud-like effect. The Japan Paper Company calls this Modu No. 3 paper in their Momoyama Papers booklet. The front board is ruled in green with red lettering, and the back features a device in green with three birds in flight. A frontispiece portrait of FitzGerald is also used in this new edition.

A small Morrisian initial "I" begins the foreword, and another larger Morris initial "I" appears here at the beginning of Hay's Address. The source for both these initials is the American Type Founders' *Specimens of type...* (Chicago, 1896). Mosher used the larger initial "I" in the

IN PRAISE OF OMAR AN ADDRESS (continued

opening of his edition of *Hand and Soul* (139). The text is printed only on the recto side of the page.

Reference: American Type Founders, p. 413, #4242; Japan Paper Company (Momoyama Papers).

173. ***INSCRIPTION FOR A FIREPLACE***. No place. No date. [Portland, Maine: Thomas Bird Mosher, November 1892].
     sheet folded once in center creating 4 pp.   25.3 x 20.5 cm.
     Privately Printed-1   H 703.   Only edition.

12 copies printed on Dutch Van Gelder paper.

Content: This 14 line unsigned sonnet was written and printed by Mosher, in this very limited edition, most likely for distribution to a few friends. It was again printed (with minor alterations) by Mosher's assistant, Flora Lamb, and appears on p. 94 of the tribute volume, *Amphora—A Second Collection*, in 1926. The *original* sonnet reads:

INSCRIPTION
FOR A FIREPLACE.

For days and nights an hundred changeful years,
My fires have flickered and fallen into cold
White ashes on these hearthstones. I endure;
Whilst you, O guests, like wav'ring tongues of flame,
You, too, go hence, nor unto me return:
Yea, I have seen fair faces vanish,—heard
Old footsteps die away that no-where left
An echo in the living world of men.
    Yet be not thou, sojourner of Today,
From over-sea or world-wide travel come,
Or thou, strayed reveler o' wintry nights,—
Less welcome to my ancient, humble warmth;
Nor fare hence cheerless even when at last
Another and a longer night is come.

The word "INSCRIPTION" appears on the front page; p. 2 is blank; p. 3 with full title and the 14 line sonnet; p. 4 is blank. In the Sheean typescript a copy is cited as having a holograph note in Mosher's hand: "Twelve copies of this sonnet (unrhymed) struck off (November 1892) T.B.M."

Comment: The sonnet is particularly meaningful in that the publisher adored his fireplaces at home and in his Exchange Street Office. A few visitors even published articles mentioning the central focus, warmth and atmosphere created by Mosher's fireplaces. The original manuscript, in Mosher's hand, is in the Bishop Collection.

First title privately printed by Mosher.

Reference: Boss XV 154; Hatch never saw a copy, but copies exist in both the Bishop Collection and at Arizona State University.

174. ***INTENTIONS*** by Oscar Wilde.   The Decay of Lying   Pen, Pencil and Poison
     The Critic as Artist   The Truth of Masks. 1904.
     vi, 237, [1] pp.   19 x 14.5 cm.
     Miscellaneous Series-25   H 286.   Only edition.

600 copies on Van Gelder: 50 numbered & signed copies on Japan vellum; 6 copies on Roman vellum in unbound folded sheets, all signed by the publisher.

Content: The source of this reprint was the 1891 edition of *Intentions*, one of 600 copies of the English edition printed for America, only with the New York,

INTENTIONS (continued)

Dodd Mead and Company title page. The actual pages that Mosher's printer followed no longer survive, but the unmistakable rose or pink canvas boards (and the London printer's statement from the back of the book) have survived. Mosher's notes and limitation instructions to the printer appear in this remnant which is now located in the Bishop Collection. Mosher's use of this edition probably explains why he never identified the source of his reprint, either in his catalogues, or in the reprint itself.

Binding & Embellishment: The Van Gelder copies are bound in Japan vellum boards with the title printed directly on the spine and front cover. The Japan vellum copies are bound in printed Japan vellum wraps over boards. Only the colophon is printed in red and black, and except for the large drop-cap initial "I" on the title page, there are no other embellishments.

This book is uniform in size and binding with Wilde's *Poems* (304). According to the 1904 catalogue, there were 75 copies (of the 600 on Van Gelder) which were "specially bound in old-style gray boards, ribbed back, with white paper labels."

Reference: Quinn 11129 & 11130; Cowan III, pp. 40-41, and IV, p. 56; Mason (*Works*), see Vol. II, No. 343 for information on the Dodd Mead binding.

---

175. ***INTIMATIONS OF IMMORTALITY AN ODE*** by William Wordsworth. [September] 1908.   *viii*, 14, [1] pp.
Golden Text Series-2   H 443.   Only edition.

925 on van Gelder; 100 on Japan vellum.

Content: The foreword is by the publisher. A selection from Thomas Traherne appears opposite the title page. The eleven-part ode appears from pp. 3-[14].

Comment: First classified by Mosher in 1908 and 1909 under the *Miscellaneous Series*, but in 1910 it was reclassified and remained under the *Golden Text Series* (see also 154).

---

176. ***IN UMBRIA: A STUDY OF ARTISTIC PERSONALITY***
by Vernon Lee. [August] 1901.   80, [1] pp. (same for second ed.)
Brocade Series-29   H 191.   First edition.

425 on Japan vellum for each edition.
First edition in separate book form.

Content: The publisher's note opposite the title page indicates that this volume is reprinted from *Belcaro: Essays on Sundry Æsthetical Questions by Vernon Lee*. London, 1882 (actually London: W. Satchell, [1881]).

Mosher printed other selections from this work in *The Bibelot* for January and February 1914 (37).

Comment: Vernon Lee is the pseudonym of Violet Paget.

See note to entry 64 which indicates which sub-series this title formed a part.

Reference: *DLB* LVII, p. 158; Vilain 28.

176.1 *IN UMBRIA: A STUDY OF ARTISTIC PERSONALITY*
by Vernon Lee. [July] 1906.
Brocade Series.   H 377.   Second edition.

177. *THE ISLE OF DREAMS* by Fiona Macleod. 1905.
      vi, 132, [1] pp. (same for second ed.)
      Old World Series-36   H 315.   First edition.

925 on Van Gelder; 50 numbered copies on Japan vellum.
First separate book appearance (revised).

Content: According to the 1905 Mosher catalogue, "Miss Macleod brings together, largely augmented and revised, the personal and legendary parts of 'Iona', " i.e., *The Divine Adventure: Iona: And Other Studies in Spiritual History* (London: Chapman & Hall, 1900).

Mrs. Sharp notes that "Iona [was] curtailed and rearranged under the title of 'The Isle of Dreams' in 1905 [Mosher's edition]."

Comment: Fiona Macleod was a pseudonym used by William Sharp who also published works under his real name.

Mosher paid Macleod $49.26 for the publication of this book in America.

Design: The cover design bears the "C" monogram of Thomas Maitland Cleland. For other Cleland designs used, see entry 6.

Reference: Quinn 8647; Vilain 7 and plate 8, p. 83 (second edition). See the Nov. 17, 1941 letter from Lamb to Yorke for Mosher's payment terms (see Appendix II); Macleod IV, p. 433.

177.1 *THE ISLE OF DREAMS* by Fiona Macleod. 1909.
      Old World Series.   H 488.   Second edition.

925 on Van Gelder. So far as is known, there were no Japan vellum copies printed.

178. *AN ITALIAN GARDEN A BOOK OF SONGS* By A. Mary F. Robinson.
      1897.   95, [1] pp. (numbered in Roman numerals)
      The Bibelot Series-10   H 37.   Only edition.

925 on Van Gelder; 100 numbered copies on Japan vellum.

Content: A poem in Italian, a Tuscan Rispetto (reverential eulogy), appears opposite the title page. Brief quotes from Sappho, Shelley, Dante, and Baudelaire appear on section titles, along with Tuscan Stornelli (folk songs). The 54 poems in this book are categorized into Nocturnes, A Garland of Flowers, Tuscan Cypress, Songs and Dreams, Vestigia, and Later Poems. This is a reprint of the T. Fisher Unwin edition (London, 1886).

A. Mary F. Robinson is the pen name of Agnes Mary Frances (Robinson) Duclaux.

Comment: In 1913 Mosher reprinted this book under the title *Songs from an Italian Garden* in the Venetian Series (365), and it also appeared in *The Bibelot* for August 1908 (31). See also *The Bibelot* (26), pp. 215-292, for an essay on the popular songs of Tuscany.

Last title published in this series.

Reference: Krishnamurti, p. 113; Boss XI 133.

179. *ITALY MY ITALY: IV LYRICS* by Robert Browning. 1910.
      viii, 34, [1] pp.
      Venetian Series-2   H 516.   Only edition.

Limitation unknown for both Van Gelder and Japan vellum copies.

Content: The foreword is by the publisher. The frontispiece reproduces Guercino's *Guardian Angel.* The four lyrics selected are "A Toccata of Galuppi's," "Old Pictures in Florence," "The Guardian-Angel / A Picture at Fano," and "De Gustibus." The 26th line in this last poem was used by Mosher for the book's title.

J

180. ***THE JOLLY BEGGARS   A CANTATA*** by Robert Burns with Introduction by William Marion Reedy. [December] 1914.

xxiii, 106, [1] pp.; port. front., music plate, 2 facsims (1 fold.)   18.5 x 14 cm.
Miscellaneous Series-70   H 610.   Only edition.

750 copies on Van Gelder; 25 numbered copies on Japan vellum.
First separate American edition.

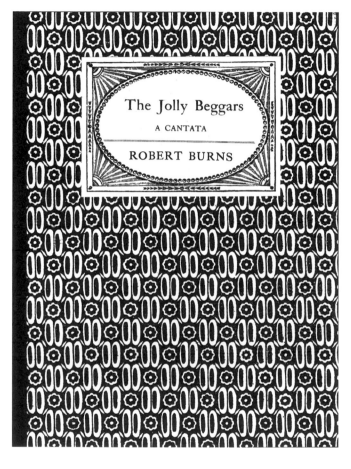

Content: The dedication to the Chicago publisher, W. Irving Way, is signed by his friend and fellow publisher, Thomas Bird Mosher. The introduction (pp. [*xiii*]-*xxiii*) is by yet another friend and fellow publisher, William Marion Reedy. Selections from Matthew Arnold, James Douglas, William Scott Douglas, and James Sime also accompany the main text (pp. [2]-28). A bibliography appears on pp. 29-33.

Following the main text is the essay "Some Aspects of Robert Burns" (pp. [51]-106) by Robert Louis Stevenson (*Cornhill Magazine* for 1879) beginning with a bibliographical note by the publisher. There are also six other entries given under "Comments," the original sources being identified by Mosher (the first three are taken from later editions containing these works):

– "Sir Walter Scott (1809)," pp. [35]-38, from a review of Cromek's *Reliques of Robert Burns*, 1808, in *The Quarterly Review* (Edinburgh, February, 1809).

– "J. G. Lockhart (1828)," pp. 38-39, from *The Life of Robert Burns* by J. G. Lockhart (Edinburgh, 1829).

– "Thomas Carlyle (1828)," pp. 39-41, from the review of Lockhart's *Life of Burns* in *The Edinburgh Review* (December 1828).

– "William Scott Douglas (1879)," pp. 41-44, from *The Works of Robert Burns*, edited by William Scott Douglas. Vol. IV (London: W. Paterson & Co., 1891, pp. 98-100).

– "William Ernest Henley (1896)," pp. 44-48, from *The Poetry of Robert Burns* (The Centenary Burns), edited by W. E. Henley and T. F. [Thomas Finlayson] Henderson. Vol. II (Edinburgh: T. C. and E. C. Jack, 1896, pp. 291-306).

– "Andrew Lang (1886-1896)," pp. 49-50, from *Letters to Dead Authors* (London: Longmans, Longmans, Green, and Co., 1886), and Lang's *Poems and Songs of Burns* (London: Methuen & Co., 1896).

Three illustrations accompany the text: a facsimile of the 1799 title page, a facsimile of the last page of Burns' manuscript from the 1823 lithographed edition, and a facsimile of the original air of the final song. The portrait frontispiece of Robert Burns is a photogravure of the Nasmyth portrait, under which reads: "Copyright A.W. Elson & Co., Boston."

Comment: Hatch mentioned that "with this title is inaugurated an almost consistent use (two exceptions) of Mosher's full name form in the imprint of *new* titles published." Instead of a middle initial, the new form becomes THOMAS BIRD MOSHER. This is correct for the regular fourteen series, but it is not the first Mosher book to so employ Mosher's full name on a title page (see 286).

THE JOLLY BEGGARS A CANTATA (continued)

Binding & Embellishment: Van Gelder copies are bound in quarter ribbed paper over green decorative boards, with white title/author labels in red and green on the spine and upper front cover. Japan vellum copies are bound in Japan vellum boards with the label designs printed directly on the boards. Title page in red and black; Chiswick ornaments; some initial letters in red outline. Text pages are ruled in black throughout.

The label design on the front cover was taken from the label appearing on Mosher's copy of *Poems Ascribed to Robert Burns, the Ayrshire Bard, not contained in any edition of his works hitherto published* (Glasgow: Printed for Thomas Stewart, 1801). See Mosher's note on p. 33 of his edition of *The Jolly Beggars*.

Reference: Quinn 1152.

K

181. *THE KASÎDAH OF HÂJÎ ABDÛ EL-YEZDÎ* translated and annotated by his Friend and Pupil, F. B. [Sir Richard Francis Burton]. 1896.

xvi, 99, [1] pp. (same for second ed.)

Old World Series-5   H 23.   First edition.

925 on Van Gelder; 100 numbered copies on Japan vellum.
First American edition.

Content: The book's text is taken from *The Kasîdah...* (London: Quaritch, 1880). The foreword is by the publisher. Opposite the title page appears the poem "The Sunburnt Poet" by Theodore Watts-Dunton. Also in this volume is a selection from a poem by Robert Browning, and quotes from Shelley and St. Augustine.

Comment: According to Lady Burton, Sir Richard Francis Burton disguised his authorship by calling this work a translation and signing it "F.B." standing for Frank Baker, taking Frank from his second name, and Baker from his mother's family name.

The word *Kasîdah* means "couplets." For further translation of the title, see comments under 182.

Penzer notes: "Besides the... English editions, there have been a great number of American ones. The "Kasîdah" has, apparently, always been more popular in America than in England. Practically all the American editions were issued in T. B. Mosher's Old World Series."

Penzer also provides an interesting note about the third London edition of 1900: "A descriptive note, written and printed by Mr. Mosher in his list of books for 1896, is used by Mr. Cook in this edition as his own publisher's note over date of April 27, 1900 (p. [3] of the preliminaries)." Mosher himself responds on p. 124 in his bibliography on *The Kasîdah* found at the end of the fifth Old World edition (181.5):

> A more surprising variant is the 'lifting' entire of a descriptive note written and printed by Mr. Mosher in his List of Books for 1896, and used by Mr. Cook in edition III [1900] as his own "Publisher's Note" under date of April 27th, 1900.

A delightful example of the pirate himself being pirated.

A bibliography of *The Kasîdah* would not appear in the Old World Series until the third edition (181.2).

THE KASÎDAH OF HÂJÎ ABDÛ EL-YEZDÎ (continued)

Special Note: There are small variations between some of the succeeding editions. For example, what is a preliminary leaf in the third edition (pp. [*xiii-iv*]) becomes a numbered leaf in the fifth edition (pp. [3-4]), the bibliography of each succeeding edition includes the previous editions, etc. These changes are relatively minor. Other changes or information are noted under the respective edition entry.

Reference: *DLB* LV, p. 26; Penzer, p. 100-101 (1-10) and the note just above; Quinn 1204.

181.1   *THE KASÎDAH OF HÂJÎ ABDÛ EL-YEZDÎ* translated and annotated by his Friend and Pupil, F. B. [Sir Richard Francis Burton]. 1898.
Old World Series.   H 85.   Second edition.

925 on Van Gelder; 100 numbered copies on Japan vellum.

Comment: In an advertisement appearing in *The Bibelot* for June 1898, mention is made of the Japan vellum copies of this second edition being limited to 50. Likewise, Mosher's bibliography in the 1906 edition of *The Kasîdah* (181.5) indicates 50 copies on Japan vellum; however, copies examined clearly state 100.

181.2   *THE KASÎDAH OF HÂJÎ ABDÛ EL-YEZDÎ* translated and annotated by his Friend and Pupil, F. B. [Sir Richard Francis Burton]. 1900.
xiv, 123, [1] pp. (same through the fourth ed.)
Old World Series.   H 163.   Third edition.

925 on Van Gelder, 100 numbered copies on Japan vellum.

Content: The notes have been expanded, and this edition is the first to contain a bibliography, pp. [119-123]. In each succeeding edition this bibliography is updated.

Comment: According to the bibliography found in the 12th edition of this work, there were 100 additional copies printed on Japan vellum.

181.3   *THE KASÎDAH OF HÂJÎ ABDÛ EL-YEZDÎ* translated and annotated by his Friend and Pupil, F. B. [Sir Richard Francis Burton]. 1902.
Old World Series.   H 234.   Third edition.

925 on Van Gelder; 100 numbered copies on Japan vellum.

Comment: *NUC* lists a copy of this 1902 "third edition" at Harvard. An error in edition note? A reprint of the previous entry?

181.4   *THE KASÎDAH OF HÂJÎ ABDÛ EL-YEZDÎ* translated and annotated by his Friend and Pupil, F. B. [Sir Richard Francis Burton]. 1903.
Old World Series.   H 267.   Fourth edition.

925 on Van Gelder. No Japan vellum copies printed.

181.5   *THE KASÎDAH OF HÂJÎ ABDÛ EL-YEZDÎ* translated and annotated by his Friend and Pupil, F. B. [Sir Richard Francis Burton]. 1906.
xii, 126, [1] pp. (same through the seventh ed.)
Old World Series.   H 369.   Fifth edition.

925 on Van Gelder. No Japan vellum copies printed.

181.6   *THE KASÎDAH OF HÂJÎ ABDÛ EL-YEZDÎ* translated and annotated by his Friend and Pupil, F. B. [Sir Richard Francis Burton]. 1908.
Old World Series.   H 446.   Sixth edition.

925 on Van Gelder; 50 numbered copies on Japan vellum.

181.7   *THE KASÎDAH OF HÂJÎ ABDÛ EL-YEZDÎ* translated and annotated by his Friend and Pupil, F. B. [Sir Richard Francis Burton]. 1909.
Old World Series.   H 482.   Seventh edition.

925 on Van Gelder. No Japan vellum copies printed.

181.8 *THE KASÎDAH OF HÂJÎ ABDÛ EL-YEZDÎ* translated and annotated by his
      Friend and Pupil, F. B. [Sir Richard Francis Burton]. 1911.
      xvi, 124 pp.; port. front. (same through the ninth edition)
      Old World Series.   H 547.   Eighth edition.

925 on Van Gelder; 50 copies printed on Japan vellum.

Content: First Old World edition to contain the frontispiece portrait etching of
Sir Richard F. Burton by Léopold Flameng, used in subsequent editions. Also,
this is the first Old World to contain Swinburne's 6-page "Elegy 1869-1891" to
Richard Burton appearing on pp. *xi-[xvi]*. The elegy is reprinted from *Astrophel and Other Poems* (London: Chatto & Windus, 1894). Both these new
contents will appears in all subsequent editions.

181.9 *THE KASÎDAH OF HÂJÎ ABDÛ EL-YEZDÎ* translated and annotated by
      Friend and Pupil, F. B. [Sir Richard Francis Burton]. 1913.
      Old World Series.   H 597.   Ninth edition.

925 on Van Gelder. No Japan vellum copies printed.

181.10 *THE KASÎDAH OF HÂJÎ ABDÛ EL-YEZDÎ* translated and annotated by his
       Friend and Pupil, F. B. [Sir Richard Francis Burton]. 1917.
       xvi, 125 pp.; port. front. (same through the twelfth ed.)
       Old World Series.   H 659.   Tenth edition.

925 on Van Gelder (20 of which are specially bound); 50 numbered copies Japan vellum.

Comment: In a variant issue, a printed leaf before the half-title indicates:

> TWENTY COPIES OF THIS, MY TENTH OLD WORLD EDITION OF THE KASI-
> DAH, HAVE BEEN BOUND IN JAPAN VELLUM BOARDS FOR THE SPECIAL
> PURPOSE OF PRESENTATION TO THOSE ASSEMBLED AT THE ANNUAL SES-
> SION OF THE OMAR KHAYYAM CLUB OF AMERICA, BOSTON, SATURDAY,
> MARCH 31, 1917. THIS COPY [NO.   ] BELONGS TO [name typed in] "VIVI,
> VALEQUE!" [*Mosher's signature*].

This limitation note is numbered and signed by Mosher, with the number and
the recipient's name typed on the page. Apparently the text block of the 20
copies is part of the 925 copies printed on Van Gelder because the limitation
statement still appears in its usual place on the verso of the title page. A copy
of this variant issue is located in the Bishop Collection.

Binding: In this variant issue, the front cover's title and design, and the spine's
title and date, are all printed in purple ink rather than the usual brown ink.

181.11 *THE KASÎDAH OF HÂJÎ ABDÛ EL-YEZDÎ* translated and annotated by his
       Friend and Pupil, F. B. [Sir Richard Francis Burton]. 1920.
       Old World Series.   H 682.   Eleventh edition.

1,500 copies on Van Gelder paper. No Japan vellum copies printed.

Comment: This limitation of 1500 copies is the largest limitation ever recorded
in a Mosher book. Mosher's own bibliography appearing at the end of each Old
World *Kasîdah* only gives the limitation as 925, contrary to the limitation
statement in the volume itself.

181.12 *THE KASÎDAH OF HÂJÎ ABDÛ EL-YEZDÎ* translated and annotated by his
       Friend and Pupil, F. B. [Sir Richard Francis Burton]. 1923.
       Old World Series.   H 702A.   Twelfth edition.

925 on Van Gelder; 25 numbered copies on Japan vellum.

Comment: This edition was not listed in the Hatch *Check List*, but was later
added by Hatch in his 1972 unpublished addenda and corrigenda, later published in Vilain.

Reference: Vilain, p. 67.

————— *Same Title, Change of Series* —————

182. RICHARD F. BURTON *THE KASÎDAH*. Edited by William Marion Reedy. 1905. *viii ℓ*, 55, [1] *ℓ*.; port. front. Large 4to: 32.5 x 25.5 cm. Miscellaneous Series-30 H 321. First thus.

Content: The introduction is by William Marion Reedy. Selections from Robert Browning, "The Sunburnt Poet" by Theodore Watts-Dunton, Shelley, and St. Augustine comprise the preliminary matter. All pages are printed on the recto side only. For further bibliographic information, see beginning of entry 181.

Comment: This is the largest book produced by Mosher and is set in 14-point old-style Roman type, each couplet in unbroken lines across the page. The frontispiece is a Bierstadt reproduction of the etching by Léopold Flameng after Lord Leighton's portrait, the exact size of the original plate, 7" x 8 1/2".

The former librarian at Brown University, Dr. Lyman Koopman, refers to this and other such large Mosher productions as examples of what he calls "tribute typography," presumably meaning a particularly fine printing of a classic work, in a limited edition. Koopman classified the Kelmscott Press books in this class of imprints.

In a Sept. 26, 1905 letter to Mosher, Koopman explains the Arabic words gilt stamped on the front cover: "At last I have gotten at the Arabic professor in regard to the Kasîdah. The words read from right to left & are without vowels. They are Abdû Hâjê Al Kasîdah. Abdû is a name, meaning *servant*. Hâjî is a title, like Mr.; it means *one who has made the journey to Mecca*. I find his Arabic name given in the *Dictionary of National Biography* as Al-Haj (= the traveler) Abdullah (which must mean the servant of God)." (The Houghton Library, bMS Am 1096 [820]). One may also add that "Kasîdah" is simply an Arabic word for couplets, and the name described above is the *non-de-plume* of Sir Richard Burton.

Binding & Embellishment: The Van Gelder copies are bound in quarter white faux-vellum over blue Fabriano boards with title/author/date in gold on the spine. The Japan vellum editions are bound Japan vellum wraps over boards with the spine information printed directly on the spine. The front covers of both issues have three lines of Arabic inscription in gilt printed directly on the cover. Title page and colophon in red and black. The large, red capital letters used throughout may be designed by Goudy (also used in 183).

Reference: Penzer, p. 101; Quinn 1203 (incorrectly catalogued date of 1895); Koopman, p. 137; Vilain, p. 22; the manuscript for the Reedy introduction is at the Houghton Library (bMS Am 1096).

182.01 RICHARD F. BURTON *THE KASÎDAH*. Edited by William Marion Reedy. 1905. *viii ℓ*, 55, [1] *ℓ*.; port. front. Large 4to: 32.5 x 25.5 cm. Miscellaneous Series-30 H 321. Variant of entry 182 above.

Content: Same as 182, except: (1) the imprint information at the bottom of the title page reads PORTLAND MAINE PRIVATELY PRINTED MDCCCV and the large double-dolphin publisher's devise that appears in the colophon of 182 is now in red beneath the title, and (2) the colophon reads: TEN COPIES OF THIS BOOK PRIVATELY PRINTED ON VAN GELDER HAND-MADE PAPER ROYAL QUARTO AND THE TYPE DISTRIBUTED NUMBER.... and the same double-dolphin device used in the colophon of 182 appears here, only now printed in black ink.

Comment: Penzer notes that there were also "10 copies with 'Privately Printed' imprint for England..." Mosher himself in his 1912 catalogue in states: "10 copies on hand-made paper, with privately printed imprint for England." It is not known for whom the volumes were privately printed.

125 copies on Van Gelder; 15 numbered and signed copies on Japan vellum; 5 on Roman vellum in sheets, signed by the publisher; 10 copies marked "privately printed" for England (see 182.01).

THE KASÎDAH (continued)

Binding & Embellishment: The binding is the same as the regular Van Gelder edition (182), but the copy examined is in green rather than blue Fabriano covered boards.

Reference: The only copy located is in the Bishop Collection. No copy is recorded in RLIN or *NUC*.

183. *THE KASÎDAH OF HÂJÎ ABDÛ EL-YEZDÎ* translated and annotated by his Friend and Pupil F. B. [Sir Richard F. Burton]. [October] 1915.
xxvii, 72, [1] pp.; port. front., 2 facsims.   Large 4to: 31 x 23 cm.
Miscellaneous Series-75   H 624.   New edition/same series.

250 on Van Gelder; 20 numbered copies on Japan vellum, signed by the publisher.

Content: A selection from James Thomson's *The City of Dreadful Night* appears on the verso of the half-title. The introduction (pp. *xi*-[*xiv*] by William Marion Reedy is preceded by a selection from Robert Browning (p. [*x*]). There are four Tributes in Verse ([*xv*]-*xxvii*): "The Sunburnt Poet / F.R.B." by Theodore Watts-Dunton; and "To Sir Richard F. Burton / (On his Translation of The Arabian Nights)," "Elegy / 1869-1891," and "On the Death of Richard Burton," the latter three all by Algernon Charles Swinburne. Selections from Robert Browning, Shelley, and St. Augustine also precede the title text. A facsimile of the original 1880 title page appears on p. [3]. For further bibliographic details, see beginning of entry 181. Contains a bibliography on pp. [69-72].

Mosher has also included a memorial tribute (p. [*v*]) to Charles Freeman Libby, a Portland resident and close friend of Mosher's, and at one time president of the American Bar Association. He was known as a cultivated man with a flair for the French.

Comment: Penzer notes: "This volume is set in 12- and 14-point old-style Roman type, each couplet in unbroken lines across the page, and follows the arrangement, with additional matter and facsimiles of the first quarto edition of 1905. With Flameng portrait on Japan vellum... The facsimiles given are those of the wrapper design and title-page of the first edition (Quaritch, 1880)." One of these is printed on the front free endpaper. The large, red capital letters may be designed by Frederic Goudy.

A copy in the Bishop Collection includes an inscription by Mosher to the Smith & Sale (Mosher's Portland printers) pressman, Frank Mangum: "My dear Frank, I ask your acceptance of this volume, which with your press work to make it so, I consider one of my best. Your friend, Thomas Bird Mosher. Feb. 29, 1916 [a leap year]."

Binding & Embellishment: Van Gelder copies are bound in quarter white faux-vellum over blue boards with white faux-vellum board tips and a gilt-stamped blue label on the spine. As with the previous entry, the Arabic inscription taken from the front wrapper of the first edition is stamped in gilt on the front cover. The Japan vellum copies are bound in Japan vellum boards. Title page and colophon in red and black. The large, red capital letters used throughout may be designed by Goudy (also used in 182).

Reference: Penzer, p. 101 (under 1915); Quinn 1214 & 1215; Vilain, p. 22.

184. RUSKIN *THE KING OF THE GOLDEN RIVER*. [November] 1914.
viii, 61, [1] pp.   18.5 x 13.5 cm.
Privately Printed-34   H 735.   Only edition.

300 copies printed on Van Gelder paper; 25 numbered copies on Japan vellum.

Content: A five-part fairy tale. The bibliographical note on pp. [*v*]-*vi* is unsigned, and mentions the many American and English reprints following the third edition of 1856.

Comment: Privately printed for Edward A. Woods of Sewickley, PA. Some copies will have a loosely inserted presentation slip, from Mr. and Mrs. Woods, bearing the family coat of arms and the title of the book.

Binding & Embellishment: Bound in blue charcoal boards with white title/author on the spine. Title page in red and black; Chiswick ornaments; initial letters in red outline; pages ruled in black. Japan vellum copies bound in Japan vellum boards.

L

185. *A LADY OF SORROW* by James Thomson. [October] 1901.
104, [1] pp. (same for second edition)
Brocade Series-30   H 192.   First edition.

425 on Japan vellum for each edition.

Content: The brief bibliographical note opposite the title page indicates that this work first appeared in *The National Reformer* during 1867, and reappeared as the first work in Thomson's *Essays and Phantasies* (London: Reeves and Turner, 1881), a copy of which was in Mosher's library. The introductory note, also by James Thomson, sets the stage for the three-part work divided into sections named "The Angel," "The Siren," and the longest section, "The Shadow."

185.1 *A LADY OF SORROW* by James Thomson. [June] 1913.
Brocade Series.   H 602.   Second edition.

186. *THE LAND OF HEART'S DESIRE* by William Butler Yeats.
[October] 1903.   *vi*, 33, [1] pp. (same through the twelfth ed.)
Lyric Garland Series-1   H 260.   First edition.

950 copies on Van Gelder for each edition. For the first edition, 100 numbered copies on Japan vellum and signed by the publisher; 10 numbered on Roman vellum signed by the publisher.

Content: A brief quote from William Blake is opposite the title page. Mosher's 1903 catalogue mentions this reprint was done "with Mr. Yeats' consent." –p. 60.

The text of this work was printed by Mosher in his June 1903 issue of *The Bibelot* (26).

Comment: According to Wade, this is the first "published edition of the revised version." The distinction Wade makes here involves the different appearances of this text in 1903. Its first appearance was in *The Bibelot* for June 1903 (26), but appearance in a serial publication does not count for first edition status. Next it appears in July 1903 (188) as a "privately printed" book which Wade calls the first "Revised Version." Then just three months later, in October, it appears as part of a regular Mosher series (186), which is what Wade refers to when he says it is the first "*published* edition of the revised version" (my emphasis).

THE LAND OF HEART'S DESIRE (continued)

Mosher first listed this book in 1902 under the Miscellaneous Series; however, in the next catalogue for 1903, the Lyric Garland Series was created and the title was transferred to it (see also 187).

Reference: Roth 73; Quinn 11437 & 11439; Wade 13; *DLB* XIX, p. 400; Vilain, p. 97 (plate 44 [9th edition]).

THE LAND OF HEART'S
DESIRE   BY   WILLIAM
BUTLER   YEATS

PORTLAND MAINE
THOMAS B MOSHER
MDCCCCIII

186.1　**THE LAND OF HEART'S DESIRE** by William Butler Yeats.
[December] 1903.
Lyric Garland Series.　　　H 281.　　　Second edition.

186.2　**THE LAND OF HEART'S DESIRE** by William Butler Yeats.
[February] 1904.
Lyric Garland Series.　　　H 314.　　　Third edition.

186.3　**THE LAND OF HEART'S DESIRE** by William Butler Yeats.
[March] 1905.
Lyric Garland Series.　　　H 347.　　　Fourth edition.

186.4　**THE LAND OF HEART'S DESIRE** by William Butler Yeats.
[February] 1906.
Lyric Garland Series.　　　H 386.　　　Fifth edition.

186.5　**THE LAND OF HEART'S DESIRE** by William Butler Yeats.
[December] 1906.
Lyric Garland Series.　　　H 387.　　　Sixth edition.

186.6　**THE LAND OF HEART'S DESIRE** by William Butler Yeats.
[January] 1908.
Lyric Garland Series.　　　H 459.　　　Seventh edition.

186.7　**THE LAND OF HEART'S DESIRE** by William Butler Yeats.
[June] 1909.
Lyric Garland Series.　　　H 502.　　　Eighth edition.

186.8　**THE LAND OF HEART'S DESIRE** by William Butler Yeats.
[November] 1910.
Lyric Garland Series.　　　H 529.　　　Ninth edition.

186.9　**THE LAND OF HEART'S DESIRE** by William Butler Yeats.
[March] 1912.
Lyric Garland Series.　　　H 583.　　　Tenth edition.

186.10　**THE LAND OF HEART'S DESIRE** by William Butler Yeats.
[December] 1913.
Lyric Garland Series.　　　H 604.　　　Eleventh edition.

186.11　**THE LAND OF HEART'S DESIRE** by William Butler Yeats.
[November] 1916.
Lyric Garland Series.　　　H 647.　　　Twelfth edition.

———————— *Same Title, Change of Series* ————————

187. *THE LAND OF HEART'S DESIRE* by William Butler Yeats.
[July] 1909.   *vi*, 32, [1] pp.   18.5 x 13.5 cm.
Miscellaneous Series-43   H 466.   First thus.

500 on Japan vellum only.

Comment: Colbeck indicates that "this may be considered the fourth American edition, or the third giving the revised version of 1903." This is not correct. As Wade properly notes, the first "published edition of the revised version" is the above entry 186. There were seven more Lyric Garland Series editions published (from December 1903 - June 1909) before this Miscellaneous Series edition was printed in July 1909. Colbeck may have thought the subsequent printings were re-impressions rather than editions, i.e., were reprinted from the same plates rather than re-typeset; however, close examination of the separate printings reveal alterations in the type, thereby confirming Mosher's assertion in his colophons that the "type [is] distributed."

Binding & Embellishment: Flexible Japan vellum cover printed in green with Kelmscott leaf, flower and vine cover design (re-used from p. 33 of entry 103) and taken from the Kelmscott, Coleridge's *Poems*. Yapp fore-edge. This same half-page ("L" shaped) border is found in the American Type Founders' *Specimens of type...*(Chicago, 1896). The noted American printer of Maine, Fred Anthoensen, identified the Dickinson Type Foundry of Boston (a subsidiary of the American Type Founders Company) as one of Mosher's sources. For other books using Kelmscott Press & William Morris designs, see entry 74. Pages are partially ruled throughout.

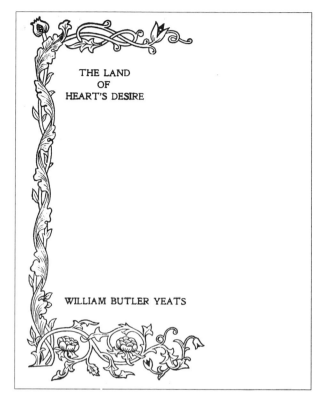

Russell's "Sword of Light" design, printed in red, also appears on both the title page and colophon (see also entry 153).

Reference: Wade 13 A; Colbeck II, p. 964 (73); American Type Founders, p. 416b, #4263.

——————— *Same Title, Change of Series* ———————

188. *THE LAND OF HEART'S DESIRE* by William Butler Yeats.
[July] 1903.   *xvi*, 29, [1] pp.   15.5 x 11.5 cm.
Privately Printed-8   H 710.   First thus.

32 numbered copies on Japan vellum printed by Mosher for presentation to his friends. First revised book edition.

Content: In addition to the main text, it contains a three-part foreword by Mosher, a brief quote from Blake ("O Rose, thou art sick") on the verso of the second half-title, and a bibliographical note at the end on p. [31].

This work was first printed by Mosher in his June 1903 issue of *The Bibelot* (26).

Comment: According to Wade, this is the first "Revised [Book] Version." It predates the Lyric Garland edition (186) which was issued three months later. See comment under 186.

Binding & Embellishment: The binding and text format is identical to the privately printed Upson's *Lyrics and Sonnets* (228).

Reference: Wade 12; Roth 72; Quinn 11438.

189. *THE LAST CHRISTMAS TREE   AN IDYL OF IMMORTALITY.*
By James Lane Allen. [October] 1914.
vi, 34, [1] pp.; port. front.   18 x 9.5 cm.
Miscellaneous Series-71   H 611.   Only edition.

950 on Van Gelder; 50 numbered copies onJapan vellum. First edition.

Content: This edition was revised and enlarged by the author and contains his approved latest portrait with facsimile of his signature. The copyright is under James Lane Allen. A somewhat different and much briefer form of this text appeared several years before in *The Saturday Evening Post.*

Comment: Lane received a 10% royalty on copies sold.

Binding & Embellishment: Bound in quarter gray paper over patterned boards, and uniform with Mosher's *Magic in Kensington Gardens* (230); darker gray title printed directly on the spine. Japan vellum copies are bound in Japan vellum boards. Title page in red, green and black; Chiswick ornaments; head-pieces of double-rowed red flowers and green leaves.

The cover design by Lucien Pissarro was taken from the 1902 Eragny Press edition of *Peau D'Ane.* The same cover design is used on the Japan vellum copy as a wrapper around boards. For other books using Eragny Press & Lucien Pissarro designs, see entry 52.

Reference: See the Nov. 17, 1941 letter from Lamb to Yorke for Mosher's payment terms (see Appendix II).

190. *LAUS VENERIS   POEMS AND BALLADS* by Algernon Charles Swinburne.
1899.   *xlvii*, 355 pp.; port. front, plates, facsim.
Quarto Series-1   H 122.   First edition.

450 on Van Gelder; 25 numbered & signed on Japan vellum; 4 numbered & signed by the publisher on Roman vellum.

Content: The unsigned preface is by the publisher. For an introduction, Mosher selected Swinburne's "Notes on Poems and Reviews" (pp. *xix*-[*xlvii*]) published in London by John Camden Hotten in 1866. The portrait frontispiece of Swinburne is from a watercolor by D. G. Rossetti, reproduced by the Bierstadt process. Three additional Bierstadt facsimiles appear: a woodcut of Cleopatra by Frederick Sandys, and two samples of Swinburne's writing taken from Nicoll and Wise's *Literary Anecdotes of the Nineteenth Century* (London: Hodder & Stoughton, 1895-96). Contains a bibliography on pages [341-350] taken from T. J. Wise's *List* in volume two of the *Literary Anecdotes...* The precise source for Mosher's reprint was a later edition of *Poems and Ballads* (London: Chatto & Windus). The original copy, edited for the printer, but now lacking the title page, preliminaries, or any bookseller ads, is now in the Bishop Collection.

Comment: Ransom indicates that this "contains the entire text of *Poems and Ballads* from the first edition, with Swinburne's rare pamphlet defense, *Notes on Poems and Reviews* [London: John Camden Hotten] (1866), and a 'very full bibliography.'"

T. J. Wise notes that "the inclusion of *Cleopatra*, which has never yet been reprinted in England, lends to the volume an especial interest..." and further comments in Vol. 6 of *The Ashley Library*: "In addition to the regular series of *Poems and Ballads* as contained in the original editions, this volume includes *Cleopatra, Notes on Poems and Reviews,* and a *Bibliography*, together with a portrait and three facsimiles. The *Bibliography* is merely a reprint of pertinent extracts taken from my own *Bibliographical List of the Scarcer Works, and Uncollected Writings of Swinburne*, printed for private circulation in 1897."

LAUS VENERIS POEMS AND BALLADS (continued)

A "revised" edition reprinted by Mosher appeared under a new title: *POEMS & BALLADS First Series*, in 1904 (see 296).

Reference: Boss VII 146; Wise I 33; Quinn 9454-9456; The Ashley Library, V. 6, p. 62; Ransom 261; Grigsby 1124 & 1125.

———————— *Same Title, Change of Series* ————————

191. ALGERNON CHARLES SWINBURNE *LAUS VENERIS.* [July] 1900.
    xi, 46 pp. (same for second ed.)
    Vest Pocket Series-3   H 156.   First edition thus.

Limitation unknown for both Van Gelder and Japan vellum copies. First separate American edition.

Content: In his 1900 catalogue, Mosher claims that "this is the first time that *Laus Veneris* has been reprinted separately since the privately issued pamphlet edition of 1866." The appendix contains a quote from William Michael Rossetti, and Swinburne's Old French quotation (with English translation) originally prefixed to the London, 1866 edition published by Moxon. A publisher's note appears on p. [*viii*], and a bibliography appears on pp. 44-46.

Comment: T. J. Wise notes that "...in 1900 Thomas B. Mosher published a dainty pocket edition of xi + 46 pages, small 8vo size. In addition to the text of the poem the little book contains a long extract [as a preface] from *Notes on Poems and Reviews*, together with a 'Bibliography' taken from my tentative volume of 1897."

Design: According to Bruckner, this is one of the first four cover designs done for this series by Frederic Goudy (see 1, 335 & 375 for the others) and subsequently used sporadically throughout the series. For other Goudy designs, see entry 1.

Reference: Livingston, p. 31; Crichton 43 and plate on p. 73; The Ashley Library, V. I, p. 99 and V. 6, p. 58; Bruckner, p. 49.

191.1 ALGERNON CHARLES SWINBURNE *LAUS VENERIS.* [June] 1909.
    Vest Pocket Series.   H 498.   Second edition.

192. *LEAVES OF GRASS* By Walt Whitman Facsimile Edition of the 1855 Text.
    1919.   15 pp., wrapper facsim.; 95 pp., back wrapper; port. front.   28.5 x 19.5 cm.
    Miscellaneous Series-87   H 667.   First edition.

250 on Old Stratford white wove; 100 numbered copies on Van Gelder; 50 numbered copies on Japan vellum, signed by the publisher.

Content: The ten-part introduction (pp. 9-15) is by the publisher. A memorial tribute to Horace Traubel (p. [5]), and Emerson's 21 July 1855 letter to Whitman (p. [7]) also precede the main work which is a typographic facsimile of the first edition of *Leaves of Grass* (Brooklyn, New York, 1855). As Mosher mentions on p. 11 of his introduction, "I am happy to reprint in type-facsimile the *Leaves of Grass*, 1855, text and *format* untampered, the original binding reproduced in all its lovely mid-century decoration..."

Facsimiles of printed colored wrappers, of some copies of the original edition, are also bound in (only colored in the Old Stratford copies). All copies contain the 1855 Samuel Hollyer engraved portrait as a frontispiece to the facsimile. The Van Gelder and Japan vellum copies have an added frontispiece portrait of Walt Whitman (often called Whitman's "King Lear" portrait) mounted opposite the title page.

Selections from the text of this work were printed by Mosher in his May 1912 issue of *The Bibelot* (35).

LEAVES OF GRASS *(continued)*

Comment: This is the first published facsimile of Walt Whitman's 1855 *Leaves of Grass*. Mosher referred to as the "Centenary Reprint." It is also the only book he co-published in his regular series, but one of three collaborations in which Mosher's name is stated along with a partner, on either the colophon or the title page. The other two are the privately printed *Rubáiyát* (337) and *The Casket of Opals* (56). Mosher's partner in this venture was the department store owner, William F. Gable of Altoona, PA .

Norman Strouse calls this book a "completely startling facsimile..., faithful even unto its binding," and Mosher's "*tour de force*, the magnificent facsimile reprint...."

In an Aug. 22, 1920 article in *The Boston Sunday Post*, Mosher mentions:

> I suppose I am best known by my Bibelot, but what I consider the most wonderful work of my life is the reproduction of Walt Whitman's 'Leaves of Grass' in the author's memorial year. I not only had the extremely great pleasure of publishing this book, but I had an equal amount of gratification in seeing this edition sold without a single word of advertising. Nor am I speaking from the commercial standpoint.

Binding & Embellishment: The Old Stratford paper copies are bound in facsimile green cloth with blind-stamping and gilt as were the 1855 copies. The Van Gelder paper copies have the same blind and gilt stamping, but on blue boards squared at the spine rather than rounded as are the green cloth spines. The Japan vellum copies are stamped and squared at the spine just like the Van Gelder copies, but bound in Japan vellum boards. The head- and tail-pieces are from the 1903 Eragny Press edition of Ronsard's *Abrégé de l'Art Poétique*, and the initial "A" on page 9 is also Eragny. For other books using Eragny Press & Lucien Pissarro designs, see entry 52. There is no colophon.

Reference: Myerson 40.I.a-c; Strouse, pp. 47 & 57; Vilain 27.

192.1. ***LEAVES OF GRASS*** By Walt Whitman Facsimile Edition of the 1855 Text.
1920.   6 pp., wrapper facsim.; 95 pp., back wrapper; port. front., facsim. (same size)
Miscellaneous Series.   H 684.   Second edition.

Content: Additions to this edition are (1) an addenda to Mosher's 1919 introduction (p. [16]), and (2) a facsimile holograph of the Ralph Waldo Emerson letter of praise.

Comment: The letter, rewritten in Whitman's hand, was in the collection of Frederick P. Hier, Jr. an attorney in New York and a friend of Horace Traubel and William Gable. Hier loaned Mosher the Whitman letter for this edition (June 10 & 18, 1920 letters to Mosher now at The Houghton Library, bMS Am 1096 [632-634]).

Binding & Embellishment: This book is bound and printed like 192, but no copies were printed on Japan vellum, nor on Van Gelder paper with the blue binding.

Reference: Myerson C 40.I.d.W; Vilain, p. 93, plate 35.

193. ***LECTURE ON THE ENGLISH RENAISSANCE*** Rose Leaf and Apple Leaf:
L'Envoi by Oscar Wilde. 1905.   *x*, 42 pp.; port. front.   17.5 x 14 cm.
Miscellaneous Series-32   H 323.   Only edition.

LEAVES OF GRASS
BY WALT WHITMAN

FACSIMILE EDITION
OF THE 1855 TEXT

PORTLAND MAINE
THOMAS BIRD MOSHER
WILLIAM FRANCIS GABLE
MDCCCCXIX

(a)

INTRODUCTION

T the forefront of this essay, mainly bibliographical, I place the words of Ernest Renan, as he contemplates the on-coming life of St. Paul; words, at the close of the second volume of his *History of the Origins of Christianity*, of peculiar beauty and fitness in connection with Walt Whitman and the first edition of *Leaves of Grass* in 1855: "*The great Christian Odyssey is about to commence. Already the apostolic barque has spread its sails the wind sighs and aspires only to carry upon its wings the words of Jesus.*"

(b)

500 on Old Stratford wove paper.

50 numbered copies on Japan vellum only.

LECTURE ON THE ENGLISH RENAISSANCE (continued)

Content: Mosher's foreword quotes from the Oscar Wilde chapter in Walter Hamilton's *The Æsthetic Movement in England* (London: Reeves & Turner, 1882), pp. 103-104, concerning Wilde's first lecture in America. There are two distinct pieces presented in this book: (1) the "Lecture," and (2) "L'Envoi" which formerly preceded Rennell Rodd's *Rose Leaf and Apple Leaf* (Philadelphia: J. M. Stoddart, 1882). Contains a bibliographical note on pp. [41-42].

The sources used by Mosher include *Poems by Oscar Wilde Together with His Lecture on the English Renaissance* (Paris: [Smithers (Wright and Jones)], 1903) and *Poems by Oscar Wilde, Also his Lecture on the English Renaissance*. The Seaside Library. Vol. 58, No. 1183 (New York: Munro, January 19, 1882, pp. 30-31). Mosher corrected his copy of the 1903 Paris 1903 edition, pp. 203-216 (in the Bishop Collection), using The Seaside Library text as "our authority" to correct the text (see Mosher's 1905 catalogue, p. 54). One of the more glaring inaccuracies corrected was "the beautiful Lady Euphonia" for "the beautiful boy Euphorion." Four other corrections were also made by Mosher for his reprint.

This title was also printed by Mosher in his July 1905 issue of *The Bibelot* (28), and the typography and content of this publication closely resembles that of its issuance in *The Bibelot*.

Comment: The portrait frontispiece of Wilde is by the photographers Ellis & Walery (same photo used in entries 304.1 & 305). This volume is one of six books in the Miscellaneous Series that form a "sub-series" uniform in style (see note to 238).

Cowan notes that Mosher's foreword is "well worth reading..."

Binding & Embellishment: Copies are bound in flexible Japan vellum boards with yapp top and fore-edges; title printed to the spine and title/author printed directly on the front cover with lead drop-cap initial in red.

Reference: Quinn 11151; Cowan IV, pp. 64-65.

---

194. *THE LEGEND OF MADAME KRASINSKA* by Vernon Lee.
[August] 1903.   77, [1] pp. (same for second ed.)
Brocade Series-41   H 255.   First edition.

425 on Japan vellum for each edition.

Content: The foreword begins with a brief statement by Mosher immediately followed by a lengthy letter by Vernon Lee to the Baronesse E. French-Cini written in 1891. The ten-part text is from Vernon Lee's *Vanitas: polite stories*. (London: Heinemann, 1892).

Comment: Vernon Lee is the pseudonym of Violet Paget.

194.1 *THE LEGEND OF MADAME KRASINSKA* by Vernon Lee.
[July] 1915.
Brocade Series.   H 633.   Second edition.

---

195. *THE LEGEND OF SAINT JULIAN, HOSPITALER*, translated from the French of Gustave Flaubert by Agnes Lee. [September] 1905.
68, [1] pp. (same for second ed.)
Brocade Series-49   H 326.   First edition.

425 on Japan vellum for each edition.
First edition of this translation.

Content: The preface is also by the translator, Agnes Lee (Mrs. Otto Freer), an American poet born in 1868 in Chicago.

195.1 ***THE LEGEND OF SAINT JULIAN, HOSPITALER***, translated from the French of Gustave Flaubert by Agnes Lee. [January] 1912.

Brocade Series. H 581A Second edition.

Comment: This edition was not listed in the Hatch *Check List*, but was later added by Hatch in 1972.

Reference: Vilain, p. 65 (second edition).

---

196. ***THE LETTERS OF A PORTUGUESE NUN*** (Marianna Alcoforado) translated by Edgar Prestage. 1900. *xli*, 54 pp. (same for second ed.)
Old World Series-22 H 139. First edition.

Content: This is a reprint of the London: D. Nutt, 1897 second edition of Prestage's English translation which first appeared in 1893. A note from the publisher appears opposite the title page. The introduction and bibliography (pp. [45-54]) are by the translator.

Reference: Quinn 7090.

196.1 ***THE LETTERS OF A PORTUGUESE NUN*** (Marianna Alcoforado) translated by Edgar Prestage. 1905.
Old World Series. H 337. Second edition.

925 on Van Gelder for both editions; 100 numbered copies on Japan vellum for first edition only.

---

197. ***LIBER AMORIS OR THE NEW PYGMALION*** by William Hazlitt. 1908. *x*, 140, [1] pp.
Old World Series-46 H 430. Only edition.

Content: The introduction (pp. 5-[10]) is by William Marion Reedy. A poem by Francis Thompson appears opposite the title page. Contains a bibliographical note on pp. [137-140], although Mosher does not identify the precise source used for his reprint.

Design: The cover design is by Thomas Maitland Cleland whose hallmark initial "C" appears in the lower left portion of the design. For other Cleland designs used, see entry 6.

925 on Van Gelder; 25 numbered copies on Japan vellum.

---

198. ***LIST OF BOOKS. Season of 1893-94.*** 8 pp. 15.3 x 10.1 cm.
Catalogue. H 4A. First Catalogue.

Content: In addition to the eight pages of the catalogue, there are four sample pages from The Bibelot Series printed on one sheet (20.0 x 20.2 cm.) with fold in center.

Comment: Hatch mentioned this list and indicated "perhaps the notation would have begun more properly with the brochure of 1893..." Later evidence reveals that Mosher himself called it "the first catalogue I ever issued... In 1891-2 I simply had announcements of the only volumes I had issued up to that date. But in 1893 I began with an 8 page affair which is a very rare thing to turn up." —Mosher to T.N. McKean, Nov. 8, 1918 (Bishop Collection). In keeping with our inclusion of Hatch cross references, it has been assigned the number "H 4A".

Binding & Embellishment: There is no wrapper around the text; however, the four sample pages from The Bibelot Series are folded around and sewn to the text.

(a)

(b)

LIST OF BOOKS. Season of 1893-94 (continued)

A red sign design advertising Mosher's books appears on the front cover (signed: "R•" in the scrollwork to the left). This design closely follows the logo used by Lane and Mathews to advertise their Bodley Head books (see preceding page). The design may be by Bruce Rogers or by Frank Rathbun, two designers used early in Mosher's career. Mosher also used this design on his business stationary. For other Bruce Rogers designs, see entry 152. For Rathbun designs, see entry 107.

Reference: Hatch, p. 42.

---

199. *A LIST OF BOOKS, MDCCCXCIV.* 1894.   16 pp.   21.5 x 10.5 cm.
Catalogue.   H 8.   Second catalogue.

Content: This list includes three reviews of the Mosher Books in the front: *The New York Tribune* (Dec. 31, 1893), *The Critic* (Feb. 10, 1894), and *The Dial* (Dec. 16, 1893). There are also two reviews from the *Springfield Republican* (no date given). Facsimiles of four printed leaves are inserted.

Binding & Embellishment: Bound in light gray paper wrappers with watermark ACAWAM BOND; title on front cover and a Florentine lily on back cover are printed in blue ink. The inner title page includes the publisher's device signed "R" (see 198). Some hard bound copies are in gray boards with paper labels on the spine and front cover. A copy examined at Yale included sample title pages from *Songs of Adieu* and *Old World Lyrics* loosely laid in.

Reference: Vilain 60.

---

200. *A LIST OF BOOKS ISSUED IN LIMITED EDITIONS.* [October] 1895.
32 pp.   17.5 x 8.5 cm.
Catalogue.   H 16.   Third catalogue.

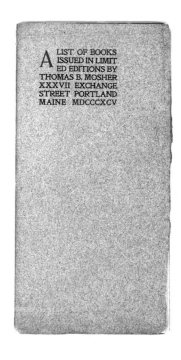

Content: The unsigned foreword is by the publisher. Selections accompanying the catalogue (other than those under specific book entries):

– Quotation from John Ruskin   – Quotation from Ralph Waldo Emerson
– Quotation from Walt Whitman   – Ten reviews of the Mosher Books

Comment: This is the first Mosher item to include the Mosher printer's mark of two stylized dolphins holding an open book which here appears in red on the back wrapper. This publisher's device was used on Mosher's stationary, other catalogues, and on the title pages of the Old World, Little Masterpieces, and Vest Pocket series.

Binding & Embellishment: Bound in red & black printed gray wrappers with red double-dolphins holding a book on the back cover; hard bound copies in gray boards with printed labels on spine and front cover. Printed in red and black throughout; decorative head- and tail-pieces similar to those used in the Old World Series.

Reference: Boss XI 138, XIII 147; Vilain, p. 103 (plate 62).

---

201. *A LIST OF BOOKS ISSUED IN LIMITED EDITIONS.* [October] 1896.
40 pp.   18.5 x 9 cm.
Catalogue.   H 28.   Fourth catalogue.

A LIST OF BOOKS ISSUED IN LIMITED EDITIONS (continued)

Content: The unsigned foreword is by the publisher. Selections accompanying the catalogue (other than those under specific book entries):

– "Confessio Amantis" by Richard Le Gallienne
– Quotation from Richard de Bury
– "How to Open a Book" by William Matthews
– Quotation from Frederic Harrison
– Nine reviews of the Mosher Books

Comment: See note to 181 for a piracy by an English publisher.

Binding & Embellishment: Pale green paper wrappers printed in dark green and red, design like a merchant's hanging sign on front cover, and Bruce Rogers' caduceus on the back cover; hard bound copies in gray boards with printed labels on spine and front cover, original wrappers bound in the back. Half-title page with publisher's design signed "R" (by Bruce Rogers?). See entry 198 for further information on this illustration. Printed in red and black throughout; decorative head- and tail-piece similar to those used in the Old World Series.

202. *A LIST OF BOOKS ISSUED IN LIMITED EDITIONS.* [October] 1897.
48 pp.   18 x 9 cm.
Catalogue.   H 51.   Fifth catalogue.

Content: The unsigned foreword is by the publisher. Selections accompanying the catalogue (other than those under specific book entries):

– Quotation from Matthew Arnold   – Quotation from Laurence Binyon

Binding & Embellishment: Light blue wraps printed in red and black with elaborate design of ornamental border, vines, and banner. Hard bound copies in gray boards with printed labels on spine and front cover; original wrappers bound in at the back. The wrappers of the Yale copy are different from those of other copies examined in that they are printed on gray paper with the title and date printed in black-letter on the front cover. Printed in red and black throughout; decorative head-piece and tail-pieces similar to those used in the Old World Series.

The cover design is by Frank Rathbun, with his "F" and double "R" monogram. For other design work by Rathbun, see entry 107. The publisher's device (a T.B.M. monogram) also appears on the back cover of the 1921 Mosher Books catalogue (entry 265).

203. *A LIST OF BOOKS ISSUED IN LIMITED EDITIONS.* [October] 1898.
64 pp.   18 x 9.5 cm.
Catalogue.   H 80.   Sixth catalogue.

Content: The unsigned foreword is by the publisher. Selections accompanying the catalogue (other than those under specific book entries):

– Quotation from William Hazlitt
– Quotation from Ralph Waldo Emerson
– Quotation from Richard Le Gallienne
– Quotation from Austin Dobson
– Unidentified quote on purchase of books

A LIST OF BOOKS ISSUED IN LIMITED EDITIONS (continued)

Binding & Embellishment: Bound in pale green wrappers printed in dark green and red with design on front cover. Hard-bound copies in gray-green boards with printed labels on spine and front cover; original wrappers bound in at the back. Printed in red and black throughout; decorative head- and tail-pieces similar to those used in the Old World Series.

Cover design by Lucien Pissarro taken from the 1896 Eragny Press publication of *The Book of Ruth and The Book of Esther*. For other publications using Eragny Press & Lucien Pissarro designs, see entry 52.

204. *A LIST OF BOOKS IN BELLES LETTRES.* [October] 1899.
   64 pp.   18 x 9 cm.
   Catalogue.   H 124.   Seventh catalogue.

Content: The unsigned foreword is by the publisher. Selections accompanying the catalogue (other than those under specific book entries):

– Quotation from Thomas Carlyle   – Quotation from Henry David Thoreau
– Quotation from Walt Whitman   – Quotation from George du Maurier

Binding & Embellishment: Bound in charcoal-blue wrappers with design in red and blue on front cover. Hard bound copies bound in blue boards with printed labels on spine and front cover; original wrappers bound in the back. Printed in red and black throughout; decorative head- and tail-pieces are similar to those used in the Old World Series.

The cover design is by Frederic Goudy and is signed with a "G". Some covers have the "G" removed. For other Goudy designs, see entry 1.

205. *A LIST OF BOOKS IN BELLES LETTRES* Issued in Choice and Limited
   Editions. [October] 1900.   68 pp.   18 x 9.5 cm.
   Catalogue.   H 160.   Eighth catalogue.

Content: The unsigned foreword is by the publisher. Selections accompanying the catalogue (other than those under specific book entries):

– Two quotations from Walter Raleigh
– Quotation from Frederick Harrison
– Quotation from Matthew Arnold
– Translation from Théophile Gautier by Austin Dobson

Binding & Embellishment: Bound in charcoal-blue paper wraps printed in red and dark blue. Hardbound copies in blue boards with printed labels on spine and front cover; original wrappers bound in at the back. Some of the hardbound copies are bound with a quarter white paper spine over blue boards (without labels) and were apparently copies for presentation. A curious inscription in the Yale copy reads, "To Mrs. Andrew Squire with the compliments of Thomas B. Mosher   Sept 18 1901. Revised Sept 18, 1909." The Spring Announcement for 1900 also bears the same Goudy design. Printed in red and black throughout; title page ruled in red; decorative head- and tailpieces are similar to those used in the Old World Series.

The cover design is by Frederic Goudy and is signed with a "G". For other Goudy designs, see entry 1.

Reference: Full page illustration in Briggs, p. [98].

206. *A LIST OF BOOKS IN BELLES LETTRES*   Issued in Choice and Limited
Editions. [October] 1901.   68 pp.   17.5 x 9 cm.
Catalogue.   H 199.   Ninth catalogue.

Content: The unsigned foreword is by the publisher. Selections accompanying
the catalogue (other than those under specific book entries):

– Two quotations from T.J. Cobden-Sanderson
– Two quotations from Gerald Stanley Lee
– Fragment from "When night fall comes, and day is done" by Lionel Johnson
– Brief unidentified quote on verso of the title page

Comment: Mosher completely drops any mention of The Bibelot Series and
The English Reprint Series from this catalogue, but he again includes them in
the 1902 and later catalogues.

Binding & Embellishment: Bound in light gray paper wrappers with cover
printed in dark blue and red. Hardbound copies are in gray boards with
printed labels on spine and front cover; original wrappers bound in the back.
Printed in red and black throughout; head- and tail-pieces are similar to those
used in the Old World Series.

The front cover design of a shelf of books is signed CRAWFORD along the spine
of the fifth book in from the right. This is the last name of the designer Earl
Stetson Crawford. For other Crawford designs used, see entry 88.

Reference: Full page illustration in Briggs, p. [90].

207. *A LIST OF BOOKS IN BELLES LETTRES*   Issued in Choice and Limited
Editions. [October] 1902.   64 pp.   23.5 x 12.5 cm.
Catalogue.   H 232.   Tenth catalogue.

Content: The unsigned foreword is by the publisher. Selections accompanying
the catalogue (other than those under specific book entries):

– Quotation from Clinton Scollard   – Quotation from Edmund Gosse
– Quotation from John Burroughs   – Quotation from Lord Lytton

Comment: This is the first time the anchor and dolphin motif appears on a
Mosher catalogue cover.

Binding & Embellishment: Bound in charcoal blue paper wraps printed in red
and dark green with a large anchor & dolphin on the front wrapper. Hardbound copies are in gray boards with printed labels on spine and front cover;
original wrappers bound in the back.

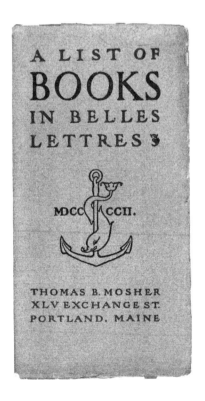

A head-piece signed "BR" (Bruce Rogers) appears upside down at the beginning of the foreword. This design was originally commissioned, along with two
others, for A.E.'s *Homeward Songs By the Way* (see entry 152 for this, and for
use of other Bruce Roger's designs). Only two of the three bands were used in
this book. The third is the one that appears in this catalogue. Another of the
BR head-pieces also appears here at the head of the index. The capital "A" on
the title page is from the Eragny Press. For other publications using Eragny
Press & Lucien Pissarro designs, see entry 52. Printed in red and black
throughout; except for the one Bruce Rogers head-piece. The head- and tail-
pieces are similar to those used in the Old World Series.

Reference: Vilain 61 (plate 63, p. 103; plate 64, p. 104).

See *THE MOSHER BOOKS* for later catalogues (entries 247-267).

208. *A LITTLE BOOK FOR JOHN O'MAHONY'S FRIENDS* by Katharine
Tynan [Hinkson]. 1909.   *x*, 56 pp.
Ideal Series of Little Masterpieces-12   H 476.   Only edition.

Limitation unknown for both Van Gelder and Japan vellum copies. First American edition.

Content: The foreword is by the publisher, in which he includes a selection of poetry from James Rhoades. A poem by Arthur Macy appears on p. *x*. The text of this book is from the privately printed work by the same title (Petersfield, Hampshire: Printed by The Pear Tree Press, 1906).

Comment: This title was first published in England by James Guthrie at the Pear Tree Press, 1906. A companion piece entitled *A Little Book for Mary Gill's Friends* was also published by Guthrie a year earlier. In his forward to the reprint, Mosher notes that "two little pamphlets lie before us, one of which we take the unasked liberty of reprinting..." According to the 1948 auction catalogue of Mosher's library, both books were present and inscribed to him by the author in January and February 1906.

Both titles appeared in Mosher's little magazine *The Bibelot* in June and Sept. 1907 (30) respectively.

Last title published in this series.

Reference: Quinn 10404; Colbeck II, p. 886 (23).

---

209. HENRY D. THOREAU *A LITTLE BOOK OF NATURE THEMES*
selected by Thomas Coke Watkins. [October] 1906.
xv, 80 pp. (same for second ed.)
Vest Pocket Series-12   H 357.   First edition.

Limitation unknown for both Van Gelder and Japan vellum copies. First edition.

Content: This volume includes 92 selections from Thoreau's works, plus a "proem" by Thoreau (pp. *xiii*-[*xv*]) taken from William Ellery Channing's *Thoreau, The Poet-Naturalist*. There is a signed foreword by Watkins. A selection from Thoreau (opposite the title page), and selections from William Wordsworth and Ralph Waldo Emerson further embellish the volume. An index of first lines is on pp. 75-[80].

Comment: According to an announcement for the Season of 1912, this title, along with three others (see 210, 211, and 212), formed a sub-series Mosher called the "Nature Thought Series" and the four volumes could be ordered as a special boxed set.

Reference: Borst E6; *BAL* 20209; Boswell 2024.

209.1 HENRY D. THOREAU *A LITTLE BOOK OF NATURE THEMES*
selected by Thomas Coke Watkins. [October] 1912.
Vest Pocket Series.   H 582.   Second edition.

---

210. RICHARD JEFFERIES *A LITTLE BOOK OF NATURE THOUGHTS*
selected by Thomas Coke Watkins. [June] 1903.   *viii*, 88 pp.
Vest Pocket Series-5   H 257.   First edition.

Limitation unknown for both Van Gelder and Japan vellum copies. First edition.

Content: This volume includes 96 selections from Jefferies' books. There is a signed foreword by Watkins, a one page selection from Walter Besant, and a selection from Henry David Thoreau (opposite the title page). An index of first lines is on pp. 83-[88].

Comment: This volume was considered part of a 4-vol. sub-series (see note to 209).

210.1 RICHARD JEFFERIES *A LITTLE BOOK OF NATURE THOUGHTS*
selected by Thomas Coke Watkins. [October] 1904.
viii, 91 pp. (same for third ed.)
Vest Pocket Series.   H 313.   Second edition.

210.2 RICHARD JEFFERIES *A LITTLE BOOK OF NATURE THOUGHTS*
selected by Thomas Coke Watkins. [July] 1907.
Vest Pocket Series.   H 425.   Third edition.

211. FIONA MACLEOD *A LITTLE BOOK OF NATURE THOUGHTS* selected
by Mrs. William Sharp and Roselle Lathrop Shields. 1908.   *xi*, 83 pp.
Vest Pocket Series-15   H 436.   Only edition.

Limitation unknown for both Van Gelder and Japan vellum copies. First edition.

Content: This volume includes 102 selections from Macleod's works, and a further selection from Macleod appears opposite the title page. Two selections from Ralph Waldo Emerson and a very brief selection from Richard Jefferies also embellish the volume. Roselle Lathrop Shields wrote the foreword, signed "R.L.S." An index of first lines appears on pp. 77-[83].

Comment: Fiona Macleod was a pseudonym used by William Sharp who also published works under his real name.

This volume was considered part of a 4-volume sub-series (see note to 209).

Mosher paid Mrs. Sharp (Elizabeth Amelia Sharp) $50 outright for the publication of this book in America.

Reference: Crichton 43 and plate on p. 73; see the Nov. 17, 1941 letter from Lamb to Yorke for Mosher's payment terms (see Appendix II).

212. WALT WHITMAN *A LITTLE BOOK OF NATURE THOUGHTS* selected by
Anne Montgomerie Traubel. 1906.   *viii*, 88 pp.
Vest Pocket Series-11   H 356.   Only edition.

Limitation unknown for both Van Gelder and Japan vellum copies. First edition.

Content: This volume contains 90 selections from the authorized edition of Whitman's prose works published in Boston by Small, Maynard & Co., 1900. The preface is by Anne Montgomerie Traubel, signed "A.M.T." A brief selection from Maeterlinck, a selection from Whitman's poetry, and full-page selection from Lafcadio Hearn further embellish the text. An index of first lines appears on pp. 83-[88].

Comment: This volume was considered part of a 4-volume sub-series (see note to 209).

Reference: Myerson C 22.I.a-b.

213. *A LITTLE BOOK OF XXIV CAROLS* by Katherine Tynan [Hinkson].
[October] 1907.   *viii*, 40, [1] pp. (same for second ed.)
Lyric Garland Series-12   H 398.   First edition.

950 copies on Van Gelder for each edition. For the first edition, 100 numbered copies on Japan vellum; 5 numbered copies on Roman vellum, signed by the publisher.

Comment: Mosher notes that these 24 "Carols were brought together by Mrs. Hinkson, and are now offered the reader oversea..." (1907 catalogue, p. 44).

Reference: Quinn 10405.

213.1 *A LITTLE BOOK OF XXIV CAROLS* by Katherine Tynan [Hinkson].
[October] 1916.
Lyric Garland Series.   H 651.   Second edition.

Binding: Some copies of this second edition are bound in blue boards rather
than the usual gray boards.

214.   *A LITTLE GARLAND OF CELTIC VERSE.* [October] 1905.
       viii, 42, [1] pp. (same through fourth ed.)
       Lyric Garland Series-7   H 330.   First edition.

Content: This anthology by Mosher contains verse chosen from the following
authors:

Lionel Johnson	Samuel Ferguson
William Butler Yeats	Nora Chesson
Eva Gore-Booth	Katharine Tynan Hinkson
Moira O'Neill	Dora Sigerson
Anna MacManus	A.E. (George Russell)

A poem by L. M. Little appears opposite the title page. The contents were
mostly based upon two issues of *The Bibelot*: August 1900 (23) & May 1903
(26) which were devoted to the Irish Renaissance. There are some additions
which were not in *The Bibelot* printing.

Comment: For Mosher's first anthology, and other anthologies assembled by
him, see 366.

Reference: Vilain 40, and p. 97, plate 44 (fourth ed.); Quinn 1529, 1530 &
7091.

950 copies on Van Gelder for each edition. For the first edition, 100 numbered copies on Japan vellum; 10 numbered copies on Roman vellum signed by the publisher.

214.1 *A LITTLE GARLAND OF CELTIC VERSE.* [June] 1907.
       Lyric Garland Series.   H 429.   Second edition.

214.2 *A LITTLE GARLAND OF CELTIC VERSE.* [October] 1913.
       Lyric Garland Series.   H 606.   Third edition.

214.3 *A LITTLE GARLAND OF CELTIC VERSE.* [July] 1916.
       Lyric Garland Series.   H 649.   Fourth edition.

Comment: Hatch did not record a Japan vellum printing. A Japan vellum copy
was located at The Houghton Library.

In addition to the Van Gelder copies, 100 numbered copies printed on Japan vellum.

215.   *A LITTLE GARLAND OF CHRISTMAS VERSE.* [October] 1905.
       viii, 48, [1] pp. (same for second ed.)
       Lyric Garland Series-8   H 331.   First edition.

Content: The poems are divided into two parts. This anthology by Mosher
lisher contains verse chosen from the following authors:

Martin Luther	Bishop Hall
Philip Doddridge	Nahum Tate
Isaac Watts	Charles Wesley
A.C. Swinburne	S. T. Coleridge
William Morris	Herbert P. Horne
Robert S Hawker	Edmund H. Sears
Phillips Brooks	Alfred Domett

950 on Van Gelder paper for each edition. For the first edition, 100 numbered copies on Japan vellum; 10 numbered copies on Roman vellum signed by the publisher.

A LITTLE GARLAND OF CHRISTMAS VERSE. (continued)

G. K. Chesterton	Fiona Macleod
Michael Fairless	Katharine Tynan [Hinkson]
Gordon Bottomley	Richard C. Trench
Robert Bridges	and old English songs & carols

A poem by George MacDonald also appears opposite the title page. The contents were based upon the *A Christmas Garland* printed in *The Bibelot* for December 1903 (26), but with the addition of a few new poems "for the first time grouped within the pages of a single book." (1905 catalogue, p. 40).

Comment: For Mosher's first anthology, and other anthologies assembled by him, see 366.

Reference: Quinn 7092.

215.1 *A LITTLE GARLAND OF CHRISTMAS VERSE.* [December] 1905.
Lyric Garland Series.   H 349.   Second edition.

215.2 *A LITTLE GARLAND OF CHRISTMAS VERSE.* [December] 1908.
viii, 50, [1] pp.
Lyric Garland Series.   H 461.   Third edition.

Content: A rearrangement of the poems in Part I, and the introduction of a new poem to Part II ("A Christmas Carol" by G. K. Chesterton), account for the greater number of pages than the first and second editions.

215.3 *A LITTLE GARLAND OF CHRISTMAS VERSE.* [December] 1914.
viii, 54, [1] pp.
Lyric Garland Series.   H 619.   Fourth edition.

Content: The two-part arrangement is dropped, and the addition of five more poems account for the expansion of this edition. Mosher added "An Old Song Re-Sung" by Katherine Tynan, "A Carol for Christmas Day Before Dawn" by Gordon Bottomley, and an untitled poem by Richard Chenevix Trench, in addition to two anonymous pieces.

216. *LITTLE WILLIE* by Eugene Field. Boston, 1904.   250 on Van Gelder; 25 on Japan
[8]pp. 11.5 x 9 cm.   vellum.
Privately Printed-9   H 711.   Only edition.

Content: The imprint on the title page reads: Boston | Privately Printed | MDCC-CCIV. This booklet consists of the a title page; four numbered, eight-line stanzas; and a note. A single red drop-cap begins each page of text.

Comment: The Sheean and Lamb typescripts indicate that *Little Willie* was published for a Mr. Weir. The pagination and edition size for the Van Gelder and Japan vellum copies likewise agree with the descriptions in the typescripts.

No colophon or other imprint information identifies these copies of *Little Willie* as being from the Mosher Press, but the designs, stylistic evidence, provenance, and agreement in collation with the Sheean and Lamb typescripts together unmistakably identify it as a privately printed Mosher Press book. In a letter to W. Irving Way dated November 25, 1914 (The Huntington Library, WY 128), Mosher indicates that "I even put in copy of the 'Willie' poem of which I was once the guilty publisher in a very limited edition."

LITTLE WILLIE (continued)

Binding & Embellishment: The cover uses an interlocking vine design with central oval by Frederic Goudy. The same design is used on the cover of the 1899 *A List of Books* (204), and the book is bound in the same style as the *List*, with gray-green charcoal paper wrappers and red silk cord sewing. For other Goudy designs, see entry 1.

A dainty flower sprig of three buds and two leaves on the title page was also used on the cover of Edwin Bolles' *Collectors & Collecting* (74) which came out six years earlier. This design appears in the American Type Founders' *Specimens of type: ornaments and borders...* (Chicago, 1896) as a Jenson Old-Style page embellishment from the Kelmscott Press. For other books using Kelmscott Press and William Morris designs, see entry 74.

According to John Taylor, the flower device on p. [8] is C. R. Ashbee's design for the Guild of Handicraft (see note to entry 30.01).

The page layout with wide leading between the lines of text, and the large Roman drop-caps, are very similar to Richard Le Galliene's *My Ladies' Sonnets* (London: Privately Printed, 1887). The Le Gallienne book was also an inspiration to John Lane of The Bodley Head in London. Mosher had a copy of the Le Gallienne work in his library (Bishop Collection) and he may have drawn upon it for his layout of this booklet.

A copy, one of "Twenty-five Copies on Japan Vellum" (verso of title page), is located at the Ekstrom Library at the University of Louisville, and was purchased from Flora Lamb's own collection. The front wrapper is printed in red and is bound with red silk thread. The booklet neatly slips into what appears to be a custom made envelope with Mosher's return address. Both a Japan vellum copy, and a Van Gelder copy (donated by Thomas Bird Mosher, Jr.), are at Arizona State University.

Reference: Taylor, p. 33 (illus. iii); American Type Founders, p. 416e, #4284. Vilain, p. 67.

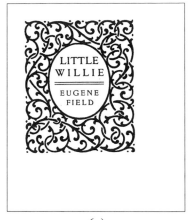

(a)

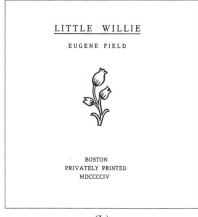

(b)

---

217. ***A LODGING FOR THE NIGHT: A STORY OF FRANCIS VILLON* by** Robert Louis Stevenson. [June] 1900.   69, [1] pp. (same through fourth ed.) Brocade Series-20   H 146.   First edition.

425 on Japan vellum for each edition.
First edition of this translation.

Content: This work first appeared in the October 1877 issue of *Temple Bar.* At the conclusion of Mosher's reprint there appears a letter from Marcel Schwob to Sidney Colvin, translated from the French by Mrs. Lucie Page.

Mosher first printed this text in the November 1895 issue of *The Bibelot* (18).

Comment: This work along with four others appeared in a sub-series (see 436). The sub-title spells Villon's first name as Francis, rather than François. This is not an error on Mosher's part, but the spelling as it appears in previous publications.

See entries 59, 268 & 394 for other translations by Lucie Page.

Reference: Not in Peckham.

217.1 ***A LODGING FOR THE NIGHT: A STORY OF FRANCIS VILLON***
by Robert Louis Stevenson. [August] 1902.
Brocade Series.   H 240.   Second edition.

217.2 *A LODGING FOR THE NIGHT: A STORY OF FRANCIS VILLON*
by Robert Louis Stevenson. [February] 1905.
Brocade Series.   H 341A.   Third edition.

Comment: This edition was listed in the Hatch *Check List* as an unlocated
trade edition, but was later added by Hatch in a 1972 (see Vilain).

Reference: Hatch, p. 168; Vilain, p. 64.

217.3 *A LODGING FOR THE NIGHT: A STORY OF FRANCIS VILLON*
by Robert Louis Stevenson. [March] 1908.
Brocade Series.   H 453.   Fourth edition.

217.4 *A LODGING FOR THE NIGHT: A STORY OF FRANCIS VILLON*
by Robert Louis Stevenson. [December] 1912.   71, [1] pp.
Brocade Series.   H 577.   Fifth edition.

217.5 *A LODGING FOR THE NIGHT: A STORY OF FRANCIS VILLON*
by Robert Louis Stevenson. [July] 1916.   69, [1] pp.
Brocade Series.   H 643.   Sixth edition.

218. *LONDON VOLUNTARIES AND OTHER POEMS* by William Ernest Henley.
1910.   *vii*, 66, [1] pp.
Lyric Garland Series-18   H 510.   Only edition.

950 on Van Gelder; 100 numbered copies on Japan vellum.

Content: The poem "The Lost Leader" by Rosamund Marriott Watson appears
opposite the title page. In his foreword, Mosher extensively quotes Henley's
comments to Henley's revised edition (*Poems*. London: David Nutt, 1898), and
Mosher notes in his 1910 catalogue that these poems were taken from "Henley's poems as revised and arranged by him in his edition of 1898."

The text was first reprinted by Mosher in his January 1902 issue of *The Bibelot*
(25).

Comment: This is the fourth volume in the Lyric Garland Series devoted to
Henley's poems. See entries 99, 165 & 323 for the other Henley Lyric Garlands. These four titles were also sold in a box slipcase with label printed in
red & black titling the contents as the "Collected Poems of W. E. Henley."

219. *LONG AGO* By Michael Field. 1897.   112 pp. (in Roman numerals); front.
The Bibelot Series-9   H 36.   Only edition.

925 on Van Gelder; 100 numbered copies on Japan vellum.
First American edition.

Content: This volume is a direct adaptation of the first and only edition of the
work. Published in London (George Bell & Sons, 1889) and limited to 100
copies. Mosher reprinted all 68 poems from that edition. A note about the
cover and frontispiece illustrations appears on p. [*cix*].

Comment: Michael Field is the pseudonym of two English
authors of lyric poetry and poetic dramas, Katherine Harris
Bradley and her niece, Edith Emma Cooper. Krishnamurti
included a copy of this book in the "Women Writers of the
1890's" exhibit held at Southern's of London, 1991, and
identified it as the First American edition.

Design: The cover design incorporates the head of Sappho
within a circle. The portrait appeared on the original 1889

LONG AGO (continued)

edition, and was itself taken from a vase nearly contemporary with Sappho's time. The frontispiece is reproduced from a figure of Sappho on a vase in the museum at Athens, and is also identical to the one used in the 1889 British edition. Title page in red and black with Minoan sea wave design below title. This publication is a prime example of both a textual *and* graphic "piracy," given a new format for an American audience.

Reference: Krishnamurti, p. 44; Vilain 4 (plate 6); Grigsby 389.

---

220. OLIVE SCHREINER ***THE LOST JOY AND OTHER DREAMS***. 1909.   Limitation unknown for both Van
    viii, 84 pp.   Gelder and Japan vellum copies.
    Vest Pocket Series-18   H 471.   Only edition.

Content: This is a reprint of eight selections taken from eleven prose poems in Schreiner's *Dreams* (London: T. Fisher Unwin, 1891). The foreword is by the publisher. A stanza from Swinburne is printed opposite the title page.

---

221. ***LOVE IN THE VALLEY*** by George Meredith. [April] 1910.   *viii*, 24, [1] pp.   925 on van Gelder; 100 on Japan
    Golden Text Series-5   H 513.   Only edition.   vellum.

Content: The foreword (pp. *v*-[*viii*]) is composed of excerpts from George Macaulay Trevelyan's *The Poetry and Philosophy of George Meredith* (London: Constable, 1906). Another excerpt from Trevelyan also appears on p. [18]. Selections from *Richard Feverel* appear opposite the title page and head the first stanza on p. 3.

Mosher reprinted both the text of the 1878 revised version (pp. [1]-[16]), and of the original 1851 version (pp. [17-24]) as it appeared among the "Pastorals" in the 1851 *Poems* (London: John W. Parker and Son). The revised and final version first appeared in *Macmillan's Magazine* for October 1878; however, Mosher used it as reprinted in Meredith's *Poems and Lyrics of the Joy of Earth* (London: Macmillan, 1883). A bibliographical statement appears on p. [2] and notes the stanzas have been numbered "for convenience in comparing the earlier form with this final recension." The two versions of 1878 and 1851 are numbered up to XXVI and XI respectively.

Reference: See Collie, p. 126; Quinn 6434; Jenkinson II, 762.

---

222. ***THE LOVE SONNETS OF PROTEUS*** by Wilfrid Scawen Blunt. 1904.   925 on Van Gelder; 100 numbered
    xii, 153. [1] pp.   copies on Japan vellum.
    Old World Series-33   H 282.   Only edition.

Content: Mosher indicates in a bibliographical note to *The Bibelot* for 1905 that "this editions follows the complete Kelmscott text [of 1892] giving in all 142 sonnets."

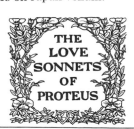

223. *LUCRETIUS ON LIFE AND DEATH* in the Metre of Omar Khayyám. By W. H. Mallock. 1919.   *xxiv*, 72 pp.   17.5 x 11.5 cm. Miscellaneous Series-88   H 668.   Only edition.

925 on Van Gelder; 25 numbered copies on Japan vellum.

Content: The 117 quatrains are taken from the final version (London: A. & C. Black, 1900) including the preface and the parallel passages translated from the original Latin text. Following the text are parallel Latin and English translations from *De Rerum Natura*, the passages after which Mallock's quatrains were formed. Contains a bibliographical note on pp. [69-72].

Mosher first printed this work in the January and February 1911 issues of *The Bibelot* (34).

Comment: W. H. Mallock is the pen name for William Hurrell.

Binding & Embellishment: Bound in blue paper boards with scored bands across the spine and going onto the front and back covers; label on the spine. Japan vellum copies are bound in Japan vellum boards. The blind-stamped circular design on the front cover is from the designs by Dante Gabriel Rossetti for Swinburne's *Songs before Sunrise*, (London: F. S. Ellis, 1871). For other Rossetti book designs, see entries 323, 325, 364 & 402. Title page printed in red and black; Chiswick head- and tail-pieces.

Reference: Warren, p. [201].

224. ROBERT BROWNING *LYRIC LOVE*. 1910.   *viii*, 88 pp. Vest Pocket Series-19   H 508.   Only edition.

Limitation unknown for both Van Gelder and Japan vellum copies.

Content: This volumes includes 37 selections from Robert Browning's poems, opening with an invocation and closing with an epilogue. There are two additional selections on p. [*ii*], and one on p. 86. There is also a table of contents on pp. *v*-[*vi*], and an index to first lines on pp. 87-[88].

225. *LYRICAL POEMS* by Lucy Lyttelton. 1912.   *viii*, 52, [1] pp. Lyric Garland Series-25   H 564.   Only edition.

950 on Van Gelder paper; 50 numbered copies on Japan vellum. First edition.

Content: According to the 1912 Mosher catalogue, "this little volume is the first bearing her [Lyttelton's] name and is issued under copyright arrangement with the author."—p. 44. The volume contains 32 titled poems, plus one untitled poem on p. [*v*].

Comment: Lucy Lyttelton is the pseudonym of Lucy Blanche Masterman, a poet who was introduced to Mosher through her friend, Katherine (Tynan) Hinkson. Mosher paid Lyttelton $25 to publish her book in America.

Reference: Boss XIII 148; correspondence from Tynan and Lyttleton is at the Houghton Library, bMS Am 1096); see the Nov. 17, 1941 letter from Lamb to Yorke for Mosher's payment terms (see Appendix II).

226. *LYRICAL POEMS* by Percy Bysshe Shelley. 1910.   *viii*, 60, [1] pp. Lyric Garland Series-20   H 512.   Only edition.

950 on Van Gelder paper; 50 numbered copies on Japan vellum.

Content: The volume contains a selection of 29 poems by Shelley. The poem "The Centenary of Shelley / July 22, 1892" by A. C. Swinburne appears on p. [5]. An index to first lines appears on pp. 59-[60].

227. *LYRICS* by Arthur Symons. [October] 1903.
viii, 37, [1] pp. (same for second ed.)
Lyric Garland Series-3   H 262.   First edition.

950 on Van Gelder paper for each edition. For the first edition, 100 numbered copies on Japan vellum; 10 numbered copies on Roman vellum, signed by the publisher.

Content: In his 1903 catalogue Mosher indicates that the first section of these poems was "reprinted with Mr. Symons' permission, from his *Collected Poems* of last year [Heinemann, 1902]." The poem "Fountain Court *à Arthur Symons*" appears in French and is signed "Paul Verlaine, Londres, November, 1894."

Comment: Mosher first listed this book in 1902 under the Miscellaneous Series; however, in the next catalogue for 1903, *The Lyric Garland Series* was created and the title was transferred to it. The format and cover did not change when the title was transferred. Mosher also printed these selection in his April 1903 *The Bibelot* (26).

Reference: Beckson A14a & b; Quinn 9772 , 9773, 9803 & 12027; Colbeck II, p. 820 (34).

227.1. *LYRICS* by Arthur Symons. [October] 1907.
Lyric Garland Series.   H 426   Second edition.

228. *LYRICS AND SONNETS* by Arthur Upson. 1909.
vi, 33 pp.   15.5 x 11.5 cm.
Privately Printed-12   H 714.   Only edition.

25 numbered copies on Japan vellum.

Content: This book includes 21 of the 26 poems included in the Lyric Garland Series edition of Arthur Upson's *Sonnets and Songs*, 1911 (see 373). The foreword, and the poem on p. [2], are signed R. S. P. (Ruth Shepard Phelps). The text of this work was printed by Mosher in his March 1909 issue of *The Bibelot* (32). A bibliography appears on p. [33].

Comment: Ruth Phelps was paid $25 for the right to reprint these sonnets.

Binding & Embellishment: Bound in flexible Japan vellum boards with yapp top and fore-edges; title/author on spine and front cover; red Chiswick initial on the front cover. Title page printed in red and black; Chiswick tail-pieces.

See *Celtic...* (entry 58) for a similarly bound and limited private printing.

Reference: Vilain 49, and p. 99, plate 51; Phelps, p. 158; see the Nov. 17, 1941 letter from Lamb to Yorke for Mosher's payment terms (see Appendix II).

229. *LYRICS FROM A LIBRARY* By Clinton Scollard. [October] 1917.
viii, 52, [1] pp.
Lyra Americana Series-4   H 656.   Only edition.

450 on Van Gelder; 25 on Japan vellum.

Content: This book of 32 poems was revised by the author from the Clinton, New York edition (G. W. Browning, [1913]) for inclusion in Mosher's reprint in the Lyra Americana Series. Two additional, untitled poems appear on pp. [*vii*] and [52].

Comment: Scollard was paid a 10% royalty on copies sold.

Binding & Embellishment: The Van Gelder copies are bound in quarter gray paper over patterned paper boards exhibiting a field of hearts with crisscrossing dots. See series in Section I for further details.

Reference: See the Nov. 17, 1941 letter from Lamb to Yorke for Mosher's payment terms (see Appendix II).

M

230. *MAGIC IN KENSINGTON GARDENS AND OTHER NATURE ESSAYS*
from the Literary Contributions of James Douglas chosen by T. B. M.
[October] 1916.   *xi*, 50, [1] pp.   18.5 x 9.5 cm.
Miscellaneous Series-77   H 636.   Only edition.

950 on Van Gelder; 25 numbered copies on Japan vellum. First edition.

Content: The foreword is signed by the publisher who selected these essays from from Douglas' journalistic work, but he offers no further information. In addition to the title essay, this book contains "A Mood without a Moral," "Kew in Flower," "In Nubibus," and "An Autumnal Idyll."

Three of these nature essays, including the title essay, were previously printed in the November 1912 issue of *The Bibelot* (35).

Binding & Embellishment: Bound in quarter blue paper over patterned boards with white spine label, and uniform with *The Last Christmas Tree* (189). The cover design by Lucien Pissarro was taken from the 1902 Eragny Press edition of *Peau D'Ane*. The same cover design is used on the Japan vellum copy as a wrapper around boards. Title page in red and black; Chiswick ornaments; some lead initial letters in red outline. For other books using Eragny Press & Lucien Pissarro designs, see entry 52.

231. *MARIUS THE EPICUREAN HIS SENSATIONS AND IDEAS*
by Walter Pater. Volume I. 1900.   *xxvi*, 211 pp.; port. front.
Quarto Series-2   H 157.   Only edition.

450 on Van Gelder; 25 numbered & signed on Japan vellum; 4 numbered copies on vellum also signed by the publisher.

Content: The text for this reprint is from the first edition of *Marius the Epicurean* (London: Macmillan and Co., 1885). The foreword (pp. [*IX*]-*XXVI*) is by William Marion Reedy. The critical "Note" (Vol. II, pp. [203]-209) by Richard Le Gallienne favors the text of the first edition, certainly one of the factors contributing to, or at least confirming, Mosher's decision to reprint the first, rather than a later edition. Mosher's brief bibliographic notes appear in Vol. I, p. [*VIII*] and in Volume II, p. [202]. A portrait frontispiece of Pater, printed on Japan vellum, is included in Vol. I

Ransom devotes one entry for both volumes, and notes that this is "the text of the first edition, with a foreword by William Marion Reedy and a note [vol. II, pp. 201-209] taken from Richard Le Gallienne's *Retrospective Reviews*." In his bibliography on Pater, Franklin Court further specifies that Le Gallienne's contribution from *Retrospective Reviews*... (London: John Lane; New York: Dodd, Mead, 1896) "was apparently first published in Oct. 1892. Its place of publication has not been determined however."

According to Mosher in his 1900 catalogue, the model for this and the following volume (232) is the work of the Chiswick Press of London. Two chapters from *Marius* were later printed by Mosher in his October 1912 issue of *The Bibelot* (35), while Chapter 12 was printed in the April 1895 issue (18).

This is the only volume in the Quarto Series with a colophon. It indicates that these volumes were printed by Thurston Print in Portland, ME.

Design: Mosher identified the graphic embellishments as "an entirely original set of head-bands [i.e., head-pieces], tail-pieces and rubricated initials." They are not signed, nor is the designer identified, but the head- and tail-pieces are most likely the work of Edward B. Edwards, a process engraver for De Vinne's

MARIUS THE EPICUREAN (continued)

shop in New York. Its style is identical to the head-pieces and letter designs in: *A Translation of Giovanni Boccaccio's Life of Dante* (New York: The Grolier Club, 1900). Edwards is credited with the Dante's cover design, and he may be the designer of the interior designs as well. These designs, in turn, very closely match those of *Marius the Epicurean*. For other designs attributed to Edwards, see 108, 132, 232, 321 & 342.

Reference: Wright, p. 163 (see also Section I , "a 36"); Vilain 54; Quinn 7588; Grigsby 897 & 898; Ransom 262; Court 73.

232. *MARIUS THE EPICUREAN HIS SENSATIONS AND IDEAS*
by Walter Pater.   Volume II.   1900.   *vi*, 209, [1] pp.
Quarto Series-3   H 158.   Only edition.

450 on Van Gelder; 25 numbered & signed on Japan vellum; 4 numbered copies on vellum also signed by the publisher.

Content: See description to 231.

Design: The original head-pieces, tail-pieces, and large decorative initials, are not signed, but on stylistic grounds, may be the work of Edward B. Edwards (see discussion above under 231). For other Edwards designs, see discussion under "Design" in entry 231.

233. *MARJORIE FLEMING* by John Brown, M.D. [September] 1899.
66, [1] pp. (same through fourth ed.)
Brocade Series-18   H 116.   First edition.

425 on Japan vellum for each edition.

Content: This portrait of a little girl was first published in 1860. The poem accompanying the work, "To Dr. John Brown" by Algernon Charles Swinburne, appears on p. [5].

Comment: This volume appears as one of three in a sub-series called "Three Idyls of Childhood by John Brown, M.D." The others in this grouping include: *Rab and His Friends* (318), and *Queen Mary's Child-Garden* (340). The latter work is paired with Richard Jefferies' *Saint Guido* and therefore appears in two different sub-series (see note to 340).

233.1 *MARJORIE FLEMING* by John Brown, M.D. [January] 1900.
Brocade Series.   H 179.   Second edition.

233.2 *MARJORIE FLEMING* by John Brown, M.D. [January] 1903.
Brocade Series.   H 276.   Third edition.

233.3 *MARJORIE FLEMING* by John Brown, M.D. [March] 1907.
Brocade Series.   H 415.   Fourth edition.

233.4 *MARJORIE FLEMING* by John Brown, M.D. [December] 1912.
67, [1] pp.
Brocade Series.   H 576.   Fifth edition.

234. *A MASQUE OF DEAD FLORENTINES* by Maurice Hewlett.
1911.   *viii*, 50, [1] pp.
Venetian Series-4   H 542.   Only edition.

Limitation unknown for both Van Gelder and Japan vellum copies. First American book edition.

Content: The foreword is by the publisher. The text is from the first edition (London: Dent, 1895). Mosher's edition was printed without the J. D. Batten illustrations. Bibliographical note on p. 49

A MASQUE OF DEAD FLORENTINES (continued)

The text of this work was also printed by Mosher in his January & February 1904 issues of *The Bibelot* (27).

Reference: Vilain 45 (plate 48, p. 98); Quinn 4131; *DLB* XXXIV, p. 189.

---

235. **MASTERPIECES** selected from the work written by the girls of The Misses Masters' School   Dobbs Ferry on Hudson. 1912.

    xv, 126, [1] pp.   19.5 x 14 cm.

Privately Printed-15   H 717.   First thus.

600 on Van Gelder paper.

Content: Consists of a brief dedication, an "Appreciation," and 47 prose and poetic contributions from the young women at the school. Three photo-illustrations accompany the text. A bookplate, designed by Euphame Mallison, is mounted inside the front cover of all copies examined.

Comment: Privately printed for The Misses Masters' School.

Binding & Embellishment: Bound in decorated Japan vellum boards printed in purple; title printed directly on the spine and front cover. The design on the front cover shows a youth perched on an oak limb playing the panpipes. This same unattributed design also appears on the back cover of Munthe's *For Those Who Love Music* (see 115), on the cover and the title page of *The Children's Crusade* (66), and on the title page of the 1909 catalogue (see 253). Title page printed in red and black; Chiswick ornaments and initial letters; pages ruled in black.

Reference: Vilain 50.

---

236. **MASTERPIECES   A DOBBS BOOK OF VERSE** by Students and Alumnae of The Misses Masters' School   Dobbs Ferry on the Hudson. 1917

    xv, 112, [1] pp.   21.1 x 13.8 cm.

Privately Printed-42   H 743.   First thus.

350 copies on Italian (Tuscany) hand-made paper.

Content: Consists of a brief dedication, an "Appreciation," a poem "To The Builders," and 93 poems by the school's students. A "Dobbs-The Misses Masters" bookplate, designed by Euphame Mallison, is mounted inside of the front cover of all copies examined.

Comment: Privately printed for The Misses Masters' School.

Binding & Embellishment: Bound in quarter white Fabriano paper spine over lavender paper boards with slightly raised bands and title label on the spine. Chiswick ornaments.

---

237. **MAURICE DE GUÉRIN** by Matthew Arnold. [July] 1903.

    76, [1] pp.

Brocade Series-37   H 251.   Only edition.

425 on Japan vellum for this edition.

Content: Mosher indicates in his foreword that this work and related studies (59, 105 & 237) were taken from Matthew Arnold's *Essays in Criticism* (First Series), but he does not cite the exact imprint.

Comment: This volume along with two others form a sub-series (see entry 59).

238. *MEMORIES OF PRESIDENT LINCOLN AND OTHER LYRICS OF THE WAR* by Walt Whitman. 1904.   *xiii*, 41 pp.; port. front.   17.5 x 14 cm.
Miscellaneous Series-26   H 287.   First edition.

50 numbered copies on Japan vellum only.

Content: This volume includes four poems from the grouping "Memories of President Lincoln" as found in the Boston *Leaves of Grass* (Osgood, 1881-2) and seven selections called "Lyrics from Drum-Taps and Songs of Parting" from *Drum Taps* (New York, 1865) and its sequel (*When Lilacs Last in the Door-Yard Bloom'd*. Washington, 1865-6).

This title was printed mostly from the plates of the August 1904 *The Bibelot* (27) with some changes. The foreword is by Horace Traubel with a bibliographical addition signed by the publisher. Selections from several other authors are also present: James Russell Lowell (p. [*v*]), John Burroughs (p. [2]), and Oscar Lovell Triggs (p. [22]).

Comment: The 1863 "war time" photo of Walt Whitman is used as the frontispiece.

The privately printed *Concerning a Pilgrimage to the Grave of Edward FitzGerald* (75) became a model for what may be stylistically looked upon as a sub-series within the Miscellaneous Series. These thin Mosher books are all the same size, bound in Japan vellum covers with yapp top and fore-edges, the title printed in black on the spine, and the title/author printed in black on the upper left corner of the front cover with first letter a red Chiswick drop-cap initial. They are all limited to just 50 copies on Japan vellum, and all (except for the initial model) appear to be printed from the plates in *The Bibelot*, with some changes. The books in this Miscellaneous "sub-series" are:

1904	*Memories of President Lincoln* (entry 238)	
1905	*Lecture on English Renaissance* (193)	
1907	*A Defence of Poetry* (85)	
1908	*The Hound of Heaven* (155)	
1909	*A Vision of Love Revealed in Sleep* (429)	
1912	*Il Pesceballo: Opera in One Act* (288)	

Reference: Myerson C 16.I; Quinn 11003; the mss. foreword by Traubel is at The Houghton Library, bMS Am 1096).

239. *MEMORIES OF PRESIDENT LINCOLN AND OTHER LYRICS OF THE WAR* by Walt Whitman. [September] 1912.
2 *p. l.*, *xii*, 13 numbered *l.*, 1 *l.*, [15]-16, [1] pp.   30 x 22.5 cm.
Miscellaneous Series-59   H 559.   New edition/same series.

300 on Italian handmade paper; 50 on Japan vellum; 10 on Roman vellum, numbered and signed by the publisher.

Content: The volume includes Whitman's "When Lilacs Last in the Dooryard Bloom'd," "O Captain! My Captain," "Hush'd Be the Camps To-day," and "This Dust was Once the Man." In addition, Lincoln's Gettysburg Address, a foreword by Horace Traubel, selections from an address by Frederick W. Lehman, selections from John Burroughs, an appreciation by William Marion Reedy, and a passage from Lowell's "Commemoration Ode" are also included. A bibliographical note appears on pp. [14]-16. The frontispiece portrait of Lincoln was taken from an original photograph and is the size as the original negative.

This work was printed by Mosher in his August 1904 issue of *The Bibelot* (27).

Comment: The 1912 Mosher catalogue mentions "taken as a whole this may be considered one of Mr. Mosher's choicest productions." Norman Strouse calls the book "an outstanding piece of fine printing, little known today and seldom to be found."

MEMORIES OF PRESIDENT LINCOLN (continued)

Binding & Embellishment: The Italian paper copies are bound in olive green Fabriano boards with title printed in dark green on the spine and front cover. The Japan vellum copies are bound in stiff Japan vellum boards with the same titling. The vellum copies are bound in Classic vellum. A regular Italian "Fabriano" paper copy bound in Japan vellum boards is in the Portland Public Library, and another regular copy in green boards without the title printed in large letters on the front cover is in the Bishop Collection. The printer's dummy for this book is in the Vilain-Wieck Collection.

The leaves of the Roman vellum copy are made of unusually thick and stiff vellum. The book's title is gilt-stamped at the top of the front cover, with green ties running through the vellum covers. It is also interesting to note that the large green drop cap "W" from the foreword (on p. *ix*) and on p. 1 of the Van Gelder copies are different in the Japan vellum and vellum copies.

The title page is printed in black and green with a large William Morris initial "M" as used in the Kelmscott Press edition of *Defense of Guenevere*; 14-point old-style Roman type is used throughout. The decorative head-piece on p. *ix*, and repeated on p. [2], also appears on the front covers of *Garlands and Wayfarings* (126) and the *Songs of the Susquehanna* (371). The triangular vine, leaf and bud tail-pieces are Goudy-like designs. The same design is found on the front cover of McGaffey's *Sonnets to a Wife* (Saint Louis: Reedy, 1901), but the same kind of work also appears in Fletcher's *English Bookbindings in The British Museum* (London: Kegan Paul, Trench, Trubner and Co., 1896) which suggests a British origin (possibly by Laurence Housman).

For other books using Kelmscott Press & William Morris designs, see entry 74.

Reference: Myerson C 30.I.a-c; Vilain 21 (plate 29, p. 91); Quinn 11024 (incorrectly indicates one of 7 copies on vellum) & 11025; Strouse, p. 57; Grolier, p. 36.

——————— *Same Title, Change of Series* ———————

240. ***MEMORIES OF PRESIDENT LINCOLN AND OTHER LYRICS OF THE WAR*** by Walt Whitman. [October] 1906.   *xii*, 43, [1] pp. (same for second ed.)
Lyric Garland Series-10   H 359.   First edition.

950 copies on Van Gelder for each edition. For the first edition, 100 numbered copies on Japan vellum; 7 numbered copies on Roman vellum, signed by the publisher.

Content: The content also includes a selection from James Russell Lowell opposite the title page, a bibliographical note on p. [*viii*], a foreword by Horace Traubel, and a brief statement by the publisher. A selection from John Burroughs appears on p. [2].

Reference: Myerson C 16.2.a-d; Quinn 11014 & 11015.

240.1 ***MEMORIES OF PRESIDENT LINCOLN AND OTHER LYRICS OF THE WAR*** by Walt Whitman. [May] 1912.
Lyric Garland Series.   H 584.   Second edition.

241. ***MICHAEL ANGELO BUONARROTI HIS SONNETS*** Now for the first time translated into rhymed English by John Addington Symonds. 1895.   109, [1] pp. (in Roman numerals); front.
The Bibelot Series-5   H 9.   Only edition.

725 on Van Gelder; 50 on Japan vellum.
First American edition of this translation.

MICHAEL ANGELO BUONARROTI (continued)

Content: The publisher's bibliographical note on p. *x* indicates that the text for this reprint was taken both from the original London edition (Smith Elder, 1878) and from Symonds' *Life of Michelangelo Buonarroti* (London: Nimmo, 1893) with textual revisions. Some copies have a facsimile of a page from Symonds' manuscript printed on Japan vellum and tipped in between pp. [*viii* and *ix*]. In addition to the "proem" and the 77 sonnets, there are seven pages of notes, a sonnet deciphered by V. de Tivoli, a madrigal, a quatrain, and a stanza by Michael Angelo.

Comment: According to the 1895 Mosher catalogue "a portrait of Vittoria Colonna has been given in artotype from a design by Michael Angelo that was reproduced in the *Gazette des Beaux-Arts* for 1875." See entry 376 for an Old World Series version .

The cover's floral design is also found on the cover of *A Free Man's Worship* (119).

Reference: *DLB* LVII, p. 321; Babington 489.

---

242. ***MIMES WITH A PROLOGVE AND EPILOGVE* by Marcel Schwob...**
Done into English by A. Lenalie. 1901.
xxviii, 97, [1] pp.; port. front   21 x 13 cm.
Miscellaneous Series-17   H 186.   Only edition.

500 on Van Gelder; 50 numbered & signed copies on Japan vellum; 6 on Roman vellum and signed by the publisher.
First edition of this translation.

Content: The volume includes the 20 mimes, prologue, and epilogue from the French edition, plus one mime not in the French edition of *Mimes: avec un prologue et un epilogue* (Paris: Mercure de France, 1894). The added mime, "Sismé" (pp. 53-55), appears here for the first time. It was originally added by Schwob to a presentation copy for William Morris, and is now placed alongside Mime XV as per the author's wishes. The foreword (pp. *xiii-xxviii*) is by the translator, Aimee Lenalie (pseudonym of Mosher's first wife, Ellie Dresser). A bibliographical note appears on p. [88], followed by a biographical note on the author which concludes the book (pp. 89-[97]). A brief selection from Oscar Wilde is found on p. [*xii*].

In his 1901 catalogue Mosher proudly mentions the author's approval of the translation "submitted before publication." In the 1901 Autumn List of Books sent to booksellers, he quotes from a May 24, [1901] letter received from Schwob (now at The Houghton Library, bMS Am 1096 [1403]):

> I have received a letter from Miss A. Lenalie in which she begs me to refer to you relatively [sic] to a proposed publication of my *Mimes* in America. The specimens Miss Lenalie has sent to me are quite masterly indeed; and it shall give me the greatest pleasure to be recalled to the minds of my American readers who may have seen *The Children's Crusade...* I hereby fully authorize Miss Lenalie and you to bring out the book under a form in which I feel a perfect trust.

Comment: See Sharp for contemporary praise of the book's form, and critical remarks with regard to the translation. Lenalie also translated Schwob's *R.L.S.' An Essay* (325), "Tell Me, Mamore" by Francis Jammes appearing in both The Mosher Books catalogue for 1909 (253) and in the *Amphora* (2), and lastly Verlaine's poem "A Une Femme" from his *Poèmes Saturniens* which appears as a supplement to *The Bibelot*, Vol. IV, No. 2, for February 1898 (21).

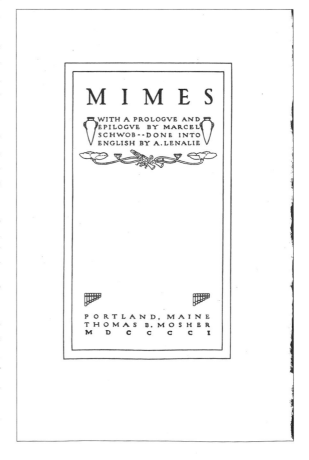

MIMES WITH A PROLOGVE AND EPILOGVE (continued)

The following inscription appears in a copy once owned by John Quinn, now located at The Free Library of Philadelphia:

> Fiona Macleod has written Mr. Mosher that a creative translation like this of *Mimes* is almost as difficult a task as that set Liban by Oisin in the Land of the Ever-Living, when he bade her take a wave from the shores and a green blade from the grass and a leaf from a tree and the breath of the wind and a man's sigh and a woman's thought, and out of them [all] make an air that would be like the single song of a bird... I can think of no sentiment more beautiful as an inscription from the translator, Aimeé Lenalie.

The spelling of Prologue and Epilogue with a "v" rather than a "u" is an historical affectation. The frontispiece oval portrait of Schwob is a reproduction of a lithograph drawn by Theodore F. Spicer Simson of Paris.

Aimee Lenalie was paid $90 for this translation.

Binding & Embellishment: Both the Van Gelder and the Japan vellum copies are bound in Japan vellum wraps over boards printed in gold and violet. There are two states of the front cover. The one uses a bluer purplish ink and the space between the outer and inner lines of the ring remain uncolored (the earliest printed vellum copies appear this way). On the other, most likely the second state, the flowers are colored in a red purplish ink and the ring connecting the two thorny plant stems is printed in color. Title page printed in red and black; red Chiswick lead initials used throughout.

The attractive art nouveau cover of gold and violet is by Earl Stetson Crawford according to the 1901 Mosher catalogue. The art nouveau title page design is signed "C" which Crichton correctly attributes to Cleland. For other Crawford designs used, see entry 88. For other Cleland designs used, see entry 6.

See color illustration on p. 369 (Plate 5).

Reference: Sharp, p. 333; *DLB* CXXIII, p. 242; Boss XIII 150; Vilain 17 (plate 25, p. 90); Crichton 45 and plate on p. 74; Quinn 8518-8521; Grigsby 993-995. See the Nov. 17, 1941 letter from Lamb to Yorke for Mosher's payment terms (see Appendix II).

---

243. ***MIMMA BELLA: IN MEMORY OF A LITTLE LIFE*** by Eugene Lee-Hamilton.
[August] 1909.   *vii*, 21, [1] l.   14.5 x 12 cm.
Miscellaneous Series-45   H 468.   Only edition.

900 on Van Gelder; 50 numbered copies on Japan vellum.

Content: The source for this book is *The Fortnightly Review* (November 1907). The signed foreword is by the publisher. The text was printed by Mosher in his June 1908 issue of *The Bibelot* (31). Mrs. Annie E. Holdsworth, the widow of the author, made alterations and returned proofs to Mosher with the comment: "the sonnets came from his heart broken by the death of our only child; and he only lived to correct the proofs for the Fortnightly." (July 10, 1909 letter at The Houghton Library, bMS Am 1096 [662]).

Comment: The following gives a glimpse into the lengths to which Mosher would go to accommodate authors (or their relatives), and the impediments he would encounter. In a June 15, 1909 letter (The Houghton Library, bMS Am 1096 [660]) addressed to Mosher, Eugene Lee-Hamilton's widow asks

> ...if it would not be possible for you to give me some monetary recognition for the Editions of his Sonnets you have recently issued—*Sonnets of the Wingless Hours*, and *Mimma Bella*. In case of the latter your issue put an end to an arrangement

MIMMA BELLA: IN MEMORY OF A LITTLE LIFE (continued)

all but concluded with an American firm; and in addition made the English publisher reluctant to touch a book the sales of which have been spoiled in the countries. This has meant a very serious loss to me; and I am dependent on my own & my husband's work.

In the July 10 letter cited above, Mrs. Holdsworth mentions how touched she is by the kindness of Mosher in wishing to meet her wishes with regard to *Mimma Bella*, but later correspondence shows that the London publisher was dead set against Mosher's publications and refused to allow her to conclude arrangements with Mosher. *Mimma Bella* was finally published in London by William Heinemann in 1909, the same year as Mosher's publication.

Binding & Embellishment: Both the Van Gelder and the Japan vellum copies are bound in flexible Japan vellum boards with yapp fore-edges. The title page is printed in red and black, and the pages are ruled in black throughout. Text pages are printed on the recto side only.

The scroll design on the front cover is by Herbert P. Horne, originally appearing on the title page of Selwyn Image's *Poems and Carols* published by Elkin Mathews (London, 1894) and printed at the Chiswick Press. For designs by Horne used elsewhere, see entry 171.

---

244. *MODERN LOVE* By George Meredith with Foreword by E. Cavazza.
 1891.   4 *l.*, *xvi* pp., 50 *l.*, [1] p.
 English Reprint Series-1   H 1.   First thus.

Content: A publisher's note appears opposite the limitation page, and a brief selection from the *Book of the Sages* appears opposite the opening lines. Mosher's reprint was extracted from the larger first edition entitled *Modern Love and Poems of the English Roadside* (London: Chapman & Hall, 1862). The foreword is by Elisabeth Cavazza.

The poetry is printed on the recto side of the leaves.

Comment: This is the first book published by Mosher.

Elisabeth Cavazza (Portland-born Elisabeth Jones) wrote verse, sketches, and book and music reviews for the *Portland Press*. She moved to Italy after marrying Signor Nino Cavazza in 1885, and after his death, returned to Portland where she married Stanley Pullen, owner and editor of the *Portland Press*. She also authored *Don Finimondone; Calabrian Sketches* (New York, 1892), and *Mr. Whitman; a Story of the Brigands* (Boston, 1902), and an earlier parody on Swinburne in *Algernon in London* (Portland, ME, 1880).

Laid in a copy of the 1862 Chapman & Hall edition of *Modern Love* was a three-page autograph letter from George Meredith to T.B. Mosher with regard to Mosher's edition of this book (Grigsby Catalogue). The letter was written March 24, 1892 and states, in part:

> I have received the copy of Modern Love, & my previous letter has come to your hands, I may suppose. Your edition of the work is most creditable. In England the sumptuous edition is devoted only to very favourite writers. I cannot say it [is] generally an example of refinement. One has to look to France for an equal to your production; & there seems a probability that Americans will rival the French in the issues of books that honour their stands.

This letter is also quoted in Forman's bibliography on Meredith, and later belonged to Emilié Grigsby. In another letter from Meredith to Frederick

400 numbered small paper copies on Van Gelder; 40 numbered large paper copies on Van Gelder; 10 numbered copies on Japan vellum, signed by the publisher.
First American edition.

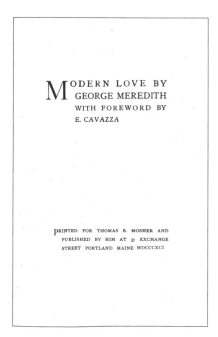

M ODERN LOVE BY
  GEORGE MEREDITH
  WITH FOREWORD BY
  E. CAVAZZA

PRINTED FOR THOMAS B. MOSHER AND
PUBLISHED BY HIM AT 37 EXCHANGE
STREET PORTLAND MAINE MDCCCXCI

MODERN LOVE (continued)

Chapman dated two days earlier, Meredith records his concern for Mosher's book selling in England:

> ...the man Mosher of Maine sent me a copy of the book. The selling of it over here is imprudent, and we might try to stop it, but why should the bother of it fall upon you? I fancy that some labour is involved in defeating these fellows, and if there is cost as well, the sale of my poetry would not cover the outlay.
>
> *(Letters*, ii, 451)

Another entry in the Grigsby catalogue includes a letter from Meredith to Mosher which eventually ended up in the hands of Norman Strouse. On March 3, 1892, Meredith writes:

> Sir, a handsome pirate is always half pardoned, and in this case he has broken only the upper laws. I shall receive with pleasure the copy of 'Modern Love' which you propose to send. I have it much at heart that works of mine should be read by Americans. Very truly yours, George Meredith.

This letter went from the Grigsby sale (1912) to the Jerome Kern sale (1929), to the Mosher sale (1948) where it was purchased by Norman Strouse, and is now at the Gleeson Library, University of San Francisco.

For advertisement purposes, Mosher gathered and printed the opinions of several bibliophiles in the fall of 1892. Among these were the comments of America's master printer, Theodore Low DeVinne, in a Dec. 23, 1891 letter to Mosher: "I am well pleased with your book. The composition and press work are well done." In the same letter DeVinne also points out that "the only fault I had to find with it was the tightness of the case in which the book was held, but that is quite a small matter." (Bishop Collection)

Binding: In what was to become a characteristic style, the binding (for both the small and large paper copies) is Japan vellum wrappers folded over boards, printed in black on the spine, and in red and black on the front cover. An early Portland newspaper review (Mosher's scrapbook in the Bishop Collection) cites Mr. Almus D. Butler of Portland as the binder. Printed dust wrapper.

Reference: *DLB* LVII, p. 173; Boss XIII 250; Vilain 1 (plate 4); Esdaile, p. 40; Grigsby 772, 786; Collie XXXVII b (see also p. 145); Forman (9) on pp. 31-32; DeVinne 1386; *CBEL* III, p. 468; Altschul, p. 84. For the standard edition of Meredith's letters, see Cline, letters 1405, 1408 & 1399.

———————— *Same Title, Change of Series* ————————

245. ***MODERN LOVE AND OTHER POEMS*** by George Meredith.   925 on Van Gelder; 100 numbered
    1898.   *viii*, 141, [1] pp.   on Japan vellum.
    Old World Series-12   H 64.   First edition.

Content: This Old World Series imprint includes selections from *Modern Love and Poems of the English Roadside with Poems and Ballads* (London: Chapman & Hall, 1862), *Poems* (London: J. W. Parker, 1851), *Poems and Lyrics of the Joy of Earth* (London: Macmillan, 1883), and from *Ballads and Poems of Tragic Life* (London: Macmillan, 1887). Also includes a brief quote from the *Book of the Sages* (?).

Reference: Esdaile, p. 45; Collie XLIII b (also p. 145); Quinn 6360, 6361 & 11936; Grigsby 803.

245.1 *MODERN LOVE AND OTHER POEMS* by George Meredith.
1904.   *vi*, 143, [1] pp. (same for third ed.)
Old World Series.   H 302.   Second edition.

925 on Van Gelder. No Japan vellum copies were printed (same for third edition).

245.2 *MODERN LOVE AND OTHER POEMS* by George Meredith. 1910.
Old World Series.   H 521.   Third edition.

246. *MONNA INNOMINATA SONNETS AND SONGS* by Christina G. Rossetti.
1899.   *viii*, 94, [1] pp.
Old World Series-17   H 105.   First edition.

925 on Van Gelder; 100 numbered copies on Japan vellum.

Content: The volume consists of the following sections: the title work of 14 sonnets (preceded by a lengthy comment in italics), "Later Life—A Double Sonnet of Sonnets" of 28 sonnets, "Songs" of 20 poems, and "Sonnets" which includes 13 more sonnets. Mosher did not identify the precise source for this book.

Design: Based upon stylistic evidence, the cover design is most likely by Frederic Goudy. For other Goudy designs, see entry 1.

246.1 *MONNA INNOMINATA SONNETS AND SONGS* by Christina G. Rossetti.
1908.   *vi*, 96, [1] pp.
Old World Series.   H 447A.   Second edition.

925 on Van Gelder. No Japan vellum copies were printed.

Comment: This second edition was printed by George D. Loring of Portland, Maine rather than the usual printer, Smith & Sale.

This edition was not listed in the Hatch *Check List*, but was later added by Hatch in 1972 (see Vilain).

Reference: Vilain, p. 65; Boss XV 155.

THE MOSHER BOOKS.
See *A LIST OF BOOKS* for entries of earlier catalogues (entries 198-207).

247. *THE MOSHER BOOKS.* [October] 1903.   64 pp.   23 x 12 cm.
Catalogue.   H 264.   Eleventh catalogue.

Content: The unsigned foreword is by the publisher. Selections accompanying the catalogue (other than those quoted by Mosher under specific book entries):

– "A Closed Book" by William P. McKenzie
– Selections from "The Library" by John Greenleaf Whittier
– Quotation from Edmund Gosse
– Quotation from Dorothy Wordsworth
– Quotation from Rosemund Marriott Watson

Comment: First catalogue to carry the name "The Mosher Books".

Binding & Embellishment: Bound in charcoal green paper wrappers printed in red and dark green with a large anchor & dolphin on the front wrapper. Hardbound copies are in gray boards with printed labels on spine and front cover; original wrappers bound in the back. Printed in red and black throughout; Chiswick and other head- and tail-pieces.

248. **THE MOSHER BOOKS.** [October] 1904.   72 pp.   23 x 12 cm.
      Catalogue.   H 300.   Twelfth catalogue.

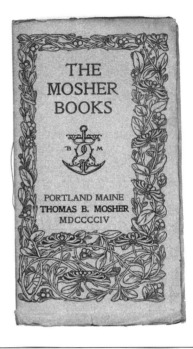

Content: The unsigned foreword is by the publisher. Selections accompanying the catalogue (other than those quoted by Mosher under specific book entries):

– Quotation from Andrew Lang
– Quotation from James John Garth Wilkinson
– Quotation from E. Nesbit
– Quotation from James Russell Lowell

Binding & Embellishment: Bound in charcoal blue wrappers printed in red and green with anchor & dolphin monogram of T.B.M. on the front cover. Hardbound copies in blue boards with printed labels on spine and front cover; original wrappers bound in back. Printed in red and black throughout; Chiswick and other head- and tail-pieces.

The cover design is by Charles Ricketts, taken from *The Poems of Sir John Suckling* (London: The Vale Press, 1896). For other publications using Vale Press & Charles Ricketts designs, see entry 47.

Reference: Vilain 62 (plate 64, p. 104).

249. **THE MOSHER BOOKS** A List of Books in Belles Lettres Issued in
      Choice and Limited Editions. [October] 1905.   64 pp.   24 x 14.5 cm.
      Catalogue.   H 333.   Thirteenth catalogue.

Content: The foreword is signed by the publisher. Selections accompanying the catalogue (other than those quoted by Mosher under specific book entries):

– Quotation from Cardinal Newman
– "Walt Whitman" by Edwin Arlington Robinson
– Quotation from A. Mary F. Robinson
– Quotation from Walt Whitman
– Quotation from John Todhunter
– Shoulder notes from Blake and Whitman

Binding & Embellishment: Bound in charcoal gray paper wrappers printed in red and black with large anchor & dolphin on the front cover. Hardbound copies are in gray boards with printed labels on spine and front cover; original wrappers bound in the back. There are also a few interleaved copies, as inscribed by Mosher in a copy at Yale:

> Mar. 3, 1906. Dear Mrs. Squire, I take pleasure in mailing you a copy of my Catalogue, of which I had a few interleaved and done up in old style boards. It may be of some use in keeping 'Notes' on the collection!

The unsigned "breasted griffins" head-piece on p. 5 is by Frank R. Rathbun of Auburn, NY, who designed T. B. Mosher's bookplate, and here uses design elements from the Mosher bookplate. For other Rathbun designs, see entry 107.

Printed in red and black throughout; Chiswick ornaments and lead letters.

250. **THE MOSHER BOOKS** A List of Books in Belles Lettres Issued in
      Choice and Limited Editions: Mdcccxci - Mdccccvi. [8 line unidentified
      quote on the title page]. [October] 1906.   68 pp.   24 x 15 cm.
      Catalogue.   H 368.   Fourteenth catalogue.

THE MOSHER BOOKS, 1906 (continued)

Content: The foreword is signed by the publisher. Selections accompanying the catalogue (other than those quoted by Mosher under specific book entries):

– "La Retraite" by John Addington Symonds
– Two quotations from J. W. Mackail
– Two quotations from John Davidson
– Quotation from Alfred J. Butler
– Quotation from John Meade Falkner
– Quotation from T. Sturge Moore
– Selection from *The Thread of Gold* by Arthur Christopher Benson

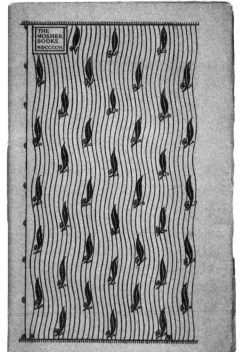

Binding & Embellishment: Bound in charcoal blue paper wrappers printed in green and red. Hardbound copies in blue boards with printed labels on spine and front cover; original wrappers and the Fall Season list bound in at the back. In some copies the cover in boards is backed with a white paper spine over blue boards, with only The Mosher Books and date found in the upper right-hand corner of the front cover. Some copies in boards come with a portrait frontispiece of T. B. Mosher. Printed in red and black throughout; ruled throughout in red; Chiswick ornaments and lead initials, and other fleuron ornaments.

The cover design is adopted from Charles Ricketts' cover for John Gray's *Silverpoints*. (London: Bodley Head, 1893). Mosher's adaptation adds five wavy lines, and an extra column of willow leaves. Expanding the design enabled him to better fill his standard size cover. Mosher also retained the monogram of Charles Ricketts, and the HLS monogram of Henry Leighton, sc. (i.e., the engraver), and inserted his catalogue title/date (in red) in place of the original title in the upper left corner. Mosher owned both the regular decorated cloth copy, and the decorated vellum copy, of *Silverpoints*. For other publications using Vale Press & Charles Ricketts designs, see entry 47.

See Wick for further explanation of the design. See also entry 366 for discussion of the influence of the *Silverpoints* format apart from the cover design.

Reference: Vilain 63 (plate 65, p. 104); Wick, pp. 8-9 (entry 8).

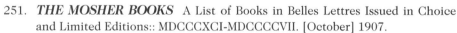

251. **THE MOSHER BOOKS** A List of Books in Belles Lettres Issued in Choice and Limited Editions:: MDCCCXCI-MDCCCCVII. [October] 1907.
68 pp.   23.5 x 15.5 cm.
Catalogue.   H 402.   Fifteenth catalogue.

Content: The foreword is signed by the publisher. Selections accompanying the catalogue (other than those quoted by Mosher under specific book entries):

– "Poetry" by Ella Heath
– "Ghosts in the Library" by Andrew Lang
– "Quatrains" by John Russell Hayes
– "After Reading 'An Italian Garden' " by Arthur Upson
– "Deservings" (anonymous)
– "A Ballad of a Book of Hours" (anonymous)
– "Finis" (anonymous)
– "The Triumph of Forgotten Things" by Edith M. Thomas
– "False Poets and True" by Thomas Hood
– Quotation from Thomas Hood
– Quotation from Edmund Gosse

THE MOSHER BOOKS (continued)

Binding & Embellishment: Bound in light blue paper wrappers printed in red and dark blue. Hardbound copies bound in light-blue boards with printed labels on spine and front cover; original wrappers bound in the back. Printed in red and black throughout; Chiswick ornaments and lead initials, and other fleuron ornaments; pages ruled in red.

The title page includes a decorative initial and a sprig of pinks (in red), the source of which remains undetermined. This device is used again on the back cover of the 1922 Mosher Books catalogue (entry 266).

---

252. ***THE MOSHER BOOKS*** [Herrick quotation of 8 lines on the title page].
　　 [October] 1908.　　　　72 pp.　　23.5 x 15 cm.
　　 Catalogue.　　　　　　 H 445.　　　　　 Sixteenth catalogue.

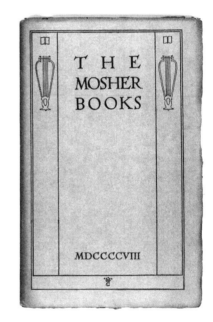

Content: The foreword is signed by the publisher. Selections accompanying the catalogue (other than those quoted by Mosher under specific book entries):

- "On an Old Song" by W. E. H. Lecky
- "Ex Libris" by Arthur Upson
- "Ballade of the Caxton Head" by Lionel Johnson
- "Sydney Pickering and Doris" by Viola Taylor
- "Aucassin and Nicolete" by F. W. Bourdillon
- "Robert Louis Stevenson" by Lizette Woodworth Reese
- "A Pagan Hymn" by J. R.
- "When the Song is Done" by Arthur Upson
- "Optimism" (anonymous)
- Quotation from John Morley
- "Within the Book, I, reading, found" (beginning line, anonymous)
- Quotation from Robert Herrick

Comment: The Sheean Typescript states: "Six of the large catalogues –1908, 1909, 1920, 1912, 1913 and 1915. These were bound up for beautiful specimens of catalogue making. The catalogue for 1910 has the head-bands [i.e., head-pieces], tail-pieces, large initials and title-page beautifully hand illuminated."

Binding & Embellishment: Bound in very light blue paper wrappers printed in dark blue and red. Hardbound copies bound in gray boards with printed labels on spine and front cover; original wrappers bound in the back. Printed in red and black throughout; pages ruled in red; Chiswick ornaments and lead letters, and other fleuron ornaments.

The cover design is by Earl Stetson Crawford with his monogram of a "C" with his stylized crown of 3 dots above 2 curved lines. For other Crawford designs used, see entry 88.

---

253. ***THE MOSHER BOOKS*** [Panpipe Player Vignette on the title page].
　　 [October] 1909.　　　　80 pp.　　24 x 15 cm.
　　 Catalogue.　　　　　　 H 480.　　　　　 Seventeenth catalogue.

Content: The foreword is signed by the publisher. Selections accompanying the catalogue (other than those quoted by Mosher under specific book entries):

- "Dust o' Books" by Arthur Upson
- "My Books" by Justin Huntley McCarthy

THE MOSHER BOOKS *(continued)*

– "Sea-Wind" by Stéphane Mallarmé translated by Arthur Symons
– "Proteus, In Memory of William Sharp" by E. R.
– "Tell me, Mamore," A. Lenalie, translator
– "The Last Journey" by John Davidson
– "The Book" by Emily Dickinson
– "The House of Cæsar" by Viola Taylor
– "Quod Semper" by Lucy Lyttelton
– "The Point of View" (I & II, anonymous)
– "A Sentimental Interlude I-II" (anonymous)
– "Toasts in a Library" (anonymous)
– "The sun and moon and stars are mine" (first line, anonymous)
– "Everything has an ending: there will be..." (first line, anonymous)
– Quotation from Wilfrid L. Randell
– Quotation from Robert Ross
– Quotation from J. W. Mackail
– Quotation from William Archer

Binding & Embellishment: Bound in light gray paper wrappers printed in darker gray. The hardbound copies are bound in gray boards with a paper spine and labels on the spine and front cover; wraps bound in at rear. Such copies contain a portrait frontispiece of Mosher on Japan vellum. Printed in red and black throughout; pages ruled in red; Chiswick ornaments and lead letters, and other fleuron ornaments.

Cover design is by Earl Stetson Crawford with his monogram of a "C" with his stylized crown of 3 dots above 2 curved lines. For other Crawford designs used, see entry 88.

The unattributed design on the title page shows a youth perched on an oak limb playing the panpipes. The same design also appears on the back cover of Munthe's *For Those Who Love Music* (see 115), the front cover of *Masterpieces* (see 235), and *The Children's Crusade* (see 66).

Reference: Vilain 64 (plate 65, p. 104); Gerstley, p. 79 (9).

---

254. **THE MOSHER BOOKS** [Maeterlinck quotation of 18 lines]. [October] 1910.
80 pp.   23.5 x 15 cm.
Catalogue.   H 519.   Eighteenth catalogue.

Content: In place of the usual foreword by Mosher is the work "George Meredith | Box Hill—May 22, 1909" by J. M. Barrie (see comment under 128). Selections accompanying the catalogue (other than those quoted by Mosher under specific book entries):

– "Lullaby" (anonymous)
– "Second Best" by Rupert Brooke
– "Distant Authors" by Mary Colborne-Veel
– "Pre-Existence" by Frances Cornford
– "The Cruiskeen Lawn" by L. A. C.
– "All Things and Roses" by Elizabeth Gibson
– "Song" by Wilfrid Wilson Gibson
– "Pain" by St. John Lucas
– "On the Fly-Leaf of the Greek Anthology" by Dora G. McChesney
– "Babylon," and "Where the Tree of Life is Blooming" by Viola Taylor

THE MOSHER BOOKS (continued)

– "May-Music" by Rachel Annand Taylor
– Quotation from Maurice Maeterlinck
– Quotation from Richard Jefferies
– Quotation from J. A. McNeill Whistler
– Quotation from William Butler Yeats
– Selection from the article "Materlinck and His Art" in *The Academy*, July 9, 1910

Comment: I have seen an extra-illuminated copy at the Portland Public Library (ME), bound in rose colored boards; wrappers bound in the rear; Mosher's portrait is printed on Japan vellum and used as a frontispiece (see comment under entry 252).

Binding & Embellishment: Bound in rose colored paper wrappers printed in a darker but matching ink; large anchor & dolphin on the front cover. Hardbound copies bound in rose boards with printed labels on spine and front cover; original wrappers bound in at the back. Printed in red and black throughout; pages ruled in red; Chiswick ornaments and lead letters, and other fleuron ornaments.

The unattributed title page design is from the Vale Press and appears, for example, on the title page of *The Tragical History of Doctor Faustus* (London, 1903). For other publications using Vale Press & Charles Ricketts designs, see entry 47.

Reference: Gerstley, p. 79 (10).

255. *THE MOSHER BOOKS* [G. H. Lewes quotation of 17 lines]. [October] 1911.
      80 pp.   23.5 x 14.5 cm.
      Catalogue.   H 545.   Nineteenth catalogue.

Content: The foreword is signed by the publisher. Selections accompanying the catalogue (other than those quoted by Mosher under specific book entries):

– "On a Country Road" by A. C. Swinburne
– "The Return" by Arthur Symons
– "Two Lyrics" by William Ernest Henley
– "The Bells of Battersea" by Russell Alexander
– "The Three Fausts" by Theodore Watts-Dunton
– "In What Vale?" by Iolo Aneurin Williams
– "The Way to Arcady" and "Strong as Death" by H. C. Bunner
– "The Stirrup-Cup" by Sidney Lanier
– "A Conclusion" by Rachel Annand Taylor
– Quotation from George Henry Lewes
– Quotation from Eden Phillpotts
– Quotation from Walter Savage Landor
– Quotation from Havelock Ellis
– Quotation from A. Mary F. Robinson
– "On Cutting Books" from *The Nation*, February 11, 1911

Binding & Embellishment: Bound in charcoal green paper wrappers printed in dark green with a large anchor & dolphin and Renaissance cartouche on the front cover. Hardbound copies in green boards with printed labels on spine and front cover; original wrappers bound in the back. Printed in black throughout; pages ruled in black; Chiswick ornaments and lead letters; and other fleuron ornaments. All further catalogues are internally printed in black only.

The unsigned anchor and dolphin publisher's device on p. 80 is also found at the back of *Ten Spiritual Designs* (entry 405). See illustration #10 on p. 72 under "Publisher's Devices." An unattributed circular illustration of an ancient lamp aside an open book appears on p. 5 of the catalogue.

256. *THE MOSHER BOOKS* [title page vignette signed e.a.c.]. [October] 1912.
80 pp.   23.5 x 14 cm.
Catalogue.   H 567.   Twentieth catalogue.

Content: The foreword is signed by the publisher. Selections accompanying the catalogue (other than those quoted by Mosher under specific book entries):

THE MOSHER BOOKS

Printed for THOMAS B MOSHER *and published by him at* XLV Exchange Street *Portland Maine* MDCCCCXII

- "Old Morality" by Edmund Gosse
- "To Lucy" by John Masefield
- "Romance" by H. H. Bashford
- "Canticles IV.8" by I. C.
- "Sunset" by W. G. Hole
- "In Passing" by Georgina B. Paget
- "The Outlaw" and "The Secret Inn" by Alfred Noyes
- "The night doth cut with shadowy knife" (poem's first line) by R.T. Chandler
- "Oh, snows so pure! oh, peaks so high!" (poem's first line) by Lewis Morris
- "Lines suggested by one of Chopin's Nocturnes" (first line, anonymous)
- Quotation from James Douglas
- Quotation from Henry Newbolt
- Selection from *The Scottish Art Review* on the binding of books

Binding & Embellishment: Bound in rose colored paper wrappers printed in matching darker ink with a Renaissance-style cartouche on the front cover and Mosher's anchor & dolphin monogram on the back cover. Hardbound copies in rose-colored boards with wrappers bound in at rear; portrait of Mosher printed on Japan vellum and used as a frontispiece. Printed in black throughout; pages ruled in black; Chiswick ornaments and lead letters; and other fleuron ornaments.

The illustrated title page signed "e.a.c." appears again, but reduced, in the 1914 catalogue. The illustration is autobiographical with images from Mosher's life and career, including a mounted stone which reads "I steer by the Stars..." The illustration is the work of a skilled amateur and is most likely the work of Elizabeth Alden Curtis, a rather mysterious figure. Mrs. Curtis authored a history, a theosophical work, and *Rubáiyát* related books (including *The Lament of Bäbä Tähir...* published by Quaritch in 1902) under the varied names of Elizabeth Brenton, Elizabeth Curtis Brenton, and Elizabeth Alden Curtis. The Hatch bibliography indicates her Mosher book, *The Norseman*, was "printed... for the author, Mrs. Elizabeth Curtis Brenton Holman," adding yet another alias. Mrs. Curtis lived in Hartford, Connecticut and in Norway, Maine (about 40 miles north of Portland). Her close proximity, the publication of her book in March 1912, her distinctive use of a lowercase "e" appearing like a capital "E" only writ small (examples in the Bishop Collection), and her friendship with Thomas B. Mosher (again as evidenced in the Bishop Collection), all point to "e.a.c." as being Elizabeth Alden Curtis. See also 432 for another design by Curtis, and 271 for a book authored by her.

Reference: Vilain 65.

257. *THE MOSHER BOOKS* ["Golden Precepts" quotation of 15 lines].
[October] 1913.   80 pp.   23.5 x 14.5 cm.
Catalogue.   H 595.   Twenty-first cat.

THE MOSHER BOOKS (*continued*)

Content: The foreword is signed by the publisher. Selections accompanying the catalogue (other than those quoted by Mosher under specific book entries):

– "The Toast" and "The Forgotten Road" by Louise Morey Bowman
– "Noel" by G. H. R. Dabbs
– "An English Gipsy Song" by L. S. Bethell
– "Reluctance"* by Robert Frost
– "Chorus at the Green Bear Inn" by Herbert Trench
– "The sunset glow is drowned" (poem's first line) by J. A. Nicklin
– "Two Boyhoods" by Alice Meynell
– "The Small Dreams" by Frances Chesterton
– "On the Road" by E. L. Darton
– "The Song of the Road" by E.G. Buckeridge
– "Ah, Chasms and Cliffs of Snow" by Sara M. B. Piatt
– Quotation from *The Book of Golden Precepts*

Comment: * "Reluctance" is the only Robert Frost poem that Mosher ever published, despite their friendship.

Binding & Embellishment: Bound in charcoal green paper wrappers printed in dark green with anchor & dolphin monogram on front cover. Hardbound copies in green boards with printed labels on spine and front cover; original wrappers bound in at rear. Printed in black throughout; pages ruled in black; Chiswick ornaments and lead letters; and other fleuron ornaments.

The cover's border design is by Frederic Goudy (for other Goudy designs, see entry 1). The headpiece on the title page is the same as that which appears on the title page to *The Germ* (132).

258. **THE MOSHER BOOKS** A List of Books in Belles Lettres issued in Choice
     and Limited Editions [Vignette]. [October] 1914.   76 pp.   23.5 x 14.5 cm.
     Catalogue.   H 613.   Twenty-second cat.

Content: The foreword, "Thomas Bird Mosher An Appreciation," is by Richard Le Gallienne (see also 39 & 408). Selections accompanying the catalogue (other than those quoted by Mosher under specific book entries):

– "Lydia" by Louise Morey Bowman
– "The Song of the Mad Prince" by Walter de la Mere [sic]
– "On a Copy of Amphora" by Sarah Evans Letchworth*
– "Hastings Mill" by C. Fox Smith
– "Time, You Old Gipsy Man" by Ralph Hodgson
– "The Beloved Vagabond" by W. G. Tinckom-Fernandez
– "Rioupéroux" and "Lord Arnaldos" by James Elroy Flecker
– Extracts from "Dominus Illuminatio Mea" by Laurence Irving

Mosher writes about the completion of *The Bibelot* (pp. 49-50) and lists its General Index in this catalogue.

Comment: The first catalogue to list Privately Printed Editions of The Mosher Press.

*Note: In a December 1, 1914 letter to W. Irving Way (The Huntington Library, WY 129), Mosher indicates that "today I am sending Mrs. Letchworth express prepaid fifty copies of her Sonnet printed on a very beautiful hand-made Batchelder writing paper..." For another example of what Mosher would do for some of his authors submitting work to *The Bibelot*, see 30.01.

THE MOSHER BOOKS (continued)

Binding & Embellishment: Bound in light colored blue-gray paper wrappers printed in dark gray with monogram anchor & dolphin on front cover and much larger monogram anchor & dolphin device on the back cover. Hardbound copies in gray boards with printed labels on spine and front cover; original wrappers bound in the rear. Printed in black throughout; pages ruled in black; Chiswick ornaments and lead letters; and other fleuron ornaments.

The cover's border design is by Frederic Goudy. For other Goudy designs, see entry 1.

The Renaissance design on top p. [76] is signed "CW" for Charlotte Whittingham, a designer for the Chiswick Press of London. For other Chiswick Press designs used, see entry 48.

Reference: Warren, p. 256 at bottom and p. 171 for Chiswick head-piece on p. 5.

---

259. **THE MOSHER BOOKS** A List of Books in Belles Lettres issued in Choice and Limited Editions [A. Cowley quotation of 13 lines]. [October] 1915.
80 pp.   23.5 x 14.5 cm.
Catalogue.   H 629.   Twenty-third cat.

Content: The foreword is from the "Conclusion" to *Studies in the History of the Renaissance* (1873) by Walter Pater. A Note by Mosher appears opposite the foreword. Selections accompanying the catalogue (other than those quoted by Mosher under specific book entries):

- "To a Poet a Thousand Years Hence" by James Elroy Flecker
- "A Litany" by Gertrude M. Hort
- "Epitaph" by Eden Phillpotts
- "Song" and three sonnets ("The Busy Heart," "Love," and "The Hill") by Rupert Brooke
- Extract from S.P.B. Mais' comment on his *The Great Lover*, with poem quote
- "The Departure" by Harold Monro
- "Rebel" by Irene Rutherford McLeod
- Quotation from Abraham Cowley
- "The Roman Road" by Rachel Annand Taylor
- Comment by James Lane Allen on Thomas S. Jones, Jr.'s *The Voice in the Silence*
- Statement attributed to William James
- Selection from the Essay on Winckelmann

Binding & Embellishment: Bound in light pink colored paper wrappers printed in red and maroon and using a new elongated anchor & dolphin device on both the front and back covers. Some copies bound in tan colored paper wrappers. Hardbound copies in tan colored boards without labels; original tan-yellow wrappers bound in, and with Mosher's portrait on Japan vellum used as frontispiece. Printed in black throughout; pages ruled in black; Chiswick ornaments and lead letters; and other fleuron ornaments.

The cover's design is by Frederic Goudy. For other Goudy designs, see entry 1.

---

260. **THE MOSHER BOOKS** A List of Belles Lettres Issued in Limited Editions by Thomas Bird Mosher at XLV Exchange Street Portland Maine
MDCCCXCI :: MDCCCCXVI. [October] 1916.   64 pp.   21.5 x 13 cm.
Catalogue.   H 640.   Twenty-fourth cat.

THE MOSHER BOOKS (continued)

Content: The foreword is signed by the publisher. Selections accompanying the catalogue (other than those quoted by Mosher under specific book entries):

– "With a Copy of Calvert's Spiritual Designs" by Wilbur Underwood
– "There's a bower of roses by Bendemeer's Stream" (poem's first line) by Thomas Moore
– "In Memory of Arthur Upson" and "At the White Gate" by Thomas S. Jones, Jr.
– "Empire" by "A. E." [George Russell]

Comment: This is the first catalogue *not* to give extensive summaries of the entries. Also showing the effect of the war upon printing, the catalogue was reduced to a 21.5 x 13 cm. format. In his note, Mosher mentions the difficulty of procuring certain paper he previously used, including the paper used for the catalogues, and the discontinuance of The Brocade Series which exclusively used Japan vellum paper.

Binding & Embellishment: Bound in light mint green, machine-made paper wrappers with an overall Renaissance-style front cover design in darker green; the back wrapper uses a new orb and cross publisher's monogram. From this point on the hard bound copies have a cloth spine over stiff boards which are decorated with the original covers in the colors as issued. This catalogue uses none of the customary ornamentation of previous catalogues, and pages are partly ruled.

The cover has an elaborate Renaissance style design of fleurons, vines, fleur-de-lys, and birds (unsigned and unattributed). The "globe and cross" publisher's device on the back cover was previously used, in reduced size, on the title page and colophon of the *Vision of Giorgione* (428).

---

261. *THE MOSHER BOOKS* A List of Books in Belles Lettres Issued in Choice and Limited Editions. [October] 1917.   44 pp.   21 x 11 cm.
Catalogue.   H 658.   Twenty-fifth cat.

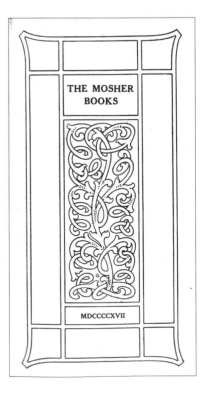

Content: The signed foreword is by the publisher. Selections accompanying the catalogue (other than those quoted by Mosher under specific book entries):

– "The Gypsies' Road" by Dora Sigerson
– "The Boys Who Never Grew Up: To the Foreign Legion" by Charles Law Watkins
– "A little island made of rocks, soft mossed" (first line, anonymous)

Comment: The first catalogue in the final format of 21 x 11 cm. (continued until 1929). The catalogue drops all entry summaries except for new books brought out for the year, and this becomes the established style for the remainder of Mosher's life.

In his foreword, Mosher notes "it is with regret that owing to the excessive advance in the price of paper, I am no longer able to send out my unique Catalogues as in former years. Instead, I have preferred to put all possible value into the books I publish."

Under the Brocade Series in the catalogue, Mosher mentions the costliness of, and difficulty in obtaining, Japan vellum, and further notes that there will be no reprints of titles in this series, repeating his announcement in the catalogue for 1916.

THE MOSHER BOOKS (continued)

Binding & Embellishment: Bound in light mint green, machine-made paper wrappers matching same paper internally, printed in darker green on wrapper and throughout. For hardbound copies see binding note to 260. Internal ornamentation is limited to a few Chiswick ornaments. All succeeding catalogue follow suit.

The entire cover design is Frederic Goudy's earlier work on the Vest Pocket Series.

For other Goudy designs, see entry 1.

262. *THE MOSHER BOOKS* A List Of Books In Belles Lettres Issued in Choice and Limited Editions [Tennyson quotation of 12 lines]. [October] 1918.
44 pp.   21 x 11 cm.
Catalogue.   H 666.   Twenty-sixth cat.

Content: The signed foreword is by the publisher. Selections accompanying the catalogue (other than those quoted by Mosher under specific book entries):

– "Ideal" by J. E. Flecker
– "A Shop in Portland Town" by Clinton Scollard
– "Beyond" by John Gibson Lockhart
– "On Looking at a Children's Book, Dated 1838" by Nancy Maude
– Quotation from Hilaire Belloc
– Unattributed selection of "Not of the sunlight" is from Tennyson's "Merlin and the Gleam"

Binding & Embellishment: Bound in light gray, machine-made paper wrappers matching same paper internally; elongated anchor & dolphin on front cover; double dolphin within a victory wreath on the back cover. For hardbound copies see binding note to 260.

263. *THE MOSHER BOOKS* A List Of Books In Belles Lettres Issued in Choice and Limited Editions [Whitman quotation of 10 lines]. [October] 1919.
45 pp.   21 x 11 cm.
Catalogue.   H 670.   Twenty-seventh cat.

Content: The signed foreword is by the publisher. Selections accompanying the catalogue (other than those quoted by Mosher under specific book entries):

– "Lady Jane Grey" by William H. Fleming
– "The Garden" by Thomas S. Jones, Jr.
– "At Thomas Mosher's" by Isabel Howe Fiske
– "A Dreamer's Epitaph" by Gertrude M. Hort
– "The Book of Pilgrimage" by Rainer Maria Rilke translated by Jessie Lemont
– Quotation from Walt Whitman's *Leaves of Grass*
– Quotation from Paul Fort
– Quotation from Alexander Smith
– Quotation from Spencer Miller, Jr.

Binding & Embellishment: Bound in manila, machine-made paper wrappers of the same paper used internally. Front and back wrappers printed in red and black (using the elongated anchor & dolphin and the front). For hardbound copies see binding note to 260.

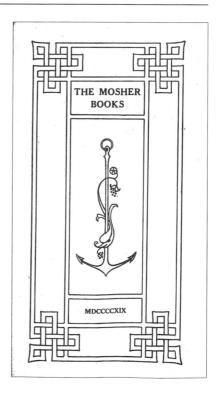

THE MOSHER BOOKS (continued)

The unsigned "breasted griffins" used as a publisher's device on the back wrapper were designed by Frank R. Rathbun of Auburn, NY. Rathbun designed similar griffins for T. B. Mosher's bookplate in 1898. They appear here for the first time on any Mosher publication.

For other Rathbun designs, see entry 107.

264. **THE MOSHER BOOKS** A List Of Books In Belles Lettres Issued in Choice and Limited Editions [Quotation of 8 lines]. [October] 1920.   45 pp.   21 x 11 cm. Catalogue.   H 681.   Twenty-eighth cat.

Content: The signed foreword is by the publisher. Selections accompanying the catalogue (other than those quoted by Mosher under specific book entries):

– "To Time" by Richard Middleton
– "Night" by William Rose Benet
– "Betrayed" by Lizette Woodworth Reese
– "Fountain Court" by St. John Lucas
– Quotation from George Gissin
– Quotation from Francis Brett Young
– Quotation from George Santayana
– Quotation from H. de Vere Stackpoole
– "Oh, Let me leave the plains behind" from "Shakespeare" by William Watson
– Quotation from A. Edward Newton

Binding & Embellishment: Bound in manila, machine-made paper wrappers matching same paper internally; wrappers printed in red and black; elongated anchor & dolphin on front cover. A new publisher's monogram device employing and anchor & dolphins appears on the back cover (see #16 in Section I, "Publisher's Devices Employed"). For hardbound copies see binding note to 260.

265. **THE MOSHER BOOKS** A List Of Books In Belles Lettres Issued in Choice and Limited Editions [*Kasîdah* quotation of 8 lines]. [October] 1921. 45 pp.   21 x 11 cm. Catalogue.   H 689.   Twenty-ninth cat.

Content: The signed foreword is by the publisher. Selections accompanying the catalogue (other than those quoted by Mosher under specific book entries):

– "Where Runs the River? Who can say" (first line) by Francis W. Bourdillon
– "Evening" by V. Sackville-West
– "Song" by William Watson
– "Clonard" by Thomas S. Jones, Jr.
– "Our phantom voices haunt the air" (poem's first line) by "R. L. S."
– "The Sabbath" (anonymous)
– Quotation from Sir Richard Burton's *The Kasîdah*
– Quotation from George Santayana
– Quotation from Robert Underwood Johnson
– Quotation from Gilbert Murray

Binding & Embellishment: Entirely printed on blue paper with matching machine-made blue paper wrappers, printed in black and red. The publisher's device on the back wrapper appeared before on the title page of the 1897 List of Books (entry 202; see also #26 in Section I, "Publisher's Devices Employed").

266. **THE MOSHER BOOKS** A List Of Books In Belles Lettres Issued in Choice
and Limited Editions [Bourdillon quotation of 8 lines]. [October] 1922.
45 pp.   21 x 11 cm.
Catalogue.   H 692.   Thirtieth cat.

Content: The signed foreword is by the publisher. Selections accompanying the
catalogue (other than those quoted by Mosher under specific book entries):

– "Vanishings," "The Song Celestial," "An Altered Chart" and "Then and Now,"
  are by Alice Buckton
– "Spring Sonnet" by Ethel Wedgwood
– "Not Yet" by Mary E. Coleridge
– "A Wasted Word" and "The Waste Garden" by Francis W. Bourdillon
– Quotation from Francis W. Bourdillon
– Quotation from Gilbert Murray

Binding & Embellishment: Bound in manila, machine-made paper wrappers of
the same paper used internally; wrappers printed in red and black; elongated
anchor & dolphin on front cover. The back cover's red flower device, a sprig of
pinks, also appears on the title page of the 1907 Mosher Books catalogue
(entry 251). For hardbound copies see binding note to 260.

267. **THE MOSHER BOOKS** A List Of Books In Belles Lettres Issued in Choice
and Limited Editions [Quotation of 8 lines]. [October] 1923.
45 pp.   21 x 11 cm.
Catalogue.   H 702.   Thirty-first cat.

Content: The foreword, "An Attempt at Appreciation of a Rare Spirit," is by
Wilbur Needham, taken from *The Chicago Evening Post* for April 20, 1923.
The article appeared in the *Post* prior to Mosher's death, but the catalogue
reached its public in October 1923, a little more than a month after Mosher's
death, so the tribute unintentionally turns into a memorial address. Selections
accompanying the catalogue (other than those quoted by Mosher under specific book entries):

– "Whither Afar?" and "The Sovereign Poet" by William Watson
– "After Dark Vapours" by John Keats
– "Rain at Night" by Helen Hoyt
– "October" by Thomas S. Jones, Jr.
– "The Kingdom of God" by Francis Thompson
– "I know the night is near at hand" by S. Weir Mitchell
– Quotation from *Dreamthorp* by Alexander Smith
– Quotation from Spencer Miller, Jr.
– Quotation from Walt Whitman

Binding & Embellishment: Bound in manila, machine-made paper wrappers of
the same paper used internally; wrappers printed in red and black; elongated
anchor & dolphin on front cover. For hardbound copies see binding note to 260.

The red sprig of flowers on the back cover was originally created by Herbert P.
Horne for the title page of *Diversi Colores* (London: Chiswick, 1891). The
same design was first used by Mosher on the front cover of *In Praise of Omar*
(entry 171). For designs by Horne used elsewhere, see entry 171.

After the year of Mosher's death, the catalogues are continued in this basic
format up to 1929 (see the Flora Lamb Checklist, entries FL 80-85, following
this bibliography).

268. *MY SISTER HENRIETTA.* Translated from the French of Ernest Renan by
     Lucie Page. 1900.   *xv*, 79, [1] pp.; plates, ports.
     Old World Series-19   H 136.   Only edition.

925 on Van Gelder; 100 numbered
copies on Japan vellum.
First edition of this translation.

Content: The preface is by the translator. An appendix gives passages from
The Life of Ernest Renan by Madame James Darmesteter (A. Mary F. Robinson), London: Methuen, 1897. A poem by Matthew Arnold appears on the
verso of the half-title, and two poems by Joseph Truman appear on pp. *viii* and
on the verso of the inner half-title. This volume includes portraits of Ernest
Renan (from an 1860 portrait by Henri Scheffer), Henrietta Renan, and five
other autotype illustrations.

The 1900 Mosher catalogue indicates that after the death of Renan, "...the
reminiscences were arranged and reprinted by Mme. Renan (Paris: [Calmann-
Lévy], 1895), from which edition a fresh translation has been especially made
for the Old World Series."

Comment: See entries 59, 217 & 394 for other works translated by Lucie Page.

Design: Based upon stylistic evidence and the time period, the design on the
front cover is most likely by Frederic Goudy. For other Goudy designs, see
entry 1.

N

269. *NATURE AND ETERNITY: WITH OTHER UNCOLLECTED PAPERS*
     by Richard Jefferies. [August] 1902.   92, [1] pp. (same for second ed.)
     Brocade Series-35   H 220.   First edition.

425 on Japan vellum for each
edition.
First edition.

Content: The unsigned foreword is by the publisher. Mosher collected these
essays from the following issues of *Longman's Magazine*: "Nature and Eternity" (May 1895), "The Spring of the Year" (June 1894), and "Vignettes from
Nature" (July 1895).

Comment: This title is part of a sub-series. See note to entry 282.

Reference: Jenkinson II, 663.

269.1 *NATURE AND ETERNITY: WITH OTHER UNCOLLECTED PAPERS*
      by Richard Jefferies. [October] 1907.
      Brocade Series.   H 417.   Second edition.

270. *THE NEW LIFE OF DANTE ALIGHIERI* translated by Dante Gabriel Rossetti.
     1896.   *xv*, 96 pp.; front. (same through third ed.)
     Old World Series-3   H 21.   First edition.

925 on Van Gelder; 100 numbered
copies on Japan vellum.

Content: The unsigned foreword is by the publisher. The frontispiece is a
reproduction of "Dante's Dream" by Rossetti. On the verso of the half-title
appears the poem "On the 'Vita Nuova' of Dante" by D. G. Rossetti. Although
Mosher never directly identifies which of the many editions of *The New Life*
he used to create this reprint, he most likely used Rossetti's *The Collected
Works* (London: Ellis & Scrutton, 1886) which he references in the appended
"notes" and a copy of which appeared in his library. In the foreword he does
mention that his reprint restores the divisions (given in Roman numerals)
given in all Italian texts.

THE NEW LIFE OF DANTE ALIGHIERI (continued)

A copy at the University of San Francisco is bound in 3/4 green morocco by Zaehnsdorf and has the printer's bookplate of C. H. St. John Hornby. See entry 290 for more information on Hornby. See also 334.

Comment: According to a letter recorded in Grigsby, Charles Eliot Norton wrote Mosher complimenting him on the publication of Rossetti's *New Life of Dante*, dated Cambridge, Dec. 3, 1896. Norton, himself an author, was a noted Harvard educator, an apostle of culture through art, a friend of John Ruskin and Dante Gabriel Rossetti, president of the Dante Society, and first president of the American Society of Arts and Crafts founded in 1897.

Design: Based upon stylistic evidence, the cover design is most likely by Frederic Goudy. For other Goudy designs, see entry 1.

Reference: Grigsby 973; Boss XIII 146 (2nd ed.).

270.1 *THE NEW LIFE OF DANTE ALIGHIERI* translated by Dante Gabriel Rossetti. 1897.
Old World Series.　　　　H 54.　　　　Second edition.

925 on Van Gelder; 100 numbered copies on Japan vellum.

270.2 *THE NEW LIFE OF DANTE ALIGHIERI* translated by Dante Gabriel Rossetti. 1899.
Old World Series.　　　　H 126A.　　　　Third edition.

925 on Van Gelder. No Japan vellum copies were printed for this and succeeding editions.

Comment: This edition was not listed in the Hatch *Check List*, but was later added by Hatch in 1972 (see Vilain).

Reference: Vilain, p. 63. See next entry.

270.3 *THE NEW LIFE OF DANTE ALIGHIERI* translated by Dante Gabriel Rossetti. 1900.
Old World Series.　　　　H 162.　　　　Third edition.

925 on Van Gelder only (same through fifth edition).

Comment: A reprint of the previous entry with change of date on the title page? An error in edition note?

270.4 *THE NEW LIFE OF DANTE ALIGHIERI* translated by Dante Gabriel Rossetti. 1905.　　　　*xiii*, 98 pp.; front. (same for fifth ed.)
Old World Series.　　　　H 334.　　　　Fourth edition.

270.5 *THE NEW LIFE OF DANTE ALIGHIERI* translated by Dante Gabriel Rossetti. 1912.
Old World Series.　　　　H 568.　　　　Fifth edition.

271. *THE NORSEMAN A DRAMA IN FOUR ACTS* by Elizabeth Alden Curtis. [March] 1912.　　　　*ix*, 96, [1] pp.　　　19.5 x 14 cm.
Privately Printed-14　　　　H 716.　　　　Only edition.

300 copies printed on Van Gelder paper.

Content: The introduction is by the author. Benton Hatch notes in his bibliography that the book was printed for the author, Mrs. Elizabeth Curtis Benton Holman. For further information, see the notes to entries 256 & 432.

Binding & Embellishment: Bound in blue charcoal paper boards with white label on the spine and on the upper right-hand corner of the front cover (with triangular Chiswick ornament). Title page in red and black; pages ruled.

O

272. **ODE ON THE MORNING OF CHRIST'S NATIVITY** by John Milton.
[September] 1909.   *vii*, 18, [1] pp.
Golden Text Series-4   H 478.   Only edition.

925 on Van Gelder; 100 on Japan vellum.

Content: The signed foreword is by the publisher. Milton's ode (pp. 3-[18]) is divided into numbered stanzas, I-XXVII.

Comment: This work was first classified by Mosher in 1909 under the Miscellaneous Series, but in 1910 it was reclassified and remained under the Golden Text Series.

273. **ODE TO GERTRUDE ON HER SIXTH BIRTHDAY** by Lloyd Mifflin.
1913.   10 *l.* (unnumbered, printed on recto side only)   18 x 10 cm.
Privately Printed-27   H 728.   Only edition.

100 copies printed on Van Gelder paper.

Content: Consists of a single ode of six pages, printed on the recto side only.

Comment: This book was privately printed for Mrs. George Woodward (i.e., Gertrude Houston Woodward) of Chestnut Hill, Philadelphia. In the early 1900's, Mifflin was known as America's sonneteer, and painter, from Columbia, PA.

Benton Hatch never saw a copy of this book.

Binding & Embellishment: According to the Lamb typescript, 85 copies were bound in blue Venetian paper boards, and 15 copies were bound in wall paper boards. A decorative label in red and black appears on the front cover. Title page printed in red and black; Chiswick ornaments; lead initial in red outline.

Reference: Vilain, p. 67 (Bishop addition); Mifflin's original manuscript is at the Houghton Library, bMS Am 1096 (965).

274. **ODES SONNETS & LYRICS OF JOHN KEATS**. Selections by Robert Bridges.
[September] 1922.   *xx*, 88, [1] pp.; port, 2 facsim.   19 x 15 cm.
Miscellaneous Series-96   H 691.   Only edition.

450 copies on Van Gelder; 50 numbered copies on Japan vellum.

Content: The signed foreword is by the publisher. The notes at the back of this volume (pp. [67]-[84]) are also by Mosher. The poem "John Keats" by Dante Gabriel Rossetti, and a selection from Albert Elmer Hancock, accompany the main text. Mosher added three lyrics and three sonnets to the text of the 1895 Daniel Press edition, while excising the revised version of "La Belle Dame sans Merci" from his reprint. Facsimiles of the Daniel Press bordered title page, the Daniel Press printer's mark, and a sample of Keats' handwriting also accompany the text. The Hollyer photoreproduction of the Keats portrait has been attributed to Joseph Severn, but was actually drawn by Severn's daughter under his supervision.

According to MacGillivray, this edition is "based on the Daniel Press edition of 1895, but with additional poems. Reissued 1924." Mosher previously printed seven of the odes in the March 1907 issue of *The Bibelot* (30).

Comment: A charming letter of November 8, 1922 was sent from Falconer Madan to R. W. Rogers (now in the collection of the University of San Frañisco):

ODES SONNETS & LYRICS
JOHN KEATS

(a)

ODES SONNETS & LYRICS OF JOHN KEATS (continued)

You could not have sent me a more *welcome* or more *opportune* book than that Mosher Keats. I did not know of its existence, and it fits into my Daniel Press Collections with great appropriateness... I am *not* fond of old Moshwig and his odious ways, but he does make his editions *interesting*. It doesn't in the least annoy me. Indeed, his edition of Keats is a Danielicum.

Mosher reprinted three other Daniel Press books: *The Growth of Love* (137 & 138), *Fancy's Following* (106), and *The Garland of Rachel* (125).

Binding & Embellishment: The Van Gelder edition is bound in blue paper boards with title/author in red and black on the spine and front cover. The Japan vellum copies are bound in Japan vellum boards with the same spine and cover information. The floral designs on the front and back covers are unattributed.

The floral art nouveau designs on the front and back covers are by George Auriol. They are found on pp. 2 & 17 of *Le Second Livre des monogrammes, marques, cachets et ex-libris composés* par George Auriol (Paris: 1, Bᵈ des Capucines, 1908). A copy of this book was in the Mosher library. For other Auriol designs, see entry 145.

Reference: MacGillivray, p. 35 (C10); Ewelme C2; Quinn 4983; Vilain, p. 58.

(b)

---

275. **OLD WORLD LYRICS: A LITTLE BOOK OF TRANSLATIONS.**
"Tout finit par des Chansons." 1893.   43, [1] pp. (numbered in Roman numerals)
The Bibelot Series-2   H 4.   Only edition.

725 on Van Gelder; 25 numbered copies on Japan vellum.

Content: Mosher selected 41 poems (including Ronsard's verse opposite the title page) for this anthology of mostly French verse which contains works by the following authors and their translators:

AUTHORS

A. V. Arnault	Charles Baudelaire
Théodore de Banville	P. J. de Béranger
Joachim Du Bellay	Remy Belleau
Lyonnet de Coismes	Théophile Gautier
Victor Hugo	Henri Murger
Gérard de Nerval	Augusto Ferrero
Pierre Ronsard	Jacques Tahureau
Niccolò Tommaseo	François Villon

...and several Old French and one Romaic poem.

TRANSLATORS

D. G. Rossetti	John Payne
Andrew Lang	A.C. Swinburne
Owen Meredith	Amelia B. Edwards
W. M. Thackeray	Walter Besant
Walt Whitman	Lafcadio Hearn
Austin Dobson	G. A. Greene

Comment: This is Mosher's second anthology. For Mosher's first anthology, and other anthologies assembled by him, see 366.

Murray notes that this volume includes "The paradox of time," and "Ars victrix," by Austin Dobson.

Design: The art nouveau floral design is an original design done for Mosher, but the artist remains unknown. For use of this same design, see entry 49.1. The title-page is printed in red & black.

Reference: Boss XI 133; Murray, p. 47.

276. *ON THE HEIGHTS WILD FLOWERS OF THOUGHT AND DREAM*   6 copies printed on Van Gelder
      GATHERED FOR ELIZABETH by Duncan Phillips. [November] 1913.   paper.
      vi, 20, [1] pp.   18.5 x 11.5 cm.
      Privately Printed-28   H 729.   Only edition.

      Content: This volume consists of 12 poems.

      Comment: Privately printed for the author, Duncan Phillips. Not seen by Hatch.

      Binding & Embellishment: Bound in charcoal blue paper boards with labels on
      spine and front cover (with Minoan sea wave design below title), housed in
      matching slipcase with label on spine. Title page printed in red and black.

      Reference: Vilain, pp. 67-68.

277. *ON THE WINGS OF THE MIND* by Elizabeth Calvert. [May] 1912.   100 copies printed on Van Gelder
      vi, 87, [1] pp.   18 x 11.5 cm.   paper.
      Privately Printed-17   H 719.   Only edition.

      Content: This work takes the form of a travel and spiritual journal kept by the
      author who dedicated the book "to the bright personalities and pleasant places
      that made my journey possible" (p. *v*).

      Comment: The book was printed for the author, Elizabeth Calvert, who is most
      likely Mrs. Elizabeth Henderson (McRobie) Calvert (b.1857), who authored at
      least four small books between 1897 and 1922, two of which were printed in
      Boston by the Roxburgh Publishing Co.: *The Two Houses* (1918) and *Little
      Christ Stories* (1922).

      Binding & Embellishment: Bound in quarter white paper over blue marbled
      paper boards. Spine with slightly raised bands and white label. Title page ruled
      and printed in red and black. Beginning initial of text in red outline.

278. *ORATIONS AND ADDRESSES* delivered by Thomas Brackett Reed.   200 numbered copies printed on
      [November] 1911.   *viii*, 170, [1] pp.; port front. 19.5 x 14 cm.   Van Gelder paper.
      Privately Printed-13   H 715.   Only edition.   First edition.

      Content: This book includes a Colby College oration of June 1885, an address
      at the Semi-Centennial of Girard College, an oration at Bowdoin College, the
      Centennial Oration at Portland in July 1886, an oration at the Grand Army
      Reunion in August 1884, and another Portland address of August 1900. There
      is a pictorial portrait frontispiece of Thomas Brackett Reed. Printed for Mrs.
      Thomas B. Reed.

      Comment: Thomas B. Reed, a Republican from Maine, served as Speaker of
      the U. S. House of Representatives under the McKinley administration. Reed
      was known for his parliamentarian prowess and for his epigrams which
      became part of the American political tradition. Mosher counted Reed as one
      of his closest friends, sharing a love for literature and books.

      According to Robinson, this book "contains many of Reed's non-political
      addresses not available elsewhere."

      Binding & Embellishment: Bound in blue boards with white label on rounded
      and blind-ruled spine. Title page in red and black; Chiswick ornaments; red
      outlined initial letters; all pages ruled.

      Reference: Robinson, p. 406.

279. **OUR LADY'S TUMBLER A TWELFTH CENTURY LEGEND** done out of
Old French into English by Philip H. Wicksteed. 1900.
xii, 30, [1] pp. (same for second ed.)   20.5 x 13 cm.
Miscellaneous Series-10   H 140.   First edition.

Content: The source for this reprint is the J. M. Dent edition (London, 1894).
The unsigned preface is by the publisher.

The text of this work was first printed by Mosher in his November 1899 issue
of *The Bibelot* (22).

Binding & Embellishment: Both the Van Gelder and the Japan vellum copies
are bound in printed Japan vellum wraps over boards. Title page printed in
red and black; pages ruled in black; Chiswick ornaments.

An inscribed copy, with the cover and spine printed in black rather than in
red and green, is in the collection at the University of San Francisco.

The Renaissance border design on cover (Warren, p. 253) is signed "CW" for
Charlotte Whittingham, designer for the Chiswick Press of London. The head-
pieces and initials are also Chiswick, including the triangular tail-pieces which
were designed by Charlotte Whittingham and engraved by Mary Byfield (Warren,
p. 314). The top and bottom elements in Mosher's cover design were switched
from the original design. For other Chiswick Press designs used, see entry 48.

Reference: Boss XIII 155; Grigsby 875 & 1314; Warren (above page references).

279.1 *OUR LADY'S TUMBLER A TWELFTH CENTURY LEGEND* done out of
Old French into English by Philip H. Wicksteed. 1900.
Miscellaneous Series.   H 167.   Second edition.

279.2 *OUR LADY'S TUMBLER A TWELFTH CENTURY LEGEND* done out of
Old French into English by Philip H. Wicksteed. 1904.
ix, 32, [1] pp. (same for fourth ed.)
Miscellaneous Series.   H 305.   Third edition.

279.3 *OUR LADY'S TUMBLER A TWELFTH CENTURY LEGEND* done out of
Old French into English by Philip H. Wicksteed. 1904.
Miscellaneous Series.   H 306.   Fourth edition.

——————— *Same Title, Change of Series* ———————

280. **OUR LADY'S TUMBLER A TWELFTH CENTURY LEGEND** done out of
Old French into English by Philip H. Wicksteed. [October] 1906.
ix, 41 pp. (same for second edition)
Ideal Series of Little Masterpieces-5   H 364.   First thus.

Content: The signed foreword is by the publisher. See 279 for the source of the text.

Comment: Mosher gave permission to E. S. Payson to use his foreword for *La
Akrobato de Nia Sinjorino. Milcentjara Legendo*. Tradukis Edward S. Payson,
Prezidanto Esperantista Asocio Norda Ameriko, [ca.1919] (Bishop Collection).
Payton was president of the Emerson Piano Company in Boston, president of
the Esperanto Association of North America, and a translator. Esperanto is an
artificial international language based on words common to the major European languages, and is still promoted by a few exponents.

Reference: Vilain 42.

450 on Van Gelder; 50 numbered
copies on Japan vellum; 4 numbered copies on American vellum,
signed by the publisher.

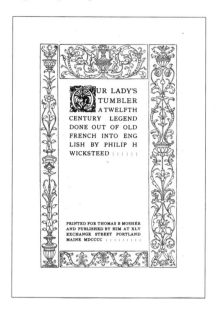

450 copies on Van Gelder for this
and succeeding editions. No Japan
vellum copies were printed after
the first edition.

Limitation unknown for both Van
Gelder and Japan vellum copies.

280.1 *OUR LADY'S TUMBLER A TWELFTH CENTURY LEGEND* done out of
Old French into English by Philip H. Wicksteed. [November] 1911.
Ideal Series of Little Masterpieces.   H 554.   Second edition.

——————— *Same Title, Change of Series* ———————

281. *OUR LADY'S TUMBLER A TWELFTH CENTURY LEGEND* done out of
Old French into English by Philip H. Wicksteed. [November] 1917.
x, 34, [1] pp.   21 x 13 cm.
Privately Printed-44   H 745.   First thus.

500 printed on Italian hand-made
paper; 50 on Japan vellum.

Content: The signed preface is by the publisher. Accompanying
the title text are two passages from Gautier de Coinci taken from
Alice Kemp-Welch's translation *Of the Tumbler of Our Lady...*
(London: Chatto and Windus, 1908), and a brief note by P. H.
Wicksteed. Essentially the same as the Miscellaneous Series editions with minor variations in page numbering, and an updated
note in the preface.

Comment: Privately printed for Edward A. Woods of Sewickley,
PA. Some copies will have a loosely inserted presentation slip, from Mr. and
Mrs. Woods, bearing the family coat of arms and the title of the book.

Binding & Embellishment: Van Gelder copies bound in blue charcoal paper
boards with title/author printed on the spine and front cover. The front cover
Renaissance-type design is most likely by Charlotte Whittingham of the
Chiswick Press. For other Chiswick Press designs used, see entry 48.

Title page in red and black; Chiswick ornaments and initials; text pages ruled
in black. Printed dust jacket.

Reference: Warren, plate opposite p. 150 (see also p. 171).

P

282. *THE PAGEANT OF SUMMER* by Richard Jefferies. [July] 1896.
50, [1] pp. (same through tenth ed.)
Brocade Series-2   H 25.   First edition.

425 on Japan vellum for each
edition.

Content: A bibliographical note appears opposite the title page and indicates
this work was first "printed in *Longman's Magazine*, June 1883, and re-issued
in the volume entitled, *The Life of the Fields* (London, Chatto & Windus,
1884). The book also includes a proem taken from Richard Jefferies' essay
"Wild Flowers."

Comment: This work, along with four others, is part of a sub-series called
"Five Idyls of Field and Hedgerow by Richard Jefferies." The other works in
this grouping include: *Hours of Spring and Wild Flowers* (157), *Bits of Oak
Bark: Meadow Thoughts* (45), *Saint Guido* (340), and *Nature and Eternity*
(269).

Binding & Embellishment: Title page and cover are printed in green & black
(most other Brocade Series title pages are printed in red and black).

Reference: Quinn 4850 (4th ed.); Vilain, p. 25 (6th ed.).

282.1 *THE PAGEANT OF SUMMER* by Richard Jefferies. [December] 1896.
       Brocade Series.   H 34.   Second edition.

282.2 *THE PAGEANT OF SUMMER* by Richard Jefferies. [May] 1897.
       Brocade Series.   H 58.   Third edition.

282.3 *THE PAGEANT OF SUMMER* by Richard Jefferies. [March] 1898.
       Brocade Series.   H 93.   Fourth edition.

282.4 *THE PAGEANT OF SUMMER* by Richard Jefferies. [August] 1899.
       Brocade Series.   H 133.   Fifth edition.

282.5 *THE PAGEANT OF SUMMER* by Richard Jefferies. [April] 1900.
       Brocade Series.   H 170.   Sixth edition.

       Binding: Parting from the usual binding material of Japan vellum, some copies
       were bound in gray paper wrappers over boards with title in black on the front
       cover (Bishop Collection). See entry 282.7 below.

282.6 *THE PAGEANT OF SUMMER* by Richard Jefferies. [May] 1901.
       Brocade Series.   H 204.   Seventh edition.

282.7 *THE PAGEANT OF SUMMER* by Richard Jefferies. [October] 1902.
       Brocade Series.   H 239.   Eighth edition.

       Comment: Benton Hatch noted a copy at Harvard bound in gray wrappers. At
       that time Hatch thought this copy to be unique, but see 282.5.

282.8 *THE PAGEANT OF SUMMER* by Richard Jefferies. [November] 1904.
       Brocade Series.   H 307.   Ninth edition.

282.9 *THE PAGEANT OF SUMMER* by Richard Jefferies. [July] 1910.
       Brocade Series.   H 524.   Tenth edition.

——————— *Same Title, Change of Series* ———————

283. RICHARD JEFFERIES   *THE PAGEANT OF SUMMER* with a preface by   Limitation unknown for both Van
      Thomas Coke Watkins. [April] 1905.   *xii*, 52 pp. (same for second ed.)   Gelder and Japan vellum copies.
      Vest Pocket-9   H 328.   First thus.

      Content: Thomas Coke Watkins' preface (pp. *vii*-[*xii*) introduces this prose-
      poem. The book includes a selection from Longfellow and one from Shelley.

283.1 RICHARD JEFFERIES   *THE PAGEANT OF SUMMER* with a preface by
      Thomas Coke Watkins. [February] 1909.
      Vest Pocket.   H 500.   Second edition.

284. *PASSAGES FROM THE PHILOSOPHY OF HERBERT SPENCER* chosen   750 on Van Gelder; 50 numbered
      by Clara Sherwood Stevens. 1910.   *xvi*, 114 pp.   19 x 14 cm.   copies on Japan vellum.
      Miscellaneous Series-48   H 505.   Only edition.

      Content: The source for these passages was the *Complete Works of Herbert
      Spencer* (New York: D. Appelton & Co., [c1860]-1904) and includes selections
      from the *First Principles*, the *Principles of Biology*, the *Principles of Psychol-
      ogy*, the *Principles of Sociology*, the *Principles of Ethics*, and miscellaneous
      works and essays. The preface is by the compiler.

PASSAGES FROM THE PHILOSOPHY OF HERBERT SPENCER *(continued)*

Comment: Although listed in Mosher's catalogues under the Miscellaneous
Series, this book may have been privately funded. The Lamb typescript carries
this title under Privately Printed Books, printed for C. S. Stevens, the compiler. Sheean lists it under the Miscellaneous Series.

Binding & Embellishment: The Van Gelder copies are bound in charcoal blue
boards with a white spine label printed in two colors. The Japan vellum copies
are bound in Japan vellum boards with label printed in red and black directly
on the spine.

Head-pieces on pp. [3] and [39], [45], and [59] all signed "CW" for Charlotte
Whittingham, designer for the Chiswick Press of London. The triangular floral
tail-piece at the back of the book is also Chiswick in origin. The book is ruled
throughout in black. For other Chiswick Press designs used, see entry 48.

Reference: Warren, p. 311 & 314.

---

285. **PASSAGES FROM THE SONG CELESTIAL** by Sir Edwin Arnold.
    1911.   *viii*, 38, [1] pp.
    Lyric Garland Series-23   H 539.   Only edition.

*950 on Van Gelder paper; 50 num-
bered copies on Japan vellum.*

Content: The foreword to these 27 selections from the *Bhagavad-Gîtâ* is by
the publisher. A Latin quote from F. von Schlegel, with its English translation,
appears opposite the title page. A list of citations for all the passages selected
is printed on p. [2].

A number of selections from these passages were printed by Mosher in the
December 1910 issue of *The Bibelot* (33).

Binding: The bindings are in two states: some copies examined are bound in
gray boards and some in a blue boards.

---

286. **PEARL**: Rendered into Modern English Verse by S. Weir Mitchell.
    1908.   *xii*, 28 pp.   16.5 x 13 cm.
    Privately Printed-11   H 713.   Only edition.

*60 copies on Van Gelder for
presentation only, of which 50
copies were given to Mr. Mitchell.*

Content: *The Pearl* was a 14th century mystical allegorical poem written in
Middle English. The introduction to the July 1908 issue of *The Bibelot* (31)
indicates Mitchell's translation draws upon the unrhymed verse translation by
Israel Gollancz (London: D. Nutt, 1891).

A note in the Old World edition (287) mentions that the translation by S. Weir
Mitchell was published in New York by The Century Co. in 1906, and
"Reprinted by Thomas B. Mosher, Portland, Maine, in *The Bibelot*, xiv, 7,
1908. Sixty copies were also printed on hand-made paper for presentation
purposes. Renders about half the poem."– p. 67

Mitchell's modern English translation was also printed in the July 1908 issue
of *The Bibelot* (31) which records an earlier copyright of 1906.

Comment: The copyright is under Weir Mitchell's name. In a July 15, 1914 letter to W. Irving Way cited by Wheeler, Mosher writes:

> As the years wander on this will be a little piece of Americana that princes may
> compete for but only Huntingtons can buy. I would say the same about the Whit-
> man on pure vellum in re 'Memories of President Lincoln'.

PEARL (continued)

According to the Lamb typescript this book was privately printed for T. B. Mosher. The Sheean typescript mentions that 50 copies were given to Mr. Mitchell, the translator.

Mosher's full name, THOMAS BIRD MOSHER, is spelled out on a title page for the first time. See also comment under entry 180.

Binding & Embellishment: The cover's title appears in the upper right-hand corner with a Chiswick design both above and below it. The title is printed vertically on the spine with the date of the publication also printed vertically. The covers are the charcoal gray used in the Lyric Garland series.

Reference: Wheeler (H.O.), p. 12.

---

287. ***THE PEARL AN ENGLISH VISION-POEM OF THE FOURTEENTH CENTURY*** done into Modern Verse by Marian Mead. 1908.   *xxiii*, 69, [1] pp.
Old World Series-48   H 432.   Only edition.

Content: The unsigned introduction is by the translator, Marian Mead of Chicago. There are three quatrains by Tennyson, S. Weir Mitchell, and Marian Mead on p. *v*. The quatrain by Tennyson is the prefatory poem in the Gollancz translation published by David Nutt in 1891. This book is an original translation of 101 sonnets, printed and copyrighted by Mosher. The translator acknowledges her debt to "Dr. Osgood's purer text..." (3 eds. were printed 1906-07) and to Mr. Gollancz's version (see 286). The volume also contains an interesting bibliographical note (pp. [63-68]) by the translator.

In a copy examined there appears a tipped in erratum slip on p. [*xxiii*].

Design: The cover design bears the "C" monogram of Thomas Maitland Cleland. For other Cleland designs used, see entry 6.

Reference: Vilain, p. 84 (plate 11); Crichton 42 and pictured on p. 73.

In addition to the 925 Van Gelder copies, there were only 25 numbered copies on Japan vellum. First edition of this translation.

---

288. ***IL PESCEBALLO: OPERA IN ONE ACT*** by Francis James Child.
[English text by J. R. Lowell] 1912.   *x*, 50 pp.   17.5 x 14 cm.
Miscellaneous Series-58   H 558.   Only edition.

Content: The signed, mostly bibliographical foreword (pp. [*vii-x*]) is by the publisher. A brief selection from Ferris Greenslet's *James Russell Lowell...* appears opposite the foreword. Mosher's reprint is based upon a collation of three distinct printings of *Il Pesceballo* in Cambridge (USA), 1862, in consultation with their appearance, elucidating their errors and variants, in *The Nation* for January 14, 1909. The opera is printed on pp. 3-31, and an appendix appears on pp. [33]-40, followed by a five-part section of notes, pp. [41]-[50].

Mosher's 1912 catalogue mentions that this volume "contains not only the complete text but gives for the first time a facsimile of the rare Programme and a portrait of Professor Lane author of the famous college song, first printed in 1855, on which the operetta was based... In its present *format* the work takes its place as a piece of genuine Americana."

The text of this work was printed by Mosher in his November 1911 issue of *The Bibelot* (34).

50 numbered copies on Japan vellum only.

IL PESCEBALLO: OPERA IN ONE ACT (continued)

Comment: This volume is one of six Miscellaneous Series books forming a uniformly styled "sub-series" (see note to entry 238).

Binding & Embellishment: Copies are bound in flexible Japan vellum boards with yapp top and fore-edges; title is printed on the spine and title/author printed directly on the front cover with the beginning drop-cap Chiswick initial in red. The title page is printed in red and black. Floral decorative head-pieces.

289. *THE PIERROT OF THE MINUTE A DRAMATIC PHANTASY*
      by Ernest Dowson. 1913.   *vi*, 38, [1] pp.
      Lyric Garland Series-26   H 592.   Only edition.

950 on Van Gelder paper; 50 numbered copies on Japan vellum.

Content: A publisher's note after the title page indicates that this edition is faithfully reprinted (with corrections to errors) from the Smithers edition (London, 1897). Printed at the end is the "Epilogue" from *Posies out of Rings and Other Conceits* by William Theodore Peters (London: John Lane, 1896).

Comment: See entry 301 for an earlier printing of *The Pierrot of the Minute* in the Miscellaneous Series *Poems of Ernest Dowson*, 1902.

Last title published in this series.

Reference: Boss XI 76: Quinn 2693 & 7093; Cevasco, p. 42 (3); *DLB* XIX, p. 149.

290. *THE PILGRIMS OF HOPE A POEM IN XIII BOOKS* by William Morris
      Author of The Earthly Paradise. 1901.
      viii, 54 pp.   22.5 x 18 cm.
      Reprints of Privately Printed Books-8   H 195.   Only edition.

400 on Van Gelder; 50 numbered copies on Japan vellum; 4 on Roman vellum in folded sheets, unbound, and signed by the publisher.
First American edition.

Content: The unsigned preface by the publisher gives a bibliographical background of the book with H. Buxton Forman's comments (pp. [*vii*]-*viii*). The work was brought together from 13 issues of *The Commonweal*, March 1885 through July 3, 1886.

Comment: This title is listed as one of the H. Buxton Forman-T.J. Wise forgeries (see Barker), but according to LeMire, the term forgery is misleading. The Foreman-Wise production is actually a piracy since it was "designed to make some claim to authorization, not priority... The attempt to deceive was to make it appear that Morris had approved, at least tacitly, of the production, to lend it a spurious authenticity..." –April 5, 1995 letter to P. R. Bishop

A copy in the collection at the University of San Francisco has the bookplate of C. H. St. John Hornby, Shelley House, Chelsea, England. Hornby was the founder of the Ashendene Press, director of W. H. Smith and Son, and one of the trustees of the William Morris estate. See also entries 270 & 334 for other references to Hornby.

Binding & Embellishment: The Van Gelder copies are bound in charcoal blue paper boards with a printed white spine label. Japan vellum copies are bound in Japan vellum wraps over boards with the label information printed directly on the wrappers. The book is not embellished with any ornamentation save the publisher's device on the title page.

Reference: *DLB* LVII, p. 195; Walsdorf 90; Boss VII 147; Barker, pp. 207-208; Quinn 7018 & 7019; Grigsby 827 & 828.

291. *PIPPA PASSES* by Robert Browning. 1902.
    viii, 92, [1] pp.; front. (same, second ed.)
Old World Series-27   H 211.   First edition.

925 on Van Gelder; 100 numbered copies on Japan vellum.

Content: Mosher's 1902 catalogue identifies the source of this poetic drama as "that of the final edition [most likely that of London, 1898, a copy of which was in Mosher's library]. A facsimile of the song, *"The Year's at the Spring,"* [frontispiece] is taken from Mr. T. J. Wise's Browning *Bibliography* [in *Literary Anecdotes of the Nineteenth Century.* London, 1895]." There is a bibliographical note on pp. 83-92.

Reference: Grigsby 139.

291.1 *PIPPA PASSES* by Robert Browning. 1908.
Old World Series.   H 449.   Second edition.

925 on Van Gelder. No Japan vellum copies were printed.

292. SOCRATES *PLATO'S APOLOGY OF SOCRATES AND CRITO WITH PART OF HIS PHAEDO* translated from the Greek by Benjamin Jowett.
[September] 1910.   *xxix*, 123, [1] pp.   19 x 14 cm.
Miscellaneous Series-50   H 507.   Only edition.

900 on Van Gelder; 25 numbered copies on Japan vellum.

Content: The introduction is by Jowett, and the text is preceded by "The Spirit of Plato" by Percy Bysshe Shelley, and by "The Voice of the Laws" by Edith Thomas.

Binding & Embellishment: The Van Gelder copies are bound in charcoal blue boards with ribs across the spine and white paper label printed in two colors. The Japan vellum copies are bound in Japan vellum boards. The Sheean typescript notes that Japan vellum copies are bound in Japan vellum wrappers over boards, but the copy examined at the State Library of Maine is in boards. Perhaps some copies were also bound in wrappers over boards. Pages of text ruled in black with Chiswick head-pieces. Title page printed in red and black; some initial letters are in red outline.

293. *PLAYING THE TANK TOWNS AND OTHER SKETCHES* by M. T. Space.
[October] 1916.   *vi*, 40, [1] pp.   14 x 9.5 cm.
Privately Printed-40   H 741.   Only edition.

300 copies printed on Van Gelder paper.

Content: This work contains seven sketches, two of which are in poetic form, and five written in a vernacular style.

Comment: Privately printed for George W. Elkins of Philadelphia. M.T. Space is the pseudonym of George W. Elkins.

Binding & Embellishment: Bound in Japan vellum wrappers over flexible boards; title/author printed on both the spine and the front cover; front cover ruled in green with green Chiswick initial. Title page in green and black; text pages ruled in green; green Chiswick lead initials.

294. *POEMS* by Dante Gabriel Rossetti. 1902.   2 *l.*, *lxxxi*, 338 pp.; port. front.
Quarto Series-6   H 229.   Only edition.

450 on Van Gelder; 25 numbered & signed on Japan vellum; 4 on Roman vellum, all signed by the publisher.

Content: The unsigned preface is by the publisher (pp. *xi-xv*). Appearing on pp. *xix-[lxxxi]* is Swinburne's 1870 essay, "The Poems of Dante Gabriel Rossetti" (*The Fortnightly Review*, May 1870, reprinted in *Essays and Studies*,

POEMS (continued)

1875), and a poem by Theodore Watts-Dunton is found on p. [x]. Rossetti's portrait frontispiece is by George Frederick Watts (Bierstadt
process). The sources for Rossetti's poems include the first edition of his
Poems (London: F. S. Ellis, 1870), and seven additional poems from the
Ellis & White edition (London, 1881). Mosher's end-notes draw heavily on
William Michael Rossetti's apparatus in the *Collected Works* (1886) and
are intended to remedy what he regarded as the ill-advised decisions of
both the poet in reprinting his poems in 1881 and his brother in attempting to reconcile the two editions, the details of which Mosher elaborates
in a preface footnote attacking WMR's editorial practices. The Notes are
divided into three sections: 1) "The Authorized Variants in Poems: 1870
taken from the edition of 1881," quoted virtually verbatim from the Preface to the *CW*; 2) "Variants from Manuscript Sources," based on three
separate sources: a variant ms. stanza of "Love's Nocturn" in William
Sharp's *Dante Gabriel Rossetti: A Record and a Study* (1882); variant
mss. readings of "Jenny" published in William Kingsland's essay on the
poem in *Poet-Lore* (January 1895), and the longer of two earlier versions
of "Ave"—"far too beautiful not to reproduce entire"—published by WMR
in "Some Scraps of Verse and Prose by Dante Gabriel Rossetti" in *Pall
Mall Magazine* (December 1898); and 3) "Notes by W. M. Rossetti,"
selected from the *CW*. Mosher's concern to issue a near definitive text of
Rossetti's poems by unraveling the complexities of the two editions of 1870 and
1881—a task "signally neglected by Rossetti's literary executor" and here accomplished by "one of his liegemen in America"—is evident throughout, as is his
anticipation of the companion volume, *Ballads & Sonnets* (B16), after whose
appearance in the following year the two volumes were sold only together.

Comment: In a letter to Mosher of August 24, 1902 (Houghton Library, bMS
Am 1096 [34]), literary critic and journalist, G. F. R. Anderson, praises
Mosher's edition for his service rendered to Rossetti's text and to criticism at
large, and commends him as being "more than a publisher" and for being "not
only a sage editor, but a minister of Beauty, Truth, and Immortality." Colbeck
calls this a "de-luxe edition."

Reference: Colbeck II, p. 697 (44); Fredeman 23.23 (p. 93); Quinn 8199 &
8200; Grigsby 971 & 972.

295. ***POEMS*** by Francis Thompson. [October] 1911.
      xx, 112 pp.; port. front. (same for second ed.)   19.5 x 14.5 cm.
      Miscellaneous Series-53   H 532.   First edition.

Content: These poems were taken from the 1893 London edition by Elkin
Mathews & John Lane, with three additional odes here collected for the first
time. Mosher wrote the foreword, and "A Word on Francis Thompson" by
Arthur Symons is reprinted from *The Saturday Review* (November 23, 1907).
A brief eulogy by James Douglas also precedes the main text.

Seven of these poems were previously printed by Mosher in the March 1908
issue of *The Bibelot* (31).

Binding & Embellishment: The Van Gelder copies are bound in charcoal blue
boards with a white spine label printed in two colors. The Japan vellum copies
are bound in Japan vellum boards with title/author/date directly printed on
spine. The portrait frontispiece on a Japan vellum leaf is a photogravure of the
poet. Title page in red and black; Chiswick ornaments.

450 Van Gelder; 50 numbered on
Japan vellum.

POEMS (continued)

The title page combines a Chiswick initial with a red-printed ornament designed by Laurence Housman for the British edition of Thompson's *Poems* (London: John Lane at the Bodley Head, 1895). For another use of Housman's designs, see 309.

Reference: *DLB* XIX, p. 384; Vilain 18 (plate 26 on p. 90); Beckson B55 notes the contribution by Arthur Symons on pp. *xvii-xx*; Quinn 10192, 10204 & 12059 (2nd ed.); not listed in Connolly.

295.1 ***POEMS*** by Francis Thompson. [October] 1914.
Miscellaneous Series.   H 616.   Second edition.

450 on Van Gelder. No Japan vellum copies were printed.

---

296. ***POEMS & BALLADS   FIRST SERIES*** by Algernon Charles Swinburne.
1904.   *xiii*, 337 pp.; port. front.
Quarto Series-9   H 294.   Second edition, revised.

450 on Van Gelder; 15 numbered & signed on Japan vellum; 4 on Roman vellum, numbered and signed by the publisher.

Content: The unsigned preface is by the publisher. The source text for this 1904 edition is Swinburne's *Poems and Ballads*. Third Edition (London: John Camden Hotten, 1868). The printer's copy, with Mosher's editorial marks, is in the Bishop Collection. The frontispiece portrait of Swinburne by Rossetti is reproduced via the Bierstadt process.

It was thought that this book was simply a reprint of Mosher 's 1899 *Laus Veneris   Poems & Ballads* (190), but examination of Mosher's source, and a page by page comparison of the two Mosher editions (190 & 296), shows this view is incorrect. *Poems & Ballads First Series* is a reprint of *Laus Veneris* with a new title and textual changes, and may still be looked upon as a "revised" edition of this Quarto Series text.

Comparisons between the 1899 and 1904 Mosher editions reveal that the preface is reduced from three pages to one, the "Notes on Poems and Reviews" in *Laus Veneris* are dropped from this 1904 edition, the lengthy Latin quote from Maistre Antoine Gaget precedes the poem "Laus Veneris" in the former edition, whereas in the 1904 edition it is relegated to the appendix along with its translation. Likewise, the "Note to the Leper" (without the translation) is taken from the appendix of the 1899 edition and placed on p. 141. The poem "Cleopatra" and the bibliography are also dropped from the 1904 edition, as are the three facsimiles which appeared in the 1899 edition. The pagination is also different, although the core text remains the same.

See entry 190 for the first Mosher edition, the Quarto Series *Laus Veneris*.

Reference: Vilain 38; Boss VII 148; Quinn 9477.

---

297. ***POEMS & BALLADS   SECOND & THIRD SERIES*** by Algernon Charles
Swinburne. 1902.   *xi*, 328 pp.
Quarto Series-5   H 228.   Only edition.

450 on Van Gelder; 25 numbered & signed on Japan vellum; and 4 on Roman vellum, all signed by the publisher.

Content: The unsigned preface by the publisher. The source text for Mosher's reprint of the 'Third Series' was the 1902, seventh edition, published by Chatto & Windus. The original copy, edited for the printer, is in the Bishop Collection. The source text for the 'Second Series' is not known, but most likely was a later Chatto & Windus edition as well. Two surviving signatures from this source are also in the Bishop Collection.

POEMS & BALLADS   SECOND & THIRD SERIES (continued)

T. J. Wise notes "in 1902 Thomas B. Mosher, of Portland, Maine, published an unauthorized edition of the Second and Third Series of Poems and Ballads together in one volume..."

The memorial verses on the "Death of Théophile Gautier," and "Ave Atque Vale" were previously printed by Mosher in the December 1898 issue of *The Bibelot* (21).

Reference: *DLB* LVII, p. 307; Vilain 38; The Ashley Library, V. 6, p. 176; Quinn 9471, 9472 & 9477; Wise I, p. 412; Grigsby 1131-32.

---

298. **POEMS IN PROSE** By Oscar Wilde. 1906.   *xvi*, 54 pp.
      Ideal Series of Little Masterpieces-2   H 361.   Only edition.

Limitation unknown for both Van Gelder and Japan vellum copies.

Content: The four-part foreword is signed by the publisher. These six prose poems were reprinted from *The Fortnightly Review* for July 1894: "The Artist," "The Doer of Good," "The Disciple," "The Master," "The House of Judgment," and "The Teacher of Wisdom."

The text of this work was printed by Mosher in his June 1904 issue of *The Bibelot* (27).

Reference: Vilain 41 (plates 45 & 46, p. 97); Cowan III, p. 69.

---

299. **POEMS IN PROSE FROM CHARLES BAUDELAIRE** translated by Arthur
      Symons. 1909.   *xiii*, 70 pp.
      Ideal Series of Little Masterpieces-11   H 475.   Only edition.

Limitation unknown for both Van Gelder and Japan vellum copies.

Content: The signed foreword (pp. [*ix*]-*xiii*) is by the publisher. A signed note by Arthur Symons is also printed on p. [*viii*]. Mosher mentions in his foreword that "it was his [Arthur Symons] expressed desire that I should publish his twelve selections from Baudelaire..."

Mosher also printed this work in the April 1909 issue of *The Bibelot* (32).

Reference: Beckson D7 notes this Arthur Symons translation; Quinn 7094.

---

300. **THE POEMS OF EDGAR ALLAN POE** with an Essay on his Poetry by
      Andrew Lang. 1901.   2 *l.*, *xxviii*, 87, [1] pp.
      Old World Series-23   H 181.   First edition.

925 on Van Gelder; 100 numbered copies on Japan vellum.

Content: The foreword by the publisher contains bibliographic information. There is an introductory essay by Andrew Lang on "The Poetry of Edgar Allan Poe" (pp. *xiii-xxviii*). Another Lang essay, "To Edgar Allan Poe," appears at the conclusion of the volume and is reprinted from *Letters to Dead Authors* (London: Longmans, Longmans, Green, and Co., 1886). A poem by John Henry Boner appears opposite the title page, and a quote from Charles Whibley (from *Studies in Frankness.* London: Heinemann, 1898) is on p. *xii*.

Though Mosher does not directly mention the precise source, he does refer to E. C. Stedman's comments from the ten volume *The Works of Edgar Allan Poe...* (Chicago: Stone & Kimball, 1894-95), "the culmination of half a century's appreciation and research" (p. *ix*). Along with the preface, dedication, and note to *The Raven and Other Poems* (New York: Wiley & Putnam, 1845), Mosher included 28 of Poe's later poems, and 12 of his poems written in youth. Mosher excluded "Tamerlane," "Al Aaraff," "Politian," and six other early poems as not fully representative, in his judgment, of Poe's poetic genius.

Reference: Not listed in *BAL*.

300.1 **THE POEMS OF EDGAR ALLAN POE** with an Essay on his Poetry by
Andrew Lang. 1906.   *xxxii*, 87 pp.
Old World Series.   H 370.   Second edition.

925 on Van Gelder. No Japan
vellum copies were printed.

301. **THE POEMS OF ERNEST DOWSON** Verses The Pierrot of the Minute
Decorations in Verse and Prose. 1902.
xxxvii, 162. [1] pp.   19 x 14.5 cm.
Miscellaneous Series-18   H 213.   Only edition.

600 on Van Gelder; 50 numbered
and signed on Japan vellum; 4 on
Roman vellum in folded sheets,
unbound, and signed by the publisher.
First collected edition.

Content: This book includes Dowson's *Verses* (London: L. Smithers, 1896), *The Pierrot of the Minute* (London, 1897), and *Decorations: in Verse and Prose* (London: L. Smithers, 1899). The two-part, unsigned foreword is by the publisher.

In addition to the works of Dowson, this book contains a poem by Anna Jameson (p. [*x*]), a poem by Arthur Symons (p. [*xvi*]), a lengthy three-part essay by Arthur Symons from *The Fortnightly Review* (June 1900) which also appeared in the October 1900 issue of *The Bibelot* (23), an epilogue by William Theodore Peters to Dowson's *The Pierrot of the Minute*, and an epilogue by Arthur Symons (p. [162]).

The text from this work appeared later in the August 1905 issue of *The Bibelot* (28) and in the March 1912 issue of *The Bibelot* (35).

Comment: See entry 289 for publication in 1913 of *The Pierrot of the Minute* in the Lyric Garland Series.

Noting several contributions by Arthur Symons, Beckson indi-cates: "See Thomas B. Mosher's 1902 edition (B28) which con-tains five brief prose selections omitted in the Lane edition."

William E. Fredeman notes that "...his [Mosher's] edition of Dow-son's *Poems*, antedating John Lane's London edition of 1905 by three years, ranks as the first collected edition."

Binding & Embellishment: The Van Gelder copies are bound in Japan vellum boards while the Japan vellum copies are bound in Japan vellum wraps over boards; both have the title printed directly on the spine and front cover. Other than the large drop-cap "T" on the title page, the book is not embellished with any ornamentation.

Reference: Beckson B28 & B36; Quinn 2686 & 2687; *PBSC*, p. 41 (Fredeman's quote); Cevasco 36, 37 & 158, and p. 41 (1); Grigsby 293 & 294; Colbeck I, p. 223 (13).

THE POEMS OF ❧ ❧
ERNEST DOWSON
VERSES
THE PIERROT OF THE MINUTE
DECORATIONS
IN VERSE AND PROSE

PORTLAND MAINE
THOMAS B MOSHER
MDCCCCII

302. **THE POEMS OF MASTER FRANÇOIS VILLON OF PARIS** now first done into English Verse in the Original Forms with a Biographical and Critical Introduction by John Payne. [October] 1900.
xvi, 261, [1] pp.; front., facsims. (same through third ed.)   19.2 x 14.5 cm.
Reprints of Privately Printed Books-6   H 153.   First edition.

725 on Van Gelder; 50 numbered
copies on Japan vellum; 4 printed
on Roman vellum and signed by
the publisher.
First American edition.

Content: Mosher indicates in the 1900 catalogue that "this reprint is based upon three editions: the rare first edition of 1878 of which but 157 copies were privately printed; secondly, the edition of 1881, issued for public sale by Reeves and Turner, London... [and] lastly the Villon Society edition of 1892, in which Mr. Payne gave his final text..." (p. 40). The foreword, with extensive bibliographical information, is by the publisher.

THE POEMS OF MASTER FRANÇOIS VILLON (continued)

A ballad to John Payne by Théodore de Banville (pp. *v-vi*), selections from Robert Louis Stevenson's *Familiar Studies of Men and Books* (p. *xii*), and extensive notes by the translator (pp. [239]-256) are also included. See Sturm's note to 302.1.

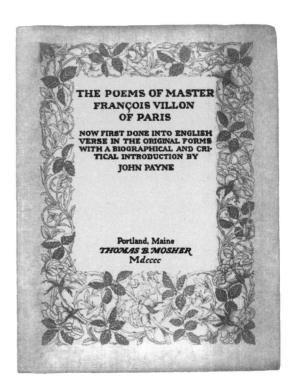

The frontispiece and the facsimiles at the rear of the volume were taken from the privately printed edition of *The Poems of Master Francis Villon...* (London: Printed for the Villon Society, 1878), to which Mosher gave credit.

Several of these ballads were printed by Mosher in *The Bibelot* for February 1895 (18).

THE "OMITTED LINES"

An eight page, privately printed addition (18.5 x 13.4 cm.) entitled "Villon / Omitted Lines" was inserted into some copies. This publication contains lines considered too risqué to be published in the Mosher edition. The sections affected are "The Complaint of the Fair Helm-maker Grown Old" (pp. 141/42 & 168/69), the "Ballad and Orison" (p. 173), the "Ballad of Slanderous Tongues" (p. 181), the "Ballad Entitled the Counterblast to Franc-Gontier" (pp. 182 & 186), the "Ballad of Villon and Muckle Meg" (p. 187), and lastly, the "Ballad of Ladies' Love" (p. 237). A total of 119 lines omitted in the Mosher edition were printed in a size which easily fit into *The Poems*. The 'Omitted Lines' was printed on Van Gelder, Japan vellum, and vellum, all copies sewn with yellow silk thread. Further details are given below.

According to the sale catalogue of The Library of Henry W. Poor, "Only a small number printed on Japanese vellum paper. Laid in is the privately printed 'Omitted Lines' printed in the same type and on Japanese vellum paper, issued by H. W. Bryant of Portland, Me." The previous Poor entry mentions that the Roman vellum edition also contains the rare omitted lines. An examination of the actual Poor Copy #2 (also once owned by Quinn, #10538) in the Bishop Collection confirms that some "omitted lines" were indeed printed on Roman vellum. Also, a boxed copy containing the eight page 'Omitted Lines' on Japan vellum was inspected in a private collection along with a letter printed on Strathmore deckle-edge paper marked confidential:

> Portland, Maine, 223 Middle St. 30 March 1901. Dear Sir. I can offer you a privately printed copy of the passages omitted from Mr. Mosher's edition of the Poems of François Villon. It is of the same format, same type and paper. Edition Limited and will be fore-warded [sic] on receipt of price, on Paper, $2; Japan Vellum, $3. Truly yours, H. W. Bryant [i.e., Hubbard Winslow Bryant].

The H. W. Bryant bookselling firm was located in Portland, ME. Bryant published a check-list of town histories, catalogues on local histories and genealogies. It is not known whether the publication of "The Omitted Lines" was immediately approved by Mosher, or whether or not it was partly his plan to print these lines, but his later letter of July 7, 1911 to W. Irving Way (The Huntington Library, WY 62) indicates he had copies:

> ...which I bought in and which fit precisely into the book of my edition of the said Villon. Now I am not going to put these out to the hoi polloi, or the general public, or into the hands of school children but I thought you would like to know of this fact because it seems to me you could do quite a little business while the copies lasted in special copies of my Villon with this added which completes the text.

THE POEMS OF MASTER FRANÇOIS VILLON (continued)

Comment: Mosher's words to E. C. Stedman on lines omitted in the Villon issue of *The Bibelot* (February, 1895) apply equally to this volume: "I'm trying to *interest* people in old literature… and to begin by disgusting them, or obliging anyone to call the police, isn't my notion of editorial duties at all at all [sic]" (see Wolf who quoted the letter at Columbia University).

Mosher's edition appears to be the first American edition. Neither Peckham nor Sturm list any previous American edition.

Binding & Embellishment: The cover design is taken from C. R. Ricketts' border design for the Vale Press. Both the Van Gelder and the Japan vellum copies are bound in the multi-color printed Japan vellum wrappers over boards. Vellum copies were bound in flexible vellum boards with ties. For other books using Vale Press & Charles Ricketts designs, see entry 47. Title page is printed in red and black; Ricketts-style lead initials in red and black.

Reference: Vilain 56; Peckham, p. 99 (Eng 1900) also includes the 1905, '09 and '15 eds.; Sturm 187 & 217 (p. 98 for 2nd ed.); Quinn 10538 & 10539; Poor IV, #930 & 931 (Feb. 23-25, 1909); Wolf, p. 100; Grigsby 1276-77.

302.1 ***THE POEMS OF MASTER FRANÇOIS VILLON OF PARIS*** now first done into English Verse in the Original Forms with a Biographical and Critical Introduction by John Payne. [November] 1905.
Reprints of Privately Printed Books.   H 345.   Second Edition.

500 copies printed on Van Gelder paper.

Comment: Hatch's pagination for this edition differed from the first and third, but copies I examined have the same pagination.

302.2 ***THE POEMS OF MASTER FRANÇOIS VILLON OF PARIS*** now first done into English Verse in the Original Forms with a Biographical and Critical Introduction by John Payne. [February] 1909.
Reprints of Privately Printed Books.   H 501.   Third Edition.

500 on Van Gelder of which 425 bound in decorated Japan vellum wrappers and 75 copies bound in old-style boards.

303. ***THE POEMS OF MASTER FRANÇOIS VILLON OF PARIS*** now first done into English Verse in the Original Forms with a Biographical and Critical Introduction by John Payne. [October] 1916.
xviii, 271, [1] pp.; port. front., facsims.
Reprints of Privately Printed Books-13   H 644.   New edition/same series.

725 copies on Van Gelder; 10 numbered copies on Japan vellum.

Content: A new frontispiece portrait of John Payne, and six additional facsimile illustrations taken from Pierre Champion's *François Villon, Sa Vie et Son Temps* (Paris: H. Champion, 1913), appear at the rear of this edition. The publisher's foreword, expanded from the preceding editions, updates information on Villon, and contains remarks in tribute to John Payne. The basic textual content outlined in 302 remains the same.

Comment: With the appearance of this new edition, *The Poems of Master François Villon* has to be classified as the 13th publication, and technically speaking, becomes the last publication of the series. The 1902 *Rubáiyát of Omar Khayyám* (B336), however, may still be regarded as the last *title* appearing in the Reprints of Privately Printed Books Series.

Some note must be made as to why this book has been assigned the last series number. The rationale for this is covered in some detail in the prefatory remarks to "The Mosher Series" in Section I. Suffice it to say here that entry

THE POEMS OF MASTER FRANÇOIS VILLON OF PARIS (continued)

303 really constitutes a *new* edition. Mosher states in his 1916 catalogue that "in this new edition a number of facsimiles of title-pages and illustrations from the original French edition of 1489 have been added, a few new notes inserted with a brief memoir, and a photo-gravure portrait of the late translator." Add to this the radically different binding, and what was really produced is a new edition for Mosher's clientele, not just a fourth reprint of the earlier editions with minor embellishments. Furthermore, to remain consistent with how post-1915 books were assigned series numbers in the Miscellaneous Series (see, for example, entries 107/8, 152/53, 171/72, 182/83, 238/39 & 403/4), this volume has been assigned a separate number in the Reprints of Privately Printed Books Series.

Binding & Embellishment: The binding was changed to plain blue boards with a paper label on the spine. Some copies were bound in Holliston Buckram with top edges gilt for library use. The Japan vellum copies are bound in Japan vellum boards. The Sheean typescript notes Japan vellum wrappers over boards, but the copy examined at the State Library of Maine is as described above. Perhaps some copies were bound in wrappers too. Textual embellishments remain the same as entry 302.

Reference: Quinn 10544.

304. ***THE POEMS OF OSCAR WILDE*** Ravenna   Poems   The Sphinx
The Ballad of Reading Gaol. [October] 1903.
viii, 297, [1] pp.   19 x 14 cm.
Miscellaneous Series-21   H 248.   First edition.

600 on Van Gelder; 50 numbered/signed on Japan vellum; 6 on Roman vellum in folded sheets unbound, also signed by the publisher.

Content: The texts drawn upon include *Ravenna* (Oxford: Shrimpton, 1878), the text of the fifth London edition of *Poems* (Bogue, 1882), *The Sphinx* (London: Mathews and Lane, 1894), and *The Ballad of Reading Gaol* (London: Smithers, 1898). Each major section is preceded by a bibliographical description of the first edition of the work represented.

Binding & Embellishment: The Van Gelder copies are bound in Japan vellum boards with the title printed directly on the spine and front cover. Japan vellum copies are bound in Japan vellum printed wraps over boards. Mason also notes that 75 copies were "specially bound in old-style gray boards, ribbed back [spine], with white paper labels." This is confirmed in Mosher's book catalogue for 1903 (247). Other than the frontispiece and the drop-cap "T" on the title page, there are no other embellishments.

This book is uniform with Wilde's *Intentions* (174) in size and binding.

Reference: Quinn 11119 & 11121; Mason (*Poems*), pp. 2, 10-11 (XII) and p. 86 (VI); Cowan III, pp. 63-65.

304.1 ***THE POEMS OF OSCAR WILDE*** Ravenna   Poems   The Sphinx
The Ballad of Reading Gaol. [June] 1905.   *viii*, 310, [1] pp.; port. front.
Miscellaneous Series.   H 341.   Second edition, augmented

750 on Van Gelder. No Japan vellum copies were printed.

Content: Mosher calls this "a Second and Augmented Edition" in his 1905 book catalogue. In addition to the contents of the first edition (304), this edition offers nine previously uncollected poems: 1. "Stanzas addressed to the poet's wife, Constance," 2. "Le Jardin des Tuileries," 3. "With a Copy of 'A House of Pomegranates'," 4. "The True Knowledge," 5. "On the Recent Sale by Auction of Keats' Love Letters," 6. "The New Remorse," 7. "The Harlot's House," 8. "Under the Balcony," and 9. "Wasted Days."

THE POEMS OF OSCAR WILDE (continued)

The portrait frontispiece of Wilde is by Ellis & Walerly taken in 1892 (for use of the same photo, see entries 193 & 305). This portrait was not used in the 1903 edition (304), being added here for the first time.

Comment: Mason (*Poems*) indicates "Methuen's edition [London, 1908] includes twenty-four poems and translations hitherto uncollected as against nine given by Mosher [in this 1905 edition]." As with the 1903 edition, Mason (*Poems*) also notes in his bibliography that "75 copies with white label in red and black... [and] No copies on Japan vellum were issued." This statement is confirmed in Mosher's catalogue for 1905.

This Mosher edition was reprinted by F. M. Buckles in 1906 (2 vols.).

Reference: Mason (*Poems*), pp. 11-12 (XIII), notes on pp. 13, 52, 54, and 57; Mason (*Works*), p. 97.

---

305. ***THE POETICAL WORKS OF OSCAR WILDE INCLUDING POEMS IN PROSE*** with Notes Bibliographical Introduction Index and Facsimiles of Title-Pages. [September] 1908.

xxiii, 396, 6 *l.*, [1] pp.; port. front., facsim.   19.5 x 14.5 cm.
Miscellaneous Series-41   H 435.   Only edition.

750 Van Gelder; 25 numbered copies on Japan vellum, signed by the publisher.

Content: Mosher called this a "Bibliographical Edition" which included all the poems of his first two *The Poems of Oscar Wilde* (304 & 304.1), plus twenty uncollected poems, four translations, and "Poems in Prose," together with the text from the authorized published works. He follows the Methuen (London 1908) edition (Vol. IX) published a few months earlier, but adds the "Poems in Prose" which the Methuen edition distributes to other volumes in the *Works of Oscar Wilde*. Mosher carefully bracketed all additional stanzas to Wilde's authorized versions which the Methuen edition failed to do.

Examination of Mosher's copy of the 1882 fifth Bogue edition of Wilde's *Poems* (Bishop Collection) also reveals several corrections in text which do not appear in his previous two reprints of *The Poems*... With these improvements Mosher felt he collected "in all probability the last windfalls recoverable from the poetic tree of Oscar Wilde's genius" and called this "the latest and only entire collection of his poetical works" (pp. *xviii* and *xxi*). Just one year later Methuen would issue a second edition in September 1909 with two newly recovered poems from Wilde's manuscript copies. So much for an *édition définitive* and Mosher's hopes of winning the game of one-upmanship with Methuen.

(a)

The three-part bibliographical introduction is signed by the publisher. A poem signed "A.D." is printed on p. [*xiv*]. The frontispiece photograph of Wilde is from the 1892 Ellis & Walery plate (also used in entries 193 & 304.1).

This volume also contains an extensive Bibliographical Index and includes bibliographical information preceding *Ravenna, Poems, The Sphinx*, and *The Ballad of Reading Gaol*. Five facsimile title pages, and a facsimile certificate reproducing Wilde's signature, are added at the rear of the book.

Comment: In Mason's preface to the *Bibliography of Oscar Wilde* (1914) thanks and acknowledgments are given, including to "Mr Thos. B. Mosher, the producer of beautiful books in America." Mason does not formally enter even one Mosher imprint throughout the bibliography (not even in the section on "Pirated Editions") as he did in his *A Bibliography of the Poems of Oscar Wilde* (1907); however, Mason did point out that "no attempt has been made

(b)

THE POETICAL WORKS OF OSCAR WILDE (continued)

to include the countless American unauthorized editions..." Still, this is an unusual turnaround.

In a letter to Mosher dated Dec. 4, 1908 (The Houghton Library, bMS Am 1096 [987]) Mason praises Mosher's 1908 edition:

> Mr. Ledger has just shown me your last edition of Oscar Wilde's Poems. It is indeed a beautiful volume, one of the most beautiful that even you have ever issued. I only wish there was a publisher over here who could have brought out the new edition [Methuen's] in as delightful a form... The facsimiles you add are most interesting; indeed, the whole book is ideal. If you only knew how obstinate Methuen is about details you would not wonder that the English edition is so unsatisfactory in parts!

Mosher was also praised in using brackets for phrases Wilde later rejected.

Binding & Embellishment: The Van Gelder copies are bound in charcoal blue paper boards; spine with slightly raised bands and white paper label printed in two colors. The front cover has the plum design in gilt on the upper right corner. The Japan vellum copies are bound in Japan vellum boards with slightly raised bands, and title label on Japan vellum printed in two colors. Hatch neglected to list the 25 copies printed on Japan vellum. The title page is printed in red and black, with a large drop-cap "T" beginning the title.

The front and back cover designs of large plum blossoms first appeared on the second edition of Wilde's *Poems* (London: David Bogue, 1881). The firm of Matthew Bell was responsible for the binding of the book. In his 1908 catalogue, Mosher points out his cover is "stamped in gold from an original design by the author." Mosher uses Wilde's design, as did Bogue, on the front and back covers, but unlike Bogue, he did not place the design on the spine of the book.

Reference: See notes in Mason (*Works*), entry 305 and pp. 198, 202 and the preface, p. *viii*; Quinn 11180; Cowan I, p. 13.

---

306. ***POLONIUS: A COLLECTION OF WISE SAWS AND MODERN INSTANCES***
by Edward FitzGerald. 1901.   *xxxii*, 109, [1] pp.; incl. facsim.   19 x 14.5 cm.
Miscellaneous Series-16   H 185.   Only edition.

450 on Van Gelder; 50 numbered copies on Japan vellum; 4 on Roman vellum in folded sheets unbound, signed by Mosher. First edition of the revised text.

Content: The unsigned foreword is by Mosher and contains a great deal of bibliographical information, including details about the unique copy from which he reprinted this edition. The comments in Mosher's 1901 catalogue (206) are illuminating:

> ... *Polonius* has never been reprinted in separate book-form since the date of its first appearance in 1852 [London, W. Pickering]... This unaccountable neglect of a golden opportunity Mr. Mosher is very glad to improve, the more so that the copy in his possession is unique. It is enriched by a number of marginalia in the author's own hand, showing that he had revised the text with a view to its possible reissue. *These additions and alterations are here included for the first time.*

FitzGerald's alterations and additions are clearly identified throughout the text. The work was reprinted in an American edition of the *Works of Edward FitzGerald* (New York & Boston: Houghton Mifflin, 1887), but this is the first reprint of the work in separate form.

Binding & Embellishment: Van Gelder copies are bound in charcoal-blue paper boards with a white spine label, and the front cover design stamped in gold. Japan vellum copies are bound in Japan vellum wraps over boards with the spine and front covers gilt-stamped directly on the wraps.

POLONIUS (continued)

The cover's wreath with Spanish motto, LA VERDAD ES SIÉMPRE VERDE. (meaning "truth is always green") is taken from the first London edition

Two head-pieces are signed "CW" for Charlotte Whittingham, designer for the Chiswick Press of London (see Warren). The book also contains a facsimile of the original title page on p. [*xi*]. For other Chiswick Press designs used, see entry 48.

Mosher saw this as a companion volume to *Edward FitzGerald: An Aftermath* (101).

Reference: *DLB* XXXII, 118; Colbeck I, p. 256 (30); Grigsby 401 & 402; Leuba 77; Warren, p. 311.

---

307. *POMPILIA* by Robert Browning with an Introduction by Arthur Symons. 1903.   *xxviii*, 70, [1] pp.
Old World Series-29   H 244.   Only edition.

925 on Van Gelder; 100 numbered copies on Japan vellum.
First separate printing in book form.

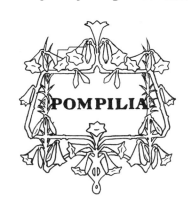

Content: Mosher does not identify the precise source text for his reprint of *Pompilia*, the seventh of Browning's famous dramatic monologues from *The Ring and the Book*. The invocation at the beginning, and the dedication at the end, are from the larger work. The introduction by Arthur Symons is a newly edited version of Symons' essay first appearing in his book: *An Introduction to the Study of Browning* (London: Cassell & Company, Limited, 1886, pp. 131-149).

In Mosher's bibliography of Arthur Symons (441) he notes that "this Introduction is not a mere reprint of passages from *The Study of Browning*." The second sale catalogue of Mosher's library (October 11 & 12, 1948, item 41) confirms this, for included in the lot of 23 Symons letters was a:

> Manuscript, in the autograph of Mrs. Symons, signed by Arthur Symons, entitled *"Introduction, for Robert Browning's Pompilia"*, published by Thomas B. Mosher. 8 pp., 4to.

Reference: Beckson B32; Quinn 1053.

---

308. *THE PORTRAIT OF MR W. H.* by Oscar Wilde. [August] 1901.
75, [1] pp. (same for all three ed.)
Brocade Series-27   H 189.   First edition.

425 on Japan vellum for each edition.
First separate edition.

Content: The publisher's note opposite the title page mentions that "this essay first appeared in *Blackwood's Edinburgh Magazine* for July, 1889, and is here reprinted entire."

Comment: This work is one of five comprising a sub-series under the group title of "Prose Selections by Oscar Wilde." Other Brocades in this grouping are: *The Happy Prince and Other Tales* (142), *The Young King : The Star-Child* (443), *The Fisherman and His Soul* (112), and *The Birthday of the Infanta* (44). Mosher not only grouped these five titles in his catalogues, but also provided a cabinet-style box for them.

Reference: *DLB* LVII, p. 355; Cowan II, pp. 56-57, III, p. 70.

308.1 *THE PORTRAIT OF MR W. H.* by Oscar Wilde. [June] 1904.
Brocade Series.   H 310.   Second edition.

308.2 *THE PORTRAIT OF MR W. H.* by Oscar Wilde. [February] 1908.
Brocade Series.   H 456.   Third edition.

309. **THE PRESENT CRISIS** by James Russell Lowell. [December] 1917.
29, [1] pp.   16.5 x 12.5 cm.
Privately Printed-45   H 746.   First thus.

Content: The signed foreword is by the publisher. The source for this little volume is the second series of "Poems," taken from the collected *Writings* (Boston: Houghton, Mifflin, 1899) which was in Mosher's library. The only change is Mosher's numbering of the stanzas. The brief selection "Richard Rumbold, on the scaffold, 1685" appears opposite the title page. A Christmas greeting personally signed by both Edward and Gertrude Woods is printed on a leaf before the half-title.

Comment: Privately printed for Edward A. Woods of Sewickley, PA.

An identical copy exists without any colophon note (Bishop Collection). Since this copy had Flora Lamb's calling card inserted along with the original Christmas greeting insert bound in, it is reasonable to assume that a few copies were produced and used for personal distribution. In a Nov. 14, 1934 letter, Oliver Sheean wrote of Edward A. Woods' books that "an edition usually runs one or two over and I always have one of the overs of the privately printed books" (Bishop Collection). Sheean was a part-time employee at the Mosher Press.

Both the Sheean and Lamb typescripts say there were 1,275 copies. Copies examined have the limitation of 1200, so possibly there were 75 other copies printed like the above copy with Flora Lamb's calling card.

Binding & Embellishment: This book is bound in bright red Toyogami paper wraps with a gold laurel wreath design enclosing the title/author on the front cover. The title page and colophon are printed in red and black.

The design on the title page is the one Laurence Housman created for the 1896 *Were-Wolf* published by John Lane at the Bodley Head. The design in the colophon is also by Laurence Housman, first used in the 1899 *The Silence of Love* also published by John Lane. For another use of Housman's designs, see 295.

Reference: Vilain 51.

——————— *Same Title, Change of Series* ———————

310. **THE PRESENT CRISIS** by James Russell Lowell. [September] 1918.
29, [1] pp.   16.5 x 12.5 cm.
Miscellaneous Series-86   H 665.   First thus.

Comment: Mosher must have been sufficiently impressed with the private printing of this book the year before (309) in that he brought out his own reprint in the Miscellaneous Series.

This book is also bound in the same bright red Toyogami wraps with the gilt laurel wreath design. The Japan vellum edition is bound in Japan vellum wraps, with the laurel wreath design on the front cover. See entry 309 for details about the designs employed in this edition.

311. **PRIMAVERA: POEMS BY FOUR AUTHORS.** 1900.
xii, 43 pp.   19.5 x 11.5 cm.
Miscellaneous Series-11   H 141.   Only edition.

Content: The four authors represented are Stephen Phillips, Laurence Binyon, Arthur S. Cripps, and Manmohan Ghose. The contents are taken from the B. H.

1,200 copies on French Arches handmade paper.

(a)

(b)

950 copies on French handmade paper; 25 numbered copies on Japan vellum.

450 copies on Kelmscott "Hammer & Anvil" handmade paper; 50 on Japan vellum; and 4 on Classic vellum, signed by the publisher.

PRIMAVERA: POEMS BY FOUR AUTHORS (continued)

Blackwell edition (London, 1890) except for the addition of a preface by John Addington Symonds excerpted from his review in *The Academy* for August 9, 1890. A 14-line poem "O Primavera" (in Italian) by Guarini (*Pastor Fido*, Atto iii, Sc. I) is also included and translates:

> O Spring, youth of the year,
> Beautiful mother of flowers,
> Of the new grass and new loves,
> It is well you return; but with you,
> The serene and fortunate days of my joy
> Do not return:
> It is well that you return, return,
> But with you return only the miserable and
> Sorrowful remembrance of my lost,
> My dear treasure.
> Thou wast in the old days
> So charming, so beautiful,
> But I am not myself what I was once,
> So dear to the eyes of others.

(a)

Binding & Embellishment: Kelmscott paper copies are bound in gray wraps over boards printed in two colors. The Japan vellum copies are printed on Japan vellum wraps over boards employing the same two-color scheme. For other books printed on Kelmscott paper, see entry 47.

(b)

The half-title design signed "SI" was done by the British artist, Selwyn Image, for the cover of the original B. H. Blackwell edition, and is attributed to him by Mosher in his bibliographical note. For other Selwyn Image designs used, see entry 57.

Mosher notes in his Catalogue for 1900 that "this is the second book (*Hand and Soul* being the first) which Mr. Mosher has printed on genuine hand-made paper such as was used by the Kelmscott Press." He also indicates that the cover is a "unique cover design in two colors" and consists of eight sinuous stylized flowers and buds in green and red with a drop-title in the upper right corner and "POEMS BY-FOUR AUTHORS" in the bottom right corner. A single flower from the cover design graces the title page. Writing about *Fancy's Following* in the Autumn List accompanying *The Bibelot* for October 1900, Mosher mentions "the cover design in colors is one of originality and great beauty and is the work of Miss Isadore B. Paine who designed the *Primavera* wrapper last spring." For other design work by Isadore B. Paine, see entries 106, 116 & 128.

See color illustration on p. 369 (Plate 3).

Reference: Vilain 16 (plate 24, p. 89); Quinn 9677; Grigsby 911-913; Japan Paper Company (Kelmscott Hand-made Paper from England).

---

312. *A PRINCE OF COURT PAINTERS AN IMAGINARY PORTRAIT*
by Walter Pater. [August] 1898.   64, [1] pp. (same for second ed.)
Brocade Series-7   H 69.   First edition.

425 on Japan vellum for each edition.
First edition in separate book form.

Content: Jenkinson notes this as a "faithful reprint of the first collected edition published in 1887 [*Imaginary Portraits* (London & New York: Macmillan)]."

Comment: See note to entry 62 for this title's appearance in a sub-series.

Reference: Wright, p. 163 (Also Section I, "a 37"); Jenkinson II, 848.

312.1 *A PRINCE OF COURT PAINTERS AN IMAGINARY PORTRAIT*
by Walter Pater. [September] 1898.
Brocade Series.   H 96.   Second edition.

312.2 *A PRINCE OF COURT PAINTERS AN IMAGINARY PORTRAIT*
by Walter Pater. [July] 1906.   65, [1] pp.
Brocade Series.   H 374.   Third edition.

---

313. **THE PRIVATE PAPERS OF HENRY RYECROFT** by George Gissing with
an Introductory Survey by Thomas Seccombe. [December] 1921.
lxiv, 246, [1] pp.   19 x 14.5 cm.
Miscellaneous Series-95   H 688.   Only edition.

700 on van Gelder; 25 numbered copies on Japan vellum.

Content: The signed foreword is by the publisher. The introductory survey,
"The Work of George Gissing" by Thomas Seccombe, is taken from Gissing's
collection of short stories in *The House of Cobwebs* (London: Constable,
1906). There are also two brief selections from Maupassant and J. M. Kennedy
on p. [*xii*]. A bibliography appears on pp. [245]-246.

Binding & Embellishment: Van Gelder copies bound in quarter Old-Style
ribbed boards (raised bands) over blue paper boards with spine label in red
and black. Japan vellum copies in Japan vellum wraps over boards with spine
label printed directly on the vellum. The title page is printed in red and black.

Reference: Garland IC (p. 20).

---

314. **PROVERBS IN PORCELAIN AND OTHER POEMS** by Austin Dobson.
1909.   *vi*, 64, [1] pp.
Lyric Garland Series-17   H 474.   Only edition.

950 on Van Gelder paper; 100 numbered copies on Japan vellum.

Content: Alban Dobson notes that "this volume... was a pirated reprint of
Proverbs in Porcelain, 1893 and 1905, without the poem 'Au Revoir,' but with
sixteen other poems selected at random from the author's works. Its existence
was apparently not known to the author..."

The text of this work was also printed by Mosher in his September 1901 and
November 1908 issues of *The Bibelot* (24 & 31).

Reference: Dobson, p. 87, no. (2).

Q

315. **QUATTROCENTISTERIA HOW SANDRO BOTTICELLI SAW SIMONETTA
IN THE SPRING** by Maurice Hewlett. [September] 1898.
54, [1] pp.; front. (same through seventh ed.)
Brocade Series-12   H 74.   First edition.

425 on Japan vellum for each edition.

Content: The unsigned foreword is by the publisher. Included are a poem by
Giacomino Fugliesi translated by D. G. Rossetti, and a reproduction of Botti-
celli's "Birth of Spring." The text is a chapter from Hewlett's *Earthwork Out of
Tuscany* which Mosher published in its entirety in 1911 (97); likewise, the
"Proem" is taken from the closing chapter of the same work.

Mosher first printed this text in the May 1896 issue of *The Bibelot* (19).

QUATTROCENTISTERIA (continued)

Comment: Ratta pictures a fictitious title page which he ascribes to Mosher for *Quattrocentisteria*. The title is pictured within a Morrisian border reminiscent of Bertram Grosvenor Goodhue's work.

Reference: Ratta. Vol. II, tavola (plate) 253.

315.1 *QUATTROCENTISTERIA HOW SANDRO BOTTICELLI SAW SIMONETTA IN THE SPRING* by Maurice Hewlett. [November] 1898.
Brocade Series.   H 101.   Second edition.

315.2 *QUATTROCENTISTERIA HOW SANDRO BOTTICELLI SAW SIMONETTA IN THE SPRING* by Maurice Hewlett. [February] 1900.
Brocade Series.   H 173.   Third edition.

315.3 *QUATTROCENTISTERIA HOW SANDRO BOTTICELLI SAW SIMONETTA IN THE SPRING* by Maurice Hewlett. [December] 1901.
Brocade Series.   H 205.   Fourth edition.

[xx]. *QUATTROCENTISTERIA HOW SANDRO BOTTICELLI SAW SIMONETTA IN THE SPRING* by Maurice Hewlett. [between 1901 and 1908].
Brocade Series.   Fifth edition.

Comment: This edition was listed in the Hatch *Check List* as an unlocated trade edition. It might exist, but it is also possible that Mosher missed this number and wrongly attributed his 1908 edition as the 6th edition. If ever found, this edition will become 315.31 in the present bibliography.

Reference: Hatch, p. 167.

315.4 *QUATTROCENTISTERIA HOW SANDRO BOTTICELLI SAW SIMONETTA IN THE SPRING* by Maurice Hewlett. [July] 1908.
Brocade Series.   H 452A.   Sixth edition.

Comment: This edition was listed in the Hatch *Check List* as an unlocated trade edition, but was later added by Hatch in 1972 (see Vilain).

Reference: Vilain, p. 65; Hatch p. 167.

315.5 *QUATTROCENTISTERIA HOW SANDRO BOTTICELLI SAW SIMONETTA IN THE SPRING* by Maurice Hewlett. [July] 1913.
Brocade Series.   H 601.   Seventh edition.

——————— *Same Title, Change of Series* ———————

316. MAURICE HEWLETT *QUATTROCENTISTERIA (HOW SANDRO BOTTICELLI SAW SIMONETTA IN THE SPRING)* by Maurice Hewlett. [October] 1904. *viii*, 60 pp.; front. (same for second ed.)
Vest Pocket Series-8   H 293.   First edition thus.

Limitation unknown for both Van Gelder and Japan vellum copies.

Content: The signed foreword is by the publisher. Included are a portrait frontispiece of Simonetta Cattaneo, a poem by D. G. Rossetti, and the "Proem" by Maurice Hewlett.

Reference: Crichton 43.

316.1 MAURICE HEWLETT *QUATTROCENTISTERIA (HOW SANDRO BOTTICELLI SAW SIMONETTA IN THE SPRING)* by Maurice Hewlett. [January] 1908.
Vest Pocket Series.   H 457.   Second edition.

317.   *A QUIET ROAD* by Lizette Woodworth Reese. [October] 1916.
        x, 64, [1] pp.   19 x 14 cm.
        Miscellaneous Series-79   H 638.   Only edition.

450 on Van Gelder; 25 numbered copies on Japan vellum.

Content: The contents consists of 52 poems (including "The Road of Remembrance" printed before the contents pages). The copyright is in the poet's name under the date of 1896.

Comment: In an inscribed copy Lizette Woodworth Reese notes that this is "my favorite book. I don't know why. L.W.R." (Bishop Collection).

Reese received a 10% royalty from all her books sold.

Binding & Embellishment: Van Gelder copies are bound in quarter cream spine over patterned boards; label in red and black on the spine. Chiswick ornaments sparingly used. A Japan vellum copy has not been located for inspection.

Reference: See the Nov. 17, 1941 letter from Lamb to Yorke for Mosher's payment terms (see Appendix II).

R

318.   *RAB AND HIS FRIENDS* by John Brown, M.D. [May] 1900.
        xvi, 17-52, [1] pp. (same through third ed.)
        Brocade Series-19   H 145.   First edition.

425 on Japan vellum for each edition.

Content: Following the title page is a poem by Robert Louis Stevenson entitled "To Doctor John Brown." The publisher's bibliographical note on p. [*x*] indicates that the preface by Dr. Brown first appeared in the illustrated quarto edition of *Rab and His Friends* (Edinburgh: Edmonston and Douglas, 1862).

Comment: This work, along with two others, is part of a sub-series (see 233).

318.1 *RAB AND HIS FRIENDS* by John Brown, M.D. [December] 1901.
        Brocade Series.   H 206.   Second edition.

318.2 *RAB AND HIS FRIENDS* by John Brown, M.D. [June] 1909.
        Brocade Series.   H 494.   Third edition.

319.   *RABBI BEN EZRA* by Robert Browning. [April] 1909.   *viii*, 22, [1] pp. (same for second ed.)
        Golden Text Series-3   H 477.   First edition.

925 Van Gelder; 100 Japan vellum.

Content: The signed foreword is by the publisher. A brief selection from Browning appears opposite the title page. A "Prospice" (pp. 3-4), and "Epilogue" (pp. 21-[22]) by Browning are added to the 32 numbered stanzas of the main poem (pp. 5-20).

Comment: First classified by Mosher in 1909 under the Miscellaneous Series, it was reclassified in 1910 under the Golden Text Series.

Reference: Grigsby 136.

319.1 **RABBI BEN EZRA** by Robert Browning. [August] 1920.
    Golden Text Series.   H 686.   Second edition.

475 copies on Van Gelder.

320. **THE RELATION OF SCHOOL AND HOME** by Anna C Brackett.
    [July] 1913.   *vi*, 13, [1] pp.   14 x 9.5 cm.
    Privately Printed-25   H 726.   Only edition.

300 copies on Van Gelder.

Content: This essay is printed from *The Christian Union* of July 26, 1890.

Comment: Privately printed for Mrs. Alice Foote McDougall.

Binding & Embellishment: Bound in dark blue charcoal boards with the front cover ruled in blue. Text pages ruled in red throughout.

321. **THE RENAISSANCE STUDIES IN ART AND POETRY** by Walter Pater.
    1902.   *xx*, 248, [1] pp.; port. front.
    Quarto Series-7   H 230.   First thus.

450 on Van Gelder; 35 numbered & signed on Japan vellum; and 4 on vellum, signed by the publisher.

Content: The reprint based on the Macmillan fourth and final edition (London, 1890) edited by Walter Pater (see comment below). The unsigned foreword is by the publisher. The frontispiece portrait of Pater is from an 1872 drawing by Simeon Solomon.

Comment: In the foreword Mosher notes that "in 1890 a Fourth, with precisely the same pagination as that in the Third Edition, but showing a few trifling textual alterations was the last that Pater revised, and this is the basis of our present reprint." In an added note to the foreword of his 1912 reprint of *The Renaissance* (322), he indicates "Later reissues [London editions] are as follows: Fourth Edition, 1893; reprinted in 1899 and 1900..."

Wright and Colebeck both record the year of the fourth edition as 1893; however, a search of RLIN reveals two fourth editions dated 1890, located at both Stanford University Libraries and at the New York Public Library.

Mosher first printed several of the studies in *The Bibelot*: "Joachim Du Bellay" in October 1896 (19), "Sandro Botticelli & Luca della Robbia" in September 1897 (20), "The Poetry of Michelangelo" in April 1898 (21), "The School of Giorgione" in September 1898 (21), and "Leonardo Da Vinci" in February 1900 (23).

Design: Mosher identified the graphic embellishments as "an entirely original set of head-bands [i.e., head-pieces], tail-pieces and rubricated initials." They are not signed nor is the designer identified, but the head- and tail-pieces may possibly be the work of Edward B. Edwards, a process engraver for De Vinne's shop in New York. Identically designed head-pieces and letter designs are found in *A Translation of Giovanni Boccaccio's Life of Dante* (New York: The Grolier Club, 1900). Edwards is credited with its cover design and he may be the designer of the interior designs as well. These designs, in turn, very closely match those of *The Renaissance*. For other Edwards designs, see discussion under Design in entry 231.

Reference: Wright, p. 163 (see also Section I, "a16" and pp. 68-69); Vilain 39 (plate 43, p. 96); Quinn 7592; Grigsby 899 & 900; Colbeck II, p. 640.

——————— *Same Title, Change of Series* ———————

322. *THE RENAISSANCE STUDIES IN ART AND POETRY* by Walter Pater.   700 on Van Gelder; 25 numbered
      [October] 1912.   *xi*, 304 pp.; port. front.   18 x 11 cm.   copies on Japan vellum.
      Miscellaneous Series-57   H 557.   First thus.

Content: The signed bibliographical foreword is by the publisher and is reprinted, with a few additional footnotes, from the 1902 Mosher edition (321). This book is essentially a reprint of Mosher's Quarto Series edition, only now in octavo format. The frontispiece portrait is changed to that of Andrea Salaino by Leonardo da Vinci.

Binding & Embellishment: The Van Gelder copies are bound in "old style green ribbed boards" with a white spine label. Japan vellum copies are in Japan vellum wrappers over boards. Title page in red and black; Chiswick ornaments and initial letters.

The bindings of *Earthwork Out of Tuscany* (97) *Roses of Paestum* (331), *By the Ionian Sea* (54), and *The Renaissance* (322) are uniform in style, and all of these titles carry the limitation statement "Limited to Seven Hundred Copies for Sale in America."

Reference: Wright, p. 163 (see also Section I , "a16"); not in Court.

323. *RHYMES AND RHYTHMS AND ARABIAN NIGHTS' ENTERTAINMENTS*   950 on Van Gelder paper; 100
      by William Ernest Henley. 1909.   *iv*, 68, [1] pp.   numbered copies on Japan vellum.
      Lyric Garland Series-16   H 473.   Only edition.

Content: Mosher notes in his 1910 catalogue (254) that these poems were taken from "Henley's poems as revised and arranged by him in his edition of 1898 [London: David Nutt]."

The poems forming the first part of the title text were printed in *The Bibelot* for January 1902 (25).

Comment: There is at least one copy bound in green Fabriano boards with the cover design similar to Mosher's *Lucretius on Life and Death* (223), and *"RLS"* (325) including the blind-stamped circular Rossetti design and blind-stamped spine bands and darts. For use of other Rossetti designs, see entry 223.

Reference: Gerstley, p. 72 (35).

324. *THE RIDING TO LITHEND A PLAY IN ONE ACT* by Gordon Bottomley.   950 on Van Gelder; 100 numbered
      1910.   *vii*, 62, [1] pp.   copies on Japan vellum.
      Lyric Garland Series-19   H 511.   Only edition.   First American edition.

Content: The text was taken from the Pear Tree Press edition of 1909, a deluxe copy of which was in Mosher's library. Bottomley and Mosher corresponded with one another on the text of this Lyric Garland edition and other matters.

Mosher's first printing of *The Riding to Lithend* was in the January and February 1910 issues of *The Bibelot* (33).

Mosher's copy of the Pear Tree Press edition (Bishop Collection) contains a single page manuscript in Bottomley's hand noting three corrections to be made to *The Bibelot* printing. These three modifications appear in this 1910 Lyric Garland Series edition and most likely represent Bottomley's final changes to this work:

THE RIDING TO LITHEND A PLAY IN ONE ACT (continued)

(References to *The Bibelot* edition.)

P.32, l.8.

After [change]

I never thought it was so fair, so fair.

to

So fair I never thought it was so fair.

P.44. l.1.

After [change]

Worn art thou to a hair's grey edge, a nothing

to

Worn art thou to a grey hair's edge, a nothing

P.14. l.9.

After [change]

Girl, girl, my son has many enemies

to

My son has enemies, girl, enemies

Comment: According to the correspondence on file at The Houghton Library, Gordon Bottomley gave Mosher *carte blanche* approval to reprint any of his works in America, and accepted any honorarium Mosher saw fit to pay. It is also interesting to note that in a Sept. 25, 1916 letter to Mosher (The Houghton Library, bMS Am 1096 [214]), Bottomley tells him that a New York publisher wants to reprint *The Riding to Lithend*, and that Mosher's copyright only covers the modifications made especially for the Mosher edition, so any American publisher may reprint "the original Pear Tree Press text without our leave." The intricacies of international copyright law were certainly exploitable by other publishers, and Mosher certainly did not stand alone in this regard.

Mosher paid Bottomley $25 for publishing this work in America. See the Nov. 17, 1941 letter from Lamb to Yorke for Mosher's payment terms (see Appendix II).

325. **"R.L.S." AN ESSAY** by Marcel Schwob done into English by the Authorized Translator A. Lenalie. [November] 1920.   *xvi*, 46, [1] pp.   18 x 10 cm. Miscellaneous Series-92   H 678.   Only edition.

950 on Van Gelder; 50 numbered copies on Japan vellum.

Content: The foreword is by the translator. A selection from Austin Dobson, "The Obsequies of Marcel Schwob" (two funeral discourses by M. Alfred Croiset and M. Michel Breal), and the poem "To Tusitala in Vailima" by Edmund Gosse, accompany the main text. The unsigned bibliographical notes are by the publisher.

Comment: Aimee Lenalie received $50 for the this translation.

A. (Aimee) Lenalie is the *nom de plume* of Ellie Dresser, Mosher's first wife. Lenalie also translated Mosher's *Mimes* by Marcel Schwob (242), "Tell Me, Mamore" by Francis Jammes appearing in both The Mosher Books catalogue for 1909 (253) and in the *Amphora* (2), and lastly Verlaine's poem "A Une Femme" from his *Poèmes Saturniens* which appears as a supplement to *The Bibelot*, Vol. IV, No. 2 for February 1898 (21).

Binding & Embellishment: The circular, blind-stamped cover design is by D. G. Rossetti from Swinburne's *Songs before Sunrise* (London: Ellis, 1871). Van Gelder copies are bound in blue boards with white spine label in two colors. Japan vellum copies are bound in Japan vellum boards with the same cover

"R.L.S." AN ESSAY (continued)

design and the spine label printed directly on the vellum. Chiswick ornamentation; large initial letters in red outline. Title page in red and black.

For use of other Rossetti designs, see entry 223.

Reference: Gerstley, p. 66 (70 & 70A); see the Nov. 17, 1941 letter from Lamb to Yorke for Mosher's payment terms (see Appendix II).

---

326. **THE ROADMENDER** by Michael Fairless. 1905.
  viii, 124, [1] pp. (same through third ed.)
  Old World Series-37   H 316.   First edition.

925 on Van Gelder for all eds.; 50 numbered copies on Japan vellum (first edition only).

Content: In addition to the title essay there are two more essays, "Out of the Shadow" and "At the White Gate." Mosher does not identify which one of the many editions (twenty in England) he used for his reprint. A London 1904 edition was in his library.

Comment: A May 9, 1905 document at The Houghton Library (bMS Am 1096) shows that Mosher had the Library of Congress search for a previous copyright on this work, and learned that no copyright existed to prevent his reprint.

Michael Fairless is the pen name for the English writer, Margaret Fairless Barber.

326.1 **THE ROADMENDER** by Michael Fairless. 1907.
  Old World Series.   H 410.   Second edition.

326.2 **THE ROADMENDER** by Michael Fairless. 1912.
  Old World Series.   H 570.   Third edition.

---

327. **THE ROMANCE OF TRISTAN AND ISEULT** retold by J. Bédier [and] translated into English by H. Belloc. 1904. *ii*, 134, [1] pp. (same through third ed.)
  Old World Series-34   H 283.   First edition.

925 on Van Gelder for all eds.; 100 numbered copies on Japan vellum (first edition only).

Content: According to Mosher's 1904 catalogue, this work is a reprint of *"The Romance of Tristan and Iseult, drawn from the best French sources and retold by J. Bédier,* (omitting the illustrations), and *translated into English by H[ilaire]. Belloc.* London [George Allen] 1903."

327.1 **THE ROMANCE OF TRISTAN AND ISEULT** retold by J. Bédier [and] translated into English by H. Belloc. 1907.
  Old World Series.   H 409.   Second edition.

327.2 **THE ROMANCE OF TRISTAN AND ISEULT** retold by J. Bédier [and] translated into English by H. Belloc. 1922.
  Old World Series.   H 695.   Third edition.

Comment: There is an interesting anecdote about a copy of this Old World edition. According to Dan Burne Jones, Rockwell Kent removed the title page and substituted a new one dated 1923 with an original wood engraving by him. It appears that a new colophon indicates that this book was printed at the Lakeside Press, Chicago under the supervision of William A. Kittredge, and bound there in full maroon niger with a binding designed by Kent stamped in gold. The book was prepared for, and given as a gift to, Frances Lee Kent, his second wife. The location of this copy is unknown.

Reference: Jones, p. 41.

328. *THE ROSE-JAR* by Thomas S Jones, Jr. [June] 1913.
      viii, 53, [1] pp.   18.5 x 11.5 cm.
      Privately Printed-24   H 725.   First thus.

Content: This book of 45 poems is the third American edition of this title, but the first Mosher printing. The book was originally published by G. W. Browning of Clinton, NY in 1906, and a second edition in 1909.

The Mosher edition includes five replacements to the 1909 edition: "As a Still Brook" is replaced by "To Song," "A Song of Life" is replaced by "Of One Who Walks Alone," "The Empty Years" is replaced by "The Piper," "Beauty" is replaced by "Träumerei," and "On the Long Road" is replaced by "At Dusk." There are also several changes to the lines of the other poems retained. The final poem "Ave atque Vale" is a memoriam to Arthur Upson. The 1909 copy revised for Mosher by Thomas Jones is in the Bishop Collection.

Comment: Privately printed for the author.

Binding & Embellishment: Copies are bound in old rose paper boards with the spine and front cover printed in darker red. Title page with crown, leaf and tudor rose device printed in red with Latin inscription: "Sub Hoc + Signo + Vinces."

See also entries 430-431.1.

——————— *Same Title, Change of Series* ———————

250 copies printed on Van Gelder paper.

329. *THE ROSE-JAR* by Thomas S Jones, Jr. [October] 1915. *viii*, 55, [1] pp.
      Lyra Americana Series-1   H 625.   First thus.

Content: Jones added one more poem to the 45 which appeared in the privately printed edition (328), "At Even" on p. 17. A bibliographical note appears on pp. [57-59].

Comment: This is the fourth edition of this title, but the second Mosher printing. The first Mosher edition was privately printed (328), and this is its the first appearance in the Lyra Americana Series.

Jones received a 10% royalty on all copies sold.

Binding: The Van Gelder copies are bound in quarter old rose paper spine over heart and dot decorated paper boards. See series in Section I for further details.

Reference: See the Nov. 17, 1941 letter from Lamb to Yorke for Mosher's payment terms (see Appendix II).

450 on Van Gelder; 25 on Japan vellum.

329.1 *THE ROSE-JAR* by Thomas S Jones, Jr. [May] 1917.   *viii*, 70, [1] pp.
      Lyra Americana Series.   H 662.   Second edition.

Content: The total number of poems increases to 58 in this edition. The poem, "Saida" of the previous edition is replaced by "One Day," "In Trinity Church-Yard" is replaced by "Dedication," and "The Hunchback" is replaced by "Denied." Furthermore, this is the only Mosher edition of *The Rose-Jar* to contain the section "From Quiet Valleys" which is comprised of eleven poems, pp. [57]-[69]. An untitled poem by Jones also appears on p. [70]. The following edition drops this section.

Comment: This is the fifth edition of this title, but the third Mosher printing. The first Mosher printing was a privately printed edition (328), and this is the second appearance in the Lyra Americana Series.

329.2 *THE ROSE-JAR* by Thomas S Jones, Jr. [June] 1920.   *viii*, 56, [1] pp.
      Lyra Americana Series.   H 687.   Third edition.

Content: This edition contains 48 poems. The poem "To Song" of the previous edition is replaced by "Endymion." "Tristesse" and "An Etude in Ivory" are replaced by "Absence" and "The Hills." The section "From Quiet Valleys" is dropped except for the untitled poem at the end which is retained on p. [56].

Comment: This is the sixth edition of this title, but the fourth Mosher printing. The first Mosher printing was a privately printed edition (328), and this is the third appearance in the Lyra Americana Series.

330. *ROSE LEAF AND APPLE LEAF* By Rennell Rodd with an Introduction by Oscar Wilde. [August] 1906.   *viii*, 100, [1] pp.   18 x 11 cm.
      Miscellaneous Series-33   H 353.   Only edition.

750 on Van Gelder; 75 numbered copies on Japan vellum; 5 copies on Roman vellum and signed by the publisher.

Content: Mosher reprinted the first edition (Philadelphia: J. M. Stoddart & Co., 1882). A quotation from E. C. Stedman's *Victorian Poets* (Boston: Houghton, Mifflin, 1889) appears on p. [92]. Mosher's lengthy bibliographical note on pp. 93-100 offers an insightful history of the origin and publication of the British edition, and is cited by Mason, who also prints part of the Stoddart-Mosher letter.

Text of this work was printed by Mosher in his July 1905 issue of *The Bibelot* (28).

Comment: Copyright for this book was transferred to Mosher from the American firm J. M. Stoddart & Co. who held the copyright from 1882. The original August 17, 1905 agreement between Stoddart and Mosher is presently in a private collection.

At the University of San Francisco there is a copy with George Charles Williamson's bookplate and with three autographed notes to Williamson from Rennell Rodd. Williamson was both a celebrated American bibliophile and author of *Behind My Door—Some Chapters on Authors, Books, and Miniatures* (New York: Dutton, 1921). See entry 110 for an account of a visit by Williamson to Swinburne's mother.

See also entry 193 for another printing of the introductory text to *Rose Leaf and Apple Leaf*.

Binding & Embellishment: The Van Gelder copies are bound in quarter white paper spine over green and purple marbled boards. Both a white title label and another white author label appear on the spine. Japan vellum copies are bound in printed Japan vellum wraps over boards. Title page and colophon printed in red and black.

Reference: Mason (*Works*), pp. 182, 184-85; Quinn 11169; Mikhail, p. 95; Cowan III, pp. 139-140.

331. *ROSES OF PAESTUM* by Edward McCurdy. 1912.   *xii*, 196 pp.   18 x 11 cm.
      Miscellaneous Series-56   H 556.   Only edition.

700 on Van Gelder "for sale in America;" 25 numbered copies on Japan vellum.
First American edition.

Content: The signed foreword is by the publisher. A selection from Theocritus (Lang, trans.) and the poem "Roses of Paestum" by William Aspenwall Bradley accompany the text. According to the 1912 Mosher catalogue, McCurdy "has now revised his text, added a pleasing little proem, *All' Italia*, and at our request has consented to the present reissue of his book..." The first British

ROSES OF PAESTUM (continued)

printing was by Grant Allen (London, 1900). McCurdy's letter of permission, and a host of changes to be made to the original London edition, and the "All' Italia" addition, are at The Houghton Library (bMS Am 1096).

Mosher also reprinted the title essay (from this work of nine essays) in the July 1904 issue of *The Bibelot* (27).

Comment: Mosher paid McCurdy $50 for the publication of this work in America. Mosher also reprinted the title poem in entry 126.

Binding & Embellishment: The Van Gelder copies are bound in old style green ribbed boards (raised bands) with a white spine label. The Japan vellum copies are in Japan vellum wrappers over boards. Title page in red and black; Chiswick ornaments and initial letters.

The bindings of *Earthwork Out of Tuscany* (97) *Roses of Paestum* (331), *By the Ionian Sea* (54), and *The Renaissance* (322) are uniform in style. Also, all of these titles carry the limitation statement "Limited to 700 Copies for Sale in America."

Reference: Vilain 20 (plate 28, p. 91) compares title page with Mosher's original editorial marks); see the Nov. 17, 1941 letter from Lamb to Yorke for Mosher's payment terms (see Appendix II).

---

332. ***RUBÁIYÁT OF OMAR KHAYYÁM THE ASTRONOMER-POET OF PERSIA.***
Rendered into English Verse by Edward Fitzgerald. [October] 1894.
79, [1] pp. (pages numbered in Roman numerals)
The Bibelot Series-3   H 6.   First thus.

725 on Van Gelder paper; 25 numbered copies on Japan vellum.

Content: This edition contains parallel texts of the first (1859) and fourth (1879) editions, and quatrains appearing only in the third edition (1868), all previously published by Quaritch of London. There is a prefatory poem "To Omar Khayyám" by Andrew Lang, and a concluding poem "L'Envoi" by Justin Huntly McCarthy.

According to Potter, this book contains the first published bibliography of the *Rubáiyát*. The bibliography (pp. *lxxv-lxxviii*), listing seven English and seven American editions of FitzGerald's translation, and four editions by other translators, was compiled by Mosher.

Comment: Entry #1205 in the Wheeler auction catalogue identifies the Boston, 1894 *Rubáiyát,* published by Houghton Mifflin, as "the copy used for Mosher's edition in The Bibelot Series, with mss. copies of the first edition, Andrew Lang's poem, etc., added." For the S. Image design on the cover, see 311.

Reference: Humphry 24; Potter 284; Wheeler (C.V.), p. 124.

---

333. ***RUBÁIYÁT OF OMAR KHAYYÁM*** Translated into English Prose by Justin
Huntly McCarthy, M.P. 1896.   131, [1] pp. (pages numbered in Roman numerals)
The Bibelot Series-7   H 19.   First thus.

925 on Van Gelder; 100 numbered copies on Japan vellum.

Content: The publisher's bibliographical note opposite the title page indicates that this reprint was taken directly from London edition published by David Nutt in 1889. McCarthy's translation contains 466 quatrains, as opposed to the 101 of FitzGerald's.

Reference: Potter 351.

———————— *Same Title, Change of Series* ————————

334. ***RUBÁIYÁT OF OMAR KHAYYÁM*** rendered into English Verse by Edward
FitzGerald. [October] 1895.   124, [1] pp. (same for second ed.)
Old World Series-1   H 11.   First edition thus.

Content: W. Irving Way wrote the biographical sketch on FitzGerald. Additionally, the book contains the poems "Omar Khayyám" by Rosamond Mariott
Watson, and a "Toast to Omar Khayyám" by Theodore Watts-Dunton. Irving
Way, a partner in the Chicago publishing firm of Way & Williams, became a
life long friend of Thomas B. Mosher, and the Los Angeles distributor for his
books. Parallel texts of the 1st & 4th London editions are printed in Italic and
Roman type. There are also variorum readings for the 2nd-4th editions, and
the omitted quatrains of the 2nd edition. A bibliography of the *Rubáiyát*
appears at the end of the book.

W. Irving Way notes that "...the Sonnet by Rosamond Marriot Watson [oppo-
site title page] is from her "Bird-Bride"; while the Sonnet by Mr. Watts [oppo-
site the colophon] is reprinted from Mr. Clodd's little 'Pilgrimage'..."

Comment: According to Franklin, the Ashendene *Rubáiyát* used Mosher's bibliography: "At the end, reprinted from Thomas Mosher's edition of 1895 (cour-
teously sent across, as we have seen, by Samuel Avery) is the descriptive bibliography of Fitzgerald's poem in its English and American appearances." In
Mosher's *Bibliographical List of the Editions of the Rubáiyát* (40) this statement appears: "This [Ashendene] reprint ends with a bibliography 'taken,
with apologies, from the Edition published at Portland, Maine, U.S.A., in the
year 1895.' " There is a letter in the Vilain-Wieck Collection, dated May 10,
1897, in which Hornby himself wrote Mosher:

> ...with regard to 'Omar', if I can at any time manage to do so I will send you a
> copy. I feel somewhat as if I owed you one, as I made use of your Bibliography of
> the English & American Editions (with an acknowledgment of the source from
> which it was derived).

Along with a copy of his *Three Poems of John Milton* (1896), Hornby also sent
Mosher a description of his own Omar for Mosher's "next Bibliography" of the
Rubáiyát (April 2, 1897 letter from Hornby to Mosher in the Bishop Collec-
tion). See entries 270 & 290 for other Mosher books in the library of C. H. St.
John Hornby, founder of the Ashendene Press.

This is the first title published in the Old World Series. The biographical
sketch by W. Irving Way is updated in later editions. The bibliography of the
Rubaiyat is also extended in each succeeding edition. These changes, and a
few other minor changes, account for the different page locations of the bibliography at the rear.

Design: The title page and backstrip were designed by Bruce Rogers (see note
to entry 334.7). The head-pieces and other designs are by Charles M. Jenckes,
including the front cover design. See entries 152 & 207 for other BR designs;
for other Jenckes designs see entries 100, 130 and many of the head- and tail-
pieces in The Old World Series.

Reference: Potter 285 & 286 note; Humphry 27; Franklin, p. 16 (see also p.
14, and Ashendene V); Humphry 33 & 34 (3rd ed.); Vilain 52; Humphry 35
(4th ed.); Humphry 44 (5th ed.). See *BAL* 7781-A for notes on the 5th edition.

925 on Van Gelder; 100 numbered
copies on Japan vellum.

(a)

RUBÁIYÁT
OF OMAR KHAYYÁM
RENDERED INTO ENGLISH VERSE
BY EDWARD FITZGERALD

Portland, Maine
THOMAS B MOSHER
M dcccxcv

(b)

(c)

334.1 *RUBÁIYÁT OF OMAR KHAYYÁM* rendered into English Verse by Edward
FitzGerald. [December] 1895.
Old World Series.   H 17.   Second edition.

925 on Van Gelder; 100 numbered
copies printed on Japan vellum.

Comment: According to the advertisements in *The Bibelot* for January & February 1896, there were 100 numbered copies printed on Japan vellum.

334.2 *RUBÁIYÁT OF OMAR KHAYYÁM* rendered into English Verse by Edward
FitzGerald. [September] 1896.   125, [1] pp. (same for fourth ed.)
Old World Series.   H 29.   Third edition.

925 on Van Gelder; 100 numbered
copies printed on Japan vellum.

Comment: According to Hatch, the 100 copies on Japan vellum have the same
collation as the 1st & 2nd editions. Contains bibliography on pp. 119-[124].

334.3 *RUBÁIYÁT OF OMAR KHAYYÁM* rendered into English Verse by Edward
FitzGerald. [May] 1897.
Old World Series.   H 52.   Fourth edition.

925 on Van Gelder; 100 numbered
copies printed on Japan vellum.

334.4 *RUBÁIYÁT OF OMAR KHAYYÁM* rendered into English Verse by Edward
FitzGerald. [February] 1898.   *xxvi*, 104, [1] pp.
Old World Series.   H 81.   Fifth edition.

925 on Van Gelder. No Japan vellum
copies were printed.

Comment: The page numbering in this edition changes from former editions.
Contains bibliography on pp. 93-[103]. The updated biographical sketch by
W. Irving Way is dated January 1898. An erratum slip inserted at p. *xxiii*
notes that the footnote should read "Edmund Gosse, in *Edinburgh Review*,
1894."

334.5 *RUBÁIYÁT OF OMAR KHAYYÁM* rendered into English Verse by Edward
FitzGerald. [November] 1898.   *xxvi*, 108, [1] pp. (same for next "sixth" ed.)
Old World Series.   H 82.   Sixth edition.

925 on Van Gelder. No Japan vellum
copies were printed.

Comment: Contains bibliography on pp. 95-[107].

334.6 *RUBÁIYÁT OF OMAR KHAYYÁM* rendered into English Verse by Edward
FitzGerald. 1899.
Old World Series.   H 125.   Sixth edition.

925 on Van Gelder. No Japan
vellum copies were printed.

Comment: In Mosher's *Bibliographical List of the Editions of FitzGerald's
Rubáiyát* (40), he notes the seventh edition as being printed in December
1899, and makes no mention of the following edition (334.7) dated 1900.
Likewise, he makes the same claim in the bibliography of the eighth Old
World edition. No copy marked "Seventh Edition" has ever been found bearing
the imprint date 1899. Mosher himself contradicts this year/edition assignment
in the "Short List of Mr. Mosher's Books" appearing in *The Bibelot* for January
1900 when he states "Seventh edition ready January 20th."

An error in edition note? A reprint of the preceding with change of date on
title page? This may be a "pseudo" edition.

334.7 *RUBÁIYÁT OF OMAR KHAYYÁM* rendered into English Verse by Edward
FitzGerald. [January] 1900.   *xxxiii*, 147, [1] pp.
Old World Series.   H 161.   Seventh edition.

925 on Van Gelder; 100 numbered
copies on Japan vellum.

Content: In his Spring Announcement of 1900, Mosher explains why this edition "differs in several important particulars from our preceding reprints of
the work."

RUBÁIYÁT OF OMAR KHAYYÁM (continued)

   (I)   Irving Way's Biographical Sketch has been revised and somewhat enlarged.
  (II)   The parallel texts of the 1st & 4th editions have been freshly collated with the original 1859 & 1879 FitzGerald issues, giving an absolutely correct text.
 (III)   In place of the Variorum readings formerly given, FitzGerald's 2nd edition has been newly collated and printed here.
 (IV)   A Comparative Table of Quatrains shows the transpositions and changes made by FitzGerald.
  (V)   The Pronouncing Vocabulary is given with some additions.
 (VI)   An updated Bibliography.
(VII)   An Appendix gives all the changes in the "so-called Fifth [FitzGerald] edition."

A preface by the publisher is added to this edition and is updated in subsequent editions.

Comment: According to the edition note in the eighth edition, the seventh was published December 1899. No copy has been located of this seventh 1899 edition, nor does that date agree with Mosher's own announcement (see *The Bibelot,* Vol. VI, which indicates a January 20th 1900 release). There is, however, the duplicate sixth edition which was dated 1899 (see 334.6).

Boss incorrectly indicates this is the first Mosher *Rubáiyát* to carry a biography of FitzGerald by W. Irving Way (see comments to 334).

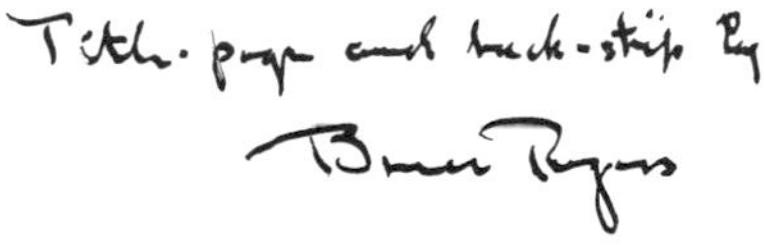

Design: On a copy of this edition Bruce Rogers inscribed on a preliminary blank, "title-page and back-strip by Bruce Rogers" (Bishop Collection). Since the title page and back-strip are identical to the first appearance of this book in the Old World Series in October 1895 (see entry 334), it is reasonable to assume the 1895 Mosher production is another Bruce Rogers incunable, the other being *Homeward Songs by the Way* printed in March 1895 (entry 152). For further confirmation, Blumenthal quotes from a letter (22 November 1943) by Rogers to Carl Weber at Colby College:

> Now to your query, I first saw some of Mosher's books in our college book-store in Indiana, while I was still an undergrad. As I was doing some lettering and book-designs in my 'art' course, I sent some on to Mosher and he gave me an order for lettering the title-page of one of his long slim volumes—I think it was the Rubaiyat. This led to several other small commissions, some after I arrived in Boston...

See also Warde's comments under entry 152. For other Bruce Rogers designs, see entries 152 & 207.

Reference: Vilain 5 (plate 7 on p. 83); Boss V, 154; Blumenthal, pp. 5, 6 and 191.

[handwritten note in right margin: "Title-page and back-strip by Bruce Rogers"]

334.8   ***RUBÁIYÁT OF OMAR KHAYYÁM*** rendered into English Verse by Edward FitzGerald. [June] 1903.   *xxxiv*, 153, [1] pp.; port. front.
Old World Series.   H 265.   Eighth edition.

925 on Van Gelder; 100 numbered copies printed on Japan vellum which are without the edition note.

Comment: FitzGerald's photographic portrait (by Cade and White at Ipswich, 1873) is added as a frontispiece to this and succeeding Old World editions. Irving Way's biographic sketch of FitzGerald is updated to January 1903.

334.9   ***RUBÁIYÁT OF OMAR KHAYYÁM*** rendered into English Verse by Edward FitzGerald. [March] 1907.   *xxxiv*, 154, [1] pp.; port. front.
Old World Series.   H 403.   Ninth edition.

925 on Van Gelder; 50 numbered copies printed on Japan vellum.

Comment: The publisher's preface is revised for this edition. The bibliography (pp. 121-153) is updated to 1906, and Mosher comments in the bibliography of this edition: "This final reissue is the most complete single volume edition extant." This bibliography is used for the privately printed *A Bibliographical List of the Editions of Edward FitzGerald's Rubáiyát... 1859-1907* (40).

RUBÁIYÁT OF OMAR KHAYYÁM (continued)

In The Free library of Philadelphia exhibition catalogue, Norman Strouse indicates that "this is an unusual edition. Although it is substantially different from any preceding editions, and contains almost twice the amount of material of the 1895 edition, mostly through the addition of considerable bibliographical data, Mr. Mosher makes no reference to this edition in any of his catalogues. Yet, both he and Mr. W. Irving Way recognized its importance, as evidenced by the inscriptions written on the blank pages preceding the half-title" (in Strouse's copy, now at the University of San Francisco):

> My dear Gable, In my opinion this is the best all-round, up-to-date edn [sic] of Omar I have, or ever will, issue. It is "all there" and in such shape that you have at a glance every variant. Sincerely yours Thomas B. Mosher Jan. 30, 1908

> My dear Mr. Harris: I entirely agree with Mr. Mosher on the relative value of this edition of Omar, and I congratulate you on the possession of this unique copy. Yours cordially W. Irving Way 5:8:'25.

For further information on William F. Gable, see entry 192.

Reference: Humphry 115; Free Library 24.

334.10 ***RUBÁIYÁT OF OMAR KHAYYÁM*** rendered into English Verse by Edward
FitzGerald. 1911.   *xxxiv*, 117, [1] pp.
Old World Series.   H 546.   Tenth edition.

925 on Van Gelder. No Japan vellum copies were printed.

Content: The bibliography was purposely omitted in this edition. Mosher notes an extensive bibliography of the *Rubáiyát* is in preparation by H.[Herman] M. Schroeter, a *Rubáiyát* collector in Los Angeles, CA.

Reference: Vilain 58; Boss VII 149.

————————— *Same Title, Change of Series* —————————

335. EDWARD FITZGERALD ***RUBÁIYÁT OF OMAR KHAYYÁM*** with preface
by Nathan Haskell Dole. [June] 1899.
xxi, 50 pp.   Pagination for variant state: *xxii*, 50 pp.
Vest Pocket Series-1   H 121.   First edition thus.

Limitation unknown for both Van Gelder and Japan vellum copies.

Content: Nathan Haskell Dole, a recognized American authority on Omar Khayyám, provided the preface, notes, and a vocabulary. Includes a poem by Thomas Bailey Aldrich. In the 1899 catalogue Mosher mentions that this *Rubáiyát* contains "a pronouncing vocabulary of all Persian names in the translation—something never before given in any edition [of Omar]."

There are two states of this 1899 Vest Pocket *Rubáiyát*: the earlier state has the preface ending on p. [*xxi*], and a vocabulary of 25 terms; the later state has a preface ending on p. [*xxii*] and a vocabulary of 38 terms. Neither copy carries any edition note on the verso of the title page. Copies of both states are located in the Bishop Collection and at Arizona State University.

Comment: First title published in the Vest Pocket Series.

A small number of copies were printed on blue-gray hand-made paper throughout, with matching blue wraps. This unusual use of blue paper can be traced to Aldus who, in 1514, issued the first book in this medium. These may very well have been unannounced rarities for a few choice buyers of Mosher books, or for presentation. Another possibility is that they were trial copies or printer's dummies. This is unlikely, however, because copies exist for other

RUBÁIYÁT OF OMAR KHAYYÁM (continued)

Mosher books that are obvious printer's dummies printed on very cheap, off-white paper, with staples used for binding.

Design: According to Bruckner, one of the first four cover designs done for this series by Frederic Goudy (see 1, 191 & 375 for the others) and subsequently used sporadically throughout the series. For other Goudy designs, see entry 1.

Reference: Vilain 33; Potter 287; Humphry 58 & 93 (6th ed.); Crichton 43; Bruckner, p. 49.

335.1 EDWARD FITZGERALD *RUBÁIYÁT OF OMAR KHAYYÁM* with preface by Nathan Haskell Dole. [September] 1899.   *xxii*, 50 pp.
Vest Pocket Series.   H 135.   Second edition.

335.2 EDWARD FITZGERALD *RUBÁIYÁT OF OMAR KHAYYÁM* with preface by Nathan Haskell Dole. 1899.   *xxii*, 50 pp.
Vest Pocket Series.   H 135A.   Third edition.

Comment: A Japan vellum copy of this 1899 Vest Pocket *Rubáiyát*, with THIRD EDITION printed on the verso of the title page, is located in the Bishop Collection. Mosher himself only identified the third edition as being printed in March 1900. The additional printing of this 1899 "third edition" was most certainly due to the unexpected high volumes of sale (see 335.3), but was not recorded anywhere in Mosher's catalogues, bibliography on the *Rubáiyát*, or in the edition notes in subsequent Vest Pocket editions.

Hatch apparently never saw a copy since no mention is made in his checklist.

335.3 EDWARD FITZGERALD *RUBÁIYÁT OF OMAR KHAYYÁM* with preface by Nathan Haskell Dole. [March] 1900.   *xviii*, 56 pp. (same through ninth ed.)
Vest Pocket Series. .   H 180.   Third edition.

Comment: The pronouncing vocabulary is moved from the end of the preface, where it appeared in earlier Vest Pocket editions, to the end of the volume (pp. 53-56). One additional term, CARAVANSERAI, is also added to the vocabulary. This placement and length were kept in all subsequent Vest Pocket editions.

An ad in *The Goose Quill* for May 15, 1900 announces a new Vest Pocket Series title, *Sonnets from the Portuguese*, adding that the previous Vest Pocket *Rubáiyát* achieved "15,000 Copies of this Edition Sold to Date." Mosher makes this same claim in his Spring 1900 announcement: "Fully 15,000 copies of the little *Omar* have been sold to date, and a third edition is now in press." The same claim and wording is used in the spring announcement in the March 1900 issue of *The Bibelot*. If true, then the preceding two Vest Pocket *Rubáiyáts* averaged a print run of 7,500 each!

335.4 EDWARD FITZGERALD *RUBÁIYÁT OF OMAR KHAYYÁM* with preface by Nathan Haskell Dole. [March] 1901.
Vest Pocket Series.   H 208.   Fourth edition.

335.5 EDWARD FITZGERALD *RUBÁIYÁT OF OMAR KHAYYÁM* with preface by Nathan Haskell Dole. [October] 1902.
Vest Pocket Series.   H 243.   Fifth edition.

335.6 EDWARD FITZGERALD *RUBÁIYÁT OF OMAR KHAYYÁM* with preface by Nathan Haskell Dole. [October] 1904.
Vest Pocket Series.   H 312.   Sixth edition.

335.7 EDWARD FITZGERALD *RUBÁIYÁT OF OMAR KHAYYÁM* with preface by
Nathan Haskell Dole. [December] 1906.

| Vest Pocket Series. | H 383. | Seventh edition. |

335.8 EDWARD FITZGERALD *RUBÁIYÁT OF OMAR KHAYYÁM* with preface by
Nathan Haskell Dole. [October] 1909.

| Vest Pocket Series. | H 497. | Eighth edition. |

335.9 EDWARD FITZGERALD *RUBÁIYÁT OF OMAR KHAYYÁM* with preface by
Nathan Haskell Dole. [October] 1916.

| Vest Pocket Series. | H 645. | Ninth edition. |

——————— *Same Title, Change of Series* ———————

336. ***RUBÁIYÁT OF OMAR KHAYYÁM THE ASTRONOMER-POET OF PERSIA.***
Translated into English Verse by Edward FitzGerald First Printed by Bernard
Quaritch London 1859 and Now Reproduced by Photo-Lithographic Process
in Exact Facsimile. 1902.

(front.) *vi*, 25 pp., 6 *ℓ*. of facsims.; 1 *ℓ*., 1 *ℓ*. (facsim.), *xiii*, 21 pp.   23 x 18 cm.

| Reprints of Privately Printed Books-12 | H 226. | First thus. |

200 numbered copies on Van Gelder; 40 numbered copies on Japan vellum; 10 numbered copies on Roman vellum copies bound in flexible vellum with silk ties. All 200 copies signed by the publisher.

(a)

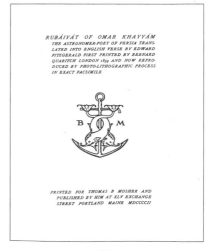

(b)

Content: The unsigned bibliographical introduction (pp. 3-23) is by the publisher, and discusses the first London edition of 1859; the second London edition of 1868; the Columbus, Ohio reprint of the second edition (1870); the third London edition (1872); the Boston reprint of the third edition, (1878); the fourth London edition (1879); and the Cleveland, Ohio, "smallest edition in the world" (1900). Facsimile title pages of all these editions are supplied, and the rest of the work is an "absolute facsimile" reprint of the 1859 *editio princeps*.

Comment: This is the first facsimile reprint of FitzGerald's 1859 translation. Thomas J. Wise produced what he called a facsimile edition (London, 1887), but this was set from the same type of the first edition, rather than a photographic facsimile.

Not all copies printed on pure Roman vellum are the same. Copies 1-5 have an original etching by Edwin Edwards, which was a canceled frontispiece to the third London edition of 1872, inserted along with a facsimile of the same. Each copy comes with a certificate of authenticity printed in red ink on the leaf preceding the etching, with Mosher's signature in red following this statement:

> Of the 10 copies of this book done on pure vellum, numbers 1 to 5 inclusive have the genuine etched frontispiece on India paper by Edwin Edwards inserted, together with a phototype reproduction of the same on skin. The publisher guarantees that this etching is one of 25 proofs only, and that the plate was destroyed after these impressions were taken in 1871. This is Number __ [signature].

Copies 6-10 contain only the phototype reproduction printed on vellum.

The canceled frontispiece is from an etching by FitzGerald's friend, Edwin Edwards. Mosher secured the five remaining copies which had come to light in 1901. The etching portrays an Indian *Fanis i Khiyal* (a very light talc cylinder) on which the figures of men and animals are painted. The cylinder is a lantern with a candle in the center providing conductive heat which makes the cylinder turn. The cylinder dangles on a string supported by, in this case, the arm of the master of the universe. This image is mentioned in quatrain XLVI of the first edition.

RUBÁIYÁT OF OMAR KHAYYÁM (continued)

Wheeler records a unique copy with a hand-written note by Mosher: "This is a unique copy made up of left-over sheets of the various editions, viz: Van Gelder hand-made paper; Japan vellum; Pure vellum; the binding is also unique, the end papers being pieces of old Venetian hand-stamped papers." A similar copy from Mosher's library was also made up of a variety of left-over sheets and is now in the Bishop Collection, but is in the regular binding and consists mostly of the facsimile title pages.

Generally speaking, this is the last *title* published in this series, but it is not the last *publication* to appear in the Reprints of Privately Printed Books Series. That distinction goes to *The Poems of Master François Villon* (303) which was published in 1916 with its title remaining the same as the former editions (B302-302.2), but with changes in format which necessitate its being classified as the 13th book of the series (see "comment" under 303).

Binding & Embellishment: The Van Gelder copies are bound in charcoal blue paper boards with printed white spine label. The Japan vellum copies are bound in Japan vellum wraps over boards with the label information printed directly on the wrapper. The title page of Van Gelder copies are in black only, while the title page of Japan vellum copies are printed in red and black.

Reference: Boss V 140, XI 144 & 145; Potter 289; Humphry 86; Grigsby 870 & 871; Wheeler (C.V.), p. 127 (#1240).

——————— *Same Title, Change of Series* ———————

337. *RUBÁIYÁT OF OMAR KHAYYÁM* Portland [Maine]. [May] 1899.

4 *p. l.*, 14 *l.*, 1 *l.*   23 x 19 cm.

Privately Printed-3   H 705.   First thus.

10 copies on vellum signed by the publisher.

Content: The limitation page reads: "This Book, of which 10 copies and no more are done on pure vellum, was privately printed by THOMAS BIRD MOSHER and EMILIÉ B. GRIGSBY at Portland, Maine, in the month of May, M•D•CCC•XCIX, and the type distributed."

The colophon reads: "Here ends the Rubáiyát of Omar Khayyám of Naishápúr rendered into English Verse by Edward FitzGerald, being the text of his Fourth Edition (1879), including the minor variants of the Fifth and final edition (1889). Done into type, and ten [numbered] copies and no more printed on pure vellum by T.B.M. & E.B.G. at Portland, Maine, during the month of May, A.D. 1899."

Comment: Emilié B. Grigsby (d. 1964) inherited part of the Charles T. Yerkes' (Chicago financier and traction magnate) fortune in 1905. She was considered one of the most beautiful and mysterious women in the world. In 1898 she lived on Park Avenue in New York, visited Boston, and sometime later moved to England where she hosted a wide circle of fashionable friends in Edwardian England, becoming a leader of Anglo-American society. Her residence was in a country cottage called Old Meadows, West Drayton, Middlesex, England. Her friends included W.B. Yeats, August Rodin, Rupert Brooke, and George Meredith who, when he met this pale beauty with golden hair, "said he had at last met the heroine of 'The Ordeal of Richard Feverel.'" –*New York Times*, February 14, 1964, p. 29. Further information on Grigsby appears in Section V, "Bibliography on Thomas Bird Mosher."

This is one of three collaborations in which Mosher's name is stated along with a partner, on either the colophon or the title page. The other two are the

RUBÁIYÁT OF OMAR KHAYYÁM (continued)

Leaves of Grass (192 & 192.1) and the privately printed, *The Casket of Opals* (56).

Benton Hatch never saw a copy, but listed the volume.

Binding: Bound in full vellum over flexible boards with yapp edges; silt ties running through the pastedowns and spine; title gilt-stamped on the spine.

Reference: Potter 288: Grigsby 869.

338. ***RUBÁIYÁT OF OMAR KHAYYÁM*** rendered into English Verse by Edward FitzGerald. [November] 1923.
   xxxii, 61, [1] pp.; port. front.   19 x 14.5 cm.
   Privately Printed-60   H 760.   First thus.

350 on Van Gelder paper; 50 numbered copies on Japan vellum.

Content: The preface is signed by E. A. W. (Edward A. Woods). The title text is that of the third London edition. Selections from Justin Huntly McCarthy, Tennyson, and John Hay are also present. Notes, and Nathan Haskell Dole's vocabulary, are at the back of the volume. The portrait frontispiece is of FitzGerald.

Comment: Privately printed for Mr. and Mrs. Edward A. Woods of Sewickley, PA. Some copies will have a loosely inserted presentation slip, from Mr. and Mrs. Woods, bearing the family coat of arms and the title of the book.

Binding & Embellishment: Van Gelder copies bound in charcoal blue paper boards with the title printed on the spine and the front cover. The cover design is from the 1903 Eragny Press edition of Ronsard's *Abrégé de l'Art Poétique*. Japan vellum copies are bound in Japan vellum boards with the same cover design. Title in red and black; Chiswick ornaments; text pages ruled in black. For other books using Eragny Press & Lucien Pissarro designs, see entry 52.

Reference: Not listed in Potter.

339. ***RUNES OF WOMAN*** [by] Fiona Macleod. [October] 1915.
   xvi, 45, [1] pp.   19 x 14 cm.
   Miscellaneous Series-72   H 621.   Only edition.

450 on Van Gelder; 25 numbered copies on Japan vellum.
First edition.

Content:. The brief preface and the prelude were both written by Anne Montgomerie (Mrs. Horace Traubel). Selections from Dante, 'The Book of White Magic,' and Nietzsche also accompany the text. The book is mostly printed on the recto side of the pages.

Comment: Fiona Macleod was a pseudonym used by William Sharp who also published works under his real name

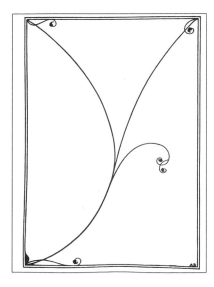

A vertically elongated and modernized anchor and dolphin appear here on the title page for the first time (see device #15 in "Publisher's Devices Employed"). This device was used by New York's McClure, Phillips & Co (1900-1907) and it appears, for example, on the cover of Charles Wagner's *The Simple Life*, and on the title page of Lewis Einstein's privately printed *The Relation of Literature to History* (New York: Privately Printed, 1903). This same device is used on the front and back cover of Mosher's 1915 catalogue, on the title-page of the 1917 catalogue, and on catalogue covers from 1918 onward. Mosher also used it on the title page of *In Memoriam* of 1920 (169). Since McClure, Phillips, later The McClure Co., was dissolved in 1908, Mosher may have felt he had free use of the design. Edmund Gress attributes the design to William Aspenwall Bradley.

RUNES OF WOMAN (*continued*)

Binding & Embellishment: Both the Van Gelder and the Japan vellum copies are bound using the Beardsley design printed directly on Japan vellum boards. The book also came with a printed glassine dust jacket.

The cover design by Aubrey Beardsley was taken from the 1896 edition of Dowson's *Verses* published by Leonard Smithers of London (reused on *The Poems of Ernest Dowson*. London: John Lane, 1905); however, the design on the Mosher imprint is slightly narrower than that of the London edition, and there are other slight variations between the two designs. The binding is of near-white Japan vellum boards with "three sinuous gold lines rising from the lower left corner of the gold frame that surrounds the cover... [giving] the book restrained elegance and vivacity" (Vilain). See also entry 52 for use of this design. Title page in red and black; Chiswick ornaments. The "cupid and ball" device, printed on the page before the half-title, is used on several other books including 52, 69, 87 & 129 (see entry 69 for details).

Reference: Vilain 24 (plate 32, p. 92); Gress, p. 72; the correspondence, the prelude, and the preface by Mrs. Horace Traubel reported under "Content" are at The Houghton Library (bMS Am 1096).

S

340. *SAINT GUIDO* by Richard Jefferies. *QUEEN MARY'S CHILD-GARDEN*
      by Dr. John Brown. [May] 1901.   60 pp. (same for all three eds.)
      Brocade Series-25   H 187.   First edition.

425 on Japan vellum for each edition.

Content: The unsigned foreword is by the publisher. "Saint Guido" is presented on pp. 11-[49], while "Queen Mary's Child-Garden" occupies pp. 53-[60].

The text of *Saint Guido* was first printed by Mosher in his July 1898 issue of *The Bibelot* (21).

Comment: This appears to be a rather odd combination, but in the foreword Mosher explains that he decided to place these two stories side by side in the same volume because 'Guido' and the 'Baby Queen' are two children made immortal by literature.

This book was counted by Mosher under two sub-series, since its contents are split between two authors. The volume is counted as one of five Brocade Series books forming a sub-series (282), and as one of three Brocades forming yet another sub-series (233).

340.1 *SAINT GUIDO* by Richard Jefferies. *QUEEN MARY'S CHILD-GARDEN*
       by Dr. John Brown. [October] 1903.
       Brocade Series.   H 278.   Second edition.

340.2 *SAINT GUIDO* by Richard Jefferies. *QUEEN MARY'S CHILD-GARDEN*
       by Dr. John Brown. [October] 1908.
       Brocade Series.   H 455.   Third edition.

341. ***SALOMÉ A TRAGEDY IN ONE ACT*** translated from the French of Oscar
Wilde by Alfred Bruce Douglas. 1911.

xxiii, 76, [1] pp.; plate	19.5 x 14 cm.	
Miscellaneous Series-51	H 530.	Only edition.

500 on Van Gelder; 50 numbered
copies on Japan vellum.

Content: The signed foreword is by the publisher. Pierre Louÿs' version of a
letter (in sonnet form) from Wilde first printed in *The Spirit Lamp* (May 4,
1893), and "A Critical Review" by Lord Alfred Douglas, are included.

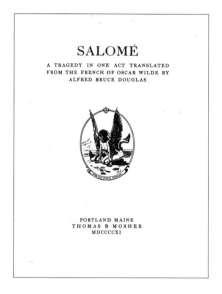

The title page bears the Felicien Rops illustration which appeared in the first
French edition (Paris: Librairie de l'art indépendant, 1893). The text is from
the 1894 Bodley Head edition without Aubrey Beardsley's illustrations, except
for one which is printed on Japan vellum and retained at the rear of the book:
a faun and a grotesque laying the dead Salome down upon a gigantic powder-
puff. Mosher disliked the Beardsley illustrations and thought they contributed
to the unsavory reputation of Oscar Wilde and his play.

Binding & Embellishment: Van Gelder copies bound in gray boards with bands
ruled across the spine; white paper label on spine. Japan vellum copies bound
in Japan vellum boards with title label printed directly on the spine. The title
page and colophon are printed in red and black.

Reference: Vilain 19 & 59 (plate 27, p. 90); Quinn 11187 & 12076; Cowan III,
p. 75.

---

342. ***SANCTUARY: POEMS*** by Margaret Carter Metcalf. 1920.

viii, 45, [1] pp.	16 x 11 cm.	
Privately Printed-53	H 753.	Only edition.

100 copies printed on old Stratford
paper.

Content: This small volume contains 28 poems.

Comment: According to the Lamb typescript, the book was privately
printed for Mrs. G. C. Metcalf (Sheean says Mrs. G. P. Metcalf).

SANCTUARY ❧ POEMS BY
MARGARET CARTER METCALF

Binding & Embellishment: Bound in Japan vellum boards with black decoration and title on the front cover; title printed on the spine. The
designer of the front cover is not identified, but it may be the work of
Edward B. Edwards, a process engraver for De Vinne's shop in New York.
Identically styled design work is found in *A Translation of Giovanni Boccaccio's Life of Dante* (New York: The Grolier Club, 1900). Edwards is credited
with the Dante's cover design and he may be the designer of the interior designs
as well. These designs, in turn, very closely match those of *Sanctuary*. For other
Edwards designs, see discussion under design in entry 231.

---

343. ***THE SAYINGS OF THE LORD JESUS CHRIST*** as recorded by His Four
Evangelists collected and arranged by J W Mackail. [October] 1905.

xx, 130, [1] pp. (same for second ed.)	19 x 13.5 cm.	
Miscellaneous Series-31	H 322.	First edition.

450 on Van Gelder; 25 numbered
copies on Japan vellum.
First edition "printed" in America.

Content: The preface is by J. W. Mackail, and the 1905 Mosher Books catalogue mentions that the *Sayings* "are now reissued with a new preface and
some slight revision of the text [London: Reeves & Turner, 1894], in hopes of
making them more widely known to America." The original seven page, edited
typescript of the preface is in the Bishop Collection.

Comment: Mackail was a British classical scholar and professor of poetry at
Oxford. He was also the first biographer of William Morris (see 435), and the
son-in-law of Edward Burne-Jones.

THE SAYINGS OF THE LORD JESUS CHRIST (continued)

Mosher had been planning to create a "Breviary Series," but he never carried this plan to completion. In his "Daily Reminder, 1906" he wrote *"Breviary Series* I Parables, The II Ecclesiastes III Circum Præcordia" on the page for January 15 (Bishop Collection). Nevertheless, he did publish *The Sayings of the Lord Jesus Christ,* 1905 (343), *Circum Præcordia,* 1906 (71), *Ecclesiastes or the Preacher,* 1907 (98), and *The Sermon on the Mount,* 1913 (345).

A London & New York second edition was published by Longman, Green in 1897; but Mosher's edition is the first to be printed in America.

Binding & Embellishment: The Van Gelder copies are bound in charcoal blue paper boards with white label printed in two colors on the spine. The Japan vellum copies are bound in Japan vellum wrappers over boards with title printed on the spine. Chiswick drop-cap initials used throughout.

Reference: Quinn 5900; relevant letters of permission, etc., are now at The Houghton Library (bMS Am 1096).

343.1. *THE SAYINGS OF THE LORD JESUS CHRIST* as recorded by His Four Evangelists collected and arranged by J W Mackail. [October] 1919. Miscellaneous Series.   H 671.   Second edition.

450 on Van Gelder. No Japan vellum copies were printed.

344. *SEBASTIAN VAN STORCK   AN IMAGINARY PORTRAIT* by Walter Pater. [August] 1898.   59, [1] pp. (same for second ed.) Brocade Series-9   H 71.   First edition.

425 on Japan vellum for each edition.
First edition in separate book form.

Content: Jenkinson notes that this as a "faithful reprint of the first collected edition published in 1887 [*Imaginary Portraits* (London & New York: Macmillan)]." The publisher's bibliographical note appears on p. [5].

Comment: See note to entry 62 for this work's inclusion in a sub-series.

Reference: Wright, p. 163 (see also Section I, a 41); Jenkinson II, 849.

344.1 *SEBASTIAN VAN STORCK   AN IMAGINARY PORTRAIT* by Walter Pater. [September] 1898. Brocade Series.   H 98.   Second edition.

345. *THE SERMON ON THE MOUNT.* 1913.   29, [1] pp.   16.5 x 10 cm. Miscellaneous Series-62   H 586.   Only edition.

900 copies on Kelmscott "Hammer & Anvil" handmade paper; 50 numbered copies on Japan vellum.

Content: The title text is reprinted from the King James Version of the Gospel According to Saint Matthew, Chapters V-VII.

Binding & Embellishment: The binding for the Kelmscott paper copies is in old-style blue boards with white paper spine and title on the spine and front cover highlighted with Kelmscott dingbats; Japan vellum copies in similarly designed Japan vellum boards. For other books printed on Kelmscott paper, see entry 47.

This book employs the American version of Morris "Golden" typeface, Jenson. The title page and its conjugate page are ruled in red. The decorative initial "A" is taken from the opening of *The Descent of Ishtar,* designed and printed by Lucien Pissarro at his Eragny Press in 1903. Red Chiswick initial letters. For other books using Eragny Press & Lucien Pissarro designs, see entry 52.

THE SERMON ON THE MOUNT (continued)

Mosher had been planning to create a "Breviary Series" which would have included this title. For more information on this, see the comment under 343.

Reference: Vilain 23 (plate 31, p. 92).

---

346. ***SESAME AND LILIES TWO LECTURES*** by John Ruskin. 1900.

    xxviii, 130, [1] pp. (same for second ed.)

    Old World Series-21   H 138.   First edition.

925 on Van Gelder; 100 numbered copies on Japan vellum (1st ed. only).

Content: This reprint contains both the preface to the 1865 edition (London: Smith, Elder) and the new preface to the edition of 1882 (Sunnyside, Orpington, Kent: G. Allen). It also includes the first two lectures: "Of Kings' Treasures," and "Of Queens' Garden."

346.1 ***SESAME AND LILIES TWO LECTURES*** by John Ruskin. 1905.

    Old World Series.   H 336.   Second edition.

---

347. WILLIAM BLAKE *XVII DESIGNS TO THORNTON'S VIRGIL* reproduced from the Original Woodcuts MDCCCXXI. 1899.

    xx, 59 pp. (incl. illus.)   26 x 16.5 cm.

    Miscellaneous Series-9   H 110.   Only edition.

450 on Van Gelder; 25 numbered copies on Japan vellum.
First separate edition of these woodcuts.

Content: The unsigned three-part introduction is by the publisher and includes extensive quotes from Alexander Gilchrist and Samuel Palmer. Selections from William Blake and Matthew Arnold also accompany the work.

Mosher later printed these plates in his December 1914 issue of *The Bibelot* (37).

In his edition of Calvert's *Ten Spiritual Designs* (405), Mosher reveals that these proofs came from a small scrapbook in his possession with the first leaf written in manuscript: "Eleven Subjects by Edward Calvert and Seventeen Woodcuts by William Blake, (ca. 1831-1835)."

Comment: Levis, in his work on the most important English language books related to engraving, calls this "a beautifully printed volume." The Blake authority, A. G. B. Russell notes that "the whole seventeen [woodcuts] were fairly well reproduced by the Unicorn Press [London, 1902]... They were also done, better, by Thomas B. Mosher, (Portland, Maine, U. S. A.)."

Aside from the appearance of three of these Blake woodcuts in the 1888 *The Century Guild Hobby Horse*, this is their first issuance *en masse* since their original publication in 1821. Keynes notes that "on p.xvi is a reproduction of Blake's third design recut by another, which first appeared in the *Athenæum*, 1843." Also, in the introduction to *The Illustrations of William Blake for Thornton's Virgil*...(The Nonesuch Press, 1937), Keynes notes that "the woodcuts were first reproduced and published by Thomas B. Mosher, Portland, Maine, in 1899." –p. 19.

WILLIAM BLAKE

XVII DESIGNS TO THORNTON'S VIRGIL
REPRODUCED FROM THE
ORIGINAL WOODCUTS
MDCCCXXI

PORTLAND, MAINE
THOMAS B. MOSHER
MDCCCXCIX

(a)

XVII DESIGNS TO THORNTON'S VIRGIL *(continued)*

Mosher presented his original manuscript used for the publication of this edition, with proof impressions of the reproductions, to Emilié B. Grigsby with an autograph inscription. This copy of Mosher's planning dummy is now located in the Special Collections of the Dartmouth College Library, NH.

(b)

Binding & Embellishment: Van Gelder copies are bound in blue boards with white spine and cover labels. Japan vellum copies are bound in Japan vellum wraps over boards with the spine and cover title/author/date (with red dingbats) printed directly on the Japan vellum rather than on separate labels as with the Van Gelder copies. Printed dust jacket.

(c)

A Japan vellum slip in some copies contains the legend: "The vignettes used as head-bands [i.e., head-pieces] and tail-pieces in this book were cut on the wood by Mr. Selwyn Image, and are taken from *The Century Guild Hobby Horse*, London, 1884-1892. The three initial letters are from original designs." Though the vignettes are all attributed by Mosher to Selwyn Image, the design element on p. *xi* is by Arthur Heygate Mackmurdo from the April 1884 *Hobby Horse*. For the use of other Selwyn Image designs, see entry 57.

Reference: Vilain 55; Bentley 505 (see also Bentley 508); Keynes, p. 300 (#223); Quinn 734; Levis, p. 154; Russell, p. 100; Jenkinson II, 364; Grigsby 102.

---

348. **SHAKESPEARE'S SONNETS.** 1901.   *iv*, 156, [1] pp. (same for second ed.)
Old World Series-25   H 183.   First edition.

925 on Van Gelder; 100 numbered copies on Japan vellum (1st ed. only).

Content: The poem by Edmund Gosse, "With a Copy of Shakespeare's Sonnets," appears opposite the title page, and a dedication signed "T.T." is opposite the first sonnet. Mosher does not give the precise source he used for these 154 sonnets.

Design: Based upon stylistic evidence and the time period, the design on the front cover is most likely by Frederic Goudy. For other Goudy designs, see entry 1.

348.1 **SHAKESPEARE'S SONNETS.** 1907.
Old World Series.   H 407.   Second edition.

---

349. **SHELLEY AN ESSAY** by Francis Thompson. [August] 1909.
xviii, 67, [1] pp. (same for second ed.)   19 x 14 cm.
Miscellaneous Series-44   H 467.   First edition.

900 on Van Gelder; 25 numbered copies on Japan vellum.

Content: Mosher's signed preface follows "The Quiet Singer" by Charles Hanson Towne (printed with the permission of Messrs. B. W. Dodge & Co.), and there is a brief selection from Swinburne. The notes at the end include a quote from *The Nation* (London, March 27, 1909), Thompson's "Stray Thoughts" from the first book edition of *Shelley* (London: Burns & Oates, 1909), and a selection from *The Athenæum* for July 10, 1909.

The source for this essay is *The Dublin Review* for July 1908 (Vol. 143, No. 286), pp. 25-49, as noted by Mosher in his preface. The bracketed passages in Mosher's reprint are lines that appear in *The Dublin Review*, but were omitted in the first edition in book form (London, 1909). Mosher's editorially marked copy is in the Bishop Collection.

SHELLEY AN ESSAY (continued)

Binding & Embellishment: The Van Gelder copies are bound in gray paper boards with white spine and front cover labels printed in two colors. The Japan vellum copies are bound in Japan vellum wrappers over boards. The triangular floral design on the front cover is Chiswick in origin, designed by Charlotte Whittingham and engraved by Mary Byfield. Text pages are ruled throughout in black. For other Chiswick Press designs used, see entry 48.

Reference: Quinn 8807, 8813 & 10194 (2nd. ed.); Warren, p. 314; Connolly XXXVII (B).

349.1 *SHELLEY AN ESSAY* by Francis Thompson. [November] 1912.
Miscellaneous Series.   H 573.   Second edition.

---

350. *A SHROPSHIRE LAD* by A. E. Housman. 1906.
iv, 91, [1] pp. (same for second ed.)
Old World Series-40   H 351.   First edition.

925 on Van Gelder (all editions); 100 numbered copies on Japan vellum (first edition only).

Content: Mosher's edition faithfully follows—down to the original errors—the first Kegan Paul edition (London, 1896). An index of first lines is also included.

Comment: In spite of his reputation, Mosher was not the only publisher of pirated editions. Carter shows that no fewer than five other publishers issued unauthorized editions of this title before Henry Holt's authorized edition of 1922.

Design: The cover design bears the "C" monogram of Thomas Maitland Cleland. For other Cleland designs used, see entry 6.

Reference: Carter, pp. 9 and 10.

350.1 *A SHROPSHIRE LAD* by A. E. Housman. 1913.
Old World Series.   H 599.   Second edition.

350.2 *A SHROPSHIRE LAD* by A. E. Housman. 1922.   *iv*, 91 pp.
Old World Series.   H 696.   Third edition.

---

351. *SIENA* by Algernon Charles Swinburne. 1910.   *vi*, 28, [1] pp.; front.
The Venetian Series-1   H 515.   Only edition.

Limitation unknown for both Van Gelder and Japan vellum copies.

Content: The foreword is by the publisher. The frontispiece reproduces D. G. Rossetti's "La Pia." The main text was first published in *Lippincott's Magazine* for June 1868, but the textual source for Mosher's reprint is "Siena" in *Songs before Sunrise. A New Edition* (London: Chatto and Windus, n.d.). The copy edited by Mosher for the printer is in the Bishop Collection (see 364 for an extended discussion on this printer's copy). A bibliography appears on p. [22], followed by six pages of notes (pp. [23]-28).

The notes are divided into two parts. Notes from pp. [23]-25 are those accompanying the edition of *Songs before Sunrise*, and the "Additional Notes" (pp. 26-28) are from *Siena* (Philadelphia: J. B. Lippincott & Co., 1868).

Comment: First title published in this series.

Reference: Quinn 9537 & 9538.

352. *THE SILENCE OF AMOR PROSE RHYTHMS* by Fiona Macleod.

[October] 1902.   *xvi*, 42, [1] pp.   21 x 12.5 cm.
Miscellaneous Series-20   H 215.   First thus.

400 on Van Gelder; 50 numbered copies on Japan vellum, signed by the publisher.
First separate appearance (revised).

Content: The foreword for this edition is by Fiona Macleod who therein distinguishes prose-rhythms from prose poems. "During the summer and autumn [of 1902] he [Sharp] had, as F.M.,... prepared a revised and augmented edition of *The Silence of Amor* for publication in America by Mr. Mosher" (Sharp). In the preface to the 1912 edition (353), Mosher states: "As written in 1895, *The Silence of Amor* originally formed the concluding section of the first edition of *From the Hills of Dream*, (Edinburgh [Patrick Geddes], 1896). By arrangement with the author a revised and enlarged text with foreword was published by us (Portland, 1902)." See also entry 121.

Comment: Fiona Macleod was a pseudonym used by William Sharp who also published works under his real name.

Mosher paid Macleod $48.70 outright for the publication of this book in America.

The Grigsby copy, #1 of 50 on Japan vellum, contains a 4 pp. A.L.S. from William Sharp, dated 4 December 1901, with regard to a proposal for Mosher's publication of a Greek Anthology compiled by his "cousin," Fiona Macleod (Bishop Collection). Mosher never published the proposed Greek Anthology.

Binding & Embellishment: Both the Van Gelder and the Japan vellum copies are bound in green printed wraps over boards. Renaissance border on cover signed "CW" (some copies drop the "CW") for Charlotte Whittingham, a designer for the Chiswick Press. For other Chiswick Press designs used, see entry 48.

The circular Celtic device in the center of the front cover is from the front cover of the first English edition of *From the Hills of Dream* published in Edinburgh by Patrick Geddes in 1896.

The whole cover design is very similar to *The House of Usna* (160).

Reference: Colbeck II, p. 741 (33); Quinn 8649; Sharp, p. 345; Jenkinson II, 947; Grigsby 1019; see Warren, p. 252 to see Mosher's exchange of design elements. See the Nov. 17, 1941 letter from Lamb to Yorke for Mosher's payment terms (see Appendix II); Macleod VI, p. 412.

——————— *Same Title, Change of Series* ———————

353. *THE SILENCE OF AMOR PROSE RHYTHMS* by Fiona Macleod.

[October] 1912.   *viii*, 40, [1] pp.
Lyric Garland Series-24   H 563.   First thus.

950 on Van Gelder; 50 numbered copies on Japan vellum.

Content: Same as the 1902 edition (352).

Comment: Although this is the first printing in the Lyric Garland Series, Mosher's edition note on the verso of the title page indicates that the first edition of 1902 (352) was an octavo of 400 copies, while this second edition is a foolscap octavo of 950 copies. Mosher copyrighted the 1902 version and continues that copyright in this edition. The newly added preface is by the publisher and gives a bibliographic overview of the origin of *The Silence of Amor*.

354. *SILHOUETTES* by Arthur Symons. 1909.
Old World Series-49   H 463.
xv, 95, [1] pp.
Only edition.

925 on Van Gelder; 25 numbered copies printed on Japan vellum. First American edition.

Content: The publisher's note opposite the title page indicates that this volume includes the entire text of the collected *Poems* of Arthur Symons (London: Heinemann, 1902), and also includes poems omitted there, but found in the first edition (London: Elkin Mathews & John Lane, 1892) and the second edition (London: Leonard Smithers, 1896), plus one poem, "In Carnival," only found in the third, complete edition. Arthur Symons' preface from the second edition, "Being a word on Behalf of Patchouli," is also used.

Design: The cover design is by Earl Stetson Crawford with his monogram of a "C" and his stylized crown of 3 dots above 2 curved lines. For other Crawford designs used, see entry 88.

Reference: *DLB* LVII, p. 330; Vilain, p. 84 (plate 12); Beckson A3c; Quinn 9837.

355. *THE SIRE DE MALÉTROIT'S DOOR* by Robert Louis Stevenson.
[August] 1900.   58, [1] pp. (same for all four eds.)
Brocade Series-23   H 149.   First edition.

425 on Japan vellum for each edition.

Content: The unsigned foreword is by the publisher. This work first appeared in the literary magazine, *Temple Bar,* for January 1878.

Mosher first printed this text in his July 1896 issue of *The Bibelot* (19).

Comment: This work along with four others is part of a sub-series (see entry 436).

Reference: Gerstley 17 N (3rd ed.).

355.1 *THE SIRE DE MALÉTROIT'S DOOR* by Robert Louis Stevenson.
[August] 1902.
Brocade Series.   H 241.   Second edition.

355.2 *THE SIRE DE MALÉTROIT'S DOOR* by Robert Louis Stevenson.
[February] 1906.
Brocade Series.   H 376A   Third edition.

Comment: This edition was not listed in the Hatch *Check List,* but was later added by Hatch in 1972 (see Vilain).

Reference: Vilain, p. 64.

355.3 *THE SIRE DE MALÉTROIT'S DOOR* by Robert Louis Stevenson.
[August] 1912.
Brocade Series.   H 577A.   Fourth edition.

Comment: This edition was not listed in the Hatch *Check List,* but was later added by Hatch in 1972 (see Vilain).

Reference: Vilain, p. 65.

356. *SIRENICA* By W. Compton Leith With an Introduction by William Marion Reedy. [October] 1915.   xvi, 142, [1] pp.   19.2 x 14 cm.
Miscellaneous Series-74   H 623.   Only edition.

450 on Van Gelder; 25 numbered copies on Japan vellum.

Content: The author of the introduction (pp. [xi]-xvi), William Marion Reedy, was both a fellow publisher and close friend of T. B. Mosher. Selections from Pindar and Virgil also precede the text, along with the poem, "The Ivory

SIRENICA (continued)

Gate," (pp. [*v*]-*vii*) by Mortimer Collins. *Sirenica* was published in London and New York by John Lane in 1913.

Comment: W. Compton Leith is the pseudonym of Ormonde Maddock Dalton, the classical scholar, medieval archaeologist, and keeper of British and medieval antiquities at the British Museum. O. M. Dalton never fully acknowledged writing three glimpses of his inner life: *Apologia Diffidentis* (1908), *Sirenica* (1913) and *Domus Doloris* (1919), written aside from his scholarly works published under his real name.

How Mosher managed to publish this title without repercussion, when Lane published it in London & New York just two years earlier, and then again published a second London & New York edition in 1915 (the same year as Mosher's reprint), is puzzling.

Binding & Embellishment: Van Gelder copies are bound in blue old-style boards with ribbed spine and gold stamping on the spine and the front cover. The Japan vellum copies are bound in Japan vellum boards with the gilt stamping the same as the regular copies. Title page in red and black; Chiswick ornaments; some lead initials in red outline. Pages ruled throughout. Printed dust jacket.

The cover design with coins or medallions is by D. G. Rossetti and was taken from the cover of Swinburne's *Atalanta in Calydon* (London: Moxon, 1863).

Reference: Vilain 25 (plate 33, p. 92); Quinn 2282 & 2283.

---

357. VERNON LEE *SISTER BENVENUTA AND THE CHRIST CHILD   AN EIGHTEENTH-CENTURY LEGEND.* 1911.   *ix*, 58 pp.
Vest Pocket Series-22   H 536.   Only edition.

Limitation unknown for both Van Gelder and Japan vellum copies

Content: The foreword is by the publisher. The source was the London edition published by E. Grant Richards in 1906.

The text of this work was printed by Mosher in his December 1907 issue of *The Bibelot* (30).

Comment: Vernon Lee is the pseudonym of Violet Paget.

---

358. *SNOW-BOUND A WINTER IDYL* by John G Whittier. [September] 1911.
vi, 42, [1] pp.
Golden Text Series-7   H 540.   Only edition.

925 on Van Gelder; 100 on Japan vellum.

Content: In his foreword Mosher is careful to mention, "copyright having expired some years ago it became public property for whoever desired to reprint it; the result was a foregone conclusion." Selections from Cornelius Agrippa's *Occult Philosophy*, and from R. W. Emerson's "The Snow-Storm" accompany the principal text.

Reference: Vilain 44 (and plate 47, p. 98); Currier, p. 184; *BAL* 22410.

359. ***SOME GREAT CHURCHES IN FRANCE THREE ESSAYS*** by William
Morris and Walter Pater. [September] 1903. 108, [1] pp. (same for all three editions)
Brocade Series-39   H 253.   First edition.

425 on Japan vellum for each edition.

Content: The unsigned foreword, with bibliographic details, is by the publisher. The first essay, "Shadows of Amiens," is by William Morris, taken from
The Oxford and Cambridge Magazine for February 1856. The second two
essays, "Notre-Dame D'Amiens" and "Vézelay," were written by Walter Pater
and were taken from *The Nineteenth Century*, March and June of 1894.

Comment: Morris' essay also appears as a title in the Reprints from "The
Bibelot" Series (70) and appeared in the March 1901 issue of *The Bibelot* (24).

Reference: Walsdorf 106; Wright, p. 163 (see also Wright Section I, "a 91" &
94); Quinn 7037 & 7095; not in Court.

359.1 ***SOME GREAT CHURCHES IN FRANCE THREE ESSAYS***
by William Morris and Walter Pater. [December] 1905.
Brocade Series.   H 344.   Second edition.

359.2 ***SOME GREAT CHURCHES IN FRANCE THREE ESSAYS***
by William Morris and Walter Pater. [November] 1912.
Brocade Series.   H 579.   Third edition.

360. ***A SONG OF ITALY*** by Algernon Charles Swinburne. 1904.   *vi*, 36, [1] pp.
Lyric Garland Series-5   H 297.   Only edition.

950 on Van Gelder paper; 100
numbered opies on Japan vellum;
10 numbered copies on Roman
vellum signed by the publisher.

Content: Swinburne's work first appeared in 1867 (London: John Camden
Hotten). Mosher's reprint includes only the poem, with the dedication to
Joseph Mazzini (p. [*v*]). No foreword, introduction, or other textual embellish-
ments accompany the text.

Reference: Quinn 9478 & 9479.

361. ***A SONG TO DAVID*** by Christopher Smart. 1900.   *vi*, 40 pp.; port. front.
Reprints from "The Bibelot"-7   H 151.   Only edition.

50 copies only printed on Japan
vellum.

Content: The unsigned introduction is by the publisher. Also included are
selections from Robert Browning, William Michael Rossetti and Edmund
Gosse which embellish the text. The text was taken from *A Song to David*.
Edited with Notes, etc. by J. R. Tutin (London, 1898). The portrait frontispiece of Christopher Smart was taken from the edition of 1791

This work was first printed by Mosher in his May 1900 issue of *The Bibelot*
(23) where the bibliographical details are given.

Comment: See note under entry 109 for details on this series.

362. ***SONGS AND SONNETS*** by Mary Ballard. 1914.   *vi*, 23, [1] pp.   14 x 12 cm.
Privately Printed-31   H 732.   Only edition.

100 copies on Van Gelder.

Content: The volume contains 16 poems.

Comment: Privately printed for Ellis Ames Ballard.

Binding & Embellishment: The layout of this book is the same as the Venetian
Series, including the anchor device on the title page and colophon, and the
ruled pages throughout. The binding is quarter white paper over Venetian decorated paper boards.

363. ***SONGS BEFORE BIRTH*** by Isabelle Howe Fiske [later Conant]. [May] 1912.
x, 39, [1] pp.   14.5 x 12 cm.
Privately Printed-16   H 718.   Only edition.

300 copies on Van Gelder.

Content: The short dedication and introduction are by the author of these 27 poems.

Comment: Printed for Mrs. Isabelle Fiske Conant. See 124 for another Fiske book.

Binding & Embellishment: Bound in Japan vellum boards. The layout of this book is very similar to those of the Venetian series, including the anchor device on the title-page and colophon, and the ruled pages throughout. The scroll design on the front cover is modeled after a design from Herbert Horne's *Diversi Colores* (London: Chiswick, 1891). For designs by Horne used elsewhere, see entry 171.

364. ***SONGS BEFORE SUNRISE*** by Algernon Charles Swinburne. 1901.
viii, 286 pp.; port. front.
Quarto Series-4   H 197.   Only edition.

450 on Van Gelder; 25 numbered & signed copies on Japan vellum; 4 numbered & signed copies on vellum.

Content: The textual source for Mosher's reprint is *Songs before Sunrise. A New edition.* London: Chatto and Windus, [n.d.]. A bibliography appears on pp. [277]-282, including the "Additional Notes" from *Siena* (Philadelphia: J. B. Lippincott & Co., 1868).

The printer's copy for Mosher's edition (now in the Bishop Collection) is an unrecorded, disbound and undated copy from his personal library, published by Chatto & Windus and bearing the imprint of Savill, Edwards and Co. The copy contains all the errors Swinburne, in two letters of January 3rd & 9th, 1875, instructed Andrew Chatto to correct in the "first issue of a new edition, which you told me some time since was not too far off" (Lang, *Letters* 583 & 585). Most of the errors are minor, and all but two (both pertaining to dropped letters in the final poem, "Epilogue") are retained in Mosher's edition, including the mistitling of "A Watch in the Night" in the contents:

   1) On p. 268, a capital "M" has been supplied in the word "Master" introducing the second line of Stanza 12;
   2) On p. 258, however, instead of inserting the exclamation "O" followed by a comma (first line of Stanza 2), Mosher compounded the error by substituting the word "For" to introduce the line "For whatsoever of life or light."

Mosher supplied the date 1877 for this printer's copy, which unfortunately has no adverts. All the dated reprints contain dated Chatto & Windus adverts, so no further evidence can be advanced to support Mosher's date, but his copy must be reasonably early.

The prelude to *Songs before Sunrise* was later printed by Mosher in the June 1914 issue of *The Bibelot* (37).

Comment: In the 1901 *A List of Books in Belles Lettres*, this title is listed as Miscellaneous Series XVI. In the catalogues from 1902-04, it is entered as The Quarto Series III. Mosher finally positioned the book as the 4th book of The Quarto Series. This is an example of Mosher's fluidity in assigning books to a series.

SONGS BEFORE SUNRISE (continued)

Design: The portrait frontispiece of Swinburne is by George Frederick Watts, R.A. The three circular designs on the cover are from the D.G. Rossetti cover design for the first edition of Swinburne's *Songs before Sunrise* (London: Ellis, 1871), and were attributed to Rossetti by Mosher in his 1901 catalogue. For use of other Rossetti designs, see entry 223.

Reference: Vilain 57; Boss XIII 152; Quinn 9464 & 9465; Grigsby 1129 & 1130.

---

365. ***SONGS FROM AN ITALIAN GARDEN*** by A Mary F Robinson.
1913.   *viii*, 48, [1] pp.
The Venetian Series-7   H 593.   Only edition.

Limitation unknown for both Van Gelder and Japan vellum copies.

Content: The signed foreword is by the publisher. The volume consists of 14 selections from *An Italian Garden: A Book of Songs* (London: T. Fisher Unwin, 1886), plus an untitled selection opposite the title page. There is a bibliographical note to the editions of A. Mary F. Robinson's books on pp. [47]-48.

The text was also printed by Mosher in his August 1908 issue of *The Bibelot* (31).

Comment: Last title published in this series. See 178 for this book in The Bibelot Series under the title, *An Italian Garden*.

Reference: Vilain, p. 98 (plate 48).

---

366. ***SONGS OF ADIEU: A LITTLE BOOK OF "FINALÉ AND FAREWELL".***
Mais où sont les neiges d'antan! [ca. November], 1893.
63, [1] pp. (pages numbered in Roman numerals)
The Bibelot Series-1   H 3.   First thus.

725 on Van Gelder; 25 numbered copies printed on Japan vellum.

Content: A selection from Percy Bysshe Shelley appears opposite the title page. Included in this slim volume is the first American book publication of Ernest Dowson's "Non Sum Qualis Eram Bonae Sub Regno Cynarae" ('I am not as I was under the control of beautiful Cynara'), the poem from which Margaret Mitchell selected the line "I have forgot much, Cynara! gone with the wind!" Mosher republished this poem many times in various publications: *The Bibelot*, August 1905 (28), *Cynara* in the Lyric Garland Series in 1907, '15, and '16 (78-78.2), and in the *Poems of Ernest Dowson*, 1902 (301).

The poem first appeared in the *Hobby Horse* for April 1891, the source of Mosher's selection (Bishop Collection). Mosher mentions in *The Bibelot* for August 1905 (28): "and so far as we are aware was first reprinted by us in *Songs of Adieu...* 1893." It was reprinted with minor changes in punctuation.

The book contains verse by the following authors:

Pakenham Beatty	W. E. Henley	Stephen Phillips
F. W. Bourdillon	Herbert P. Horne	A. Mary F. Robinson
Robert Bridges	Andrew Lang	Arthur Symons
William Canton	Amy Levy	John Addington Symonds
H. E. Clarke	Justin H. McCarthy	William Watson
Lord DeTabley	"Owen Meredith"	Augusta Webster
Austin Dobson	Alice Meynell	Margaret L. Woods
Ernest Dowson	Arthur O'Shaughnessy	...and anonymous
Paul H. Hayne	John Payne	

SONGS OF ADIEU (continued)

Comment: This is the first anthology compiled by Thomas Bird Mosher, and the first book of The Bibelot Series. It was also the third book published by him. According to Mosher's 1893 *List of Books* (198) for the 1893-94 season, *Songs of Adieu* would be ready by November 1893. Mosher's original mock-up for the book (Bishop Collection) shows that he first contemplated publishing it as compiled by R.M. (Richard Merrill), a pseudonym once used by Mosher for his early poetry.

For other anthologies compiled by Mosher, see entries 2, 18-37 (*The Bibelot*), 110, 111, 179, 214, 215, 275, 367 & 382. One may also look upon the Mosher Book catalogues as anthologies.

Design: Arthur Stedman mentions in the December 16, 1893 issue of *The Dial* that Mosher got the idea for the design of this book (and consequently for the design format of whole series) from Pollard's *Last Words on the History of the Title-page* (London: J. C. Nimmo, 1891, the 1519 *Horace* discussed on p. 26, illustrated opposite p. 28). A more likely model, however, is John Gray's *Silverpoints*, designed by Charles Ricketts and issued by the Bodley Head in early March 1893, two copies of which Mosher had in his library. Ricketts said that his format was based on the work of the Venetian printer, Aldus Manutius; Mosher said The Bibelot Series was "modelled [sic] on the Aldine format." (1902 catalogue).

Anyone comparing *Silverpoints* with Mosher's *Songs of Adieu* cannot help but see the similarities in format. The size and dimensions are the same. Both use an italic type, and pages are numbered using Roman numerals. Both employ left-justified titles (set in even capitals) to the poems. Both use a large capital letter to begin each poem, the top of which extends above the other letters of the line. Both begin the first word of all the other lines of verse with an upright Roman capital letter followed by all italic letters (e.g., *Rude* or *Then*). Both books are printed on Van Gelder paper, and the limitation statement in Mosher's Japan vellum version of *Songs of Adieu* is worded and positioned on the page in a fashion similar to *Silverpoints*. These comparable eccentricities are more than mere coincidence, and show that *Silverpoints* was certainly the model behind The Bibelot Series. The book must have had a lasting influence, for Mosher used its cover design for the cover of his 1906 catalogue (250). Mosher's cloth copy of *Silverpoints* is in the Bishop Collection. For other books using Vale Press & Charles Ricketts designs, see entry 47.

Reference: Vilain 3 (plate 5); Boss XI 133; Murray, p. 47.

———————— *Same Title, Change of Series* ————————

367. ***SONGS OF ADIEU   A LITTLE BOOK OF FINALE AND FAREWELL.***
Mais où sont les neiges d'antan! [September] 1913.   18 x 9.5 cm.
x, 59, [1] pp.
Miscellaneous Series-61   H 585.   First thus.

925 on Van Gelder; 50 numbered copies on Japan vellum; 5 on Roman vellum bound in Classic vellum.

Content: This is essentially a reprint of the 1893 anthology by Mosher, with some minor rearrangement of the material for this new format. The author of two previously unattributed poems (in 366) is now identified as Rosamund Marriott Watson.

Comment: For Mosher's first anthology, and other anthologies assembled by him, see 366.

SONGS OF ADIEU (continued)

Binding & Embellishment: The Van Gelder copy in blue boards uses the same front cover decoration as the above 1893 edition, except that now the title is separated from the leaf and stem decoration and placed at the top of the cover with the floral decoration at the bottom. The Japan vellum copies repeat the same design, only on Japan vellum boards. All title information is printed directly on the boards. The title page is printed in red and black; Chiswick ornaments.

Reference: Boss XIII 151; Quinn 7096, 7097 & 7098.

---

368. **SONGS OF INNOCENCE** Lyrics from the Works of William Blake. 1904.
viii, 111, [1] pp.
Old World Series-35   H 284.   Only edition.

925 on Van Gelder; 100 numbered copies on Japan vellum.

Content: Keynes notes that this book "contains *Songs of Innocence and of Experience* and most of the *Poetical Sketches*; texts printed are those of "EY" [*The Works of William Blake, Poetic, Symbolic and Critical*. Edited by E. J. Ellis and W. B. Yeats, 3 vols., London, 1893]." Mosher also included selections from *Ideas of Good and Evil*. The poem by James Thomson, "William Blake," appears opposite the title page.

Comment: Some of these poems were printed in *The Bibelot* for January 1895 (18).

Reference: Bentley 150; Keynes, p. 279 (#163); Quinn 738.

---

369. **SONGS OF THE GLENS OF ANTRIM** by Moira O'Neill. 1911.
vi, 43, [1] pp.
Lyric Garland Series-22   H 538.   Only edition.

950 on Van Gelder; 50 numbered copies on Japan vellum.

Content: A publisher's note appears opposite the title page. There are 25 entries which were originally contributed to *Blackwood's Magazine* and the *Spectator*. The first was published in Edinburgh by William Blackwood, 1900, and went through many impressions. Mosher indicated he reprints "them entire and in the order arranged by Moira O'Neill" (1911 catalogue, p. 46).

---

370. **SONGS OF THE SUSQUEHANNA** by Frederic Brush. [February] 1914.
vi, 49, [1] pp.   17.5 x 11 cm.
Privately Printed-29   H 730.   First edition.

250 copies printed on Van Gelder paper.

Content: Consists of 11 poems, each preceded by its own half-title.

Comment: Privately printed for the author, Dr. Frederic Brush. In an inscribed copy (Bishop Collection), Brush alters line 14 of the last poem ("When Winter Comes") from:"Through frosted forest-aisles cadence low." to: "Through frosted forest-aisles a cadence slow."

Binding & Embellishment: Bound in gray-green Fabriano boards with title in dark green on the spine and title/author printed in dark green on the front cover. Title page is print in red and black; Chiswick ornaments and red initial letter.

The binding is uniform with the privately printed *From the Foothills* (120), and *Sprays of Shamrock* (381).

371. *SONGS OF THE SUSQUEHANNA* by Frederic Brush. [May] 1920.   500 on Glaslan handmade paper.
      vi, 60, [1] pp.   19 x 12.5 cm.
      Privately Printed-52   H 752.   Second, enlarged ed.

      Content: Expanded to 32 poems, including the poems previously printed in
      370. Some of the original poems have also been expanded, and "When Winter
      Comes" has been altered as noted above.

      Comment: Privately printed for the author, Dr. Frederic Brush.

      Binding & Embellishment: Bound in gray-green Fabriano boards with the
      title/author printed on the spine and the front cover. Title page printed in red
      and black; Chiswick ornaments and red initial letter.

      The Chiswick cover design at top is printed upside down, i.e., the bird and
      other portions of the design were mistakenly inverted by the printer. This
      same unattributed design appears right side up on entries 126 & 239.

372. *SONGS WITH TEARS* [by] Forbes Rickard Jr. 1919.   450 copies printed on Shogun paper.
      xxviii, 65, [1] pp.; port. front.   19 x 14 cm.
      Privately Printed-47   H 747.   Only edition.

      Content: This is a memorial tribute to Forbes Rickard Jr. who was killed in
      action during WW I. The text includes verse, prose and letters written by
      Rickard, and is preceded by tributes from several friends. The text from
      Rickard's bronze memorial tablet appears at the rear. A selection from R. R.
      Greenwood appears on the verso of the half-title. There is a frontispiece por-
      trait photograph of Forbes Rickard Jr.

      Comment: Privately printed for Mrs. Forbes Rickard.

      Binding & Embellishment: Bound in light blue charcoal paper boards with
      bands blind-ruled across the spine with white label. Title page printed in red
      and black; Chiswick ornaments.

373. *SONNETS AND SONGS* by Arthur Upson. 1911.   *x*, 48, [1] pp.   950 on Van Gelder; 50 numbered
      Lyric Garland Series-21   H 537.   Only edition.   copies on Japan vellum.

      Content: This edition of Upson's poems contains five additional poems not
      present in the 1909 privately printed edition (228).

      The poem "His Lovers to Arthur Upson" by Ruth Shepard Phelps appears on
      p. [*vii*]. A bibliographical note by Phelps explains that "this little group of son-
      nets and songs, chosen from *The Collected Poems of Arthur Upson* [Min-
      neapolis: The Upson Memorial Committee, 1909], is almost identical with a
      selection made at the poet's request a few weeks before the end of his life
      [*Lyrics and Sonnets* (228)]. It bears the title and the dedication he intended
      for it. Acknowledgment of their kind permission to reprint these poems is ten-
      dered to Mrs. Julia Claflin Upson, Mr. Edmund D. Brooks, and *The Bellman*."
      –p. [2]

      Binding: There are both gray and blue board bindings of this issue.

      Reference: Boss XIII 154 A; Phelps, p. 159; the correspondence surrounding
      this publication is at The Houghton Library (bMS Am 1096).

374. *SONNETS FROM THE PORTUGUESE* by Elizabeth Barrett Browning.
      1897.   *vi*, 68, [1] pp. (same through the fifth ed.)
      Old World Series-10   H 41.   First edition.

925 on Van Gelder; 100 numbered copies on Japan vellum.

Content: The three-part preface (pp. 1-[21]) by Edmund Gosse was first printed as a preface to an illustrated edition of the *Sonnets* (London: Dent & Co., 1894), afterwards revised and included by Gosse in his *Critical Kit-Kats* (London: Heinemann, 1896). A shortened version of the preface appears in the Vest Pocket Series (375). No precise source has been identified for the 44 sonnets which were available in a variety of editions.

Comment: Barnes lists a 1913 Mosher edition (E391) at Yale, but all searches for any copy (either in the Old World Series or the Vest Pocket Series) have been fruitless.

Design: The cover design bears the "C" monogram of Thomas Maitland Cleland. For other Cleland designs used, see entry 6.

Reference: Grigsby 139 (3rd ed.); Vilain 8 (5th. ed., plate 9, p. 83); Barnes E230, E238 & E351 (1st, 2nd & 5th).

374.1 *SONNETS FROM THE PORTUGUESE* by Elizabeth Barrett Browning.
       1898.
       Old World Series.   H 86.   Second edition.

925 on Van Gelder. No Japan vellum copies were printed.

374.2 *SONNETS FROM THE PORTUGUESE* by Elizabeth Barrett Browning.
       1899.
       Old World Series.   H 129.   Second edition.

925 on Van Gelder; 100 numbered copies on Japan vellum.

Comment: An error in edition note? A reprint of the preceding edition with a change of date on the title page only?

374.3 *SONNETS FROM THE PORTUGUESE* by Elizabeth Barrett Browning.
       1901.
       Old World Series.   H 202.   Third edition.

925 on Van Gelder; 100 numbered copies on Japan vellum.

374.4 *SONNETS FROM THE PORTUGUESE* by Elizabeth Barrett Browning.
       1904.
       Old World Series.   H 301A.   Fourth edition.

925 on Van Gelder. No Japan vellum copies were printed.

Comment: This edition was listed in the Hatch *Check List* as an unlocated trade edition, but was later added by Hatch in 1972 (see Vilain).

Reference: Vilain, p. 64; Hatch, p. 167.

374.5 *SONNETS FROM THE PORTUGUESE* by Elizabeth Barrett Browning.
       1909.
       Old World Series.   H 484.   Fifth edition.

925 on Van Gelder. No Japan vellum copies were printed.

———————— *Same Title, Change of Series* ————————

375. ELIZABETH BARRETT BROWNING *SONNETS FROM THE PORTUGUESE* with preface by Edmund Gosse. [February] 1900.
      xviii, 46, [1] pp. (same through the fifth ed.)
      Vest Pocket Series-2   H 155.   First edition.

Limitation unknown for both Van Gelder and Japan vellum copies.

Content: In a note opposite the preface, Mosher mentions that "this essay, of which the larger portion is here given, was first printed as a preface to an

SONNETS FROM THE PORTUGUESE (continued)

illustrated English edition of the *Sonnets* (London, 1894). It was afterwards revised and included by Mr. Gosse in his *Critical Kit-Kats* (London: [Heinemann], 1896)...” In the present edition the preface was edited and shortened from the preface appearing in Mosher's 1897 edition (374).

Comment: For an interesting note on the expected popularity of sales for this first Vest Pocket issue of the *Sonnets from the Portuguese* based on sales of the Vest Pocket Omar, see the note to entry 335.2.

Design: According to Bruckner, the cover design is one of four done for this series by Frederic Goudy (see 1, 191 & 335 for the others) and subsequently used sporadically throughout the series. For other Goudy designs, see entry 1.

Reference: Barnes E270, E277, E298 & E330 (1st-4th), and E359 (5th) which Barnes mistakenly designates the sixth edition; Bruckner, pp. 48-49.

375.1 ELIZABETH BARRETT BROWNING **SONNETS FROM THE PORTUGUESE**
with preface by Edmund Gosse. [June] 1901.
Vest Pocket Series.   H 209.   Second edition.

375.2 ELIZABETH BARRETT BROWNING **SONNETS FROM THE PORTUGUESE**
with preface by Edmund Gosse. [February] 1903.
Vest Pocket Series.   H 279.   Third edition.

375.3 ELIZABETH BARRETT BROWNING **SONNETS FROM THE PORTUGUESE**
with preface by Edmund Gosse. [March] 1906.
Vest Pocket Series.   H 384.   Fourth edition.

375.4 ELIZABETH BARRETT BROWNING **SONNETS FROM THE PORTUGUESE**
with preface by Edmund Gosse. [September] 1910.
Vest Pocket Series.   H 527.   Fifth edition.

376. *THE SONNETS OF MICHAEL ANGELO BUONARROTI* translated by
John Addington Symonds. 1897. *viii*, 103, [1] pp. (same through fourth ed.)
Old World Series-7   H 38.   First edition.

725 on Van Gelder; 100 numbered copies on Japan vellum.

Content: The brief note on p. [2] is by the publisher. In his 1897 catalogue, Mosher offered “... this Old World reprint, which is now done with the very kind assent of Mr. Symonds' literary executor–Mr. Horatio F. Brown, author of an authoritative monograph upon *The Venetian Printing Press*.” In addition to the 75 numbered sonnets, Michaelangelo's poem “On His Father's Death” (p. [*ii*]), and his “Proem” (p. [*vii*]) appear before the main text. There are also seven pages of notes (pp. 91-[97]) and appendices (pp. 101-[103]).

Comment: This reprint follows the same text as The Bibelot Series version (241).

Reference: Babington 489.

376.1 *THE SONNETS OF MICHAEL ANGELO BUONARROTI* translated by
John Addington Symonds. 1899.
Old World Series.   H 128.   Second edition.

925 on Van Gelder. No copies were printed on Japan vellum.

376.2 *THE SONNETS OF MICHAEL ANGELO BUONARROTI* translated by John Addington Symonds. 1901.
Old World Series.   H 201.   Second edition.

925 on Van Gelder. No copies were printed on Japan vellum.

Comment: An error in edition note? A reprint of the previous edition with change of date on the title page?

376.3 *THE SONNETS OF MICHAEL ANGELO BUONARROTI* translated by John Addington Symonds. 1903.
Old World Series.   H 268   Third edition.

925 on Van Gelder; 100 numbered copies printed on Japan vellum.

376.4 *THE SONNETS OF MICHAEL ANGELO BUONARROTI* translated by John Addington Symonds. 1909.
Old World Series.   H 483.   Fourth edition.

925 on Van Gelder. No copies were printed on Japan vellum.

377. *SONNETS OF THE WINGLESS HOURS* by Eugene Lee-Hamilton.
1908.   *viii*, 117, [1] pp.
Old World Series-47   H 431.   Only edition.

925 on Van Gelder; 25 numbered copies on Japan vellum.

Content: Mosher states in his 1908 catalogue that the "sonnets published by Elliot Stock in 1894, [are] far less known than they should be to readers of verse in America." This Old World edition contains 84 poems.

The text of this work (17 poems) was partially printed by Mosher in his June 1902 issue of *The Bibelot* (25).

Comment: See comment under *Mimma Bella* (243)

378. *THE SOUL OF MAN UNDER SOCIALISM* by Oscar Wilde. 1905.
iv, 90, [1] pp.; port. front. (same for second ed.)   16.5 x 13 cm.
Miscellaneous Series-28   H 319.   First edition.

600 on Van Gelder; 50 numbered copies on Japan vellum.

Content: The text was taken from *The Fortnightly Review* for February 1, 1891. A brief selection from Wilde's *De Profundis* (1905) appears on p. [2].

Binding & Embellishment: The Van Gelder copies are bound in charcoal gray paper boards with title/author printed in two colors directly on the spine, the title printed in red directly on the front cover, and a boxed anchor device printed in red on the back cover. The copy at the University of Louisville is bound in gray wraps over boards. The Japan vellum copies are bound in Japan vellum wraps over boards with the wording printed on the covers, except the spine is printed in one color only and the front cover has the addition of the author's name at the bottom. Title page and colophon are printed in red and black. A Chiswick head- and tail-piece, and a Chiswick drop-cap initial, also adorn the text.

This book is one of only two Mosher books with a color frontispiece, the other being *Sylvie* (394). The portrait of Wilde is from a drawing made by Thomas Maitland Cleland, who did other work for Mosher. For other Cleland designs used, see entry 6.

Reference: Quinn 11159; Cowan III, pp. 83-84.

378.1 *THE SOUL OF MAN UNDER SOCIALISM* by Oscar Wilde. 1907.
Miscellaneous Series.   H 413.   Second edition.

600 on Van Gelder only for this and subsequent editions.

378.2 *THE SOUL OF MAN UNDER SOCIALISM* by Oscar Wilde. 1909.
   iv, 90 pp.; port. front. (same for fourth ed.)
   Miscellaneous Series.   H 490.   Third edition.

378.3 *THE SOUL OF MAN UNDER SOCIALISM* by Oscar Wilde. 1915.
   Miscellaneous Series.   H 631.   Fourth edition.

379. *THE SOURCES OF THE POWER OF MUSIC* by Ella White Custer.
   [October] 1917.   *x*, 63, [1] pp.   26.5 x 20.5 cm.
   Privately Printed-43   H 744.   Only edition.

600 on Blue Hill Text paper; 400 "deluxe" on Italian (Tuscany) handmade paper.

Content: The seven chapters herein cover dynamics (primeval force), rhythmics (regulation), harmonics (beneficent combinations), the significance of the scale of C major (relationships), the psychological sources of art (compound influences), and beauty (ethereal essence). Three full-page musical charts accompany the text. In the Italian paper copies examined there is an extra suite of the charts folded and loosely inserted.

Comment: The Lamb typescript indicates that this book was printed for Miss J.R. Custer of Scarborough Beach, Maine.

Binding & Embellishment: The 600 copies on Blue Hill Text are bound in blue Herculean heavy covers; the 400 printed on Italian paper are bound in Ancona blue paper boards.

The large decorative initials are the same as those used in the Quarto Series' *The Renaissance* by Pater, 1902 (321); the head-pieces are Chiswick. The large (5 x 4.5 cm.) capital "T" on the title page was first used by Robert Estienne in 1544 (Eusebius' *Ecclesiasticae Historiae*), and has been traditionally ascribed to Geofroy Tory.

The lyre design used on the front cover is by Earl Stetson Crawford and first appeared on the cover of Mosher's 1908 catalogue. For other Crawford designs used, see entry 88.

380. *THE SPHINX* by Oscar Wilde. 1911.   *viii*, 27, [1] pp.
   Venetian Series-5   H 543.   Only edition.

Limitation unknown for both Van Gelder and Japan vellum copies.

Content: The foreword (pp. [*v*]-*vii*) is by the publisher who quotes Ingleby's *Oscar Wilde* (London: T. Werner Laurie, 1908) at length. There is a bibliographical note on p. [*viii*] describing the Bodley Head edition of 1894. The 13-part poem covers pp. [3]-27.

Reference: Vilain, 98 (plate 48); Quinn 11188 & 12077; Cowan III, pp. 85-86.

381. *SPRAYS OF SHAMROCK* by Clinton Scollard. [March] 1914.
   vii, 66, [1] pp.   18 x 11 cm.
   Privately Printed-30   H 731.   Only edition.

250 copies on Van Gelder paper.

Content: This volume contains 52 Irish poems, plus a poem on the verso of the half-title.

Comment: Privately printed for the author.

Binding & Embellishment: The title page is printed in green. Chiswick ornaments and a green Chiswick capital initial. The binding is uniform with *From the Foothills* (120), and *Songs of the Susquehanna* (370). Bound in green Fabriano paper boards with darker green lettering on spine and front cover.

382. ***SPRING IN TUSCANY AND OTHER LYRICS.*** 1912. *viii*, 46, [1] pp.
Venetian Series-6   H 565.   Only edition.

Limitation unknown for both Van Gelder and Japan vellum copies.

Content: The foreword is by the publisher who assembled this anthology. The works of verse include: "Proem" and "Florentine May" by A. Mary F. Robinson; "Relics" and "Spring in Tuscany" by Algernon C. Swinburne; "With a Poetry Book" and "In An Arbour, Asolo" by Percy E. Pinkerton; "Umbria" and "Ricordi" by Laurence Binyon; "In Florence" by Cora Fabbri; "In a Gondola" by Aureolus Paracelsus (John Todhunter); "La Retraite" by John Addington Symonds; and "O Primavera, Gioventù de L'Anno" by Giovanni Battista Guarini as translated by Leigh Hunt.

Comment: Swinburne's entry became the title for this anthology.

For Mosher's first anthology, and other anthologies assembled by him, see 366.

Reference: Quinn 7099 & 7100 (mistakenly catalogued date of 1892).

383. RALPH WALDO EMERSON ***STARS OF THOUGHT*** selected by Thomas
Coke Watkins. 1907.   *xvii*, 79 pp.
Vest Pocket Series-14   H 396.   Only edition.

Limitation unknown for both Van Gelder and Japan vellum copies.

Content: In addition to the 106 selections from Emerson's works in the main section, there are three more selections from Emerson embellishing the preliminaries, and two more lengthy selections in the "Proem" (pp. *xiii*-[*xvii*]). The foreword is also by Watkins.

Reference: Myerson C58; *BAL* 5480.

384. ***THE STORY OF AMIS & AMILE*** done out of the Ancient French into English
by William Morris. [August] 1896.   47, [1] pp. (same through sixth ed.)
Brocade Series-3   H 26.   First edition.

425 on Japan vellum for each edition.
First American edition.

Content: The source for this volume was most likely *Old French Romances* edited by Joseph Jacobs (London: George Allen, 1896). In tandem with this reprint of four Morris tales, Mosher may have also consulted the Kelmscott Press edition of *The Story of Amis & Amile* (Hammersmith, 1894), a copy of which was in his personal library. A bibliographical note appears opposite the title page; the unsigned foreword is by the publisher.

Comment: Forman mentions this edition in his bibliography. He describes the cover "with the title printed in capitals imitated from those of Morris' golden type, and a brown ornamental capital T badly imitated from one of his [Morris]. The tiny volume has a slip case of card-board covered with a paper imitation of brocade: its two companions in this misery of transatlantic fussiness, *The Child in the House* and *A Pageant of Summer*, are similarly treated; and the three volumes are enclosed in a box covered with the same paper."

Some copies lack the brown printed portion of the title page: "The Story of Amis & Amile" & the date. This title along with three others formed a sub-series (see note to 396).

Reference: Walsdorf 65; Forman 152.

384.1 ***THE STORY OF AMIS & AMILE*** done out of the Ancient French into
English by William Morris. [December] 1896.
Brocade Series.   H 35.   Second edition.

384.2 *THE STORY OF AMIS & AMILE* done out of the Ancient French into
English by William Morris. [October] 1897.
Brocade Series.   H 59.   Third edition.

384.3 *THE STORY OF AMIS & AMILE* done out of the Ancient French into
English by William Morris. [November] 1898.
Brocade Series.   H 94.   Fourth edition.

384.4 *THE STORY OF AMIS & AMILE* done out of the Ancient French into
English by William Morris. [November] 1899.
Brocade Series.   H 134.   Fifth edition.

384.5 *THE STORY OF AMIS & AMILE* done out of the Ancient French into
English by William Morris. [February] 1909.
Brocade Series.   H 491.   Sixth edition.

385. *THE STORY OF CUPID AND PSYCHE* done out of the Latin of Apuleius   425 on Japan vellum for each
by Walter Pater. [April] 1897.   52, [1] pp. (same for second ed.)   edition.
Brocade Series-4   H 44.   First edition.

Content: This is a direct reprint of the original text in *Marius the Epicurean*
(London: Macmillan, 1885). The unsigned foreword is by the publisher, but
mostly contains quotes from others.

Reference: Wright, p. 163 (see also Wright, Section I, "a 3"); Jenkinson II,
850; not in Court.

385.1 *THE STORY OF CUPID AND PSYCHE* done out of the Latin of Apuleius by
Walter Pater. [December] 1897.
Brocade Series.   H 60.   Second edition.

385.2 *THE STORY OF CUPID AND PSYCHE* done out of the Latin of Apuleius by
Walter Pater. [October] 1898.   54, [1] pp.; front. (same for the fourth ed.)
Brocade Series.   H 95.   Third edition.

385.3 *THE STORY OF CUPID AND PSYCHE* done out of the Latin of Apuleius by
Walter Pater. [June] 1900.
Brocade Series.   H 171.   Fourth edition.

385.4 *THE STORY OF CUPID AND PSYCHE* done out of the Latin of Apuleius by
Walter Pater. [October] 1903.   58, [1] pp.; front. (same for the sixth ed.)
Brocade Series.   H 272.   Fifth edition.

385.5 *THE STORY OF CUPID AND PSYCHE* done out of the Latin of Apuleius by
Walter Pater. [January] 1909.
Brocade Series.   H 492.   Sixth edition.

386. *THE STORY OF DAVID GRAY* By Robert Buchanan. [October] 1900.   400 on Van Gelder; 50 numbered
2 *l.*, *xxii*, 85, [1] pp.; port. front.   19.5 x 15.5 cm.   copies on Japan vellum; 4 on Roman
Miscellaneous Series-14   H 144.   Only edition.   vellum, and signed by the publisher.

Content: The text is reprinted, together with Buchanan's poems "To David in
Heaven" and "Poet Andrew," from the same source: Buchanan's *David Gray,
and Other Essays: Chiefly on Poetry* (London: Sampson, Low, Son, and

THE STORY OF DAVID GRAY (continued)

Marston, 1868). The unsigned preface is by the publisher, and the portrait frontispiece is enlarged from the small woodcut on the title page of the 1868 edition. A brief selection from David Gray's "The Luggie" appears on p. [2].

Comment: The 100*th* title published by Mosher. The portrait frontispiece was reproduced by the Bierstadt process from the small woodcut on the title-page of Buchanan's original edition.

Binding & Embellishment: Both the Van Gelder and the Japan vellum copies are bound in Japan vellum wraps over boards, printed in black, green, red and white.

The Renaissance design on title page and p. [67] are signed "CW" for Charlotte Whittingham, a designer for the Chiswick Press of London. Head-pieces for the title-page and pages [v], [xi], [3], and [67] all appear in Warren on p. 311, and the two large tail-pieces appear in Warren on p. 314. For other Chiswick Press designs used, see entry 48.

The striking front cover design consists of a border of blackberries with green serrated leaves, thorny stems, and a few white blossoms at the top. Inside the design is the title, publisher information and logo printed in red and black. The thorny stems are again used on the spine. The proportions of the border design are like those on Kelmscott Press books. This design is unsigned and unattributed.

See color illustration on p. 369 (Plate 4).

Reference: Quinn 1108; Grigsby 145 & 146.

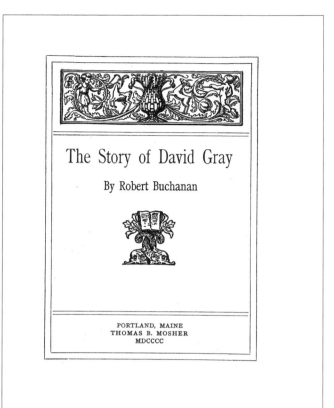

---

387. *THE STORY OF IDA   EPITAPH ON AN ETRURIAN TOMB*
by Francesca Alexander. [Edited by John Ruskin] 1899.
x, 75, [1] pp. (same for second ed.)
Old World Series-15   H 103.   First edition.

925 on Van Gelder; 100 numbered copies on Japan vellum.

Content: The preface is by John Ruskin. Mosher never clearly identified from which edition he reprinted: the British or the American edition of 1883. Since copyright problems were most likely avoidable by reprinting the British edition, it most likely was the G. Allen edition (Sunnyside, Orpington, Kent, 1883).

Comment: The portrait frontispiece is by the author, Francesca Alexander, the American artist who spent much of her life in Italy, befriended John Ruskin, and published much of her work in the 1880's and 90's. She died in 1917.

Design: Based upon stylistic evidence, the cover design is most likely by Frederic Goudy. For other Goudy designs, see entry 1.

Reference: Vilain, p. 84 (plate 10).

387.1 *THE STORY OF IDA   EPITAPH ON AN ETRURIAN TOMB*
by Francesca Alexander. 1904.
Old World Series.   H 303.   Second edition.

925 on Van Gelder. No copies were printed on Japan vellum.

388.   *THE STORY OF MY HEART   MY AUTOBIOGRAPHY* by Richard Jefferies.
        1898.   *viii*, 147, [1] pp. (same for second ed.)
        Old World Series-13   H 65.   First edition.

925 on Van Gelder; 100 numbered copies on Japan vellum.

Content: The preface is by the publisher. A poem by H. H. von Sturmer appears opposite the title page, and a poem by William Wordsworth is opposite p. 1. Although not specifically identified, the source was most likely the original edition of 1883 (London: Longmans, Green and Co.), a copy of which was in Mosher's library.

Comment: Selections from this work first appeared in the March 1896 issue of *The Bibelot* (19).

Reference: Quinn 4851.

388.1   *THE STORY OF MY HEART   MY AUTOBIOGRAPHY* by Richard Jefferies.
        1900.
        Old World Series.   H 164.   Second edition.

925 on Van Gelder. No copies were printed on Japan vellum.

388.2   *THE STORY OF MY HEART   MY AUTOBIOGRAPHY* by Richard Jefferies.
        1905.   *vi*, 149 pp.
        Old World Series.   H 335.   Third edition.

925 on Van Gelder; 25 numbered copies on Japan vellum.

388.3   *THE STORY OF MY HEART   MY AUTOBIOGRAPHY* by Richard Jefferies.
        1909.   *vi*, 149, [1] pp.
        Old World Series.   H 485.   Fourth edition.

925 on Van Gelder. No copies were printed on Japan vellum.

389.   *THE STORY OF THE UNKNOWN CHURCH AND OTHER TALES*
        by William Morris. 1902.   *viii*, 77 pp.
        Reprints from "The Bibelot"-11   H 222.   First thus.

35 numbered copies on Japan vellum.
First edition.

Content: In addition to "The Story of the Unknown Church" (pp. 5-22), the other tales in this book are "Lindenborg Pool" (pp. 25-[40]) and "A Dream" (pp. 47-[77]). The introductory remarks (pp. [1-2]) to the volume are selections from J. W. Mackail's and Aymer Vallance's biographies of Morris. Mosher's preface to "A Dream" appears on pp. [43-45]. The source for these works was *The Oxford and Cambridge Magazine* for January and September 1856.

This work was printed by Mosher in his March 1902 issue of *The Bibelot* (25).

Comment: The Quinn catalogue notes: "These scarce little booklets are not the regular Mosher publications, but are separates in book form from the original setting in the *Bibelot*. They constitute the First Editions of these pieces in book form, being mainly Morris' contributions to the *Oxford and Cambridge Magazine*, discerned by Mosher to be writings meriting a more permanent dress than the pages of a magazine..."

See also comment under entry 109.

Reference: Quinn 6984; mentioned in Walsdorf 101; Vilain 29 (plate 37, p. 94); Jenkinson II, 811.

THE STORY OF THE
UNKNOWN CHURCH
AND OTHER TALES BY
WILLIAM MORRIS

Portland, Maine
THOMAS B. MOSHER
Mdccccij

——————— *Same Title, Change of Series* ———————

390.   **THE STORY OF THE UNKNOWN CHURCH AND OTHER TALES** by
William Morris. [July] 1902   97, [1] pp. (same for second ed.)
Brocade Series-34   H 219.   First edition.

Content: The foreword is by the publisher. In addition to the title work, the
volume includes the tales "Lindenborg Pool" and "A Dream." For more information on the content and source, see 389.

Comment: This work is one of four which forms a sub-series. See note to entry
150 for the listing of all four titles.

Reference: Walsdorf 101.

425 on Japan vellum for each
edition.

390.1   **THE STORY OF THE UNKNOWN CHURCH AND OTHER TALES**
by William Morris. [July] 1906.
Brocade Series.   H 379.   Second edition.

391.   **THE STORY WITHOUT AN END** translated from the German of F. W.
Carové by Sarah Austin. [August] 1897.   1 ℓ., 59, [1] pp. (same for second ed.)
Brocade Series-5   H 45.   First edition.

Content: The unsigned foreword is by the publisher. The book includes the
dedication by Sarah Austin to her daughter (pp. [3-4]). A brief selection from
this work appears at the beginning of the May 1911 issue (p. [161]) of *The
Bibelot* (34).

Comment: The title page and front cover are printed in green & black rather
than the usual red & black of most other Brocade Series books (59 & 282 are
also exceptions).

425 on Japan vellum for each
edition.

391.1   **THE STORY WITHOUT AN END** translated from the German of F. W.
Carové by Sarah Austin. [December] 1897.
Brocade Series.   H 61.   Second edition.

391.2   **THE STORY WITHOUT AN END** translated from the German of F. W.
Carové by Sarah Austin. [March] 1900.   62, [1] pp. (same for fourth ed.)
Brocade Series.   H 172.   Third edition.

391.3   **THE STORY WITHOUT AN END** translated from the German of F. W.
Carové by Sarah Austin. [June] 1904.
Brocade Series.   H 308.   Fourth edition.

Comment: Some copies have a red & black title page.

392.   **STUDIES IN SENTIMENT** Apple-Blossom in Brittany—The Eyes of Pride—
Countess Marie of the Angels—The Dying of Francis Donne by Ernest Dowson.
1915.   *xvi*, 108 pp.   18 x 11 cm.
Miscellaneous Series-73   H 622.   Only edition.

Content: The essay "Apple-Blossom in Brittany" first appeared in *The Yellow
Book* (October 1894), while the other three essays appeared in *The Savoy*
(January, April and August 1896 respectively). To these essays Mosher added
"In preface" from *Verses* (1896), and the heretofore unpublished lyric, "To the
River Aven," inscribed in a book owned by Dowson's publisher, Leonard
Smithers. The foreword is signed by the publisher, and a selection from
Rabindranath Tagore appears opposite the title page.

450 on Van Gelder "for sale in
America;" 25 numbered copies on
Japan vellum.

STUDIES IN SENTIMENT (continued)

"The Eyes of Pride" and "Countess Marie of the Angels" previously appeared in *The Bibelot*, September 1912 (35), and "The Dying of Francis Donne" in *The Bibelot*, March 1912 (35).

Binding & Embellishment: The Van Gelder copies are bound in ribbed (raised bands) old-style blue paper boards with a white paper spine label printed in two colors. Japan vellum copies are bound in Japan vellum wraps over boards with title/author/date on spine in black and red. The title page is printed in red and black; Chiswick ornaments.

Reference: Quinn 2695 & 2696; Cutler & Stiles, p. 38; not separately listed in Cevasco.

---

393. *THE SWEET MIRACLE OF EÇA DE QUEIROZ* done into English by
      Edgar Prestage. [April] 1906.   *viii*, 33 pp.
      Ideal Series of Little Masterpieces-1   H 360.   First edition.

Limitation unknown for both Van Gelder and Japan vellum copies.

Content: The prefatory note on pp. [*vii*]-*viii* is by the translator. A brief quote from *Evangelium secundum Matthacum*, caput IX, appears on p. [2].

The text of this work already appeared as part of Mosher's December 1905 issue of *The Bibelot* (28).

Comment: A September 1, 1906 letter from Prestage (Colby College Collection) notes that he was surprised to find his translation in the Ideal Series, but praises Mosher for the book's beautiful execution: "your volume is beautifully got up and I hope it may give pleasure to many in its new country and lead Americans to pay attention to the literature of Portugal." Mosher remunerated Prestage by sending him Mosher books, including several copies of *The Sweet Miracle*.

First title published in this series.

393.1 *THE SWEET MIRACLE OF EÇA DE QUEIROZ* done into English by Edgar
      Prestage. [November] 1914.   *viii*, 33, [1] pp.
      Ideal Series of Little Masterpieces.   H 620.   Second edition.

---

394. *SYLVIE: SOUVENIRS DU VALOIS* translated from Gérard de Nerval by
      Lucie Page. 1896.   *xv*, 86 pp.; color front.
      Old World Series-6   H 24.   First edition.

925 on Van Gelder; 100 numbered copies on Japan vellum.
First edition of this translation.

Content: The preliminary unsigned notes (entitled GÉRARD DE NERVAL) are by the publisher. The translator, Lucie Page, includes Nerval's lengthy dedication to Alexander Dumas "now done into English for the first time" (appendix). Also included are the poems "Gérard de Nerval," "An Old Tune," "Sylvie et Aurélie," and "El Desdichado" by Andrew Lang, as well as two brief selections from Ludovic Halevy and Walter Pater. The translation is of *Sylvie; Souvenirs du Valois* (Paris: L. Conquet, 1886).

See entries 59, 217 & 268 for other translations by Lucie Page.

Design: Sylvie is one of only two Mosher books with a color frontispiece, the other being *The Soul of Man Under Socialism* (378). The original *aquarelle* was painted by Andhré des Gachons and secured by Mosher for 100 francs through the artist's brother, Jacques. In his Autumn announcement for

(a)

(b)

SYLVIE: SOUVENIRS DU VALOIS (continued)

1896, Mosher states "the frontispiece is in collotype from an original *aquarelle* commissioned by the publisher from the young French artist, Andhré des Gachons, 1896 whose delicate work will presently be more widely known in this country." Another painting, in sepia, was secured by Mosher for 50 francs from the same artist, and appears as a loosely laid-in supplement to "Lyrics from Paul Verlaine" in *The Bibelot*, in February 1898 (21). The original watercolor for Sylvie, and letter from the artist's brother (dated 23 July 1896), are in the Bishop Collection.

Reference: Quinn 7195.

394.1 *SYLVIE: SOUVENIRS DU VALOIS* translated from Gérard de Nerval by Lucie Page. 1899.   *xv*, 88 pp.; color front.
Old World Series.   H 127.   Second edition.

925 on Van Gelder. No copies were printed on Japan vellum.

394.2 *SYLVIE: SOUVENIRS DU VALOIS* translated from Gérard de Nerval by Lucie Page. 1904.   *xv*, 85, [1] pp.; color front.
Old World Series.   H 301   Third edition.

925 on Van Gelder; 25 numbered copies on Japan vellum.

Comment: The change in pages is due to a slight re-arrangement of the text.

There seemed to be some problem with the color frontispiece for the Japan vellum issues. Hatch wondered whether some copies came without the frontispiece. No copies were found without the frontispiece; however, at least one copy has the frontispiece for the Old World Series' *The Story of Ida* incorrectly applied to *Sylvie* (Bishop Collection).

T

395. *THE TALE OF CHLOE AN EPISODE IN THE HISTORY OF BEAU BEAMISH* by George Meredith. 1899.   *iv*, 116 pp.
Old World Series-18   H 106.   Only edition.

925 on Van Gelder; 100 numbered copies on Japan vellum.

Content: A poetic selection from "Captain Chanter's Collection" appears opposite the title page. Mosher did not identify the precise source for this reprint.

Comment: Forman indicates: "In 1899, Mr. Thomas Bird Mosher of Portland, Maine, issued a pretty edition of *The Tale of Chloe* in his 'Old World Series' ..."

Design: Based upon stylistic evidence, the cover design is most likely by Frederic Goudy. For other Goudy designs, see entry 1.

Reference: Esdaile, p. 35; Forman, p. 95; Crichton 42 and pictured on p. 73; Quinn 6368; Grigsby 803.

396. *THE TALE OF KING COUSTANS THE EMPEROR* done out of the Ancient French into English by William Morris. [April] 1899.
xxxvi (initial leaf blank), 28, [1] pp. (same for second ed.)
Brocade Series-13   H 111.   First edition.

425 on Japan vellum for each edition.
First American edition.

Content: The publisher's bibliographical note appears opposite the title page. The lengthy six-part introduction (pp. *ix-xxxvi*) is taken from *Old French Romances* edited by Joseph Jacobs (London: George Allen, 1896), which also

THE TALE OF KING COUSTANS THE EMPEROR (continued)

contains the text to *The Tale of King Coustans the Emperor*. In tandem with this reprint, Mosher may have consulted the Kelmscott Press edition of *The Tale of the Emperor Coustans* (Hammersmith, 1894), a copy of which was in his library.

Comment: This work is one of four comprising a sub-series "Old French Romances" translated by William Morris. Other Brocades in this grouping are: *The Story of Amis & Amile* (384), *The Tale of King Florus and the Fair Jehane* (397), and *The History of Over Sea* (148). Mosher not only grouped these four titles in his catalogues, but also provided boxed sets with labels.

Reference: Walsdorf 74.

396.1   *THE TALE OF KING COUSTANS THE EMPEROR* done out of the Ancient French into English by William Morris. [August] 1900.
Brocade Series.   H 174.   Second edition.

396.2   *THE TALE OF KING COUSTANS THE EMPEROR* done out of the Ancient French into English by William Morris. [June] 1912.   *xxxiv*, 28, [1] pp.
Brocade Series.   H 575.   Third edition.

397.   *THE TALE OF KING FLORUS AND THE FAIR JEHANE* done out of the Ancient French into English by William Morris. [September] 1898.
73, [1] pp. (same through third ed.)
Brocade Series-11   H 73.   First edition.

425 on Japan vellum for each edition.
First American edition.

Content: A publisher's bibliographical note appears opposite the title page. The foreword, pp. [5-6], is from *Old French Romances* edited by Joseph Jacobs (London: George Allen, 1896), as is the text for this reprint of the Morris tale.

Comment: This title along with three others formed a sub-series. See note to 396.

Reference: Walsdorf 69; Thompson, p. 194.

397.1   *THE TALE OF KING FLORUS AND THE FAIR JEHANE* done out of the Ancient French into English by William Morris. [November] 1898.
Brocade Series.   H 100.   Second edition.

397.2   *THE TALE OF KING FLORUS AND THE FAIR JEHANE* done out of the Ancient French into English by William Morris. [January] 1904.
Brocade Series.   H 309.   Third edition.

397.3   *THE TALE OF KING FLORUS AND THE FAIR JEHANE* done out of the Ancient French into English by William Morris. [December] 1915.   74, [1] pp.
Brocade Series.   H 632.   Fourth edition.

398.   *THE TALE OF THE FOUR WHITE SWANS* by Fiona Macleod.
[April] 1904.   97, [1] pp. (same for all three eds.)
Brocade series-43   H 288.   First edition.

425 on Japan vellum for each edition.
First separate book edition.

Content: The poem opposite the title page is from *The Three Sorrows of Story Telling*: "The Children of Lir," translated by Dr. Douglas Hyde (London: T. Fisher Unwin, 1895). "The Tale of the Four White Swans" first appeared as one of the tales in the *Laughter of Peterkin* (London: Archibald Constable & Co., 1897).

THE TALE OF THE FOUR WHITE SWANS (continued)

Comment: Fiona Macleod was a pseudonym used by William Sharp who also published works under his real name.

See note to entry 53 for identification with a sub-series.

Reference: Macleod I, p. viii.

398.1 *THE TALE OF THE FOUR WHITE SWANS* by Fiona Macleod.
[February] 1907.
Brocade series.   H 419.   Second edition.

398.2 *THE TALE OF THE FOUR WHITE SWANS* by Fiona Macleod.
[December] 1911.
Brocade series.   H 552.   Third edition.

---

399. *TAM O'SHANTER   A TALE* by Robert Burns. [January] 1913.
29, [2] pp.   17.5 x 10 cm.
Privately Printed-22   H 723.   Only edition.

500 on Van Gelder paper. Some copies do not have the limitation stated.

Content: The text for this edition was taken from *The Poetry of Robert Burns* ("The Centenary Burns") edited by Henley and Henderson (Edinburgh: T. C. and E. C. Jack, 1896). The signed foreword is by the publisher. The introduction "To Robert Burns" by Andrew Lang, is reprinted from *Letters to Dead Authors*, (London: Longmans, 1886) and appears on the verso of the inner half-title. Selections from A. C. Swinburne and Gawin Douglas accompany the volume.

Comment: On the verso of the colophon page is the printed statement: From Ghaisties, Ghoulies and long-leggity Beasties and Things that go Bump in the night— Good Lord, deliver us!

The book was commissioned by John McF. Howie of Buffalo, New York for presentation to his hotel guests on the 154th anniversary of the birth of Robert Burns on January 25, 1913.

Binding & Embellishment: Bound in gray and white shadow paper wraps with ruled lines superimposed over the overall background. The cover design of waves closely resembles the Gelett Burgess design for Yone Noguchi's *Seen & Unseen...* (San Francisco: Burgess and Garnett, 1897), but it is clearly identified by the Japan Paper Company as "San ban" shadow paper. The title page's illustration is signed "W.B." A Chiswick headpiece is used on p. [10].

Reference: Crichton 67; Japan Paper Company (Japanese Shadow Paper).

---

400. *TARES   A BOOK OF VERSES* by Rosamund Marriott Watson 1898.
viii, 27 pp.
Reprints from "The Bibelot"-4   H 76.   First thus.

25 numbered copies only printed on Japan vellum.
First American edition; author's first book.

Content: The unsigned introduction is by the publisher. The 15 poems used by Mosher are from the first and only edition published in London by Kegan

TARES A BOOK OF VERSES (continued)

Paul, Trench & Co. in 1884. There is also an untitled poem by Watson accompanying the main text.

These verses first appeared in Mosher's May 1898 issue of *The Bibelot* (21).

Comment: See note under entry 109 for more information on this series.

———————— *Same Title, Change of Series* ————————

401. ***TARES A BOOK OF VERSES*** by Rosamund Marriott Watson
[October] 1906.   *xii*, 60, [1] pp.
Lyric Garland Series-9   H 358.   First thus.

950 on Van Gelder; 100 numbered copies on Japan vellum; 7 numbered copies on Roman vellum and signed by the publisher.

Content: The two-part foreword is by the publisher. In addition to the original 15 poems in the 1884 *Tares*, Mosher added 18 later lyrics taken from Watson's books: *The Bird-Bride* (London: Longmans Green, 1889), *A Summer Night* (London: Methuen, 1891), and *Vespertilia* (London: John Lane, 1895), all of which were in Mosher's personal library. There is also an untitled poem by Watson which accompanies the main text on p. [2]. The quote "Mais où sont les neiges d'antan?" appears opposite the title page.

Comment: Krishnamurti included this edition in the 1991 Sotheran's of London exhibition, "Women Writers of the 1890's," perhaps because the poetry in it was originally published from 1884-1895, although one still has to ask what is a book from 1906 doing in an 1890's exhibit? Krishnamurti also apparently missed the fact that this edition contains additional poems beyond those of 1884. He also identified it as the first American edition. That "honor" belongs to entry 400 above which would have more appropriately fit into the exhibit.

Reference: Krishnamurti, p. 88.

402. ***THE TENDER MEMORIES*** Laval 1918 E S H. [March] 1920.
By E.S.H. [Elmer Stetson Harden].   74, [1] pp.   17.5 x 11.5 cm.
Privately Printed-51   H 751.   Only edition.

450 on Shogun handmade paper.

Content: This volume contains reminiscences of a soldier wounded in the war, describing some of his experiences while recovering from his wounds in the hospital.

Comment: According to the Lamb typescript, this book was privately printed for H. H. Crops (Sheean spells it Crapo).

Binding & Embellishment: Bound in dark blue charcoal paper boards with blind-ruled spine bands and darts wrapping around to the covers; white spine label. Blind-stamped Rossetti design on front cover. Title page in red and black; Chiswick ornaments and initial letter. For use of other Rossetti designs, see entry 223.

403. ***"TEN O'CLOCK" A LECTURE*** by James A. McNeil Whistler. [October] 1916.   *xii*, 54, [1] pp. (same for second ed.)   22 x 18 cm.
Miscellaneous Series-80   H 639.   First edition.

450 on Van Gelder; 25 numbered copies on Japan vellum (first edition only).

Content: Selections from Arthur Jerome Eddy, and Elizabeth R. and Joseph Pennell, appear opposite the title page. A brief eulogy, also by the Pennells, appears on p. [8] before the bibliographical foreword written by Don C. Seitz

"TEN O'CLOCK" A LECTURE (continued)

of Cos Cob, CT (pp. [ix]-xii). There is a selection from Arthur Symons on p. [2]. Whistler's lecture is on pp. [3]-30. The appendix (pp. [31]-54) begins with a note from Mosher (signed T.B.M.), and includes the following four selections:

- Swinburne's "Mr. Whistler's Lecture on Art" from *The Fortnightly Review* for June 1888, accompanied by Whistler's *An Apostasy* with his marginal "Reflections" as they appeared in *The Gentle Art of Making Enemies* (London, 1890).
- Whistler's "Et tu, Brute!" taken from *The Gentle Art of Making Enemies* (1890).
- Whistler's "Freeing a Last Friend" taken from a letter to *The World*, June 3, 1888.
- Swinburne's poem, "Before the Mirror (Verses Written Under a Picture) Inscribed to J. A. Whistler" (source unidentified), prefaced by a note on the poem, signed T.B.M.

Comment: Mosher notes in his 1916 catalogue that the expired copyright permitted him to publish the Whistler lecture. The Mosher edition is copyrighted under his own name.

Binding & Embellishment: Van Gelder copies are bound in stiff brown paper boards with gold title printed on the spine. Whistler's distinctive butterfly signature is printed in gold on the front cover along with the book's title. Japan vellum copies bound in Japan vellum boards with the same gilt stamping. Title page is printed in red and black, as are some pages of the text in the appendix.

Reference: Quinn 10883.

403.1 **"TEN O'CLOCK" A LECTURE** by James A. McNeil Whistler. [January] 1917.
Miscellaneous Series.   H 660.   Second edition.

---

404. **"TEN O'CLOCK" A LECTURE** by James A. McNeil Whistler. [September] 1920. *xii*, 64, [1] pp., port. front., 2 plates   Size was increased to 24 x 16 cm.
Miscellaneous Series-93   H 679.   New edition/same series.

450 on Van Gelder; 25 numbered copies on Japan vellum.

Content: This new edition is an enlargement of entry 403, with an additional four writings by Whistler which seemed "fitting addenda to the *Ten o'Clock*." Mosher drops the nomenclature, "Appendix," and inserts these four writings before the other four selections he used in 403, the whole spanning pp. [31]-64, and including:

- "The Red Rag" was taken from "Mr. Whistler Cheyne Walk" in *The World*, May 22, 1878
- "Propositions" Mosher only identifies these eleven propositions as "with compliments to the Committee of the 'Hoboken' Etching Club upon the occasion of receiving an invitation to compete in an etching tourney whose first condition was that the plate should be at least two feet by three."
- "Propositions—No. 2" was taken from a lithograph made in Paris for Whistler's students, c. 1885
-"A Further Proposition" was taken from the *Art Journal*, 1887.

Binding & Embellishment: Bound in stiff brown paper boards with gold title printed on the spine. Whistler's distinctive "butterfly signature" is printed in gold on front cover along with the book's title. Japan vellum copies bound in cream Japan vellum with the same gilt stamping. The cover is also a lighter shade of corn colored paper than is found on 403. The title page is printed in red and black, as are many of the pages after p. [41].

"TEN O'CLOCK" A LECTURE (continued)

This enlarged edition also newly includes three illustrations. The first is the frontispiece photo of Whistler taken c. 1885 by the London Stereoscopic Co. and lent by Earl Stetson Crawford; the second is a fold-out facsimile of the "Propositions—[No. 2]" lithograph (again lent by Crawford); and the last, Whistler's Tomb, is from the original 1916 etching by George T. Plowman, with an adjacent printed tissue leaf with a description of the etching from the *Boston Transcript* of January 20, 1917.

405.   EDWARD CALVERT *TEN SPIRITUAL DESIGNS* enlarged from Proofs of the Originals on Copper, Wood and Stone MDCCCXXVII-MDCCCXXXI. [October] 1913.   33.5 x 25.5 cm.

400 on Van Gelder; 25 numbered copies on Japan vellum. In the Van Gelder copies, the 10 plates are mounted on blue paper portfolio.

ix, 15, [1] pp., portfolio of 10 mounted plates with cover-title and end-page
Miscellaneous Series-65   H 589.   Only edition.

Content: The signed foreword is by the publisher, and the essay "A Brief Notice of Edward Calvert, Painter and Engraver" by Herbert P. Horne is reprinted from *The Century Guild Hobby Horse* for July 1891, pp. 113-118. Also preceding the plates is a selection from Charles S. Ricketts, the notice of Calvert's death (*The Athenæum*, August 18, 1883), a sketch of Calvert's life by George Richmond (*The Athenæum*, August 25, 1883), and select passages from *A Memoir of Edward Calvert...* by Calvert's son, Samuel (London: Sampson, Low, Marston, and Co., 1893). The ten designs are from copper, wood and stone engraved proofs owned by Mosher in a portfolio scrapbook. His decision to enlarge the designs was based upon another book he examined: Frederick H. Evans' *William Blake's Illustrations to Thornton's Pastorals...* Lmtd. to 25 copies. (London: Privately Printed, 1912).

(a)

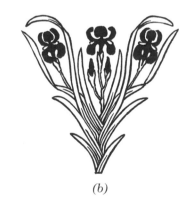

(b)

Comment: One of Mosher's larger productions: 33.5 x 25.5 cm. Other large volumes in the Miscellaneous Series include Burton's *The Kasîdah* (182 & 183), Blake's *XVII Designs to Virgil* (347) and Whitman's *Leaves of Grass* (192).

Binding & Embellishment: Van Gelder copies are bound in old-style blue boards with quarter white paper spine; white labels printed in two colors on both the spine and on the front cover. The illustrations are tipped on blue paper. Japan vellum copies also bear the label information directly printed on the Japan vellum boards, and the illustrations are tipped onto Japan vellum sheets which have blue ruled borders around each illustration. The title page is printed in red and black.

A legend slip found in some volumes notes "the head-bands [i.e., head-pieces], tail-pieces and initials used in this book were cut on the wood by Lucien Pissarro and are reproduced from volumes issued by the Eragny Press, London, 1901-03." Most are from the 1903 Eragny Press edition of Ronsard's *Abrégé de l'Art Poétique*, including the three iris flowers at the back of the book. The anchor and dolphin device at the back is also used in the 1911 Mosher Books catalogue (255). For other books using Eragny Press & Lucien Pissarro designs, see entry 52.

Reference: Vilain 22 (plate 30, p. 91); Quinn 7101 & 7102.

406. ***THÉ DANSANT IN THE BOWERY*** By M. T. Space. [August] 1915.

6, [1] *l.* (numbered) 14 x 9.5 cm.

Privately Printed-36 H 737. Only edition.

300 copies printed on Van Gelder paper.

Content: This brief story is written in the vernacular of New York City street language, e.g., "De other night I puts on me glad rags an' I sashshays up to Lizzie Maloney..." From the French, "thé dansant" literally means "tea dance."

Comment: Privately printed for George W. Elkins of Philadelphia. M. T. Space is the pseudonym of George W. Elkins of Philadelphia.

Binding & Embellishment: Bound in blue charcoal paper wrappers over flexible boards; front cover ruled in blue with title and author printed on both the spine and the cover. The title page is printed in red and black; text printed on recto side only; all page sides are ruled in red. Chiswick lead initial.

---

407. ***THEODORE ROOSEVELT A TRIBUTE*** by William Hard. 1919.

viii, 15, [1] pp. (same for second ed.) 18.5 x 14.5 cm.

Miscellaneous Series-89 H 669. First edition.

550 on Van Gelder; 50 numbered copies on Japan vellum.
First edition.

Content: In his brief bibliographical note Mosher mentions that this work was first published in *The New Republic* for January 25, 1919 under the title "Roosevelt Now." Selections from the Book of Daniel, John Bunyan's *The Pilgrim's Progress*, James G. Blaine's "Eulogy on Garfield," and a poem by Michael Angelo (translated by J. A. Symonds), accompany the text.

Comment: Mosher paid $25 for the right to reprint this work.

Mosher's original edited copy of *The New Republic* article is located at The Houghton Library (bMS Am 1096), as is the letter of permission from *The New Republic*.

Binding & Embellishment: Van Gelder copies are bound in blue boards with title/author printed directly on the spine and front cover. Japan vellum copies are bound in Japan vellum boards with the same printed spine and front cover.

The design surmounting the title on the cover is from Ronsard's *Abrégé de l'Art Poétique*, designed by Lucien Pissarro (London: Eragny Press, 1903). For other books using Eragny Press & Lucien Pissarro designs, see entry 52.

The "TR" design on the front cover is by George Auriol. It is found on p. 50 of *Le Second Livre des monogrammes, marques, cachets et ex-libris composés* par George Auriol (Paris: 1, B^d des Capucines, 1908), originally designed as a monogram for Richard Troller. A copy of this book was in the Mosher library. For other Auriol designs, see entry 145.

There are also two pictorial designs accompanying the text, one of which is by Selwyn Image (p. 14). For the use of other Selwyn Image designs, see entry 57. The title page is printed in red and black.

Reference: Wheelock, p. 23; see the Nov. 17, 1941 letter from Lamb to Yorke for Mosher's payment terms (see Appendix II).

407.1 ***THEODORE ROOSEVELT A TRIBUTE*** by William Hard. 1920.

Miscellaneous Series. H 685. Second edition.

550 on Van Gelder; 50 numbered copies on Japan vellum.

408. *THOMAS BIRD MOSHER   AN APPRECIATION* by Richard Le Gallienne.
Privately Printed for their Friends : Portland   Maine   : : : : MDCCCCXIV.
[September] 1914.   *iv*, 18, [1] pp.   14 x 9.5 cm.
Privately Printed-33   H 734.   Only edition.

Edition size is unknown; printed on Van Gelder paper.
First edition.

Content: A note opposite the title page reads "reprinted from *The Forum,* for January, 1914, by kind permission of the publisher, Mr. Mitchell Kennerley."

Comment: As indicated on the title page, this book was privately printed for both Mosher and Richard Le Gallienne. Neither the Lamb nor the Sheean typescripts record it. See also entries 39 & 258 for other appearances of this "appreciation."

Binding & Embellishment: Copies are bound in green paper wrappers; title/author printed in red and black on front cover; cover ruled in black. The title page is printed in red and black; red Chiswick lead initial; all pages ruled.

Reference: Colbeck I, p. 484 (59); Lingel 65.

409. *THRAWN JANET: MARKHEIM   TWO TALES* by Robert Louis Stevenson.
[September] 1903.   75 [1] pp. (same for second ed.)
Brocade Series-40   H 254.   First edition.

425 on Japan vellum for each edition.

Content: The contents of this volume consists solely of the two tales: "Thrawn Janet" (pp. 7-[32]), and "Markheim" (pp. 35-[75]).

Comment: The word "thrawn" is Scottish meaning lacking in pleasing or attractive qualities.

This work along with four others appeared in a sub-series. See entry 436 for details.

Reference: Beinecke, I 425 & 426; Gerstley 33 K.

409.1 *THRAWN JANET: MARKHEIM   TWO TALES* by Robert Louis Stevenson.
[November] 1906.
Brocade Series.   H 380.   Second edition.

410. *THREE LEGENDS OF THE CHRIST CHILD* By Fiona Macleod. 1908.
xi, 41 pp.
Ideal Series of Little Masterpieces-10   H 441.   Only edition.

Limitation unknown for both Van Gelder and Japan vellum copies.

Content: The foreword was written by Anna M. Batchelder. The three legends, "The Children of Wind and the Clan of Peace," "The Lords of Wisdom," and "How Deep Knowledge Came to the Child Jesus," were taken from the prose works of Fiona Macleod.

Comment: Fiona Macleod is a pseudonym used by William Sharp who also published works under his real name.

This volume, along with *The Distant Country* (90) and *The Wayfarer* (433), formed a sub-series that could be bought together in a cabinet style box.

411. *THRENODY AND OTHER POEMS* by Ralph Waldo Emerson. [Sept.] 1911.
x, 44, [1] pp.
Golden Text Series-8   H 541.   Only edition.

925 on Van Gelder; 100 on Japan vellum.

THRENODY AND OTHER POEMS (continued)

Content: The foreword (pp. *v*-[*x*]) is by the publisher. A selection from E. C. Stedman appears opposite the title page. In addition to "Threnody" which appeared in Emerson's first volume of *Poems* (1847), there are the following poems: "Dirge," "The Past," "Experience," "Give all to Love," and "Terminus."

Comment: Of the 925 copies printed on Van Gelder, 725 were bound in colored wrappers, and 200 were bound in marbled paper. The cover title of the Japan vellum and regular edition reads: *Threnody and Other Lyrics*, but the label on marbled paper copies reads: *Threnody and Other Poems*.

Last title published in this series.

Reference: Vilain 43; Myerson A 18.21; *BAL* 5486.

---

412. ***THYRSIS: A MONODY AND THE SCHOLAR-GIPSY*** by Matthew Arnold.
[September] 1910.   *vi*, 31, [1] pp.
Golden Text Series-6   H 514.   Only edition.

925 on Van Gelder; 100 on Japan vellum.

Content: The signed foreword is by the publisher. A selection from E. C. Stedman's translation of "Moschus, Idyl III" appears on p. [2]. "Thyrsis" appears on pp. 3-15 with an extensive note on p. [16]; "The Scholar-Gipsy" occupies pp. 19-[31] with a long quote from Glanvill's *Vanity of Dogmatizing*, 1661, preceding the poem on p. [18].

Mosher first printed this text in his October 1897 issue of *The Bibelot* (20).

---

413. ***THE TIME OF ROSES*** by John Vance Cheney. [September] 1908.
vi, 56, [1] pp.   14.5 x 12.5 cm.
Miscellaneous Series-40   H 434.   Only edition.

900 on Van Gelder; 50 on Japan vellum.
First edition.

Content: There are 35 poems by Cheney. A brief quote from Thomas Hood ("Ballad") appears on the title page. Some of the conjugate pages have text in italics.

Comment: John Vance Cheney was librarian of the Newberry Library in Chicago, and a founding member of The Caxton Club of Chicago. He also edited many of The Club's publications.

Mosher paid Cheney a 10% royalty on the sale of Van Gelder copies only.

Binding & Embellishment: Both the Van Gelder and the Japan vellum copies are bound in flexible Japan vellum boards with yapp fore-edges; spine and front cover printed in brown.

The cover's scrollwork design was taken from Herbert Horne's title page design for *Diversi Colores* (London: Published by the Author at the Chiswick Press, 1891). The text pages are ruled throughout in black. For designs by Horne used elsewhere, see entry 171.

Reference: See the Nov. 17, 1941 letter from Lamb to Yorke for Mosher's payment terms (see Appendix II).

414. *TO-MORROW'S ROAD AND LATER POEMS* by Gertrude M Hort.
[August] 1916.   *vi*, 67, [1] pp.   21 x 13 cm.
Miscellaneous Series-78   H 637.   Only edition.

500 on Van Gelder; 25 numbered copies on Japan vellum. First edition.

Content: This book includes the thirteen poems of *To-Morrow's Road*, the foreword poem, "Taking the Road," and sixteen "Later Poems".

Comment: Mosher paid Hort $25 for the publication of this work.

Correspondence from Hort to Mosher is preserved at The Houghton Library (bMS Am 1096).

Binding & Embellishment: The Van Gelder copies are bound in quarter dark-blue paper over blue decorated paper boards with the same pattern as that of *The Jolly Beggars* (180). The title is directly printed on the spine in gilt; the spine is slightly ribbed. The Japan vellum copies are bound in Japan vellum boards and gilt-stamped on the spine. The title page and colophon are printed in red and black; upper portion of text pages ruled.

Reference: See the Nov. 17, 1941 letter from Lamb to Yorke for Mosher's payment terms (see Appendix II).

415. ROBERT G. INGERSOLL *TOWARD HUMANITY* arranged by Anne
Montgomerie Traubel. 1908.   *viii*, 86 pp.
Vest Pocket Series-16   H 437.   Only edition.

Limitation unknown for both Van Gelder and Japan vellum copies.

Content: The foreword is signed A.M.T.(the editor). There are 150 selections taken from the works of Ingersoll. The book is also embellished by selections from Walt Whitman, Edward Carpenter, and Emile Zola. An index of first lines appears on pp. 77-86.

416. *TRISTRAM OF LYONESSE AND OTHER POEMS* by Algernon Charles
Swinburne. 1904.   *xi*, 389 pp.   (*vii*, 193 pp. for second vellum set)
Quarto Series-10   H 295.   Only edition.

450 on Van Gelder; 25 numbered & signed on Japan vellum; 4 on Roman vellum, signed by the publisher; 4 more copies on vellum of just of the Tristram poem. First American edition.

Content: Livingston notes: "The entire poem, Prelude and nine cantos, was published in the volume 'Tristram of Lyonesse and other poems,' 1882 [Chatto & Windus]. Thomas B. Mosher issued the poem separately in 1904." –p. 23 The source for Mosher's reprint is indeed the 1882 Chatto & Windus edition as evidenced by Mosher's copy, edited for the printer (Bishop Collection).

Comment: The "Prelude" was later printed by Mosher in the June 1914 issue of *The Bibelot* (37). This is the last title published in this series.

Despite Colbeck's comment that this volume is typographically distinctive but "without bibliographical significance," no previous American edition has been found.

In addition to four copies of the entire text printed on vellum, there were four additional vellum copies of just the title poem (see Section I, "Mosher Books Printed on Vellum" for a fuller explanation).

Reference: Colbeck II, 804 (83); Jenkinson 246; *DLB* LVII, pp. 306-07; Livingston, pp. 23 and 31; Quinn 9480 & 9481.

417. *TWENTY-ONE POEMS* written by Lionel Johnson: Selected by William Butler Yeats. 1908.　　*vi*, 55, [1] pp.
Lyric Garland Series-14　　　H 439.　　　Only edition.

950 on Van Gelder; 100 numbered-copies on Japan vellum.
First American edition.

Content: In a bibliographical note on p. [2], Mosher notes that the source for these poems is *XXI Poems* printed by the Dun Emer Press (Dublin, Ireland, 1904), plus seven additional poems of his own choosing (precise sources undisclosed).

Twelve of these poems were previously printed by Mosher in the March 1904 issue of *The Bibelot* (27).

Reference: Wade 231 indicates this is the First American edition; Quinn 4888 & 11895; Cevasco, p. 273 (1).

---

418. *TWICE TOLD TALES* by George C Chase. [November] 1923.
xvii, 60, [1] pp.　　　18.5 x 14 cm.
Privately Printed-61　　　H 761.　　　Only edition.

50 copies printed on Van Gelder.

Content: The unsigned introduction is by the author. The volume contains memories of the author's life which are "twice told," i.e., once to his children, and now to his grandchildren.

Comment: Printed for Elizabeth D. and Caroline W. Chase.

This is the last title privately printed for a client by Mosher.

Binding & Embellishment: Bound in gray paper boards with title/author on the front cover below the Eragny Press design which was taken from the 1903 edition of Ronsard's *Abrégé de l'Art Poétique*. Title page in red and black; Chiswick lead initial letters. For other books using Eragny Press & Lucien Pissarro designs, see entry 52.

TWICE TOLD TALES

BY GEORGE C CHASE

---

419. *THE TWO SIDES OF THE RIVER AND OTHER POEMS* by William Morris. 1899.　　*vi*, 24 pp.
Reprints from "The Bibelot"-6　H 118.　　　Only edition.

25 numbered copies only on Japan vellum.
First American edition.

Content: Besides the title poem, this volume includes "Hapless Love," "The First Foray of Aristomenes," and "Winter Weather." The unsigned bibliographic preface is by the publisher. Apparently the source for this volume was the Wise-Forman imprint of 1876. To this Mosher added "Winter Weather" taken from *The Oxford and Cambridge Magazine* for 1856.

These poems were first printed by Mosher in the September 1899 issue of *The Bibelot* (22).

Comment: Quinn notes that "these scarce little booklets are not the regular Mosher publications, but are separate in book form from the original setting in the *Bibelot*. They constitute the First Editions of these pieces in book form, being mainly Morris' contributions to the *Oxford and Cambridge Magazine*, discerned by Mosher to be writings meriting a more permanent dress than the pages of a magazine..." Quinn's note is not fully accurate here; only "Winter Weather" came from *The Oxford and Cambridge Magazine*. The others came from other periodicals, and the privately printed pamphlet, *The Two Sides of the River...* appeared in London, 1876.

THE TWO SIDES OF THE RIVER AND OTHER POEMS (continued)

See also comment under entry 109 for an explanation of the printing procedure.

According to Barker, this title was one of the H. Buxton Forman-T.J. Wise forgeries. It appeared as a privately printed pamphlet of crown octavo size, noted and described by Mosher in *The Bibelot* and in this reprint.

Reference: Quinn 6984; Walsdorf 76; Barker, pp. 210-212.

U

420. ***ULAD OF THE DREAMS*** by Fiona Macleod. [September] 1904.
70, [1] pp. (same for second ed.)
Brocade Series-46   H 291.   First edition.

425 on Japan vellum for each edition.

Content: The publisher's bibliographical note appears opposite the title page, indicating that his reprint is taken from the first "complete form, as here reprinted, in *The Dominion of Dreams* (London, 1900 [sic, 1899])." The 1899 edition, which was the first of the "complete form," was published in Westminster (London) by A. Constable, a copy of which was in Mosher's personal library.

Comment: Fiona Macleod was a pseudonym used by William Sharp who also published works under his real name.

See note to entry 53 which indicates the sub-series of which this title formed a part.

420.1 ***ULAD OF THE DREAMS*** by Fiona Macleod. [December] 1907.
Brocade Series.   H 420.   Second edition.

421. ***UNCOLLECTED ESSAYS*** by Walter Pater. 1903.
vi, 161, [1] pp.   18 x 11 cm.
Miscellaneous Series-22   H 249.   Only edition.

450 on Van Gelder; 50 numbered copies printed on Japan vellum. First edition.

Content: This volumes brings together twelve previously uncollected articles by Walter Pater:

– "Symonds' *Renaissance in Italy*" (*The Academy*, July 31, 1875)
– "M. Lemaître's *Serenus, and Other Tales*" (*Macmillan's Magazine*, November 1887)
– "The Life and Letters of Gustave Flaubert" (*The Pall Mall Gazette*, August 25, 1888)
– "Wordsworth" (*The Athenæum*, January 26, 1889)
– "A Poet with Something to Say" (*The Pall Mall Gazette*, March 23, 1889)
– "It Is Thyself" (*The Pall Mall Gazette*, April 15, 1889)
– "Fabre's *Toussaint Galabru*" (*The Nineteenth Century*, April 1889)
– "Correspondence de Gustave Flaubert" (*The Athenæum*, August 3, 1889)
– "A Century of Revolution" (*The Nineteenth Century*, December 1889)
– "A Novel by Mr. Oscar Wilde" (*The Bookman*, November 1891)
– "Mr. George Moore as an Art Critic" (*The Daily Chronicle*, June 10, 1893)
– "Shadwell's Dante" (Introduction to Charles L. Shadwell's *The Purgatory of Dante Alighieri*. London & New York: Macmillan, 1892)

The unsigned note is by the publisher.

Comment: Selections from this edition appear in Dennis Donoghue's new biography, *Walter Pater* (New York, 1995). Mosher's edition of *Uncollected Essays* uses the same format as *Essays from the "Guardian"* (104) also published as a Chiswick Press facsimile.

UNCOLLECTED ESSAYS (continued)

Binding & Embellishment: The Van Gelder copies are bound in charcoal blue boards with a white spine label. The Japan vellum copies are bound in Japan vellum wraps over boards with the label information printed directly on the spine. The title page is printed in red and black; Chiswick ornamentation and lead letters. Printed dust wrapper.

Reference: Wright, 163 (I a 101); *DLB* LVII , p. 217; Quinn 7591; not in Court.

---

422. *UNDER A FOOL'S CAP: SONGS* By Daniel Henry Holmes.
    [October] 1910.   *xvi*, 99, [1] pp. (same for all three eds.)   17.5 x 11 cm.
    Miscellaneous Series-49   H 506.   First edition.

900 on Van Gelder: 75 numbered copies printed on Japan vellum. First American edition.

Content: Daniel Henry Holmes, an American, originally published his twenty-four nursery rhymes in London (Kegan Paul, Trench and Co., 1884), and Mosher reprinted the rhymes, the author's own amplifications, and the original epilogue. The signed foreword is by the publisher and the review at the back is by Norman Roe, reprinted from *The Cornhill Magazine* (August, 1909). A poem from another Holmes book, *A Pedlar's Pack* (New York: E. D. North [Trow Press], 1906), also appears on p. [*x*]. Contains a bibliographical note on pp. [97]-99. Comments on arrangements made with Mosher can be found in the correspondence from Mrs. Rachel (Gaff) Holmes, at The Houghton Library (bMS Am 1096).

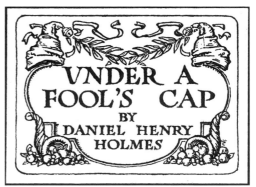

Comment: Mosher published both Roe's review and thirteen of the nursery rhymes in the May 1910 issue of *The Bibelot* (33). The response from his readership was quite encouraging, so he reprinted the book in the same year.

In a letter to Elizabeth Butterworth (Jan. 28, 1914), Mosher indicates that "the book was duly approved of by Mrs. Holmes and I think the family was much pleased to know he had at last come into his just due as an author of something that seems to me unique in American literature" (Bishop Collection). *DAB* mentions that "Holmes' works would probably have remained unknown for a longer time but for their discovery by Thomas Bird Mosher, who was the first to identify the authorship of his early poems."

Binding & Embellishment: The Van Gelder copies are bound in lavender paper boards with white spine and front cover labels printed in salmon. The Japan vellum copies are bound in stiff Japan vellum boards with the spine and front cover information printed directly on the Japan vellum. The ruled title page, and colophon, are printed in red and black. Pages ruled at top.

The front cover design is by Earl Stetson Crawford with his "C" monogram of a stylized crown of three dots above two curved lines. For other Crawford designs used, see entry 88.

Reference: *DAB*, IX, pp. 161-62.

422.1 *UNDER A FOOL'S CAP: SONGS* By Daniel Henry Holmes.
    [November] 1911.
    Miscellaneous Series.   H 550.   Second edition.

900 on Van Gelder. No copies were printed on Japan vellum. Colophon unchanged from first edition.

422.2 *UNDER A FOOL'S CAP: SONGS* By Daniel Henry Holmes.
[November] 1914.
Miscellaneous Series.   H 614.   Third edition.

900 on Van Gelder; 100 special copies printed on Van Gelder paper. No copies were printed on Japan vellum.

Comment: A variant of this edition at the University of Louisville has a note on the verso of the half-title: "One hundred copies of this book have been printed on Van Gelder hand-made paper for the Oakwood binders of Pittsfield Massachusetts and the type distributed." The 100 copies are bound in half-suede leather over light brown paper boards. The leather extends 4.5 cm. onto the board with the endpapers of the same paper. The edition note on the verso of the title page is identical to that of the 900 Van Gelder copies. It is not known if these 100 copies were part of the regular run, or if they were in addition to the 900 copies printed.

423.   *UNDER THE MICROSCOPE* by Algernon Charles Swinburne. 1899.
xi, 97 pp.   23.5 x 15 cm.
Reprints on Privately Printed Books-5   H 120.   Only edition.

450 on Van Gelder; 50 numbered copies printed on Japan vellum. First American edition.

Content: The unsigned preface (pp. *vii*-[*x*]) is by the publisher. Swinburne's text, reprinted from the first edition published by D. White (London, 1872), runs from pp. 1-[85], which is then followed by three appendices. All but one of the selections are by Robert Buchanan, most famous for his pamphlet, *The Fleshy School of Poetry and Other Phenomena of the Day* (London: Strahan, 1872), a work attacking Rossetti and Swinburne and prompting Swinburne's rejoinder in *Under the Microscope*. Mosher's appendices (pp. 89-[97]) include:

Appendix I:

Buchanan's "The Session of the Poets," a satiric attack on contemporary poets, including Swinburne (reprinted from *The Spectator*, September 15, 1866) in which he disingenuously includes himself.

Appendix II:

The diatribe, "The Monkey and the Microscope," Buchanan's rejoinder to *Under the Microscope* (reprinted from *Every Saturday*, Boston, August 31, 1872).

Appendix III:

– "Buchanan's *Apologia*," beginning with a retraction quoted from a letter addressed to T. Hall Caine, and printed in Caine's *Recollections of Dante Gabriel Rossetti* (London: E. Stock, 1882, pp. 71-72).

– W. M. Rossetti's comment on Buchanan's retraction, reprinted from *Dante Gabriel Rossetti: His Family Letters, with a Memoir by William Michael Rossetti*. 2 vols. (London: Ellis & Elvey, 1895, Vol. I, p. 301), summarizing the controversy.

– Buchanan's dedication "To an Old Enemy" (two quatrains), prefixed to Buchanan's *God and the Man A Romance* (London: Chatto & Windus, 1881).

– Two further stanzas, "To Dante Gabriel Rossetti," which were added to the above dedication in the 1894 edition of *God and the Man*, also published by Chatto & Windus.

Comment: T. J. Wise notes: "In 1899 a handsome but unauthorized edition... was published by Thomas B. Mosher..."

Colbeck calls this "a handsome but unauthorized reprint of the book first printed in 1872."

Livingston notes: "*Under the Microscope* was never reprinted in England, but Mosher published an edition in 1899, which gives the text of the reprinted leaf, not the original." Apparently Livingston is referring to the cancel leaf (pp. 41/42) of the 1872 edition.

UNDER THE MICROSCOPE (continued)

Binding & Embellishment: The Van Gelder copies are bound in charcoal blue paper boards with printed white spine label. Japan vellum copies are bound in Japan vellum wraps over boards with the label information printed directly on the wrapper. Aside from the publisher's mark on the front page, there is no other ornamentation.

Reference: *DLB* LVII, p. 306; Quinn 9459 & 9460; Colbeck II, p. 804 (81); Boss XIII 153; Livingston, pp. 21, 30; Wise 56 (see note) and Vol. I, p. 220; The Ashley Library VI: 104; Grigsby 1126.

---

424. *UNDERNEATH THE BOUGH   A BOOK OF VERSES* by Michael Field.
1898.   *viii*, 93, [1] pp.
Old World Series-14   H 66.   Only edition.

925 on Van Gelder; 100 numbered copies printed on Japan vellum. First American edition, and first appearance of this preface and several of the poems.

Content: The work is divided into five books of song, each with its own table of verses, for a total of 99 entries. In a prefatory note to Mosher's edition, Michael Field writes:

> Meanwhile, readers from further England [America]—if they will pardon my so classing them—have given me that joy of listening denied to me in my own island; and to them I offer this book of lyrics, adding such new songs as I count my sweetest to those of "The Old World Series," some of which, I have reason to hope, have won place in their hearts. September 8th, 1898.

Mosher notes in his 1898 catalogue "the Old World Edition is now put forth under Michael Field's authorization, and is the First American reprint of these exquisite lyrics. A large number of new poems are here given for the first time, and the entire volume has been re-arranged by the author."

Comment: Michael Field is the pseudonym of two English co-authors of lyric poetry and poetic dramas: Katherine Harris Bradley and her niece, Edith Emma Cooper.

Colbeck notes that "though not so certified, this is [overall] the Third Edition of the work; there is a new preface by the authors dated 8 September 1898, and the contents are considerably revised."

William E. Fredeman notes that "Michael Field's *Underneath the Bough* contains a new preface and authorial revisions, giving first edition status."

Reference: Vilain 53; Colbeck I, p. 249 (21); Boss IX 131, *PBSC*, p. 41 (for Fredeman's comment); Grigsby 389-395.

---

425. *UNDERWOODS* by Robert Louis Stevenson. 1900.   *xix*, 101, [1] pp.
Old World Series-20   H 137.   First edition.

925 on Van Gelder; 100 numbered copies on Japan vellum (first edition only).

Content: The 38 poems in "Book I" are in English, while the 16 poems in "Book II" are in Scots with a "Table of Common Scottish Vowel Sounds" preceding the first poem. Mosher does not list the precise source for his reprint.

Design: Based on stylistic evidence and the time period, the design on the front cover is most likely by Frederic Goudy. For other Goudy designs, see entry 1.

425.1 *UNDERWOODS* by Robert Louis Stevenson. 1908.   *xviii*, 103, [1] pp.
Old World Series.   H 448.   Second edition.

V

426. ***VERSES AND A DREAM***. [author unidentified].   [March] 1922.
      viii, 26, [1] pp.   18 x 12 cm.
      Privately Printed-56   H 756.   Only edition.

3 copies printed on Van Gelder paper.

Content: The book consists of 14 poems by an unidentified American WW I soldier (pp. 1-15), and a prose piece entitled "A Dream" (pp. 17-26). Each of these two sections is preceded by a personal note, printed in italic. The first is addressed to "My Father" and mentions that the occasion for this writing was "the mobilization in 1917 [which] cut us off at one stroke from that outward beauty of circumstance... Thereafter we ate from tin and raw boards. We slept in crowded sheds..."

Comment: The author's name does not appear on the work. The Sheean typescript indicates that this book was printed for Josephine B. Pressey.

Hatch had not seen a copy and took his information from the Sheean typescript where it is described as 30 pp. The copy examined is at the Ekstrom Library at the University of Louisville (Flora Lamb's copy). The title page information reads, in part: PORTLAND MAINE | THE MOSHER PRESS | MDCCCXXII

Binding & Embellishment: Bound in charcoal gray boards with white printed label on the spine. The overall appearance, including the title page, is like the Lyric Garland Series. Title page is printed in red and black; the publisher's device of two dolphins around an anchor is printed in red.

427. ROBERT LOUIS STEVENSON ***VIRGINIBUS PUERISQUE***. [March] 1904.
      ix, 94 pp. (same for second ed.)
      Vest Pocket Series-7   H 292.   First edition.

Limitation unknown for both Van Gelder and Japan vellum copies.

Content: In addition to the four-part essay "Virginibus Puerisque," this volume includes Stevenson's dedicatory epistle from the first edition published by C. Kegan Paul (London, 1881). A publisher's note appears opposite the dedication.

Comment: This volume is part of Mosher's Vest Pocket Series publication of twelve essays collectively known as *Virginibus Puerisque and Other Papers*, which first appeared in 1881 (London, C. Kegan Paul & Co.). See entries 1, 5 & 76 for the other Vest Pocket titles containing essays from this collective work, and thereby forming a sub-series in the Vest Pocket Series.

Reference: Beinecke I, 97; Prideaux, p. 15; Gerstley 12 L-M.

427.1 ROBERT LOUIS STEVENSON ***VIRGINIBUS PUERISQUE***. [November] 1906.
       Vest Pocket Series.   H 385.   Second edition.

427.2 ROBERT LOUIS STEVENSON ***VIRGINIBUS PUERISQUE***. [November] 1910.
       ix, 95 pp.
       Vest Pocket Series.   H 528.   Third edition.

428. ***A VISION OF GIORGIONE THREE VARIATIONS ON VENETIAN
      THEMES*** by Gordon Bottomley. [April] 1910.   *viii*, 46, [1] pp.   19 x 14 cm.
      Miscellaneous Series-47   H 504.   Only edition.

500 on Van Gelder; 50 on Japan vellum.
First edition with all three scenes.

Content: This edition includes the text originally published in *The Gate of Smaragdus* (London: The Unicorn Press and Elkin Mathews, 1904), now augmented by a third, and new, scene. The related correspondence between Bottomley and Mosher is at The Houghton Library (bMS Am 1096).

A VISION OF GIORGIONE (continued)

Comment: Mosher paid Bottomley $24.65 for the publication of this book in America. See comment under 324 for further information on Bottomley's arrangements with Mosher.

The first complete British edition, with all three scenes, would not appear until it was published in London by Constable in 1922. In that edition, Gordon Bottomley's Bibliographical Note on p. [*ix*] indicates that "the whole was first published in 1910 in the United States of America [by T. B. Mosher], and is now issued (with alterations and additions) in Great Britain for the first time."

Binding & Embellishment: The Van Gelder copies are bound in gray paper boards with white paper spine and cover labels printed in salmon. The Japan vellum copies are bound in Japan vellum wraps over boards with the same colored label information printed directly on the wraps. The title page and colophon are printed in black and mauve. Drop-cap initial "T" outlined in color. Pages are partially ruled throughout.

Cover design is by Earl Stetson Crawford with his monogram of a "C" with his stylized crown of 3 dots above 2 curved lines. For other Crawford designs used, see entry 88. The "globe and cross" publisher's device used on the title page and the colophon also appear on the 1916 catalogue (entry 260). The text pages are ruled throughout.

Reference: Colbeck I, p. 77 (9); see the Nov. 17, 1941 letter from Lamb to Yorke for Mosher's payment terms (see Appendix II).

---

429. *A VISION OF LOVE REVEALED IN SLEEP* by Simeon Solomon.
1909.   *viii*, 64 pp.   17.5 x 14 cm.
Miscellaneous Series-42   H 465.   Only edition.

50 numbered copies on Japan vellum only.
First American edition.

Content: The source for the main text (pp. 3-[53]) is the work by the same title, privately printed in London by Simeon Solomon (carried by F. S. Ellis) in 1871. The signed foreword is by the publisher, and a review by J. A. Symonds from *The Academy* (Vol. II, April 1, 1871, pp. 189-190) concludes the work (pp. 57-[64]). A bibliographical note appears on p. [2].

This work also appeared in the January & February 1909 issues of *The Bibelot* (32), including Symonds' review.

Comment: For information on this book being one volume of a "sub-series," see the note to entry 238.

Though not in the book, Mosher also published Swinburne's essay, "Simeon Solomon: Notes on 'His Vision of Love' and Other Studies" in *The Bibelot* for September 1908 (31).

Binding & Embellishment: Copies are bound in flexible Japan vellum boards with yapp top and fore-edges; title printed on the spine and title/author printed directly on the front cover with lead drop-cap initial in red. Title page printed in red and black. Chiswick ornamentation; small floral ornamental head-piece on p. 3.

Reference: Reynolds, p. 37 & 102; Fredeman 61.2.

A VISION OF LOVE
REVEALED IN SLEEP
BY SIMEON SOLOMON

PORTLAND MAINE
THOMAS B MOSHER
MDCCCCIX

430. *THE VOICE IN THE SILENCE* by Thomas S. Jones, Jr. [April] 1915.   275 copies printed on Van Gelder.
      With an Introduction by James Lane Allen.   *xii*, 49, [1] pp.   18.5 x 11.5 cm.
      Privately Printed-35   H 736.   First thus.

      Content: James Lane Allen's introduction, pp. [7-9], was added here for the
      first time. The volume contains 36 poems.

      Comment: This is the third American edition of the title, but the first Mosher
      edition. The book was published by G.W. Browning of Clinton, NY in 1912 and
      in a second edition in 1913.

      Privately printed for the author. See also entries 328-329.2 for another Jones
      title both privately printed and in the Lyra Americana Series.

      Binding & Embellishment: Bound in dark blue charcoal paper boards, and
      designed like the Lyra Americana Series.

      ———————— *Same Title, Change of Series* ————————

431. *THE VOICE IN THE SILENCE* by Thomas S. Jones, Jr. [October] 1917.   450 on Van Gelder; 25 on Japan
      With an Introduction by James Lane Allen.   *xii*, 49, [1] pp.   vellum.
      Lyra Americana Series-5   H 657.   First thus.

      Content: Contains 37 poems and a bibliographical note: p. [49]. There were
      several changes between 430 and this edition. Two poems were dropped and
      several were newly added.

      Comment: Jones received a 10% royalty on copies sold.

      Binding & Embellishment: The Van Gelder copies are bound in quarter blue
      paper over patterned paper boards exhibiting a field of hearts with crisscrossing
      dots. See series in Section I for further details.

      Reference: Vilain 46; See the Nov. 17, 1941 letter from Lamb to Yorke for
      Mosher's payment terms (see Appendix II).

431.1 *THE VOICE IN THE SILENCE* by Thomas S. Jones, Jr. [September] 1919.
      x, 52, [1] pp.
      Lyra Americana Series.   H 676.   Second edition.

      Content: Four sonnets are added at the end of this edition: "Sanctuary," "The
      Last Spring," "The Garden," and "The Path of the Stars." The original press copy,
      with Jones' manuscript changes for this edition, is in the Bishop Collection.

      Comment: In 1922 Mosher also became the distributor of Thomas Jones' book
      entitled *Sonnets of the Cross*, published by London's Society of SS Peter and
      Paul (1922), but did not get clearance to publish it before his death. His assis-
      tant, Flora Lamb, published it in 1927.

W

432. *A WALLED GARDEN AND OTHER POEMS* by Margaret Root Garvin.   250 on Van Gelder paper.
      1913.   *viii*, 58, [1] pp.   18 x 11 cm.
      Privately Printed-23   H 724.   Only edition.

      Content: This volume consists of 49 poems.

      Comment: This book was privately printed for the author.

A WALLED GARDEN AND OTHER POEMS (continued)

Binding & Embellishment: Bound in green Fabriano paper boards with darker green ink title/author on front cover and title on spine. Green ornamental initial on p. 3 and another ornament of heart-shaped design following the last poem.

The green printed illustration of a water fountain on the title-page is signed "e.a.c." (Elizabeth Alden Curtis) who also did the illustration work for the 1912 Mosher Books catalogue (256). See also 271 for a book authored by Curtis.

---

433. *THE WAYFARER* By Fiona Macleod. 1906.   *xi*, 47 pp.   Ideal Series of Little Masterpieces-4   H 363.   Only edition.

        Limitation unknown for both Van Gelder and Japan vellum copies. First separate publication in book form.

Content: The signed foreword is by the publisher. "The Wayfarer" first appeared in *Cosmopolis: An International Review* for June 1898, and a revised version was prepared for *The Winged Destiny* (London: Chapman and Hall, 1904). The revised version was the source for Mosher's separate reprint. The poem "Fiona Macleod" by Alfred Noyes is used as a preface to the text, and was taken from *The Fortnightly Review* of 1906.

Comment: Fiona Macleod was a pseudonym used by William Sharp who also published works under his real name.

This volume, along with the *Three Legends of the Christ Child* (410) and *The Distant Country* (90), formed a sub-series that could be bought together in a cabinet style box.

Reference: Macleod VII, p. 454.

---

434. *A WAYSIDE LUTE* by Lizette Woodworth Reese. [October] 1909. *viii*, 66, [1] pp. (same for all three eds.)   19 x 14 cm. Miscellaneous Series-46   H 469.   First edition.

        450 on Van Gelder for each edition; 25 numbered copies printed on Japan vellum (first edition only). First American edition.

Content: This work contains 51 poems by Reese.

Comment: Reese received a 10% royalty on all her books sold.

Binding & Embellishment: The book is bound in quarter white paper over a green decorative paper with a field of flowers and circular designs. The paper label on the spine is printed in two colors. Two Chiswick head-pieces are the only adornments.

Reference: *DLB* LIV, p. 344; Wirth, p. 10; the correspondence and several mss. poems are at The Houghton Library (bMS Am 1096); see the Nov. 17, 1941 letter from Lamb to Yorke for Mosher's payment terms (see Appendix II).

434.1 *A WAYSIDE LUTE* by Lizette Woodworth Reese. [October] 1916. Miscellaneous Series.   H 642.   Second edition.

434.2 *A WAYSIDE LUTE* by Lizette Woodworth Reese. [August] 1922. Miscellaneous Series.   H 697.   Third edition.

---

435. *WILLIAM MORRIS AN ADDRESS* By J. W. Mackail. 1902.   *iv*, 41 pp. Reprints from "The Bibelot"-12   H 223.   Only edition.

        50 numbered copies only printed on Japan vellum. First American edition.

Content: The reprint is taken from the Doves Press edition of April 1901. The introductory remarks are by the publisher.

WILLIAM MORRIS AN ADDRESS (continued)

The text of this work was also printed by Mosher in his September 1902 issue of *The Bibelot* (25).

Comment: Mackail, a British classical scholar and professor of poetry at Oxford, was the first biographer of William Morris and the son-in-law of Sir Edward Burne-Jones. For other Mackail entries, see 100, 130-31 & 343.

Quinn mistakenly calls this a first appearance in book form. As noted above, it was first printed in separate book form by The Doves Press in 1901; however, we have not been able to find any other American edition prior to 1902.

Last title published in this series. See also comment under entry 109.

Reference: Quinn 6984; Walsdorf 102.

---

436. **WILL O' THE MILL** by Robert Louis Stevenson. [September] 1899.
       68, [1] pp. (same through sixth ed.)
       Brocade Series-17   H 115.   First edition.

    425 on Japan vellum for each edition.

Content: This work first appeared in the January 1878 issue of *Cornhill Magazine*.

Comment: This work is one of five which form a sub-series called "Five Tales and a Study by Robert Louis Stevenson." The other Brocades in this grouping include: *The Sire de Malétroits Door* (355), *A Lodging for the Night* (217), *François Villon* (118), and *Thrawn Janet: Markheim* (409). Not only were these titles grouped together in Mosher's catalogues, but he also provided the lot in a boxed set.

Reference: Gerstley 33 H; Beinecke I, 427 (5th ed.).

[xx]. **WILL O' THE MILL** by Robert Louis Stevenson.
       Published between Sept. 1899 and March 1900.
       Brocade Series.   Second edition.

Comment: This edition was listed in the Hatch *Check List* as an unlocated trade edition. If ever found, this will become 436.01 in the present bibliography. Unlocated trade edition. Possibly the next entry was meant to be the second edition and was wrongly labeled "Third".

Reference: Hatch, p. 168.

436.1 **WILL O' THE MILL** by Robert Louis Stevenson. [March] 1900.
       Brocade Series.   H 178.   Third edition.

436.2 **WILL O' THE MILL** by Robert Louis Stevenson. [January] 1903.
       Brocade Series.   H 275.   Third edition.

Comment: Error in edition note? Reprint of previous edition with change of date on title page?

436.3 **WILL O' THE MILL** by Robert Louis Stevenson. [December] 1904.
       Brocade Series.   H 309A.   Fourth edition.

Comment: This edition was listed in the Hatch *Check List* as an unlocated trade edition, but was later added by Hatch in 1972 with the results printed in Vilain.

Reference: Vilain, p. 64; Hatch, p. 168.

436.4 **WILL O' THE MILL** by Robert Louis Stevenson. [September] 1907.
       Brocade Series.   H 414.   Fifth edition

436.5 *WILL O' THE MILL* by Robert Louis Stevenson. [September] 1910.
Brocade Series.   H 525.   Sixth edition.

——————— *Same Title, Change of Series* ———————

437. ROBERT LOUIS STEVENSON *WILL O' THE MILL.* 1911.   73 pp.
Vest Pocket Series-21   H 535.   First thus.

Content: This work first appeared in the January 1878 issue of *Cornhill Magazine*.

Comment: The popularity of Stevenson's *Will o' the Mill* encouraged Mosher to
continue printing this title which, until this Vest Pocket edition, went through
six editions in the Brocade Series. This edition exhibits how Mosher further
capitalized on a title by transferring it to another series, a sales strategy that
often worked in his favor.

Reference: Vilain 37 (plate 42, p. 96); Beinecke I, 428 & 429.

Limitation unknown for both Van
Gelder and Japan vellum copies.

——————— *Same Title, Change of Series* ———————

438. STEVENSON *WILL O' THE MILL*. [November] 1915. With a preface by
Thomas B. Mosher.   *xii*, 63, [1] pp.; port. front.   19 x 14 cm.
Privately Printed-38   H 739.   First thus.

Content: The signed foreword is by the publisher. Also preceding the title text
is the selection, "R.L.S. to W. E. Henley," and another from Walter Raleigh.
The frontispiece portrait of Stevenson is a photograph once owned by
Edmund Gosse.

Comment: Privately printed for Edward A. Woods of Sewickley, PA. Some
copies will have a loosely inserted presentation slip, from Mr. and Mrs. Woods,
bearing the family coat of arms and the title of the book.

Binding & Embellishment: The Van Gelder copies are bound in blue charcoal
boards with white spine label. Japan vellum copies are bound in Japan vellum
boards. Title page and colophon in red and black; Chiswick ornaments; lead
initials outlined in red; all pages ruled in black.

Reference: Gerstley 33 M.

300 copies printed on Van Gelder
paper; 25 copies on Japan vellum.

439. *WINE WOMEN AND SONG   MEDIEVAL LATIN STUDENTS' SONGS*
now first Translated into English Verse with an Essay by John Addington
Symonds. [October] 1899.   *viii*, 190, [1] pp.   19 x 14 cm.
Reprints of Privately Printed Books-4   H 119.   First edition.

Content: There are 60 songs numbered in Arabic numerals, and 22 explana-
tory notes by Symonds interspersed throughout and numbered in Roman
numerals (the first 13 of which go up to p. 47). The first student song begins
on p. 48. A two-line quote from Martin Luther, the reprint of the May 1884
dedication to Robert Louis Stevenson, and an extensive appendix (including
notes, a table of songs translated, and a list of "Books on Goliardic Literature") also supplement this volume. This work is a reprint of the London edition (Chatto and Windus, 1884), and is largely composed of translations from
Carmina Burana.

Several of these songs were previously printed by Mosher in *The Bibelot* for
March 1895 (18).

725 on Van Gelder: 50 numbered
copies on Japan vellum; 4 on Roman
vellum and signed by the publisher.
First American edition.

WINE WOMEN AND SONG (continued)

Binding & Embellishment: Both the Van Gelder and the Japan vellum copies are bound in the same multi-color decorated Japan vellum wraps over boards.

In some copies a printed slip appears on Japan vellum: "The [cover] border of violets on wrapper was designed and cut on the wood by Charles Ricketts, and is taken from an edition (210 copies only) of *Fifty Songs by Thomas Campion*, London: The Vale Press, Mdcccxcvi." The red decorative initial on the first page of text is by Lucien Pissarro. Title page in red and black.

For Lucien Pissarro designs used elsewhere, see entry 52. For other books using Vale Press & Charles Ricketts designs, see entry 47.

Color facsimiles of these designs (front cover and spine) are reproduced on two extra leaves at the end of the book in copies printed on Roman vellum.

Reference: Babington 493; Colbeck II, p. 815 (60); *DLB* LVII, p. 321; Vilain, p. 93 (plate 34 [of cover]); Quinn 9674; Grigsby 1158, 1180-81.

————— *Same Title, Change of Series* —————

440. ***WINE WOMEN AND SONG   MEDIEVAL LATIN STUDENTS' SONGS***
now first Translated into English Verse with an Essay by John Addington Symonds. [September] 1918.
xvi, 189, [1] pp.; port. front., plates   18.5 x 14 cm.
Miscellaneous Series-84   H 663.   First thus.

500 on Van Gelder; 50 on Japan vellum.

Content: A signed foreword by the publisher was added to this edition. A Latin quote from Walter Mapes is printed in red on tissue paper and appears opposite p. [2], just before the second engraving by William Strang. There is also a brief quote from Martin Luther and a dedication to William Marion Reedy. Two illustrations by William Strang appear opposite pp. 84 and 162. A four-page table of contents is also added to this edition.

The frontispiece portrait of J. A. Symonds is from an original 1890 pen and ink drawing by the American artist Samuel Richards, now at the Art Institute of Indianapolis. A note opposite the portrait not only gives this credit, but also directs the reader to an article about the artist and J. A. Symonds in *The Reader*, (NY), June 1903.

Binding & Embellishment: The Van Gelder copies are bound in plain blue paper boards with ribbed spine; black and red spine label. Japan vellum copies are bound in Japan vellum wraps over boards using the same Ricketts border design as used on the earlier edition (439), with the addition of a "youth on a fool's stick" device in the center of the front cover (same device newly appears on the title page) and no date printed at the base of the spine.

The engraved title page is printed in black within an ornamental border (red within black border in the Japan vellum copies), the ornamental border on p. [3], the tail-piece at the book's conclusion, and the two illustrations are all William Strang designs cut on wood by Bernard Sleigh.

On p. *xiv* of the foreword Mosher indicates that "the two border designs and tailpiece are taken from the Essex House Press edition (London 1901) of Erasmus on *The Praise of Folie*, while the two full page illustrations come in

WINE WOMEN AND SONG (continued)

reduced form out of *The Doings of Death*, a series of twelve woodcuts (140 copies only and blocks destroyed, London 1901)." *The Doings of Death* is also from the Essex House Press, and the year of publication is 1902, not 1901 as Mosher recorded.

The book's two decorative initials, printed in red, were designed by Charles Ricketts for his Vale Press. For other books using Vale Press & Charles Ricketts designs, see entry 47.

Reference: Vilain 26 (plate 34 of title page, p. 93).

---

441. ***THE WORKS OF ARTHUR SYMONS: A BIBLIOGRAPHICAL NOTE***
by T. B. M. 1912.   *ii*, 8 pp.   15.5 x 11.5 cm.
Privately Printed-20   H 722.   Only edition.

Only 5 copies printed on Bachelor & Kent imported blue laid writing paper.

Content: Under the poetry section Mosher lists 9 entries, plus 5 of his own reprints. Under prose he lists 19 entries. He also included 5 entries under translations, numerous magazine articles (including those which, to date, appeared in *The Bibelot*), 5 entries under the editorial section, plus various introductions, and a description of Symons' contributions to *The Savoy*. This same bibliography appears in *The Bibelot* for February 1912 (35).

Comment: Under the prose section Mosher first lists a copy of Arthur Symons' *An Introduction to the Study of Browning* (London, 1886), originally inscribed by Symons to Browning using the following unpublished quatrain:

> *To draw no envy, Browning, on thy name,*
> *Am I thus ample to thy book and fame;*
> *While I confess thy writings to be such,*
> *As neither man nor muse can praise too much.*

What Mosher didn't record is that this very copy was re-inscribed to himself:

> I am happy to offer this copy of the first edition of my "Introduction' (which had been inscribed for Browning himself, but held back in order to have a copy specially bound) to Thomas B. Mosher, printer of beautiful books. Arthur Symons March 1903

Quite obviously, Symons held a special place in the heart of Thomas B. Mosher, and Symons admired Mosher's work. This copy is now located in the Bishop Collection.

Binding: Bound in blue marbled boards with title/author label on the front cover.

Reference: Quinn 9841 (see also 9845).

Y

442. *A YEAR'S LETTERS* by Algernon Charles Swinburne. 1901.
viii, 220, [1] pp.   21 x 12.5 cm.
Reprints of Privately Printed Books-9   H 196.   Only edition.

450 on Van Gelder; 50 numbered copies on Japan vellum.
First edition.

Content: The unsigned preface is by the publisher. The text was taken from *The Tatler* for August-December 1877.

Comment: *The Tatler* series appeared under Swinburne's pseudonym, Mrs. Horace Manners.

A YEAR'S LETTERS (continued)

Livingston notes: "In 1877, Swinburne published a serial story 'A Year's Letters' in the 'Tatler,' Vol. II, August to December. It was not copyrighted in America. Foreign authors could not claim copyright in the United States until after July 1, 1891. In 1901, twenty-four years after its appearance in the periodical, Thomas B. Mosher reprinted this story. This was the first edition in book form, but it is omitted from the [Wise] Bibliography."

Sypher writes: "[Mrs. Horace Manners'] fame was alive in America, where in Portland, Maine, T. B. Mosher brought out a small, unauthorized edition of *A Year's Letters*—with Swinburne's name on the title page... A copy of this edition eventually came into Swinburne's hands, and Watts-Dunton [poet, novelist, and very close friend of Swinburne], perhaps anxious about the copyright, persuaded him to republish it. He still felt awkward about the book which, as he wrote in the Dedication [to Watts-Dunton], 'would never have revisited the light or rather the twilight of publicity under honest and legitimate auspices, if it had not found in you a sponsor and a friend.' But relations between the piratical Mosher and 'The Pines' [Watts-Dunton's famous villa in Putney where Swinburne lived] must have been cordial enough, to judge from letters written by Watts-Dunton to Mosher. Swinburne made a few small corrections in his copy of Mosher's edition, and sent it to press for publication with Chatto and Windus..."

T. J. Wise notes that this is "the First Edition in book form... Although this edition of *A Year's Letters* was unauthorized, it is of interest as being the first edition of the work in book form, and also as being the only individual form in which the original text of the novel is available. It was reprinted directly from the pages of *The Tatler*, and therefore does not present the changes and alterations which Swinburne introduced when preparing his own edition of 1905."—V. 6 of *The Ashley Library*: p. 202. In the second entry Wise notes: "This copy of *A Year's Letters* was employed by Swinburne as 'copy' for his own edition entitled *Love's Cross-Currents* first published in 1905. For this purpose it was corrected throughout, and several pages were marked for deletion. On page 41 Swinburne has written, '*Cancel all that passage about la monnaie de sa vertu.*'"

The August 5, 1905 *Saturday Review* write-up on *Love's Cross Currents* (the London:Chatto & Windus, 1905 edition) notes: "This letter [letter to the author on English virtue], which is one of the most interesting and characteristic parts of the book, is not republished in the new edition; its mere presence makes Mr. Mosher's unauthorized American reprint [of *The Tatler* sequence] more valuable than the authorized English reprint." The added letter appears on pp. 3-5 in the Mosher edition.

The alternative title for this book, *Love's Cross-currents–A Year's Letters* (New York and London: Harper & Bros., 1905) is often erroneously cited as the first American edition; however, Mosher published the work four years earlier (the London firm of Chatto & Windus also published an edition in 1905).

Binding & Embellishment: The Van Gelder copies are bound in quarter white paper spine over blue boards with printed white label on the spine. The Japan vellum copies are bound in Japan vellum wraps over boards with the label information printed directly on the wrapper. The title page is printed in red

A YEAR'S LETTERS

BY

ALGERNON CHARLES SWINBURNE

PORTLAND MAINE
THOMAS B MOSHER
MDCCCCI

A YEAR'S LETTERS (continued)

and black; beyond the publisher's device on the title page, there are no other adornments.

Reference: *DLB* LVII, p. 307; Sypher, pp. *xxx-xxxi*, and *xxxv-xxxvi*. The Ashley Library, V. 6, pp. 202 & 203 (two entries); Quinn 9466; Livingston, p. 30; Grigsby 1128; Metzdorf 2037; the copy of Mosher's edition with the printer's notations and Swinburne's manuscript alterations is located in the J. A. Symington Collection, Special Collections Department, Rutgers University Library.

443. *THE YOUNG KING AND THE STAR-CHILD* by Oscar Wilde.
[July] 1904.   80, [1] pp. (same for all four eds.)
Brocade Series-45   H 290.   First edition.

425 on Japan vellum for each edition.

Content: The publisher's note opposite the title page indicates that these two tales were taken from Oscar Wilde's *A House of Pomegranates* (London: Osgood & McIlvaine, 1891).

Comment: See note to entry 308 which indicates which sub-series this title formed a part.

443.1 *THE YOUNG KING AND THE STAR-CHILD* by Oscar Wilde.
[February] 1906.
Brocade Series.   H 382.   Second edition.

443.2 *THE YOUNG KING AND THE STAR-CHILD* by Oscar Wilde.
[February] 1909.
Brocade Series.   H 496.   Third edition.

443.3 *THE YOUNG KING AND THE STAR-CHILD* by Oscar Wilde.
[June] 1913.
Brocade Series.   H 603.   Fourth edition.

444. *THE YOUNG KING AND OTHER TALES* by Oscar Wilde.
[November] 1922.   *vi*, 116, [1] pp.   18.5 x 14 cm.
Privately Printed-58   H 758.   Only edition.

300 on Van Gelder; 50 numbered copies on Japan vellum.

Content: In addition to the title text, this work contains two other tales: "The Birthday of the Infanta," and "The Star-Child." The text comes from Wilde's *A House of Pomegranates* (London: Osgood & McIlvaine, 1891).

Comment: Printed for Edward A. Woods of Sewickley, PA. Some copies will have a loosely inserted presentation slip, from Mr. and Mrs. Woods, bearing the family coat of arms and the title of the book.

Binding & Embellishment: Bound in blue charcoal boards with the title/author in red and blue on the spine and front cover. The Renaissance-style design on the front cover is a Chiswick design. Title page in red and black; Chiswick ornaments and red initial letters; pages ruled in black (except for the title page).

ADDENDUM

445. *AN APPRECIATION* [caption title] by Jessie B. Rittenhouse. 1917.   Number of copies printed
     [3], [1] pp.   20.5 x 13.1 cm.   unknown.
     Privately Printed-46   H 746A.   Only edition.

Content: The three pages of text were taken from *The Bookman* for December 1917. Rittenhouse writes an appreciative overview of the poetry of Thomas S. Jones, Jr.

Comment: This publication is a single sheet folded once to make four pages. The verso of the second leaf contains *The Bookman* source and the publisher's imprint notation: PORTLAND MAINE / THOMAS BIRD MOSHER / MDCCCCXVII. Benton Hatch never recorded a copy.

The use of this piece is unknown. Perhaps it served as a promotional flyer or may have been privately mailed to a few friends as a keepsake. Whatever the case, there is precedent to include such briefly printed items (see *Inscription for a Fireplace*, #173), and since it does bear the publisher's imprint of 1917 and is completely without any advertising, it was decided to give it a separate listing under privately printed books.

Two copies have been located, one in the Bishop Collection and one in the Baker Special Collections at the Dartmouth College Library.

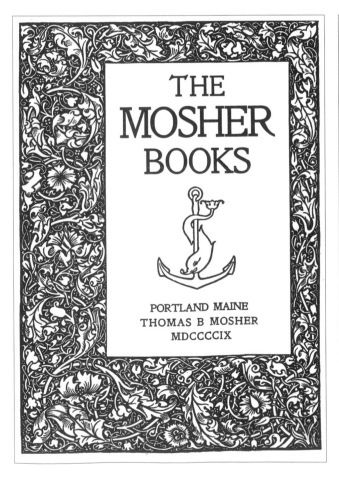

Section III

CHECKLIST OF THE MOSHER PRESS PUBLICATIONS
UNDER FLORA MACDONALD LAMB AND MRS. MOSHER
1924–1941

After Mosher's death in 1923, Flora Lamb continued as manager of The Mosher Press. Mosher's will stipulated that no new books were to be brought out, and only reprints of earlier titles were supposed to be printed, but the following list is a testimonial to the contrary. Many of the 137 publications listed below were privately printed works which Flora Lamb sold along with the regular Mosher books. One new work, the second *Amphora*, was even published by Lamb over the objections of Mrs. Mosher. Several lists were sent out to customers, and sales continued through the mails up to 1941 when the Press was sold to The Williams Book Store.

The books below are listed in alphabetical order by author. This arrangement contrasts as much as possible with the Mosher books bibliography of the books published from 1891-1923. The prefix of "FL" (Flora Lamb) identifies these post-Mosher books. The following entries have no stated limitation, and are not recorded in the Sheean or Lamb typescripts: FL24, 34, 41, 63, 65, 70, 104, 117, 126, and 132.

FL 1   *Amphora—A Collection of Prose and Verse* Chosen by the Editor of The Bibelot. [Fifth edition] 1926. *xvi*, 190, [1]pp. Bound in blue paper boards with red and black spine label as with previous Mosher editions. 18 x 12 cm. Limited to 925 printed on Van Gelder paper. Printed dust wrapper. Copies could be ordered bound in three-quarters red, green, blue, or brown levant. Some copies bound in three-quarter leather have a binder's stamp for The Monastery Hill Bindery.

FL 2   *Amphora—A Second Collection of Prose and Verse* Chosen by the Editor of The Bibelot. 1926. Portrait frontispiece, *xviii*, 137, [1]pp. The volume includes several tributes to Mosher, and ten selections from Mosher's catalogue introductions and poetry. Bound in blue paper boards with red and black spine label as with previous *Amphorae* from the Mosher Press. 18 x 11.5 cm. Limited to 925 printed on Van Gelder paper; 50 printed on Japan vellum with Japan vellum boards. Copies could be ordered bound in three-quarters red, green, blue or brown levant matching the binding on the first *Amphora*. The original Certificate of Copyright Registration of Oct. 1926, No. 950891, lists Flora M. Lamb as editor while Anna L. Mosher is the claimant (University of San Francisco). In a Feb. 26, 1927 letter to Mrs. Butterworth, Flora Lamb mentions: "I had a great deal to do in the making of the first Amphora—in fact Mr. Mosher said he would never have had the patience to have done it without me—and the second I did in his memory so that I hope when you read these volumes you will not only think of Mr. Mosher but of me who is striving to keep the good work going." (Bishop Collection)

FL 3   Anon, ed. [Abbe, Dr. Robert]. *In Memory of Dr. Robert Abbe.* 1928. Frontispiece portrait, *iv*, 32 pp. Cream colored paper wraps over cardboard with title framed in black: "In Memory of Dr. Robert Abbe 1851-1928." 14.4 x 9.5 cm. No limitation given (Sheean typescript states 400 copies, but the Lamb typescript states 100 copies on Van Gelder paper, bound in tinted plate paper wrappers for Mrs. W. G. Ladd, and adds that there was another edition of the same book in the same year).

FL 4   (Anthony, Alfred Williams). *For Sale, An Extra-Good Birthday—Somewhat Used But Thoroughly Reconditioned.* 1931. *vi*, 14, [1]pp. Blue paper wraps, stapled. Title printed on front cover. 12.7 x 10 cm. Limited to 250 numbered copies printed on Van Gelder paper. No copyright given.

FL 5   Anthony, Alfred Williams. *A Venture in Good Will—An American and Some English Cathedrals.* Entente Cordiale. 1931. *vi*, 35, [1]pp. Dark blue paper boards with title/author on spine and front cover (title in red on cover) under Eragny Press design. 19.2 x 14.7 cm. Limited to 215 numbered copies printed on Van Gelder paper. No copyright information given.

FL 6   Aughiltree, Ruth Maxson. *Stars on a Chain*. 1935. Frontispiece portrait, *vii*, 114, [1]pp. Bound in green cloth with title/author in gilt on spine and front cover. 19.4 x 15 cm. Limited to 100 copies printed on Old Stratford paper.

FL 7   *Autumn Leaves from Maple Cottage*. 1926. The only reference for this is the Lamb typescript. The number of copies printed is given as 4,000 and it is described as 16mo., in decorative wraps, printed on Van Gelder paper. An earlier edition was privately printed by Mosher in 1919.

FL 8   Ballard, Ellis Ames and Nina Schwefel. *From Generation to Generation.* 1928. Frontispiece portrait, *viii*, 99, [1]pp. (plus 3 portrait plates). Dark blue charcoal boards; title/author on spine, and title on front cover with large red "F" drop cap. 19 x 14.7 cm. Limited to 100 copies on Van Gelder paper printed for Mr. and Mrs. Ellis Ames Ballard.

FL 9   Ballard, Ellis Ames. *Seventy-Six Years of Life in a Changing World.* A Record for My Descendants Unto the Third and Fourth Generations. 1937. Portrait frontis, 2 *ℓ*, 120, [1]pp. Bound in blue charcoal paper boards with title/author in blue on spine and front cover which has a large "S" drop cap. 19 x 14.8 cm. In printed dust jacket. Limited to 50 copies on Van Gelder paper for Ellis Ames Ballard of Roxborough, PA.

FL 10   Barrie, J. M. *George Meredith A Tribute*. 1929. *vii*, 11, [1]pp. Light purple wraps over boards with title/author printed on spine and front cover which is ruled. Limited to 750 on Van Gelder paper. This is the fifth edition issued under The Mosher Press continuing the Miscellaneous series.

FL 11   Bennet, Florence Mary (Mrs. Louis Francis Anderson). *Spindrift*. 1930. *ix*, 85, [1]pp. Bound in Dutch blue charcoal paper decorated boards; title in red on spine and front cover; author's name printed in dark blue, Chiswick design (printed upside down) with criblé background on front cover. 19.3 x 14.8 cm. Limited to 500 copies printed on Van Gelder paper. Acknowledgments include: *Art and Archeology, The Living Church, The Phi Beta Kappa Key, The New Unitarian, The Christian Register;* also *A Half-Century of Song, The American Poetry Anthology,* and *Independent Poetry Anthology.* Florence Benet is also listed as being the author of three books: *An Off-Islander, The Garland of Defeat,* and *Religious Cults Associated With the Amazons.* Copyright under the author's name.

FL 12   *The Bibelot.* In "The Mosher Books" catalogue for October 20, 1932 there appears the following statement on p. 11: "The issues [of *The Bibelot*] listed below have been so much in demand that we have put some into old-style blue boards [about 15 x 11.5 cm] with pasted label..." Technically, the text block of each booklet is from each original issue of *The Bibelot*, but it was decided to place these newly bound issues in this post-1923 checklist since their binding and issuance is a later production.

FL 12.1	**Lyrics** from Paul Verlaine
FL 12.2	**Three Dreams in a Desert** by Olive Schreiner
FL 12.3	**XVII Woodcut Designs to Thorton's Virgil** by William Blake
FL 12.4	**Lyrics** from William Blake
FL 12.5	**Fragments from Sappho**
FL 12.6	**Three Selections from *Vagaries*** by Axel Munthe
FL 12.7	**Poems in Prose** from Charles Baudelaire translated by Arthur Symons
FL 12.8	**Father Damien** by R. L. Stevenson
FL 12.9	**Poems in Verse and Prose:** (Cynara) by Ernest Dowson
FL 12.10	**Three Greek Idylists**: Theocritus, Bion and Moschus
FL 12.11	**A Flower of Laurium:** Translated from Meleager and other Greek Lyrists
FL 12.12	**Proverbs in Porcelain and Other Lyrics** by Austin Dobson

Additionally, it should be noted that Flora Lamb continued to sell copies of the original set of Mosher's *The Bibelot*, and also acted as agent for the New York: Wm. H. Wise & Co reprint.

FL 13   Brush, [Dr.] Frederic. *Susquehanna*. [Third Edition]. 1924. *vii*, 140, [1]pp. Blue paper over boards with title (in red)/author on spine and front cover under an Eragny Press design. Limited to 550 copies printed on Van Gelder paper. 19 x 14.7 cm. Copyright under author's name. Previous Mosher Press editions were under the title *Songs of the Susquehanna* in 1914 and 1920.

FL 14   Candler, Beatrice Post. *Life's Garden*. 1930. *x*, 55, [1]pp. Blue charcoal paper boards with title on spine and front cover along with Eragny Press design; floral design on rear cover. 19 x 14.7 cm. 500 copies printed on Van Gelder paper bound in blue Fabriano boards. Copyright under the author's name.

FL 15   Child, Leslie. *Dream-Forest—Afternoon of a Faun and a Flower*. 1928. *viii*, 40 pp. Green paper wraps over boards with title/author on spine and title on front cover under a Selwyn Image design. 15.7 x 12.4 cm. Limited to 200 copies printed on Aurelian paper for Isabel Fiske Conant (according to the Lamb typescript). Copyright under The Mosher Press.

FL 16   Clark, Marguerite Dixon. **Wind Free**. 1924. *ix*, 52 pp. No colophon; no limitation given (Sheean and Lamb typescripts state 500 copies for Mrs. M. Clark). Gray paper boards with title on cover and spine; decorative device on front cover. 19 x 14.8 cm. Van Gelder paper. The acknowledgments include: "*The Bowling Green, The New York Evening Post, Casements, The Garden Bulletin, The Smith College Monthly, The Smith Alumnæ Quarterly, The Sun Dial, New York Evening Sun, The Lariat, The Measure, Voices, and others...*" Copyright under The Mosher Press.

FL 17   Conant, Isabel Fiske. *Frontier*. With a Foreword by Corinne Roosevelt Robinson. 1924. *x*, 70 pp. No colophon; no limitation given (Sheean and Lamb typescripts state 500 copies for I. F. Clark). Blue paper boards with title in red on spine and front cover along with an Eragny Press design. 19 x 14.9 cm. Van Gelder paper. The acknowledgments include: "*American Poetry Magazine; Casements; Circle; Fugitive; Lyric; Monitor; New York Herald; New York Post; New York Sun; New York Times; The Lantern of the New York Tribune; Poetry; Psychology; Unbound Anthology; Voices.*" Copyright under The Mosher Press.

FL 18   Conant, Isabel Fiske, [editor]. *Scrapped Silver*. 1928. *x*, 37 pp. Blue charcoal paper wraps over boards. Title labels on spine and front cover. 15.4 x 12.4 cm. Limited to 260 copies (Sheean states 270) on American white wove paper (Blue Hill Text paper). Lamb states 260 on Blue Hill Text and 10 on Aurelian paper for I. F. Conant. Acknowledgments made to *Voices* and the *Stratford Monthly*. Copyright under The Mosher Press. This is a book of verse by the pupils of the Scoville School.

FL 19   Conant, Isabel Fiske. *Aisle-Seat; Lyrics, Sonnets, Quatrains*. 1937. *vi*, 55 pp. Green paper boards with title on spine and front cover with Eragny Press design. 19 x 14.7 cm. Blue Hill text paper. No colophon; no limitation stated. Contains the acknowledgments to "*The Commonweal, The Harpoon, The New York Herald-Tribune Books, The Gypsy, The London Poetry Review, The Lyric, Palms, The Poetry Society of America, The Poetry Society of Georgia, The New York Times, The New York Sun, Poetry, The Saturday Review of Literature, Scribner's, Shards, Talaria, The Troubadour, Voices*, and others." Copyright under The Mosher Press.

FL 20   Coughlin, Anna Emma. *Knots of Straw and Other Verses*. 1926. *viii*, 85, [1]pp. Green paper boards with title on spine and front cover with cover design from the Old World Series. 19 x 14.7 cm. Limited to 300 copies on Van Gelder paper. Copyright under author's name.

FL 21   Cramer, Ruth. *And All My Life*. 1928. *v*, 38, [1]pp. Green Strathmore paper wrappers over boards with title/author on spine and front cover (title in red on cover below a Chiswick design). 15.1 x 12.4 cm. Limited to 300 copies on American white wove paper (Blue Hill Text paper). According to the Lamb typescript, this book was printed for Isabel Fiske Connant. Copyright under The Mosher Press name.

FL 22   Curtis, William John. *Memoirs of William John Curtis.* 1928. [*iv*], [5]-209, [1]. Photographic portrait used as frontispiece. Limited to 25 numbered copies printed by The Mosher Press for Mrs. William John Curtis (Lamb states 20 copies). 22.7 x 17 cm. A copy examined at Bowdoin College is bound in 3/4 blue leather over blue cloth, and is signed by Walter Hughson Jr. on the limitation page.

FL 23   Drummond, Henry. *The Greatest Thing in the World.* 1927. Portrait frontispiece, *xl*, 53, [3] pp. Blue paper boards with title printed in red on spine and front cover; all other design & print in blue; printed dust jacket. 19 x 14.5 cm. Colophon indicates 250 copies printed on Van Gelder, 50 copies on Japan vellum, and privately printed for Mr. and Mrs. Edward A. Woods of Sewickley, PA.

FL 24   Edey, Birdsall Otis. *Butter Money.* 1931. *ix*, 59 pp. Yellow Marlowe paper boards with title/author on spine and front cover; jar design on cover. 19.1 x 14.7 cm. Acknowledgments are made to "*The Commonweal; The Evening Sun; The Sketch Book Magazine; Book and Craft Bulletin; Oracle Anthology.*" Printed on Van Gelder paper; no limitation statement. Copyright under the author's name.

FL 25   Edey, Birdsall Otis. *Rivets.* 1928. *viii*, 53 pp. Orange Mayan-Marlowe paper boards with title on spine and front cover. 19 x 14.7 cm. No colophon; no limitation given. According to the Lamb typescript, there were 300 copies printed on Van Gelder paper and bound in Mayan-Marlowe boards for B. O. Edey. Acknowledgments are made to "*The Commonweal; Harp; Sun; Sketch Book Magazine; Book and Craft Bulletin; Braithwaite Anthology; Bronxville Review; Oracle Anthology.*" Copyright under author's name.

FL 26   Evans, Jessie Benton, trans. *Giulietta and Romeo.* A Story from the Original Italian of Luigi da Porto of Vicenza Illustrated with Pictures Painted in Italy by the Translator. 1934. Color-frontispiece, special title page, *xviii*, 50, [1]pp.; plus 5 four-color and 9 black & white half-tone plates not part of collation. Bound in Japan vellum boards with title/author on spine and front cover; multi-colored and gilt decorative initial "G" on front cover printed in four-color process. 19.2 x 14.8 cm. Printed dust jacket. Plates with titled tissue guards. Some in-text illustrations and colored decorative initials. Special title page printed on Japan vellum. Limited to 1000 copies printed on Van Gelder paper. Copyright under the author's name.

FL 27   Fort, Adèle Brooks. *Splendor in the Night—Recording a Glimpse of Reality by a Pilgrim.* With Foreword by Rufus M. Jones, M.A., D. Litt. Professor of Philosophy, Haverford College, Pennsylvania, [May] 1933. *xxii*, 65, [1]pp. Dutch blue pictorial wraps with design and letters printed in dark blue and orange. 17 cm. 500 copies on Blue Hill text.

FL 28   Fort, Adèle Brooks. *Splendor in the Night—Recording a Glimpse of Reality.* With Foreword by Rufus M. Jones, M.A., D. Litt. Professor of Philosophy, Haverford College, Pennsylvania. [December] 1934. *xxii*, 65, [1]pp. Blue pictorial wraps over boards. 16.7 x 11.1 cm. Title on spine and front cover which is printed in yellow and brown. 500 copies printed on Blue Hill text. Copyright 1933 under The Mosher Press.

FL 29   French, Elizabeth Short. *Once Upon a Time.* 1932. Frontispiece, *v*, 168, [1]pp., 28 photo-plates. Charcoal blue boards with label on spine. 19.2 x 14.8 cm. Colophon indicates that 7 copies of this book were printed on Van Gelder "...arranged with the Mosher Press..." Apparently a copy was printed for each of the seven grandchildren named on the dedication page.

FL 30   (Frost, Robert). *The Arts Anthology. Dartmouth Verse 1925.* With an Introduction by Robert Frost. 1925. *xiv*, 57, [1]pp. Quarter white paper spine over blue paper boards with title/date printed in black and red; dingbats on spine. 17.8 x 11.6 cm. Limited to 500 numbered copies on Van Gelder paper for *The Arts Dartmouth College* Hanover, New Hampshire. "COPYRIGHT 1925 BY THE ARTS *All Rights Reserved*".

FL 31   Fryer, Eugénie M [Mary]. *Unending Quest.* 1932. *viii*, 30, [1]pp. Dark blue Dutch Charcoal paper boards with title/author labels on spine and front cover (title in red with Chiswick designs on cover). 18.1 x 11.7 cm. Limited to 500 copies on Van Gelder paper. In the style of the Lyric Garland Series. Copyright under the author's name.

FL 32   Gissing, George. ***The Private Papers of Henry Ryecroft.*** With an Introductory Survey by Thomas Seccombe. [Second edition] 1928. *lxiv*, 246, [1]pp. This volume is the same size and design as Mosher's previous 1921 edition in the Miscellaneous Series. 19.1 x 14.7 cm. Limited to 500 copies on Van Gelder paper. Printed dust wrapper.

FL 33   Glines, Ellen. ***Garden Untended.*** 1933. *xii*, 116, [1]pp. Dark green Ingres paper boards with red author/title labels on spine and front cover. 19 x 14.7 cm. Limited to 500 copies printed on Van Gelder paper. Acknowledgments include: "*Poetry: A Magazine of Verse, Palms, Lyric, Century Magazine, Plain Talk (New York), Voices, Midland, True Confessions, Youth's Companion, Carillon, Fugitive, College Humor, Kaleidoscope, Japm, Palo Verde, Bozart, Skyline, Oracle, Porto Rico Progress, and El Tiempo... The Lantern of the New York Tribune... Evening Post... and to The Poetry Society of South Carolina for permission to reprint for One Who Cannot Forget.*" Copyright under the author's name.

FL 34   Hamlin, Simon Moulton. ***The Hamlins of New England.*** Descendants of James and Anna Hamlin Barnstable County Massachusetts 1639-1936. Privately Printed [The Mosher Press], 1936. Frontispiece, *xiii*, 65, [1]pp., 10 photo-plates. Red cloth with title in gold on spine. 22 x 15.7 cm. Colophon indicates this book was printed on Blue Hill paper, but no limitation is given. Copyright under author's name. In printed dust jacket.

       Hart, Robert-Edward. *The Poet of the Indian Ocean.* (see Underwood)

FL 35   [Healy, Rev. Walter]. ***Lucena Marion Downer Buswell.*** No place, no date [ca. 1929]. 8 pp. Bound in same paper as wrappers with black cord; title and birth/death dates on front wrapper. 14.8 x 10.8 cm. April 11, 1928 tribute by Rev. Healy. The Sheean typescript indicates there were 100 small quarto pamphlet copies of this memorial printed on heavy Van Gelder paper, with portrait sewn with silk.

FL 36   Hewlett, Maurice. ***Quattrocentisteria—How Sandro Botticelli Saw Simonetta in the Spring.*** 1927. Frontispiece, *ix*, 67, [1] pp. Light blue paper boards with spine's title in red and title/author in red on front cover within green rules. 15.6 x 9.4 cm. Limited to 975 copies on Van Gelder paper. No edition note given and may either be seen as a continuation of the Vest Pocket or the Brocade series, but the present volume does not resemble either style. The volume is bound like the 1928 Wicksteed translation of *Our Lady's Tumbler* (FL 135).

FL 37   Higginson, Mary Thacher. ***Fugitives.*** 1929. *vii*, 74, [1]pp. Green charcoal paper boards with author/title printed on spine and front cover. 16.5 x 12.5 cm. Limited to 200 copies privately printed on Blue Hill paper. Copyright under the author's name.

FL 38   Holmes, Daniel Henry. ***Under a Fool's Cap.*** [Fourth edition] 1925. *xvi*, 99, [2] pp. 18 cm. Limited to 900 copies printed on Van Gelder paper.

FL 39   Hoskier, H. C. [Herman Charles] ***"The Bronze Horses"—A Comment on the Prose-poem of Amy Lowell.*** 1930. 18, [1]pp. Green Strathmore paper boards with red title/author printed on spine and front cover; Old World Series device on front cover. 19.1 x 14.7 cm. Limited to 500 copies on Blue Hill Text paper. Copyright under author's name.

FL 40   Hoskier, H. C. ***What is Nirvana?*** 1930. 13, [1]pp. Blue paper boards with title on spine and front cover along with a decorative device from the Old World Series. 19 x 14.5 cm. 500 copies on Van Gelder paper. Copyright under the author's name.

FL 41   Johnson, Crawford. ***Hunters of the Moon.*** 1931. *x*, 62 pp. Quarter white paper spine over blue boards done in the style of Mosher's *Sermon on the Mount* with same cover decorations and page layouts. 17 x 10.9 cm. A hand-painted flag and a photo-portrait are part of the preliminary pages. No limitation given.

FL 42   Jones, Thomas S. [Samuel], Jr. *Akhnaton and Other Sonnets*. 1928. *iii*, 25, [1]pp. Light blue paper
         boards; title on spine and title (in red)/author on front cover under Mackmurdo design as on Under-
         wood's *Attic Twilights* (1928). 15.3 x 12.7 cm. Limited to 500 on Van Gelder paper. Sometimes in blue-
         gray paper covered slipcase (label on spine) with Jones' *Sonnets & Quatrains*. Copyright under
         author's name.

FL 43   Jones, Thomas S., Jr. *The Image and Other Sonnets*. 1932. [14]pp. Light red paper boards with
         title/date on front cover with the Sword of Light device. 15.4 x 12.9 cm. A hand-written colophon in
         the author's hand indicates: "One of six special copies printed on Van Gelder paper in the Month of
         May, and published on Saint Columba's Day, June 9, 1932" (Bishop Collection). Regular copies limited
         to 450 on Blue Hill paper, [14+1]pp., bound as before. Copyright under the author's name.

FL 44   Jones, Thomas S., Jr. *Jeanne d'Arc*. 1929. 12 pp. Bound in decorated dark blue Dutch charcoal paper
         wrappers. 15 cm. Limited to 500 copies on Van Gelder paper.

FL 45   Jones, Thomas S., Jr. *Leonardo Da Vinci and Other Sonnets*. 1930. [12], [1]pp. Pale pink charcoal
         wrappers with silk thread tie; title/author printed in pink on front cover over a design from the Old
         World Series. Also copies bound in stiff pink boards. 15.2 x 12.8 cm. Limited to 500 copies on Van
         Gelder paper. Copyright under the author's name.

FL 46   Jones, Thomas S., Jr. *Quatrains*. [1928]. 4 pp. "Caption title and colophon. Printed on outside of dou-
         ble leaf cut at top" and "8 pp." according to *NUC*. A copy examined shows that only four of the eight
         sides are actually printed. The booklet is formed by twice folding a single sheet which has only been
         printed on one side. The result is a slim booklet of four printed pages on a rather heavy paper stock
         with chain lines. 15.4 x 12.3 cm. The Lamb typescript indicates 500 copies in wisteria covers for T. S.
         Jones. A copy at Arizona State University is bound in purple "wisteria" wraps stitched with a purple
         silk cord.

FL 47   Jones, Thomas S., Jr. *The Rose Jar*. [Seventh edition] 1924. *viii*, 56, [1]pp. Bound in quarter light pur-
         ple paper over pink heart-designed paper (same style as the original Lyra Americana Series) with
         title/author on spine. 18 x 11.7 cm. Limited to 750 copies on Van Gelder paper. Copyright under
         author's name. Often offered in slipcase with *The Voice in the Silence*.

FL 48   Jones, Thomas S., Jr. *The Rose Jar*. [Eighth edition] 1928. *viii*, 56, [1]pp. Bound in quarter light purple
         paper over old rose heart-designed paper (same style as the original Lyra Americana Series) with
         title/author on spine. 18 x 11.7 cm. Limited to 750 copies on Van Gelder paper. Copyright under
         author's name.

FL 49   Jones, Thomas S., Jr. *Saint Christopher*. 1927. [4]pp. with only the first page printed, the others being
         blank. Printed in green and black for Jones as a 1927 Christmas greeting. 14.1 x 11.3 cm. No place of
         publication, but much like a Mosher publication in style. The copy at Arizona State University is
         inscribed to Mrs. Mosher from the author.

FL 50   Jones, Thomas S., Jr. *Six Sonnets*. 1926. [8], [1]pp. Light green charcoal Fabriano wraps bound with
         red thread, title/author and design from the Old World Series on front cover. 15.2 x 12.8 cm. Limited
         to 600 copies printed on Glaslan hand-made paper. Copyright under author's name.

FL 51   Jones, Thomas S., Jr. *Sonnets and Quatrains*. 1928. *v*, 21, [1]pp. Green paper boards with title on
         spine and title (in red)/author on front cover under Chiswick design. 15.3 x 13 cm. Limited to 600 on
         Van Gelder paper. Copyright under author's name.

FL 52   Jones, Thomas S., Jr. *Sonnets of the Cross*. [4th, enlarged edition]. 1927. *vii*, 62, [1]. Bound in deco-
         rated Wisteria Marlowe paper over boards. Title on spine and title/author on front cover over a design
         from the Old World Series. 15.2 x 13 cm. Limited to 750 copies on Van Gelder paper. Other editions

listed for 1922, 1923 and 1926 on verso of the title page. These three former editions (size: 12.5 x 9.5 cm. in paper covers of different colors) were published in London by the Society of SS. Peter & Paul. The copyright to this edition is under the author's name. The previous London editions of this title were officially distributed by Mosher in America since 1922 according to that year's catalogue (see 431.1). *Sonnets of the Cross* and *Sonnets of the Saints* are sometimes found together in a single slip case.

FL 53   Jones, Thomas S., Jr. *Sonnets of the New World*. 1930. [21]pp. 15.5 x 18 cm. Decorated corn color boards with George Russell's sword of light device on the front cover. Limited to 500 copies printed on Van Gelder paper.

FL 54   Jones, Thomas S., Jr. *Sonnets of the New World*. With dedicatory Forward by John L. Foley. [Second edition] 1935. [27]pp. 15 x 13 cm. Limited to 500 copies printed on Blue Hill paper.

FL 55   Jones, Thomas S., Jr. *Sonnets of the Saints*. [Second edition]. 1926. *vii*, 34, [1]pp. Green Strathmore paper boards with title/author on spine and front cover; design from Old World Series on front cover. 15.3 x 13 cm. Limited to 400 copies on Shogun paper, and 100 copies on Glaslan paper. Copyright under the author's name. *Sonnets of the Saints* and *Sonnets of the Cross* are sometimes found together in a single slip case. The first edition was published in 1925, London: SS. Peter & Paul.

FL 56   Jones, Thomas S., Jr. *Sonnets of the Saints*. [Third, enlarged edition]. 1929. *ix*, 34, [1]pp. Light green Strathmore paper boards with title/author on spine and front cover; design from Old World Series on front cover. 15.3 x 13 cm. Limited to 750 copies on Van Gelder paper. Copyright under the author's name.

FL 57   Jones, Thomas S., Jr. (edited by John L. Foley) *Sonnets of Saint Francis and Saint Clare*. With Foreword by John L. Foley. 1934. [20], [1]pp. Brown paper boards with title/author on front cover between which appears George Russell's "Sword of Light" design. 15.4 x 12.7 cm. Limited to 450 copies on Blue Hill paper. Copyright under the name of the executor of the Thomas Jones estate, John L. Foley.

FL 58   Jones, Thomas S., Jr. *The Unicorn and Other Sonnets*. 1931. [19], [1]pp. Stiff Japan vellum boards with title (in red & black) and author on front cover above a small triangular Chiswick design. 15.2 x 13 cm. Limited to 450 copies printed on Van Gelder paper. Copyright under the author's name.

FL 59   Jones, Thomas S., Jr. *The Voice in the Silence*. [Sixth edition] 1924. *x*, 52, [1]pp. Quarter blue paper spine over blue heart patterned paper boards with title on spine. 18 x 11.7 cm. 750 copies on Van Gelder paper. Copyright under the author's name.

FL 60   Jones, Thomas S., Jr. *The Voice in the Silence*. [Seventh edition] 1929. *xi*, 54, [1]. Quarter blue paper spine over blue heart patterned paper boards with title on spine. 18 x 11.7 cm. Limited to 750 copies on Van Gelder paper. Copyright under the author's name. Often offered in slipcase with *The Rose Jar*.

FL 61   Jordan, David Starr. *The Philosophy of Hope*. 1926. *xxxii*, 46, [1]pp. Blue paper boards with title/author on spine and front cover (titles in red), and floriated design at top of cover. 19.2 x 14.7 cm. Printed dust jacket. Limited to 360 copies privately printed for Mr. and Mrs. Edward Woods; 40 copies were also printed on Japan vellum in Japan vellum boards. Lists three copyrights: Copyright 1902 David Starr Jordan; copyright 1907 Paul Elder and Company; copyright 1926 Edward A. Woods. Also: "Reprinted by Permission of The Beacon Press, Inc."

FL 62   Keats, John. *Odes Sonnets & Lyrics of...* 1924. Frontispiece, *xx*, 88, [1]pp. Blue paper boards author/title on spine and front cover in black and red, and cover floral design. 19 x 14.7 cm. Limited to 450 on Van Gelder paper. Same binding as the former Mosher Press edition.

FL 63   Kellogg, Lois. **Opposites.** 1933. 29, [1]pp. Multi-colored Sagan paper boards with title/author label on front cover. 19.5 x 12.5 cm. Printed on Blue Hill paper; no limitation given. Copyright under the author's name. Another copy examined was bound in multi-colored mock marbled boards with labels. Yet another copy examined is in the former binding but printed on a white wove paper. All are the same size with the same text.

FL 64   Kinsolving, Sally Bruce. **Grey Heather.** 1930. x, 90, [1]pp. Decorated gray Georgian paper boards with title on spine and front cover which also has a seagull design signed "C.K." 19 x 14.6 cm. 500 copies printed on Van Gelder paper. Acknowledgments are made to "*American Poetry Magazine; The Baltimore Evening Sun; Book of American Verse; The Black Swan; The Carillon; The Commonweal; Contemporary Verse; The Crisis; The Echo; The Grub Street Book of Verse; The Harp; Japm; The Larial; The Literary Lantern; The Lyric; The North American Review; The Norfolk Virginian Pilot; Patterns for Pan; The Personalist; Poetry; Poetry World; The Quota Quarterly; The Reviewer; Star-Dust; Will o' the Wisp; The Witness.*" The copyright is under The Mosher Press.

FL 65   Ladd, Kate Macy. **The Story of My Life.** Written at the suggestion of my husband and begun November twenty-six Nineteen hundred twenty-nine, 1930. Portrait frontispiece, *vi,* 269 pp., illustrated with 11 additional portraits. Bound in multi-colored cloth with red gilt-stamped spine label. 19.3 x 13.5 cm. No limitation given.

FL 66   Lang, Andrew, trans. **Aucassin & Nicolete.** Done into English by... [Tenth edition] 1929. Frontispiece, *xxii,* 66, [1]pp. (Several copies examined have this improper pagination: Frontispiece, xvi, 43-59, 11-66). From the Old World Series, bound in both the regular Japan vellum flexible boards and the old world style with quarter white paper spine over blue boards. Limited to 925 copies on Van Gelder. In slipcase.

FL 67   Le Gallienne, Richard. **An Appreciation.** 1934. This entry comes from a list at Colby College, compiled by Oliver Sheean and covering a collection of Mosher Books he assembled.

FL 68   Leith, W. Compton (pseud. Ormonde Maddock Dalton). **Sirenica.** With an Introduction by William Marion Reedy. 1927. *xvi,* 142, [1]pp. Blue paper boards with Rossetti cover design same as the 1915 Mosher edition. 19.3 x 14.3 cm. The colophon indicates that 450 of this "second edition" printed on Van Gelder paper. Continuation of the Miscellaneous Series.

FL 69   Lemont, Jessie. **White Nights.** 1930. *ix,* 75, [1]pp. Bound in light green paper boards with title/author on spine and front cover; woodcut designs on front and back cover by Tonkin Williams. 18.9 x 14.6 cm. Limited to 500 copies on Van Gelder paper. Acknowledgments to the editors of "*Harper's Magazine, The Century Magazine, The Measure, Poetry—A Magazine of Verse, Poet Lore, Voices, The Commonweal, The Lyric West, The Catholic World, Contemporary Verse...*" Copyright under author's name. Printed for Jessie Lemont Trausil.

FL 70   Lewis, Elizabeth. **You Take the Glory.** 1932. *x,* 38 pp. Blue charcoal boards with title/author on spine and front cover which also has a triangular design of intertwining vines. 19 x 14.6 cm. No limitation given. Copyright under the author's name.

FL 71   McGiffert, Gertrude Huntington. **Cast in Bronze.** 1929. *ix,* 97, [1]pp. Blue charcoal boards with title, etc., printed on spine and front cover. 19 x 14.7 cm. The colophon indicates that 500 copies were printed on Van Gelder. The volume also indicates that another book by McGeffert was *A Florentine Cycle and Other Poems* and further contains the statement: "Some of the poems in this volume are reprinted by permission from *The Phi Beta Kappa Key; Art and Archaeology; Contemporary Verse; Voices; The Step Ladder; The Congregationalist; The Craftsman's Year Book;* Mrs. Waldo Richards' anthology, *The Magic Carpet.*" Copyright under author's name.

FL 72   McKean, Katharine. **Le Poulet de Cristal—Pensées Vagabondes.** [1934]. [21], [1]pp. Blue paper wraps with title/author in darker blue on front cover, bound with a red cord. 15.4 x 13.1 cm. Limited to 200 copies printed on Aurelian paper. Copyright under the author's name.

FL 73   *Masterpieces   A Dobbs Book of Verse and Prose Edited by the Seniors of the Masters School.* Dobbs Ferry on Hudson: The Masters School, 1927. The Sheean and Lamb typescripts list this edition as being 600 copies printed on Aurelian paper, and bound in decorated Wisteria Strathmore paper boards.

FL 74   *Masterpieces   A Dobbs Book of Verse and Prose Edited by the Seniors of the Masters School.* Dobbs Ferry on Hudson: The Masters School, 1928. Two frontispieces, 138, [1]pp. (plus 20 photo plates and numerous illustrations). Bound in Dutch charcoal ochre paper boards with framed title and date in purple on front cover; matching dust jacket. 22.7 x 16.7 cm. Limited to 525 copies on Aurelian paper. Title page carries the Mosher double-dolphin publisher's mark.

FL 75   *Masterpieces   A Dobbs Book of Verse and Prose Edited by the Seniors of the Masters School.* Dobbs Ferry on Hudson: The Masters School, 1929. 121, [1]pp. (plus 30 photo-plate pages; numerous illustrations). Bound in blue paper boards with paper labels on spine and front cover. 22.8 x 16.6 cm. Limited to 600 copies.

FL 76   *Masterpieces   A Dobbs Book of Miscellany and Memories edited by the Seniors of the Masters School.* Dobbs Ferry on Hudson. The Masters School, 1930. Line-illustrated frontispiece, 128, [1]pp. Bound in Dutch light plum charcoal boards with title and date on front cover. 22.8 x 16.5 cm. 425 copies printed on Cameo Plate paper.

FL 77   Morley, Christopher. *A Golden String* [caption title] by Christopher Morley. [ca. 1925]. 4 pp. (single sheet folded once to make four pages). 21.5 x 11.7 cm. Limitation unknown. Last page indicates the text was taken from the July 11, 1925 issue of *The Saturday Review of Literature.* This publication may have been a promotional flyer for selling the Wm. H. Wise printing of *The Bibelot,* or a keep-sake privately printed and mailed to a few friends.

FL 78   Morrill, Alice McGuffey. *Verses.* 1940. *ix,* 77, [1]pp. Bound in dark-blue paper boards with title/author in black on spine and front cover; front cover incorporates an illustration by A. H. Mackmurdo above the title (see entry 347). 19.2 x 14.5 cm. Limited to 250 copies printed on White Wove paper. The acknowledgments include the *Christian Science Monitor, Catholic Poetry Society's Spirit, Nantucket Harpoon,* and the *Golden Gate Anthology.* Copyright under the author's name.

FL 79   *The Mosher Books*—A List of Books in Belles Lettres Issued in Choice and Limited Editions. 1924. [i]. 44, [1]pp. Printed wraps, basically same design & size as 1923 Mosher catalogue.

FL 80   *The Mosher Books*—A List of Books in Belles Lettres Issued in Choice and Limited Editions. 1925. [i], 44, [1]pp. Printed wraps, basically same design & size as 1923 Mosher catalogue. Introduces the category "Privately Printed Editions" which were offered for sale to the general public.

FL 81   *The Mosher Books*—A List of Books in Belles Lettres Issued in Choice and Limited Editions. 1926. [i], 44, [1]pp. Printed wraps, basically same design & size as 1923 Mosher catalogue.

FL 82   *The Mosher Books*—A List of Books in Belles Lettres Issued in Choice and Limited Editions. 1927. [i], 44, [1]pp. Printed wraps, basically same design & size as 1923 Mosher catalogue.

FL 83   *The Mosher Books*—A List of Books in Belles Lettres Issued in Choice and Limited Editions. 1928. [i], 44, [1]pp. Printed wraps, basically same design & size as 1923 Mosher catalogue, but the color of the paper was changed from beige to blue and the date on the front cover was changed from Roman numerals to Arabic numbers.

FL 84   *The Mosher Books*—A List of Books in Belles Lettres Issued in Choice and Limited Editions. 1929. [i], 44, [1]pp. Printed wraps, basically same design & size as 1923 Mosher catalogue, but the color of the paper was changed from beige to pale green and the date on the front cover was changed from Roman numerals to Arabic numbers.

FL 85   *The Mosher Books.* October 20, 1930. Single sheet measuring 43 x 28 cm. (twice folded) with listing of book titles still available in quantity for sale.

FL 86   *The Mosher Books.* October 20, 1931. Single sheet of blue paper measuring 43 x 28 cm. (twice folded) with listing of book titles still available in quantity for sale.

FL 87   *The Mosher Books.* October 20, 1932. Single sheet of blue paper measuring 43 x 28 cm. (twice folded) with listing of book titles still available in quantity for sale.

FL 88   *The Mosher Books.* 1933-1934. Single sheet of paper measuring 43 x 28 cm. (twice folded) with listing of book titles still available in quantity for sale, including duplicates from Mr. Mosher's library.

FL 89   *The Mosher Books.* 1935-36. 16 pp. The catalogue is completely redesigned from the previous catalogues, and what would serve as a front cover is now the first page of entries.

FL 90   Nickerson, Paul Sumner. *Surf.* 1931. *ix*, 68, [1]pp. Bound in dark green Ingres paper boards with title information printed in silver on spine and front cover which also contains an illustration in silver. 19 x 14.7 cm. There were 500 numbered copies printed on Van Gelder paper. The colophon page indicates that "the cover was designed and drawn by the author. Drawings in the text by Edna Brucker." Contains the acknowledgments to the editors of "*Contemporary Verse, Second Contemporary Verse Anthology, The Lyric, Voices, The Measure, The Double Dealer, The Wave, The Emerson Quarterly, The Boston Globe, The Boston Herald,* and the *Springfield Republican.*" Copyright under the author's name.

FL 91   Nix, James Thomas. *Mother-Love Sketches in Prose and Verse.* 1928. *xv*, 93, [1]pp. (plus one portrait plate). Dark blue charcoal paper boards with gilt title/author on spine and on front cover; gilt laurel wreath around title/author on front cover. 19 x 14.3 cm. Limited to 300 copies on Van Gelder paper for James Thomas Nix MD, New Orleans, Louisiana. Frontispiece of Dr. Nix's mother. In slipcase.

FL 92   Oliver, Wade. *Fantasia, A Book of Poems by...* 1938. *x*, 98. [1]pp. Colophon indicates 500 printed on Aurelian paper. Blue boards with blue print and design; title printed in red on spine and front cover. 18.1 x 11.7 cm. Copyright under author's name.

FL 93   Oliver, Wade. *Sky-Rider.* 1928. *viii*, 44, [1]pp. Decorated blue charcoal paper boards. 18 cm. Limited to 500 copies on Aurelian paper for Isabel Fiske Conant (according to the Lamb typescript).

FL 94   Ouida (Louisa De La Ramée). *A Dog of Flanders.* 1924. *vi*, 84, [1]. Title/author in blue on spine (dingbats in red); title in red, author in blue on front cover all beneath an Eragny Press design. 19.4 x 14.9 cm. Limited to 300 copies on Van Gelder paper and 25 copies on Japan vellum for Mr. and Mrs. Edward A. Woods of Sewickley, PA.

FL 95   Page, George Hyde. *Verses.* 1925. *ix*, 48 pp. Blue paper boards with gilt title and author's initials running vertically down the spine; gilt Rossetti design on the front cover. 18.1 x 11.8 cm. Limited to 50 copies printed on Van Gelder paper for Mrs. G. H. Page. The copyright is under the name Mary Hutcheson Page.

FL 96   Paillou, Francesca. *A Handful of Songs.* 1930. *xvii*, 241, [1]pp. Green Ingres paper boards stamped in gold on front cover and spine; cover with gold wreath. 19.2 x 14.5 cm. Limited to 500 copies printed on Van Gelder paper.

FL 97   Pater, Walter. *The Renaissance—Studies in Art and Poetry.* 1924 (second edition of entry 322). *xi*, 304 pp. Frontispiece of Andrea Salaino by Da Vinci. Old-style green ribbed boards. Limited to 900 copies on Van Gelder paper.

FL 98   Peck, George Record. ***The Kingdom of Light.*** 1925. *xxx*, 32, [1]pp. Japan paper boards; title/author printed in red and black on spine and front cover; Eragny Press design at top of front cover. Limited to 450 copies printed on Van Gelder and 50 numbered copies printed on Japan vellum and privately printed for Mr. and Mrs. Edward A. Woods. Regular copy in blue paper boards with title printed in red on spine and front cover, and author's name in blue on same; design in blue above cover's title; printed dust jacket. 19.1 x 14.6 cm. Reprinted through the courtesy of the author's daughter, Mrs. Isabel Peck Wilson, and the publishers, G. P. Putnam's Sons. Copyright under the 1907 G. P. Putnam's Sons, New York and London.

FL 99   Perot, Mary E. B., compiler. ***The After Glow.*** *Selections Chosen for Each Day of the Year.* No date [around 1938]. Portrait frontispiece, 191, [1]pp. No colophon; no limitation given. Blue Fabriano paper cover with title on spine and front cover. 16.4 x 12.5 cm. According to the Sheean typescript, 1,000 copies were printed on American white wove (Blue Hill Text) paper..

FL 100   Reese, Lizette Woodworth. ***A Quiet Road.*** [Second edition] 1924. *x*, 65 pp. 19 x 14 cm. Limited to 450 copies [*NUC* records 550 copies]. Continuation of the Miscellaneous Series.

FL 101   Reese, Lizette Woodworth. ***A Wayside Lute.*** [Fourth edition]1929. *viii*, 67 pp. 19 x 14 cm. Limited to 550 copies on Van Gelder paper.

FL 102   Roe, William W. ***Saint Francis and the Birds.*** 1939. [9], [1]pp. Corn color boards with Chiswick decorative design, title/author in blue on front cover. 15 x 13 cm. Limited to 250 copies printed on Aurelian paper. Copyright is under author's name.

FL 103   Russell, Bertrand. ***A Free Man's Worship.*** With a Special Preface by Bertrand Russell. [Second edition]. 1927. *xvii*, 28, [1]pp. Blue paper boards with title on spine and front cover (in red) and floral device at top. 18.5 x 10.3 cm. Colophon notes 950 copies on Van Gelder paper. Copyright of 1923 is under Thomas Bird Mosher.

FL 104   Russell, Sydney King. ***Lost Warrior.*** 1931. *vii*, 101 pp. No colophon; no limitation given. Gray paper boards with title on spine and front cover which also has a decorative device on it. In printed dust jacket with reviews from *The Saturday Review, The American Mercury, Voices,* the *Boston Globe,* and several others. 19 x 14.7 cm. Printed on American white wove paper. The acknowledgments include "*New Yorker, Poetry, Voices, The San Franciscan, New York Sun, New York World, Game and Gossip, Opinion, Los Angeles Saturday Night,* and *Braithwaite's Anthology of Magazine Verse.*" Copyright under the author's name.

FL 105   Sanborn, Marjorie. ***Through the Emerald—A Modern Novel in Traditional Verse.*** 1939. *iv*, 26, [1]pp. Light green paper boards with title/author on front cover under a Chiswick design. 19.1 x 13.8 cm. Limited to 250 copies on American white wove paper.

FL 106   Scollard, Clinton. ***Songs Out of Egypt.*** [September], 1930. *vii*, 50, [3]pp. Bound in decorated Mayan-Marlowe paper boards. 19 cm. Limited to 350 copies printed on American white wove (Blue Hill Text) paper.

FL 107   Scollard, Elisabeth. ***Candle and Cross.*** 1925. *xii*, 82, [1]pp. Blue paper boards with title/author on spine and front cover (titles in red) and Chiswick design above cover's title. 18.3 x 11.7 cm. Limited to 500 copies on American white wove paper (Blue Hill Text paper). The acknowledgments include "*The Munsey, Ainslee's Magazine, The Poetry Review, Town Topics, The New York Herald, The New York Sun, The Columbian Crew* and *The New York Times.*" Copyright under the author's name.

FL 108   Shedd, John A. ***Salt From My Attic.*** 1928. 63, [1]pp. Charcoal blue paper boards with title in red on spine and title/author in red on front cover all within ruled front cover (same as *Our Lady's Tumbler.* Mosher Press, 1928). 15.5 x 9.3 cm. Limited to 500 copies on Aurelian paper for John A Shedd. The acknowledgments included are: "A few of these aphorisms have been printed in *Current Literature, The Bible To-day, The Christian Advocate* and *The Guide to Nature.*"

FL 109   Sinkler, Louise Elkins. *Judas Tree*. 1933. 12, [1] pp. Blue paper wraps bound with a red cord; dark blue title/author above and below George Russell's "Sword of Light" design on front wrapper. 15.1 x 12.8 cm. Limited to 100 copies printed on Van Gelder paper. Copyright under the author's name.

FL 110   *The Spence School*. 1930. According to the Sheean typescript, 239 copies were printed on Aurelian paper and bound in green Ingres paper boards. Printed for Zoe Warner and Beatrice Trostel.

FL 111   *Spring Blossoms from Maple Cottage*. 1928. *ix*, 42 pp. Pink paper wraps with pictorial front cover of a meadow path. 14.5 x 9.6 cm. No limitation; no colophon. Printed on Van Gelder paper. The foreword of this book is signed "KML" (presumably the initials of Mrs. Ladd name). This is the same Mrs. Walter G. Ladd who had *Autumn Leaves from Maple Cottage* printed in 1919 and 1926. There were 4,000 copies ordered (The Houghton Library), but the Sheean and Lamb typescripts state there were 5,000 printed, bound in "fancy" printed wrappers.

FL 112   Stewart, Elinor C. [Cochran], compiler. *Promises of Hope and Gladness, An Anthology*. 1927. *viii*, 32, [1]. French blue-gray charcoal paper boards with title on spine and title/compiler name in red on front cover within monument design; similarly printed dust jacket on Japan vellum paper. 14.8 x 10 cm. Limited to 975 copies on Van Gelder paper (Sheean and Lamb typescripts state 1,000 copies). The colophon notes this is [privately] printed by The Mosher Press for Elinor C. Stewart. The 1927 Mosher catalogue notes these selections are from the American Standard Bible.

FL 113   Taylor, Mary Atwater. *Ropes and Threads*. 1925. *x*, 70 pp. No colophon; no limitation statement (Sheean and Lamb typescripts state 300 copies for Mrs. G. H. White). Gray paper boards with title labels on spine and front cover. 18.9 x 14.5 cm. Printed on Van Gelder paper. A typed page of Taylor's poetry, tipped in at the back of a copy examined, carries the note: "This cd [could] be trimmed down and pasted in the back of the book, if you wished. Several have done that." The acknowledgments include: "*Current Opinion; Contemporary Verse; The Literary Review of the New York Evening Post; The New York Sun; The New York Times; The Examiner; Book and Craft Bulletin; The Circle; The Step Ladder; The Measure; Voices; Eleven Poets*." Copyright under The Mosher Press.

FL 114   Thompson, Francis. *The Hound of Heaven*. [Sixth Edition]. 1926. *x*, 16, [1]pp. Marbled paper boards with title label on spine and title/author label on front cover. Limited to 925 copies on Van Gelder paper. A continuation of the Golden Text Series.

FL 115   Thompson, Francis. *Poems*. [Third edition] 1924. Portrait frontispiece, *xx*, 112 pp. Same blue boards and design as the previous 1911 and 1914 Mosher editions from the Miscellaneous Series. 19 x 14.8 cm. Limited to 750 copies on Van Gelder paper. Printed dust jacket.

FL 116   Thompson, Francis. *Shelley: An Essay*. [Third edition] 1929. *xviii*, 67 pp. Bound in old-style gray boards with white labels printed in red & black. Limited to 600 copies printed on Van Gelder. This edition contains a new tribute to Thompson by Mr. Charles Hanson Towne entitled "The Quiet Singer."

FL 117   Underwood, Edna Worthley, trans. *Anthology of Mexican Poets: From the Earliest Times to the Present Day*. 1932. *xxxiii*, 331, [1]pp., plus errata slip. 19 x 14.6 cm. Printed on American white wove paper. Strathmore green and quarter red vellum cloth boards; labels on spine and front cover. Copyright under author's name. No limitation given.

FL 118   Underwood, Edna Worthley. *Attic Twilights*. 1928. 13, [1]pp. Beige-ochre Georgian paper wraps over boards. 15.9 x 12.5 cm. Title in red on front cover beneath the A. H. Mackmurdo design once used in the 1899 Mosher copy of Blake's *XVII Designs to Thornton's Virgil* (also used by Lamb on copy of Jones' *Akhnaton*). Limited to 500 copies on American white wove paper (Blue Hill Text paper). Credits are given to *Cross Currents* and *The International Studio*. Copyright under author's name.

FL 119   Underwood, Edna Worthley. *The Book of Seven Songs by Tu Fu.* Translated by Edna Worthley Underwood and Chi-Hwang Chu. 1928. 11, [1] unnumbered pages. Bound in decorated yellow-orange Triglaff paper wrappers. 16.1 x 13.3 cm. Limited to 500 copies printed on American white wove paper (Blue Hill Text paper). The 1928 catalogue claims, "This is the only translation in any language of this autobiographical song."—p. 42, and opposite the title-page appears: "This is the only translation in any language of this autobiographical song of Tu-Fu, written when an exile and homeless wanderer of the wars. Tu-Fu ranks as one of the greatest poets of the world. He lived in the Tang Dynasty: his dates are 712-770 A.D."

FL 120   Underwood, Edna Worthley. *Egyptian Twilights.* 1928. 11, [1]pp. Multi-colored English paper (St. Albans paper) wraps over boards with title on front cover. 15.5 x 12.3 cm. 500 copies printed on American white wove paper. Contains the statement: "Acknowledgment is given to the *International Studio*, where Twilights was first published under title of *Ars Egpytiea*, for permission to reprint." Copyright under the translator's name.

FL 121   Underwood. Edna Worthley. *Improvisations.* Volume I: Africa [and] The Mediterranean. Volume II: South America [and] The Carib Sea. Paintings by A. Hyatt Verrill. 1929. Color-frontispiece, *xv*, 46, [1]pp., 1 black & white plate; color-frontispiece, *xi*, 69, [1]pp., 2 black & white plates. 450 copies printed on Van Gelder; 100 copies printed, numbered and signed on Japan vellum. Volume I is bound in Chinese Brocade jade-green silk; Volume 2 is bound in Chinese Brocade yellow silk, with label on each volume's spine. 12.6 x 8.2 cm. Copyright under author's name. Housed in green decorated slipcase with label. There were 75 Japan vellum copies bound in Chinese gold and silver brocade, and 25 Japan vellum copies bound in antique Benáres brocade.

FL 122   Underwood, Edna Worthley. *Maine Summers; Sonnets to My Mother.* 1940. Portrait frontis, *vi*, 26 pp. Bound in orange paper boards with title/author label on front cover. 19.1 x 14.5 cm. Copyright under the author's name.

FL 123   Underwood, Edna Worthley. *Masque of the Moons.* 1928. *viii*, 22, [1]pp. Green Ingres paper boards with title on spine and front cover; front cover title in red with Chiswick design on top. 18.1 x 11.7 cm. Colophon reads 500 copies printed on American white wove paper (Blue Hill Text paper). Credits given to "*Smart Set, Art and Life, Shadowland,* and *Poetry Magazine.*" Copyright under author's name.

FL 124   Underwood, Edna Worthley, trans. *Nuevo Amor by Salvador Novo.* 1935. 26 leaves, only printed on one side of each leaf. 19 cm. Printed on Blue Hill paper. Cinnamon orange laid boards or wraps with label on front cover. According to the publisher's note, this work is the first individual volume by a Mexican poet to appear in English.

FL 125   Underwood, Edna Worthley, trans. *The Poet of the Indian Ocean* by Robert-Edward Hart. Translated by Edna Worthley Underwood, Correspondante de l' Institut. 1937. *xvi*, 28, [1]pp. Gray paper boards with title/author label in red and black. 19.1 x 14.7 cm. Printed on Blue Hill paper; no limitation given. Includes 5 woodcuts of Indian Ocean Island scenes by Marcel Cabon, Jacques Desmarais, André Atger, and Xavier Le Juge de Ségrais. Copyright under the translator's name.

FL 126   Underwood, Edna Worthley, trans. *The Poets of Haiti 1782-1934.* 1934. *xlii*, 159, [1]pp. Woodcuts by Pétion Savain. Glossary by Charles F. Pressoir. 1934. Quarter yellow cloth spine over cinnamon paper boards with labels on spine and front cover. 18.8 x 14.5 cm. Printed on Blue Hill paper; no limitation given. Copyright is under the translator's name.

FL 127   Underwood, Edna Worthley, trans. *The Slav Anthology.* Russian, Polish, Bohemian, Serbian, Croatian, translated by... 1931. *xviii*, 346 pp. Charcoal-black Fabriano and quarter yellow cloth boards; label on spine; title/trans. on front cover. 23 x 16.5 cm. Printed on Van Gelder paper; no limitation given (according to the Sheean typescript, 500 copies were printed).

FL 128   Underwood, Edna Worthley, trans. *Spirit of the Andes by José Santos Chocano.* Poems translated by...1935. Frontispiece, *xviii*, 44 pp. Bound in red charcoal paper boards with title/author on front cover label. 18.7 x 14.5 cm. Printed on American white wove paper (Blue Hill Text paper). Frontispiece portrait caricature of Chocano by H. Lavalle. Copyright under the author's name.

FL 129   Underwood, Edna Worthley. *Taste of Honey: The Note Book of a Linguist.* 1930. 4 *p.l.*, 202 pp. 23 x 16.5 cm. Printed on American white wove paper (Blue Hill Text paper). Sheean typescript states there were 500 copies printed. Yellow Fabriano paper boards decorated in purple ink; title/author on spine and front cover which also has an illustration. In printed dust jacket. Copyright under author's name.

FL 130   Underwood, Edna Worthley, trans. *Three Chinese Masterpieces.* Translated into English by Edna Worthley Underwood and Chi-Hwang Chu. 1927. [12], [1]pp. Orange Marlowe (Lamb says Mayan) paper wrappers (stapled) with title and translator information printed on front cover along with the Lawrence Housman design previously used on *The Present Crisis.* 16.2 x 13.3 cm. Limited to 500 copies printed on American white wove paper (Blue Hill text paper). Copyright under The Mosher Press name.

FL 131   Underwood, Edna Worthley, trans. *TU FU—Wanderer and Minstrel Under Moons of Cathay.* Translated by Edna Worthley Underwood and Chi-Hwang Chu. 1929. Portrait frontispiece, *liv*, 247, [1]pp.; 19 plates not part of collation. Bound in charcoal-black and Chinese lacquer-red [cloth] old-style boards with line portrait in gold on front cover. Japan vellum copy bound in quarter white vellum over gold and silver Chinese brocade silk with title and translators in gilt on spine. 18.8 x 15 cm. Opposite the foreword is this statement: "This is the first edition in the world of Tu Fu to be printed outside of China, likewise it is the first edition of any one individual Chinese poet." Limited to 1000 copies on American white wove paper (Blue Hill Text paper); 50 numbered & signed copies on Japan vellum (with slipcase). Copyright under the translator's name.

FL 132   Underwood, Edna Worthley, trans. Yergath, Arsène. *The Weaver by the Nile.* Done into English by Edna Worthley Underwood *Correspondante de l'Institut.*, 1936. Portrait frontispiece, *vii*, 16, [1]pp. Light green paper boards with title/author on front cover. 19 x 14.7 cm. Printed on Blue Hill paper. Copyright under Edna Worthley Underwood. No limitation given.

FL 133   Whistler, James A. McNeill. *"Ten O'Clock."* 1925. Frontispiece, *xii*, 64, [1]pp. (plus 2 plates). Tan paper boards with title in gilt on spine and title/butterfly signature in gilt on front cover. 24 x 16.3 cm. Limited to 450 copies on Van Gelder hand-made paper, but the paper seems to be other than Van Gelder with an oval paper watermark of a laurel wreath head and the monogram of "PU." Copyright under Thomas Bird Mosher 1916, but edition notice at bottom says: First Edition, September 1920; Second Edition, September 1925. Mosher published three editions in 1916, 1917, and 1920. This edition is based on Mosher's third "enlarged" edition.

FL 134   White, Grace Hoffman. *Wings to Dare.* 1925. *x*, 46 pp. No colophon; no limitation given (Sheean typescript states 500 copies). Blue paper boards with labels on spine and front cover. 18 x 11.6 cm. Printed on Van Gelder paper. Contains these acknowledgments: "Certain of these poems were reprinted through the courtesy of *The Minaret, The Year Book of the League of American Pen Women, Voices, Book and Craft, Eleven Poets, Interludes, The Lyric, The Harp* and other publications." Copyright under author's name.

FL 135   Wicksteed, Philip H., trans. *Our Lady's Tumbler—A Twelfth Century Legend.* 1928. *xi*, 37, [1] pp. Blue paper boards with title in red on spine and title/author in red on front cover; blue rules on front cover. 15.5 x 9.5 cm. Limited to 975 copies on Van Gelder paper. Verso of the title page lists this as the third edition, and gives the other editions as 1906 and 1911; therefore, this must be the third edition in the Ideal Series of Little Masterpieces, although the binding and size is different. Bound in the same manner as FL 36, Hewlett's *Quattrocentisteria* (1927).

FL 136   ***Writing and Speaking–A Craft***. 1929. According to the Sheean typescript, there were 500 copies printed on Victory bond, in sheets, for The Masters School.

FL 137   Yeats, W. B. ***The Land of Heart's Desire***. [Thirteenth edition]. 1925. *vi*, 33, [1]pp. Light gray boards and two-color paper labels on the front cover and the spine (as produced in the Lyric Garland Series). Decorative head- and tail-piece and Chiswick ornaments. 18 x 1.5 cm. Limited to 950 copies on Van Gelder paper.

—End of 1924-1941 Checklist—

THE WILLIAMS BOOK STORE PUBLICATIONS
UNDER THE MOSHER PRESS NAME
1941–1970s

The Mosher Press book stock was purchased by one time friend of Mosher's, Joseph G. Williams of The Williams Book Store in 1941, and new Mosher Press publications were given the address: "The Mosher Press, 81 Washington Street, Boston, Massachusetts (Publishers of Fine Books for over Half a Century)." Williams announced his acquisition:

> The glory, the legend, and the romance still abound in its rafters, as mute evidence of the master craftsman. Never before, and perhaps never again, will so composite a genius appear in the annals of bookmaking. He was a great editor, a great compiler, and a master builder of beautiful books, in every detail. He won fame for selecting the choice morsels from not only the famous authors, but those of unknown and unsung ones as well. From obscure and forgotten periodicals, and out of the way channels, he found little crumbs of beauty and banded them together in beautiful settings to make them works of art.
>
> —George Williams (newspaper clipping in Bishop Collection, source unidentified)

In addition, the firm's wooden typecase with Mosher's ornaments, decorative initials, publisher's devices, headpieces, tail-pieces, and plates for cover designs, were also transferred to The Williams Book Store.

When The Williams Book Store went out of business in the mid 1970's, the remaining Mosher book stock was placed in storage. A few years later the books, and the typecase, were sold to a New York book dealer who marketed a collection of the remaining stock in 1979. It is rumored among some booksellers that many of the unsold Mosher books stock was later pulped. The typecase with Mosher's ornaments was sold to another New York City bookseller. A past owner of The Williams Book Store retained some choice books which were received when they originally bought the stock in 1941, but in all likelihood, the very last vestige of those holdings were sold in Boston at public auction in October 1995.

The following list of books is not claimed to be complete, and there are most likely other later "Mosher Press" titles floating around out there; however, a complete listing serves no purpose. The following list is sufficient to show readers that they still may indeed come across post-1941 books with The Mosher Press imprint. The last book which we have found published under "The Mosher Press" name is surprisingly late: Bradford Johnson's *Pulpits to the North* (Boston, 1974). The days of the true Mosher Press ended in 1923, and its residual publication program under Mosher's long-time manager, Flora Lamb, surely ended with its sale in 1941. Beyond that, not much need be said.

WB 1   Bliss, Donald Thayer. *The Seasons.* 1944. Limited to 100 copies. 21 pp. 15 cm.

WB 2   Boardman, Ruby. *The Abbess and the Troubador Ten Poems and a Portrait.* [1957]. 36 pp. Limited to 100 numbered copies. 36 pp. Bound in red paper loosely fitting over stiff boards, with label in red and black on front cover. 30.8 x 24.7 cm. The book's pages are printed on stiff, card-thick paper. Printed in red and black throughout.

WB 3   Dunham, Elizabeth Marie. *How to Know the Mosses. A Popular Guide to the Mosses of the Northern US.* 1951. xxv, 289 pp. Bound in green cloth with gold print on front cover and spine. 19.5 x 13 cm.

WB 4   Grebanier, Bernard D. N. *Mirrors of the Fire.* Poems and Translations by... 1946. xiv, 124 pp. Yellow paper boards with title/author/publisher on white spine label. 19.8 x 14.5 cm. Rust colored pictorial dust jacket designed by Lionel Ziprin. The colophon indicates 2000 copies of this first edition were printed, and a limited edition of 300 were numbered and signed by the author. The yellow copies are the limited edition of 300 while copies in red paper boards carry no limitation or colophon page and are most likely those of the higher limitation. Copyright under The Mosher Press name.

This book is a virtual panoply of various Mosher printer blocks including several different Chiswick head- and tail-pieces, the use of a garland design which once encircled Mosher's publisher's device only now appearing sideways to encircle a sectional title (p. 59), the appearances of the panpipe-playing youth, a Laurence Housman design which once appeared on a Mosher Press title, borders from the covers of the Vest Pocket Series now being used to frame sectional titles, likewise title borders for labels on the Venetian Series covers (now serving as frames for sectional titles), three different samples publisher's devices now appearing at different locations, and some of the original head-pieces are used as tail-pieces. This is quite a concatenation of ornaments once fittingly placed in The Mosher Books.

WB 5   Grebanier, Bernard D. N. *Fauns, Satyrs and a Few Sages: Songs, Epigrams and Pieces After the Greek.* 1945. *xiv,* 136 pp. Blue-green paper boards with title/author/ publisher/date label. 19.7 x 14.9 cm. The colophon states there were 2000 copies printed of this first edition. Copyright under The Mosher Press name. There is also another state of the book (nearly identical with the preceding book save for the omitted printer's design) in which the limitation is 300 copies numbered and signed by the author.

WB 6   Hatson, Constance Elinore. **Who Know Not Leaf.** 1947. *ix,* 63, [1]pp. Blue cloth binding with gilt title/author/publisher on spine and gilt title/author on front cover with leaf dingbat. 20.9 x 14.7 cm. White illustrated dust jacket with cover design by Charles Lathuras; inner flaps include lists of Mosher Books available to the public; back cover includes photo of author and a brief write-up. Colophon states limitation of 1000 copies, with a limited edition of 500 numbered and signed by the author. Copyright under The Mosher Press name.

WB 7   Hickcox, Percy Merriman. **Mine Eyes Have Seen.** 1950. *xv,* 109 pp. Illustrated, portraits. Limited to 500 copies numbered and signed by the author. 23 cm.

WB 8   Jacobs, Nancy. **Love and Happiness: Your Real Identity.** 1947. *v,* 42 pp. 21 cm. Limited to 1000 copies. Green cloth in dust jacket.

WB 9   Johnson, Bradford. **Pulpits to the North.** Poems by... 1974. *viii,* 55, [1]pp. Gray cloth binding with title/author printed in green on front cover and spine. 20.3 x 13.7 cm. Illustrated with several differently styled head- and tail-pieces. Stated first edition. The printed dust jacket has a Selwyn Image sunrise and tree design on the front. The colophon reads that "the first twenty-five copies of this edition are hors commerce and have been signed and numbered by the author. *Limited Edition Published in Boston by The Mosher Press.*"

WB 10   Leigh, Leila M., pseud. (Leila A. M. Assanger). **This Clarion Call for Peace.** c.1945. 12, [1]pp. Limited to 500 copies. 17 cm.

WB 11   Miriam, Sister. **Woven of the Sky.** Introduction by Odell Shepard. Boston, 1946. *xiii,* 55 pp. Red cloth with gilt on the spine and front cover. 21 cm. Limited to 1000 copies of a de luxe edition, 200 copies of which were numbered and signed by the author.

WB 12   Sherwood, Grase. **Lift Up Your Heart.** 1947. [*xiv*], 63, [1] pp. Limited to 500 copies. Stated first edition. Bound in green cloth with gold stamping on the spine and front cover; printed dust jacket with Chiswick designs. 21.5 x 14 cm. Uses several Chiswick ornaments throughout the text.

WB 13   Teresa, Sister Frances, editor. **The Snob and the Saint; Essays Selected and Edited with Permission from Periodicals.** 1947. *xiii,* 151 pp. Red cloth in dust jacket. 23.5 x 16 cm. There were 4,000 copies printed.

WB 14   Urn, Althea [pseud. for Ford, Consuelo (Urisarri)]. *Trophies of Artemis.* 1951. x, 68, [1]pp. Black or pink paper boards, white spine label with title/author/publisher printed in red & black. 19.8 x 15 cm. Colophon notes that 1000 copies of this first edition were printed and a limited edition of 300 copies were numbered and signed by the author. The copyright is under The Mosher Press name.

Note: Two books were advertised on dust jackets or in announcements, but copies have not been located in any collections or in any databases if, indeed, they were ever published at all. The two volumes are Bernard D. N. Grebanier's *The Triumph of Love,* and Fritz Helmuth Schwanke's *Desire, Joy, and Sorrow* (the typescript and advertisements for which are in the Bishop Collection).

A somewhat dreadful looking book carrying the Mosher Press name has also been uncovered, but the subject matter, place of publication, poor quality of paper, uneven type impressions, and lack of all Mosher Press ornamentation (internally the book looks more like a common paperback than anything else), surely place it outside any Mosher connection save for the press name. For the sake of general awareness, however, the listing is given below:

Gropper, Milton Herbert. *Ladies of the Evening.* Arlington, New Jersey: Mosher Press, 282 Davis Ave., [1947]. [*iv*], 172 pp. Blue horizontally striped cloth with gilt on spine, including "Mosher Press" at the tail of the spine; dark brown endpapers. 19.2 x 12.5 cm. Verso of the title page reads: "MOSHER PRESS EDITION / First Printing - September 1947 / This MOSHER PRESS EDITION is published by arrangement with GREENBERG, Publishers. / Copyright 1931 by Milton Herbert Gropper."

—End of 1941-1970s Checklist—

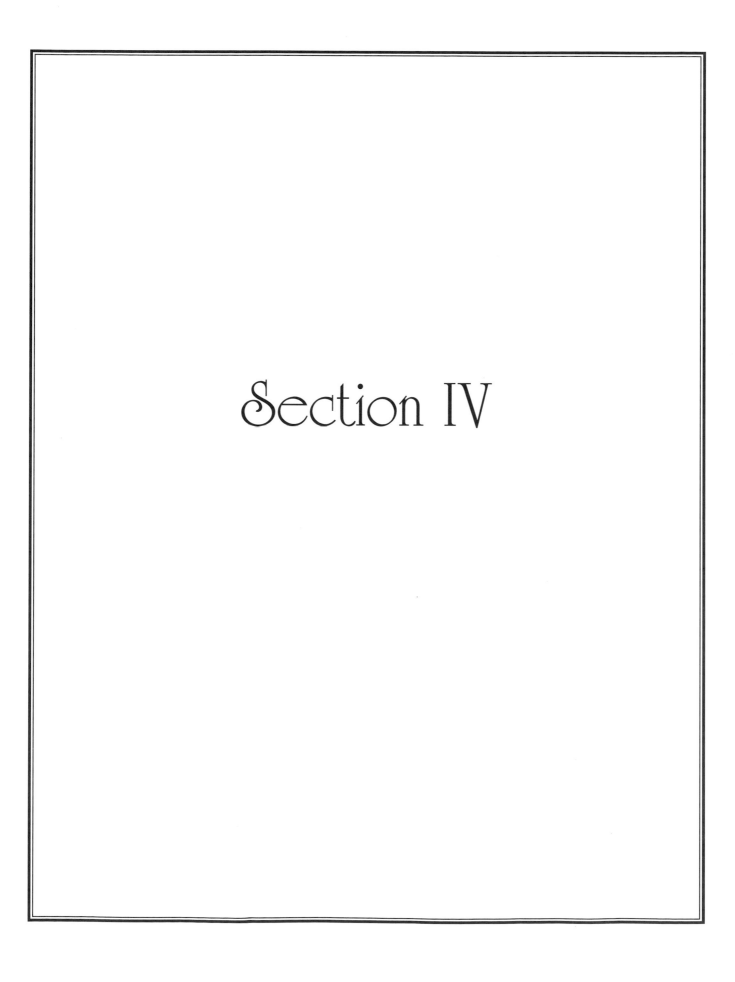

Section IV

BINDINGS AND ILLUMINATED COPIES
OF THE MOSHER BOOKS

One of the ways to pay tribute to an author or publisher is to have his work covered in a luxurious binding. Such tribute was paid the Mosher Books time and again. Mosher himself even commented on this phenomenon:

> In this connection it may not be inappropriate, or devoid of interest, to mention the fact that American and foreign binders have chosen many of these books whereon to lavish their skill. In America, Mr. Otto Zahn, the Misses Nordholf and Bulkley; in London, Miss Prideaux and the Guild of Women Binders have re-clothed in exquisite bindings not a few of the special copies of Mr. Mosher's editions.   – "A List of Books in Limited Editions" 1898, p.6

Yet another way, popular in the 19th and early 20th centuries, was to extra-illustrate or illumine them. Illumination could mean just coloring the title page and the head- and tail-pieces, or more elaborate productions of flowers, mini-scenes, and full-page illustrations. Mosher himself encouraged the illustration of his books, either by announcing in his catalogue that a certain book had ample margins for adding illustration, or by corresponding with persons interested in illuminating as a hobby, for special presentation to a loved one or friend, or for some remuneration. Work like this was done on a regular basis on the early Roycroft books; however, unlike the Roycroft Print Shop, Mosher never hired a team of illuminators to carry out the work. Independent parties were involved, and examples of illumination can be seen on books decorated by Rookwood artist, Clara Chipman Newton of Cincinnati, and yet another illuminator only known by the initials E.M.S., or by a Mrs. Kate Townsend of Milwaukee, Wisconsin, with whom Mosher discussed extra-illumination through his correspondence with her.

In 1906 the Grolier Club held "AN EXHIBITION OF SOME OF THE LATEST ARTISTIC BINDINGS DONE AT THE CLUB BINDERY." The Club Bindery was set up by a select few members of the Grolier Club to bind their most precious books following the finest standards of European binderies. Mosher was a member of the Grolier Club since December 1895, and eight of the one-hundred thirty eight bindings exhibited were on Mosher imprints–more than any other American publisher represented at the exhibition. Most bindings were very limited editions (fewer than ten) on Roman vellum, and belonged to Henry William Poor.

Another important creative binder of Mosher's books was Otto Zahn. His monograph, *On Art Binding*, was prepared for the 1904 St. Louis Exposition where products of his bindery, Toof and Company of Memphis, Tennessee, were on display at the Fine Arts Building. Included in Zahn's monograph were twelve photo-reproductions of the firm's finest work. Among those were bindings on original manuscripts by Tennyson, Dickens, and Napoleon, two Kelmscott books and two of "Thomas B. Mosher's beautiful publications." Mosher referred his clients wishing fine bindings directly to the binders, as he did in a March 21, 1898 letter to a wealthy patron:

> I also send you some photos of binding done by Mr. Otto Zahn. You will see an article on his work in Scribner's Book Buyer for March. I have written him giving your address, and hope if you decide to bind the set, you will permit him to do it for you–in part at least–as I believe he is without an equal on this side the waters.
> –Mosher to Emilié Grigsby, March 21, 1898, pp. [1-2], at the Donohue Rare Book Room of the Gleeson Library, University of San Francisco
> (quoted here with permission)

Various "job" binderies entered the picture, and many Mosher books were bound in 3/4 morocco by English and American firms for the retail market. Zaehnsdorf, Sangorski and Sutcliffe, and R. R. Donnelley all provided elegant dress for the Mosher books. Such firms as Boston's Rose Bindery, J. W. Meyers, Chicago's Monastery Hill Bindery, and New York's MacDonald's Bindery also provided bound Moshers for Brentano's, Putnam's and the Lord and Taylor bookshops, especially for the holiday seasons. A fuller list appears at the end of this section.

Section IV documents a few examples of the fine bindings placed on Mosher Press imprints. They range from bindings contemporary with the book's publication to more recently executed modern bindings. In many instances the binding was personally examined by me, and the location or collection in which the book resides is given at the end of the listings. When available, some information about the binder or illuminator is also given. In other instances the binding is only known through a secondary source such as an exhibition catalogue or some other publication. The following books are printed on Van Gelder paper unless otherwise specified. The list is in alphabetical order by binder's last name. Illuminators are listed under the entry: (Illuminator). In cases where there is more than one notable example of a binder's work, multiple listings are given. Entry numbers are prefixed with an "R" (the "R" standing for "relieure," the French for book binder) to eliminate any confusion with the bibliography in Section II.

❦ Binding descriptions with this mark are color-illustrated in this section.

R1.   **(Adams Bindery)** Schwob, Marcel. *Mimes*. (Miscellaneous Series) 1901. Copy No. 5 of 6 on vellum. Bound in full dark navy morocco signed THE ADAMS BINDERY (20.5 x 13.3 cm.); five raised bands with gilt dots across each; spine panels boxed in gilt with decorative corners of panels; red onlay flowers in spine panels; title and author in other panels. Covers with single fillet around perimeters and an inner frame of two fillets with gilt roll-tool between them and within the inner frame; central diamond shaped design of red onlays on front and back covers. All board edges gilt roll-tooled; 1 cm. turn-ins with vellum inner panel: front inner panel with book's original spine design printed on Japan vellum mounted in the center. Book's original vellum printed cover and spine bound in at the rear. ❦ See Plate 23 on page 374 (Illustrated with permission from the Donohue Rare Book Room, Gleeson Library, University of San Francisco)

R2.   **(Arnold, Frances)** Macleod, Fiona. *By Sundown Shores*. (Brocade Series) 1902. Bound in full light brown morocco (12.9 x 8.7 cm.) and signed FA 1903 at foot of inside back cover. Covers with dark brown and gilt-tooled boards with gilt lettering on covers and date on the other side; gilt-tooled spine with raised bands. Gilt tooled board edges and turn-ins; all page edges gilt. (Special Collections, Bryn Mawr College)

   Frederick Maser's book on *Bookbinding in America, 1680-1910* (Bryn Mawr, 1983) indicates: "Inspired in part by the Arts & Crafts Movement and in part by the Cornish Colony which grew up around the sculptor Augustus Saint-Gaudens, Frances Arnold (1874-1975) was one of a group of American women who early turned their hands to bookbinding."–p.108

R3.   **(Baer, Cuneo Press Bindery)** Gissing, George. *The Private Papers of Henry Ryecroft*. (Miscellaneous Series) 1921. One of 700 on Van Gelder. Bound in full brown morocco (19 x 15 cm.), gold-tooled, tooled slip-case by George Baer of the Cuneo Press Bindery, Milwaukee, WI. (Gift from Norman Strouse to the Donohue Rare Book Room, Gleeson Library, University of San Francisco)

   In the 1960's, George Baer and his associate, William Anthony, directed the Cuneo Fine Binding Studio. The Studio was founded around 1925/26 by Leonard Mounteney, who later became director emeritus and consultant (also see entries R49-50). Baer received his initial training in Germany, directed his own studio in Europe, and served on the faculties of several schools in Germany, Greece and Switzerland. He also executed commissions for two popes, and President Auriol of France, among others. The bindery was apparently located in Milwaukee, WI (according to information at the University of San Francisco), and at the Chicago plant of The Cuneo Press, Inc. For samples of their work, see the brochure "Cuneo Fine Binding" Chicago, The Cuneo Press, Inc., 1964. The bindery ceased operation in the late 1970's.

R4.   **(Baer, Cuneo Press Bindery)** Rossetti, Dante Gabriel. *Poems*. (Quarto Series) 1902. One of four copies on vellum. Copy No. 4 signed by Mosher and from his library. Bound in full light brown morocco (22.3 x 18.2 cm.), gold and blind-tooled, double slip-cased on commission (1964) from Norman Strouse by George Baer of the Cuneo Press of Milwaukee, WI. Spine with double raised bands with blind-tooled fillet between each double set and also flanking them on top and bottom. Gilt title and author on the second and third panels; other panels with gilt heart, swerving lines and eye design. Front cover with double hearts, swerving line design and eye in the middle. Top page edges red; blind-tooled turn-ins. ❦ See Plate 24 on page 374 (Illustrated with permission from the Donohue Rare Book Room, Gleeson Library, University of San Francisco)

R5.   **(Bat with wings extended and the initial "S")** Rossetti, Dante Gabriel. ***Hand and Soul.*** (Miscellaneous Series) 1899. Small quarto bound in full red morocco (14.8 x 10.8 cm.). Spine with raised bands and stylized gilt ornamentation. Covers with triple rule enclosing a fourth inner rectangular space (8 x 3.5 cm.) with vines and leaves filling the space and the initials •H•F•R• in the center front cover and •C•L•R• (the book's owners) in the center back cover. Gilt fillet along board edges; gilt turn-ins with bat stamp of binder; a.e.g. The binder is unknown. (Donohue Rare Book Room, Gleeson Library, University of San Francisco)

R6.   **(Bellefroid, Micheline de)** Swinburne, Algernon Charles. ***Tristram of Lyonesse.*** (Quarto Series) 1904. Copy No. 4 of 4 on vellum, signed by the publisher. Bound in full black morocco (22.3 x 18 cm.) by Micheline de Bellefroid, with white and silver inlays forming an abstract design on the front and back covers. Housed in matching chemise and slipcase. ❋ See Plate 20 on page 373 (Gift from Norman Strouse to The Bancroft Library; illustrated with permission, shelf mark TYP AA49 .B4 S9 1904)

> Micheline de Bellefroid is listed in Philip Ward, ed. *Contemporary Designer Bookbinders, An Illustrated Directory* (Cambridge, England: The Oleander Press, 1995), pp. 8-9, as living in Brussels, Belgium. She studied binding at l'Ecole Nationale Supérieure d'Architecture et des Arts Visuels de La Cambre, Brussels. Bellefroid taught binding at the l'Ecole de La Cambre from 1966-87, and established a photographic archive of historic books and bindings. She has participated in a number of international expositions, and her bindings can be found at The British Museum, the Royal Albert Library in Brussels, and at the Royal Library at The Hague. She has also written on fine bindings and on the history of the book.

R7.   **(Bickers & Son, London)** Burton, Sir Richard. ***The Kasîdah of Haji Abdu El-Yezdi.*** Second edition. (Old World Series) 1898. Full red morocco binding (18.2 x 10 cm.) signed BICKERS & SON, LONDON on lower inside front cover. Two raised bands on the spine, gilt floral panels at top and bottom of spine, central panel with full title running horizontal; spine panels boxed in gilt. Front cover with gilt floral designs at each side and top/bottom of front cover; double gilt rules running the perimeter, gilt rule along board edges; t.e.g. Gilt inner dentelles of 1 cm.; cloudy pink marbled endpapers. With Anna L. Mosher's bookplate (the publisher's wife). (Special Collections, Arizona State University)

R8.   **(Bradstreets)** Swinburne, Algernon Charles. ***Laus Veneris; Poems and Ballads.*** (Quarto Series) 1899. One of 25 copies on Japan vellum. Bound in full blue crushed levant morocco, floral tooling on sides and back, ornate inside borders, gilt top, uncut. (Poor Sale, IV, 757)

R9.   **(Broca, L.)** Symonds, John Addington. ***The Sonnets of Michael Angelo Buonarroti.*** Second edition. (Old World Series) 1901. Bound in full dark blue crushed morocco (18 x 10 cm.) by L. BROCA. Inlays of red stylized tulips with green leaves within a field of gilt dots at all corners; boards framed and inner-framed with double gilt fillets; tulip inlay in the center of each board. Spine with gilt across raised bands and tulip onlays in compartments. Gilt along all board edges and turn-ins; t.e.g. Bookplate of F. T. Hubbard. Slipcase. ❋ See Plate 8 on page 370 (Bishop Collection; photography by Joan Broderick)

> R9.1   Lang, Andrew. ***Ballads & Lyrics of Old France with Other Poems***. Second edition. (Old World Series) 1898. Bound in full crimson crushed levant by L. Broca, front and back covers with an elaborate design of gilt stamped flowers and leaves within a double gilt-ruled border. Doublures of blue morocco with inlays of small red flowers; t.e.g. Enclosed in a full red morocco slipcase. (Houle Gallery & Bookshop, Los Angeles, CA)

> L. Broca is the same Frenchman, Lucien Broca, who ghosted all of Sarah Prideaux's later more successful bindings. He was trained under Chatelin and later partner with Simon Kaufmann until he took up his own premises in the West End trading as an "art binder." The fascinating account of Broca's secret involvement with Prideaux's bindery is given in Marianne Tidcombe's book, *Women Bookbinders 1880-1920*, p. 109, where she indicates Broca was "a superb trade finisher." Over the last two decades, 26 bindings by "L. Broca" or "Broca" have been recorded in *American Book Prices Current*, including fine bindings on second and fourth Shakespeare folios.

R10. **(Chambolle-Duru)** Lang, Andrew. ***Aucassin & Nicolete*** done into English by Andrew Lang. (Old World Series) 1895. Bound in "Lemon morocco, with panel formed of roulette side bands, diapered top and bottom, with twining rose sprays, bees, and birds. Linings and ends of silk brocade" – Entry No. 150 in the *Catalogue of an Exhibition of Nineteenth Century Bookbindings* (Chicago: Caxton Club, 1898), p. 68.

René Chambolle called his Paris bookbinding studio "Chambolle-Duru," adopting the surname of the celebrated bookbinder, Hippolyte Duru, under whom he had once apprenticed. He retired in 1898 and his son
followed in the business.

R11.   **(Club Bindery)** Henry William Poor had a marvelous library in which appeared at least two hundred and
forty-six imprints (including some sets) bound exclusively for the collector by New York's Club Bindery,
including the following thirty Mosher titles. Descriptions of these bindings are given in the 1908-09, five
part "Henry W. Poor Library" sale catalogue. Each catalogue volume and entry number is given for reference. In many instances the copy is one of a very limited edition printed on vellum. Poor's copy of *The
Germ* (R11.27 below) is described by Henri Pène du Bois and photo-featured opposite p. 40 in *American
Bookbindings in the Library of Henry William Poor* (New York: George D. Smith, 1903).

R11.01 Bridges. *The Growth of Love*, 1894 (Part I, No. 215)	R11.16 Wilde. *The Poems of...*, 1903 (III, 1004)
R11.02 Henley. *In Hospital,* 1903 (I, 627)	R11.17 Wilde. *Intentions*, 1904 (III, 1005)
R11.03 Pater. *Marius the Epicurean*, 1900 (I, 876)	R11.18 Wilde. *Ballad of Reading Gaol*, 1904 (III, 1007)
R11.04 Pater. *The Renaissance*, 1902 (I, 877)	R11.19 Meredith. *Modern Love*, 1891 (IV, 420)
R11.05 Phillips, et.al. *Primavera*, 1900 (I, 888)	R11.20 Stevenson. *Father Damien*, 1905 (IV, 726)
R11.06 Whitman. *Book of Heavenly Death*, 1905 (I, 1030)	R11.21 Swinburne. *Songs before Sunrise*, 1901 (IV, 758)
R11.07 Hay. *In Praise of Omar*, 1898 (II, 555)	R11.22 Swinburne. *Poems & Ballads*, 1902 (IV, 759)
R11.08 Rossetti. *Ballads and Sonnets*, 1903 (II, 890)	R11.23 Swinburne. *Tristram of Lyonesse*, 1904 (IV, 761)
R11.09 Thomson. *City of Dreadful Night*, 1892 (II, 973)	R11.24 Symonds. *Fragilia Labilia*, 1902 (IV, 771)
R11.10 Burton. *The Kasidah*, 1905 (III, 207)	R11.25 Symons. *Lyrics,* 1903 (IV, 774)
R11.11 Lang. *Ballads and Lyrics of Old France*, 1896 (III, 700)	R11.26 Villon. *Ballads...*, 1904 (IV, 932)
R11.12 Fitzgerald. *Polonius*, 1901 (III, 471)	R11.27 Rossettl. *The Germ*, 1898 (V, 951)
R11.13 Morris. *Pilgrims of Hope*, 1901 (III, 804)	R11.28 Rossetti. *Poems by...*, 1902 (V, 955)
R11.14 *Little Garland of Christmas Verse*, 1905 (III, 811)	R11.29 Swinburne. *Tristram of Lyonesse*, 1904 (V,1057)
R11.15 *Little Garland of Celtic Verse*, 1905 (III, 812)	R11.30 Swinburne. *A Song of Italy*, 1904 (V, 1058)

The Club Bindery was founded in 1898 by Edwin Holden, and a few other wealthy members of the Grolier Club, to bring the
art of fine bookbinding to America. One of the more outstanding binders and finishers was Léon Maillard who studied under
France's finest, including Marius Michel. The bindery ceased its operation in 1909. Further detailed descriptions for select
Club bindings are given in the following entries R12-R17. *Note:* Entries R11.23 and R11.29 above appear to be the same book, but
one included only the title poem, "Tristram of Lyonesse," while the other included that poem plus several others (for further explanation,
see this title in Section I on "Mosher Books Printed on Vellum").

R12.   **(Club Bindery)** Symonds, John Addington. ***Fragilia Labilia***. (Miscellaneous Series) 1902. Copy No. 2 of 5
copies on vellum signed by the publisher. Full gray-brown polished morocco (19.4 x 11.6 cm.) signed CLUB
BINDERY 1905 and finished by Léon Maillard with floral inlay design in the center of the front cover in red,
orange, white, lavender, green, tan, black and gray; small bud in similar design on center of back cover.
Polished gray morocco doublures with red inlays at corners; a.e.g. Housed in a chemise and slipcase of
mottled purple boards with spine of purple morocco. The Henry W. Poor - Cortlandt F. Bishop - John
Roland Abbey - Norman H. Strouse copy. ✿ See Plate 18 on page 373 (11.24 above; Gift from Norman Strouse to
The Bancroft Library; illustrated with permission, shelf mark TYP AA13 .S95 1902)

This copy was also displayed (see No. 123) in *An Exhibition of Modern English & French Bindings from the
Collection of J.R. Abbey* ([London]: The Arts Council, 1949).

R13.   **(Club Bindery)** Pater, Walter. ***The Renaissance***. (Quarto Series) 1902. Copy No. 2 of 4 printed on vellum
and signed by the publisher. Bound in full brown morocco (22 x 18 cm.) by THE CLUB BINDERY, 1905 with
inlays of four shades of tan, green, bone, brown and red in a stylized Renaissance design; spine has raised
bands and similar geometric design. Polished brown morocco doublures. Housed in chemise and slipcase
of mottled purple boards with purple morocco spine. ✿ See Plate 19 on page 373 (R11.04 above; Gift from Norman Strouse to The Bancroft Library; illustrated with permission, shelf mark TYP AA13 .P35 1902)

This book was displayed in the 1967 "An Exhibition of Books from the Press of Thomas Bird Mosher from
the Collection of Norman H. Strouse" held at The Free Library of Philadelphia. The Poor catalogue notes
"this is, perhaps, one of the finest specimens of modern American mosaic bookbinding."

R14. **(Club Bindery)** Swinburne, Algernon Charles. ***Songs Before Sunrise.*** (Quarto Series) 1901. One of four printed on vellum. Portrait frontispiece. Bound by the Club Bindery-Léon Maillard, finisher. Full old rose crushed levant morocco with "symbolic mosaic decorations" in dark green morocco on the sides. Doublures with maroon levant morocco; a.e.g. (R11.21 above; present location unknown)

> The Poor catalogue calls this "a very beautiful specimen of modern American bookbinding" and is pictured in Part IV, opposite p. 80.

R15. **(Club Bindery)** Swinburne, Algernon Charles. ***Tristram of Lyonesse.*** (Quarto Series) 1904. Copy No. 2 of 4 on vellum, signed by Thomas B. Mosher and from his library. Bound in full polished red morocco (22.3 x 18 cm.) signed The Club Bindery 1908. Both covers have deep green, tan, and bone colored inlays on a tapestry-like design, lightly gilt; spine with a similar pattern with raised bands. Polished red morocco doublures with gilt around the edges. Marbled brown and violet boards, in chemise and slipcase with brown morocco spine. From the Library of Henry William Poor. See Plate 21 on page 373 ❀ (Gift from Norman Strouse to The Bancroft Library; illustrated with permission, shelf mark TYP AA13 .S9 1904).

> This book was displayed in the 1967 "An Exhibition of Books from the Press of Thomas Bird Mosher from the Collection of Norman H. Strouse" held at The Free Library of Philadelphia.

R16. **(Club Bindery)** Fitzgerald, Edward. ***Polonius.*** (Miscellaneous Series) 1901. Copy No. 3 of 4 copies on vellum from library of Henry W. Poor, bound at the Club Bindery in 1904, in full polished turquoise morocco (19.2 x 14.8 cm.); both covers have gilt morocco border and rectangular inlay of rust morocco gilt with floral garlands and flourishes; spine has raised red bands and floral gilt panels; matching turquoise doublures and vellum fly-leaves. Housed in a chemise slipcase of marbled boards with violet morocco spine. (R11.12 above; Gift from Norman Strouse to The Bancroft Library)

R17. **(Club Bindery)** Pater, Walter. ***Marius the Epicurean.*** (Quarto Series) 1900. Two volumes. Copy No. 2 of 4 printed on vellum. Bound for Henry W. Poor in full green morocco (both vols. 22.1 x 17.9 cm.) by the CLUB BINDERY 1902. Both covers are heavily gilt in garlands and flourishes, with red and tan morocco design of inlays and gilt. Brown polished morocco doublures and green silk fly-leaves. Each volume is housed in a chemise of mottled purple boards with purple morocco spine; slipcase of dark brown marbled boards. (R11.03 above; Gift from Norman Strouse to The Bancroft Library)

R18. **(Coverly, Roger de)** ***Aucassin & Nicolete*** done into English by Andrew Lang. (Old World Series) 1895. Copy No. 85 of 100 on Japan vellum. Bound in full morocco by Roger de Coverly; richly tooled corners and center piece; inside border. (location unknown)

> When Cobden-Sanderson decided to take up bookbinding at the age of forty-three, he learned the tasks of forwarding under Roger de Coverly for several months from 1883-84. De Coverly died in 1915. Though he executed a binding on at least one Mosher book, his pupil, Cobden-Sanderson, refused to do so (see note to R23).

R19. **(Diehl, Edith)** Buonarroti, Michel Angelo. ***The Sonnets of Michael Angelo Buonarroti.*** Translated by John Addington Symonds. (Old World) 1897. The binding, by the "ED Bindery" (Edith Diehl), is off-white morocco with onlays of olive green, black, and brown with gilt tooling. The doublures are an off-white with an onlaid frame of black and brown with gilt; vellum endleaves. The book is enclosed in a case of brown morocco with gilt tooling. (Spencer Collection, The New York Public Library)

> This binding was displayed as entry No. 24 of The Guild of Book Workers 75th Anniversary Exhibition and is described in the exhibition's catalogue (NY: The Guild of Book Workers, 1981) on p. 27.

> Edith Diehl (1876-1953), a graduate of Wellesley College, first learned to bind at the Nordhoff Bindery in 1902, and also took lessons in Paris, Brussels and London. When she returned to New York she set up a small bindery and employed two binders from the former Club Bindery. She later ran the edition bindery at William E. Rudge in Mt. Vernon, NY. Throughout her binding career Diehl lectured on and taught bookbinding. She is the author of the well-known two volume work on *Bookbinding: Its Background and Technique*, published in 1946.

R20.   **(Donnelley, R. R.)** Swinburne, Algernon Charles. *Songs before Sunrise*. (Quarto Series) 1901. Copy No. 4 of 25 on Japan vellum signed by Mosher. Bound in full dark blue morocco (22.5 x 17.5 cm.) with gilt tooling in Jansenist style signed DONNELLEY - CHICAGO. Double gilt fillets around each cover, raised bands and gilt tooling on spine. Gilt-decorated turn-ins of 1.2 cm.; blue paper endpapers. The very small pencil lettering "C P Hill" (the sewer of the binding?) appears in the gutter on one of the back Japan vellum endpapers. Housed in matching morocco backed slipcase. This book was exhibited at the 1992 "Thomas Bird Mosher and the Art of the Book" Exhibit hosted at Temple University. (Bishop Collection)

   R20.1   An exact mate to the above Donnelley binding was also put on a copy of Swinburne's *Tristram of Lyonesse*. (Quarto Series) 1904. Copy No. 5 of 25 copies on Japan vellum signed by Mosher. (private collection)

   R20.2   ENTRY NO. 10 – Richard Garnett's *De Flagello Myrteo*. (Miscellaneous Series) 1906. Bound in three-quarter red niger goatskin.

   R20.3   ENTRY NO. 17 – Rossetti's *The House of Life*. (Old World Series) 1898. Bound in three-quarter red niger goatskin.

   R20.4   ENTRY NO. 21 – John Hay's *In Praise of Omar*. (Miscellaneous Series) 1898. Bound in three-quarter blue niger goatskin.

   R20.5   ENTRY NO. 39 – *The Sayings of the Lord Jesus Christ*. (Miscellaneous Series) 1905. One of 25 on Japan vellum bound in tooled and inlaid full brown levant.

   ───────────

   R. R. Donnelley & Sons operated the Extra Bindery (founded in 1921) at the Lakeside Press in Chicago. Alfred de Sauty, who had worked at Rivière as a finisher, was responsible for binding design and management of the bindery from 1923-1935. From December 9-13, 1924 the Donnelley Bindery held an exhibition of 80 of their better bindings at the Blackstone Hotel in Chicago, including bindings on first editions, and on Kelmscott, Eragny, Riccardi, and Essex House Press books. Four of the bindings presented were on Mosher imprints (see entries R20.2-20.5 above).

XX.   **(Doves Bindery)** See note to Florence Foote, entry R23.

R21.   **(Eddington Bindery – Plumley)** Pater, Walter. *The Renaissance*. (Quarto Series) 1902. Copy No. 11 of 35 copies on Japan vellum signed by Mosher. Bound in full light green morocco (22.5 x 17.5 cm.) signed BRUCE B. PLUMLEY EDDINGTON BINDERY 1981. Flat spine with gilt title running vertically along the spine. Covers with darker green leaf and stem design running across the covers and the spine; front cover includes a yellow rising sun disk with horizontal gilt lines abutting it two-thirds of the way down. Full inner leather doublures are actually a continuation of the cover leather almost seamlessly attached; a.e.g, marbled endpapers with first endpapers laminated with suede facing the doublures. Housed in black clamshell case.
   ❦ See Plate 34 on page 376 (Gift from Norman Strouse to the Donohue Rare Book Room, Gleeson Library, University of San Francisco; illustrated with permission)

R22.   **(Eddington Bindery)** Pater, Walter. *The Renaissance*. (Quarto Series) 1902. One of four copies on vellum. Bound in full brown morocco (22.8 x 19 cm.) signed EDDINGTON BINDERY with geometric design in gold on both covers and across the flat spine (with gilt title on an angle). Green velvet paste downs. A note with the binding indicates it was done by David K. Stevens who, while visiting Norman Strouse on November 3, 1979 along with the Eddington Bindery's patroness, Lady Formoy, received the commission that day. Housed in clamshell box. (Gift from Norman Strouse to the Donohue Rare Book Room, Gleeson Library, University of San Francisco)

R23.   **(Foote, Florence)** FitzGerald, Edward. *Rubáiyát of Omar Khayyám*. (Vest Pocket Series) 1900. Bound in full brown morocco (13.3 x 7 cm.) and stamped F •1901• F at the foot of the inside back cover. Spine with raised bands and gilt decorated compartments with flowers and roundels. Upper and lower caps over head-bands. Covers decorated with gilt-ruled frames enclosing a field of gilt dots. Gilt decorated turn-ins of 1 cm.; paper endpapers. Double head-bands; all page edges gilt with dot-gauffering along the sides. The binding was restored by Denis Gouey of Norfolk, MA. (Bishop Collection)

Florence Foote was one of Cobden-Sanderson's prized pupils, and continued her binding career in New York City where she ran the Evelyn Nordhoff Bindery. Foote gives us an insight into why we have never been able to locate any Mosher imprint in a Doves binding. In a letter to Mosher dated October 22, 1900 (Houghton Library) she states, "I returned from England a few days ago, and as my Bindery has started its autumn work, we want more of your beautiful books to bind... I took three copies of your 'Hand and Soul' to bind while I was with Mr. Cobden-Sanderson—but he would not let me do any of them because he said it was a 'piracy' to have printed them over here! I suppose you are used to hearing that?"

R24. **(GAZ)** FitzGerald, Edward. ***Rubáyát of Omar Khayyám.*** With Preface by Nathan Haskell Dole. (Vest Pocket Series) 1909. Bound in full blue crushed morocco (14.1 x 7.5 cm.) signed •GAZ• (George A. Zabrinskie). Spine with two raised bands with gilt dots across each band. Horizontal title in gilt in central panel with red painted, gilt flowers in top and bottom panels; gilt rules flanking each band and at top and bottom of spine. Covers with gilt rule around perimeters and inner blind-tooled frame of flowers and other decorations emanating from the inner rule of the frame. The letters of the word RUBÁIYÁT are vertically arranged and gilt-stamped in the center of both covers. Gilt dots along board edges ending with a star at head and tail. Turn-ins of 1.2 cm. consisting of gilt-tooled leafy vines and flowers within two gilt rules. This is reportedly Mosher's own copy, and the owl bookplate of Oliver Sheean appears at the back of the volume. (Special Collections, Arizona State University)

R25. **(G.E.S.)** Morris, William. ***A Dream of John Ball.*** (Old World Series) 1902. One of 925 on Van Gelder paper. Contemporary dark blue morocco, elaborately gilt decorated front and back covers with overall design of diagonal lattice, each space of which incorporates a flower made up of point tools; spine gilt in six compartments. Inside turn-ins gilt decorated and signed "G.E.S." who is identified as Miss Sherringham in the Thomas Thorp catalogue. (Thomas Thorp, Antiquarian Bookseller, 1994 listing)

R26. **(Guild of Women-Binders, London)** Rossetti, Dante Gabriel, et.al. ***THE GERM: Thoughts Towards Nature in Poetry, Literature, and Art. MDCCCL.*** (Miscellaneous Series) London: Guild of Women-Binders, 61 Charing Cross Road [Printed by Mosher for the Guild], 1898. Full brown morocco binding (23.5 x 16.2 cm.) elaborately blind and gilt tooled with GUILD OF WOMEN-BINDERS stamped in gold at bottom of inner front cover. Design by Constance Karslake, and tooled by Florence de Rheims? The limitation page reads "25 copies only of this book have been printed on Japan vellum, for England. Acquired by the Guild of Women-Binders, 61 Charing Cross Road, London. This is No. 6 *Thomas B. Mosher.*" Overall design of inverted blind-tooled heart-shaped leaves with straight stems, each with three blind-tooled floral devices. Space between leaves is filled with gold dots. Design within a single blind-tooled rule. Flat spine with elements of the cover design and three single blind-tooled flowers; title in gilt on spine. Gilt decorated turn-ins of 1.4 cm. with blind-tooled hearts and gilt dots filling space between the heart shaped leaves; green cloudy marbled inlay panel and flyleaves. Top page edges gilt and gauffered. This copy does not include the 16 pages of facsimiles of the title pages and contents Mosher printed at the end of the other copies of the rest of the edition (see entry 132 in Section II). ❀ See Plate 14 on page 371 (Illustrated with permission from the Special Collections, Arizona State University; photography by Gene Valentine)

    R26.1 Another copy has also been recorded. The Curtis Hidden Page catalogue entitled "List of association books, first editions, book-plates, autographs, limited editions from special presses... from the library of Curtis Hidden Page... offered for sale by C. H. Page, Gilmanton, New Hampshire" (ca. 1931). Entry No. 242 on p.71 notes: "Only 25 copies of this issue were printed for the Guild of Women Binders, London, to be specially bound by hand. This is [copy] No. 7 with the autograph signature of Thomas Bird Mosher, authenticating the above. Printed on Japanese vellum and bound in full crushed levant morocco with exquisite blind tooling, by the Guild of Women Binders. 'Out of Print and rare' the moment it was issued. Perhaps this is the hardest to find of all Mosher items–as well as being a rarely beautiful example of the binder's art, (each being unique); and a first edition (in book form) of Rossetti." Curtis Hidden Page assembled this undated sales catalogue around 1931. Page was a professor of English at Dartmouth, authored a book on Japanese poetry, translated numerous French works, and was a book collector turned bookseller.

The Guild of Women Binders was founded by Frank Karslake (who also founded The Hampstead Bindery) in 1898. It operated until 1904 as a loosely-knit federation of women binders from such groups as the Edinburgh Social Union, the Kirkby Lonsdale Handicraft Class, the Chiswick Art Workers' Guild, and Miss Bassett's Leighton Buzzard Handicraft Class for crippled girls, among others. Some of the more outstanding women binders represented by the Guild included Miss Constance Karslake, Miss Edith de Rheims, Florence de Rheims, Miss Helen Schofield, Mrs. Frances Knight, Mrs. Macdonald, Miss Lilian Overton, and Miss Edwards. The Guild, together with its counterpart, The Hampstead Bindery, published *The Bookbindings of To-morrow* in 1902, and held both exhibitions and sales of their bindings at Sotheby's. It is also interesting to note that Mosher copied a Karslake binding design for the design he employed on bindings in the Ideal Series of Little Masterpieces (see Section I).

R27.   **(Guild of Women-Binders, London)** Fitzgerald, Edward. *Rubáiyát of Omar Khayyám.* (Old World Series) 1897. Binding of full light brown modeled pigskin (18 x 10 cm.) with illustrated tooling in relief signed THE GUILD OF WOMEN BINDERS incised at the foot of the inside front cover; the Guild's stamp is also affixed on the last free end leaf. The bindery work is that of Miss Gaskell. The front cover shows Omar and his beloved while the back cover illustrates grape vines. Gilt-lined turn-ins and marbled endpapers; all page edges green. ❀ See Plate 7 on page 370 (Illustrated with permission, Collection of Jean-François Vilain and Roger S. Wieck; photography by Roger Wieck)

   This book was displayed at the 1992 Mosher Press exhibit at Temple University, and is pictured in the exhibition catalogue, *Thomas Bird Mosher and the Art of the Book* (Philadelphia: F. A. Davis, 1992), pp. 40-41 and illustration 54 on p. 100.

R28.   **(Hamilton, Christine)** Wilde, Oscar. *The Happy Prince and Other Tales.* (Old World Series) 1907. Bound in full red-brown morocco (17.5 x 10.6 cm.); gold and blind tooled covers with plum morocco onlays. French oil-marbled paper doublures in red, black and gold; morocco hinge and gold sewn headbands; t.e.g.

   This binding, displaying bold geometric design and color combinations, was part of The Guild of Book Workers' 75th Anniversary Exhibition and is described in the exhibition's catalogue (NY: The Guild of Book Workers, 1981). It appears as entry No. 34 and is color illustrated on p. 39, and was lent to the exhibition by the Graphic Arts Collection, Princeton University Library.

   Christine Hamilton was a member of the Guild for over 25 years. She studied with Eleanore Van Sweringen and Charles Pannier. Her bindings were exhibited at the San Francisco World's Fair in 1939, at the Argent Galleries in New York ten years later, and at the Firestone Library at Princeton University in 1951. Her bindings are located at Princeton University, the New York Public Library, the Pierpont Morgan Library, and at Dartmouth College.

R29.   **(Hampstead Bindery)** Rossetti, Dante Gabriel, et. al. *The Germ: Thoughts Towards Nature in Poetry, Literature, and Art. MDCCCL.* (Miscellaneous Series) London: Guild of Women-Binders, 61 Charing Cross Road [Printed by Thomas Bird Mosher for the Guild], 1898. Copy No. 9 of 25 on Japan vellum. Bound in full green levant morocco (23.3 x 15.8 cm.) by P. A. Savoldelli for The Hampstead Bindery. Front and back covers decorated with gold-tooled vines and stalks bearing flowers in groups of three and inlaid in orange, purple, green, pale blue and white morocco; t.e.g. with a symmetrical abstract pattern of gauffering that goes 4.7 cm. from the spine toward the fore-edge. Full doublures in green leather and center panel of ivory vellum with gold and blind stamping of tendrils, heart-shaped leaves, and inlaid disks; vellum endpapers. This copy includes the sixteen pages of facsimiles of the title pages and contents Mosher printed at the end of the book. The binding was donated to Brown University in 1924 by the widow of William Henry Hoffman who collected Napoleona and fine bindings. It was presumably acquired by Hoffman from the dealer, Gabriel Weis of New York, whose description is included in the volume. ❀ See Plate 13 on page 371 (Illustrated with permission, Napoleon Collection, The John Hay Library, Brown University)

   R29.1   Johnson, Charles. *From the Upanishads.* (Miscellaneous Series) 1897. No. 35 of 50 copies on Japan vellum. Bound in full dark brown morocco (15.6 x 9 cm.) signed THE HAMPSTEAD BINDERY which appears in gilt on the lower inner panel of the inner front cover. Gently rounded spine with title vertically lettered in gilt and a stem topped with a leaf at the bottom half. Covers elaborately gilt tooled with leaf, stem, and gold dot design particularly concentrated at each of the four corner areas, with double gilt rules curving toward the center of the cover's outer boundaries with gilt dots filling the overlapping areas; gilt rule about the perimeter of each cover. Board edges with single gilt rule. Turn-ins of 1.3 cm. with leaves outlined in gilt around the inner board within two gilt rules; central white inlay panel with gilt rule around perimeter. Gilt rule around perimeter of first and last flyleaf; t.e.g. (Special Collections, Arizona State University).

R29.2　Another Mosher book, Dante's ***The New Life***. (Old World Series) 1896, was bound by the Hampstead Bindery around 1900 and is photo-illustrated in Howard M. Nixon's *British Bookbindings presented by Kenneth H. Oldaker to the Chapter Library of Westminster Abbey* (London: Maggs Bros., 1982, pp. 118-119).

England's Hampstead Bindery was founded in 1898 by the antiquarian bookseller and founder of the *Book Auction Records*, Frank Karslake. It operated until 1904 as a closely-knit workshop of binders including the likes of Alfred de Sauty (chief designer), P. A. Savoldelli, Samuel Tout, and Thomas Edward Caley. It was considered the male counterpart to the Guild of Women-Binders. Several of P. A. Savoldelli's bindings (see R29 above) are pictured in *The Bookbindings of To-morrow* (London, 1902).

R30.　**(Harcourt Bindery)** Morris, William. ***Child Christopher and Goldilind the Fair***. (Miscellaneous Series) 1900. Large 8vo. (23.7 x 16.7 cm.) Full red morocco signed HARCOURT BINDERY with gilt stamped decorated borders of leafy vines and dots surrounding a large inner rectangular panel on the front and back covers. Spine with raised bands and elaborate gilt in the compartments. Wide inner dentelles gilt-stamped with an ornamental border composed of flowers and leaves; t.e.g. Bookplate of F. T. Hubbard (see R33). Housed in a red buckram slipcase. ❧ See Plate 35 on page 376 (Bishop Collection; photography by Joan Broderick)

R31.　**(Hillbourne)** Holmes, Daniel Henry. ***Under a Fool's Cap***. (Miscellaneous Series) 1911. Bound in full orange crushed morocco (17.7 x 11 cm.) signed HILLBOURNE. Spine with raised bands and gold and blind-tooled compartments (gold flowers above blind-tooled leaves). Blind-tooled fillets around covers with inner panel of a double fillet rectangle filled with a field of the same blind-tooled leaves and gilt dots with two vertical rules dividing the field into three columns. Narrow turn-ins, paper endpapers and paste downs; a.e.g. In this copy there has been inserted an oval portrait frontispiece with *"Benjamin Copy 1909"* written below it in pencil. (Gift from Norman Strouse to the Donohue Rare Book Room, Gleeson Library, University of San Francisco)

R32.　**(Hillside Bindery)** Along with the Nordhoff Bindery, Mosher also mentions Miss Mary Bulkley as a binder of his books in the foreword to his 1898 catalogue. Bulkley called her workshop the 'Hillside Bindery' at Hillside, St. Louis County, Missouri. No example has been seen. See Tidcombe's *Women Bookbinders 1880-1920* (Oak Knoll Press & The British Library, 1996), p. 186.

R33.　**(Hubbard, F. T.)** Arnold, Matthew. ***Empedocles on Etna***. (Miscellaneous Series) 1900. One of fifty copies on Japan vellum. Bound in full orange-brown morocco (22.6 x 15.7 cm.) and signed in gold at the foot of the spine: F.T.H. 1900. The binding is reminiscent of the more chaste and linear designs of Charles Ricketts's: gently rounded spine with gilt fillet around the perimeter; the title/author is tooled in imitation of the original Japan vellum spine including three leaves used as space fillers. Front and back covers with single gilt fillet around the perimeter of the boards; front cover is gilt tooled with an asymmetrical and vertical double-fillet rectangle which is bordered on the left and bottom with an elaborate triple tooled network of straight and curved lines with heart, leaf and dot embellishments, the whole of which forms a large "L" on the cover. Single gilt rule along board edges. Wide turn-ins (1.5 cm.) with single gilt fillet; inner green morocco doublure outlined with a double gilt fillet and floral devices at each corner; t.e.g.; green ribbed silk endpapers. Housed in a custom leather mouthed and fleece lined slipcase. ❧ See Plate 16 on page 372 (Bishop Collection; photography by Joan Broderick)

F. T. Hubbard was a well-to-do Boston area collector of finely bound books who tried his hand at the book-binding art. This binding was very possibly executed by Hubbard with his initials "F.T.H." appearing at the base of the spine, and represents rather accomplished skill, if somewhat eccentric tooling. Incidentally, a number of Mosher books in fine bindings were in Hubbard's collection (see entries R9, R30 and R82).

R34. **(Hunt, Rachael MacMasters Miller)** Six fine bindings on Mosher books are listed in Marianne Fletcher Titcombe's *The Bookbinding Career of Rachel McMasters Miller Hunt* (Pittsburgh, PA: The Hunt Botanical Library, 1974). Mrs. Hunt was a student of Cobden-Sanderson's pupil, Euphemia Bakewell, and became a noteworthy American binder in her own right (also see entry 74, Utley).

    R34.1 ENTRY NO. 7 *The Garland of Rachel, by Divers Kindly Hands* (Reprints of Privately Printed Books) 1902. (Mrs. Hunt's first full-leather binding). Green levant morocco (21.4 x 13.6 cm.) signed "R Mc M M, 1905," plain endpapers, t.e.g.. Title tooled within a wreath of leaves and flowers on the covers.

    R34.2 ENTRY NO. 12 Maurice Hewlett. *Quattrocentisteria.* (Vest Pocket Series) 1904. Maroon calf (13.3 x 8.6 cm.) signed R Mc M M 1906." Pink and green marbled endpapers, edges gilt. Covers blind-tooled with panel of pomegranates and heavy gouges; gilt title on spine.

    R34.3 ENTRY NO. 68 Robert Browning. *Pippa Passes.* (Old World Series) 1908. Copper colored niger morocco (17.7 x 10 cm.) signed "R Mc M M • 1912." Blind tooled with squares and gold trillium flowers. Cloudy orange endpapers, all page edges gilt. ❀ See Plate 9 on page 370 (Illustrated courtesy of the Hunt Institute for Botanical Documentation-Carnegie Mellon University, Pittsburgh, PA)

    R34.4 ENTRY NO. 77 François Villon. *Poems.* (Reprints of Privately Printed Books) 1909. Green levant morocco (size unknown). Rose and green marbled endpapers. Covers with border of dots and lines and central medallion with mother-of-pearl inlays. Finished February 22, 1913. "Sold to Margaret Barr as a wedding gift for Jean Oliver."

    R34.5 ENTRY NO. 110 James M. Barrie. *George Meredith.* (Miscellaneous Series) 1904. Bound in gray crushed levant morocco (13.8 x 9.7 cm.) with dark blue onlaid border and signed "R Mc M M 1918" with her mark of a lamb between initials and date. Front cover of two dark blue panels, title and Roman date tooled in panels.

    R34.6 ENTRY NO. 118 '**Poems of Italy**' (six titles from the Venetian Series all bound together) 1910-1913. Bound in mulberry crushed levant morocco (14 x 12.4 cm.) and signed "R Mc M M 1918" using her mark of a lamb between name and date. Covers with border of dots, stars and Florentine fleurs-de-lys; front cover with framed quotation from Browning surmounted by a green morocco inlay "from Florence" inside a wreath of oak leaves. Italian woodblock endpapers. All board edges gilt tooled; all page edges gilt.

R35. **(Illumination–unidentified)** *The Bibelot.* Volume II, No. I. Portland, Maine: Thomas Bird Mosher, January 1896. Extra-illustrated with seventeen pen and ink drawings, three of which are hand-colored. (Gift from Norman Strouse to the Donohue Rare Book Room, Gleeson Library, University of San Francisco)

R36. **(Illumination–William Cushing Bamburgh)** Fitzgerald, Edward. *Rubáiyát of Omar Khayyám.* (Old World Series) 1911. Original covers wrapped in a jacket protector with pochoir decorations in red, blue, maroon, and yellow in the Moorish or Persian style, signed Wm Cushing Bamburgh Illuminator Boston 1916 on the front inner flap. Spine with blue leaves and vine on a dark maroon background; design continues onto the back cover. ❀ See Plate 31 on page 375 (Bishop Collection; photography by Joan Broderick)

    Bamburgh was an illuminator who worked for Frederick H. Hitchcock's Grafton Press and for the private press of Robert Grier Cook, both of New York City. This book was exhibited at the 1992 Mosher Press exhibit at Temple University and is described and pictured in the exhibit catalogue, *Thomas Bird Mosher and the Art of the Book* (Philadelphia: F.A. Davis, 1992), pp. 42 and 102 (#60).

R37. **(Illumination–Bertha Avery)** Arnold, Matthew. *Empedocles on Etna.* (Miscellaneous Series) 1900. ❀ See Plate 28 on page 375 (Illustrated with permission, Collection of Jean-François Vilain and Roger S. Wieck; photography by Roger Wieck)

According to Jean-François Vilain's description of this piece displayed at the Temple University exhibition, "This copy, from the library of Flora Lamb, has a title page and two initials (on the preliminary title page and on page 49) sumptuously hand-illuminated by Bertha Avery in a style strongly reminiscent of the work of Cora J. Cady and Emilie M. Whitten for the Craftsman Guild's *The Perfect Woman* and *Love Songs*. Hand illumination, less common among British private presses, had a prominent role in American presses; it was used most successfully by the Roycrofters. Illuminated Mosher books are very rare, and seem to have been commissioned mostly by Lamb. (Two other volumes in this exhibition, The Mosher Books, 1909 and Upson's *Sonnets and Songs*, also from Lamb's library, have more modest hand illuminations.)" –Vilain & Bishop. *Thomas Bird Mosher and the Art of the Book*, pp. 18-19. The same book also appears as entry 156 in Kaplan. *"The Art that is Life": The Arts & Crafts Movement in America, 1875-1920*, p.295. It was also exhibited at the 1992 Mosher Press exhibit at Temple University.

R38.   **(Illumination–Clara Chipman Newton)** Wilde, Oscar. ***Poems in Prose***. (Ideal Series of Little Masterpieces) 1906. This delightfully illuminated copy contains numerous full-page, intricate watercolor decorations, signed by Clara Chipman Newton. ❧ See Plate 29 on page 375 (Illustrated with permission, Collection of Jean-François Vilain and Roger S. Wieck; photography by Roger Wieck)

> R38.2   Another signed example of Clara Chipman Newton's illumination appears on Mosher's Vest Pocket edition of Richard Jefferies, *A Little Book of Nature Thoughts* (1907) in the Huston Collection at Kalamazoo College.

> Clara Chipman Newton (1848-1936) was both secretary and decorator at Rookwood Pottery of Cincinnati, OH. This book was shown at the 1992 Mosher Press exhibit at Temple University and one of the pages is described and illustrated in the exhibit catalogue, *Thomas Bird Mosher and the Art of the Book* (Philadelphia: F. A. Davis, 1992), pp. 32-33 and p. 97 (#45). Illumination by Newton on a Mosher book provides a unique conjunction between several branches of the Arts and Crafts Movement: pottery, Mosher's publications of the period, and the art of illumination.

R39.   **(Illumination–E.M.S.)** Burton, Sir Richard F. ***The Kasîdah***. (Miscellaneous Series) 1905. Large quarto. Limited to 125 copies. With photogravure portrait frontispiece. Contains an original water-color drawing of leaves, stems and two large pomegranates (at the bottom) and at large banner with the wording, "the Tinkling of the camel's bell" at the top, the whole watercolor filling the 33 x 25 cm. page. The water-color is signed "E.M.S. 06" at the lower right. The book was purchased by Norman H. Strouse from the London bookseller, Ifan Kyrle Fletcher. The original Leopold Flameng etching is also loosely laid in. ❧ See Plate 30 on page 375 (Gift from Norman Strouse to the Donohue Rare Book Room, Gleeson Library, University of San Francisco; and illustrated with their permission)

R40.   **(Illumination–Mrs. Kate Townsend)** The following is a list of several of the works which were once in the Norman Strouse collection. The present location of these volumes is unknown. Several pieces of the 1902-04 correspondence between Mosher and Mrs. Townsend are housed at the Gleeson Library, University of San Francisco. Mosher mentions Mrs. Townsend's illumination of *The Growth of Love* and recommends her doing the 1895 *Homeward Songs by the Way*.

> R40.1   Jefferies, Richard. *Story of My Heart*. Second edition. (Old World Series) 1900. Vellum cover, hand-illuminated by Mrs. Kate A. Townsend.

> R40.2   Jefferies, Richard. *Bits of Oak Bark and Meadow Thoughts*. Second edition. (Brocade Series) 1901. Hand-illuminated cover by Kate A. Townsend.

> R40.3   Morris, William. *The Tale of King Florus and Fair Jehane*. Second edition. (Brocade) 1898. Hand-illuminated cover by Kate A. Townsend.

(Illumination) See also R46.

R41.   **(Kamph, Jamie)** Keats, John. ***Odes Sonnets and Lyrics***. (Miscellaneous Series) 1924. Bound in full red (dark russet) Niger goatskin (18.4 x 14.5 cm.) by Jamie Kamph, signed "Stonehouse Bindery." Tan "frieze" onlays of gold-tooled classical figures similar to figures of warriors from a Greek vase. Titled in gold within a Greek-key border. Twinrocker endsheets; red, tan, and gold head- and tail-bands. In textured natural linen solander case with gold-tooled leather strip with title on spine. ❧ See Plate 36 on page 376 (Illustrated with permission from the Spencer Collection, The New York Public Library; Astor, Lenox and Tilden Foundations)

> This binding is pictured as Entry #53 in *Contemporary American Bookbinding–An exhibition organized by the Grolier Club at the invitation of Les Amis de la Reliure Originale.* Compiled and edited by Mary C. Schlosser. (NY: The Grolier Club, 1990). It was bound in 1987 and later purchased by the New York Public Library. Even though the Mosher imprints included in this section are on bindings dated prior to 1923, the book is essentially a reprint of Mosher's earlier 1922 edition and represents an exquisite example of the binder's art. Kamph has also bound Mosher's editions of *Quattrocentisteria* and Thoreau's *A Little Book of Nature Themes* (both of the Vest Pocket Series) in dark brown oasis goatskin with onlays in multi-colored goatskin vaguely representing garden landscapes.

> The binder, Jamie Kamph, was born in Princeton, NJ in 1946. She studied with Hope Weil, and established the Stonehouse Bindery, Lambertville, NJ, in 1973 where she continues the art of design, fine binding and restoration. She has taught several workshops on binding, and has authored several articles and *A Collector's Guide to Bookbinding* (Oak Knoll Books, 1982). Her bindings are to be found in several prestigious institutions and in many private collections.

(The Knickerbocker Press). See R84.

R42. **(Lakeside Press)** Rossetti, Dante Gabriel. ***Ballads & Sonnets.*** (Quarto Series) 1903. Copy no. 4 of 4 on vellum, signed by Mosher and from his library. Bound in full green morocco (23.2 x 18.5 cm.), gold tooled by Harold Tribolet of THE LAKESIDE PRESS–CHICAGO. Spine with high raised bands and gilt tooling across each; gilt decorated panels. Cover outlines with double gilt fillets with dots between the rules; 1.3 cm. turn-ins with Cockerell paper paste downs and endpapers. Housed in green slip-case. Bound on commission for Norman Strouse in 1964. (Gift from Norman Strouse to the Donohue Rare Book Room, Gleeson Library, University of San Francisco. For other related bindings, see Donnelley entry R20)

R43. **(Monastery Hill Bindery)** Swinburne, Algernon Charles. ***Laus Veneris.*** (Quarto Series) 1899. One of 450 copies. Bound in full orange morocco (22.7 x 18.2 cm.), elaborately and densely gold-tooled by THE MOSTERY HILL BINDERY. Spine with raised bands, gilt rule across each; panels richly gilt tooled. Gilt rule along board edges; 2.3 cm. turn-ins elaborately decorated; moiré inner panels and endpapers; t.e.g. Blind stamp indicating this copy was from the library of Dana C. Bradford. ❧ See Plate 25 on page 374 (Gift from Norman Strouse to the Donohue Rare Book Room, Gleeson Library, University of San Francisco; illustrated with permission)

> R42.1 Another Monastery Hill binding appears on Rossetti's *Ballads & Sonnets.* (Quarto Series) 1903. One of 450 copies, bound in full dark green morocco and elegantly tooled in gold on both covers with an art nouveau design of stylized thorny branches emanating from a central rose and forming four panels on each cover; t.e.g. Dentelles tooled in gilt with file fillets. This binding was photo-illustrated in Boss's *The Turn of the Century*, 1993, opposite p. 302, item 131. (Bishop Collection)

The Monastery Hill Bindery operated out of Chicago and did numerous bindings for Mosher Press books. It was also the bindery selected to do the 3/4 morocco bindings for post-1923 editions of the *Amphora*.

R44. **(Morgan Seaford)** Symonds, John Addington. ***Fragilia Labilia.*** (Miscellaneous Series) 1902. Copy No. 4 of 5 on vellum. Bound in England for Norman Strouse in full green morocco (20.1 x 12.5 cm.) signed MORGAN SEAFORD. Raised bands with gilt stars and rules. Covers with single fillet around perimeter, and front cover with off-center gilt box with title and author in gilt; field of widely spaced stars both blind- and gilt-tooled on front, and only blind-tooled on the back cover. Gilt hatch marks on board edges. Wide gilt decorated turn-ins; paper panels and Cockerell endpapers. (Gift from Norman Strouse to the Donohue Rare Book Room, Gleeson Library, University of San Francisco)

R45. **(Morgan Seaford)** Watson, Rosamund Marriott. ***Tares: A Book of Verses.*** (Lyric Garland Series) 1906. Copy No. 1 of 7 on vellum. English binding in full blue morocco (18.2 x 11.2 cm.) with red leather flower onlays on spine and front cover (5 flowers) and back cover (1 flower). Wide turn-ins with central panel of vellum. Top page edges gilt-in-rough. Cockerell endpapers. (Gift from Norman Strouse to the Donohue Rare Book Room, Gleeson Library, University of San Francisco)

> This book was shown in the 1967 "An Exhibition of Books from the Press of Thomas Bird Mosher from the Collection of Norman H. Strouse" held at The Free Library of Philadelphia.

R46. **(Morrell)** Rossetti, Dante Gabriel. *The House of Life. A Sonnet Sequence.* (Old World Series) 1898. No. 66 of 100 copies on Japan vellum. Bound in full mauve morocco (18 x 10 cm.) signed MORELL, BINDER for the Charles Lauriat Co. of Boston. Spine in French style with two raised bands; horizontal title in gilt in second panel; upper and lower panels with stems and leaves; date at bottom. Both covers within gilt ruled border and stylized vine, leaves and flowers in gilt forming an inner frame. Gilt rule along board edges; t.e.g. Decorated 1.5 cm. turn-ins; central panel of moiré silk matching moiré endpapers. This copy specially hand-colored and illuminated by "H.H.T July 1902." (Gift from Norman Strouse to the Donohue Rare Book Room, Gleeson Library, University of San Francisco)

R47. **(Morrell Bindery)** Fitzgerald, Edward. *Rubáiyát of Omar Khayyám.* (Old World Series) 1900. Small 8vo. One of 100 on Japan vellum. Full brown morocco by Morrell, tooled in a gilt art nouveau design of sweeping lines with leaf and floral ornaments on the front cover; rear cover is panel-ruled with floral ornaments. Spine with one raised band and with gilt title and leafy vines; t.e.g.; gilt turn-ins with yellow silk doublures and endsheets. The design for this cover by Morrell is almost a direct imitation of the cover design for the 1884 *Rubáiyát* illustrated by Elihu Vedder, using his design on the front cover. (private collection)

R48. **(Morrell Bindery)** Symonds, John Addington. *Fragilia Labilia.* (Miscellaneous Series) 1902. 8vo. Limited to 50 copies on Japan vellum. Bound in full brown morocco by Morrell with art nouveau design in gilt on front and back covers. Central panel with stylized design of a bouquet of flowers using green and blue leather onlays. Gilt-tooled dentelles; t.e.g. Housed in a fleece-lined buckram slipcase. (Listed in Thomas G. Boss "The Turn of the Century," Catalogue One, and now in a private collection)

R49. **(Mounteney, Leonard)** Rossetti, Dante Gabriel, et.al. *The Germ: Thoughts Towards Nature in Poetry, Literature, and Art. MDCCCL.* (Reprints of Privately Printed Books) 1898. 8vo. (22.8 x 15 cm.). Copy No. 4 of 4 printed on vellum, with proofs of original cover and spine with Ricketts designs bound in. Bound in full orange mahogany morocco signed MOUNTENEY, BINDER. Ornately tooled in gilt with three-color onlays. Spine with gilt dots across raised bands; panels double-rule framed with black onlays between the rules; in the center of each panel is a gilt stem with black onlay leaf, two white rose onlays flank either side of the vertical stem, and a field of dots fills out the space of each panel. Gilt title and box on second panel, gilt publisher/date in box at the foot of the sixth panel; widely spaced gilt dots across head- and tail-caps. Front and back covers ornately gilt decorated in the same fashion with onlays: widely spaced double fillets frame the outer board, deep blue onlay with gilt flower and vine roll-tool, decorative gilt corners. An inner frame of a swirling roll-tool with two more gilt fillets inside that tool. Persian-like central lozenge with deep blue oval center and gilt leaf and stem device in the center; outer part of the lozenge with fourteen white onlays of roses and three black leaves at the top and the bottom. Whole inner panel filled with crisscrossing gilt dot fillets. All board edges with gilt dot fillet. Ornately tooled dentelles. Royal blue moiré silk doublures with matching moiré endpapers. Double-sewn silk head- and tail-bands; a.e.g. Housed in a fleece-lined slipcase. ✤ See Plate 12 on page 371 (Bishop Collection; photography by Joan Broderick)

> R49.1 **(Mounteney, Leonard)** Swinburne, Algernon Charles. *Poems and Ballads.* (Quarto Series) 1903. One of four copies on vellum. Bound in full brown morocco by Mounteney; t.e.g. Bound by Mounteney while in London, and before his work at Lakeside's Donnelley Bindery-Chicago. This binding was in the Norman Strouse Collection (p. 17 of his private catalogue dated August 20, 1970), but its present location is unknown.

> Leonard Mounteney was from Nottingham, England, and served a seven year apprenticeship there with Messrs. G & J. Abbott. He also studied ornamental design at the Battersea Polytechnic, was hired by R. Riviere & Sons of London as an exhibition finisher, and attended several lectures on bookbinding by Cobden-Sanderson. The above book was most likely bound by Mounteney while in London, before he worked as a finisher at the Donnelley Bindery-Chicago under Alfred de Sauty. Mounteney was engaged by Douglas Cockerell for R. R. Donnelley & Sons Company in October 1923, but only started in September 1924. He left a year or so later to work for the Cuneo Fine Binding Studio of Milwaukee, WI (also of Chicago), of which he was the founder, director, director emeritus and consultant (see entry R50).

R50.   **(Mounteney, Leonard - Cuneo Press Bindery)** Schwob, Marcel. *Mimes*. (Miscellaneous Series) 1901. Copy 20 of 50 on Japan vellum, signed by the publisher. Bound in full wine-red morocco (20.8 x 13.5 cm.) signed BOUND BY CUNEO on the lower inside front cover, and MOUNTENEY, FINISHER on the lower inside back cover. Spine with raised bands; gilt lined compartments of black diamonds, dots, and roundels. Front and back covers with an elaborate design of gold tutor roses, diamonds, and blind-tooling; central cross formed by thirteen black diamonds, gilt dots and roundels; t.e.g. Gilt ruled turn-ins, with the Japan vellum covers from the original Mosher edition used as doublures. The Cuneo Press Bindery operated out of Milwaukee, WI. ❀ See Plate 15 on page 372 (Illustrated with permission, Rare Book Department, The Free Library of Philadelphia)

R51.   **(Peller, Hugo)** Morris, William, trans. ***The Story of Amis & Amile***. (Brocade Series) 1899. Bound in full brown morocco (13.2 x 8.9 cm.) signed H. PELLER as stamped on the lower inside of the back cover. Front cover with onlays of red and purple and white forming an abstract design of two entities (representing the two friends, Amis and Amile) linked together and rising from a seven gilt line-and-dot field of 1.5 cm. which wraps across the front cover, across the spine, and then fully across the back cover. Peller's characteristic large gilt mark appears between the two abstract figures. Gilt lettering both across and down the flat spine. Gilt rule along all board edges. Gilt decorated turn-ins of 0.7 cm. Doublures and endpapers of bright red leather with a field of gold dots filling each doublure. Alternating gold and graphite on all page edges. Housed in a brown morocco, hinged box inner-lined with red leather and containing a gilded case attached with a ribbon which activates by "popping up" the book when the case is opened. ❀ See Plate 33 on page 376 (Bishop Collection; photography by Joan Broderick)

> Hugo Peller (b.1917) studied in Strasbourg and began an apprenticeship in 1934. In the 1940's he also studied at the École Estienne in Paris where he was taught finishing by Professor A. Jeanne. Afterwards he became a teacher at the Gewerbeschule, Solothurn until 1967. He is known internationally as an outstanding master teacher and bookbinding artist. His teaching at his bindery in Ascona, Switzerland has produced many outstanding binders, and his work appears in major binding collections throughout the world. Examples of his work are vividly illustrated in Franz Bauman's, et. al., *Der Buchbinder Hugo Peller* (Bern; Stuttgart: Paul Haupt, [1990]).

R52.   **(Powell, Roger)** Burton, Richard F. ***The Kasîdah***. Edited by William Marion Reedy. (Miscellaneous Series) 1905. One of five on vellum. Bound in full blue morocco (32.5 x 25.7 cm.) by Roger Powell in 1974. Gold tooled with a series of perpendicular and slanting lines on both covers with inlays of yellow and green morocco; spine has raised bands with title in gilt. Front pastedown and fly leaf have star pattern which is a symmetrical inversion of the pattern on the book's pastedown and fly leaf in gilt; back pastedown and fly leaf have a pattern of letters in gilt that spell out the title of the work and which, when read in proper order, read: "Bound for Norman and Charlotte Strouse by Roger Powell, The Stade, Foxfield, Petersfield, MCM 74." Housed in a gray cloth box with blue morocco spine lettered in gilt. ❀ See Plate 17 on page 372 (Gift from Norman Strouse to The Bancroft Library; illustrated with permission, shelf mark fTYP AA11 .B9 1905)

> Roger Powell was born in 1896 and came from a family of craftsmen influenced by William Morris and the Arts and Crafts movement. He started bookbinding in 1930 at London's Central School of Arts and Crafts where his instructors included Douglas Cockerell, Peter McLeish and William Mathews. He was a partner in the firm of Douglas Cockerell & Son from 1935-1947. From 1943-1956 Powell was also in charge of bookbinding instruction at the Royal College of Art. He has a fine reputation for rebinding vellum manuscripts, including the world famous *Book of Kells*. Just two years after binding Norman Strouse's copy of the above 1905 *Kasîdah* (originally issued in sheets), Powell received the Order of the British Empire in 1976 for his contributions to the preservation of books. His work is recorded in *Bookbinders in the British Isles*, in *Modern British and French Bindings from the Collection of J.R. Abbey*, and in *The Tradition of Fine Bookbinding in the Twentieth Century*.

R53.   **(Preston, Eleanor)** FitzGerald, Edward. ***Rubáiyát of Omar Khayyám***. (Old World Series)1895. Tall 12mo, full green crushed levant morocco, gilt tooled and inlaid with floral designs in citron, cream, and crimson morocco. Doublures of mauve morocco inlaid and gilt tooled with green, purple, and crimson morocco in grape design; gilt edges (Item No. 411 in the Marsden J. Perry Sale. NY: American Art Association, March 11 & 12, 1936).

R54.   **(Prideaux, Sarah T.)** There are two entries in Miss Prideaux's *A Catalogue of Books Bound by S. T. Prideaux Between MDCCCXC and MDCCCC* (Spring Valley, NY, 1979 reprint of the original London edition) which, though not identified as such, are indeed bindings on Mosher imprints:

> R54.1 PAGE 12 Andrew Lang. *Ballads and Lyrics of Old France with Other Poems.* (Old World Series) 1896. Narrow foolscap octavo. Two copies.

> R54.2 PAGE 13 William Morris. ***The Defence of Guenevere. A Book of Lyrics Chosen from the Works of William Morris.*** (Bibelot Series) 1896. Narrow octavo.

These are the only entries in the whole Prideaux catalogue that are without publisher and place of publication. Prideaux did not wish to incur the wrath of some of England's publishers who were dead set against the Mosher piracies and who backed the ban of the sale of Mosher books in England. Even some of her fellow binders, e.g., Cobden-Sanderson, refused to bind the Mosher imprints (see note under entry 23, Florence Foote). Mosher himself mentioned Prideaux as a binder of his books in the foreword to his 1898 catalogue.

Using Prideaux's notes, Marianne Tidcombe confirms the above entries (R54.1 & R54.2) as being Mosher books. In *Women Bookbinders*, p. 197, Tidcombe identifies *three* copies (No. 101-103) of *Ballads and Lyrics of Old France*, and one copy (No. 140) of *The Defence of Guenevere* as being Mosher imprints.

Prideaux was noted as one the most competent of all women binders in England at the time (having trained under Zaehnsdorf in London and Gruel in Paris) and was the first British woman to really deserve the title of professional bookbinder. Her career spanned from 1888 to 1904. Her bindings have been displayed in numerous exhibitions and are to be found in many major binding collections. She also wrote several books on both historical and contemporary bookbinding. Subsequent research into Prideaux's work (see Marianne Tidcombe's *Women Bookbinders 1880-1920* [Oak Knoll Press & The British Library, 1996, pp. 107 & 109]), however, reveals that her finer work was most likely due to the skill of Lucien Broca (see previous entries R9 & R9.1).

R55   **(Pye, Sybil)** Lang, Andrew, trans. ***Aucassin & Nicolete.*** (Old World Series) 1895. Bound in red goatskin, blind and gold tooled. Bound around 1919.

> This book is recorded by Marianne Tidcombe in her book *Women Bookbinders 1880-1912* (Oak Knoll Press and The British Library, 1996, p. 209, entry No. 30), and is now in a private American collection.

> Sybil Pye was a self-taught British binder who learned her craft from Douglas Cockerell's *Bookbinding and the Care of Books* manual, beginning her career ca. 1906. The influence of the design work of Charles Ricketts is evident in her binding designs. She exhibited regularly from 1910 to about 1946, and is best known for her elaborate curvilinear, architectural designs with the use of inlays and onlays of bright colors. Major Abbey, a noted collector of bookbindings, commissioned many of her bindings which were exhibited in a separate case at the exhibition "Modern English and French Bindings from the Collection of J. R. Abbey..." Her binding career ended in 1955.

R56.   **(Rennie, Silvia)** Fitzgerald, Edward. ***Rubáiyát of Omar Khayyám.*** (Old World Series) 1895. Bound in full blue oasis goatskin (18 x 10 cm.). Oriental-style onlays of gold, black, and blue leathers with multi-colored tooling. Double end bands of gold, red, and green silk. Gold Japanese paper end sheets. Gilt and decorated head edge; fore-edge and tail-edge colored red. (The binding was bought by a Ms. Magerstadt of New York City, but its current location and ownership is unknown)

> R56.1 Other Mosher books bound by Rennie include an unusual dos-a-dos binding of ***The Eclogues*** (now at Princeton) in green morocco with gold and silver leather onlays, pictured on pp. 5-6 in the 1985 catalogue of an exhibit at Kroch's & Brentano's in Chicago.

> R56.2 A copy of ***Immensee*** in quarter vellum over marbled papers, also pictured on pp. 5-6 in the 1985 catalogue of an exhibit at Kroch's & Brentano's in Chicago.

> R56.3 A copy of a Rennie binding on Baudelaire's ***Poems in Prose*** (1909) is pictured in "A. R. A." 2[e] Forum Internatl. De la Reliure d'Art, Bêle, 1990.

The above binding of the *Rubáiyát* is pictured in Ritzenthaler and Spitzmueller's *80 Years Later. [An] 80th Anniversary Exhibition of the Guild of Book Workers* (Washington, D.C.: The Guild of Book Workers, 1986, pp. 152-153). The binder mentions, "I aimed for a sumptuous, jewel-like effect reminiscent of fabulous Oriental tales."

Swiss by birth and British through marriage, Silvia Rennie became a resident of the United States in 1967. She studied under Hugo Peller of Ascona, Switzerland. Now retired from the profession, she operated her studio out of Madison, Wisconsin. Her bindings appear in numerous private and institutional collections.

R57. (S & S) Rossetti, Dante Gabriel. *Hand and Soul.* (Miscellaneous Series) 1899. Small quarto bound in full red morocco (15.4 x 11.2 cm.) with raised bands and gilt tooling on spine and covers. The book has "S&S / 1899" stamped on the spine signifying the collaborators for this binding: Mary Crease Sears who designed the cover, and Agnes St. John who was the binder.

This binding was entry No. 108 in the 1997-98 exhibit, "Inspiring Reform: Boston's Arts & Crafts Movement," held at the Davis Museum and Cultural Center (Wellesley College) from February 28-July 14, 1997 and at the Renwick Gallery of the National Museum of American Art (Smithsonian Institution) from March 6-July 6, 1998. It is also pictured in the exhibit's extensive catalogue assembled under the direction of the consulting curator, Marilee Boyd Meyer (Wellesley, MA: Davis Museum and Cultural Center. Wellesley College; New York: Distributed by Harry M. Abrams, 1997), and is described on pp. 190-91, and color illustrated in Nancy Finlay's chapter on "A Millennium in Book-Making: The Book Arts in Boston," p. [128]. The binding was on loan from the Department of Printing & Graphic Arts at The Houghton Library, Harvard University (the gift of Oliver C. Sheean).

Mary Crease Sears (d.1938) began design studies at the Museum School in Boston, and she also secured lessons from P. S. Sanford of Sanford & Sons Bindery. Sears left for Paris in 1889 and studied under M. Provost, first assistant to Leon Gruel, and also studied gold tooling with Jules Domont. While in Paris she met Agnes St. John who had just completed three years of design work at the school of Industrial Arts in Philadelphia. Together, these two women returned to Boston where they collaborated on many projects, including an entry which received a gold medal award at the 1904 St. Louis Exposition. Sears first exhibited with the Society of Arts & Crafts, Boston (SACB) in 1899 and continued her involvement with the SACB in different capacities throughout her lifetime. She also earned a certificate of Master Craftsman in 1914. She operated her own Sears School of Bookbinding for many years. More information on Sears can be found in Joseph Newman's article, "Mary Crease Sears Rediscovered" in the *Guild of Book Workers Journal*. Vol. XXXIII, No. 1. Spring 1995, pp. 32-51.

R58. (Sangorski & Sutcliffe) Scollard, Clinton. *Lyrics from a Library*. (Lyra Americana Series) 1917. Bound in full Hewit calf by SANGORSKI & SUTCLIFFE as stamped on the front end paper. Spine with five raised bands with gilt dots across each. Gilt roll at top and bottom of each panel; second and third panels with green morocco labels. Covers with double gilt rules around perimeters of boards; gilt title stamped on front cover. Double rules along edge of boards; t.e.g.; gilt turn-ins of 0.8 cm. Mustard and blue woodblock endpapers. White oval leather bookplate of "EMC." (Special Collections, Arizona State University)

The London firm of Sangorski and Sutcliffe was founded in 1901 by Francis Sangorski and George Sutcliffe, both of whom studied under Douglas Cockerell at the London Central School of Arts and Crafts. The firm's reputation was built on ostentatious and elaborate jeweled bindings, but it also produced a wide variety of satisfying leather bindings for the English and American public. Sangorski and Sutcliffe is still considered to be England's leading firm for bookbinding.

A gift book catalogue by Edmund D. Brooks, publisher, bookseller and importer at the Handicraft Guild Building in Minneapolis, MN (ca. 1914), gives some insight into the American import trade for bindings. There are fifteen Mosher books listed on p. 7, along with two full-page illustrations of Sangorski & Sutcliffe bindings on Mosher books. The Old World Series books are listed for $10 each, and the smaller Vest Pocket and Brocade series books in fine bindings are priced at $5 each.

R59. (Sangorski & Sutcliffe) Wilde, Oscar. *The Happy Prince and Other Tales*. Second Edition. (Old World Series) 1911. Bound in full dark brown deerskin (18.2 x 10 cm.) by Sangorski & Sutcliffe for G. M. Millard (a prominent bookseller in Pasadena, CA in the 1920's) with the tipped in statement: "This book is bound in Scotch deer skin, which has been specially tanned and dyed for Messrs. Sangorski and Sutcliffe, of No.

I, Poland Street, London, W.1. Deerskin is a good-looking and durable leather which has rarely been used for bookbinding purposes since the Middle Ages. It has been prepared free from injurious acids and the natural grain preserved. The deer was killed owing to shortage of food during the Great War." The spine has five raised bands with gilt dots atop each, and gilt-decorated panels. The binding is ornately tooled with the covers decorated with a quadruple gilt fillet border framing a field of stylized gilt flower petals interspersed with dots and circles. Board edges with single gilt rule; top page edges gilt. Gilt turn-ins (8 mm.) with three gilt rules; floral designed endpapers. (Gift from Norman Strouse to the Donohue Rare Book Room, Gleeson Library, University of San Francisco)

R60. **(Sangorski & Sutcliffe)** Holmes, Daniel Henry. *Under a Fool's Cap.* Third edition. (Miscellaneous Series) 1914. Bound in full red morocco (18 x 11.5 cm.) by SANGORSKI & SUTCLIFFE; spines with raised bands and double gilt boxed panels; covers decorated with a sextuple gilt fillet border framing a field of hearts and diamonds; front cover has the addition of the title and a fool's cap done in gilt at top. All board edges with single gilt fillet; 9 mm. turn-ins. Marbled end-papers; top page edges gilt. (Gift from Norman Strouse to the Donohue Rare Book Room, Gleeson Library, University of San Francisco)

> This copy bears the inscription to William F. Gable: "Dear Gable: When reading these Songs I can think of only two other Americans–Eugene Field and Whitcomb Riley. Isn't that enough to say of any man that he is worthy of such fellowship? Thomas Bird Mosher March 1916." Gable was owner of the Gable Department Store in Altoona, PA, and was a passionate collector of rare books. He also co-published the facsimile edition of *Leaves of Grass* (1919) with Mosher.

R61. **(Sangorski and Sutcliffe)** DeQuincey, Thomas. *Ann: A Memory.* (Ideal Series of Little Masterpieces) 1908. Bound in full brown crushed levant morocco (14.1 x 9.6 cm.), signed BOUND BY SANGORSKFI AND SUTCLIFFE LONDON. Raised bands with dot on each; thin double gilt fillets in panels. Covers with mixture of gilt fillets and wider blind fillet between the gilt ones. Darts extending from the bands to the covers where each is connected to an inner gilt panel with dots along the box; t.e.g., other edges uncut. Inscribed by a noted book dealer to a noted collector: "William F. Gable, a gift from George D. Smith, New York, Christmas, 1913." (Gift from Norman Strouse to the Donohue Rare Book Room, Gleeson Library, University of San Francisco)

> This book was exhibited in the 1967 "An Exhibition of Books from the Press of Thomas Bird Mosher from the Collection of Norman H. Strouse" held at The Free Library of Philadelphia.

R62. **(Sangorski and Sutcliffe)** Wilde, Oscar. *Poems in Prose.* (Ideal Series of Little Masterpieces) 1906. Bound in full cerulean blue calfskin (14.2 x 9.6 cm.) by SANGORSKI AND SUTCLIFFE, with simple gilt fillet, inner gilt dentelles; t.e.g. With pencil inscription by Mosher: "In just these few things Oscar will live when much else has 'gone into the waste of time' TBM" (Gift from Norman Strouse to the Donohue Rare Book Room, Gleeson Library, University of San Francisco)

R63. **(Sauty, Alfred de)** Guérin, Maurice de. *The Centaur and the Bacchante.* Translated by Lucie Page. (Brocade Series) 1897. Bound in full green crushed morocco; spine with the title in descending letters; covers with a formal design of five parallel stems curving from a common source with each terminating in a flower suggestive of a thistle blossom; wide turn-ins with repetition of tools used on the cover, and with the binder's signature. (The John Work Garrett Library of The Johns Hopkins University)

> This binding was part of the groundbreaking Walters Art Gallery binding exhibition held at the Baltimore Museum of Art from November 12, 1957 to January 12, 1958. It is entry No. 583 in *The History of Bookbinding 525-1950 A.D.* (Baltimore: The Walters Art Gallery, 1957, p. 231).

> De Sauty trained for a couple years with Rivière in London, set up on his own, and later on made designs for The Hampstead Bindery. He taught at the London County Council School of Arts and Crafts until he came to the United States around 1908. De Sauty became manager of the R. R. Donnelley Bindery of Chicago in 1923.

R64. **(Scheer, Bruno)** Rossetti, Dante Gabriel *The Blessed Damozel.* Second edition. (Miscellaneous Series) 1902. Bound in red morocco gilt, wide border on covers incorporating the first eight lines of the poem around both covers; paneled spine; a.e.g., slipcase, by Bruno Scheer of Berlin. (Library of John Roland Abbey, and now at The Bancroft Library)

R65.   (Schultz, Otto) *A Little Garland of Celtic Verse.* (Lyric Garland Series) 1905. Bound in full green crushed morocco (17.5 x 11.5 cm.) signed •BOUND BY OTTO SCHULTZ & Cº EDINBURGH• Spine with raised bands, gilt ruled compartments with shamrock in center of each panel. Single gilt fillet around perimeters of covers. Gilt fillet on board edges; t.e.g. Gilt decorated turn-ins. Front cover with a field of shamrocks interspersed with dots and a title at the top of the cover within a gilt rectangle. Ex Libris of John McCormack. (Gift from Norman Strouse to the Donohue Rare Book Room, Gleeson Library, University of San Francisco)

R66.   (Steburdess) Rossetti, Dante Gabriel. ***Ballads and Sonnets.*** (Quarto Series) 1903. Copy No. 3 of 4 on vellum. Bound in full brown crushed morocco (23.1 x 18.5 cm.) with the stamp: BOUND BY [owl mark] STEBURDESS. Spine with raised bands and gilt across each. Gilt tooling within panels. Cover with triple fillets and inner frame; 1.2 cm. gilt decorated turn-ins; vellum pastedowns and end papers. Slipcase in cloth. (Gift from Norman Strouse to the Donohue Rare Book Room, Gleeson Library, University of San Francisco)

R67.   (Strouse, Charlotte A.) FitzGerald, Edward. ***Polonius: A Collection of Wise Saws and Modern Instances.*** 1901. One of 450 copies. Bound in full burnt orange morocco with gilt top edges and insert leather design.

> This binding is listed as entry no. 33 in Norman Strouse's exhibition catalogue, *Ladies in My Library–Books and Letters from the Collection of Norman H. Strouse.* (Philadelphia, PA: The Free Library of Philadelphia. 1968, p. 33). Charlotte Strouse was the wife of the noted Mosher collector, Norman Strouse, who referred to his wife as "my favorite binder" and adding that "my most expensive bindings come from that captive atelier." Other examples of her work (signed C.A.S.) are in the Mosher Collection at the Donohue Rare Book Room, Gleeson Library, University of San Francisco.

R68.   (Toof & Co.) Lathrop, George Parsons. ***The Casket of Opals*::: (Privately Printed Books) 1900. Copy No. 6 of 15 printed on Roman vellum. Bound in elaborately decorated full green crushed morocco (19 x 14.3 cm.) by "Toof & Co." of Memphis, TN. The spine has five raised bands with gilt lined compartments; white onlays of violets in center of each compartment with curved gilt lines and dots filling the space; title/author in the second panel while the date is near the tale of the spine. Covers with gilt rule around perimeter and filled-in with an elaborate design of gilt leaves and tendrils and flower onlays of red and white violets and large stylized five-point red flowers; the book's title is framed in the center of the front cover only (back frame blank). All board edges single gilt rule interrupted with gilt roundels. Full leather doublures with outer frame in dark green and inner panel in light green matching the moiré endpapers; uses same tools from the covers with white, red, and purple violets; t.e.g. The first leaf of text is printed with a Chiswick drop cap and a full Ricketts-style border of leaves, vines and flowers. The border is hand-illuminated with purple, white, red and yellow violets, leaves are shaded in greens, and the vines are of burnished gold. The drop cap is also illuminated. Tipped in is a three page A.L.S. from G. P. Lathrop to Stoddart, the publisher, in which Lathrop discusses his plays. Enclosed in a full leather solander case.
✿ See Plate 27 on page 375 (Gift from Norman Strouse to the Donohue Rare Book Room, Gleeson Library, University of San Francisco; illustrated with permission)

> This copy appears in the book sale catalogue for Victor Thrane of Chicago (New York: American Art Association, April 14 & 15, 1926).

> At the Houghton Library there is a letter dated October 31, 1898 from Otto Zahn to Mosher (No. 1638) with twenty-seven photographs of bindings on Mosher books (twenty-six covers and one doublure). The titles identified from the pictures are: from the Old World Series *Helen of Troy* (two copies), *Sonnets from the Portuguese, Sylvie,* the *Rubáiyát, The Kasîdah, The Sonnets of Michael Angelo, Aucassin and Nicolete* (three different copies), *Félise, The New Life of Dante Alighieri,* and *Ballads and Lyrics of Old France* (two copies). Bindings on The Bibelot Series include *Long Ago, The Defense of Guenevere* and the *Rubáiyát* (1894). Bindings on books from the Brocade Series are *The Hollow Land, The Story of Cupid and Psyche,* and *The Story of Amis and Amile.* There are also: *Father Damien* (Reprints from "The Bibelot"), *Essays from the "Guardian"* (Reprints of Privately Printed Books), *In Praise of Omar* (Miscellaneous Series), *From the Upanishads* (Misc. Series), and a sample binding on one of the bound volumes of *The Bibelot.* All these bindings represent a wide array of styles ranging from art nouveau to more Grolieresque designs.

In yet another letter at the Houghton dated April 27, '97 (No. 1638a), Zahn tells Mosher he has sent ten copies of Old World Series books "to the Nashville Centennial, put up in elaborate art bindings. I bought the books from the Mansford Co. here." He further remarks, "I also have bound some of your editions for booklovers in San Francisco, Cal. and Minneapolis, Minn. The prices of the bindings you saw at the Grolier Club are as follows: Sylvie: $30.00 The Kasidah $27.00. All the others: $20.00. I will be glad to dress your beautiful editions in a garb befitting their worth, should you chose to entrust me with them." Mosher highly prized Zahn's work and recommended the Toof & Co. to some of his more special customers (see the introduction to this "Section IV" on bindings, and entry R70 below).

Otto Zahn apprenticed under T. A. Franke in Arnstadt, Germany (ca. 1872-73) and also spent a year developing his skills in fine binding at the Zaehnsdorf bindery in London. Zahn came to America in 1883 and in one year he permanently settled in Memphis, Tennessee. He went to work with S. C. Toof & Co. around 1884, eventually becoming foreman and then, in 1918, president of the company until his death in 1928. The Toof firm and Otto Zahn were highly respected by Mosher who indicated "...I believe he [Otto Zahn] is without an equal on this side the waters." –Mosher to Grigsby ALs, March 21, 1898, p.2. More information on Zahn and photos of some of the Toof bindings can be found in Don Etherington's article, "Will the Real Otto Zahn Please Stand Up?" in the *Guild of Book Workers Journal*. Vol. XXXIII, No. 1. Spring 1995, pp. 21-31.

R69. **(Toof & Co.)** Field, Michael. *Underneath the Bough, A Book of Verses.* (Old World Series) 1898. Binding of full green, highly polished crushed morocco (18 x 10 cm.) signed S. C. TOOF & CO. ZAHN at the foot of the front inside cover. Front cover with gilt art nouveau flower and vine motif, including dragonflies on the front cover and on the compartments of the spine. (Bishop Collection)

This book was shown at the 1992 "Thomas Bird Mosher and the Art of the Book" Exhibit at Temple University.

R70. **(Toof & Co.)** Symonds, John Addington. *Wine, Women and Song.* (Reprints of Privately Printed Books) 1899. Copy No. 2 of 50 on Japan vellum. Binding in full crimson super-extra crushed levant (19 x 14.6 cm.); raised bands with floriated spine panels decorated with gilt vines, flower, leaves and onlays. Front and back covers strikingly decorated with a central nouveau panel of vines, tendrils, and flowers (with small gold hearts between lines) all emanating from an onlaid dark-brown heart and green leaves. The central panel is placed on what appears to be the lines of a far larger leaf whose veins radiate beyond the far reaches of the cover. Elaborately gilt decorated turn-ins with a central moiré doublure and matching red silk endpapers. ✳ See Plate 32 on page 376 (Illustrated with permission, Rare Book Department, The Free Library of Philadelphia)

This binding (along with a binding on *The Bibelot* for 1899 "in chaudron super-extra crushed levant, inlaid in white, brown, and bluish gray") was "among those which won the highest award at the Pan-American Exposition, Buffalo, NY, May 1-Nov.1, 1901." It was originally bound for Mrs. Gertrude Cowdin (Mosher had privately printed *The Casket of Opals* for her).

Also according to Briggs, "In 1884 Otto Zahn came to the United States and established himself in Memphis, Tennessee, where he is now a member of the firm of S. C. Toof & Company. Examples of his work were shown at the Pan-American Exposition and obtained the highest award."
–*Twentieth Century Cover Design* (Plymouth, MA: Briggs & Briggs, 1902), pp. 23 and [74]

R71. **(Toof & Co.)** Pater, Walter. *Marius the Epicurean-His Sensations and Ideas.* (Quarto Series) 1900. Two volumes bound in one, each being copy No. 3 of 4 on Roman vellum. Bound in full mauve morocco (22.3 x 17.8 cm.) signed TOOF & CO. at foot of inner front doublure. Covers with rich art nouveau design of gilt-tooled roses and vines. Gilt inner dentelles and silk doublures. Housed in a specially designed, full black morocco clamshell case with blind- and gilt-tooling signed 19 SAN 94 (S. A. Neff, Jr., a bookbinder in Sewickley, PA). ✳ See Plate 26 on page 374 (Bishop Collection; photography by Joan Broderick)

This binding is illustrated as exhibition binding No. 8 in Otto Zahn's monograph *On Art Binding*, prepared for the 1904 Louisiana Purchase Exposition at St. Louis. In this same monograph Zahn also displays Mosher's *An Italian Garden* (binding No. 4), "...one of Thomas B. Mosher's beautiful publications, bound in myrtle-green crushed levant, mirror-polished and exquisitely hand-tooled; designed and bound by Toof & Co., Memphis." The book was also shown at the 1992 "Thomas Bird Mosher and the Art of the Book" Exhibit at Temple University, and is illustrated in the exhibit catalogue on p. 101 (#56).

R72   **(Truslove and Hanson)** Rossetti, Dante Gabriel. *The Blessed Damozel.* (Miscellaneous Series) 1905. Bound in full dark blue crushed morocco (14 x 13 cm.) with front cover design, signed TRUSLOVE AND HANSON 8 SLOAN STREET. The front cover's art nouveau design consists of seven stars, four leaves, and three lilies all incorporated into an overall tree-like structure with gilt fillets around the perimeter of the front and back covers. Spine with two raised bands, panels gilt ruled in outline, and title longitudinally gilt-stamped. Blue endpapers; t.e.g. (Special Collections, Carnegie Mellon University)

R73.   **(Ullman, Charlotte)** Fitzgerald, Edward. *Rubáiyát of Omar Khayyám.* (Reprints of Privately Printed Books) 1902. Copy No. 9 of 10 on vellum. Binding signed C. M. ULLMAN 1969 in full light brown morocco (21.5 x 17.5 cm.), beautifully gold-tooled upper and lower covers with triple fillets and triple elongated fleur-de-lys at each corner, and elaborate gold tooled doublures (gilt stamped turn-ins of 1.5 cm.) in two colors of leather; inner panel with a field of the same elongated fleur-de-lys. Spine with raised bands, gilt ruling across the bands and flanking the bands with three fleur-de-lys in panels. Gilt rule along board edges; t.e.g. Feather marbled endpapers. Quarter leather and cloth case. (Gift from Norman Strouse to the Donohue Rare Book Room, Gleeson Library, University of San Francisco)

   This work was commissioned by Norman Strouse, and was completed in March 1969.

   Charlotte Ullman studied binding with Kathryn and Gerhard Gerlach and first practiced binding part-time with Jacques Nosco in New York City. She later set up her own studio and was hired by one of her clients, The Pierpont Morgan Library. In 1963 she was awarded a Ford Foundation grant and her travel and work abroad included work with colleagues in Toulouse, at the Bibliothèque Nationale and at the Ecole Estienne in France. She also worked with Roger Powell and Sidney Cockerell, and at the British Museum.

R74.   **(Utley, Elizabeth M.)** Rossetti, Dante Gabriel. *The Blessed Damozel.* (Miscellaneous Series) 1901. Square 8vo. Exhibition binding in full dark navy morocco (14.5 x 13.5 cm.) and signed on lower inside rear cover: E• M• U•–1906. Spine with raised bands and stars intertwining from the top to the bottom of the spine. Gilt drop-title in second panel; date at bottom. Front and back covers with outer double gilt-ruled box with stars between the rules. Green onlays of 2.4 cm. flanking either side of a central panel of a field of gold stars; onlays have three long vertical stems with leaves and terminating in a flower at top. Title in gilt at lower part of inner box; rear cover without the title but with an extension of a field of gold stars. Gilt rule along far edges of the boards; 1.3 cm. gilt decorated turn-ins with stars between two widely separated rules. Blue marbled endpapers; a.e.g. ❦ See Plate 22 on page 374 (Bishop Collection; photography by Joan Broderick)

   This binding was exhibited along with seventy-three others in the Guild's first exhibition at the old Tiffany Studios, 333 Fourth Avenue, New York City. Later the book was also shown in The Art Society of Pittsburgh's Exhibit of Artistic Industries at the Carnegie Institute in 1912, and at the Associated Artists of Pittsburgh's (Crafts Group) annual exhibition at the Carnegie Institute Galleries in 1935. It was also most recently exhibited by the Craftsman Farms Foundation in their exhibit "Women's Work: The Role of Women in the Arts and Crafts Movement," July 7 - Oct. 6, 1996. The greater majority of the Utley bindings are at the Mariam Coffin Canaday Library, Bryn Mawr College (Utley-Thomas' alma mater), including nearly all her training bindings.

   This binding was executed by Elizabeth Minerva Utley (later Mrs. Isaac B. Thomas) of Pittsburgh under the supervision of Euphemia Bakewell who, in turn, trained under England's master-binder, T. J. Cobden-Sanderson. Utley's closest friend, Rachael McMasters Hunt, also trained under Bakewell. All three women became charter members of the newly formed Guild of Bookworkers (1906) and were listed as professional bookbinders. Utley also corresponded with Cobden-Sanderson, and met with him when he visited America.

R75.   **(Verburg, Peter)** Walter Pater. *The Child in the House An Imaginary Portrait.* (Brocade Series) 1902. Bound in royal blue morocco (ca. 13.5 x 9 cm.) with both covers having double rule gilt borders, elaborate stylized floral gilt designs at each corner with onlaid brown leaves and two gilt panels intersecting the floral designs. Gilt lettering on the front cover along the perimeter and between gilt fillets. Spine with raised bands and six gilt compartments; a.e.g. Corner of inner dentelles with stylized floral gilt designs with green and red onlaid leaves. Back cover is signed "P.V. 1903." (Edward D. Nudelman Catalogue Sixteen)

Peter Verburg was the protégé of the Chicago binder, Ellen Gates Starr, who trained directly under Cobden-Sanderson. Verburg further trained with Douglas Cockerell in England for six months, and upon return "entered into partnership" with Starr in 1902 (Hull House semi-annual bulletin, Vol. 5, #2). He departed sometime around 1904 and set up a business in "Fine-Binding in Special Designs" in Boston, doing work for Scribner's and for D. B. Updike of the Merrymount Press. Around 1912 he moved to New York City. A photo of Verburg with Ellen Gates Starr is found in Marianne Tidcombe's *Women Bookbinders 1880-1920* (Newcastle, DE: Oak Knoll Press, and London: The British Library, 1996, p. 184).

R76. **(Walter, Florence)** Dowson, Ernest. ***The Poems of Ernest Dowson.*** (Miscellaneous Series) 1902. One of four printed on vellum, signed by Mosher. Bound in purple morocco (19 x 14.5 cm.), with sunburst design from center on inset red circles with leather chemise and case, by Florence Walters. (Gift from Norman Strouse to the Donohue Rare Book Room, Gleeson Library, University of San Francisco)

This binding was executed in 1955 by Florence Walters, an outstanding binder of San Francisco, who studied bookbinding in San Francisco and Paris. It was shown in the "Ladies in My Library" exhibit (entry 30) during fall 1968 at The Free Library of Philadelphia. This exhibition included books and letters from the collection of Norman H. Strouse, as well as several bindings (including one binding on Mosher's *Polonius: A Collection of Wise Saws*) by Charlotte A. Strouse, the wife of the collector (see R67 above). A similar binding in full brown morocco also appears in The Bancroft Library.

R77. **(Yerkes, Lawrence)** Mead, Marian, trans. ***The Pearl. An English Vision-Poem of the Fourteenth Century Done into Modern Verse...*** (Old World Series) 1908. Bound in full light brown oasis goatskin with five raised bands: blind-tooled title on spine; blind-tooled bands forming darts extending onto the covers; each dart culminates in a roundel. Front and back boards with an overall blind-tooled diaper pattern forming a grid of diamonds all enclosed within a vertical rectangular box. (In the binder's private collection)

Yerkes is a book conservator and binder in Iowa City, Iowa, and apprenticed under William Anthony (see discussion under R3) at the University of Iowa Conservation Department. He has been binding for the past ten years as a member of the Guild of Bookworkers. Yerkes has bound several Mosher books, including the Vest Pocket Series *Aucassin and Nicolete* (1903) in green goatskin with onlays, and a copy of the Brocade Series *Gertha's Lovers* (1905) in limp vellum with alum tawed goatskin ties.

R78. **(Young, Belle McMurtry)** Burton, Sir Richard F. ***The Kasîdah.*** Edited by William Marion Reedy. (Miscellaneous Series) 1905. One of 125 copies printed on Van Gelder paper. Bound in full blue morocco (33.3 x 26 cm.) with color onlays in floral pattern, and blind-tooling on front and back covers. Blue silk panels on inside front and back covers, within inlaid borders. Marbled free end-papers; t.e.g. Housed in a custom box of purple Chinese silk and lined with purple satin. (Heller Rare Book Room, Olin Library, Mills College in Oakland, CA)

> R78.1 Whitman, Walt. *Memories of President Lincoln*, 1912. Bound in full maroon levant morocco (30.3 x 22.7 cm.) with color onlays forming a leaf pattern, and gilt tooling of concentric frames on front and back covers. Marbled end-papers, t.e.g.

Belle McMurtry Young (1875-1943) was a Bay Area bookbinder and instructor. She trained with Octavia Holden in San Francisco and in France with Rose Adler, Henri Houlhac, Adolphe Cuzin, and Emile Maylander. She was a charter member of the Guild of Book Workers and her work was represented in their 75th Anniversary Exhibit in 1981.

R79. **(Young, Henry & Sons)** Pater, Walter. ***Essays from the "Guardian."*** Second edition. (Miscellaneous Series) 1898. Three-quarter crushed brown morocco signed HENRY YOUNG & SONS, LIVERPOOL whose stamp appears at the top of the first free endpaper; light marbled paper boards. Spine with five raised bands with gilt dots across each, and gilt floral decorations (central bloom with a bud on either side) in panels one and panels four to six; the second and third panels contain the title and author; all panels gilt boxed; date gilt boxed at bottom. Original book's blue paper spine bound in at rear. (Special Collections, Arizona State University)

R80. **(Zaehnsdorf)** Hay, John. *In Praise of Omar*. (Miscellaneous Series) 1898. Limited to 925 copies printed on Van Gelder paper, signed BOUND BY ZAEHNSDORF 1898 in full green crushed morocco (14.9 x 11.9 cm.), gilt decorated, silk doublures, original wrappers bound in; covers with twelve gilt boxes nested within one another. With the bookplate of Pearl Craigie (John Oliver Hobbes), and a note indicating it was bought from the London book dealer, Ifan Kyrle Fletcher. (Gift from Norman Strouse to the Donohue Rare Book Room, Gleeson Library, University of San Francisco)

> This long-standing British firm was founded by Joseph Zaehnsdorf in 1842 and was widely renowned for its fine bindings. The son of the founder, Joseph William Zaehnsdorf, directed the firm while his father still lived, and continued it after his father's death in 1886. By the turn of the century Joseph William Zaehnsdorf was considered by many to be the leading English binder, and he authored the influential *The Art of Bookbinding* (1880), a standard textbook for novice binders and apprentices. The bindery continued under the founder's grandson, Ernest, who oversaw the operations until 1945. *Note:* This copy contains two manuscript corrections to the text, one altering a misprint, the other changing "pouring" on p.8 to "frowning".

R81. **(Zaehnsdorf)** Field, Michael. *Underneath the Bough. A Book of Verses*. (Old World Series) 1898. Full black morocco (17.6 x 9.6 cm.) signed BOUND BY ZAEHNSDORF with richly gilt-tooled covers with field of tulip and leafy vines all within a single gilt-fillet surrounding the perimeter; matching gilt-tooled spine also with gilt-fillet around the whole spine. Turn-ins of 1 cm. tooled with leaf ornaments. Fine double gilt fillet on all board edges. Marbled endpapers; a.e.g. Special Zaehnsdorf gilt oval medallion mark on inside of rear cover denoting a superior binding. ❧ See Plate 6 on page 370 (Bishop Collection; photography by Joan Broderick)

> This binding was photo-illustrated in Boss's *The Turn of the Century*, 1993, opposite p. 217, item 131.

R82. **(Zaehnsdorf)** Swinburne, Charles. *Atalanta in Calydon*. (Old World Series) 1897. Copy No. 21 of 100 on Japan vellum. Bound in full tan crushed levant morocco (17.9 x 10 cm.) by Zaehnsdorf (dated 1902) with a stunning art nouveau design of lilies, poppies, leaves and twining tendrils on the front cover, heightened with pointillé above each flower; all within a widely spaced double gilt fillet. Back cover replicating (in reverse) the lower portion of the front cover's design. Spine with raised bands and gilt-stamped floral designs. Tan silk doublures; t.e.g.; uncut. Oval medallion mark in blind on inside rear cover, signifying a superior binding by this firm. Bookplate of F. T. Hubbard (also see entries R9, 30 and 33). Enclosed in a faux tortoise shell board slipcase. ❧ See Plate 10 on page 370 (Bishop Collection; photography by Joan Broderick)

R83. **(Zaehnsdorf)** William Blake. *XVII Designs to Thornton's Virgil*. (Miscellaneous Series) 1989. Full crushed brown morocco (25.9 x 17 cm.) marked BOUND BY ZAEHNSDORF at foot of inner front cover; with special oval medallion mark on inside of rear cover denoting a superior binding. Classical gilt tooling around the perimeter of the covers; gilt tooling across the spine's wide raised bands with floral motifs used in the compartments. Gilt turn-ins (1.2 cm.) with silk endpapers. Fine double-gilt rules along all board edges; t.e.g. Striking art nouveau bookplate of Alexandra Helen Murray Baillie. (Bishop Collection)

ADDENDUM

R84. **(The Knickerbocker Press)** Arnold, Matthew. *Empedocles on Etna*. (Miscellaneous Series) 1900. One of fifty copies on Japan vellum. Bound in full green crushed French levant (22.3 x 15.6 cm.) with G. P. PUTNAM'S SONS stamped on the inside front cover, and THE KNICKERBOCKER PRESS stamped on the inside of the back cover. Elaborate gold-tooled design with red, brown, and white onlays on both covers and the spine. Each cover with central red, octagonal cartouche of scalloped edges within which a brown, almond shaped quadriform and leaves and stems appear; outer rectilinear and curvilinear gold tooling with four red and white flowers; single gilt fillet along board perimeters. Richly gilt-tooled spine with onlays; double gilt rule along all board edges; t.e.g. Wide turn-ins (2.5 cm.) tooled to resemble portions of the outer binding. Cloudy red, green and purple doublures of marbled paper with matching endpapers. (Bishop Collection)

> Little is known of The Knickerbocker Press' in-house bindery and its personnel. It apparently operated out of New York City or New Rochelle, NY around the turn of the century into the twentieth century, and many of its bindings carry both the stamps of G. P. Putnam's Sons and The Knickerbocker Press. That they were

capable of very fine work is evidenced by the Art Nouveau binding on Maria Francesca Rossetti's *A Shadow of Dante* (London, 1871), which appears as entry 34 in Christie's November 9, 1990 catalogue, "The Chevalier Collection of English Twentieth-Century Bookbindings..." They seemed to have borrowed many of their design motifs from Prideaux, Doves, Rivière, and other English binderies.

OTHER BINDERS RECORDED

The following binders have applied quarter, half, three-quarter, or full bindings to Mosher books. Since the bindings examined are not as significant as the full leather bindings mentioned above, but still represent skillful and respectable work, their makers are listed below. It is altogether possible that they did finer work on Mosher books, but such has not been seen in the collections examined.

John P. Gray & Son, Ltd., Cambridge, England.
The Rose Bindery of Boston, MA
P. B. Sanford
J. W. Meyers
Elizabeth B. Bruce
W. Roach of New York
Bogardus of the Huntington Library
Root & Son
Stikeman & Co. of New York City
Hatchards in Picadilly, England
The Harvard Co-operative Society, Cambridge, MA
True Love and Hanson   S. Sloan St. W.
Smith, Binder
Bayntun. Binder. Bath, England
A. Casciani - Roma
E • I • v • S - 1919
J. MacDonald–Binder, New York
Stanley Clifford, Deer Isle, Maine
Grabau, John F. (binder for the Roycrofters)
Ramage of London
Gruel of Paris
W. B. O. Field
William Anthony
Hazel Dreis
Scroll Club of New York
Otto Schultz (on *An Idyl of First Love*)
Stern & Dess
L. Averill Cole (Mrs. Howland) did full leather bindings for Wm. F. Gable in
   Altoona, PA.

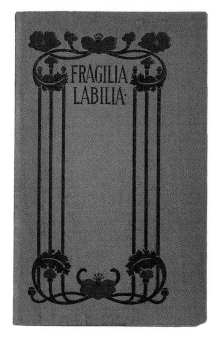

Plate 1
Cover of *Fragilia Labilia,* 1902
(B116)

Plate 2
Cover of *Fancy's Following,* 1900
(B106)

Plate 3
Cover of *Primavera,* 1900
(B311)

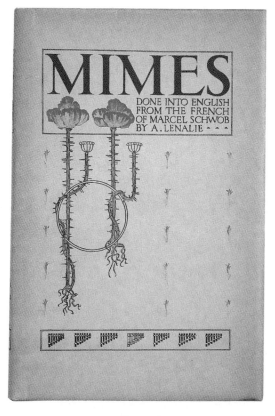

Plate 4
Cover of *The Story of David Gray,* 1900 (B386)

Plate 5
Cover of *Mimes,* 1901 (B242)

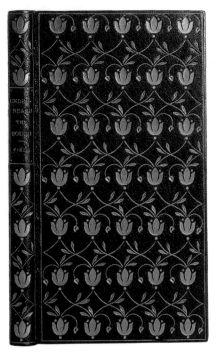

Plate 6
Michael Field's *Underneath the Bough,*
1898 (R81) Bound by Zaehnsdorf
(17.6 x 9.6 cm.)

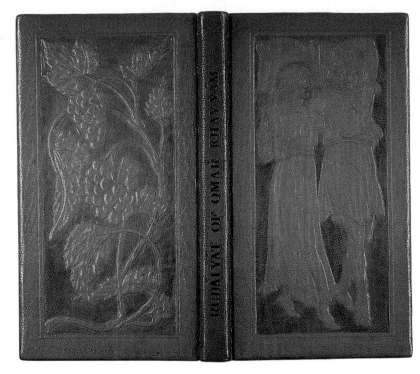

Plate 7
Edward FitzGerald's *Rubáiyát of Omar Khayyám,* 1897 (R27)
Bound by Miss Gaskell of the Guild of Women-Binders (18 x 10 cm.)

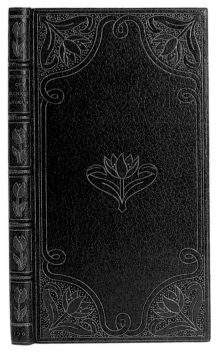

Plate 8
J. A. Symonds, trans., *The Sonnets of
Michael Angelo,* 1901 (R9)
Bound by Lucien Broca
(18 x 10 cm.)

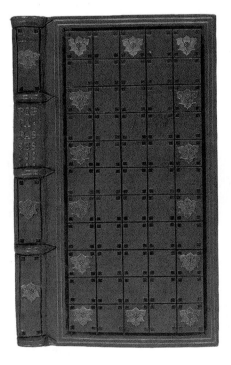

Plate 9
Robert Browning's *Pippa Passes,*
1908 (R34.3)
Bound by Rachel MacMasters Miller
Hunt (17.7 x 10 cm.)

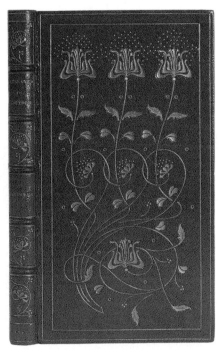

Plate 10
A. C. Swinburne's *Atalanta in
Calydon,* 1897 (R82)
Bound by Zaehnsdorf
(17.9 x 10 cm.)

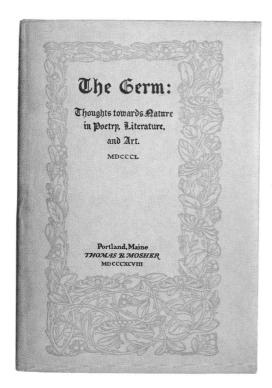

Plate 11
Cover of *The Germ,* 1898 (B132)

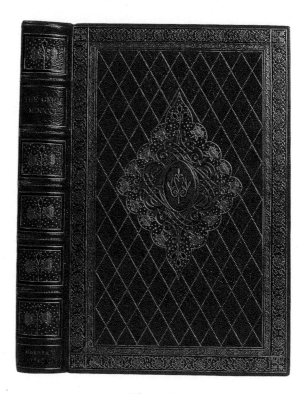

Plate 12
D. G. Rossetti, et al, *The Germ,* 1898 (R49)
Bound by Leonard Mounteney (22.8 x 15 cm.)

Plate 13
D. G. Rossetti, et al, *The Germ,* 1898 (R29)
Bound by P. A. Savoldelli for the Hampstead Bindery
(23.3 x 15.8 cm.)

Plate 14
D. G. Rossetti, et al, *The Germ,* 1898 (R26)
Bound by the Guild of Women-Binders (23.5 x 16.2 cm.)

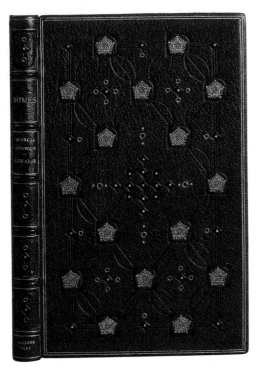

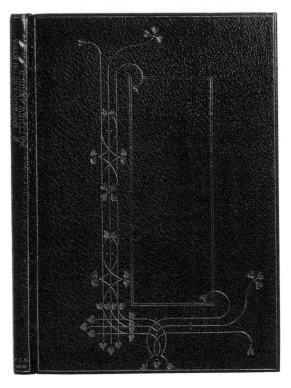

Plate 15
Marcel Schwob's *Mimes,* 1901 (R50)
Bound by Leonard Mounteney-Cuneo Press Bindery
(20.8 x 13.5 cm.)

Plate 16
Matthew Arnold's *Empedocles on Etna,* 1900 (R33)
Bound by F. T. Hubbard (22.6 x 15.7 cm.)

Plate 17
Richard Burton's *The Kasîdah,* 1905 (R52)
Bound by Roger Powell (32.5 x 25.7 cm.)

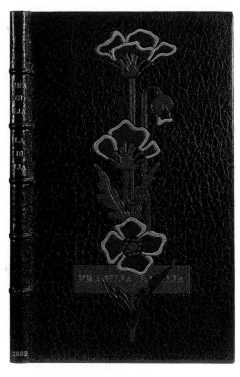

Plate 18
J. A. Symonds' *Fragilia Labilia,* 1902 (R12)
Bound by The Club Bindery, Léon Maillard–finisher
(19.4 x 11.6 cm.)

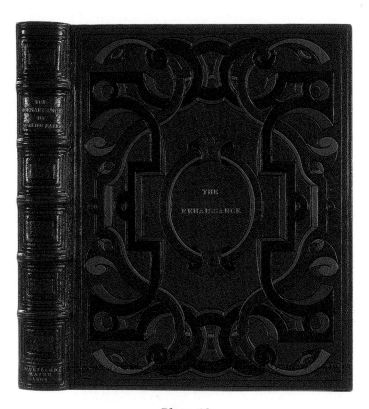

Plate 19
Walter Pater's *The Renaissance,* 1902 (R13)
Bound by The Club Bindery (22 x 18 cm.)

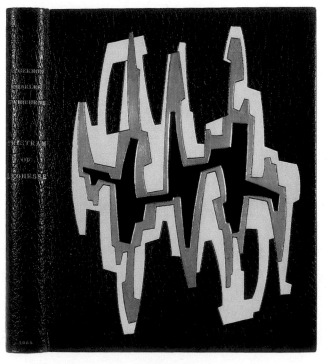

Plate 20
A. C. Swinburne's *Tristram of Lyonesse,* 1904 (R6)
Bound by Micheline de Bellefroid (22.3 x 18 cm.)

Plate 21
A. C. Swinburne's *Tristram of Lyonesse,* 1904 (R15)
Bound by The Club Bindery (22.3 x 18 cm.)

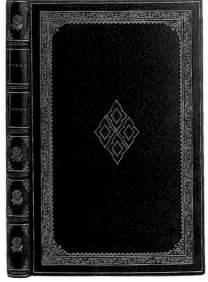

Plate 22
D. G. Rossetti's
The Blessed Damozel,
1901 (R74) Bound by
Elizabeth M. Utley
(14.5 x 13.5 cm.)

Plate 23
Marcel Schwob's
Mimes, 1901 (R1)
Bound by The
Adams Bindery
(20.5 x 13.3 cm.)

Plate 24
D. G. Rossetti's *Poems,* 1902 (R4)
Bound by George Baer at the Cuneo Press Bindery (22.3 x 18.2 cm.)

Plate 25
A. C. Swinburne's *Laus Veneris,* 1899 (R43)
Bound by The Monastery Hill Bindery (22.7 x 18.2 cm.)

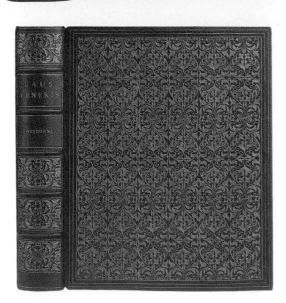

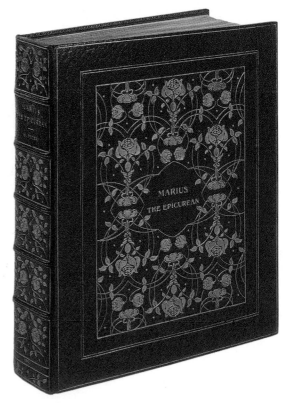

Plate 26
Walter Pater's
*Marius the
Epicurean,*
1900 (R71)
Bound by Toof
and Co. under
Otto Zahn
(22.3 x 17.8 cm.)

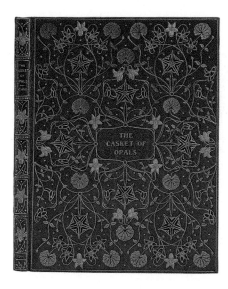

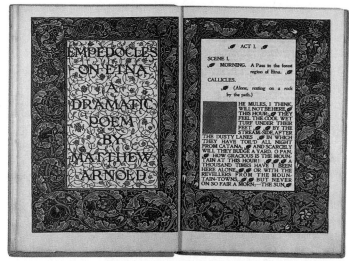

Plate 27
George Lathrop's
*The Casket of
Opals,* 1900
(R68) Bound by
Toof and Co.
under Otto Zahn
(19 x 14.3 cm.)

Plate 28
Matthew Arnold's *Empedocles on Etna,* 1900 (R37)
Hand-illuminated by Bertha Avery

Plate 29
Oscar Wilde's *Poems in Prose,* 1906 (R38)
Hand-illuminated by Clara Chipman Newton

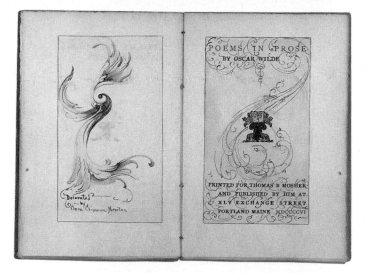

Plate 30
Richard Burton's *The Kasîdah,* 1905 (R39)
Hand-illuminated by "E.M.S."

Plate 31
Edward FitzGerald's *Rubáiyát of Omar Khayyám,* 1911 (R36)
Pochoir cover by William Cushing Bamburgh

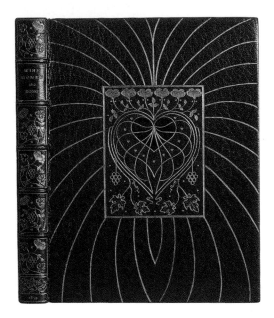

Plate 32
J. A. Symonds, trans.,
Wine Women and Song, 1899 (R70)
Bound by Otto Zahn of Toof & Co.
(19 x 14.6 cm.)

Plate 33
William Morris, trans., *The Story of Amis & Amile*, 1899 (R51)
Case and binding by Hugo Peller (13.2 x 8.9 cm.)

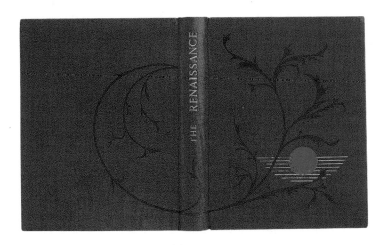

Plate 34
Walter Pater's *The Renaissance*, 1902 (R21)
Bound by Bruce Plumley of the Eddington Bindery (22.5 x 17.7 cm.)

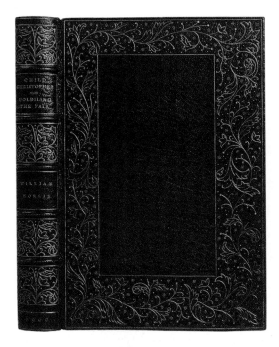

Plate 35
William Morris' *Child Christopher and
Goldilind the Fair*, 1900 (R30)
Bound at the Harcourt Bindery
(23.7 x 16.7 cm.)

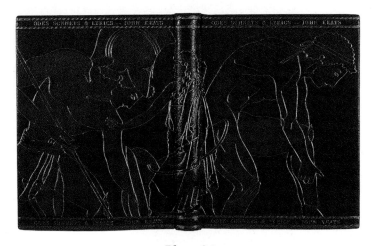

Plate 36
John Keats' *Odes Sonnets and Lyrics*, 1924 (R41)
Bound by Jamie Kamph at the Stonehouse Bindery (18.4 x 14.5 cm.)

Section V

STATEMENTS, REVIEWS, AND
MEMORIAL TRIBUTES TO MOSHER

EARLY REVIEWS

A NOD FROM AMERICA'S MASTER PRINTER

I am well pleased with your book [*Modern Love*]. The composition and press work are well done...

I have to thank you for your kind remembrance in the gift of the "City of Dreadful Night." It is a very good bit of book-making.

> The first comment by Theodore Low DeVinne was taken from "Opinions of Bibliophiles" gathered and printed by Mosher in fall 1892. DeVinne was the preeminent master printer in America, founder of the DeVinne Press in New York City, and esteemed author and member of the Grolier Club. The second quote is taken from a letter to Mosher from DeVinne dated Jan. 12, 1892 (Bishop Collection).

C. B. FOOTE

I have received today the large paper copy of your beautiful production [*Modern Love*]. You deserve great credit for the taste displayed and the remarkably clean and artistic typography...

> Early review from C. B. Foote of New York, recorded in Mosher's "Opinions of Bibliophiles" printed in the fall 1892 catalogue.

DEAN SAGE

The book [*Modern Love*] is a better one than could have been published by any press in the country ten years since, or by very, very few now.

> Dean Sage of Albany, NY, recorded in Mosher's catalogue under "Opinions of Bibliophiles" printed in the fall of 1892. Sage was a wealthy lumber merchant, benefactor of Cornell University, and a distinguished book collector.

GEORGE MEREDITH

Sir, a handsome pirate is always half pardoned, and in this case he has broken only the upper law. I shall receive with pleasure the copy of *Modern Love* which you propose to send. I have it much at heart that works of mine should be read by Americans.

> Letter from Meredith to Mosher, March 3, 1892. George Meredith was the author of *Modern Love*.

ARTHUR STEDMAN IN *THE DIAL*

As to books for book lovers, *editions de luxe*, etc., printed in this country, I have been much impressed in recent letters from English friends to find frequent mention of—the Riverside Press, Mr. DeVinne, or the University Press, say you?—no, indeed, Mr. Thomas Bird Mosher of Portland, Maine. He stirred up the younger English "illuminati" mightily with his beautiful reproductions of Meredith's "Modern Love," and Thompson's "City of Dreadful Night,"...

> Arthur Stedman in *The Dial*, December 16, 1893. Also reprinted by Mosher in his 1894 *A List of Books*.. Stedman was a supporter of Mosher in the piracy controversy.

THE CRITIC

To Mr. Thomas B. Mosher, of Portland, Maine, belongs the distinction of publishing a book whose general style and make-up are a departure from the regulation book and a departure that may be commended. His editions of Meredith's "Modern Love," and Thomson's "City of Dreadful Night," were charming in every respect, and the same must be said of two dainty *bibelots* which he published during the last holidays. Mr. Mosher is a pioneer in the same direction that Messrs. Elkin Mathews and John Lane, of London, are pioneers; and if he can only find suitable books among the writings of our own authors, we venture the opinion that his will become one of the leading houses of the country. The manufacturing of fine books, of books of artistic workmanship, has until recently been but little cultivated here; we have depended for such things upon English houses like David Nutt, Lawrence & Bullen, and the one mentioned above... We hope the publisher will find the generous welcome for his pretty volumes which they deserve. And we shall congratulate the first American poet who gets Mr. Mosher to introduce him to the public.

> *The Critic* (New York), February 10, 1894. Also reprinted by Mosher in his 1894 *A List of Books*...

SPRINGFIELD REPUBLICAN

That curious elegancy of bookmaking which Mr. Mosher has himself devised and which is quite apart from *fin de siecle* oddities.

> *Springfield Republican*, November 18, 1894, as quoted in Mosher's 1895 *A List of Books*...

NEW YORK TRIBUNE

Fragility sometimes blossoms in the strangest places! The daintiest of bookmaking has commonly come from centres like Paris, London, or New York; but from the town of Portland, Maine, there have been recently issued, under the title of "The Bibelot Series," some little paper-covered volumes of poetry which are as luxurious and artistic as anything that hails from France or England. Mr. T. B. Mosher is the publisher of these bits of clever workmanship.

> The *New York Tribune*, December 31, 1894. Reprinted by Mosher in his 1894 *A List of Books*...

THE BOSTON *BEACON*

It is hard to envision that the most artistic books of the year could come out of Portland, but conviction comes with the first glance at these captivating volumes.

> *The Beacon* (Boston) December 1894, as quoted in the 1895 Mosher *A List of Books...*

THE BOSTON *TRANSCRIPT*

Thomas B. Mosher has shown conclusively that all fine bookmaking in this country is not confined to the great cities or famous publishers.

> *The Transcript* (Boston) December 24, 1894, as quoted in the 1895 Mosher *A List of Books...*

THE PHILADELPHIA *PUBLIC LEDGER*

The daintiest specimens of bookmaking come from Thomas B. Mosher. He seems to have solved the problem of how to present a choice poem in choice dress at a very small cost.

> *The Public Ledger* (Philadelphia) December 12, 1894, as quoted in Mosher's 1895 *A List of Books...*

THE *NEW YORK TRIBUNE*

In the city of Portland, where one would hardly expect to run bibliomania to the earth, Mr. Thomas B. Mosher has been attempting to rival the most fastidious of English publishers in the perfection of the books he issues.

> *New York Tribune*, February 3, 1895, as quoted in the Mosher's 1895 *A List of Books...*

FIVE MORE NEWSPAPER OPINIONS ON *THE BIBELOT* QUOTED IN MOSHER'S 1895 CATALOGUE

The difference between William Blake and François Villon is sufficient to indicate the catholicity of taste of the Portland publisher who is offering rare flowers of old literature in the attractive little BIBELOT. —*Boston Transcript*

Book-lovers owe Mr. Mosher a debt of gratitude. He has shown what could be done in the way of dainty settings to delicate jewels. —*Philadelphia Evening Bulletin*

A dainty and delightful little literary monthly is THE BIBELOT... It is exquisitely printed on fine papers, and the broad margins are captivating... Book-lovers will hereafter have a tender spot in their hearts for Portland, Maine.
—*The Buffalo Enquirer*

Mr. Thomas B. Mosher, the Portland publisher, is creating a place for his dainty little periodical, THE BIBELOT. Each month's issue is devoted to some more or less unfamiliar pro-duction in prose and verse, and the selections are made with commendable discrimination. —*New York Tribune*

Literary *gourmets* find in each number of THE BIBELOT the evidence of a very refined taste in its compiler and publisher, who in the various brief introductions shows an ability far beyond the ordinary in saying a great deal very gracefully in very small space. —*St. Louis Mirror*

FROM THE *HARTFORD COURANT*

We know of no one in the country who is doing more for the higher interests of book-making and select literature than Thomas B. Mosher, the Portland, Maine, publisher... Both invention and cultured taste go to the making of such books, and it is remarkable that a publisher so far away from the great book centres should have the courage and devotion to do such work—work which is destined to be appreciated wherever the love for books exists.

> Richard Burton in the *Hartford Courant*, quoted in Mosher's 1896 autumn announcement.

FROM THE *SAN FRANCISCO CHRONICLE*

One of the new men who have shown what rare beauty can be put into artistic printing and binding is Thomas B. Mosher of Portland, Maine. For several seasons he has brought forth books that were a revelation of the resources of the printer's art... They are noteworthy for their scholarly judgment shown in their selection as for the perfect taste of their dress.

> From the *San Francisco Chronicle*, and reprinted in Mosher's 1896 autumn announcement.

A SENSITIVE REVIEW IN *THE ARTIST*

While upon the subject of artistic book-making, it is a pleasure to allude to the delightful editions of choice literary morsels issued by Thomas B. Mosher of Portland, Maine. Each volume is confined in a parchment wrapper, sealed with a gold wafer, upon which a *fleur de lis* is embossed. This at once sets the key to our appreciation. Instinctively, we feel that something precious is therein, and begin to use our finger tips. We are *en rapport* with Mr. Mosher's own thought. It was just because the literary morsel was precious that he selected it; and feeling it to be a gem, has striven to give it a worthy setting. With a mind attuned to this impression, we pass a paper-knife beneath the seal and find inside the wrapper a daintily decorated slide-case, out of which we draw the enticing volume. It is printed on Van Gelder paper, stout and smooth, and bound in flexible Japan vellum. If you are a book-lover, you realize by this time that Mr. Mosher has done something for you that no other publisher accomplishes in the same way. Not by costliness, for the volumes are extraordinarily cheap, but by the reverence which he has for the text and the rare discrimination with which he gives expression to it, he has given a garnish to the volume that affords the most refined enjoyment to the reader. If you are not a book-lover and have hitherto regarded a book as a mere receptacle of matter to be read, you will get your first lesson in that deeper, personal affection which should exist between the reader and the book. You value your friend for his own sake as well as for the joy of his conversation, and volumes such as these will grow to be precious to you quite apart from their contents. Appropriateness is the sign-manual of all good craftsmanship, and, as far as may be, Mr. Mosher's editions certainly fulfill this condition. Their make-up is in spirit with the text.

> Charles H. Caffin in *The Artist*, December 1898. *The Artist* was an illustrated monthly magazine review of Arts, Crafts and Industries, and especially concentrated on the Arts and Crafts movement in America. It was published by Truslove, Hanson & Comba of NY.

THE SKETCH

Why should we allow the Americans to beat us in the *format* of books? Mr. Mosher, of Portland, Maine, at least, can do that. For instance, he has just issued a beautiful 'vest-pocket' edition of Omar Khayyám, edited by Mr. Nathan Dole... As an enthusiast for the book beautiful, I thank Mr. Mosher.

The Sketch (London) August 2, 1899.

CONTEMPORANEOUS ACCOUNTS

BRUCE ROGERS

I did mean the reference to Aldus seriously—for you have (to the despair of us all) succeeded in doing just what he did 400 years ago, almost to a year, i.e., making beautiful little editions of the best writers in inexpensive form. The last is the most annoying feature of it all—and how you do it I can't see—unless, indeed, you pocket the loss—which I don't believe.

> Letter from Bruce Rogers to Mosher, Dec. 30, 1909 (excerpt printed with the permission of The Houghton Library, bMS Am 1096, 1357 & 1358). In this letter Rogers discusses his freelancing plans and offers his services as a designer. Bruce Rogers is considered by many to have been America's finest book designer. Rogers also inscribed a book he designed, Wordsworth's *IV Sonnets*, "To the Aldus [Thomas Bird Mosher] of the XIX Century from an amateur printer." (Item #378 of Mosher's library sale in 1948). Aldus was a famous 15th century printer/publisher, and disseminator of classical editions in inexpensive format.

E. V. LUCAS

These cheap books [the series of English standard works published by Cassell for threepence, and the Walter Scott shilling edition of the poets], however, though they delivered the goods, were not beautiful. It was not till the rise of the American pirate Thomas B. Mosher that I was able to possess beautiful books. So far as I can recollect, the circumstance that he disregarded the law of copyright did not disturb me in the least. I liked his distinguished little pamphlets too much—and even more I liked the new territories to which they pointed the way, the unknown palaces of which they were single stones. I suppose Thomas B. Mosher was a scamp, but his nefariousness was very gracious and stimulating. And he did not stimulate merely readers; many an honest publisher must have been spurred to better deeds by the Terror of the (Portland) Maine.

> Edward Verrall Lucas. *Reading, Writing, and Remembering*, 1932, p. 118. Lucas was a well known British essayist, novelist, anthologist, and writer of light verse.

RICHARD LE GALLIENNE'S
THOMAS BIRD MOSHER—AN APPRECIATION

Criticism has latterly been promoted to a place among the creative arts. Somewhat tardily, it has become recognized that the contemplation of one work of art by what may be called skilled enthusiasm results not infrequently in another. There is necessarily an artistic principle at work in all appreciation, for appreciation implies selection, and may be defined as selection creatively vitalized by praise. Then taste actively employed must result in some form of personal rearrangement of its objects which gives one the sense of a new harmony. Thus an individually selected library often becomes the artistic embodiment of its owner's personality. A real book-lover, that is one whose books are each and all sensitively related to himself, is known by the books that he buys. His library is a microcosm of his individual cosmos. The catalogue of a man's library is a form of autobiography. Now, this principle has been carried one step further in our time by one who has shown us that not only the criticism and collection of books may belong to the creative arts, but the publication of them also. The history of printing and book-selling records other instances of a like nature. Pickering and Moxon and Russell Smith, to mention only two or three recent names, are examples of publishers who impressed their businesses with a personal artistic character. But none of these better deserves the description of creative publisher than Thomas Bird Mosher, of Portland, Maine. Many publishers we have who know and love and publish good literature, and take pride, too, in the building of beautiful books. But such books are only a small part of their general output. Their catalogues are impersonal, *omnium-gatherum*, lists of unrelated volumes. There is evident in them no selective principle, save that of a general merchant to purvey such creditable wares as the reading public is likely to purchase. You do not say immediately as you take up one of their books: "This is a Pickering book!" or some one's else as the case may be. Their name on a title-page stands for nothing distinctive, nothing beyond general respectability, or the reverse. With Mr. Mosher it is delightfully different; and, as a result of twenty years' devotion to a certain personal ideal of literary appeal and perfection, he is able, with perfect propriety, and without need of explanation, to entitle his catalogue—"The Mosher Books."

As one looks back over Mr. Mosher's publishing career, one is struck by the fact that he began right away as he meant to go on. Already the line he meant to mark out for himself was clear in his mind, the result of a well-defined maturity of taste and judgment. For I believe I am right in thinking that the first issue from his press was an edition of George Meredith's *Modern Love*—at that time of day all but unknown outside the secret society of fanatic Meredithians. I remember well the grateful surprise and curiosity with which in London I received Mr. Mosher's present of that now rare imprint. It is always delightful to catch the windfall of a beautiful book, as it were, out of the air; and then one was thankful to this unknown enthusiast oversea, first, for having discovered for himself that great unappreciated poem, and then for his courage in reprinting it. "Portland, Maine," meant nothing to me in those days, or I should have been still more surprised at this good thing coming out of that particular Nazareth. Even more exotic to me would have seemed another publication that soon followed—Andrew Lang's translation of *Aucassin and Nicolete*.

Andrew Lang was very angry over that act of charming "piracy"; never, in fact, got over it. Possibly, I take an immoral view of such so-called literary piracy; yet it seems to me mere childishness, when one has neglected properly to protect one's literary property, to complain if some one exercises his undoubted legal right of taking a fancy to it. Actually, I rejoice no little that so much exquisite literature would seem to have been thus left unprotected; for in that neglect has been the opportunity of Mr. Mosher's enthusiasm, and by reason of it many lovely things that, in the indifferent hands of their "legitimate" sponsors, stood a fair chance of oblivion, have been rescued and displayed for our "delight in widest commonalty spread." One English writer, at all events, who had the common sense to take this view of Mr. Mosher's "piracy," William Sharp, has had good reason to congratulate himself on his association with "The Mosher Books"; for it is hardly too much to say that the fame of *Fiona Macleod*, in its inception, at all events, was largely due to that devoted appreciation in far-away Portland, Maine. So William Sharp would have been the first to admit.

But Mr. Mosher as an exquisite Claude Duval of publishing is but an almost forgotten parenthesis in his career. If, as Kipling says, he has taken his good where he found it, 't is all to the gaiety of bookmen, and here I am not so much concerned with the so-called piracy as with the creative taste which inspired it. Of this creative taste Mr. Mosher's catalogue is one really exquisite expression. *The Bibelot* is the other. The catalogue has the charm of a delicately made anthology. It is indeed a garland of fragrant names, names that "bring a perfume in the mention." It is a veritable "box where sweets compacted lie."

Every book-lover knows the evocative power that lies in the mere names of his favorite authors, and the titles of his favorite books. As he looks around his shelves, and his eyes fall upon them, gleaming in morning sun, or evening lamplight, what a music of association streams out to him from the well-loved backs. There is no need to take them down. Those names and titles are eloquent to him as the faces of familiar friends—aye, no few of them are as the faces of passionately loved women. They thrill him through with an indescribable imaginative ecstasy: as Justin Huntly McCarthy sang of Omar Khayyám, one can say "my youth lies buried in thy verses." They hold so much of our lives, as a poignant gloss, between their leaves. Some of them have been pressed close to dead bosoms, and still keep their perfume. That *Theocritus*, that *Villon*, that *Keats*, that *Well at the World's End!*

Now, in his catalogue, Mr. Mosher has collected more such names than I know where else to find together. Often I take it down and turn over its leaves, as I would walk in a garden of old-world flowers; or press to my nostrils some pomander of precious evocative spices. It is at once a lachrymatory, a honey-pot or a potpourri jar, for in it are collected together, as in precious vials, all the tears, all the honey, all the blossom of literature. Or, to compare it again to a garden, how one admires the charming, conceited arrangement of the garden, its quaint walks, and the inscriptions scattered here and there on dial and bower. It is the *catalogue raisonné* lifted into the region of poetry. It is a similar triumph in bibliography to that of Villon or Rossetti in poetry, when of a string of beautiful names they make a new harmony, the names of the fair ladies of old time, or of the five handmaidens of Mary —

"whose names
Are five sweet symphonies
Cecily, Gertrude, Magdalen,
Margaret and Rosalys."

So Mr. Mosher has brought together the names whose mere mention at once suggests the beauty, the passion, the pathos of existence, all that in literature which we connect especially with such writers as Theocrites, Villon, Omar, DeQuincey, Pater, Morris, Rossetti, and with such books as *The Greek Anthology*, *The Book of Ecclesiastes*, *The Vita Nuova*. Yet his garden is not all set with elegiac or epicurean blooms, it is not without its austerer walks, and sturdier sunlit groves, over which preside such names as Milton and Wordsworth, Matthew Arnold and Browning, Meredith and Whitman.

To the making of the library which this catalogue represents Mr. Mosher has brought not only the creative selective taste of a rare lover of literature, but the delight in the fair craftsmanship of books which marks the bibliophile, so that his issues are become proverbial for the exquisiteness of their format. Still, while thus solicitous for the outside of the platter, it has grown more and more evident that his publishing has had a deeper purpose than either the production of dainty editions, or the commercial gain resulting from their purveying, and that he has combined with both those very proper aims a certain missionary enthusiasm for the dissemination of the more spiritual and exquisite forms of literature. Long ago (1895) in his prefatory note to the first issue of *The Bibelot*—to me the most fascinating miscellany of lovely thought and expression ever compiled—Mr. Mosher thus defined a purpose which he has pursued no less in his book-publishing than in the little magazine in question: "To bring together the poesies of other men bound by a thread of one's own choosing is the simple plan of the editor of *The Bibelot*. In this way those exotics of literature that might not immediately find a way to wider reading, are here reprinted, and, so to speak, resown in fields their authors never knew."

The tiny, delicately worded prefaces to each issue of *The Bibelot* revealed that Mr. Mosher possessed a sensitive pen of his own, and these and the occasional introductions to his catalogue vibrate with a passion for literature that speaks for itself, and clearly differentiates Mr. Mosher from his publishing brethren. With what a "sad sincerity" Mr. Mosher has devoted himself to his dream, some words of an almost valedictory wistfulness from a recent "foreword" of his bear witness. He has been quoting one of Whitman's affirmations of the spiritual nature and destiny of man. "And would you," he says. "call this *a lost point of view?* If it is, then my scheme of things has an insubstantial value, and any 'tidings of great joy' I thought inherent in the books I have chosen to offer you is but a mirage of the mind, the baseless fabric of a vision that fades and leaves no trace. . . . At times I may have unduly insisted upon the fact that it was not merely a commercial adventure with me, but the possession of ideals in book-publishing, with the implication that the thing done was for a purpose beyond itself: 'seeing finally with inexorable vision the way that life comes and the way that life goes whatever may happen with words.' "

Recently, in a volume called *Amphora*—a sort of private breviary of prose and verse—Mr. Mosher has included several such little essays of his own, among them one which I find especially delightful for the glimpses it gives of the bookish ardors and adventures of his youth— "The Books I shall not read again." "No! I shall never again read books," he says, "as I once read them in my early seafaring when all the world was young, when the days were of tropic splendor, and the long evenings were passed with my books in a lonely cabin dimly lighted by a primitive oil-lamp, while the ship was ploughing through the boundless ocean on its weary course around Cape Horn." This glimpse of bookish seafaring is as tantalizing as it is fascinating. I want some more of those old memories. Won't Mr. Mosher be persuaded to take his pen in hand and go seafaring and book-faring once more? I am persuaded that he could write us a new *Bibliomania* with a spiritual-human thrill in it entirely missing from the old.

Richard Le Gallienne. *Thomas Bird Mosher An Appreciation* by... Privately Printed for Their Friends. Portland: [The Mosher Press], 1914. Reprinted from *The Forum* for January 1914 with the permission of Mitchell Kennerley. This appreciation was again reprinted at the end of *The Bibelot*'s Index volume and in the 1914 Mosher catalogue. Le Gallienne was a British poet, author, and essayist/critic whose career included relationships with John Lane of The Bodley Head, Mosher, Elbert Hubbard of the Roycrofters, and the New York literary society.

WILLIAM MARION REEDY ON THE ENDING OF *THE BIBELOT*

For twenty years no month has passed that I have not had one certain joy. It was in the reading of the dainty, gray-blue covered *Bibelot* that came from Mr. Mosher, of Portland, Maine. And now the end. The last number of the twentieth volume appeared in December. For all that time, though I have been pretty strenuously engaged in the game of life, the *Bibelot* has always arrived with its message of beauty to win me for a while away from issues and from crises. The fears and hopes, the angers and despairs of the tide of battle have come and gone. The things of the *Bibelot* remain—they perish never. They are a recurrent inspiration, consolation, sustenance to the soul. Beautiful verse by the masters of song, rescued from books little known; treasures of delicate or virile prose, the cadences of which set the heart to marching; voices of joyous memory and sweet-lingering regret; clairvoyant and clairaudient perspicacities of interpretation of life and letters and art; jewellery [sic] work in words that carry an over-soul of sense and thought; the exquisitries of the little masters otherwise lost to remembrance; exhumed splendors from books and authors unaccountably committed to neglect bordering on oblivion; a whole world of literature which has concern only for life of the heart and spirit—all this was, nay is, the *Bibelot*. But this literature is more than merely "precious." It is vital. It concerns the very essence of the only life we know—the individual life. It deals with the things that give life its pattern: the splendor and the sadness of it; the mystery of it and those hints that sometimes come to all of us of the meaning of the world and its pageantry sumptuous or sordid—all the "intimations of immortality." Two hundred and forty issues of such inner-life-stuff presented always sympathetically, never in contempt of the world of here and now, and never in insensibility to the something without the world and space and time, are a body of literature which, but for the resurrectionist Mosher, we might never have known. Burns in it all the flame of the spirit in the urn of form. The perfect marriage of thought or feeling with expression was what Mosher sought—and found, and gave to us. And to that union he added another element—beautiful, chastely beautiful printing. His idea, beautifully carried out, has been to make the *Bibelot* a means to setting and leading people in the way of culture—not the culture that has for object one's superiority over others, but the culture that is inclusive in its effect, the culture that is essentially sympathy [sic] with all the living. In the wide range of the *Bibelot's* contents one finds a *fugue* consistent. Each selection conforms to an underlying, informing purpose—to touch the soul to finer issues, to acquaint it with the ecstasies of life lived and contemplated. To think that this labor of years is come to an end is a sadness very great. For we readers of the *Bibelot* came to know and to love Mosher—his work made such a beautiful exhibition of his own soul. The introductions he wrote for each number were gems of expository lucidity, touched with color, vibrant with music—"the still, sad music of humanity" and its mightier, diapasonic organ tones. He did not preach to us this or that. He taught us to see, to hear, with spirit's eye, its ear. And in so far as we learned from him and his expositions none of us is dead to the message the world and life convey to us of duty to love one another. The complete *Bibelot*, in twenty volumes, is an encyclopedia of the literature of rapture with the spirit of beauty. That Mr. Mosher has decided to end his labors is a deep regret to those who followed them. That the effects of those labors will go endlessly on and on in lives made better, saner, more "in tune with the Infinite," is his exceeding great reward.

> Reedy, William Marion. "The Ending" Index volume to *The Bibelot*, 1915. Reprinted by Wm. H. Wise in *An Outline of Distinguished Reading*, 1925. Reedy was the editor of the St. Louis *Mirror*, an author, and friend of T. B. Mosher.

"An Attempt at Appreciation of a Rare Spirit"

(I)

He has done what every true booklover who is also a litterateur would like to do. He has done it so well that, like the work of the old masters, it is really not worth doing again. I think that the books of Thomas Bird Mosher,—books he never wrote but which are his because he has put upon them the imprint of his taste in book-craft and his selective genius in literary matters,—are meant for immortality. Some one is bound, after he has finished his work here, to take it up and spread broadcast the little volumes he has produced in small quantities for those who care. That will not matter, however, and it will come about naturally, easily.

(II)

For those who do not know Thomas Bird Mosher, I quote a few titles in the list of books which has been steadily growing since 1891: *Odes, Sonnets and Lyrics* of John Keats, the Daniel Press edition; *The Private Papers of Henry Ryecroft* by George Gissing; *Dreamthorp* by Alexander Smith. Some were limited editions, or did not get a reprinting for one reason or another, and these are now out of print and very scarce. Others that I do not mention may be quite as unobtainable. The rest are reprinted whenever exhausted, in the same form usually as the original. There are more than three hundred titles in the list; and besides this Mr. Mosher has a set of books which he calls *The Bibelot*, a twenty volume collection of prose and poetry ranging from François Villon to Stephen Mallarmé, and from William Blake to Maurice Hewlett. His separate volumes are issued in series with charming names: The Brocade, the Old World, and the Venetian. One finds in many the name of Fiona Macleod; haunting titles like *From the Hills of Dream* and *The Four White Swans*.

Mr. Mosher, indeed, was among the first, if not the first, to discover William Sharp's delicate things, and it was he who was practically responsible for the pen name that Sharp assumed for part of his work, Fiona Macleod.

The format of every book is exactly in the spirit of the author—and in the Mosher spirit, too. Most of them, not to speak of leather bindings for those who do not fear the rot of years, are in old-style boards and in a cream cover of vellum, stamped in brown, and inclosed in a slip case to preserve from dust.

(III)

"The literary journals," says Mr. Mosher, "are so full of details about works that sell by the carload that any attempt of mine would be like the needle in the haymow—'lost to sight' even if to memory dear! I shall hope to go on with my work, small as it is, however, until, to quote from another—'the end is ended—the infinite begun'."

There has been nothing quite like Thomas Bird Mosher before this day—he is not, he asserts, a "second William Morris"—and there will be, we suspect, nothing like him after this day is gone, and he with it.

> Wilbur Needham. *The Chicago Evening Post*, April 20, 1923. Reprinted as the introduction in the 1923 *The Mosher Books* catalogue.

J. M. Stuart-Young, Friend of Oscar Wilde

I have noticed that you make a speciality of Oscar Wilde's books, and I have one of your sumptuous editions on my shelves. I wonder if you would care to undertake an edition of my "Osrac"? The copyright is my own, and I should like to see it known across the Atlantic.

Wilde and I were great friends,—with that friendship which he declared to be the finest possible, for I was a boy of fifteen in 1894, the year when calamity came to him....

Trusting to hear from you soon, and thanking you cordially for the great work which you are doing for tasteful literature in these commercial times, I remain, Yours sincerely...

> Excerpts from a letter of J. M. Stuart-Young to Mr. Mosher dated 24th January, 1907 (Bishop Collection). The book mentioned was privately printed in England under the title *Osrac, the Self-Sufficient* in 1905, and sent to Mosher for his review and hopeful publication. Mosher kept the book in his library, but never published it.

WILLIAM DANA ORCUTT

The influence which a publisher can exert upon the Art of the Book is shown by the series of classics issued in exquisite form by Mr. Thomas B. Mosher at prices within the reach of all. These volumes are distinct evidences of his own taste and knowledge, rather than triumphs of the printer, for Mr. Mosher has expressed himself in the type, margins, paper and the general format of his admirable publications.

> From William Dana Orcutt's brief chapter on America in "The Art of the Book." Special number of the London *Studio* for Spring 1914. Also quoted in *Thomas Bird Mosher of Portland, Maine.* Portland: The Southworth-Anthoensen Press, 1941, pp. iii-iv.

TWO OF MOSHER'S OWN SUMMARIES

MOSHER, THOMAS BIRD, publisher, editor; *b.* Biddeford, Me., Sept.11, 1852; *s.* Benjamin and Mary Elizabeth (Merrill) M.; ed. pub. schs. Biddeford, Me., and Boston; (hon. A.M. Bowdin Coll., 1906); *m.* Anna M. Littlefield, of Saco, Me., July 2, 1892. Began publishing choice and limited edits. of books in belles lettres, Oct., 1891; began editing and publishing The Bibelot, Jan., 1895, a reprint of poetry and prose, largely from scarce editions and sources not usually known. Edited and published Am. edit. of The Germ, 1898; Swinburne's Poems and Ballads, 1899; Rossetti's Poetical Works, 1901; the first absolute facsimile reprint of Fitzgerald's Omar Khayyam of 1859, 1902; besides editing and compiling bibliography in Old World edit. of Fitzgerald's entire texts of Omar. Mem Bibliog. Soc., London. *Clubs:* Grolier (New York), Author's, Omar Khayyam (Boston), Caxton, Dofobs (Chicago). *Home:* 40 Highland St. *Office:* 45 Exchange St., Portland, Me.

Mosher's own submission to *Who's Who.* 4th ed. 1906-07.

As for my character, dear boy, I can only say that it has been slowly forming lo these many years until at last I am one of the choicest specimens in the publishing world and compared with Harper's, Scribner's, or The Dodd, Rot & Company. I am as a star that dwells apart! Seriously, old man, all that I felt it necessary to have said of me is in "Who's Who"... My escapades in business have been many. I once went through bankruptcy proceedings... I then emerged in '71 [sic '91] all by my lonesome, began publishing with "Modern Love" and from that day I have had no more failures but have managed to scrape up about enough to pay the taxes, educate my eldest and if I die to-day go to Hobo-Moko and leave a trail of glory behind me...

> Extracts from a July 28, 1914 letter to fellow publisher, W. Irving Way, formerly of Chicago's Way and Williams publishing firm. Printed in *Excerpts from Letters of Thomas Bird Mosher.* Intro. by Audrey Arellanes. Pasadena, CA: Bookworm Press, 1972.

"THE MOSHER BOOKS" FROM AN ENGLISH POINT OF VIEW

A far off in the northeast corner of Yankeedom, "away down in Maine," in the city of the birth of the poet Longfellow, there is one Mosher, who publishes books along new lines. Not that he advocates new authors or any very new departures in the manufacture of choice printed things. Simply that he combines as many of those tried and proved excellencies of design, typography, format, etc., as go to make up the nearest approach to the perfect book: Old Style types, Chiswick headbands (or some satisfactory substitute therefor), handmade, English, Dutch or Japanese papers, and an absolute freedom from those fads and eccentricities of glaring vulgarity which disgrace so many modern "De Luxe" books printed in the English language. Generally speaking, they do this thing better in France, where they seem to understand and appreciate delicacy and symmetry in the printed page without the suggestion of effeminacy.

The product of Portland, the children of Mr. Mosher's good taste and perspicacity, now number some 140 volumes, in range from the "Laus Veneris" of Swinburne to the "Child's Garden of Verses" of Stevenson, and "The Story of David Gray" to "The Dream of John Ball." Many of them, in fact the majority, are in strictly limited editions.

Mr. Mosher is what we are wont to call from our distant view-point a pirate, though we note *en passant* that our English publishers who lift the good things of American literature without fee or "by your leave," we designate merely as "Publishers of Reprints." As Whistler, he of the butterfly hallmark, has it, "It's a case of 'other minds other lines.' "

The foreword to Mr. Mosher's charming "List of Books in Belles Lettres" is an admirable essay in praise and favour of the private collectors of books "whose," as Mr. Gosse says, "glimmering hearths were the haunts of learning over which Knowledge spread her cold fingers."

"The ideal library," Mr. Mosher says, "is perhaps, after all, a small one, where the books are carefully selected and thoughtfully arranged according to one central code of taste." For twelve years Mr. Mosher's aims have been to develop, if possible, a theory of bookmaking; a theory which at no time had the most remote relevance to any scheme "of one hundred (or one thousand) best books;" a large output of popular selections, nor a relatively small one of an arbitrary choice; but rather to converge on a definitely thought-out and preconcerted plan of "careful selection according to this one central code of taste."

One series, the Quartos, is an attempt at forming a representative collection of the English Üsthetic School of Poetry and Prose, and includes, among other volumes, "Laus Veneris" of Swinburne, "Marius the Epicurean" of Pater, "The Poems of Rossetti," etc., set throughout in pica old style roman, and printed on Van Gelder handmade paper, with an original set of headbands, tailpieces, and initials. The volumes may well be said to rival, if not excel, the best contemporary productions. They range in price from sixteen shillings to some five pounds for copies on Japanese vellum; from which regal examples, to the Vest Pocket Series on GENUINE HANDMADE PAPER AT A SHILLING PER VOLUME, is a wide range in price. And so, too, is exemplified in a measure the importance of the method of choice and arrangement of Mr. Mosher's general scheme. Not that the volumes of this latter series are in any sense of a contrasting quality or even value, as a consideration of such titles as FitzGerald's Fourth Translation of "The Rubáiyát," "Laus Veneris" again (this time, mark you, at a shilling), and the "Sonnets from the Portuguese," etc., will show.

Continuing this most delightful preamble to his "List," Mr. Mosher says, further, that he has been asked to define his attitude towards this development in what, for want of a better phrase, may be called "cooperative bookmaking."

"Paint, chisel, or write, the law of survival shall decide which shall last, and what by its own weakness will be forgotten." There is today noticeable in America to a marvellous degree, far more so than its existence here in England, the interest of the "young person" in the broadening influence of the æsthetic movement in life, literature, and art. The public, the great big generous public, to whom they look for the rise and development to a far greater degree than it could ever have been with their elders of a generation ago, is to be made up of "THE YOUNG MEN AND WOMEN OF TO-DAY." It is they—in America—who in the main desire and demand joy in one's daily round, comradeship in one's work and one's loves, and a desire to possess and surround themselves with Things Beautiful.

Our protest therefore is against the indiscriminate collection of books big or little, arguing, as certain wise men have done before, that a few books well read are worth many unread. But we believe also that the choice of selection is often a very faulty choice on the part of many a publisher who has lumbered up his catalogue with many an incoherent and unrelated list of so-called Classics. Not infrequently a publisher's name does not stand for what it once did: there are too few Bentleys, Ballantynes, and Smiths left to grace the profession as it stands today; but there is no reason why every publisher, be he great or small, cannot hold out for a "scheme of publication" and a "code of choice" which should at least stand for a great deal more than the indiscriminate grouping of "Robinson Crusoe" and "The Vicar of Wakefield" in a series, and calling it the "Twentieth Century Library." What may be the "best books" to one mind, may be, if not poison to another's, perhaps a violent dissenting note. Therefore, let us hail the "new" publisher who come before us with his wares, whether they be reprints or what not, so long as he confines himself to a certain set purpose which in his prospectuses and printed matter he defines in an appealing fashion, so much so that it appeals to us at all events; and let us welcome with joy the opportunity to gather unto ourselves a modest and attractive collection of dainty books which will not only be a pride to posses, but which in reality will be worth to us, by making them our intimates, vastly more than yards of shelf room encumbered with the redundant essays and theories of mere pedants or cyclopÊdia makers. Inasmuch as this screed is in the nature of a free and unsolicited advertisement of Mr. Mosher's books, we advise all and sundry who may be interested and who may care to know more of his truly beautiful books to send to him for his "List of Books in Belles Lettres," in itself a beautiful book, and enjoy its perusal for themselves.

> From *THE PROTEST, A Journal for Philistines*; No. 5. (Kent, England: Published for the Proprietors from the Sign of the Hop-Pole, Crockham Hill, Eden Bridge, January 1903). Reprinted as an ad in *The Bibelot* for May 1903 (not in yearly bound copies).

MEMORIAL TRIBUTES

THE INLAND PRINTER

There are some names that will always stand out in the history of printing in New England, such as Stephen Day [sic, Daye], the first printer in Cambridge; Isaiah Thomas, the great printer-publisher of Worcester, and the publishers of the works of the poets, authors, and historians of the last century. Among the later notables there should be included one whose name is not so

widely known, as his works had a limited sale. I refer to T. B. Mosher, of Portland, Maine. Mr. Mosher was a bookseller who edited and published "Belle Lettres" on his own account. He had discriminating literary taste, to which he
added ability in planning formats of his books. Every collector of fine printing in
the United States should acquire some representative Mosher works.

> *Inland Printer*, 1933. Reprinted in *The Mosher Books* catalogue of
> 1935-1936, p.[2].

A. E. NEWTON

It is curious to remember that the two men who have so influenced the style
of the modern book, William Morris and Thomas Mosher, began their work quite
independently of each other, in the same year, 1890 [sic]. It is now almost forty
years ago that I bought, immediately upon its appearance, the first Kelmscott
Press book, *The Story of the Glittering Plain*. I bought it from E. D. North, who
was then with Scribner's, because it interested me rather than because I thought
it beautiful. The book created a sensation at the time: it was hailed as a great
achievement. Mosher's first book, whatever it was [*Modern Love*] created no comment. He, so far as I know, made no pronouncement; he merely went to work,
and with the limited means at his disposal—and they were extremely limited in
Portland, Maine, in the early nineties—produced books which were beautiful in
type and format, were easy to read and easy to hold; moreover, they had this great
merit: they were published at a price which put them within reach of all. Mosher
did not prate about art for the masses or the beauty of democracy, and then produce books which only rich men could buy; but by the sheer force of his good
taste and good judgment he got the results he set out to secure. He was never a
printer himself, but he had ideas and ideals, and he was able to impress them
upon others; with the passage of time he came to command the best types, paper,
and ink that could be had, and he used them like the artist that he was.

I have before me as I write two of the catalogues which, before the war, he
used to issue annually. One is dated 1906: it is a slender catalogue of sixty-eight
pages; the cover is of dark blue paper printed in an allover design in dark green,
while in a small panel in the upper left-hand corner, in vermilion, is the title
The Mosher Books, and the date. I have called it a catalogue: it is more—it is an
anthology. Even more beautiful is the pamphlet issued four years later: it is now
a booklet of eighty pages; the cover is old rose with the printing in two shades of
the same color. Nothing could be more daintily simple than these brochures
which were intended for gratuitous distribution. But I have only suggested their
greatest, their most enduring charm. Never before or since, I believe, has a man
made such a delicate appeal to the reader and the book-lover. With exquisite
quotations in verse and in prose, from every source under the wide and starry
sky, he called attention to the literary merit of his wares, saying just enough
about type and size and binding to enable one to order by letter—for practically
he sold only by mail.

Occasionally, not often,—not often enough,—someone went to Portland and
asked where his shop or printery or office was, and practically no one knew.
When he was at the height of his fame, known all over the world, someone went
to Portland, registered at the hotel, and then asked where he could find T. B.
Mosher. The clerk didn't know, had never heard of him, but he would inquire;
after a time he returned, saying nobody knew; if he had ever lived in Portland
he must be dead. A prophet is not without honor, and so forth.

Mosher's books have another merit which one looks for in vain elsewhere. I
refer to their literary quality. I don't think he ever printed a book merely

because it would sell, although I have no doubt that many people bought his books because he printed them—and they never regretted doing so. His selective taste was as unerring as his knowledge of the practical side of his business. He made the best literature of all time and of all countries popular, if so be a book may be called popular which in a nation of a hundred millions sells in hundreds only. But mass production was not for him.

Simplicity—what may be called readability—he kept ever before him. Whether a Mosher book was of large format or small, bound this way or that, one could always tell it at a glance—or could until every printer and publisher in the country copied more or less his style. Morris has his disciples,—Rudge, Rogers, Nash, Updike, Goudy,—but no less a debt is owed Mosher by those who may be called commercial publishers, and it is these who disseminate the taste of the nation; indeed, it seems to me our printers owe as much to Mosher as to Morris. Mosher may have thought of himself as democratic; he would have laughed to have heard himself called an aristocrat of publishers; but he was an aristocrat in his mind and in his method. All of us who love books, inside and out, are and will ever be in debt to Thomas Bird Mosher. I feel no hesitation in speaking of him. I never saw him, and I had only one letter from him, and that was when, some ten years ago, I wrote in the *Atlantic Monthly* a few lines of appreciation of the work he was doing in the making of fine books. I am glad I did; I am glad I spoke while yet he was alive; after his death, to say what I thought would merely have been to join in the chorus.

Some of the best writing brains of this country are functioning in the art of advertising. A cigarette advertiser has said, "There is a little Turkish in all good cigarettes, but"—some cigarette or other "is all Turkish." In like manner, I should say that there is a little Mosher in all well-printed books, but the best-printed books are all Mosher. Bruce Rogers remarked to a lecturer who had paid a tribute to Mosher in the Grolier Club one evening, "I would rather have done his work than mine." It was generously said, but Bruce Rogers can afford to let others look after his fame: it is secure. But there is, I fear, some danger—because Mosher was a publisher and not a printer and because, as a publisher, he paid few or small royalties—that his real service to the book-lover will be forgotten.

Comparisons are always odious. There is glory enough for all. Both men are dead, but their work still lives after them; both in England and in this country we have not one supreme, but many excellent printers—and this is as it should be. It is absurd to suppose that if you want a finely printed book it must, necessarily, come from the press of so-and-so. There are many excellent printers... The lines of Tennyson occur to me: —

> Most can raise the flowers now.
> For all have got the seed.

And the seed was planted by William Morris in England and by Thomas Bird Mosher in this country.

> A. Edward Newton. *This Book Collecting Game* (1928), pp. 119, 122-25. Large excerpts reprinted as "The Book Itself" in *The Mosher Books* catalogue of 1929, pp. 3-4. Newton was an author and distinguished collector.

From *Scribner's Magazine*

I have before my eyes a beautiful volume dedicated to the memory of Thomas B. Mosher, of Portland. It is called "Amphora. A Second Collection of Prose and Verse Chosen by the Editor of the Bibelot." It is embellished with a portrait and contains some original verse by Mosher himself. Mr. Mosher loved good books, and loved to make them. He was an excellent critic with a flair for beauty that enabled him to discern what was worth preservation in the work of writers both living and dead, and he preserved it in a beautiful way. A Mosher book came to mean a book invariably good and invariably well printed. There are thousands of book-lovers who will never forget this man, who will always hold his name in reverence...

> William Lyon Phelps. *Scribner's Magazine*, February 1927. Reprinted in *The Mosher Books* catalogue for 1927, pp. 3-4. Phelps was an American essayist, professor of English at Yale, and author.

A BRITISH PUBLISHER'S VIEW

Writing of Frank Murray just now I wrote the name of Mosher. Thomas B. Mosher was an American publisher who, fitly enough, carried on business at Portland, Maine, a state whose coast, indented, according to my atlas, with creeks and rich in islands and rivers, is, apart from its climate, the very place for pirates. He produced charming little books and a periodical *The Bibelot*. Yes, Andrew Lang was not incorrect in calling him a "pirate" in that he made full use of the fact that at the time he greatly flourished the English writer had little or no copyright protection in the United States. But it is difficult to see why the word "pirate" should be used in any opprobrious sense, since all that he did was to avail himself of his legal rights. Besides, much of what Mosher printed was "chosen from scarce editions and from sources not generally known", while at all times he used material that was, according to the law of his country, within the public domain. However, pirate or honest man, Mosher was more or less a scholar and had as high a standard of book production and, apparently, as fine a sense of literary values, as any bookmaker or publisher working in the United States of his day. He did much, in that long dreary period which Miss Dorothy Dudley so well describes in *Dreiser and the Land of the Free* [in America this book was called *Forgotten Frontiers*], to keep the literary torch alight in the forty-five States of the Union...

Frank Murray of Derby, I suppose, had not such financial strength as Mosher, and, moreover, he had the cares of three bookshops. But he did make his mark although he was at the business of book production for only a short time. He helped to keep William Sharp on the map, for instance—he published *Vistas* at the Moray Press in 1904—and was surely the first man to put Fiona Macleod between covers—yes, Murray did that, no doubt on Sharp's advice. It is a coincidence that Le Gallienne, writing about Mosher after his death, was able to state that the inception of Fiona Macleod's fame was largely due to the American pirate's devoted appreciation. Mosher and Murray were linked in that enthusiasm.

Mr. Mosher irks me because he prints better books than I do.

> The first and largest selection is from Grant Richards. *Author Hunting*, 1934, pp. 88-90. Richards was a British publisher and writer. The last one-line excerpt is from Grant Richard's letter to the *London Times*, March 13, 1914, defending Mosher against piracy charges.

A BROWN UNIVERSITY LIBRARIAN

We may recall with satisfaction that one of the leaders in American fine printing issued his first book also in 1891, and that, save for a single volume which was frankly an imitation, Thomas B. Mosher published his charming and significant books all on classical lines, regardless of the weight of ink and the startling types that were being employed by other American book-designers. So our discussion of modern fine printing in America may well begin with the work of Mosher.

He was not a printer in the sense of owning a press, but he worked with printers to get the results that he desired. He followed classical lines in type, paper, ink and press work, and every book of his was a genuine composition. His publications varied in size from the impressive quarto edition of Burton's *Kasidah* to the tiny quarto leaflet of John Hay's *In Praise of Omar*. Mr. Mosher's printing, or rather book-design, cannot be separated from his publishing, for which he deserves no less credit. It was his service to his countrymen to introduce to them a selection of choice but not popular literature that was an excellent corrective of provincialism and of content with the commonplace. To each book chosen by him for publication he endeavored to give an ideal dress. In thought he was something of a come-outer, but in printing he was a decided conservative, so that even his innovations were always in the interest of the finest elements of the old order.

> Harry Lyman Koopman. *The American Mercury,*. May 1924. Reprinted in *Amphora* II, pp. 98-99. Koopman was an author, librarian and bibliographer at Brown University, and fellow member of the Grolier Club. The above comments came from a speech he gave to the Grolier Club in 1924 which was twice reprinted.

EDWARD LAROCQUE TINKER

In the same year that William Morris in England launched his Kelmscott Press that was to inspire a movement circling the globe, William [sic] Bird Mosher in Portland, Me., matured his plans to provide a better standard of printing on this side of the Atlantic by manufacturing well-made, beautifully designed books at prices within the reach of the general public—prices ranging from $1.50 to $5.

With his hawkeye for the fine and unusual, he selected for his first venture George Meredith's "Modern Love and Other Poems," then almost unknown. Choosing excellent materials, he stood over a Portland printer until he had worried him into producing an approximation of the book that Mosher could see in his mind's eye. It was far superior in taste and design to anything then being done in this country and became the cornerstone of that long series of 500 reprints—as excellent in their choice of text as in the execution of their typography.

Soon these book were sought by bibliophiles all over the world and Mosher became far better known in Bombay, London, Melbourne or San Francisco than he was in Portland; and the catalogues he issued once a year were treasured as collector's items, for not only were they fascinating typographically but there were also delightful literary jewels, culled from his wide reading, inserted here and there wherever there was room. Richard Le Gallienne described them as "the catalogue *raisonné* lifted into the region of poetry"...

His ideas of typography were sane and charming, and the only criticism might be the smallness of type and the fragile daintiness of covers. In spite of this, his books and the issues of the "Bibelot" as well are important collectors' items because they mark the beginning, and were the inspiration of, the renaissance in printing that took place in this country at the turn of the last century.

> Edward Larocque Tinker. *The New York Times Book Review*, October 5, 1941, p.28. Tinker was an American author and critic for *The New York Times Book Review*.

A Private Press Printer & Bibliographer

With a very modest demeanor, Thomas Bird Mosher of Portland, Maine, devoted many years and an exquisite taste to offering the writings of men who, at the time, were little known. His *forte* was literary content, yet his ideas of typography were eminently sound, or at least sane, with a distinctly individual character... Many of the most delightful stylists among modern authors came into our ken in the tiny pages of *The Bibelot* and the Vest Pocket Editions, and the not much larger formats of the Mosher books. How many people there must have been who, through Mosher's kindly offices, first made acquaintance with William Morris's Romances, Maurice Hewlett's *Earth-work Out of Tuscany*, and Fiona Macleod's prose lyrics, to mention only a few viands of the feast.

In typography and format the Mosher books justly may be called both sane and charming. With almost the restraint of Cobden-Sanderson, Mr. Mosher used very little decoration. Even color appears very seldom. And that choice took strength of character and a certain conviction in those days when typography was running pretty wildly to decorative and colorful, even weird, effects.

> Will Ransom in *The Publisher's Weekly*, March 24, 1928. Reprinted under the heading "In the Tradition" in *The Mosher Books* catalogue for 1928. Ransom was a printer/designer in the American private press movement, and became, as Susan Otis Thompson calls him, "the dean of writers about private presses."

Maxwell Steinhardt's Quarto Club Paper

It was here [in Portland] that he published the Mosher books and accomplished creative results in literature the value of which is bound to be permanent and ever growing. Some one said of Mosher and Portland that it was "the city he made famous throughout the literary world." The observation is not exaggerated, for his influence has spread fruitfully through that rather indeterminate territory...

No publisher has ever maintained such an unbroken record for excellence of substance and form. Each volume justifies itself. We may not like this or that choice, but we must agree that the entirety is a monument to creative publishing, to use the phrase someone tacked on to Mosher. He printed what he loved and that is perhaps the secret of his triumph...

It is useless to attempt to speculate over Mosher's influence in and upon our literature. It has been important and possibly as important as that of any other American critic or publisher. He was a pioneer and planted over extended and untouched areas the seed of appreciation of fine letters. Accurate is the estimate that "few men have done more for literature, and done it so understandingly." He loved books and his affection for them is expressed imperishably. As an artist he served his calling without shame or lust. His memory will not die in after days.

> Excerpted from Maxwell Steinhardt's "An Appreciation of Mosher" in the *Quarto Club Papers 1926•1927*. NY: Printed for the Members, 1927, pp. 45, 48, and 54. Steinhardt was a prominent New York attorney and secretary of New York's The Quarto Club. His paper was read before the Club on July 13, 1926.

JOHN FOLEY'S FOREWORD IN *AMPHORA II*

My aim has been, and is, to print only those things informed by the spirit of beauty—of the souls of books—not hackneyed, by reason of constant use or display. If the book has any demonstrable raison d' Être, it is more especially that I have got out of the beaten highway and wandered into bypaths, seeking for fine flowers of the forest rather than for floral displays of the classical literary garden. [T. B. Mosher]

That Thomas Bird Mosher accomplished his difficult task of gathering "the lesser known, but imperishable utterances" which earlier editors "had never found or had never set out to find," is clear not only from the gratifying response to the first *Amphora*, which he brought out in 1912, but also from the singular measure of praise which it has won from judicious critics. It had long been Mr. Mosher's purpose to make a second collection of rare prose and verse championed by him from writers of distinction, many of whom had had to wait for just recognition. These selections which he had included in his catalogues from 1912 to 1923, he was intending to publish in a satisfying format when death frustrated his plan. Since that time many persons have requested that these choice passages, as yet scattered, be brought together under one cover, and many have asked for some account of Mr. Mosher's life.

Amphora: A Second Collection, while fulfilling his purpose, also preserves his Forewords, which are essays in themselves, and three of his poems not heretofore printed over his name; presents an admirable likeness of him; and records several distinguished tributes to his life and work. This volume, then, rightly takes on the character of a memorial.

But no memorial volume can have any claim to being complete unless it defines Mr. Mosher's position as an editor and publisher, and unless it sets forth his personality among his friends. The former is established by the very individual and creative publishing he achieved and sustained in America over many years; the latter can really be appreciated only by those who knew him in the intimacy of his remarkable library. There he lived in an other-worldliness of ideal beauty—to him the essential reality—and this escape he offered to many other seekers through the exquisite reprints which he put within their reach.

Entirely independent of what the public wanted, Thomas Bird Mosher published what he liked—and no more. While other publishers were, and are, satisfied to supply very profitably the latest variation in public preference, he set himself, in his own words, "to awaken a passion for *the language of the absolute* which from the reading of my books is discoverable in ever living beauty." To follow such an elusive ideal was to travel a lonely way in a young nation and in an age which must be busied about the insistent material needs of a swiftly changing world. Of the men in his field, however, no one held more steadfastly than he to a venture which must go unappreciated by the majority of his contemporaries, for he was a fearless soul who dared to do the unpopular, one of those who are weavers of intellectual and spiritual beauty against the need of a newer day. He was, in fact, a publisher who turned poet in the making of beautiful books, and for this he holds in the history of American publishing a place apart.

Quickened by the flame which stirred William Morris, Rossetti, Burne-Jones, and Ruskin, he began in the Eighteen-Nineties a pilgrimage to the spirit of beauty. As Arthur Symons says in his conclusion to *Studies in Prose and Verse*, "Art begins when a man wishes to immortalize the most vivid moment he has ever lived." Mr. Mosher immortalized his highest moments as a pilgrim along the road "to the best that is thought and known in the world" in his reprints and in *The Bibelot*, both fast becoming classics. And what better single evidence of his craftsmanship can one offer than his beautiful edition of Sir

Richard Burton's *The Kasidah*? What more conclusive proof of his exact literary judgment and unerring taste in editing than the fruits of his many years, which William Marion Reedy commended thus: "The complete *Bibelot*, in twenty volumes, is an encyclopedia of the literature of rapture with the spirit of beauty"? Similarly, his first *Amphora* and this his second *Amphora* together bring to a consummation the record of his distinctive work in publishing those things which from his viewpoint possessed permanence in literature.

His genius for discerning the durable and less known excellence in books was paralleled by his kindliness and keen humor. Those who knew him best will always see him as the booklover and humanist before his hearthfire in his immense library at home, a large oblong room solid with unusual books from floor to ceiling. There the man whom readers of his *Amphora* must know indirectly, roamed at will, drawing down from shelf on shelf, times without number, some edition long sought by collectors, and immediately opening it to humorous or illuminating sections, laughing like a boy, yet serious in an instant and alert to champion, as ever, unrecognized worth, or to right some wrong to literary fame. Lover of beauty and stoic, he may be imagined as writing in his second *Amphora* as he wrote in the first selection of 1912:

> My *Amphora*, then, O friends whom I may never meet nor greet other than in these words, is not a cinerary urn such as Sir Thomas Browne discovered..... but rather a vessel still containing in unspoiled solution a genuine and generous juice of the most high Muses!

Indeed, this second collection reveals once more the gifts and personality of Thomas Bird Mosher whose editing and publishing of fine books has helped to make the best in literature available in America, and whose work may be described in Walter Pater's words on art, as devoted "to such presentment of new or old truth about ourselves and our relation to the world as may ennoble and fortify us in our sojourn here."

> John Foley. "Foreword" in *Amphora: A Second Collection*, pp. *xiii-xviii*. Foley was a New York newspaperman and writer.

COLONEL W. F. PRIDEAUX'S LETTER

I was very pleased with the "Garland," [*The Garland of Rachel*, 1902] which I look on as having attained the high-water mark of production, or rather, <u>repro</u>duction. I fear I must regretfully allow that typography and the general build of a book takes a higher level on your side of the Atlantic then on ours. Of course we have our Kelmscott Press and so on, but their output is only for the bookshelves of the rich, whereas your dainty reprints may be purchased by any one who cares to have the best of literature presented in the most attractive guise, and at the most moderate price.

> Colonel W. F. Prideaux's letter to Mosher dated 2 Dec. 1902. Prideaux was the English bibliographer of Robert Louis Stevenson.
> (Printed with permission from The Newberry Library).

CHRISTOPHER MORLEY'S "A GOLDEN STRING"

Here and there, leavened in among masses of populace, are those few to whom the name of the late Thomas Bird Mosher still carries a special vibration. Mr. Mosher spent more than thirty years in betrothing books and readers to one another; like the zooming bumble-bee and with a similar hum of ecstasy he sped from one mind to the next, setting the whole garden in a lively state of cross-fertilization.

The famous twenty volumes of the *Bibelot* are Mosher's testament, both the greater and the less as his friend Villon would have said. These are twenty books—yes, and duly stamped in black and red—that any clerk of Oxford would be glad to have at the head of his couch.

"The resurrectionist Mosher" his kinspirit Billy Reedy called him. Aye, how many exquisite things he disinterred, and how far ahead of the thundering herd to see the good things coming. In one of his crisp little prefaces he spoke of "that saving remnant who when they see a good thing know it for a fact at first sight." As early as 1900 he was hailing the Irish literary renaissance in Yeats, Lionel Johnson, Moira O'Neill and others; and coming to the defence of *vers libre*. It was in those little grey-blue *Bibelots*, chance-encountered in college days, that Mistletoe first met Fiona Macleod, Francis Thompson, Synge, Baudelaire, H. W. Nevinson, William Watson, Arthur Upson, Richard Jefferies, Arthur Symons, Alexander Smith.... one could carry on the list *ad lib*. What was there in this hardy sea-bred uncolleged downeaster that made him open so many magic portholes? He had the pure genius of book-fancy; an uneducated man, as uneducated as Chaucer and Lamb and Conrad; and I like to think that when he took Aldus's device for himself there was some memory of the time when an anchor meant more to him than an emblem printed on a title-page.

I like to think of the good luck of the people who had the fun of learning in the *Bibelot* something of the extraordinary thrills that literature can give. I think it is not extravagant to say that as a collection of a certain kind of delicacies, this cargo of Mosher's is unrivalled. I suppose it is the most sentimental omnibus that ever creaked through the cypress groves of Helicon. Like all men of robust, gamesome, and carnal taste, Mosher had a special taste for the divine melancholies of ink. Gently tweaked by subscribers for his penseroso strain, he replied "We shall prove that a humorous *Bibelot* is not, as we have been informed, out of our power to produce." But, speaking from memory, I believe he exhumed only the somewhat Scollay Squareish hilarities of James Russell Lowell's operetta about the fish-ball. Its title, *Il Pesceballo*, is the best of it.

I think indeed that a too skittish and sprightly *Bibelot* would have been out of the picture. Mosher's sentiment was of the high and fiery kind, the surplus of some inward biology that made him the rare Elizabethan he is said to have been. He was by no means the indiscriminating all-swallower; his critical gusto was nipping and choice; in those brief prefaces you will find many a live irony, many a graceful and memorable phrase. The particular task that he set himself in the *Bibelot* was, moreover, not prone to casual mirth. He was the seeker among "spent fames and fallen lights." the executor of unfulfilled renowns. The poets he loved were those who were "torches waved with fitful splendor over the gulfs of our blackness."

Take it in beam and sheer, the *Bibelot* is an anatomy of melancholy. It has been called an encyclopedia of the literature of rapture, but it is that kind of rapture which is so charmingly indistinguishable from despair. Mosher loved the dark-robed Muse: he emprisoned [sic] her soft hand and let her rave; he fed deep upon her peerless eyes. He was the prince of editors: he did not come to his task until he had tried other ways of life and found them dusty. He was almost forty when he began publishing, and what did he begin with? Meredith's "Modern Love!" Think of it, gentles [sic]. Would not that have looked like a lee shore to most bookmen in Portland, *arida nutrix* of publishers? But it was what he called the "precious minims" that interested him. There was in him more than the legal 1/2 of one per cent of Hippocrene. In 1895 he began his *Bibelot* and carried it through monthly numbers for twenty years. As editor he never obtruded himself. When he died I don't think there was a newspaper in America that had a photo of him available in its files. He was the potential author of one of the most fascinating autobiographies that were never written.

So it was that there came to us, from what has been called the stern and hidebound coast, this most personal and luxurious of anthologies. These twenty little grey briquettes pile up into a monument. He was always, in the phrase he loved to apply to his favorite writers, "touched to finest issues." He knew lapidary work when he saw it. Once he spotted a poem written by a contributor to the old Bowling Green. At once he wrote for permission to reprint it in his catalogue. "It is one of the few things," he said, "that to me seem almost absolutely perfect." May I tell you, without breach of manners, what it was? Life is very short anyhow for paying one's respect to the things that need admiration. The poem was "Night" by William Rose Benét.

In these twenty volumes there is enough material even for those of us who never knew him to guess fairly closely into Mosher's own tastes. He was all for "songs gotten of the immediate soul, instant from the vital fount of things." And however sharp his taste for the fragile and lovely, there was surely a rich pulse of masculine blood in his choices. He was often accused of piracy. If it be piracy to take home a ragged waif of literature found lonely by the highway, to clothe her in the best you have and find her rich and generous friends—if this be piracy, then let any other publisher who has never ploitered a little in the Public Domain cast the first Stone and Kimball. The little upstairs fireside on Exchange Street, Portland, is one of the most honorable shrines that New England can offer to the beadsman of beauty.

They pile up, I repeat, into a monument that any man might envy, these twenty little fat books. No one reader will agree with all Mosher's choices, but surely never did any editor of genius ramble with so happy an eye among the hedgeflowers of literature. A Scottish critic has said there is only one enduring test of a book: is it aromatic? These beautiful books, from beginning to end, are fresh with strange aroma and feed more senses than the eye. Words of Arthur Upson's, printed here by Mosher, describe them:

> Wine that was spilt in haste
>   Arising in fumes more precious;
> Garlands that fell forgot
>   Rooting to wondrous bloom;
> Youth that would flow to waste
>   Pausing in pool-green valleys—
> And passion that lasted not
>   Surviving the voiceless tomb!

The *Bibelot* began and ended with selections from William Blake. And like Blake, Mosher gave us the end of a golden string.

> Christopher Morley. *John Mistletoe*, 1931, pp. 316-321. Reprinted in *The Saturday Review of Literature* for July 11, 1925, p. 892; and again reprinted in the second *Amphora*, 1926, pp. 109-113 (with some minor changes), and in *An Outline of Distinguished Reading* (1925), pp. 89-94. Morley was an American journalist, essayist, and novelist.

Laurence Gomme's
Little Book-Shop Around the Corner

In the early beginnings of the shop, arrangements were made with Thomas Bird Mosher to act as his agent in New York. He was at the peak of his popularity. From his house in Portland, Maine, came forth the *Bibelot*, a magazine devoted to the most significant in English letters of the last fifty years, the familiar series of volumes clothed in their simple raiment of gray boards, and an annual catalogue which any keen collector would today be proud to place among his choicest. He was scornfully referred to in England as "The Pirate of Portland." Whether a deserved appellation or not, it must be recorded that many an English author reached a very great reading public that would never have been his but for the selectiveness of T.B.M. and the elegance with which he clothed his "victims." It was Andrew Lang, I think, who declared with asperity that in order to protect his rights from the "Pirate" it would soon be necessary to copyright his laundry list. Be that as it may, he produced "only those things informed by the spirit of beauty—of the souls of books—not hackneyed by reason of constant use or display," and in doing this he was frankly out to express his own taste and opinions, not only in what he published but also in the manner of his publishing.

I only met T.B.M. once. It was on one of his very infrequent visits to New York, and early in our start. I had heard that he was the son of a sea captain and had accompanied his father around Cape Horn in his sailing vessel. I hardly expected to meet a sea captain but that is what he seemed to be rather than a publisher of belles-lettres. He was a quiet but hearty fellow, with a ready story, all the better for the Rabelaisian touch. Some years later, at the invitation of Mrs. Mosher, I had the privilege of examining his library. As was to be expected it was a personal collection of the choicest quality. Mostly first editions of the authors he had sought to popularize in his publishing business. Many of the volumes bore inscriptions to him, and let it be said many of these were grateful acknowledgments to his genius and generosity.

> Lawrence J. Gomme. "The Little Book-Shop Around the Corner," in *The Colophon*. New Series—A Quarterly for Bookmen. Vol. II, No. 4. (New York: Pynson Printers, Inc., Autumn 1937, pp. 574-575). First run by Mitchell Kennerley, Lawrence Gomme ran one of New York's most famous bookshops which operated from 1907-1917. Many an author, publisher, celebrated book person, photographer, thespian, and typographer frequented Gomme's little shop. As the place became a center of literary activity, Gomme himself published over thirty books under his imprint at The Little Book-Shop.

FREDERICK A. POTTLE'S
ALDI DISCIPULUS AMERICANUS

Eight years ago, Thomas Bird Mosher placed opposite the little foreword with which he ended *The Bibelot* the first and last stanzas of one of Robert Frost's most beautiful poems [see Index, Volume XXI]. I can think of no other words which would express more completely the thought which he would have chosen to stand at the end, not only of *The Bibelot*, but of his work as a whole:

> *Out through the fields and the woods*
> *And over the walls I have wended;*
> *I have climbed the hills of view*
> *And looked at the world and descended;*
> *I have come by the highway home*
> *And lo, it is ended.*
>
> ....
>
> *Ah, when to the heart of a man*
> *Seemed it ever less than a treason*
> *To go with the drift of things,*
> *To yield with a grace to reason*
> *And bow and accept the end*
> *Of a love or a season?*

Thomas Bird Mosher, publisher of rare and limited editions of books in *belles-lettres*, died at his home in Portland, Maine, on August 31, 1923, at the age of seventy-one. I thought as I read the news story in the *Portland Evening Express* of another story Mr. Mosher once told me of a clerk in one of Portland's largest hotels who told a Mosher enthusiast, who had come from afar in the hope of seeing the master personally, that he believed he had heard of a man named Mosher who carried on some kind of business in Portland, but that he thought he was dead. It is too true now. I imagine that the present citizens of Portland (the event of the story took place some years ago) barely noticed this news of the passing of their most illustrious citizen. Most of them had probably never heard of him. Part of the headline of the article in the *Express* reads, "Little Known Here Though His Works Were Widely Read in Foreign Countries." If the Mayor or the Chief of Police had died, the papers would have given him most of the front page and arranged a civic memorial. But this man, whose name was known in San Francisco and London, in Bombay and Sydney, the publisher of the finest series of editions ever produced in America, and whose work as a whole surpasses anything since the days of the Kelmscott Press, slipped out of the life of their city without causing so much as a ripple of excitement. The truth is that he never really lived in Portland. He resided there almost continuously for over fifty years, and he published his books there from the same address for thirty-two, but he actually lived in a city of wider horizons. Portland was the place where he published his books, but he was not of it. In an unpretentious room on the second floor of a building on one of its lesser thoroughfares he breathed the air of a city which was the world.

I cannot believe that I shall never see him again. Truly, the happiest moments of my life have been spent in that room at 45 Exchange Street. You found the place the first time by the number. There was no sign which could be seen across the street; only a two-line legend on the jamb of the door stating that T. B. Mosher, publisher of fine books, had his office within. You opened the door and found yourself at the foot of a narrow and much worn staircase going straight up two flights. From above (in regions I never explored) came the peculiar grating and rolling sound of a press. You ascended the stairs and suddenly and unexpectedly found on the landing to your right a door with the announcement, "Thomas B. Mosher, Publisher." You hesitated, wondering whether to knock or to enter boldly. The glass of the door was frosted so that you could not see in; you had no idea what to prepare yourself for; whether a large bare room with a press, or a little cubby-hole of an office, where you would find yourself confronting a busy and annoyed person across a large desk. You reflected that, at all events, Mr. Mosher could hardly be like that. You finally pushed the door timidly and it opened, rubbing at the bottom, making a sound like the press, which was still rolling and grating upstairs. Nothing happened. You waited a moment, your courage gone, and then a kind and genial voice called, "Come in!" You entered.

Oh, that room! The warmth, the dusk, the fragrance of it! Lighted on the front by windows opening over the street, but in the corners at the back dim with a mellow duskiness. . . Books all around you to a height easily reached from the floor. . . Facing you as you entered, a great fireplace of brick with blue plates on the mantel ledge, a fire of hard wood smoldering and glowing, the fragrance of maple smoke in the air. . . . In the centre of the room, facing the fireplace, a great comfortable davenport, and backed up to it a little bookcase with all the Mosher books. . . . Around the walls, small framed pictures of authors; you recognized Yeats, Swinburne, J. A. Symonds, an unusual Lincoln. . . . But, then from a desk by the window a man rose and came forward towards you, his hand extended in greeting. You knew at once that it was Mr. Mosher.

Those who own the full set of *The Bibelot* have an excellent portrait of Mr. Mosher as frontispiece to the index volume. It is the only one I have ever seen. If, like me, you did not meet Mr. Mosher until near the end of his life, you saw him as he appears in that photograph. A thick-set, rather portly figure, of middle height, dressed in a plain dark suit; a full, clear-skinned face, with nothing of a bookish pallor, brown hair (later quite white), thin and downy on top, but soft and abundant over the temples; a gray mustache, beautifully curling upwards at the ends; blue eyes with drooping lids and eyebrows going up at a quizzical angle. . . . You notice the passion of the full lips, the laughter in the quizzical eyes, the alertness, even youth of his bearing. He spoke to you again, you stammered something about his books, he laughed and pointed at the bookcase—and in a moment you were out of Portland and in his city of the world.

Oh, the afternoons I have spent in that magic place! Days when the fog hung heavy over the docks, and a gloomy drizzle washed the deserted cobbles of Exchange Street, shut in from the gray cold of out of doors, sitting on the great davenport before the quiet fire, reading or listening to that voice going on and on in its talk of books and authors. His voice (how can it be silent for ever?) was indescribable. It went with the laughter in the eyes and the lips; a quizzical, throaty voice with a velvet-soft rasp to it and a frequent chuckle—not a laugh; only a single note of amusement deep in the throat. "The Prophet says that the heart of mankind is desperately wicked." I hear him say, "I think it would be better to say that the heart of mankind is desperately stupid." A chuckle. "The reformers will never completely divorce genius from vice, I fear." Another chuckle. "A dretful [sic] thing," he would say of some unfortunate work of author or publisher; "A dretful thing."

Those exquisite forewords which are the glory of the Mosher editions contain the passion and rapture of his talk, but they do not contain the humor, the sunny irony, the racy colloquial quality of his conversation. The gleam of his eye is there, but not the twinkle. We talked always of books. I do not remember that I ever asked him a direct question about his own life. But in the course of those magic afternoons, in chance allusions and broken sentences, I learned enough so that I could construct the general outlines of his history.

He was born in Biddeford in 1852. His father was the master of a sailing vessel. I never heard him say much about his father, but I can easily imagine him as a skipper of the old days; of Portland as it was when the boy Longfellow haunted the docks enthralled with

> *The Spanish sailors with bearded lips,*
> *And the beauty and mystery of the ships,*
> *And the magic of the sea.*

The boy Mosher attended school for a few years in Biddeford and later in Boston. But at a very early age (before he was sixteen, certainly; I think before he was fifteen) his father took him out of school forever and carried him away to sea. I do not know the reason for this step, unconventional even in those days, but I have no doubt that it was because his father happened by a miracle to be a man of such unusual insight and sympathy that he was able to form a correct appreciation of his son's peculiar talents. The boy was probably not doing especially well under the stifling routine of the public school, and his father had the courage to try a better method.

It may surprise those persons who think of education as solely the work of the schools to learn that Thomas Bird Mosher never went beyond the grammar grades. Yet what an education he built the foundation for on that clipper of his father's as it ploughed its course through the seven seas! No critic or editor that America has produced ever had a more effective education in literature, if the work he did is to be taken as the test. He was never sorry for his lack of schooling; indeed, though he gave his sons a conventional education, he remained a frank and unconverted skeptic as to the values of mass education. "Having had little of school," he once said, "it is no wonder that I loved literature." When he left school to go to sea his favorite reading was the terrific romances of Sylvanus Cobb—*The Smugglers of King's Cove, Bion the Wanderer*, etc.—and dime novels. He once told me that he left behind him a barrel completely filled with his dime novel library. "I wish I had that barrel now," he added; "I have no doubt it would be worth a thousand dollars." His father snatched him away from the public school, the trashy literature, the college education ("I am particularly grateful to my father for saving me from a college education," he used to say) and left him for four years with the sea and one short shelfful of books—all good.

"No! I shall never again read books as I once read them in my early seafaring," he wrote in one of those too rare personal essays of his printed in his miscellany, *Amphora*, "when all the world was young, when the days were of tropic splendor, and the long evenings were passed with my books in a lonely cabin dimly lighted by a primitive oil lamp, while the ship was ploughing through the boundless ocean on its weary course around Cape Horn." What scenes, what visions, those casual allusions evoke for me! That slender lad, with passionate lips and eyes, leaning over the rail, gazing in a dream back along the white track of the vessel through the green calm, or lying on his back on the deck, with the snowy canvas billowing between him and the sun! What sights of foreign ports and strange people, what glimpses of land looming up beyond the bow after days and weeks of unbroken horizon, bringing the grateful tears into the eyes; what fury of tempest, what calm after the storm. . . . Why did I not talk to him of these things? Did he first read *The Ancient Mariner* out of sight of land? Did he stumble by chance upon Keats's lines, and then read them again and again with a growing and incredulous rapture:

> *Charmed magic casements, opening on the foam*
> *Of perilous seas, in faery lands forlorn.*

One of the experiences of those years must have made an especially strong impression on him, for I remember hearing him mention it more than once. That was the time he sailed with his father into New Orleans with men for Gen. Butler's garrison.

Four years of that glorious life of the sea, and then the days of his seafaring were over forever. I think he never again left this country except for one memorable trip to England, when he met York Powell (a man he held in especial reverence) and William Michael Rossetti. It may have been at that time that he first met William Sharp, whose Fiona Macleod writings he did so much to introduce. To those who know and marvel at the catholicity and range of his taste and the true scholarship of his work it seems incredible that he could read no language save English, and that, apart from those brief stops in foreign ports during his boyhood, he never visited any foreign country except England. I know that this was a great disappointment to him. I remember once, as I was looking at his edition of *The Hollow Land,* I told him how I once saw the Hollow Land itself. "It is as you come out of the Auvergnes and look down from the rim of the mountains upon the plain of Clermont Ferrand. Have you ever seen it?" I shall never forget the wistfulness of his tone as he said quietly: "I have never been in France." Then he added, after a long pause: "And now I shall never go there."

His four years of happy idleness were soon ended, and his circumstances demanded that he now make a way for himself. He was, I suppose, about eighteen when he began the struggle to make a living. And for the next twenty years he met with disappointment and failure. I can imagine him with the glory of those early years still upon him, his heart singing to the melodies of those immortal strains he had come to know so well, his eyes rapt with visions. . . . . What could he do? He knew only vaguely what he wanted to do, and no way to do it. I suppose he drifted irresolutely into connection with the publishing house he finally entered because of his fondness for books. His choice of occupation was no more his own than was Lamb's. Like Lamb, he became a book-keeper. But, unlike Lamb, he found a way of escape.

For twenty years he kept up that sort of thing. He left Portland for a year or two, only to come back to enter a newly formed partnership—a publishing business. "I had made a failure of everything else," he said, "and I had to borrow money to go into business. The man who lent it to me thought he would lose it, but he lent it to me because he loved me."

For eight years he worked with this firm, learning the practical details of publishing. All the while it was becoming clearer and clearer to him how he could do the thing he wished to do. He had held to that desire with unyielding tenacity. Through disaster and disappointment and failure he had clung to his dream of what he wanted. In October, 1891, when he was almost forty years old, and had, by his own admission, failed at everything else he had tried, he began the publishing of The Mosher Books. "Do what you know you would like to," he said to me once. "You can't succeed at anything else." His first book was George Meredith's *Modern Love*.

As I ponder it I, who have not the courage of genius, wonder how he could have succeeded. Forty, a failure at business, with no regular schooling, and to begin with *Modern Love*! Why, of all the books he had to choose from, all the books he later published, did he choose that particular one? I am glad that I know. It was because the last line of that poem sequence expressed the idea which all his life had gripped him so mightily—the soul of The Mosher Books:

To throw that faint, thin line upon the shore!

Faint? Thin? I suppose so, for the circumference of the shore is large. But the line is there. No part of the world where English-speaking people live in any numbers is without those to whose feet it has borne its foam. It will delight the lovers of his work, I think, to know that, in accordance with his wish, the business will go on. No new titles will ever be added, but those books for which there is a call will be kept in print in exactly the form which he gave them.

Thomas Bird Mosher was the pioneer in the making of beautiful and inexpensive reprints of not-easily-accessible masterpieces of literature. To-day the advertising pages of our periodicals shriek with the proclamations of cheap classics. But all those who know The Mosher Books know that as he was a pioneer so was he always in a class by himself. Mere cheapness he abhorred. Expensive books he would not make. In choosing titles he was guided by only one principle: whether he loved the book or not. Every book he made a work of art, lavishing on it every attention to make it perfect in size and shape, in texture of paper, in type, in binding. And these exquisite things he sold for the price of ordinary books. He was, in these days of quantity production and cheap manufacture, a craftsman and an artist, a true disciple of Aldus, whose anchor and dolphins he placed upon his title pages.

Frederick A. Pottle. *The Literary Review*, December 29, 1923. Reprinted in the second *Amphora*, 1926, pp. 117-126. Pottle was a professor of English at Yale University, and is widely known today as the editor of the Boswell books.

MITCHELL KENNERLEY

Mr. Mosher made popular in America such authors as Walter Pater, Andrew Lang, Arthur Symons, Maurice Hewlett and a host of others many years before they would have otherwise become known... there is no doubt that he did more for the cause of pure literature in America than any other publisher America ever had.

> Mitchell Kennerley. "Recollections of Thomas B. Mosher." [New York] *Evening Telegram*, Sept. 5, 1923. Kennerley, who started as an assistant to John Lane, was a New York City publisher, and later, director of the American auction house, the Anderson Galleries. He was also a close friend of Mosher's.

CLEMENT SHORTER

Dreamthorp [has never been] presented before in so perfect a form... many English publishers would do well to acquire his books and make then a standard for typography and general 'get-up'.

> Clement Shorter. *Literary Digest*, May 9, 1914. Shorter was a noted British literary critic who defended Mosher at the height of the piracy controversy.

A VIEW FROM AN AMERICAN EDUCATOR & WRITER

The Mosher editions, and the Riverside Press special editions designed by Bruce Rogers, are the two high spots of American printing and publishing. Other presses may have issued more pretentious work, much more elaborately decorated books, or even in some cases more beautiful single volumes. But these two series of publications are the most distinguished—by their simplicity, sincerity, beauty, wise selection of content, readability, appropriateness of the form to the substance, and uniformly fine design. Bruce Rogers had more opportunity of showing historical knowledge and varied adaptability to work representing different periods. But even he, with his wide range, did not surpass Thomas Bird Mosher in the simple beauty and fitness of his work.

It should be the ambition of every American collector to possess a complete set of these two finest series yet issued by Special Presses in America—the two most distinguished in content as well as in form.

He [Mosher] was a publisher who turned poet in the making of beautiful books; and for this he holds in the history of American publishing a place apart.

> This was written by Curtis Hidden Page (1870-1946) in an undated sales catalogue of books Page assembled in the 1930's, the quote being from Volume I, No. 1, p. 66. Page was a professor of English at Dartmouth, authored *A History of Japanese Poetry* (1923), and translated numerous French works.

FROM THE EDITOR OF *THE ATLANTIC MONTHLY*

Any one to whom the tradition of fine books is precious, owes you much gratitude, and, perhaps you will not take it amiss if, out of a very sincere admiration for the new standards you have introduced into American publishing, I take the liberty of writing this letter.

> January 6, 1922 letter to Mosher from Ellery Sedgwick, editor of *The Atlantic Monthly*.

RALPH FLETCHER SEYMOUR COMMENTING ON
MOSHER'S ROLE IN THE AMERICAN PRINTING REVIVAL

It was not long before book makers began to compromise with simon pure handwork by substituting power press printing and machine made, rag paper for hand work. Copeland & Day, of Boston, did a few good books in this class. Thomas Bird Mosher, of Portland, Maine, became the most interesting exponent of this American way. His editions were however, printed on Van Gelder paper. He used small type, bound many editions in paper boards with blue charcoal wrappers, and all his editions were limited. Although he was an admirer of Morris his books did not look like Kelmscott Press ones except the few which were deliberately copied. His books were priced remarkably low and lovers of well made volumes who bought them got more for their money than they could anywhere else. Their contents sometimes were original contributions but oftener were reprints of belles-lettres and hard-to-find small literary masterpieces. Mosher intended to make interesting literary gems printed in charming formats available at low prices, an idea something like the one hit on by the house of Aldus, who undertook to publish literary masterpieces and useful books in large editions at low prices, giving the common man, who until then had hardly been permitted to read the Bible, his first chance in this world to get somewhere by reading books. Mosher thought literature should be free as air and when he ran across something interesting to both himself and others he was liable to reprint it in what is known as a pirated edition, unless it was protected by an air-tight copyright. Both he and I had reprinted Whistler's "Ten O'Clock," which had equivocal copyright protection, at best. I had sent a couple of copies of my edition to Charles Freer, of Detroit, who had assumed the role of protector of Whistler's interests in this country, and he had demanded that I send the edition to him at once, for destruction. I had done so, after talking it over with an attorney. Mosher could not believe I had been such a fool. Thomas B. Mosher did a great deal to acquaint and interest many in good book making and in literature of distinction. He was a stocky, quiet, unpretentious man, with a big "wallop", and a very interesting talker, if one could get him to talk. The flare for his publications faded somewhat before he died, due partly to the noticeable improvement in book making which appeared here, and to the great increase in human interest our literary people put into current writing.

> Ralph Fletcher Seymour. *Some Went This Way—A Forty Year Pilgrimage Among Artists, Bookmen and Printers*, 1945, pp. 107-08. Seymour was an important figure in the Chicago book world. He established the Alderbrink press, designed type, and produced books in both the Aesthetic and in Arts & Crafts style, but his later work leaned toward commercial production. Some of the correspondence between Mosher and Seymour is now located at the University of San Francisco.

A TRIBUTE FROM INDIA

Thomas Bird Mosher, for nearly half a century publisher of rare editions of books in *belles lettres* and dean of the world's book lovers, died on the 31st August, 1923.

Beginning life as a book-keeper Mr. Mosher lived to establish a business which has no equal. He was a writer of fine discernment, a critic and an authority in the branch of literature to which he devoted his life.

Mr. Mosher occupied a unique position, in that he was so busy supplying the people of distant lands and places with books that his townspeople were scarcely familiar with him. Beloved by the comparatively few who were privileged to know him in the City of Portland, Maine, U. S. A., where he practically spent his life, his name is a household word in the cities and towns of the West and South, in which there is apparently a greater demand for books of the quality published by Mr. Mosher than in Portland. It might even be said in this connection that the distinguished bookman was better known in Australia and in India than he was to the people of Exchange Street, where in 1871 he entered the publishing business as a clerk in the store above which his office was afterwards located.

It was here, however, that Mr. Mosher was able to throw himself into the work which made life for him "the sunlit road," which he declared he had found it. Here he lived surrounded by his books, pictures and bric-a-brac, receiving his patrons and friends from the literary centres of the world, attending to his immense correspondence and to a still greater extent finding companion-ship with the great men of letters of the past. Broadminded and with a literary outlook of the widest, he was also ready to welcome the good work of men of today, as well as to help preserve and to send down the productions of the great authors and scholars of the past. His own scholarship was exact and comprehensive along special lines and it would be hard to set any bounds to his field of literary observations and research.

Mr. Mosher was born in Biddeford, September 11, 1852, the son of Benjamin and Mary Elizabeth (Merrill). He was educated in the public schools of Biddeford and Boston and in 1906 Bowdoin College conferred the honorary degree of A. M. upon him. He married Anna M. Littlefield of Saco, July 2, 1892. He is survived by his wife and two sons, Harrison Hume and Thomas Bird Jr. and by one sister, Mrs. Elizabeth Cowan of Biddeford.

He began publishing choice and limited editions of books in *belles lettres* in October, 1891. His work of editing and publishing the Bibelot [titles not italicized in this article] was begun in January, 1895; he thus completed a reprint of poetry and prose, largely from scarce editions and sources not usually known, in twenty-one volumes with index, in 1915. He edited and published an American edition of The Germ, 1898; Swinburne's Poems and Ballads, 1899; Rossetti's Poetical Works, 1902. The first absolute facsimile reprint of Fitzgerald's Omar Khayyam of 1859 was produced by Mr. Mosher in 1902. He also edited and compiled a bibliography in Old World editions of Fitzgerald's entire texts of Omar.

It is of interest to know that the first time Mr. Mosher ever heard a word about the Rubaiyat was in 1879 and the man who quoted "the moving finger writes" was a doctor of medicine, F. H. Gerrish, of Portland who was very well known in the medical profession. It was in a little lecture room in Congress Street on the subject of hygiene that the latter quoted those four lines, and from that time to the last day of Mr. Mosher's life, as it were, Omar was with him. "I think I need Omar every hour," he was fond of saying.

At that time Mr. Mosher's day had not dawned. He was a hard working bookkeeper who was carrying burdens and had not seen his way to publish the "Mosher books," or indeed any books except the ordinary folios used in his professional career. From 1882 to 1890 he was one of the partners of the firm which was known as McLellan, Mosher and Co. Leaving Portland in 1879, he returned to Maine and went into business with the late Reuel T. McLellan in 1882.

He came in touch with the particular interest which proved to be the ruling hobby of his life through wanting to publish things according to his idea of how they should be published. He intuitively felt that such work would have place. Then, too, expression was doubtlessly a motive,—the impulse which shows itself in the desire for good workmanship. These combined with perseverance, the faculty which gives one the power to accomplish a piece of work without allowing one's self to be turned aside from purpose, either by the initial difficulties involved or by the obstacles that multiply as one progresses with his task, led to the goal.

Mr. Mosher's first book was Modern Love by George Meredith. It faithfully reproduced the text of 1862 and was later revised with other poems by Meredith in his Old World Series. The closing words of that poem better than anything else, tell what Mr. Mosher tried to do as a publisher, as he once said,—"To throw that faint, thin line upon the shore." He considered the greatest achievement of his career to be, not his Bibelot, by which he was best known, but the reproduction of Walt Whitman's Leaves of Grass, in the author's memorial year. Mr. Mosher not only had the extremely great pleasure of publishing this book, but he had an equal amount of gratification of seeing the edition sold out without a word of advertising, although this interest was in no sense from the commercial standpoint. It was simply a case of "throwing out that faint, thin line upon the shore." His last published work was Odes, Sonnets and Lyrics of John Keats.

Mr. Mosher once made the statement that he rarely ever read the newspapers for the reason that he could not indulge in the habit without enfeebling his taste for literature, although he admitted that his early dreams were of a newspaper.

He claimed it was his father who gave him his greatest education when he allowed him to go to sea for five years. He often declared that he was grateful to his father for saving him from a college education. He attributed his love of reading to the fact that having little school training, he needed and loved literature.

Mr. Mosher published nearly 500 titles reproducing upon the finest papers, by means of the most beautiful fonts of type and in the most artistic bindings, some of the most exquisite editions of literary works. Thus the best traditions of English literature have been preserved, and through "the faint, thin line" which the Portland publisher eminently succeeded in throwing, these traditions should and undoubtedly will pass into the possession of coming generations whose pleasure it will be to cherish them and whose duty it will be to perpetuate them. Much also might be said of Mr. Mosher's cultured home life, and of the gaiety, optimism and irony, combined in his delightful personality. He lived profoundly, which indeed was the secret of his producing greatly. But it is as a publisher of unique volumes, as an editor and poet that he will be remembered, and this will be as he wished, if one may judge from the preface of one of his own works in which he wrote in part as follows:

"To you who have bought and loved my books and know what they have signified during the past years I need give no stronger assurance as to the tenor of my way than is set forth in these solemn affirmations. To believe that literature is the lasting expression in words of the meaning of life, has been and will ever remain an ideal as long as I am permitted to publish at all."

"And when the curtain comes down for the last time, I want not a few half-wearied spectators and a fast emptying house, but a still appreciable audience."

> "I know the night is near at hand,
> The mist lies on the hill and bay,
> The autumn leaves are drifting by,
> But I have had the day."

Wilbur Needham has made the following fine attempt at appreciation of the rare spirit which pervaded all that Mosher did:

[quotes Needham's three-part article, *in toto*, from *The Chicago Evening Post*]

The latest books which Mosher lived to place in the hands of his readers were in his best style. One of these is "a Freeman's Worship" [sic] with special preface by Bertrand Russell, the other is "a Children's Crusade" [sic] translated from the French of Marcel Schwob in the same format as originated by him.

We are delighted to find that although no more new books will be published in these series, the Mosher books will be reprinted as called for. Truly may the words of William Watson be applied to Mosher:

In light, in night, in twilight,
        I sought for very Thee:
But my light, was it 'Thy light?
        I sought, and nought could see.

I strove by inward eyesight
        To gaze on things to be:
But my sight, was it Thy sight?
        I gazed, and nought could see.

Along Thy starlit highway
        Thou lead'st me, bound or free!
If my way, then, be Thy way,
        O whither lead'st Thou me?

> The above memorial tribute is taken from: Alphamu. "Thomas Bird Mosher (1852-1923)" in *The Calcutta Review*. Vol. 9, No. 3. (Third Series). Calcutta, India, December 1923, pp. 459-465. Alphamu is perhaps a pen name play on the initials "A" and "M" (in Greek, "alpha" and "mu").

SPENCER MILLER, JR., CRITIC

The law of excellence and the law of democracy stand in apparent conflict one with another in our modern age. They seem outwardly to have little in common. Yet Thomas Bird Mosher resolved this conflict through a sharing of enduring prose and poetry with his fellow-men. It was his gift to know what was excellent; it was his passion to share this excellence as widely as possible; it was his destiny to attain the realization of his ideal. He linked beauty which is ageless in art with the desire for the best which is timeless in the spirit of man.

His place among great American publishers is secure. This position he made unique through his unerring genius in selecting those things of established worth which are "a lasting expression in words of the meaning of life," and in sending forth each piece of literature in a manner appropriate to the nature of the work itself. Every volume was printed from hand-set type on hand-made paper and was hand-bound in paper boards. The human hand runs through all his work—a symbol of the human touch of mankind.

When we shall view the fullness of his achievement in an historical perspective, we shall regard it with an unceasing admiration. For he has done what all fine artists seek to do—to increase truth and beauty in the world. His quest of this ideal will be the measure of his own inheritance in the memory of men.

> The above tribute by the critic, Spencer Miller, Jr., is quoted from a twenty-six page paper read by Henry O. Wheeler before the Zamorano club at Los Angeles, CA, on September 30, 1936, p. 3. It was taken from "To Thomas Bird Mosher" in *Amphora—A Second Collection...* (Portland, ME, 1926), pp. *vii-viii*.

MODERN ASSESSMENTS (1930-1992)

CARL P. ROLLINS, YALE UNIVERSITY PRINTER

I am still of the opinion that Mosher was less noteworthy for his printing than for his skill in selection of material. For instance, Sidney Kramer in his recent bibliography of Stone & Kimball says: "*The Bibelot* derived directly from the eclectic publications with which 'The Portland Pirate' had begun, in 1891, his publishing career, and Stone & Kimball were always polite to Captain Mosher." The Stone & Kimball publications, including *The Chap Book*, if not an influence in themselves, typographically, were at least very much in the spirit of the times, part of the renaissance of printing in America.

As for Koopman's criticisms, I cannot agree with him. I knew Harry Koopman, a lively, kindly, appreciative man, who wrote interestingly on many bookish subjects. Nevertheless I do not think that he thought out what he said about Mosher. To speak of him as a leader in fine printing is to quite ignore DeVinne and Gilliss and even H. O. Houghton—and they were at work before Mosher.

I do not want to depreciate Mosher's work, only to point out that charming as his printing was, it was not the printing but the stuff he printed which gave him fame. And I am quite elated that you have put your finger on the essential fact of that fame: its appeal to the romantic nostalgia of the time. If I were asked to describe the effect which his books had on me when I was in my early twenties (you see?) I would quote Wordsworth:

> Will no one tell me what she sings?
>   Perhaps the plaintive numbers flow
> From old, unhappy, far-off things,
>   And battles long ago.

I sometimes wonder if my interest in those books and the *Bibelot*, shared with few to my knowledge, but obviously shared by many, was not as much a sadness for what was coming as for what had gone. *Meccanismo* and science were gathering speed for their approaching blitzkrieg; the rottenness of the post Civil War prosperity was beginning to smell; perhaps we felt a slight shiver at the premonition that we too belonged on

> The far, forgotten fields of flight and faery,
>   O loves and hates deceased long ago....

We were not esthetes. I for one was as busy as a one-armed paper hanger, at printing. But I had read my Morris, and I was troubled about the world. I did not like "successful" people like my uncle who went west and ran a big brick company in Illinois: I preferred that other uncle whose passions were laying stone walls, haying, and raising strawberries. I found consolation and elation and incentive in Mosher's discoveries of small, choice bits of literature. I liked the minor note in them, my Quaker heritage found, I suppose, something more quieting in them than in the more usually accepted "classics."

Maybe I am suffering from a Freudian difficulty of some sort—but I never analyse myself in that direction. I think I could tell you something of the reaction of a man born in 1880 to the new stresses of the twentieth century, but it has been done better. Only I lived through those years and they had something to offer—something which I rather think the world would be better off with today...

> This is a major portion of a July 23, 1941 letter from Carl P. Rollins in New
> Haven, CT to Dean Yorke who was writing a biography of Mosher's early
> life (Bishop Collection). Carl Purington Rollins (1880-1960) was a printer

associated with the Yale University Press as an advisor in typography and as a printer to Yale University since 1918. He served in an editorial capacity with several publications and held numerous honorary memberships.

JAMES VAN TRUMP & ARTHUR ZIEGLER

Mosher... bravely published *Modern Love* even though it had secured little recognition in its English edition; he attested to Oscar Wilde's worth by bringing out some of his work when he was in disrepute. Searching into the back numbers of *The Germ*, *The Oxford and Cambridge Magazine*, and *The Dark Blue*, he discovered already neglected essays, poems, and stories of the Pre-Raphaelites, especially Morris, Swinburne, and Rossetti. He took work from *The Yellow Book* and *The Century Guild Hobby Horse*, which were limited in circulation. The aesthetes, such as Ernest Dowson, Lionel Johnson, Francis Thompson, Vernon Lee, and Lord Alfred Douglas unexpectedly found their work circulating in America while it had a restricted public in England. Mosher presented very fully the Irish literary revival to America by printing Yeats, Thomas Moore, James Clarence Mangan, Sir Samuel Ferguson, and A.E. He printed Ernest Rhys, Stopford Brooke, and all the work of Fiona Macleod. Through English editions Mosher introduced the prominent figures of the as yet little known French Symbolist Movement.

While this small list witnesses to Mosher's discriminating taste, it also demonstrates that Mosher was printing literature of which other publishers were unaware or which they did not trust as profitable or worth protecting at Washington. Without Mosher's audaciousness the authors not only would have received no royalties but also no publication in America for probably some time. There Mosher's worth will stand: he printed in unique and worthy dress, at clear risk of financial loss and personal discredit, work which was unpopular or unproven but which has since won a secure place in our literary heritage. Seeking to 'increase truth and beauty in the world', Mosher, with 'missionary enthusiasm', acquainted the American public with writing that merited its attention.

> James D. Van Trump and Arthur P. Ziegler, Jr. "Thomas Bird Mosher— Publisher and Pirate" in *The Book Collector*. Vol. II, No. 3. Autumn, 1962, pp. 310-311. Both authors are noted Pittsburgh historians, writers, and architectural preservationists.

NORMAN H. STROUSE, MOSHER COLLECTOR EXTRAORDINAIRE

Basic to the delight one experiences in handling Mosher books is the exquisite hand made paper on which he exercised his rare talent for book making. Although Mosher drew on sympathetic craftsmen to print his books, every volume spoke eloquently of a personal dedication to the concept of a private press. Mosher books were a simple extension of the personality of Thomas Bird Mosher and his compulsive delight in the spiritual treasures of literature...

It is a reassuring peculiarity of American civilization that during the last century, a period during which there have been such intense drives toward mechanization and mass production, there have been those who have found a way to live quiet and modestly successful lives while seeming to defy the normal rules for success. In fact, it would appear almost as though their achievements, and their influence within their own sphere of action, can be attributed to their serene disregard for such rules.

Often as not, these seemingly eccentric individuals have been found living in places quite isolated from our vast centers of population, and though only one in ten thousand may ever have heard of them, they have provided a singular and permanent leaven in our cultural life.

Such a man was Thomas Bird Mosher, whose name is almost as unfamiliar to most people as it has been important in American publishing. He is little discussed today for his influence on the development of fine printing and the private press in this country; yet, wherever in the world the English Language is spoken, and men have succumbed to the love of books as artifacts as well as for content, the Mosher colophon is still to be found in the libraries of a select few. I was about to say in the libraries of Mosher collectors, but possessors of Mosher books are not necessarily book collectors as such. In fact some might even be puzzled by the word "collector." They have simply found in Mosher books an essential and deeply satisfying beauty which springs from the combining of exquisite physical appearance and choice literary content into inseparable harmony. They have been attracted by that philosophy-by-selection, so to speak, which provides a quiet, shaded retreat from the harsh achievements of the modern world.

> Norman H. Strouse. *The Passionate Pirate* (North Hills, PA: Bird & Bull Press, 1964). Excerpts are from the introductory note, p.12 and the prologue, pp. 14-15. Many of these same comments also appeared in The Free Library of Philadelphia's 1967 Mosher Press exhibition booklet. Strouse was Mosher's main biographer and proponent, president of the J. Walter Thompson Advertising Agency, and an ardent bibliophile who assembled major book collections donated to several U. S. institutions.

SUSAN OTIS THOMPSON

His ability to combine the two enthusiasms [a love of literature and of fine printing] in a long series of titles published at modest prices is what makes him an enduring figure in the history of American bookmaking... Mosher had disseminated his books wider than any private press, while investing in them a degree of personal conviction no trade publisher could possibly emulate.

> Susan Otis Thompson in Wendy Kaplan's *The Art That is Life* (Boston, Museum, 1987). Thompson, a professor at Columbia University, is also author of the landmark volume, *American Book Design and William Morris* (New York: Bowker, 1978).

LEONARD BASKIN

The intersticed densities of the prodigious Portland pirate, Thomas Bird Mosher, here all set forth in bibliographical order, caused a call on my subtlest typographical skills. The immense, dense & complex index is reflective of Mosher's endless manipulation of the same texts, set & issued in various sizes in divers series; it resolved itself into forty one pages set in eight point type. This is not the place to discuss or assess Mosher, but he was influential & important on many different levels. The book was needed & its bibliographical avowals & endless index illuminate the tangled growth of his publishing tendencies.

> This note is by Leonard Baskin in *The Gehenna Press—The Work of Fifty Years 1942-1992* (Dallas, TX: The Bridwell Library & The Gehenna Press, 1992), p.66, entry 48 referring to Baskin's publication of Benton Hatch's *A Check List of the Publications of Thomas Bird Mosher of Portland Maine* (1966). Baskin is a world-renown artist, book illustrator, sculptor, and private printer.

From the Director of the Spiral Press

Thomas Bird Mosher of Portland, Maine, was not a participant in the Boston-Cambridge burst of typographic fervor. Neither was he touched by the tidal wave from Kelmscott. He is the first American to have established and sustained a program, over thirty-two years, of splendid literary output in consistently felicitous typographic form... They were bought by thousands of literate men and women whose pleasure in reading was enhanced by fine paper, good workmanship, and an unassuming and quiet typographic elegance.

> Joseph Blumenthal. *The Printed Book in America* (1989), p.41. Blumenthal served as director of the Spiral Press. He also authored the catalogue for the 1973 "Art of the Printed Book" exhibit at New York's Pierpont Morgan Library, in which Mosher received honorable mention.

Thomas Bird Mosher and the Art of the Book

When Mosher published his first book in 1891, thereby founding the first significant private press in America, the printing arts on this continent as well as in England were in ferment... Mosher was aware of the reform of printing brought about by the Arts and Crafts movement, probably through the Hobby Horse, of which he owned a complete set, and the Inland Printer; he was aware as well of Morris (he owned seven Kelmscott books and published nineteen titles by Morris) and his conception of what a book should be. With Morris, Mosher shared a concern for the beauty and design of the page, an attention to details, and the idea of a book as a unit rather than a series of pages. But, unlike Morris, he aimed at simplicity and quiet elegance, taking as his models the unassuming books printed in Oxford between 1845 and 1906 by the Reverend Daniel; the books, printed for William Pickering, by the Chiswick Press (to which he admitted his debt); those of the Bodley Head; and those of Aldus. Mosher's choice of a dolphin as an element of his logo is an homage both to Aldus and to Pickering. Mosher became *the* foremost proponent of the Aesthetic style in America.

> Jean-François Vilain in *Thomas Bird Mosher and the Art of the Book* (1992), pp. 5-6. Vilain is a publisher at F. A. Davis Co. in Philadelphia, a collector of books from the Arts & Crafts period, and a writer and lecturer.

The Antiquarian Book Monthly Review

Bruce Rogers called him "The Aldus of the nineteenth century." Norman Strouse praised him as the "first American to publish distinctive books in limited editions." This unique bookman was Thomas Bird Mosher, the celebrated reprint "pirate" who, in the early 1900s, produced over 400 titles in 32 years of successful book publishing. In an age indifferent to fine printing he stood almost alone—concocting charming volumes of tasteful typography, at what he called, "a price so moderate as almost to cause incredulity"...

Although Mosher's books are sometimes criticized for too small print, datedness, fragile bindings, and too chaste a look, his total production was substantial, and his simple crisp press-work proved an enduring influence on later publishers. The Trovillion Press (1930s-60s) acknowledged its debt to Mosher, and I feel a kinship exists between him and certain contemporaries—particularly the Peter Pauper Press. Although Beilenson sold through retail stores, and stressed illustration and graphic interest, there are obvious similarities. Aspects like small, concise format, sophisticated titles, quality paper, slipcases, distinguished typography, an extremely modest price, and an overall understated, but tasteful look all hark back to Mosher's ideal...

Mosher's paradoxical career was truly an American phenomenon—the unschooled, self-made businessman, who put Portland, Maine on the literary map. In spite of his significant contribution both to publishing, and to the bettering of American life, he now seems relatively unknown, or over-looked. Today, when conglomerates are busy taking over small publishers (and producing only sure money makers), it is satisfying to recall Thomas Mosher and his courageous zeal in disseminating fine literature. As Carl Purington Rollins said in a later tribute, "We may know more about typography now, but I doubt if we know more about sanity in publishing."

> Extracts from Kay MacKay's " 'A Pirate Half Pardoned...'—Thomas Bird Mosher" in the *Antiquarian Book Monthly Review* 14. [January 1987], pp. 16 and 21. MacKay's background is in journalism and library science. She works for Omnigraphics, has a small antiquarian book business, and is newsletter editor and program chairperson for the Book Club of Detroit.

"A MODERN LOVE OF LITERATURE"

One hundred years ago, bibliophile Thomas Bird Mosher (1852-1923) published his first book, *Modern Love* by George Meredith. Motivated by his "modern love" of literature and fine books, Mosher made his mark on the publishing world by bringing to the American public the fine printing revival which had begun in Britain only a few years earlier...

As an independent publisher, Mosher could offer the American book lover a chance to own well-made books, and works of literature which were previously unobtainable. Since he was not operating a commercial press, Mosher was unconstrained by the demands of the marketplace, and because the United States was not participating in the International Copyright Convention, he was free to reprint British authors as he liked...

Looking back on the one hundredth anniversary of The Mosher Books, the determination of one man to bring quality books and literature to America is to be admired, and his works continue to instill a modern love of literature in new generations of book lovers.

> Excerpts from the 1991 exhibition booklet for "A Modern Love of Literature—One Hundredth Anniversary of Mosher Books" curated by Leslie M. Parsons and held at the A. M. Todd Rare Book Room of Kalamazoo College, Michigan.

THE UNVEILING OF A COMMEMORATIVE PLAQUE

> Just above, on the second floor of this building, was the office of T. B. Mosher who published over 775 books of fine literature from 1891 to 1923. Mosher's beautiful books helped to influence a generation of printers and designers in the American printing arts.

The above words are printed on a brass plaque erected at Mosher's business location in Portland, Maine. The following remarks were made at the unveiling ceremony:

It has been 67 years since Mosher's death and Portland has not formally recognized this world famous publisher known in San Francisco and New York, in London and as far away as Bombay, India and Sydney, Australia. Barely a ripple was caused here in Portland when he died on August 31, 1923. Why even while Mosher was alive and vibrant, an outside traveler on pilgrimage from some distance finally arrived in Portland only to hear a hotel clerk answer his inquiry: "Mosher? Let's see, I believe there was a man of that name lived here but I think he died some time back." Mosher used to chuckle over this from time to time. Well... today Portland finally offers some small token of recognition and appreciation to the man at the site of one of the two literary shrines he left behind in this city.

Rather than to try to recount the many facets of Mosher's life including his seafaring days, several life tragedies, and his Horatio Alger climb to fame, I encourage those of you here today to find out what stuff this man was made of, who attracted friends the likes of Nathan Haskell Dole of the *Atlantic*; Booth Tarkington; Thomas Brackett Reed nicknamed 'Czar Reed', the most powerful man of the U. S. Congress during the McKinley administration; authors Austin Dobson, Edmund Gosse, William Butler Yeats, Richard LeGallienne, Christopher Morley, and of course, Robert Frost who openly admitted that Thomas Bird Mosher was one of only three men who stirred a biographical impulse in him. What was it that attracted people to enter these very doors, poets like Frost and Thomas Jones, editors like St. Louis's William Marion Reedy, and C. Lewis Hind of the London Academy, and famous actors and actresses like C. S. Williams, Julia Marlowe, Ellen Terry, Ethel Barrymore, and many others?

Along the way in your search and investigation of this man, you'll find such praises as those given by world renowned typographer and book designer, Bruce Rogers who called Mosher "the Aldus of the XIX Century." You'll most certainly come across Joseph Blumenthal's recent book entitled *The Printed Book in America* in which he proclaims Mosher as "the first American to have established and sustained a program... of splendid literary output..." And once you pick up steam, you'll read Norman Strouse's *The Passionate Pirate* in which he lauds Mosher as the "first American to publish distinctive books in limited editions."

But even if you don't have the time to consult these sources and delve into minute historic fact, at least treat yourself to some of the wonderful productions from the heart and mind of Mosher. Just down the street you can visit the Portland Public Library which has a large collection of Mosher Press books. Mosher published over 400 titles in 14 different series, totaling in excess of 750 books when you tally all the different editions. Maybe you'll only be impressed by his first ever facsimile of Walt Whitman's 1855 *Leaves of Grass* published to commemorate Walt's 100th birthday anniversary. Or you might marvel at his first absolute facsimile of the first edition of FitzGerald's *Rubáiyát of Omar Khayyám*. Perhaps you'll be struck by three of the books which most closely resemble William Morris' Kelmscott Press productions. You might even get hooked on the beautifully worded forewords to Mosher's famous catalogues, or to many of his introductions in *The Bibelot*, Mosher's successful small literary magazine. However, most importantly, *read* some of these or other books in the Mosher cornucopia and discover why Mosher said:

> Confessedly, my work has opened the gates of a luminous
> world to me. And for this very reason, I would transmit
> what I may, to others, even as in races of old, relays of run-
> ners passed on the burning torch.
>
> I am convinced that in literature alone is to be found
> and cherished the element which brings together vanished

past and living present. Hence, what I have learned of
storm and sun, may I not in my books make over to the
men and women who reach out through intellectual sympathy and touch hands with me. Its poets and prophets are
forever creating a divine unrest which must unite us all as
Brethren of the Book.

Here we stand, and up there is where he once stood, and out through these
doors poured the steady stream of Mosher's labors—these things of beauty he
called "The Mosher Books." Now, at long last, Portland begins to remember one
of its most illustrious citizens—Thomas Bird Mosher.

The remarks are by Philip R. Bishop in an address given at the unveiling of a plaque erected at Mosher's business location at 45 Exchange
Street in Portland, Maine, on August 16, 1990.

Nash's Essay in the Hatch Bibliography

The first Mosher Book, like those to come, was his because it expressed his
thought and feelings and moreover because he cared enough for the adopted
text (by no means all were actually orphaned or deserted waifs of literature) to
dress it in his own handsome livery and to promote it with enthusiastic publicity. He was an ardent salesman who knew well what he was about; he was a literary evangelist who rejoiced in every soul saved for his society of booklovers.
He was neither an exponent nor purveyor of bogus and hardly deserves the
careless linking of his name with Elbert Hubbard's...

So, though much hyperbole has been lavished on Mosher as a printer, admiration on other points would have been more grateful to him. He considered
himself a literary gentleman, a bibliophile, and by profession an editor and publisher... The work of Arthur B. Turnure—another Grolier Club founding father
with De Vinne—and his Art Age Press of the eighties has closer affinities with the
Mosher production. The Portland Pirate, as he was pleased to be called, took no
part in the Boston renascence of printing as an art sponsored by Henry Lewis
Johnson's arts and crafts activity in the nineties and the Society of Printers a little later. He came closest in having some ornaments drawn by Bruce Rogers...

In a number of instances Mosher claimed as his models books produced by
the Pickering-Whittingham team in England. His adoption of a dolphin and
anchor device was doubtless suggested by the Chiswick Press's more modest use
of it as well as the salt-water allusion. He was justified in taking Aldus, implic-
itly, as spiritual master too, for were not both primarily interested in perfecting
editions of favorite texts and turning them into compact, appealing, little
books? A principle difference someone has pointed out is that the Aldine press
was bedeviled by rivals pirating the output, whereas Mosher did not scruple to
appropriate the "flotsam and jetsam" of British publishers, and rights be
damned. In 1895 and again preceding the first World War there were indignant
flare-ups about what was termed the Mosher Method. The unrepentant Mosher,
as champion of the impecunious republic of booklovers, adroitly fanned the fuss
into valuable publicity.

Extracts from Ray Nash's "Thomas Bird Mosher: His Life and Work," a
biographical essay in Benton Hatch's *A Check List of the Publications of
Thomas Bird Mosher...* (Northampton: The Gehenna Press, for The University of Mass. at Amherst, 1966), pp. 23, 25 and 26. Nash was a news-
paperman, and became a professor in the Art Department of Dartmouth
College where he specialized in printmaking and printing history.

E. Byrne Hackett
First Director of Yale University Press

He had excellent taste in his selections of material; in this he bordered on genius—and he secured the right to reprint some of Symons, Yeats, A.E., Lionel Johnson, Ernest Dowson, Katherine Tynan and others. He was not a pirate, and I believe paid the authors whose works he published, a small royalty or an outright sum, to publish their work in his "Bibelot", a well-printed journal which ran to about twelve small volumes. Mosher had good taste typographically; within a very narrow range all his work was marked by over-nicety and sameness and gentility, but he undoubtedly helped English and Irish men of outstanding ability, to secure a larger audience than they could have secured without his help. Arthur Symons valued Mosher's friendship.

> Undated letter from E. Byrne Hackett to Roger Lhombreaud in whose book this letter appears: *Arthur Symons—A Critical Biography* (Phila.: Dufour Editions, 1964), pp. 186-87. The publisher, Edmund Byrne Hackett (1879-1953), was associated with Double-day, Page & Co. for several years, and headed the publishing department of The Banker & Taylor Co. of New York. Hackett became the first director of the Yale University Press, and later founder and president of Brick Row Book Shop of New York.

Glaister's Glossary of the Book

Mosher Press: established as a publishing imprint in 1891 at Portland, Maine, by Thomas Bird Mosher (1852-1923)... From 1894 to 1914 he published as 'gift books' a series of anthologies called 'The Bibelot'. The books he published were small, usually 12mo, printed mostly on Van Gelder paper, and prettily tricked out with decorative title pages, slip cases and limitation notices. They were made to be sold cheaply, which his critics claimed could only be done because he pirated English texts by authors who had failed to register them in Washington. Andrew Lang, Francis Thompson, Robert Louis Stevenson and Robert Bridges were but a few of those affected. The British trade referred to him as the 'Portland Pirate'.

Mosher argued with reason that what he printed was unknown in America since others were unaware of it or considered it unprofitable to publish, and he certainly extended the reputation there of the writers he chose. By 1923 he had issued some 800 editions. After his death Flora Lamb ran the Press for his widow until 1938. In 1941 it was sold to a Boston bookshop.

> Geoffrey Ashall Glaister. *Glaister's Glossary of the Book*. Second ed., revised. (London: George Allen & Unwin Ltd., 1979), p. 333.

Charles P. Everitt's
The Adventures of a Treasure Hunter

The man from whom Hubbard probably stole most of his ideas about bookmaking (except for the ooze leather, which was original) was an interesting character of a very different type, Thomas Bird Mosher, of Portland, Maine. Mosher had a delicate, *fin-de-siècle* taste in literature, and introduced such people as Lionel Johnson and William Ernest Henley to America in dainty little volumes invariably printed from hand-set type on Van Gelder handmade paper...

Two things distinguished Mosher as a publisher, aside from his unerring though rather precious taste: he was probably the first in this country who was, and made other people, conscious of books as physical things; and he made a great deal of money doing it. He found a way of turning taste and personality into cash that has been the despair of "fine book lovers" in the trade ever since.

> Charles P. Everitt. *The Adventures of a Treasure Hunter* (Boston: Little Brown Co., 1951), p.160-161.

AN AUTHORITY ON PRINTING IN AMERICA

Thomas Bird Mosher had shown a very unusual flair for delicate and appetizing bookmaking... Not lacking in commercial enterprise and fully as individual and discriminating as the young men just discussed [Stone & Kimball, Way & Williams, etc.] was Thomas Bird Mosher, the much discussed sea captain [sic] and literary pirate in Portland, Maine. Nonchalantly he disregarded the rights of British authors and proceeded with the good old custom of printing anything that pleased him without asking for permission and without paying a cent of royalty... Mosher was a fanatic believer in the value of cultivated and individually thought-out book designing. His diminutive volumes are most inviting, agreeable to hold and to read... Without asking too much what the public liked, he indulged in the luxury of following his own taste, and he was successful—obviously so because his taste was good...

> Hellmut Lehmann-Haupt. *The Book in America—A History of the Making and Selling of Books in the United States.* Second edition. (New York: R. R. Bowker, 1951), pp. 277-278, and 326.

CHARLES MADISON'S ASSESSMENT

Thomas Bird Mosher of Maine was the first to devote himself to fine printing. In 1891 he began to bring out beautifully printed books, and he continued to publish small attractive volumes until his death in 1923. His English Reprint Series and his Bibelot Series were famous among lovers of beautiful books.

> Charles A. Madison. *Book Publishing in America* (New York: McGraw-Hill, 1966), p. 150.

A NOTE FROM PAUL JOHNSTON

Both D. B. Updike and Bruce Rogers owe some debt to [William] Morris, yet their attention had already been directed to the art in books when they first heard of him. Thomas Bird Mosher, the American disciple of Pickering, and Pickering himself were probably as much of a source to them as was Morris... Thomas Bird Mosher set out to publish a series of books, quite obviously with Pickering's editions in mind.

> Paul Johnston. *Biblio•Typographica—A Survey of contemporary Fine Printing Style.* (New York: Covici, Friede, 1930), p. 5.

KENNETH DAY'S JUDGEMENT

The aesthetic movement appeared in America, as in Europe, considerably before the *fin de siècle*; Oscar Wilde had made his famous American lecture tour in 1882, and *Patience* had scored as resounding a success in New York, as in London. During the 1890's it reached its peak, quickly going out of favour as an aftermath of the Wilde scandal; during its heyday in the '90's it made up in intensity what it lost in longevity. Like the arts and crafts revival, the aesthetic movement attracted its *poseurs* and imitators, but it also numbered among its young and enthusiastic members a number who showed genuine originality and talent. Among these were the publishing firms of Stone and Kimball, Way and Williams, and Copeland and Day, all of which published small books of great originality and charm, bearing a certain family resemblance, and yet each with its own house style and originality. More significant, perhaps, was Thomas B. Mosher, literary pirate and publisher, of Portland, Maine.

> Kenneth Day, ed. *Book Typography 1815-1965   In Europe and the United States of America* (Chicago: The University of Chicago Press, 1965), p. 341.

THE MOSHER BOOKS AT SOTHEBY'S AUCTIONS

Thinking of books on view before a sale calls to mind the curious changes that are wrought by time. Whenever Sotheby's had a sale that included modern books of which the copyright had not expired, for the three days that they could be looked at the sale-room was visited by inspectors, who had come to make sure that there were no illegal Mosher imprints in the collection. Mr. Mosher, a printer [sic] in the United States, was making himself a nice profit by printing editions of English books copyrighted in England, but not in the United States, so that, although he was breaking no law in his own country, he was depriving the authors and copyright owners of their rightful dues. Mosher imprints were illegal in England at that time, and could not be sold at auction. I am writing, of course, of over forty years ago, and the copyright law has since been changed. The interesting thing is that the same situation exists now, or did until very recently, not between England and the United States, but between the United States and Russia! A few years ago, when the late Mr. Adlai Stevenson was in Moscow, one of the problems with which he had to cope was the publication by Russian printers of books copyrighted in the United States, but not in Russia, so that by the sale of these books the American authors were being deprived of the royalties due to them, as the English authors had been cheated by Mr. Mosher in the past!

> E. Millicent Sowerby. *Rare People & Rare Books* (Williamsburg: The Bookpress, 1987), p. 70. Sowerby worked for Voynich, Sotheby's, and for A. S. W. Rosenbach.

JAMES NELSON ON THE BODLEY HEAD'S INFLUENCE

Two other avant-garde publishing houses [in addition to Copeland and Day] of the nineties brought out American editions of Bodley Head books: Stone and Kimball and Way and Williams, both of Chicago. And although Thomas B. Mosher of Portland, Maine, never published Bodley head books under a joint imprint, he published attractive editions of some of their authors which in their subject matter, format, and letterpress reflected the influence of the London firm.

To [Ezra] Pound the books of the Bodley Head were no strangers: during his college years in America he had read Fiona Macleod, Dowson, and Symons, and had been guided in his reading by "Mr. Mosher," and he later described himself during this time as having been "drunk with 'Celticism', and with Dowson's 'Cynara', and with one or two poems of Symons."

> James G. Nelson on *Elkin Mathews-Publisher to Yeats, Joyce, Pound* (Madison, Wisconsin: The University of Wisconsin Press, 1989), pp. 131-32. Nelson is an authority on the Bodley Head's publications and its authors.

LAWRENCE WROTH ON PRINTING IN THE MAUVE DECADE

From William Morris to Thomas Bird Mosher seems an unusual jump, and yet it is perfectly clear that while Morris was performing the service which we have described above [Morris's impact on printing, and turning the book into an object of art], and while Elbert Hubbard in the United States was trying to smuggle himself into Morris's mantle, Mosher was attempting a revivification of the typographical tradition, applying to the task a narrow but exquisite taste. Then and now his friends have claimed too much for him. The tradition of good printing had not died out in the United States; Joel Munsell, John Wilson, Theodore Low DeVinne, and Walter Gilliss, were among those, past and present, who had kept it alive; D. B. Updike was about to set up the Merrymount Press, and Bruce Rogers, already known, was soon to be at the Riverside Press. None the less, the normal reader of good literature felt that a new delight had entered his life when the first number of the "Bibelot," Mosher's monthly reprint of prose and poetry was put into his hands. The large number of "Mosher books," embodying reprints and first publications of verse and other forms of belles lettres, which the reader saw in the next twenty years continued to give him delight. Here was a publisher who, employing for his books the type faces of common use, required that they be set with thoughtfulness and care, and printed faultlessly upon selected paper, and who carried to fulfillment the requirements thus established by the closest supervision of his printers. If the pattern of the typical Mosher book seldom varied, neither did the excellence of its production. Occasionally when he stepped off the accustomed path Mr. Mosher's taste failed him. Blowing up Edward Calvert's matchless miniature wood engravings and copperplates to twice their size and printing them from photo-engravings was an instance in point. But within the limits set by the general rum of his books he did a superb service, unforgotten by his readers, in a period when even the best typography was struggling with the illness caused by too much complacency on the one hand and by undigested William Morris on the other.

> Lawrence C. Wroth. "Printing in the Mauve Decade" ("Notes for Bibliophiles" column) in the *New York Herald*, February 8, 1942, p. 18.

JOHN BIDWELL AT R.I.T.

However, what really distinguished Mosher from Stone & Kimball (or from any other of the new turn-of-the-century publishers for that matter) was a consistent and deliberate refinement in his choice of texts and typography. Above all else, Mosher was an admirer of good taste, and, having arrived at a precise, personal understanding of what it should be, he imposed it rigorously on every one of his books... At a time when the only other direct mail purveyor of inexpensive fine printing was Elbert Hubbard (now more appreciated for the wit and audacity of his huckster-ism than for his typographical craftsmanship), the air of good breeding and elegance in the Mosher books could note help but be appreciated... To be more precise, Mosher was not really a printer. Although he was responsible for typefaces, papers, and layouts, the actual printing was done in local Portland shops. Decorative materials, for instance, were the property of the publisher and were loaned out to the printers—usually Smith & Sale or George D. Loring—for each job. Nevertheless, trial title-pages, even dummies for entire books surviving with his annotations, attest to his meticulous concern for the look of his publications.

> John Bidwell, then Curator of The Melbert B. Cary, Jr. Collection at the Rochester Institute of Technology's School of Printing, wrote these comments in the April 1978 issue of the *New York-Pennsylvania Collector*, pp. 4-6.

BIBLIOGRAPHY OF THOMAS BIRD MOSHER

(WORKS ON, ABOUT OR MENTIONING MOSHER)

— SELECTIVELY ANNOTATED —

INCLUDING SOURCES REFERENCED IN SECTION II

☞ = Those works referenced in Section II appear in bold.

☞ (Adler, Elmer) Slater, John Rothwell. *Catalogue of an Exhibition of the History of the Art of Printing—1450-1920*. Rochester, New York: The Memorial Art Gallery, 1920, p. 53. This exhibition was collected and arranged by Elmer Adler who is famed as one of America's outstanding printers. He was also noted as a publisher, designer and collector. He founded the Pynson Printers in New York, and created the memorable typographic and bibliophilic publication, *The Colophon: A Book Collector's Quarterly*. His concern with typography led him to form a collection of enough scope to justify the Art of Printing Exhibition held, not at a library, but at Rochester's Memorial Art Gallery, in "recognition of the fact that really good printing is itself a beautiful thing." (p. 3). The Mosher publication, *Circum Praecordia* (entry 193), appears in the section "The Revival of Fine Printing" along with twenty-four other books from the Kelmscott, Essex House, Doves, Elston, Merrymount and other presses. The catalogue was written by John Rothwell Slater, professor of English at the University of Rochester (certainly annotated in cooperation with Adler). The write-up below Mosher's book states that "Mr. Mosher was one of the earliest American publishers to issue small books printed in small but good type in small editions for booklovers with small incomes. Though there has been no striking novelty in his typographical methods, his service to the cause of literature and of printing has been not inconsiderable." **See entry 71**.

Alphamu. "Thomas Bird Mosher (1852-1923)" in *The Calcutta Review - An Illustrated Monthly*. Vol. 9, No. 3 (Third Series). Calcutta, India: Calcutta Review, December 1923, pp. 459-465. This monthly literary periodical was distributed through agents in London, New York, Bombay, New Delhi, Patna, and Calcutta. Most of the text of this article is printed in ""Memorial Tributes" in Section V, pages 407-10.

☞ Altschul, Frank. *A Catalogue of the Altschul Collection of George Meredith in the Yale University Library*, compiled by Bertha Coolidge with an introduction by Chauncy Brewster Tinker. [Boston]: Privately Printed [D. B. Updike, Merrymount Press], 1931. **See entry 244**.

☞ American Type Founders Company. *Specimens of type: ornaments and borders, brass rules and dashes, business cuts, society emblems, initial letters, card and billhead logotypes, newspaper headings, check lines, and other materials necessary in the printing office*. Chicago, IL: The Company, [1896]. The noted printer of Maine, Fred Anthoensen, identified the Dickinson Type Foundry of Boston as one of Mosher's (or his printer's) sources of type. This foundry was one of fourteen old-line foundries which merged with the American Type Founders Company headquartered in Newark, NJ in the 1890's. Designs found in this source include the "Jenson Old-Style Series" of initials, page embellishments and borders used in Mosher publications like *Empedocles on Etna* (103), *Collectors and Collecting* (74), *Little Willie* (216), *Hand and Soul* (139), *The Land of Heart's Desire* (187), and *In Praise of Omar* (172). **See entries 74, 103, 139, 172, 187, 216**.

Amphora—A Second Collection of Prose and Verse Chosen by the Editor of The Bibelot. Portland, ME: The Mosher Press, 1926. The second *Amphora* is meant to be a companion piece to the first one published in 1912, and contains ten contributions by Mosher. The several tributes to Mosher include the sonnet "October, in Memory of Thomas Bird Mosher" by Thomas Jones; a dedication "To Thomas Bird Mosher" by Spencer Miller, Jr.; a tribute entitled "Forewords" by John L. Foley; another tribute "A Golden String" written by Christopher Morley; and a character sketch of Mosher entitled "Aldi Discipulus Americanus" written by Frederick A. Pottle. A full page notice on this second *Amphora* appeared as "In Memory of Thomas Bird Mosher" in *The Publisher's Weekly*, November 20, 1926, p. 1991.

Anon. "Books and Authors—Thomas Bird Mosher" in *The Bulletin of the Maine State Library*. Vol. XII, No. 3. Augusta, ME, January 1927, pp. 62-65. The library boasts owning a complete set of the Mosher books, but this article consists mostly of extracts from the second *Amphora*, including a lengthy quote from *Publisher's Weekly* of September 15, 1923. There is also a brief sketch of Mosher's life.

Anon. "The Mosher Books" in *The Protest, A Journal for Philistines*. No. Five. Kent, England: Published for the Proprietors from the Sign of the Hop-Pole, Crockham Hill, Eden Bridge, January 1903. Reprinted as an advertisement accompanying *The Bibelot* for May 1903 (not to be found in yearly bound copies). The full text of this selection is printed under "Contemporaneous Accounts" in Section V, pages 390-91.

Anon. *An Outline of Distinguished Reading*—With which are combined several appreciations of the work of Thomas Bird Mosher. New York: Wm. H. Wise & Co., 1925. The section "An Approach to Distinguished Reading" (pp. 7-14) serves as an introduction to Mosher's life and his publication, *The Bibelot*. The three essays at the end of the book are "The Joys of Books" by Alexander Smith, "A Golden String" by Christopher Morley, and "The Ending of the Bibelot" by William Marion Reedy. This little tome was meant as both an advertisement, and as a companion guide, to the reprint of *The Bibelot* of 21 volumes, also published by Wm. H. Wise & Co. in 1925.

Anon. "Portland Librarian Collects Thomas Bird Mosher's Books" in the *Portland Press Herald*. January 5, 1968. Included under the "Clearing House" section, the focus of this multi-column article is Miss Frances Lombard, a secondary school teacher and past president of the New England School Librarian's Association. Excerpts were taken from Lombard's paper on Mosher presented before "the College Club." The article presents no new information on Mosher, and mentions titles in her collection of Mosher books, in addition to quotes from her talk.

Anon. "Publisher on Rural Culture" in the *Boston Sunday Post*. (single, sixteen-inch column with photograph) Boston, August 22, 1920, p. [40]. The title of this interview is a bit deceiving, but derives from Mosher's remarks: "It is a dream of mine to see literature carried to the farms. Is there any reason why a man with a milk route should not read Shelley?" Looking back over his publishing career, he also mentions that "the books which I have published are my contribution to the end which I would bring about... From the books I have read of prose and verse I have sought to extract the life-blood of the ages and would, by the books I publish, together with my method of publishing, persuade others to seek in them the same kinship I have found. We are now so situated by the compulsion of the hour that we cannot make a book of the same high quality at the old low price. Yet I won't make any other kind of a book." The interviewer remarked that "An hour spent with Mr. Mosher and his books reveals the fact that he has not only produced greatly but he has lived profoundly." (see also the Caswell entry below)

Anon. "A Publisher Who Saw His Dream Come True" in *Current Opinion* 76. [February 1924], 177-79. Extensively quotes Charles Dunn article (see below).

Anon. "Revival of Printing" in *Craftsman Homeowner*. Vol. III, No. 4. Winter 1992, p. 7. This press release announces the Temple University exhibition "Thomas Bird Mosher and the Art of the Book" and gives a brief overview of Mosher's publishing career. The exhibition was also overviewed in *Bookman's Weekly*. Vol. 89, No. 21. Clifton, NJ: AB Bookman Publications, May 25, 1992, p. 2149.

Anon. "Sermones." "Thomas Bird Mosher" in *Bookman's Journal and Print Collector*. Vol. II, No. 35. June 25, 1920, p. 135.

Arellanes, Audrey Spencer, ed. *Excerpts from the Letters of Thomas Bird Mosher*. Pasadena, CA: Bookworm Press, 1972. This miniature twenty-nine page press book, limited to 215 copies, consists of an introduction by Arellanes, a facsimile frontispiece of Mosher's bookplate, a reproduction of W. Irving Way's monogram at the end of the book, and seventeen excerpts of letters at the Huntington Library from Mosher to W. Irving Way, the contents ranging from the profound to the humorous. One of these letters is printed under "Contemporaneous Accounts" in Section V, page 389.

☞ Arlen, Shelley. *The Cambridge Ritualists: An Annotated Bibliography of the Works by and About Jane Ellen Harrison, Gilbert Murray, Francis M. Cornford, and Arthur Bernard Cook*. Metuchen, NJ: The Scarecrow Press, Inc., 1990. See entry 3.

☞ (Ashley Library) Wise, Thomas James. *The Ashley Library*. A Catalogue of Printed Books, Manuscripts and Autograph Letters. 11 vols. London: Printed for Private Circulation Only. 1922-36. Volume six is the only volume to contain references to the Mosher Press books present in The Ashley Library. **See entries 190, 191, 297, 423, 442.**

☞ Babington, Percy L. *Bibliography of the Writings of John Addington Symonds*. London: J. Castle, 1925 (reprint, New York: Burt Franklin, 1968). **See entries 116, 125, 241, 376, 439.**

☞ (BAL) Jacob Blanck, compiler. *The Bibliography of American Literature*. 9 vols. New Haven and London: Yale University Press, 1955-1991. *BAL* includes references to Mosher imprints under John Hay, John Greenleaf Whittier, Ralph Waldo Emerson, and Henry David Thoreau. Although Walt Whitman appears in *BAL*, reprinted Whitman books and selections published after 1900 were not included, therefore there are no later Mosher editions in *BAL* for Whitman. No note on any Mosher publication is listed under the Edgar Allan Poe, James Russell Lowell, or the James McNeill Whistler entries. The American poets Lizette Woodworth Reese, Arthur Upson, John Vance Cheney, Daniel Henry Holmes are not included as entries in *BAL*. **See entries 171, 209, 300, 334, 358, 383, 411.**

☞ Barker, Nicholas and John Collins. *A Sequel to An Enquiry into the Nature of Certain Nineteenth Century Pamphlets by John Carter and Graham Pollard. The Forgeries of H. Buxton Forman & T. J. Wise Re-examined*. New Castle, DE: Oak Knoll Books (and Scholar Press), 1992. Mosher printed four of the Wise forgeries, *The Two Sides of the River* (419), *Dead Love* and *Unpublished Verses* (81), and *The Pilgrims of Hope* (290). The reader may also wish to consult John Carter and Graham Pollard's pioneering work which first appeared in 1934: *An Enquiry into the Nature of Certain Nineteenth Century Pamphlets*. Second Edition. With an Epilogue by John Carter and Graham Pollard. Edited by Nicholas Barker & John Collins (London & Berkeley: Scolar Press, 1983). **See entries 81, 290, 419.**

☞ Barnes, Warner. *A Bibliography of Elizabeth Barrett Browning*. Austin, TX: The University of Texas & Baylor University. [1967]. Barnes' Mosher citations are confusing as he stops giving series identifications after the first three of the nine entries he cites in the index under publishers, and he misses some of the Mosher editions. Additionally, his entry E359 is listed as a 1910 "sixth" edition which is probably a misattributed edition note; it should read the 1910 "fifth" edition (referring to 375.4 of the Vest Pocket Series). The other problematic citation in Barnes is E391 which he lists as a 1913 Mosher edition at Yale. In checking the *National Union Catalogue*, the Library of Congress Online Catalogue, RLIN, and Yale's online catalogue (OPAC), no 1913 edition has been located. **See entries 374, 375.**

Baskin, Leonard and Hosea. *The Gehenna Press—The Work of Fifty Years 1942-1992*. Dallas, TX: The Bridwell Library & The Gehenna Press, 1992, p. 66. Baskin's remarks on Mosher are quoted under "Modern Assessments" in Section V, page 413.

☞ Beckson, Karl, et. al. *Arthur Symons: A Bibliography*. Number Five in the 1880-1920 British Authors Series. [Greensboro, NC: Elt Press (Dept. of English at the Univ. of North Carolina)], 1990. **See entries 154, 227, 295, 299, 301, 307, 354.**

☞ (Beinecke) McKay, G. L., compiler. *A Stevenson Library—Catalogue of a Collection of Writings by and about Robert Louis Stevenson formed by Edwin J. Beinecke*. New Haven: Yale University Library, 1951. For the purposes of a Mosher bibliography, only the first two volumes on "Printed Books, Pamphlets, Broadsides, etc." were applicable. **See entries 1, 5, 67, 76, 107, 108, 113, 409, 427, 436, 437.**

☞ Bentley, G. E. Jr. *Blake Books—Annotated Catalogues of William Blake's Writings... Reproductions of his Designs, Books with his Engravings...* Oxford: The Clarendon Press, 1977. **See entries 347, 368.**

Bidwell, John. "The Publishing Career of Thomas Bird Mosher" in the *New York-Pennsylvania Collector*. April 1978, pp. 4-6. The author, John Bidwell, was curator of The Melbert B. Cary, Jr. Collection at the Rochester Institute of Technology's School of Printing. The article pictures several designs of Mosher's books and his bookplate. The information covered is basically taken from Strouse's *Passionate Pirate* and from the Hatch bibliography. Extracts from this article are found in Section V, "Modern Assessments," page 421.

Bishop, Philip R. "Thomas Bird Mosher—Publishing Prince...or Pirate?" in *BIBLIO-The Magazine for Collectors of Books, Manuscripts, and Ephemera*. Vol. 2, No. 7. Eugene, OR: Aster Publishing Corporation, July 1997, pp. 38-45. The front cover call-outs advertise the article inside as "The Princely Picaroon of Publishing." This illustrated article presents a general overview of Mosher's life, motivations, publishing program, and selling techniques. Two sidebars present the 1997 retail market prices for key Mosher imprints, and sources for additional information on the Mosher Press.

—. "Thomas Bird Mosher—A Remembrance" in *The National Book Collector*. Vol. II, No. 3, May/June 1991. This is the text of a brief address given at the August 16, 1990 unveiling of a commemorative brass plaque at Mosher's publishing office at 45 Exchange Street in Portland, ME. For the full text see "Modern Assessments" in Section V, pages 415-17.

—, ed., and Scott Anderson, website designer and coordinator. *The Mosher Press*. 1997-98. Online. Internet. 15 June 1998. Available HTTP: www.millersv.edu/~mosher/index.html (hosted by Millersville University). This site is comprised of a variety of material. The table of contents lists the following sections: Biography of Mosher, Printing History, Books in Series, Piracy Dispute, Exhibitions, Book Samples, Fine Bindings, Bibliographies, Mosher Press Collections, Visitor Registration, and Sites of Related Interest. The site is illustrated, contains material for scholars to access, and is updated periodically.

☞ Blackwell, Kenneth and Harry Ruja, et. al. *A Bibliography of Bertrand Russell*. Volume I, "Separate Publications 1896-1990." London & New York: Routledge, [1994]. This three volume bibliography on Bertrand Russell lists both the first Mosher issue of *A Free Man's Worship* in 1923 (A44.1a) and the second edition of 1927 (A44.1b). The first entry indicates that there is correspondence between Russell and Mosher in the Houghton Library, Harvard. Correspondence and the galley proofs are also listed as being in The Bertrand Russell Archives of the William Ready Division of the Archives and Research Collections, Mills Memorial Library, McMaster University, Hamilton, Ontario. There are also two letters catalogued in Volume II on pp. 530 and 545: J84.01 being a letter to Flora M. Lamb thanking her for sending five copies of the 1923 edition of *A Free Man's Worship*, (catalogued in the booksellers catalogue James F. O'Neil; List 85-C, Boston, April 1984, p. 9, item 79), and Hh90.02 being a letter to Blanco White from Flora Lamb reproduced in facsimile in Sheila Turcon's "Recent Acquisitions: Correspondence." *Russell*, n.s. 10 (summer 1990), pp. 30-67. **See entry 119.**

Blank, Jacob. "News from the Rare Booksellers" in *The Publisher's Weekly* 141. [January 19, 1942], pp. 210-11. Discusses the transfer of the Mosher Press assets to the Williams Book Store in Boston.

Block, Andrew. *The Book Collector's Vade Mecum*. London: Denis Archer, 1932, pp. 49-50. Block mentions Mosher in his fourth chapter on Modern Presses wherein he lists the Ashendene, Doves, Golden Cockerel, Kelmscott, Nonesuch, Vale, etc. When he turns to America he makes mention of the Merrymount Press, et.al, and comments: "For really charming editions we must turn to the books published by the late Thomas B. Mosher; they can nearly all be purchased at nominal prices, but are well worth acquiring."—p.49.

☞ Bloomfield, B. C. "T. B. Mosher and the Guild of Women Binders" in *The Book Collector*. XVI. Spring 1967, p. 82 (Note 285). Here given in its entirety: "May I offer the following small footnote to the articles on Mosher (*The Book Collector* Autumn 1962, pp. 295-312) and 'English Bookbindings LVI' (*The Book Collector*, Spring 1966, p.46). My copy of Mosher's reprint of *The Germ* has the following statement on the page facing the title-page: '25 copies only of this book have been printed on Japan vellum, for England. Acquired by the Guild of Women-Binders, 61 Charing Cross Road, London. This is No. 8 Thomas B. Mosher'. [The number and signature are manuscript]. The imprint on the title-page reads: London GUILD OF WOMEN-BINDERS [in red] 61 Charing Cross Road MDCCCXCVIII.' Since this copy is in paper covered boards the Women-Binders never seem to have got to work on it." Bloomfield was apparently unaware of any copies bound by the Guild of Women-Binders. The present bibliography locates two copies (see Section IV, entry R26), and yet another copy bound by the Hampstead Bindery (R29). Others may still survive. **See entry 132.**

Blumenthal, Joseph. *Art of the Printed Book 1455-1955—Masterpieces of Typography Through Five Centuries from the Collections of the Pierpont Morgan Library New York*. Boston: David R. Godine, 1973. pp. 45-46.

A brief sketch on Mosher is presented in the section "The Printed Book in the United States" along with Benjamin Franklin, Isaiah Thomas, Theodore Low DeVinne, Daniel Berkeley Updike, John Henry Nash, Elmer Adler, Dard Hunter, Victor Hammer, and Bruce Rogers. Blumenthal notes that Mosher published "some four hundred titles, modest in format, price, and design, with forthright charm—the first American to sustain a consistent program of fine bookmaking."

☞ —. *Bruce Rogers A Life in Letters*. Austin, TX: W. Thomas Taylor, 1989. Blumenthal notes: "The first book with the name Bruce Rogers in the colophon was Homeward Songs by the Way (plate 2) by A.E. (George Russell), with a few decorations by Rogers, published in 1895 by Thomas B. Mosher in Portland, Maine. (Mosher was the first American to have established and sustained a program, over thirty-two years, of splendid literary output in consistently felicitous typographical form.)" Also in this book Blumenthal quotes a November 22, 1943 letter from Bruce Rogers to Carl Weber in which Rogers discusses some of his early work for Mosher, including "lettering the title-page of one of his long slim volumes—I think it was the Rubaiyat. This led to several other small commissions, some after I arrived in Boston...." —pp. 5-6. **See entries 152, 334.7.**

—. *The Printed Book in America*. Boston: David R. Godine, 1977, pp. 41-43, and illustration 31. A portion of this text is printed under "Modern Assessments" in Section V, page 414.

—. *Typographic Years—A Printer's Journey Through a Half Century 1925-1975*. New York: Frederic C. Beil, [1982], p. 3. Blumenthal writes, "In 1891, when Morris completed his first Kelmscott book, *The Story of the Glittering Plain*, Thomas B. Mosher in Portland, Maine, published George Meredith's *Modern Love*, the first of Mosher's long list of attractively designed small books of impeccable literary taste. The next forty years would witness the production of many beautiful books. Volumes were printed and published that compare favorably with the best work produced during the five centuries since the appearance of Gutenberg's great legacy to mankind."

Born, Edward. *General Catalogue of Bowdoin College... A Biographical Record of Alumni and Officers, 1900-75*. Brunswick, Maine: Bowdoin College, [1978], p. 659. The section on "Honorary Degree Recipients" lists Mosher as receiving a Master of Arts degree (one of ten recipients of honorary degrees during 1906—six doctorates and four masters degrees). According to Bowdoin librarians, the actual college record of Mosher's honorary degree is absent due to college president, William Dewitt Hyde, who was in office in 1906. He burned or otherwise destroyed all his correspondence and records upon leaving Bowdoin.

☞ Borst, Raymond R. *Henry David Thoreau—A Descriptive Bibliography*. Pittsburgh: University of Pittsburgh Press, 1982. **See entry 209.**

☞ Boss, Thomas G., John William Pye and Judith Nelson. *The Turn of the Century*. 1/100 copies. Boston: Published by Thomas G. Boss Fine Books [Printed by the Firefly Press of Sommerville, MA], [1993]. This book is actually the composite of six bookseller's catalogues (V, VII, IX, XI, XIII, and XV) reprinted on special paper and bound in cloth by Boston's Harcourt Bindery, and comes with an index. The contents includes numerous Mosher publications, is well illustrated, and gives the reader a good feel for the type of book material being published around the time of Mosher's publishing efforts. With regard to Mosher, the only major mistake in this book is the entry for the *Rubáiyát* in Catalogue V, #154 (see entry 334.7 of the primary bibliography). **See entries 16, 18, 47, 48, 61, 72, 74, 87, 98, 103, 108, 116, 132, 137, 146, 147, 153, 160, 165, 171, 173, 178, 190, 200, 225, 242, 244, 246.1, 270, 275, 279, 289, 290, 296, 334.7, 334.10, 336, 364, 366, 367, 373, 423, and 424.**

☞ (Boswell & Crouch). Boswell, Jeanetta, and Crouch, Sarah. *Henry David Thoreau and the Critics: A Checklist of Criticism, 1900-1978*. Metuchen, NJ: Scarecrow Press, 1981, p. 176. **See entry 209.**

☞ Bowles, J. M. "On the Early Work of Bruce Rogers" in *The Colophon—A Book Collectors Quarterly*. Part 11. September 1932, pp. [5] and [11]. Bowles notes that "what is of more importance to us is the fact that he lettered one or two title-pages for Thomas B. Mosher, the publisher (or re-publisher) of Portland, Maine, whose charming little paper-bound books were making a sensation just then..."—p.[5], and "it has always been a toss-up as to which was the first book with Rogers decoration, this [R. B. Gruelle's *Notes: Critical & Biographical* (Indianapolis: J. M. Bowles, 1895) about the art collection of W. T. Walters] or the 'Homeward songs by the Way' by A.E. (George Russell), published by Mosher the same year. It doesn't matter: anyway, the Walter's book is more important. Also in the little

'Homeward Songs' some of the decorations were either drawn too large as size for the space in which they were to be used, or their reduction was too great, for some reason, for the lines in the design are crowded. In the Walter's book the designs blend better with the type. Both books carry Rogers' name in the colophon. Although worked on in 1894, these books bear the publication date of 1895."—p. [11]. **See entry 152.**

Brewster, Stella F. "Late T. B. Mosher: One of World's Foremost Lovers of Belles-Lettres" in the *Portland Sunday Telegram and Sunday Press Herald* (three columns). Portland, ME, April 9, 1933. This is a general article touching on many familiar facts and reprinting often used quotes from Mosher's catalogues and *The Bibelot*. Perhaps the most telling feature is that the author was a resident of Portland, ME, and a member of the Portland Junior League, but never had heard of Mosher until a 1929 meeting with the poet, Thomas S. Jones, Jr.

☞ [Briggs brothers]. *Twentieth Century Cover Designs*. Arranged, compiled, printed and published by Victor H. and Ernest L. Briggs. Plymouth, MA: Victor H. & Ernest L. Briggs, 1902, pp. [63, 67, 72, 74, 90, 98, and full page ad in rear]. Several pages within this book exhibit design work done either directly for Mosher, or extra-binding designs placed on Mosher's books. Unfortunately the publisher information for many of the bindings is not given, but given the date and dimensions of the book, some are most likely on Mosher imprints, for example, the Ralph Randolf Adams binding on *Ballads and Lyrics of Old France* (illustrated on p.63) and the binding on the *Rubáiyát* by Emily Preston (illustrated on p. 67). Mosher's two catalogues for 1900 (Goudy design) and 1901 (Crawford design) are given full-page illustrations on pp. 98 and 90 respectively. **See entries 205, 206.**

Bruccoli, Matthew J. *The Fortunes of Mitchell Kennerley, Bookman*. New York: Harcourt Brace Jovanovich, [1986], pp. 8, 10, 12-14, 24-25, 106-107. Bruccoli notes that Kennerley was an early collector of Mosher's books. He also mentions the unfortunate label of literary pirate given Mosher, and indicates "Kennerley would later emulate certain aspects of the Mosher imprint" (and like Mosher, Kennerley would also bring out an edition of *Modern Love* by George Meredith). Important mention is also made of Kennerley's and Mosher's shared interest in Aimee Lenalie (but apparently unknown to Bruccoli, Lenalie was actually Mosher's first wife, Ellie Dresser). An interesting quoted letter from William Marion Reedy (*St. Louis Mirror*) to Mosher reveals the circle of familiarity surrounding Reedy, Mosher, Kennerley, William Bixby, and John Quinn.

☞ Bruckner, D. J. R. *Frederic Goudy*. (Masters of American Design) New York: Harry N. Abrams, Inc., 1990, p. 48-49. Reference is made to Goudy's commission for designing the covers of the first four books in the Vest Pocket Series. **See entries 1, 191, 335, 375.**

Burke, Harry R. *A Visitation at Thatchcot*. Herrin, IL: Trovillion Press, 1944, pp. 4 and 8. Mention is made of Mosher in two locations: " 'A counsel of wisdom guides them,' written to Hal W. Trovillion long ago by Thomas B. Mosher, whose beautiful books are treasured by booklovers everywhere: "Remember what a great man once said; 'don't try to die rich, but live rich!' " –p. 4 [and] "It [*Francine's Muff*] was printed in the chaste tradition of the Mosher Books—small wide margined, of graceful clear-faced type. Simple, charming, beautiful, inviting."—p. 8 (see also Herman Schauinger entry below).

Burke, W. J. and Will D. Howe. *American Authors and Books 1640 to the Present Day*. Augmented and Revised by Irving R. Weiss. New York, Crown Publishers, Inc., [1962], p. 511. "The fine editions of literary classics which he published and the monthly periodical, *The Bibelot*, which he edited, are noteworthy exemplars of the graphic arts in America."

Caffin, Charles H. Review in *The Artist*. New York: Truslove, Hanson and Comba, December 1898. For the text of this selection, see "Early Reviews" in Section V, page 382.

☞ Carter, John and John Sparrow. *A.E. Housman—A Bibliography*. Second edition revised by William White. Godalming, Great Britain: St Paul's Bibliographies, 1982. For the particulars on the many publishers of the authorized and unauthorized editions of *A Shropshire Lad*, Carter references William White's *The Library*. Fourth Series. XXIII, June 1942, pp. 33-34; and Fifth Series. VII, September 1952, pp. 202-204; and the appendix to Carl J. Weber's 'Jubilee Edition' [of *A Shropshire Lad*], Waterville, Maine, 1946. **See entry 350.**

Caswell, Mina H. "Would See Literature Carried to the Farms—Why Shouldn't the Milkmen Read Shelley?" in the *Portland Evening Express & Advertiser*. Portland, ME, May 5, 1920, p. 21. This article, filled with personal accounts by Mosher, is the result of a face-to-face interview in his office. For example, he mentions that the first time he ever heard of the *Rubáiyát* was during a hygiene lecture in Portland in 1879 by Dr. F. H. Gerrish. There is also mention of his early work on an historical volume on bookkeeping, "with special reference to Charles Lamb and his clerkship at the India House." He points out, in some detail, that his greatest achievement in his publishing career was not *The Bibelot*, but rather the reproduction of Whitman's *Leaves of Grass*. The description of Mosher's behavior, while the interview is being conducted, is captivating. Obviously Mosher was an intriguing personality.

Catalogue of Special & Private Presses in the Rare Book Division. The Research Libraries. The New York Public Library. Vol. 2. Boston, MA: G. K. Hall & Co., 1978, pp. 66-76. This catalogue lists 214 Mosher entries (G. K. Hall & Co. also published specialized catalogues like this for other major research institutions in America).

Cave, Roderick. *The Private Press*. Second Edition. New York & London: R. R. Bowker Company, 1983, pp. 101 and 200. Surprisingly, Mosher is only mentioned in passing, and in discussing the Daniel Press production of *The Garland of Rachel*, Cave mentions, "the book had the distinction (if that is the right word) of being pirated in a sort of type facsimile by Thomas Bird Mosher at Portland, Maine, in 1902." Cave also indicates that Mosher's "little bibelot editions" helped to inspire Hal Trovillion to print his own publications of the Trovillion Press.

☞ (*CBEL*). Bateson, F. W. *The Cambridge Bibliography of English Literature*. 4 vols., plus supplement. New York: The Macmillan Company, 1940-41. **See entries 116, 125, 132, 137, 147, 244.**

☞ Cevasco, G. A. *Three Decadent Poets, Ernest Dowson, John Gray, and Lionel Johnson—An Annotated Bibliography*. New York: Garland Publishing, Inc, 1990. **See entries 78, 289, 301, 392, 417.**

Chapman, Alfred C. "Thomas Bird Mosher" in the *Colby Library Quarterly*. Series IV, No. 13. [February 1958], pp. 229-44. This article is most derivative, drawing upon memorial tributes in the second *Amphora*, Mosher's catalogues, and other authors cited in this bibliography. The conclusion of the article presents a useful overview of the relationship between Robert Frost and Mosher.

☞ Chielens, Edward E. *American Literary Magazines—The Eighteenth and Nineteenth Centuries*. New York, Greenwood Press, 1986, pp. 63-65. Though the entry on *The Bibelot* is generally good, there are two glaring mistakes. E. Kate Stewart, who wrote the entry, states that Mosher ceased publication of this little magazine in 1915 "because of retirement." Mosher never retired from the book business until he died in 1923. In a letter from Mosher to Elizabeth Butterworth dated August 19, 1914 (Bishop Collection), Mosher states on p. 3: "This completion of The Bibelot by no means indicates that I am to retire from business. On the contrary, I hope to devote even more time than was possible in the past years to the making of choice printing and beautiful editions." Stewart's mistake is forgivable though, since Mosher did indeed slow down production. The second mistake, however, is bibliographical. Stewart indicates that *The Bibelot* "carried no advertisements." This is patently untrue and makes one wonder if Stewart ever examined the original issues in monthly parts. *The Bibelot* did indeed carry numerous advertisements. The ads were dropped when the magazine was bound in blue boards covering each year. **See entry 18.**

Cirker, Hayward and Balanche, eds. *Dictionary of American Portraits—4045 Pictures of Americans from Earliest Times to the Beginning of the Twentieth Century*. New York: Dover Publications, Inc., [1967], p. 440. Mosher's portrait, taken around the age of 49, appears on the lower right side. This is the same portrait that appears in some of Mosher's specially bound copies of his book catalogue.

☞ Clark, Robert Judson, editor. *The Arts and Crafts Movement in America 1876-1916*. Princeton: Princeton University Press, [1972], pp. 117 and 132. This is a catalogue for an exhibition organized by the Art Museum, Princeton University, and The Art Institute of Chicago. The section on "The Arts and Crafts Book" was written by Susan Otis Thompson, and pictures Mosher's edition of *Fancy's Following*, of which she says "occasionally, a welcome flourish makes a title stand out,... [and] the bold lines of the floral decoration relate it to turn-of-the-century modes [of cover design] elsewhere."—p. 132. In her introduction to this section (p. 117), she mentions Mosher as one of the "avant-garde amateurs" and "literary publishers" of the 1890's. **See entry 106.**

Clary, William W. *Fifty Years of Book Collecting*. Los Angeles: The Zamorano Club (Printed by Grant Dahlstrom of Pasadena, CA), 1962, pp. 13-14, and 21. Clary formed a number of collections, including Shelley and Keats which included imprints by publishers W. Irving Way and Thomas Bird Mosher. The book is essentially the text (with illustrations) of Clary's talk before members of the Zamorano Club on May 27, 1961. He discusses the friendship between Mosher and W. Irving Way. Clary mentions that Robert Burns' *The Jolly Beggars* was one of Mosher's favorites, having a "strong affinity for the vigor as well as the ribaldry of Burns." He also mentions that "before his death Way gave me a package of 142 letters written to him by Mosher... These letters, of course, would be of great value to any student of the period.... They contain some blunt and outspoken comments on Los Angeles booksellers, whom Mosher did not like, and some equally outspoken remarks about the Boston highbrows who, he thought, high-hatted him because he had not attended Harvard University." Clary gave the entire collection of letters to the Huntington Library.

☞ Cline, C. L., ed. *The Collected Letters of George Meredith*. 3 vols. Oxford: Clarendon, 1970. This source contains four letters related to Mosher. Selections from letter 1405 (MS: Harvard), 1408 (MS: Yale), and 1399 (MS: University of San Francisco), have already been quoted. In letter 1409, dated 29 March 1892 (MS: Messrs Macmillan, but now should be in the Macmillan Papers in the British Library), George Meredith writes: "The enclosed shows our American Pirate invading my native land to despoil me. / Is it worth any expense required for a move to attack him at the Customs? Have we any sale for Modern Love? If not, then both English and American Editions may huddle together in the shades.—I have another Volume ready [*Poems: The Empty Purse*], after which I hope to stop this flux. / ..." **See entry 244.**

☞ Colbeck, Norman. *A Bookman's Catalogue—The Norman Colbeck Collection of Nineteenth-Century and Edwardian Poetry and Belles Lettres* in the Special Collections of The University of British Columbia. 2 volumes. Compiled with a Preface by Norman Colbeck. Edited by Tirthankar Bose with an Introduction by William E. Fredeman. Vancouver: University of British Columbia Press, 1987. This is a compilation of a distinguished collection of Romantic, Victorian, and Edwardian books. **See entries 18, 62, 88, 97, 101, 104, 104.1, 125, 132, 152, 156, 164, 171, 187, 208, 227, 294, 301, 306, 321, 352, 408, 416, 423, 424, 428, 439.**

Collie, Michael. *George Gissing*... (see note under Garland entry).

☞ Collie, Michael. *George Meredith, A Bibliography*. Toronto and Buffalo: University of Toronto Press, [1974], pp. 123, 132, 141, and 144-45. The text mentions Mosher several times; however, it doesn't include references for any other Meredith titles by Mosher, except for editions of *Modern Love*. A reference to Mosher's printing of *Love in the Valley* is made in a chart on p. 126, but no further information is given in the actual entry (LIV) for this title. **See entries 221, 244, 245.**

☞ Connolly, Rev. Terrence L., ed. *An Account of Books and Manuscripts of Francis Thompson*. Chestnut Hill, MA: Boston College, [n.d.]. **See entries 154, 155, 295, 349.**

☞ Court, Franklin E., comp. and ed. *Walter Pater—An Annotated Bibliography of Writings About Him*. De Kalb, IL: Northern Illinois University Press, 1980. Contains lightly annotated references to prefaces in Mosher's books on Pater (see Court 73, 145-46, 168, 177-78, 185-86, 190-91, 242-43, 250, 263). No mention or record is made of Pater's *Uncollected Essays* published by Mosher in 1903 with a note by Mosher, though more extensive comments were probably needed for inclusion in Court; however, Mosher's catalogue write-ups would have been useful. Emphasis seems to be on appearances and comments in *The Bibelot*. **See entries 127, 231, 322, 359, 385, 421.**

☞ Cowan, Robert Ernest, and William Andrews Clark, Jr., et. al., comps. *The Library of William Andrews Clarke, Jr.—Wilde and Wildeiana*. 6 vols. San Francisco: Printed by John Henry Nash, 1922. These volumes are difficult to use in that there is no comprehensive index. In addition to the reference locations cited in Section II, there are also two references to *The Bibelot* in Cowan IV, pp. 18-19. **See entries 13, 44, 112, 142, 143, 159, 174, 193, 298, 304, 305, 308, 330, 341, 378, 380.**

☞ Crichton, Laurie W. *Book Decoration in America 1890-1910*. A Guide to an Exhibition by Laurie W. Crichton. Revised by Wayne G. Hammond [and] Robert L. Volz. Williamstown, MA: Chapin Library, Williams College, 1979, pp. 17-18, 45-47, and plates on pp. 73-74. Crichton's book is a most useful reference. While generally a reliable work on book design of the period, Crichton omits the cover designer of *Mimes* (242) and missed the clear reference Mosher gives to the designer of the pictorial frontispiece and the two headband illustrations (plus a tail-piece) in *Aucassin & Nicolete* (10). Both of these designers were easily identified from Mosher's own readily available sources. Mosher's 1901 *A list of Books...* provides the cover designer's name for *Mimes*: Earl Stetson Crawford. With regard to the Old World *Aucassin & Nicolete*, the designer's "PH" monogram is cited in Crichton, but there is no further identification. The information on the designer is found in Mosher's own explanation of the monogram as standing for P. Jacomb Hood (see his "Note" on the verso of the half-title). **See entries 10, 130, 161, 191, 211, 242, 287, 316, 335, 395, 399.**

☞ Currier, Thomas Franklin. *A Bibliography of John Greenleaf Whittier*. Cambridge, MA: Harvard University Press, 1937. **See entry 358.**

☞ Cutler, B. D. *Sir James M. Barrie, A Bibliography. With full collations of the American unauthorized editions*. New York: Burt Franklin, 1968 (reprint of 1931 text). **See entry 128.**

☞ (Cutler & Stiles) Cutler, B. D. and Villa Stiles. *Modern British Authors: Their First Editions*. London: George Allen & Unwin Ltd., 1930. **See entries 78, 392.**

☞ (*DAB*) Sargent, George Henry. "Thomas Bird Mosher" in the *Dictionary of American Biography*. Edited by Dumas Malone. Vol. XIII. New York: Charles Scribner's Sons, 1934, pp. 278-79 (see also the *Concise Dictionary of American Biography*. New York: Charles Scribner's Sons, [1964], p. 709). Mosher's entry is about 1½ columns in length and says little about the books published save for *Modern Love, The Bibelot*, and the *Amphora*. There are a few corrections to the biography. The phrase "trip to the Rhine" should read "trip to the Elbe..." The return from the world voyage was in spring 1870, not the winter of that year. The article strongly suggests Mosher took out on his own, "uninfluenced by the revival in printing... led by William Morris in England in 1890." In fact, Mosher was influenced by several of the British presses and publishers throughout his career, including Morris' Kelmscott Press, the Bodley Head, the Chiswick Press, the Daniel Press, and the Vale and Eragny Presses. In the references section at the end, Koopman's article should read "Modern Am. Printing," not "Modern Am. Painting." **See entry 422.**

Day, Kenneth, ed. *Book Typography 1815-1965. In Europe and the United States of America*. Chicago: The University of Chicago Press, 1965, p. 341 For a quote from this selection, see "Modern Assessments" in Section V, pages 419-20.

Denson, Alan, ed. *Letters from AE*. New York: Abelard-Schuman, [1961], pp. 50-51, 55-56. This book of George W. Russell's (AE's) letters includes two letters written to Mosher in March 1904 and April 1905. Included in the first letter is the comment: "I have to thank you for the very charming little edition of Yeats *Land of Heart's Desire* and for other Bibelots... I notice you announce a new edition of *Homeward Songs* in the spring at which I am much pleased. I will never be so charmingly bound and printed anywhere again unless you undertake to improve on your past." At the conclusion of the second letter represented, Russell mentions, "I heard great praises of you from a Mrs. Simeon Ford of New York who was over here lately as the only American publisher of any independence who only published what he liked." Mrs. Simeon Ford is Julia Ellsworth Ford, the American lady whose book on Simeon Solomon was published in 1908.

☞ —-, comp. *Printed Writings by George W. Russell (AE)—A Bibliography*. With Some Notes on His Pictures and Portraits. Foreword by Padraic Colum. Evanston, IL: Northwestern University Press, 1961, pp. 48-49. **See entries 152, 153.**

☞ (DeVinne). "The Library of the Late Theodore Low De Vinne." New York: The Anderson Galleries, 1920. Five Mosher books were recorded in the library sale of America's foremost printer of the day: *The House of Usna*, 1903 (#1113); *Modern Love*, 1891 (#1386); *The City of Dreadful Night*, 1892 (#1424—presentation copy); *Child Christopher and Goldilind the Fair* (#1422); and *Essays from the "Guardian"*, 1907 (#1502). In the fall of 1892 Mosher gathered and printed opinions from several bibliophiles including Theo. L. DeVinne who is quoted as writing: "I am well pleased with your book [*Modern Love*]. The composition and press work are well done." In response to the presentation copy of *The City of Dreadful Night* sent to him, De Vinne wrote (on his letterhead dated January 12, 1892) that "I have to thank you for your kind remembrance in the gift of the "City of Dreadful Night." It is a very good bit of book-making. Allow me to ask your acceptance of our "Columbus Letter" sent by this mail." Certainly a pair of pleasing nods from this master printer. **See entries 61, 72, 104, 160, 244.**

☞ (*DLB*) Various editors. *Dictionary of Literary Biography*. Vols. 9, 32, 34, 35, 55, 57, 123. Detroit, MI: A Bruccoli Clark Layman Book. Gale Research Co., 1984. In addition to articles on authors and publishers, entries in this multi-volume work have a listing on first British and American editions of an author's publications. There is a remarkable omission in the series. Although the *DLB* has two volumes devoted entirely to *American Literary Publishing Houses, 1638-1899*, there is not one mention of Thomas Bird Mosher or The Mosher Press. Many small or obscure publishers are mentioned, and even the Roycrofters receive a lengthy section, but Mosher is left entirely out of the American publishing picture. **See entries 60, 61, 64, 65, 103, 104, 107, 116, 152, 176, 181, 186, 234, 241, 242, 244, 289, 290, 295, 297, 306, 308, 354, 416, 421, 423, 434, 439, 442.**

☞ Dobson, Alban. *A Bibliography of the First Editions of Published and Privately Printed Books and Pamphlets by Austin Dobson*. With a Preface by Sir Edmund Gosse, D. B. New York: Burt Franklin, 1970 (reprint of 1925 text). **See entries 125, 314.**

Dunn, Charles. "Thomas Bird Mosher" in *The Publisher's Weekly*. September 15, 1923, p. 466. Reprinted in *Maine Library Bulletin*. Vol. XII, No. 3, pp. 62-63. A portion of this recollection also appeared in *The Literary Review* for September 22, 1923 under the "Book Sales and Rare Books" section by Frederick M. Hopkins.

Ellis, Estelle, Caroline Seebohm, and Christopher Simon Sykes. *At Home with Books—How Booklovers Live With and Care For Their Libraries*. New York: Carol Southern Books, [1995], p. [i]. This attractively color-illustrated book surprisingly pictures a slightly enlarged and color-tinted reproduction of Mosher's personal library bookplate with the book's half-title "At Home with Books" superimposed on the bookplate. Even today the Mosher bookplate is strongly associated with the formation of a fine personal library.

☞ Esdaile, Arundel. *Bibliography of the Writings in Prose and Verse of George Meredith, O.M.* London: Walter T. Spencer, 1907 (Norwood Editions, 1979). **See entries 244, 245, 395.**

Everitt, Charles P. *The Adventures of a Treasure Hunter*. Boston: Little Brown Co, 1951, pp. 160-61. See "Modern Assessments" in Section V, pages 418-19, for an extensive quote from this selection.

☞ (Ewelme) Kable, William S, comp. *The Ewelme Collection of Robert Bridges—A Catalogue*. Bibliographical series, No. 2. [Columbia, SC]: University of South Carolina, Department of English, 1967. **See entries 125, 137, 274.**

Foley, John. "Foreword" in *Amphora—A Second Collection*. Portland, ME: Mosher, 1926, pp. *xiii-xviii*. Foley's remarks are printed in full under "Memorial Tributes" in Section V, pages 397-98.

Foley, John L., ed. *Shadow of the Perfect Rose: Collected Poems of Thomas S. Jones, Jr*. With a Memoir and Notes by John L. Foley. New York: Farrar & Rinehart, Inc., [1937], pp. *xxiii-xxiv, xxvi*. The newspaper man, John Foley, recalls that the "tie between publisher and author [Thomas Jones] was one of mutual admiration and cordiality." A selection from a Jones to Mosher letter is quoted. It is also mentioned that Flora MacDonald Lamb, Mosher's assistant, would continue to publish Jones' work after Mosher's death.

☞ Forman, Henry Buxton. *The Books of William Morris*. New York: Burt Franklin, [1969]. Originally published in 1897, numerous quotes from this work can be found under individual Morris titles given in the Mosher Books bibliography of Section II. **See entries 149, 384.**

☞ Forman, Maurice Buxton. *A Bibliography of the Writings in Prose and Verse of George Meredith*. New York: Haskell House Publishers Ltd., 1971 (first published in 1922). **See entries 244, 395.**

☞ Franklin, Colin. *The Ashendene Press*. Dallas, TX: Bridwell Library—Southern Methodist University, 1986, pp. 14 and 16. These pages refer to Mosher's *Rubáiyát* being sent to Hornby, and to his use of Mosher's Old World *Rubáiyát* bibliography in the Ashendene edition. Actual correspondence from St. John Hornby to Mosher can be found in the Vilain/Wieck and the Bishop Collections. **See entry 334.**

Franklin, Colin, and John R. Turner. *The Private Presses*. Second Edition. Hants, England: Scolar Press, [1991], p. 155. Though this work is devoted to the English private presses, brief mention is made of Mosher: "The mock-Morris manner of the Vincent Press appears more commonly in early American echoes of the printing revival. Thomas Bird Mosher of Portland, Maine, used it conspicuously in his edition of Arnold's play *Empedocles on Etna*. The fashion had traveled east to west by slow boat and established itself as a fresh movement unworried by comparisons. Portland and Hammersmith were far apart in those days. Mosher printed in other ways over the years and made his own style of neat reprint, often taking his notions from the English private presses—sometimes pirating against anyone's will, as in his edition of *Garland of Rachael*, sometimes making useful reprints of scarce works, as when he re-issued the Pre-Raphaelite journal from 1848, *The Germ*. Mosher reprints are quite pleasant little books now, but not a vital part of the printing renaissance."

☞ Fredeman, William E. *Pre-Raphaelitism—A Bibliocritical Study*. Cambridge, MA: Harvard University Press, 1965. A well known and excellent source on Pre-Raphaelite authors. **See entries 16, 47, 132, 294, 301, 429.**

Fredeman, William E. See (*PBSC*).

☞ (Free Library) Strouse, Norman H. "An Exhibition of Books from the Press of Thomas Bird Mosher—From the Collection of Norman H. Strouse. January 16th - March 12th, 1967." [Philadelphia, PA]: The Free Library of Philadelphia, 1967. This sixteen-page exhibition catalogue is a record of the first major exhibition of Mosher's books in the twentieth century. The text of Strouse's three-page introduction is basically taken from his own book on Mosher, *The Passionate Pirate*. There were 156 exhibits distributed among the thirteen exhibit cases, including many copies on Japan vellum (some from Mosher's own library), twelve copies of Mosher publications on vellum, numerous letters from Mosher (including seven to Miss Emilié B. Grigsby), Richard Le Gallienne's original autograph manuscript *Thomas Bird Mosher—An Appreciation*, and many Mosher books in fine bindings. **See entries 152, 334.9.**

(Frost, Robert) The following books and articles include information on the relationship between Mosher and Robert Frost, and correspondence exchanged between the publisher and the poet:

Blumenthal, Joseph. *Robert Frost and His Printers*. Austin, TX: W. Thomas Taylor, [1985], pp. 1, 4-7, and plate 2. Blumenthal discusses the Mosher/Frost correspondence, the printing of Frost's poem, "Reluctance," and Mosher's tardy demurral to Frost's request to print his first book in Mosher's Lyric Garland series. The plate illustrates the 1913 Mosher catalogue cover and the page where that poem is printed.

Burch, Francis F. "Mosher and Baxter: Robert Frost's Early Supporters" in *The New England Quarterly—A Historical Review of New England Life and Letters*. Vol. LXIV, No. 1. March 1991, pp. 179-181 (Also in *American Notes and Queries—A Quarterly Journal of Short Articles, Notes, and Reviews*. Vol. 3, No. 4. Lexington, KY, October 1990, pp. 179-181). Burch writes that "At one point, Mosher appears to be the only editor who expressed confidence in Frost's talents and urged him to try to make a go of poetry." He also notes Louis Untermeyer's labeling of Mosher as an "arty publisher" (Untermeyer. *The Letters of Robert Frost to Louis Untermeyer*. New York: Holt, 1963, p. 18).

Crane, Joan St. C. *Robert Frost—A Descriptive Catalogue of Books and Manuscripts in the Clifton Waller Barrett Library University of Virginia*. Charlottesville, VA: Published for the Associates of the University of Virginia Library by the University Press of Virginia, 1974. The entries included in this mammoth Frost collection include: A3.1 (Barrett copy 592719-Mosher's copy of *North of Boston*), E44 (Mosher's comment in an inscription: "Thomas Bird Mosher said Reluctance was all I had ever written and all I needed to have written."), F16-16.6 (six ALS from Robert Frost to Thomas Bird Mosher, 1912-1915), and F35.1-2 (two ALS from Frost to Mosher's assistant, Flora Lamb, extending permission to "use *Reluctance*" in the second *Amphora*, and Frost comments: "I have a special feeling for that poem from the way it bound me in friendship to Tom Mosher...").

Gould, Jean. *Robert Frost: The Aim Was Song*. New York: Dodd, Mead & Company, [1964], pp. 107-108, 121, 123, 143-145, and 237. One of the more interesting insights is Mosher's last minute request to publish Frost's first book, just after Frost had committed himself to the British publisher, David Nutt. Gould indicates Frost gave permission to publish the poem "Reluctance" in Mosher's book catalogue, and also mentions the American publication of Frost and Mrs. Nutt's annoyance with Mosher.

Lincoln, Franklin P. "Frost Had Great And Good Friend in Portland Publisher" in the *Portland Press Herald* (four columns). Portland, ME, June 22, 1960, p. 8. This is a good general overview of Frost's relationship with Mosher.

Myers, Jeffrey. *Robert Frost*. New York: Houghton Mifflin, 1996, p. 341. Mosher is mentioned at several places, but on p. 341 Myers describes a talk given by Frost at the National Poetry Festival in Washington, D. C. on October 23, 1962, during which Frost generously praised old friends who supported him through his career, including the Maine editor, Thomas Bird Mosher.

Nash, Ray. "The Poet and the Pirate" in *New Colophon* II, part 8. [February 1950], pp. 311-321. This is a very insightful article on Robert Frost's friendship with Mosher, quoting the complete text of four Frost-Mosher letters, and selections from many others at Dartmouth College Library. Nash also relates several stories Frost himself would tell about their curious relationship. The relationship was "curious" because in all their dealings with one another, Mosher never produced one book of Frost's poetry. Yet Frost's admiration for Mosher was certain, for he was to exclaim that Mosher was one of only three persons that stirred a biographical impulse in him.

Sergeant, Elizabeth Shepley. *Robert Frost—The Trial by Existence*. New York: Holt, Rinehart and Winston, 1960, pp. 98, 109-10, 112, 130, 139, 143-45, and 259. Most of these pages are quotes from the Frost to Mosher letters later printed in Thompson's *Selected Letters*.

Thompson, Lawrance. *Robert Frost—The Early Years 1874-1915*. New York: Holt, Rinehart and Winston, [1966], pp. 389-90, 401-03, 421, 428 and 591. This work contains portions of letters from Frost to Mosher along with some commentary surrounding the purchase of the poem "Reluctance," the publishing of Frost's first book by the firm of David Nutt & Company in London, and Frost's comments on Ezra Pound to Mosher. "Reluctance" was the only poem of Frost's Mosher ever published, and that was only in his 1913 catalogue. After Mosher's death, the Mosher Press reprinted the same poem in the second *Amphora* (1926) and Frost's Introduction in *Dartmouth Verse* (1925).

—, ed. *Selected Letters of Robert Frost*. New York: Holt, Rinehart and Winston, 1964, pp. 46-47, 55-56, 70, 73-75, 83-84, 96-97, 109, 119, 129, 137, and 139. Ten letters from Frost to Mosher are quoted. As part of a short introduction to Frost's February 19, 1912 letter to Mosher, Thompson portrays Mosher as, "a picturesque gourmet, dilettante, and book collector, with a taste for blue-china, poetry, fine printing, and pornography..." An interesting remark on Mosher's books appears in a letter (4 April 1913) from Frost to his former Pinkerton Academy student and later newspaper reporter in Canada, John Bartlett, in which Frost proclaims, "I had hardly signed this contract [for *A Boy's Will*, and other books] when I had requests for a book from two American publishers, one a most flattering thing from Mosher of Portland, whose letterpress is considered perhaps the most beautiful in the States."—p.70. In his letters to Mosher, Frost seems to try to tantalize the American publisher with his successes in England. Mosher apparently does bite from time to time, but Frost writes back that Mosher's requests to publish Frost are too late. This little cat and mouse game occasionally surfaces in Frost's letters. One such letter revealing what Americans thought of Mosher appears in the Frost to Mosher letter dated 27 July 1914 in which Frost mentions, "I have thought of you in connection with my new book several times since its appearance. It has done so well here that I should almost venture to send you a copy in spite of your well-known predilection for the manner of the nineties."— p. 129. These letters from Robert Frost to Mosher are often quoted in publications on Frost, the most recent occurrence being in Walter Jost's "Lessons in the Conversation That We Are: Robert Frost's 'Death of the Hired Man' " (*College English*. Vol. 58, No. 4. April 1996, p. 413).

Walsh, John Evangelist. *Into My Own—The English Years of Robert Frost*. New York: Grove Press, 1988, pp. 45, 75, 117, and 153. Includes four references to Mosher and quotes from letters mainly with regard to Frost's projection of his own self-importance. For example, Frost writes to Mosher: "You are not going to make the mistake that Pound makes of assuming my simplicity is that of the untutored child. I am not undesigning."—p. 117.

Weintraub, Stanley. *The London Yankees. Portraits of American Writers and Artists in England 1894-1914.* New York and London: Harcourt Brace Jovanovich, [1979], pp. 304-305, 311, 314, 316, 317, 318, and 362. The references to Mosher are all in connection to Robert Frost.

• End of Robert Frost material •

Fuller, Marion Cobb. "Thomas Bird Mosher" in the *Maine Library Bulletin.* Vol. XII, No. 3. [January 1927], pp. 62-65. Mostly quotes from the Charles Dunn article.

☞ Garland, Bruce. "Checklist of George Gissing's Appearances in Mosher Press Publication" in *The Gissing Newsletter.* Vol. XII, No. 1 (January 1976), pp. 19-21. This checklist was listed in Michael Collie's *George Gissing—A Bibliographical Study.* Winchester, England: St. Paul's Bibliographies, 1985, p. 154 (No further reference to Mosher appears in Collie's bibliography). The opening of Garland's checklist states: "Thomas Bird Mosher chose the books he published with loving care. An occasional piracy now and then seemed justified when one beheld the end product—a privately printed book, simply beautiful and beautifully simple. Gissing was among those authors honored by Mosher's selection."—p.19. Garland's checklist covers books by Gissing in the Mosher corpus up to 1928, books containing references to or quotations from books by Gissing up to 1926 (basically in the *Amphora* and Mosher's catalogues), and Gissing's appearances in *The Bibelot.* **See entries 49, 54, 313.**

☞ [Gerstley]. Stevenson, Robert Louis. *A Catalogue of the Henry E. Gerstley Stevenson Collection, the Stevenson Section of the Morris L. Parrish Collection of Victorian Novelists, and Items from Other Collections in the Department of Rare Books and Special Collections of the Princeton University Library.* Princeton, NJ: Princeton University Library, 1971. **See entries 1, 5, 76, 108, 113, 118, 253, 254, 323, 325, 355, 409, 427, 436, 438.**

Glaister, Geoffrey Ashall. *Glaister's Glossary of the Book.* Second edition. London: George Allen & Unwin Ltd., 1979, p. 333. This concise entry is fully quoted in "Modern Assessments" in Section V, page 418.

Gomme, Laurence J. "The 'Pirate of Portland'—Thomas Bird Mosher" in the *Maine Digest.* Vol. 2, No. 1. [Fall-Winter 1967], pp. 88-93. A brief version of this article also appears in the *Maine Digest.* Vol. I, No. 4. [Summer 1967], pp. 105-106. Though mostly a general overview, Gomme does mention a few things of interest, including the fact that as proprietor of The Little Book-Shop Around the Corner, he felt privileged to be an agent for the Mosher Books in New York City from 1909-1917. He also mentions that Mosher sent him a letter about how the piracy controversy in England helped sell books. In one letter Mosher sent Gomme, he reveals that "since the letter of Richards [the British publisher, Grant Richards, who came to Mosher's defense] was printed I had several letters from England, and they are continuing to come in so that it was really very good advertising."—p.92

—. "The Little Book-Shop Around the Corner" in *The Colophon New Series—A Quarterly for Bookmen.* Vol. II, No. 4. New York: Pynson Printers Inc., Autumn 1937, pp. 574-575. Gomme later used some of this material for his article in 1967 in the *Maine Digest* (see previous entry). Gomme's remarks on Mosher are printed under "Memorial Tributes" in Section V, pages 400-01.

Gordon, Ruth I. *Paul Elder: Bookseller-Publisher (1897-1917): A Bay Area Reflection.* Unpublished dissertation. Berkeley, CA: University of California at Berkeley, 1977, p. 36. Gordon explains the exclusive place and high regard for the Mosher books at Paul Elder's establishment: "In this room, which was the roofed-over former backyard, one cabinet had the jewelry of a local craftsman, Ferdinand Heiduska, as well as the jewelry of W. S. Hadaway of London. These objects were displayed on Japanese brocades and ooze leather, a substance with a suede-like finish that also was popular for book binding at the time. It was there, too, that the books of reprint publisher Thomas B. Mosher were shown, an indication of Elder's high regard for these books. Elder & Shepard, and later Elder alone, were the West-Coast agents for Mosher."

☞ Green, Roger Lancelyn. *Andrew Lang—A Critical Biography with a Short-Title Bibliography of the Works of Andrew Lang.* London: Edmund Ward, [1946]. This Oxford scholar includes only three entries on Mosher's publication of Lang, all being selections which appeared in *The Bibelot:* the 1903 appearance of "Lyrics," the 1908 inclusion of "Three Poets of French Bohemia," and the 1910 entry entitled "Does Ridicule Kill?" In all three entries Green records the American publisher of each work: "Pirate Edition by Moscher [sic]." None of the book forms of Lang's works appears here, and one can only speculate as to why Green consistently refers to Mosher as "Moscher." **See entries 26, 31, 33**.

Greif, Martin. *The Gay Book of Days: An Evocatively Illustrated Who's Who of Who Is, Was, May Have Been, Probably Was, and Almost Certainly Seems to Have Been Gay During the Past 5,000 Years*. Secaucus, NJ: Lyle Stuart, Inc. (A Main Street Press Book), [1982], p. 18. The following appears under the entry for Marsden Hartley, the early American modern abstract painter: "Among Hartley's acquaintances were a telephone directory of contemporary homosexuals, including William Sloan Kennedy, the biographer of Longfellow, Whittier, and Holmes; Thomas Bird Mosher, the publisher of Whitman and one of the earliest American publishers of Oscar Wilde; Horace Traubel, socialist editor of the Conservator and Whitman's secretary; Peter Doyle, Whitman's trolley conductor lover; Gertrude Stein; the American painter Charles Demuth; writer and publisher Robert McAlmon... Although few seem to know it, Hartley was also a fine poet..." Though Mosher had several close friendships with men throughout his life, including Horace Traubel, William Marion Reedy, W. Irving Way, and an early relationship with Leopold Lobsitz, there is no corroborating evidence for Mosher's inclusion in *The Gay Book of Days*. In fact, there is a vast amount of evidence to prove the contrary. The key to Mosher's contact with Hartley probably resided in their mutual love of poetry.

☞ Gress, Edmund G. *The Art & Practice of Typography*. New York: Oswald Publishing Co., 1917. Gress shows a title-page from McClure's 1903 publication, *Records of Shelley, Byron and the Author*. The elongated anchor and dolphin device is the same as used by Mosher in his publications *The Runes of Woman* (1915), *In Memoriam* (1920) and on many of his catalogues, especially those after 1917. **See entry 339**.

☞ Grigsby, Emilié B [Busbey]. "The Art and Literary Collections of Emilie B. Grigsby of New York City." New York: The Anderson Auction Company, January 22 and 29, 1912. This two-volume catalogue is divided into "Part I: Objects of Art" and "Part II—Books and Carbon Prints." Grigsby collected nineteenth-century authors, purchased fine bindings including those from the Doves Bindery and Sarah Prideaux, and assembled collections of several of the English private presses including Kelmscott, Essex House and the Vale Press. A substantial number of the Mosher books on Japan vellum were sold to Grigsby by Mosher himself who first assembled a complete collection of his books up to 1897 and thereafter continued to supply Japan vellum copies of all his newly published books.

Several of the copies listed in this sale either were inscribed or had association letters inserted, e.g., there are several letters cited from the John Addington Symonds biographer, Horatio F. Brown, to Mosher (see Grigsby 1158, 1172 & 1180). Grigsby was also one of the few people who ever co-published a book with Mosher, a limited edition of only ten copies of the 1902 *Rubáiyát* printed on vellum. She also purchased many of Mosher's other limited editions on vellum, usually acquiring copy #1 of each very limited edition.

Grigsby owned several items which had a bearing on the Mosher piracy dispute including several of Mosher's Andrew Lang imprints with letters from Edmund C. Stedman relating to these publications, and a whole portfolio on the Mosher and Lang controversy over the *Aucassin and Nicolete* piracy. This 3/4 blue morocco portfolio includes autograph letters from Lang, Mosher, and David Nutt (Lang's London publisher), the original autograph manuscripts of Mr. Mosher's side of the question called "An open Letter to Mr. Andrew Lang"(14 pp. dated June 26, 1896, with an opening quote from Emerson: "The profoundest thought or passion sleeps as in a mine, until an equal mind and heart finds and publishes it."), and the ALS of Mr. Hatch (L. W. Hatch; not Benton Hatch, the Mosher bibliographer) who published a criticism of the Mosher publication. There are six items in the portfolio, representing about twenty-eight manuscript pages (see Grigsby 688, 690, and 691). This portfolio collection is now at Arizona State University (Box 2, F1). There are several large lots of Mosher Books (829-839, 872-873, 1042-43, 1050, 1134, 1185, 1200-1201) not separately cited in the bibliography. For biographical information on Emilie B. Grigsby, see Bruccoli's *The Fortunes of Mitchell Kennerley*, pp. 57-58, 75-77. **See entries 10, 46, 47, 56, 58, 61, 72, 75, 101, 104, 104.1, 106, 116, 121, 132, 137, 147, 152, 161, 171, 190, 219, 231, 242, 244, 245, 270, 279, 290, 291, 294, 297, 301, 302, 306, 311, 319, 321, 336, 337, 347, 352, 364, 374, 386, 395, 423, 424, 439, 442**.

☞ (Grolier). *The Lengthened Shadow... An Address By Norman H. Strouse at an Opening of an Exhibition of Modern Fine Printing at the Grolier Club April 19, 1960*. New York: Philip C. Duschnes, 1960, pp. 15-18 and p. 36. As Norman Strouse mentioned in his opening remarks, the majority of the books presented in this exhibit were of a sort, "edging in spirit toward the amateur, and in professionalism somewhat toward the commercial. We might say that these are the presses representing that labor of love that also make a living. If they are not 'private,' they are at least very personal enterprises... The presses which seem to capture the special fancy of most discriminating collectors of fine printing are those which are as Emerson defined an institution, 'the lengthened shadow of one man.' " Strouse devoted several pages to Mosher, and Mosher books were exhibited along with fifty-five other categories of presses, club publications, and individual printers and designers totaling 117 entries. Three Mosher books were selected: A.E.'s *Homeward Songs by the Way* (1895) with the Bruce Roger's designs, Rossetti's *Hand and Soul* (1898), and Whitman's *Memories of President Lincoln* (1912), all listed on p. 36. **See entries 139, 152, 239.**

Groome, Francis Hindes. *Edward FitzGerald: An Aftermath. With Miscellanies in Verse and Prose.* Freeport, NY: Books for Libraries Press, [1972]. This is a reprint of Mosher's 1902 edition.

Gully, Anthony Lacy. "Scholarly Resources: Pre-Raphaelite and Victorian Publisher Collections of the Charles Trumbell Haydon Library, Arizona State University" in *The Journal of Pre-Raphaelite Studies.* New Series 5. (Spring 1996), pp. 95-97. The article deals with Arizona State University's Pre-Raphaelite Collection and three large collections of "innovative" Victorian presses: the Vale Press, the Edwin Gilcher Collection of George Moore (though it's difficult to see how this collection ranks as a Victorian press), and the Mosher Press. In the last two paragraphs of the article (p. 97), Gully mentions that the Mosher collection was formed from the Root Collection and members of the Mosher family "whose ancestor established this notorious press." He gives a brief synopsis of the content and quantity of Mosher's publishing program and notes that "the Mosher Press was the first large private press in America." Professor Nicholas Salerno is credited with being instrumental in attracting the "Mosher Family Bequest" to Arizona State University.

(Haberly, Loyd) *Loyd Haberly—A Centennial Exhibition.* Madison, NJ: Florham-Madison Campus Library [Keepsake printed at the Bullnettle Press], March 1996, p. [12-13]. Rhodes scholar, poet, printer, typographer and artist (Seven Acres Press, Gregynog), and finally dean at Fairleigh Dickinson University, Loyd Haberly wrote "My last press— now in the Florham-Madison Campus Library—was bought at a Boston sale of the effects of Thomas Bird Mosher, the Portland, Maine, printer who had earned the undying enmity of Robert Bridges by pirating his preciously-guarded sonnets." Haberly's remarks (pp. [7-13]) were delivered on the occasion of the presentation of his Stansbury Press to the Florham-Madison Campus Library in 1972, and are reprinted from *The Printing Art* (London), Vol. I, No. 3. Autumn 1973.

Hart, James. *The Oxford Companion to American Literature.* With Revisions and Additions by Phillip W. Leininger. Sixth edition. New York: Oxford University Press, 1995, p. 449. "Mosher, Thomas Bird (1852-1923), Maine publisher, whose Mosher Books, a series begun in 1891, were attractively printed, cheap editions of great works of literature little known in the U.S. *The Bibelot* (1895-1915) was a monthly reprint of prose and poetry from obscure but significant works, which both in selection and in printing were marked by his usual good taste."

☞ Hatch, Benton L, compiler and editor. *A Check List of the Publications of Thomas Bird Mosher of Portland Maine •MDCCCXCI MDCCCCXXIII•* Amherst, MA: Printed at the Gehenna Press for the University of Massachusetts Press, 1966. A pioneering effort and the primary bibliography for many years. Finely printed by The Gehenna Press with tipped-in title page facsimiles. Entries are arranged chronologically by year of publication. This work should be consulted for extensive details on pagination. There is an excellent biographical essay on pp. 9-39 by Ray Nash (unfortunately Nash does not give the location sources for three critical documents cited or quoted at length), and a comprehensive index. A prime source for some information contained in the new bibliography. Additions to Hatch were included in the 'Addenda & Corrigenda' which appeared in the Temple exhibition catalogue by Jean-François Vilain and Philip R. Bishop. A lengthy quote from Nash's biography is given under "Modern Assessments" in Section V, page 417. **In addition to all the Hatch numbers cited with each and every entry, the following entries mention Hatch somewhere in the annotations: 10.2, 10.5, 10.6, 10.7, 12, 15, 39, 62.11, 67.2, 74, 82, 117, 118.1, 121.4, 122.1, 124, 154.3-154.5, [xx] after 157.[xx], 159.2, 167, 171, 171.7, 173, 181.12, 195.1, 198, 217.2, 246.1, 256, 270.2, 271, 276, 282.7, 302.1, 305, 315.[xx], 315.4, 334.2, 335, 335.2, 355.2, 355.3, 337, 374.4, 394.2, 426, 436.[xx], 436.3, 445.**

(Hoyle, John Thomas, comp.) *In Memoriam—Elbert and Alice Hubbard.* East Aurora, NY: The Roycrofters, [c. 1915], p. 66. Following the death of Elbert and Alice Hubbard on the Lusitania (May 7, 1915), the Roycrofters published this memorial tribute ("Collected and arranged, secundum artem, by John T. Hoyle" and with a preface signed by Elbert Hubbard, II) listing 328 contributors which included letters from people like Robert H. Ingersoll,

Richard Le Gallienne, William Marion Reedy, and Mitchell Kennerley. One contributor was Thomas Bird Mosher who wrote: "The friendship that Elbert Hubbard had for me, and which it is possible I may not have as deeply considered as I should, was none the less something not overlooked and which now, when these words to you can mean nothing to him, was real and lasting. Some few of his letters I have before me, the earliest being dated December Second, Eighteen Hundred Ninety-five. I shall place it with a copy of his first volume received by me so many years ago. I well remember the impression that his "Message to Garcia" produced not only upon the millions but upon a single individual, myself. It is one of the minor masterpieces, but it is a masterpiece that I hope will go on making its appeal for many a year to come."

☞ Hume, Robert Ernest. *The Thirteen Principal Upanishads Translated from the Sanskrit.* With an Outline of the Philosophy of the Upanishads and an Annotated Bibliography. Second edition, revised. London, New York: Oxford University Press—Humphrey Milford, 1934, pp. 461-465. Mention to Mosher's edition is in Section I on "Translations of Collected Upanishads." **See entries 122, 123.**

☞ (Humphry) Weber, Carl J. *Fitzgerald's Rubáiyát—Centennial Edition.* Edited with an Introduction and Notes by Carl J. Weber and with a check-list of the Rubáiyát Collection in the Colby College Library compiled by James Humphry III. Waterville, Maine: Colby College Press, 1959. **See entries 332, 334, 334.9, 335, 336.**

Huntress, Keith G. "Thomas Bird Mosher: A Bibliographical and Literary Study." Unpublished dissertation. Urbana, IL: University of Illinois, 1942. The major contribution of this 211 page dissertation is its second chapter "The Bibelot" on pp. 43-136 (the others being a "Biography" from pp. l-42, "The Mosher Books" from pp. 137-84, and a "Conclusion" from pp. 173-81). This still remains the only extensive study ever done of *The Bibelot.* There is also a brief appendix (pp. 182-85), and a chronological title list of *The Bibelot* and the Mosher books from pp. 186-208. Pages 209-211 are a general bibliography. Huntress notes that "Mosher should be known as the first publisher in this country to bring to the business of printing something of the feeling of the artist... He is also important as the printer of first editions of AE, Swinburne, Fiona Macleod, and Walter Pater"—p. 176.

Inland Printer, 1923. Reprinted in *The Mosher Books* catalogue, 1935-36, p. [2]. A lengthy quote from this issue is printed in "Memorial Tributes" in Section V, pages 391-92.

☞ Jacob, Gertrude, comp. "Bertrand Russell, An Essay Toward a Bibliography" in the *Bulletin of Bibliography...* Vol. 13. No. 10. Boston: F.W. Faxon Company, September 1926-December 1929, p.198. **See entry 119.**

☞ (Japan Paper Company) "Hand Made Paper." Numbered portfolio. New York: Japan Paper Company, [ca. 1913-1916]. The Japan Paper Company, with offices in New York, Boston and Philadelphia, was America's leading importer of hand-made papers for private editions, deluxe books, club books, and for a whole host of others book arts needs. This company's large client portfolio (15" x 11") of loosely inserted material was distributed to printers, book binderies, and others concerned with the printed, bound, or calligraphed page, and was updated on an ongoing basis. Some of the most interesting inserts are the slim bound booklets with titles like Japanese Shadow Paper; Momoyama Papers; and Italian Hand Made End and Side Paper. There are numerous price lists for soft Japan papers, Italian Fabriano cover paper, French "Arches" papers, Imperial Japan velum, parchments & vellums, Kelmscott "Hammer & Anvil" paper, and many, many more. Though direct evidence of Mosher's use of this particular company has not been found, the samples and availability through Boston and New York strongly suggest his use of this company in selecting his papers (even if he acquired his papers elsewhere in America, it speaks to the ready availability of such stock to the artful minded publisher). It provided a sort of one-stop-shopping, so to speak. For example, all the papers used throughout Mosher's Venetian Series are neatly mounted and numbered in "Italian Hand Made End and Side Paper." In the "Japanese Shadow Paper" booklet one finds the endpapers in the *Amphora*, and on the cover of *Tam O'Shanter*. In "Momoyama Papers" we find the cloudy grey paper used on the 1920 *In Praise of Omar*. The portfolio does not include Dutch Van Gelder paper. **See entries 2, 47, 66, 103, 106, 116, 139, 172, 311, 399.**

☞ (Jenkinson) *The Richard C. Jenkinson Collection of Books—Chosen to Show the Work of the Best Printers.* Newark, NJ: The Public Library by Order of its Board of Trustees, 1925. This is an exhibition catalogue commemorating a major gift of modern finely printed books Jenkinson gave to the Newark Library. Included are Kelmscott, Officina Bodoni, Bruce Rogers designed books, Merrymount Press, DeVinne, Chiswick, small private presses from England, and a variety of others. Included with this august company are Mosher's *The Germ*, and *Tristram of Lyonesse*. **See entries 132, 416.**

☞ (Jenkinson II) *The Richard C. Jenkinson Collection of Books—Chosen to Show the Work of the Best Printers*. Book II. Newark, NJ: The Public Library by Order of its Board of Trustees, 1929. This is a continuation of the first volume which appeared in 1925. It includes a dozen books from The Brocade Series, three titles from the Reprints from "The Bibelot" Series, *Love in the Valley* from the Golden Text Series, and four books from the Miscellaneous Series: *The Heptalogia, The House of Usna, The Silence of Amor*, and *William Blake XVII Designs to Thornton's Virgil*. **See entries 45, 62, 89, 96, 102, 133, 135, 147, 148, 150, 157, 160, 221, 269, 312, 344, 347, 352, 385, 389.**

Johnson, Bruce E. "More Than Words" in *Country Living*. Vol. 20, No. 2. New York: The Hearst Corporation, February 1997, p. 40. Johnson's article (on pp. 38, 40, and 63) centers on Hubbard and The Roycrofters, but mentions Mosher as one of the private presses of Arts & Crafts Books in America: "The Arts and Crafts Movement found many dedicated followers in America. Between 1895 and 1910 more than 50 private presses were established to produce handmade, artistic books. In Portland, Maine, Thomas Mosher published limited editions of Arts and Crafts books of the finest design. In some instances, such as his 1897 edition of the *Rubáiyát of Omar Khayyám*, Mosher printed a mere 100 copies on the highest quality Japan vellum, a stiff, long-fibered paper recognized for its exceptional printing capabilities."

Johnston, Paul. *Biblio • Typographica—A Survey of Contemporary Fine Printing Style*. New York: Covici, Friede, 1930, pp. 5 and 15. For a quote from this selection, see "Modern Assessments" in Section V, page 000.

☞ (Jones, Dan Burne). *American Book Collector*. Vol. XIV, No. 10 (Special Rockwell Kent Number). Summer 1964, p. 41. This entry appears along with several others appending an article by Rockwell Kent on the Asgaard Press, but this portion is clearly by Dan Burne Jones who follows with a list of books illustrated by Kent. The specific entry is worded: "Tristan and Iseult, 1923. Small octavo, the Mosher edition of 1922, title p. and binding removed, new title p. with wood engraving by Kent, printed at the Lakeside Press under the supervision of Wm. A. Kittredge, and bound there in full maroon niger with binding design by Kent stamped in gold. Given as a gift to Frances Lee Kent [Kent's second wife]." **See entry 327.2.**

Jones, Louise Seymour. *The Human Side of Bookplates*. Los Angeles, CA: The Ward Ritchie Press, 1951, p. 132. Brief mention is made of Mosher in the company of other fine printers and publishers: "Then there are the master printers, men who with stars in their eyes design and create books and handle them tenderly: William Morris, Daniel Berkeley Updike, Tom Mosher, Hal Trovillion, John Johnson, John Henry Nash, Ward Ritchie, Bruce Rogers, all hard-working creative book lovers and not a dilly-dally aficiona do-da-do in the lot!"

Jordan-Smith, Paul. *I Salute the Silver Horse—The Story of the Trovillion Private Press, America's Oldest Private Press Whereonto is Added an Account of Its Founding by Hal W. Trovillion*. Herrin, IL: Trovillion Private Press at Sign of Silver Horse, 1958, pp. 6 and 7. Paul Jordan-Smith relates a story about his education at Lombard College in Galesburg, IL. It was there that he met Carl Sandburg's teacher, guide and inspirer, Philip Green Wright. Wright taught economics and ran a private press he called the Asgaard Press. Jordan-Smith recalls how Wright, "...tried to inspire in his students creative activity. He spoke often of William Morris and Cobden-Sanderson. He showed his students the dainty little books from the private press of Thomas Bird Mosher and told them that if a book was worth reading it was worth keeping, and, to that end it should be well printed on durable paper. He praised the small book as something to be carried about through the day as an amulet against evil." Influenced by Wright, Jordan-Smith began collecting "those memorable little pocket books printed by Mosher." Hal Trovillion was also influenced by the Mosher Press and often related how those books became his model for printing (see Herman Schauinger entry).

☞ Kaplan, Wendy, editor and contributor. *"The Art that is Life": The Arts & Crafts Movement in America, 1875-1920*. Boston: Little, Brown and Company (Boston Museum of Fine Arts), 1987, pp. 294-95. Susan Otis Thompson prepared the section on graphics (quoted under "Modern Assessments" in Section V, page 413 of this Mosher bibliography). Entry No. 156 shows a copy of *Empedocles on Etna: A Dramatic Poem* by Matthew Arnold. This is the Vilain/Wieck copy specially hand-colored, but pictured in black and white in *The Art that is Life*. **See entry 103.**

Keith, Elizabeth. "Thomas Bird Mosher: Internationally Appreciated Publisher and Lover of Books—Once a Resident of Portland, Maine" in *Sun Up, Maine's Own Magazine*. June 1927, pp. 5, 42-44. This is a general overview of Mosher's life and work as a publisher, and one which Mosher's assistant, Flora MacDonald Lamb, enjoyed as a tribute to Mosher.

Kennerley, Mitchell. "Recollections of Thomas B. Mosher" in the *New York Evening Telegram*. September 5, 1923. A selection from Kennerley's letter is quoted under "Memorial Tributes" in Section V, page 406.

☞ Keynes, Geoffrey. *A Bibliography of William Blake*. New York: The Grolier Club, 1921 (Kraus reprint of 1969). The particular references are to Mosher's 1914 reprint of the *Songs of Innocence* (Keynes 163) and to *XVII Designs to Thorton's Virgil* (Keynes 223). **See entries 347, 368.**

Koopman, Harry Lyman. "Modern American Printing" in *The American Mercury*, May 1924, pp. 25-28. Reprinted in *Amphora: A Second Collection*, pp. 98-99. A selection from this text is printed in "Memorial Tributes," Section V, pages 394-95. This essay was read before members of The Grolier Club in 1924.

☞ —. *The Booklover and His Books*. Boston: The Boston Book Company, 1917, p. 137. Koopman mentions, "...we can imagine a popular series that should deserve the name of tribute typography. Certain recent editions of the German classics, perhaps, come nearer to justifying such a claim than any contemporary British or American work. In more expensive publications some of Mr. Mosher's work, like his quarto edition of Burton's *Kasîdah*, merits a place in this class... [and] the work of the Kelmscott Press obviously falls within this class." Dr. Koopman was then librarian of Brown University. **See entry 182.**

Kramer, Sidney. *A History of Stone & Kimball and Herbert S. Stone & Co.* Chicago, IL: Norman W. Forgue, 1940, pp. 26 & 40. Brief mention is made of Mosher advertising his reprint series in *The Chap-Book*. Kramer also notes that "*The Bibelot* derived directly from the eclectic publications with which 'The Portland Pirate' had begun, in 1891, his publishing career, and Stone & Kimball were always polite to Captain Mosher."

Kraus, Joe W. *A History of Way & Williams...* Philadelphia: George S. MacManus Co., 1984, p. 17. Brief mention is made of W. Irving Way writing, "a long biographical introduction for the Thomas B. Mosher edition of *The Rubaiyat* in 1898" which leaves the reader with the impression that it was only with the 1898 edition that Irving Way's biographical introduction begins. Way's biographical sketch of FitzGerald first appeared in the 1895 Old World Edition of *The Rubáiyát* and continued, in updated form, throughout subsequent editions until the tenth and last edition of 1911.

☞ Krishnamurti, Dr. G., comp. *Women Writers of the 1890's*. With an introduction by Margaret Drabble. London: Henry Sotheran Limited [and the 1890s Society], 1991, pp. 44, 88, and 113. Three entries in this Sotheran exhibit were Mosher publications: (1) Michael Field's *Long Ago*, 1897, (2) Rosamund Marriott Watson's *Tares: A Book of Verse*, 1906, and (3) A. Mary F. Robinson's *An Italian Garden; A Book of Songs*, 1897. The above date of 1906 is not a misprint. For some inexplicable reason Krishnamurti included the 1906 "Lyric Garland," rather than Mosher's 1898 Reprint from "The Bibelot" edition. Krishnamurti was responsible for an 1890s exhibition eighteen years earlier compiled in catalogue form: *The Eighteen-Nineties—A Literary Exhibition September 4-21, 1973.* London: National Book League and the Francis Thompson Society, 1973. Mosher receives no mention whatsoever, either in the catalogue and in its supplement, but with the advent of *Women Writers of the 1890's*, we have several nods in Mosher's direction, certainly a recognition of Mosher's role in the 1890's literary movement and its authors. **See entries 178, 219, 401.**

Labbie, Edith. "Mosher Books Were Works of Art" in the *Lewiston Evening Journal* (Magazine Section). Lewiston, ME, March 17, 1979, pp. 1 and 8. Though this well illustrated newspaper feature article in the magazine section covers much familiar territory, there are a few things which add to Mosher's story. Labbie mentions that some booklovers actually referred to Portland as "Mosher Town." The article draws heavily from an interview of Mosher written in 1904 by Alice Frost Lord, then staff member on the *Lewiston Evening Journal Magazine*. The underlying philosophy of Mosher's style of printing and book design, and his *modus operandi* as a publisher, which Lord appealingly labels a 'Love Affair with Publishing,' is set forth with clarity and candor in Mosher's response to one of the questions Lord put to him in the interview: "...I have never done much with illustrations. Thus far [up to 1904] the lettering of my title pages has been drawn by New York artists, but hereafter type will suffice for I believe it is more simple and truly artistic. My style of typography is open to anybody from the types anyone can secure." Mosher also told Miss Lord that "the silk ribbons for book marks, I purchased in England." A 1979 interview with Francis M. O'Brien, one of Maine's outstanding booksellers, is also included in this issue in which he reveals he was asked by one of Mosher's sons to "come out and help appraise it [Mosher's personal library]."

☞ (Lamb Typescript of The Mosher Books). This twelve-page typescript, plus title (about 10" x 11 1/2") is located at Dartmouth College and was probably prepared by Flora Lamb up to 1928, the date of its last entry. Flora Lamb was Mosher's long-time assistant who managed The Mosher Press after Mosher's death (1923) until 1941. The typescript's cover title is "A bibliographical list of the Mosher Books compiled by Miss Flora MacDonald Lamb," and the final page bears the signature of Steven Barabas (an assistant?). In the 1924 Mosher Books catalogue, Flora Lamb wrote that:

> We have been asked by lovers of the work of Thomas Bird Mosher if a Bibliography of The Mosher Books was not to be issued. This was something Mr. Mosher had in mind to do, and we have all the material necessary for the publishing of such a volume. It has been suggested that through the medium of our catalogue we invite subscriptions to a limited edition, with a portrait and memorial sketch, on Van Gelder paper; also a few copies on Japan Vellum. If sufficient interest is manifested in having a Bibliography, we shall be pleased to proceed with its preparation and have it ready for publication next season.

Apparently there was not enough interest expressed, and the preparation of a Mosher bibliography remained on the back burner. Another typescript, with much of the same information, was assembled a few years later by Oliver Sheean (probably under Lamb's direction). The Lamb typescript should be used in tandem with the Sheean typescript of Mosher's books, because it does vary from the Sheean typescript on occasion, and in some instances further helps to resolve questions on limitation, paper used, or binding materials. The Lamb typescript includes:

(1) the first appearance, in chronological order, of each Mosher book (pp. 1-6) along with series and size information

(2) the books printed on pure vellum along with size, type of vellum for the leaves and for the binding, and a frequency chart by year and series (p. 7)

(3) books privately printed for T. B. Mosher (p. 8)

(4) a frequency chart showing the number of books printed by series and year (p. 9)

(5) a list, in chronological order, of privately printed books beginning in 1898 and ending in 1928 (pp. 10-12)

The following mention Lamb's typescript somewhere in the annotations to entries: 2, 12, 49.1, 55, 68, 82, 124, 166, 167, 216, 273, 284, 286, 309, 342, 379, 402, 408.

Langstaff, Eleanor de Selms. *Andrew Lang*. Boston: Twayne Publishers (Division of G. K. Hall & Co.), [1978], p. 106. A brief reference is made to Mosher and his piracy of Lang's work, though the information may be a little misleading. For example, reference is made to Mosher including "fifty-five selections from Lang," and to the "Bibelot series, a twenty one-volume..." *The Bibelot* was a magazine, not a series. I am not able to duplicate the high count of Lang's fifty-five selections. As an interesting tid-bit, there appears a phrase comparing Mosher to "the Robin Hood of publishing." Actually, this phrase first appeared in *The Sketch* for September 2, 1896 (and again in *The Critic* for October 10, 1896): "The eulogist of St. Andrews grows so angry as to speak of this piratical publisher as a 'kind of noble publishing Robin Hood' " and four times reuses the ballade line: "This [or The] literary Robin Hood. "

Lawson, Alexander S. *A Printer's Almanac—The Heritage of the Printer*. Volume II. Philadelphia: North American Publishing Company, 1966, pp. 179-180. The entry on Mosher is under his birth date of "September 11." The article mentions: "In England, William Morris was ready to embark on his own effort to promote the printer's craft, although his route was not at all that of Mosher, whose desire was to make literature readily available in tasteful format at a low price, while Morris catered to the purse of the wealthy book collector." An additional remark of interest is: "Bruce Rogers, who always disliked the American propensity to match any individual with an historical figure, thought enough of Mosher to call him a 'XIX Century Aldus' which was a fitting comparison indeed." The first volume of this set was published under the title *The Heritage of the Printer* by Dr. James Eckman in 1965.

Le Gallienne, Richard. "In Praise of a Literary Pirate" in *The Literary Digest International Book Review* 2. [October 1924], pp. 777-78. This was Le Gallienne's second public tribute to Mosher (aside from his weekly columns and book reviews). Particular attention is paid to Mosher's selective taste in literature. Le Gallienne writes that, "outside of Lamb's 'Selections' and Leigh Hunt's various miscellanies..., I know no comparable example of creative taste. We have become used to the idea that criticism can be creative, but that individual taste, undaunted faith in one's own selective judgment, can be creative too is more seldom realized." Le Gallienne borrows extensively from his 1914 tribute to Mosher, *Thomas Bird Mosher—An Appreciation*, again referring to Mosher as "an exquisite Claude Duval of publishing."

—. *Thomas Bird Mosher—An Appreciation*. Portland, ME: Mosher, 1915. Previously appeared in the *Forum 51* [January 1914], pp. 124-29; and also appeared in the Index to *The Bibelot* (1915). This text is quoted in full under "Contemporaneous Accounts" in Section V, pages 383-86.

Lehmann-Haupt, Hellmut. *The Book in America—A History of the Making and Selling of Books in the United States*. Second edition. New York: R. R. Bowker, 1951, pp. 277-78 and 326. For a quote from this work, see "Modern Assessments" in Section V, page 419.

☞ (Leuba). *A Sampler from the Library of Walter and Martha Leuba on Exhibit in the Special Collections Department of the Hillman Library. The University of Pittsburgh. November 13, 1977-January 30, 1978.* Limited to 700 copies. Pittsburgh, PA: Special Collections, The University of Pittsburgh [Davis & Wade Printer], 1977. This exhibit commemorates one of the most outstanding collections of fine presses and books exhibiting fine printing ever given to the University of Pittsburgh. Entry #77 of 170 items on exhibit was Mosher's *Polonius* on Van Gelder paper. **See entry 306.**

☞ Levis, Howard C. *A Descriptive Bibliography of the Most Important Books in the English Language Relating to The Art & History of Engraving and the Collecting of Prints with Supplement and Index.* London: Chiswick Press, 1912 & 1913 (Reprinted by Dawsons of Pall Mall, 1974). **See entry 347.**

Lhombreaud, Roger. *Arthur Symons—A Critical Biography*. Philadelphia: Dufour Editions, 1964, pp. 186-87. An undated letter from E. Byrne Hackett to Roger Lhombreaud is quoted. See "Modern Assessments" in Section V, page 418.

Lieberman, Elizabeth Koller, ed. *The Check-Log of Private Press Names*. Fifth Edition. White Plains, New York: The Herity Press, 1964, p. 16. This checklist contains an entry for the Mosher Press.

Lincoln, Franklin P. "Portland May Forget Him But Not the Graphic Arts World" in the *Portland Press Herald* (four columns). Portland, ME, December 7, 1962.

☞ Lingel, R. J. C. "Contributions Towards a Bibliography of Richard Le Gallienne" in *The American Collector*. Metuchen, NJ: Charles F. Heartman, November 1925, p. 70. **See entry 408.**

☞ Livingston, Flora V. *Bibliographical Data Relating to a Few of the Publications of Algernon Charles Swinburne*. With Notes on the Priority of Certain Claimants to the Distinction of "Editio Princeps." MA, Cambridge: Privately Printed, 1920. This source includes information on first American editions of Swinburne, as well as corrections to the Wise bibliography. It includes several Mosher editions "of especial interest to collectors." At the end of the book appears this interesting tabulation: "A list of the first American editions and publishers of the books of Swinburne shows that Ticknor and Fields of Boston, Swinburne's first American publishers, issued three books in 1866 and 1867, G. W. Carleton of New York published only 'Laus Veneris,' R. Worthington & Co. of New York published seventeen between 1866 and 1883, probably from advance sheets, and some of them perhaps before the English editions were ready. The United States Book Co. issued two books, one in 1884 and one in 1892. Thomas Bird Mosher issued seventeen between 1894 and 1912, all unauthorized. Charles Scribner's Sons, Dodd, Mead & Co., and E. P. Dutton, each printed one volume. Harper Brothers published several volumes and the collected 'Works.' " —p.[31]. **See entries 81, 110, 147, 191, 416, 423, 442.**

Lord, Alice Frost. "Artistic Book Publishing in Maine" in the *Lewiston Journal* (Illustrated Magazine Section). Lewiston, ME, December 17-21, 1904, p. 3. The sub-title reads: "Thomas B. Mosher of Portland Leads in this Phase of the Arts and Crafts Movement in This Country." Lord refers to William P. Cutter, former buyer for the Congressional Library at Washington and library authority, who concedes that in his estimation, Mosher has "first place among book publishers in this country," further qualifying that "more than anyone else, Mr. Mosher is publishing for the love of his art..." The major portion of the article is devoted to Mosher's judgment and choice literature, the thorough planning that goes into each book's materials and appearance, and the publisher's ability to keep costs down. Lord also mentions that Mosher "brags of no hand presses and workshop of his own. He thoroughly believes in the cylinder press, run by competent pressmen." Mosher is also recorded as having said that his only regrets in not having a college education was that he has no formal training in the classics, and that he would have liked training in

French so that he could have better appreciated "the delicacy of meaning in the original of much that he has seen fit to print in translation." In summary of his broadest aims, Mosher said that his books were meant to appeal to the "latent energies" of his readers, and to give them something to ponder over. As for himself, "I have tried to work so that I should not be sorry in later years that I brought out what I have and in the way I have." See also Edith Labbie's article on The Mosher Books.

—. "Two Shrines Remain in Portland to Memory of Most Distinguished Publisher of Belle's Lettres" in the *Lewiston Journal* (Magazine Section - fourteen columns). Lewiston, ME, July 7, 1928, pp. 1-2. This article covers the whole front page of the Magazine Section, and includes photographs of Mosher, his two sons, his home library, and contrasts writing samples between William Sharp and "Fiona Macleod." The two shrines mentioned are Mosher's home library at Woodfords (also called Longfellow Heights), and his Exchange Street office. There are interviews with Mrs. Mosher and with Flora MacDonald Lamb, Mosher's assistant. In speaking of his book collecting, they mention he "bought about a hundred choice books a year..., mostly from English catalogues... In buying books he always preferred second to first editions, because he knew they were likely to be better edited." The full text of a letter from "Fiona Macleod" (Aug. 5, 1901) is printed in this article, in which she mentions that "no one can know your publications and not see that apart from the beauty and charm of your reprints in point of format, they bear the impression of your own individual love of and selection of beautiful things—in fact your several series would have been impossible but for central judgment, taste, and knowledge." The story is told about how Mosher even received a photograph of Miss Macleod which he had to promptly return. The balance of the article is devoted to the new Mosher Press books printed after Mosher's death.

☞ Lowden, David W. "William Morris and the Printed Page: English Influence on American Book Design." Craftsman Farms exhibition booklet for September 8 - October 27, 1996 exhibit. Parsippany, NJ: The Craftsman Farms Foundation, 1996, pp. 14-15. This 21-page annotated checklist includes works printed at the Kelmscott and other English private and trade presses of the period. It also lists American private and trade presses displayed, including New York's Elston, Village, and Roycroft presses, Boston's Copeland & Day, the Merrymount Press, and the Craftsman Guild, Chicago's Alderbrinck and Blue Sky presses, Maine's Mosher Press, The Monadnock Press of New Hampshire, Michigan's Cranbrook Press, Wisconsin's Philosopher Press, and the California publisher, Paul Elder. Works designed by Bruce Rogers and Will Bradley were also included. Four works were selected from the Mosher Press for display. **See entries 47, 92, 103, 139.**

Lucas, Edward Verrall. *Reading, Writing, and Remembering*. New York and London: Harper & Brothers Publishers, 1932, p. 118. A quote from this is found under "Contemporaneous Accounts" in Section V, page 383.

☞ MacGillivray, J. R. *Keats—A Bibliography and Reference Guide...* Toronto, Canada: University of Toronto Press, 1949 (reprinted 1968). **See entry 274.**

MacKay, Kay. "A Pirate Half Pardoned—Thomas Bird Mosher" in the *Antiquarian Book Monthly Review*. Volume XIV. No 1. Oxford, January 1987, pp. 16-21. A lengthy quote from this article appears under "Modern Assessments" in Section V, pages 414-15.

☞ —. "In Appreciation of Dreamthorp" in the *Antiquarian Book Monthly Review*. Vol. VII, No. 9. Oxford, September 1980, pp. 430-436. At the end of this article MacKay developed "A Contribution Towards a Checklist of the Works of Alexander Smith," with nineteen British and American editions of Dreamthorp issued from 1863 to 1972. There were at least three nineteenth-century American editions and another in 1901. Mosher's friend and fellow publisher, Mitchell Kennerley, issued the title in 1907, six years before the Mosher Press edition of 1913. **See entry 95.**

McKenna, Paul. *A History & Bibliography of the Roycroft Printing Shop*. Second Edition. Grand Island, New York: Tona Graphics, 1996, pp. 12, 50, 51-52, and 64. In addition to the somewhat misleading information about Mosher never paying royalties (p. 12), on pp. 51-52 McKenna mentions Mosher's early advertising in *The Philistine* (second issue, front foldover cover). Mosher subsequently dropped this ad, and as McKenna notes, "Mosher's ad was the last any quality publisher would take in The Philistine." Mosher also included advertisements for the Roycrofters in his own little magazine, *The Bibelot*, and there are ten Roycroft titles recorded in Mosher's personal library.

☞ (Macleod, Fiona). *The Works of "Fiona Macleod."* Uniform Edition. Seven volumes. Arranged by Mrs. William Sharp. London: William Heinemann, 1910. This set includes numerous notes by both William Sharp and by his wife. Most of these notes are found at the end of each volume, along with particular comments on Mosher's American editions. There is an earlier volume published by Heinemann in 1907 entitled *From the Hills of Dream: Threnodies, Songs and Later Poems* which is called the "posthumous English edition." This volume is bound in identical fashion to the Uniform Edition, but is supplanted by Volume VII of the Uniform Edition which goes under the title *Poems and Dramas*. **See entries 53, 58, 88, 91, 121, 156, 160, 164, 177, 352, 398, 433.**

McMurtrie, Douglas C. *The Golden Book—The Story of Fine Books and Bookmaking—Past and Present.* Chicago, IL: Pascal Covici, 1927, p. 361. McMurtrie notes that "the books designed by Thomas B. Mosher, although somewhat out of the scope of this chapter [on Private Presses], deserves mention because of the influence on American typography. Mosher did not himself own a plant but he designed and supervised the printing of the many excellent books which he published."

☞ (Madan, Falconer). *C. H. O. Daniel vs. Thomas B. Mosher—A Letter from F. Madan to R.W. Rogers.* Limited to 150 copies. San Francisco: Roxburghe Club (Printed at the Nova Press by William P. Barlow, Jr.), May 17, 1983. The original letter is in the collection of the Gleeson Library at the University of San Francisco and was written on November 8, 1922. **See entry 274.**

☞ (—). *The Daniel Press.* Memorials of C. H. O. Daniel with a Bibliography of the Press, 1845-1919. Oxford: Printed on the Daniel Press in the Bodleian Library, 1921. For notes on Thomas B. Mosher and his reprints, see Madan's entries 4, 20 and 33, with amusing comments on the Mosher piracy issue. **See entries 62, 125, 137.**

Madison, Charles A. *Book Publishing in America.* New York: McGraw-Hill, 1966, p. 150. See this quoted under "Modern Assessments" in Section V, page 419.

Manuscripts. (See RLIN & OCLC, and *National Union Catalogue on Manuscript Collections* entries).

☞ Mason (*Poems*). Mason, Stuart. *A Bibliography of the Poems of Oscar Wilde.* Giving Particulars as to the Original Publications of each Poem, with Variations of Readings and a Complete List of All Editions, Reprints, Translations, &c. London: E. Grant Richards, 1907. Mosher had a copy of this bibliography upon which he specifically remarked: "Regarding the bibliographical notes and index, our indebtedness to Mr. Stuart Mason is something we desire to fully acknowledge. Without his aid it would have been impossible to carry out our plan. References to every poem annotated by Mr. Mason are given; but the minute textural [sic] changes noted by him with that patient and loving accuracy associated with a formal bibliography are omitted." —*The Poetical Works of Oscar Wilde* (Mosher, 1908), p. *xx*. Mason included several of the Mosher editions of Wilde's poetry, including the 1903 and 1905 *The Poems of Oscar Wilde* from the Miscellaneous Series, and *The Ballad of Reading Gaol* from the Lyric Garland Series. There are additional notes on Mosher's editions throughout the text on pp. 13, 52, 54, 57, 60, 63, 65, 73, 86, and 87. On these pages he provides information such as: "Volume I [of Wilde's works in German (Vienna: Wiener Verlag, 1906)], entitled GEDICHTE, contains a translation of the Poems from Mosher's edition" and the text of the *Poems* (New York: F. M. Buckles & Co., 1906), "is a reprint of Mosher's 1905 edition without the bibliographical notes." Curiously, just seven years later, Mason only mentions Mosher's editions in passing, never as actual entries in his *Bibliography of Oscar Wilde* (see below). The correspondence from Mason (Christopher Sclater Millard) to Mosher is located at the Houghton Library and shows that Mosher helped Mason in compiling portions of the bibliography, and Mason sent much information on various editions to Mosher. **See entries 13, 304, 304.1.**

☞ Mason (*Works*). Mason, Stuart. *Bibliography of Oscar Wilde.* With a Note by Robert Ross. Illustrated. London: T. Werner Laurie Ltd., n.d. (or) New York: Haskell House Publishers Ltd., 1972 (reprint of the original 1914 edition). It is interesting to note that even though Mason felt it necessary to quote or refer to Mosher's Oscar Wilde titles, he never once formally included in his bibliography any Wilde title issued by Mosher (including in the section of Pirated Editions, pp. 531-553). Mention is made on pp. *viii*, 97, 182-183, 185, 198, and 212. In all fairness, Mason did indicate in his preface that "no attempt has been made to include the countless American unauthorized editions..., a complete list of which would have extended the work to double the present size." (p. *vii*). In the same preface Mason also acknowledges "Mr. Thos. B. Mosher, the producer of beautiful books in America..." (p. *viii*). Along with the fact that Mason heavily cited Mosher's Oscar Wilde publications in his previously published bibliography of Wilde's poems, and the fact that the two men maintained friendly and mutually supportive correspondence throughout the years, one cannot surmise any negative reason why Mosher's books were not formally listed in this 1914 bibliography, except for the general unfavorable reaction of some British publishers toward Mosher.

A more serious omission of Mosher's publications occurs in Thomas Mikolyzk's compilation of *Oscar Wilde—An Annotated Bibliography* (Westport, CT: Greenwood Press, 1993), which never once mentions Mosher's editions even though he often cites other pirated or non-authorized editions (throughout the chapter on "Book Publications by Wilde," pp. 1-26. **See entries 305, 330.**

Mathews, Dr. Richard. "Morris, Mosher, and the Konglomerati Press" in *Ex Libris.—Journal of the USF Library Associates.* Vol. 2, No. 1. Summer 1978, pp. 1-3. *Ex Libris* is the quarterly publication of the University of South Florida Library Associates. The author of the article, Dr. Mathews, was then assistant professor of English at Eckerd College in St. Petersburg, the 1975 William Morris Fellow at Kelmscott House, London, and owner/operator of the Konglomerati Press in Gulfport, Florida. The article cites the influence of William Morris and Frederick Goudy on the Konglomerati Press, and acknowledges the influence of Mosher's "unconventional publishing." Examples of Mosher's influence are given by Mathews: "The 'restraint' of Mosher, it seems to us, was part of the production techniques which enabled him to produce his volumes at modest cost. He makes interesting use of simple rules rather than ornate borders for title page arrangements. That ruled effect can be seen in the Konglomerati title page design for *Goudy Presence* [Ruth Pettis. *The Goudy Presence at Konglomerati Press.* Gulfport, FL, 1978]... Konglomerati approaches the contemporary literature it publishes in much the same way [as Mosher], seeking to publish the best new writing in distinctive, high quality editions at a reasonable cost. We appreciate the simplicity of Mosher as an 'American individualistic publisher' without the 'artsy' trappings of the private presses." –p. 3. There is also an article in this issue of *Ex Libris* entitled "From Our Collections" which highlights the Mosher Press holdings at the University of South Florida (pp. 6-8), and mentions the exhibit "Thomas Bird Mosher Press, 1891-1923" (p. 15).

Matthews, Annie Harmon. *Thomas Bird Mosher of Portland, Maine.* [Keepsake No. 11]. Portland, ME: The Southworth-Anthoensen Press, 1942. The foreword and "Thomas Bird Mosher—A Portrait" (pp. 21-26) are by Edward F. Stevens. The remainder of this small book, pp. 1-19, gives a glimpse of Mosher by his friends and neighbors, Mr. and Mrs Fred V. Matthews, though it often presents quotes from other sources. A letter by Maurice Lavanoux which appeared in the *New York Evening Post* is quoted at length, giving details of a visit to Mosher in Portland. Lavanoux also remarks that he issued an account of Mosher's "special niche in the world of letters and book publishing" in *The Bowling Green.* Direct reference for either account has not been located.

Mayfield, John S, ed. *Swinburneiana—A Gallimaufry of Bits and Pieces About Algernon Charles Swinburne.* [Gaithersburg, MD: Waring Press], 1974, pp. 44-47. Part 17 is entitled "Norman H. Strouse and the Passionate Pirate." Mayfield gives both a broad overview of Mosher's work, and of Norman Strouse and his book, *The Passionate Pirate.* Of interest is a Mosher letter dated May 30, 1902 (a facsimile is illustrated) in which Mosher recounts: "The editions I have issued of Swinburne *are not* his complete works—nor should I ever think of issuing him complete. For the past ten years or more he has produced some very poor stuff, and it is no part of my plan to reprint rubbish even by Swinburne! The things I *have* printed are some of his best and rarest—and no other editions compare with mine for book-making." Mayfield indicates the original of this letter is in the private collection of the curator of Manuscripts of Rare Books of Syracuse University.

☞ Metzdorf, Robert F., comp. *The Tinker Library—A Bibliographical Catalogue of the Books and manuscripts Collected by Chauncey Brewster Tinker.* Storrs-Mansfield, CT: Maurizio Martino, no date (reprint of the New Haven, 1952 edition). **See entry 442.**

☞ Mikhail, E. H. *Oscar Wilde—An Annotated Bibliography of Criticism.* Totowa, NJ: Rowman and Littlefield, [1978], p. 95. Cites Mosher's "Bibliographical Note," in James Rennel Rodd's *Rose Leaf and Apple Leaf* (Portland, Maine: Mosher, 1906) pp. 95-100." **See entry 330.**

Miller, Spencer. "Dedication" in *Amphora: A Second Collection.* Portland, ME: Mosher, 1926, pp. *vii-viii.* Part of the text of this dedication is printed under "Memorial Tributes" in Section V, page 410.

Moore, Edward Martin. "Mosher in Maine—A Print from the Inky Fingers of Edward Martin More" in *Reading and Collecting.* Vol. I, No. 4. [March 1937], pp. 9-10. In this somewhat eccentric and entertaining overview of

Mosher's achievements, Moore comments on the 1890's plethora of short-lived little magazines, and notes that "in this welter *The Bibelot* stood out like a handsome, sedate old dog in a yard full of giddy puppies of mixed breeds... Imagine starting a five cent magazine with Lyrics from William Blake: when most of its neighbors were ready to damn anything over a year old on the score of age!" The article covers the various series produced, and the importance of the catalogues and Mosher's essays and criticisms. The last several paragraphs are devoted to questioning how much design work Bruce Rogers did for Mosher, and he wonders if the Mosher letterhead, signed R, is actually early BR, but can't confirm it because "even the management [of the Mosher Press] has no information." Moore is one of the founders of the Blue Sky Press.

——. *To Omar: Spoil of the North Wind.* Chicago: Blue Sky Press, 1901, p. 3. Moore mentions Mosher as a collector of *The Rubáiyát*: "...every edition has something of this sort [thoughts, pro and con, about *The Rubáiyát*]. I do not possess a collection of even the American editions—I gave it up long ago. Mr. Mosher of Portland, ME, is suspected of trying to keep pace with them. 'Tis told he wrote the Philosopher Ellis for a Rubaiyat. Mr. Ellis replied that the Philosopher Press had not printed a Rubaiyat. And, as this was unique he had thoughts of advertising the fact. Mr. Mosher lists in his latest bibliography [seventh Old World edition] XXXV items in American reprints alone and one of these items covers 26 editions..."

☞ Morgan, Bayard Quincy. *A Critical Bibliography of German Literature in English Translation, 1481-1927.* Second Edition. New York: The Scarecrow Press, Inc., 1965. Entries 9185 & 9186 are for Mosher's first two editions of Theodor Storm's *Immensee: An Idyll*, (1902 & 1905) as translated by Irma A. Heath. No entry is given for the second translation of *Immensee* Mosher brought out in 1912. This second translation appeared in the *Dark Blue Magazine* (London, July 1872). **See entry 162**.

Morley, Christopher. "A Golden String" in *Amphora: A Second Collection.* Portland, ME: Mosher, 1926, pp. 109-113. Reprinted from the *Saturday Review of Literature* in the July 11, 1925 issue on p. 892, and later published as "A Dogwood Tree," in Morley's *John Mistletoe* (New York: Doubleday, 1931, pp. 316-321). Morley's remarks are printed in full under "Memorial Tributes" in Section V, pages 398-400.

——. *The Haunted Bookshop.* New York: Doubleday & Page, 1919. *The Haunted Bookshop*, along with its companion piece, *Parnassus on Wheels*, has long been an American books-on-books classic. As part of the story, the radiantly lovely Titania Chapman is sent to live with the bookshop's owners by her father in order to correct the evils of a finishing school education. In the third chapter, "Titania Arrives," the Mifflins have prepared her boarding room with carefully selected books chosen for their potential influence on Titania. For example, *The Notebooks of Samuel Butler* are placed there to "give her a little intellectual jazz," *The Wrong Box*, "because it's the best farce in the language," *Travels with a Donkey* "to show her what good writing is like," and finally, "some of Mr. Mosher's catalogues: fine! they'll show her the true spirit of what one book-lover calls biblio-bliss."

——. *Thomas Bird Mosher.* (U. S.): The Attic House, 1936. This twelve page booklet is, "an essay from John Mistletoe by Christopher Morley, 'borrowed' by Emerson G. Wulling and printed with pleasure in the busy time of the year for friends, because the essay and the man it speaks of are worth special attention."—p. 2

Morris, William. *The Story of the Glittering Plain & Child Christopher.* With a New Introduction by Norman Talbot. Bristol, UK: Thoemmes Press, 1996, p. *vi.* Talbot indicates that "an American reprint, published by Thomas B. Mosher (Portland, Maine, 1900), was reprinted as A Newcastle Forgotten Fantasy Classic, ed. R. Reginald and Douglas Menville, with an interesting introduction by Richard Matthews, in 1977." The book Talbot mentions is: Morris, William. *Child Christopher and Goldilind the Fair.* New Introduction by Richard Mathews. The Newcastle Forgotten Fantasy Library, Vol. XII. North Hollywood, CA: Newcastle Publishing Company, Inc., 1977. It goes beyond being just a reprint. This is a photo-facsimile of Mosher's 1900 edition, including ruled pages, Chiswick designed head- and tail-pieces, and the large decorative initial on p. [3]. Mosher's title page and colophon are adapted to include the Newcastle Publishing Co. information. Though the size of the Mosher text block is retained, the margins are reduced, Mathew's introduction is inserted between the Table of Contents and a half-title, ads are placed at the rear, and the whole book is perfect bound with paperback cover illustrations by Robert Kline.

Mosher, Thomas B., ed. *The Bibelot.* 21 Vols. (including index). New York: Wm. H. Wise & Co., 1925. This New York reprint was done by the Wm. H. Wise & Co. who contracted with Mrs. Mosher paying her a royalty of $1 per set sold. The set is called the "Testimonial Edition" and includes 4,500 numbered sets printed for subscribers with a List of Subscribers appearing at the end of the Index volume. The set is bound in light blue boards with white spines and some sets are not numbered. Another 500 extra-illustrated sets with 104 illustrations (compared to seven in the original, including the portrait frontispiece) are not numbered and are bound in dark blue library buckram. The major feature of this set is the "Analytical Index" which greatly improves upon Mosher's index. Mosher's original index is 140 pages in length, while the Wise index is 403 pages, and includes first lines of poems when no title is given. It also has subject listings (e.g., love, life, man) and six pages of "Notes by Thomas Bird Mosher" under the entry for *The Bibelot*. Clearly, any investigation of *The Bibelot* should reference Wise's analytical index.

(Mosher, Thomas B.) "Library of the Late Thomas Bird Mosher and Examples of His Own Publications Many Printed on Vellum." *Part One.* New York: Parke-Bernet Galleries • Inc., May 10 and 11, 1948. [and] *Part Two.* "Art and Illustrated Books Autographs & Manuscripts French & German Literature Inscribed and Other First Editions - Press Books William Sharp Correspondence. Final Portion of the Library of the Late Thomas Bird Mosher and Property from the Estates of the Late D. Bertalan Nemenyi [and] Herbert S. Long." New York: Parke-Bernet Galleries • Inc., October 11 and 12, 1948. The preface to the first part is by Oliver C. Sheean, a worker at the Mosher Press, and compiler of the Sheean typescript. Marked and priced copies of both catalogues, often giving the purchaser's name, are in the Bishop Collection. A major reference on Mosher's library.

Mosher, Thomas B. "The Celtic Revival in Some of Its Lyrical Aspects." Unpublished paper. 1904, 24 page typescript. This paper was originally read before the De Burians of Bangor on February 8, 1904, at their annual meeting. The De Burians was a book club in Bangor, Maine. The typescript for this address is located in the Norman Strouse collection at the Donahue Rare Book Room, University of San Francisco.

Mott, Frank Luther. *A History of American Magazines—1885-1905.* Vol. IV. Cambridge, MA: Harvard University Press [Belknap Press], 1957, pp. 424-427. There are several well expressed passages in this four-page article on *The Bibelot.* Speaking of Mosher's first publishing of the tragic masterpiece, *Modern Love,* Mott notes its "pleasing format, with excellent typography and presswork" and that "this was a choice characteristic of his later work as publisher and anthologist, for Mosher was to show a predilection for verse and essay of a somber cast, for work that had been allowed to languish in obscurity, and for performances of high literary quality." Mott shows that this carried over into Mosher's selections of "poems, poem-sequences, one-act plays, single acts from longer dramas, essays, short stories, or prose poems," for *The Bibelot.* Mott points out that *The Bibelot* may have been suggested by the *Chap-Book,* and was only rivaled in sheer span of existence by Hubbard's *Philistine,* but that it "had something most of its rivals in this field lacked—a legitimate appeal to the self-culture motive of the nineties." Mott's essay also presents some interesting discussion on the piracy issue.

☞ Murray, Francis Edwin. *A Bibliography of Austin Dobson.* New York: Burt Franklin, 1968. Originally published in 1900, this bibliography only catalogues Dobson's works up to 1900 and therefore does not include books Mosher subsequently published including *Proverbs in Porcelain,* and *The Garland of Rachel* which included a Dobson selection. **See entries 275, 366.**

☞ Myerson, Joel. *Ralph Waldo Emerson—A Descriptive Bibliography.* Pittsburgh: University of Pittsburgh Press, 1982. **See entries 383, 411.**

☞ —. *Walt Whitman—A Descriptive Bibliography.* Pittsburgh: University of Pittsburgh Press, 1993. **See entries 48, 192, 192.1, 212, 238, 239, 240.**

Nash, Ray. "Thomas Bird Mosher" in *Grolier 75: A Biographical Retrospective.* New York: Grolier Club, 1959, pp. 67-70. As with Nash's biography in the Hatch *Check List,* this overview is well written. There is one bit of information that appears nowhere else, but characteristically, Nash never cites any reference. Nash writes on p. 69, "As an enthusiastic student of literature not only rare but also gamy he [Mosher] fought manfully against the Portland port collector's embargo on the copy of H. S. Ashbee's bibliography of suppressed and prohibited books he was trying to bring from England. He carried the cause up to the United States Senate..." The final disposition of the case is not stated. Norman Strouse, the great Mosher collector, said he never knew Mosher was a member of The Grolier Club until Nash's biographical sketch appeared in *Grolier 75.*

Nash, Ray. (See also the Hatch entry, *A Check List*, for the biographical sketch written by Nash).

National Union Catalogue of Manuscript Collections. Compiled and edited by the Manuscripts Section, Special materials Cataloguing Division. Washington, D. C.: Cataloguing Distribution Service, 1959-1993. The following yearly entries are for collections which contain correspondence to or from Mosher. For other additional manuscript holdings recorded in this bibliography, see the entries under "RLIN & OCLC"

> MS 62-398 (W. Irving Way correspondence at the Huntington Library, San Marino, CA)
> MS 72-31 (papers relating to Oscar Wilde and his circle at the Clark Memorial Library, UCLA)
> MS 80-63 (Morley papers at Haverford College-see below)
> MS 81-338 (William Stanley Beaumont Braithwaite papers at the University of Virginia Library)
> MS 81-611 (Mosher's publishing papers at the Houghton Library, Harvard University)
> MS 89-663 (Morley family papers at Haverford College Library-Quaker Collection)
> MS 93-798 (Horace & Anne Montgomerie Traubel papers at the Library of Congress)

☞ Naylor, Gillian, Patricia Bayler, et. al. *The Encyclopedia of Arts and Crafts—The International Arts Movement,, 1850-1920*. New York: E. P. Dutton, 1989, pp. 145, 146, 148, and 150. The author of chapter seven on "Graphics" is Jean-François Vilain. Though the entry for Mosher is necessarily brief, three of Mosher's books are illustrated on p. 148: *Fancy's Following*, the opening spread of *Empedocles on Etna* (this copy hand-colored by Bertha Avery and once belonged to Mosher's secretary-manager, Flora Lamb), and a binding on the 1897 Old World *Rubáiyát* executed by Christina Gaskel for the Guild of Women Binders. **See entries 103, 106.**

Needham, Wilbur. "An Attempt at Appreciation of a Rare Spirit" in *The Mosher Books* catalogue, 1923. Reprinted from the *Chicago Evening Post*, April 20, 1923, p.4. The full text is printed among "Contemporaneous Accounts" in Section V, page 388.

Newton, A. Edward. "The Book Itself" in his *This Book Collecting Game*. Boston: Little, Brown, 1928, pp. 119, 122-25. Excerpts were reprinted in *The Mosher Books* catalogue, 1929, pp. 3-4. This selection is printed in full in "Memorial Tributes", Section V, pages 392-93.

—. "The Decay of the Bookshop" in *The Atlantic Monthly*. Vol. 125. July 11, 1925, p. 892. (Reprinted in *Amphora: A Second Collection*. Portland, ME: Mosher, 1926, pp. 79-80). Newton is critical of William Morris who preached art and beauty for the masses, but then produced books only the wealthy could buy. Mosher, on the other hand, created beautiful books and sold them cheaply. Newton mentions that Mosher "comes as near to being the ideal manufacturer as any man who has ever lived."

Nowell-Smith, Simon. "Note 189: Mosher and Bridges" in the *Book Collector* 11 [1962], pp. 482-83. This note was written to contradict the claim of Van Trump and Ziegler that Mosher printed the first American edition of Robert Bridges. Macmillan & Co. of New York first published Bridges in *The Humours of the Court, a comedy, and other poems* in November of 1893. Mosher's first Bridges title was *The Growth of Love* printed in 1894.

Orcutt, William Dana. "The Art of the Book in America" in Holme, Charles, ed. *The Art of the Book*. Special Number of the London *Studio*. London & New York: The Studio Ltd., Spring, 1914 (reprinted by the Dorset Press of New York, 1990), p. 270. The quote from this book is printed under "Contemporaneous Accounts" in Section V, page 389.

Page, Curtis Hidden. "Section VIII: Mosher Press" in the Curtis Hidden Page catalogue entitled "List of association books, first editions, book-plates, autographs, limited editions from special presses... from the library of Curtis Hidden Page... offered for sale by C. H. Page, Gilmanton, New Hampshire," [ca. 1931], p. 66 and entries 218-369a following the one-page description of the Mosher Press. A quote from this source is included in "Memorial Tributes" in Section V, page 406.

Parsons, Leslie M., ed. "A Modern Love of Literature—One Hundredth Anniversary of Mosher Books." Kalamazoo, MI: Kalamazoo College, 1991. Four leaf exhibition program curated by Leslie M. Parsons and held at the A. M. Todd Rare Book Room, exhibiting the Mosher books given by Robert A. Huston to Kalamazoo College. A quote from this booklet is printed under "Modern Assessments" in Section V, page 415.

Pater, Walter. *Uncollected Essays*. New York: AMS Press, 1978. This is a reprint of the 1903 edition of Pater's *Uncollected Essays* published by T. B. Mosher of Portland, ME. Reprints of Mosher's 1903 edition seem to have had some popularity. The first recorded reprint is by the Folcroft Press of Folcroft, PA in 1969, and then by Norwood Editions of Norwood, PA in 1976, and the next year by R. West of Philadelphia, PA in 1977.

Patterson, Eleanor C. "Salve et Vale" in *The Bibelot: General Index*. Portland, ME: Mosher, 1915, pp. *v-vi*. A brief, sentimental tribute.

☞ (PBSC) Fredeman, William E. "Thomas Bird Mosher and the Literature of Rapture: A Chapter in the History of American Publishing" in the *Papers of the Bibliographical Society of Canada*. XXVI. Toronto, 1987, pp. 27-65. This paper was originally given at the 42nd Annual Meeting of the Bibliographical Society of Canada held at the University of British Columbia, in Vancouver on June 10, 1987. It not only gives an informative and ground-breaking statistical analysis of the Mosher Press productions (primarily concentrated in the appendices), but also includes an introductory overview of the cultural milieu in England (pp. 27-30), a comparison between Elbert Hubbard's and Mosher's productions (pp. 30-31), and a short but important section on Mosher's mystical literary influences (p. 34). Overall this is a well crafted and researched article by this important Pre-Raphaelite scholar. **See entries 10, 132, 152, 301, 424.**

☞ Peckham, Robert D. *François Villon—A Bibliography*. New York: Garland Publishing, 1990. **See entries 17, 118, 217, 302.**

☞ Penzer, Norman M. An *Annotated Bibliography of Sir Richard Francis Burton*. [Reprint of the first edition limited to 225 copies]. Mansfield, CT: Maurizio Martino, Publisher, no date. **See entries 181, 182, 183.**

☞ Peterson, William S. *The Kelmscott Press—A History of William Morris's Typographical Adventure*. Berkeley: University of California Press, 1991. Peterson notes: "A third American publisher, Thomas Bird Mosher of Maine, produced beautiful pirated editions of English books rather more in the Whistlerian than Morrisian vein, but in 1900 he issued a *Hand & Soul* that was a thoughtful imitation of the Kelmscott version. Unlike many of his American contemporaries, Mosher realized that the secret of Morris's success as a printer lay not in his types and ornaments (which were so easily copied by photo-engraving methods) but in patient craftsmanship. 'Mr. Irving Way who brought out the Morris edition in this country recently wrote me desiring to know how I succeeded in getting so close a duplicate [of *Hand & Soul*],' Mosher said. 'It was done by using our best efforts on the press work and by procuring special inks, which I think on comparison fully come up to the Morris ink.' "—p. 301. **See entry 139.**

☞ Phelps, Ruth Shepard, ed. *The Arthur Upson Room—The Four Addresses on the Occasion of Its Opening 21 February 1925 and A List of the Books in the Room*. Edited and compiled by R. S. P. No place: privately printed, 1928. In addition to the list of books in Upson's library, a list of Arthur Upson's own publications is given on pp. 158-159. **See entries 228, 373.**

Phelps, William Lyon. Review in *Scribners Magazine*, February 1927. Reprinted in The Mosher Books catalogue, 1927, pp. 3-4. The text is fully printed in "Memorial Tributes," Section V, pages 393-94.

Philpott, Anthony J. "Mosher of Portland, Me." in the Boston *Globe*, December 20, 1907. Purportedly an interview with Mosher covering two columns. There are two letters at the Houghton Library (#374 and #703) which strongly suggest that Philpott was a sobriquet Mosher used to write his own interview.

☞ (Poor). "Catalogue of the Library of Henry W. Poor." Parts I-V. New York: The Anderson Auction Company, November 1908-April 1909. The Henry Poor collection contained numerous press books and fine bindings, including a fine collection of the more limited publications of Thomas Bird Mosher. Poor owned at least forty-two Mosher books printed on vellum. One of these copies was bound by Bradstreets and twenty-three others were bound by the Club Bindery of New York, including one finished and signed by Léon Maillard. Poor owned yet another 142 Mosher books printed on Japan vellum plus 39 Japan vellum copies from the Brocade Series. He also owned a set of *The Bibelot* (Vol. I-XIII, plus the index) printed on Japan vellum. **See entry 302.**

☞ Potter, Ambrose George. *A Bibliography of the Rubáiyát of Omar Khayyám*. Together with Kindred Matter in Prose and Verse Pertaining Thereto. London: Ingpen and Grant, 1929. Mosher's editions appear under the sub-heading, "FitzGerald's Versions—More than One Text" on pp. 91-93; and under "Versions in English Other than FitzGerald's" on p. 113. **See entries 40, 75, 171, 332-338 (whole number entries).**

Pottle, Frederick A. "Aldi Discipulus Americanus" in *Amphora: A Second Collection*. Portland, ME: Mosher Press, 1926, pp. 117-26. Reprinted from the *Literary Review of the Evening Post*, [December 29, 1923], p.410. The complete text of Pottle's essay is printed in "Memorial Tributes," Section V, pages 401-05.

(Pound, Ezra) The following books and articles include information on the relationship between Mosher and Ezra Pound, and correspondence exchanged between the publisher and the poet:

Espey, John. "The Inheritance of Tò Kayóv" in *New Approaches to Ezra Pound; a co-ordinated investigation of Pound's poetry and ideas*. Edited by Eva Hesse. Berkeley, CA: University of California Press, 1969, 321-326. Espey was one of the first scholars to cite the importance of *The Bibelot* as part of Ezra Pound's early literary development. He notes a number of selections from *The Bibelot* that most likely helped to form "Pound's foci" while at the University of Pennsylvania, but further notes that "this is not to claim that Pound read *The Bibelot* regularly or that a student of markedly independent mind... would let himself be led by Mosher alone... But it is to suggest that, together with what one thinks of as the frequently rarefied and precious enthusiams [sic] of the Pre-Raphaelites and the Nineties and 'Celticism', Pound was absorbing additional material that helped form the standards by which he was to judge the period." (pp. 324-25). Espey also notes that in addition to Pound's requests that Mosher publish his first work, *A Lume Spento*, about six years later Pound also offered Mosher the eight poems that make up *Cathay*. Mosher returned both manuscripts and never published any of Pound's work.

Goldwasser, Thomas A. "Ezra Pound's *A Lume Spento*—A Preliminary Census" in *The Papers of the Bibliographical Society of America*. Vol. 38, New York, March 1989, pp. 18 and 30. Goldwasser includes Thomas Bird Mosher's copy of *A Lume Spento*, and mentions Ezra Pound's correspondence to Mosher with regard to having him bring out the first edition of this, the author's first book, or at least to publish the first American edition. Mosher published neither, nor did he ever publish any of Ezra Pound's work.

Ingber, Richard Geoffrey. "Ezra Pound and the Classical Tradition: Backgrounds and Formative Influences." Unpublished dissertation. Cambridge, MA: Harvard University, 1983, pp. 29-161, 195, [366]-388. This study traces the development of Ezra Pound's involvement with ancient literature from the earliest evidence through the lyrics and epigrams of Riposte and Lustra. The first part of the inquiry deals with Pound's classical education. Here it is shown how he used bilingual editions, translations, and popular guides to supplement the deficiencies in his formal training. Pound's extensive debt to Thomas Bird Mosher of Portland, Maine, is given particular attention. After a survey of Mosher's career, and a discussion of the general significance of his publications for the formation of Pound's literary imagination, an attempt is made to indicate how the young poet acquired by these means a unified understanding of the classical tradition as a whole.

Nelson, James G. *Elkin Mathews-Publisher to Yeats, Joyce, Pound*. Madison, WI: The University of Wisconsin Press, 1989, pp. 131-32. Nelson mentions that the books published by the Bodley Head influenced Mosher's books "in their subject matter, format and letterpress..." Nelson also briefly discusses Ezra Pound's early guidance in reading by Mosher, describing himself as being "drunk with 'Celticism', and with Dowson's 'Cynara', and with one or two poems of Symons." This selection is quoted more fully under "Modern Assessments" in Section V, page 420.

• End of Ezra Pound material •

☞ Prideaux, Colonel W. F. *A Bibliography of the Works of Robert Louis Stevenson*. A New and Revised Edition. London: Frank Hollings, 1917. **See entries 1, 5, 76, 108, 113, 427.**

(Publisher's Weekley) "Thomas Bird Mosher—Publisher. A Tribute from a Friend" in *The Publisher's Weekly*, September 15, 1923, pp. 786-787.

☞ (Purdue) Hepburn, William M. "Bruce Rogers of Purdue" in *The Purdue Alumnus*. Vol. XXXIII, No. 4. March-April, n.d. [1947], pp. 6-7, 21-22. The author of this article, William Hepburn, was Purdue Librarian Emeritus. On page seven he mentions, "To this period [1890-95] also belong several commissions involving the designing of title-pages of books or pamphlets and for book-cover designs, and some contacts with Thomas B. Mosher of Portland, Maine, who at that time was producing a series of books notable for their careful typography, culminating in 1895 when he designed the decorations for the Mosher edition of *Homeward Songs by the Way* by A. E. (George W. Russell)." On p. 22 Hepburn also notes, "While at Purdue he sometimes signed drawings with a Caduceus and he used this symbol in the Mosher volume of 1895, for the last time." Mosher continued to used this caduceus device on the back cover of the leather bound copies of his Vest Pocket Series from 1899 to 1913. **See entry 152.**

Putzel, Max. *The Man in the Mirror: William Marion Reedy and His Magazine*. Cambridge, MA: Harvard University Press, 1963, pp. 7, 9, 46, 61, 130-131, 156, 170, 172. The close friendship between Reedy and two other publishers, T. B. Mosher and Mitchell Kennerley, is noted. Reedy also promoted Mosher's publications through the *Mirror*, a weekly St. Louis magazine. In quoting a January 15, 1913 letter from Reedy to Theodore Dreiser (at the University of Pennsylvania), Reedy dubs Mosher as "a High Priest of Letters" and also quotes from a letter indicating the first meeting between Mosher and Reedy was in St. Louis in 1879, when "you [Reedy] were a news-paper boy and I was a poor damned book clerk in St. Louis" (source is not identified).

☞ (Quinn, John). "Complete Catalogue of the Library of John Quinn. Sold by Auction in Five Parts [November 12, 1923-March 17, 1924]." Two vols. New York: The Anderson Galleries, 1924 (Reprinted New York: Lemma Publishing Corp., 1969). John Quinn was an important figure on several fronts. He was one of the chief backers of the 1913 Armory Show, and as a superb lawyer, he defended James Joyce's *Ulysses* against censors trying to ban the book from importation into the United States. An avid supporter of numerous Irish writers, Quinn was an established friend of the Irish literary community. He provided support for Ireland's Dun Emer Press, and arranged for private editions of the works of J. M. Synge and W. B. Yeats to be brought out in America. He was friend and correspondent with many of the leading English literary figures of the day, including Joseph Conrad, Ezra Pound, and James Joyce. Quinn had a unique opportunity to amass a large and highly respected library of contemporary literature and manuscript material. Quinn also counted the publisher, T. B. Mosher among his friends, and thought highly of Mosher's publishing efforts, indicating in his library catalogue that "few men have done more for literature, and done it so understandingly." According to a Feb. 8, 1937 letter From Flora Lamb to Norman Strouse, the article in the Quinn catalogue entitled "Mosher Books" (p. 692) was written by a Charles Vale. **See entries 8, 9, 17, 47, 48, 49, 53, 58, 59, 61, 62, 70, 72, 78, 79, 84, 88, 91, 92, 97, 101, 102, 104, 106, 121, 125, 127, 132, 133, 135, 137, 138, 146, 147, 149, 152, 153, 154.4, 156, 159, 160, 164, 165, 174, 177, 180, 181, 182, 183, 186, 188, 190, 193, 196, 208, 213, 214, 215, 221, 227, 231, 234, 238, 239, 240, 242, 245, 274, 282, 289, 290, 294, 295, 296, 297, 299, 301, 302, 303, 304, 305, 307, 311, 321, 330, 341, 343, 347, 349, 351, 352, 354, 356, 359, 360, 364, 367, 368, 378, 380, 382, 386, 388, 389, 392, 394, 395, 403, 405, 416, 417, 419, 421, 423, 435, 439, 441, 442.**

Ransom, Will. "In the Tradition" in *The Publisher's Weekly*, March 24, 1928. Reprinted as "In the Tradition" in *The Mosher Books* catalogue, Portland, ME: Mosher, 1928, p. 3. The text is printed in "Memorial Tributes" in Section V, page 396.

—. *Private Presses and Their Books*. New York: R. R. Bowker, 1929. (A reprint of this title was issued in 1963 by Philip C. Duschnes of New York, in 1976 by New York: AMS Press Inc., and later New York: James Cummins, 1992), pp. 73, 126-127, and 352-356. The section "In the Tradition" notes Mosher's "forte was literary content, yet his ideas of typography were eminently sound, or at least sane, with a distinctly individual character." Ransom's criticisms are with the small type used, and the dainty bindings which "forced the books into the gift class." Later on a scant checklist of only thirty-nine Mosher titles is presented, giving title, date, size, limitation, and cost.

☞ —. *Selective Check Lists of Press Books—A Compilation of All Important & Significant Private Presses, or Press Books Which Are Collected*. New York: Philip C. Duschnes, 1945 (Reprinted New York: James Cummins, 1992), pp. 182-210. The 336 entries are divided between The Mosher Books, and privately printed books of The Mosher Press. This is the first nearly comprehensive bibliography of Mosher's publications aside from the Mosher catalogues themselves, and lists the first appearances within each series. It also cross-references to the same title published in different series. **See entries 16, 122, 125, 132, 139, 147, 190, 231.**

☞ Ratta, Cesare. *L'Arte Del Libro e Della Rivista Nei Paesi D'Europa e D'America*. Volume II. Bologna, Italy: Della Scuola d'Arte Tipografica del Comune di Bologna, 1927. **See entry 315**.

Reedy, William Marion. "The Ending of *The Bibelot*" in *The Bibelot: General Index*. Portland, ME: Thomas Bird Mosher, [1915], pp. 187-191. The full text for this selection is printed under "Contemporaneous Accounts" in Section V, page 387.

☞ Rempel, Richard A., Andrew Brink, et. al. *The Collected Papers of Bertrand Russell*. Vol. 12 "Contemplation and Action, 1902-14." London: George Allen & Unwin, 1983. **See entry 119**.

☞ Reynolds, Symon. *The Vision of Simeon Solomon*. Stroud, Glos.: Catalpa Press Ltd., 1984. Reynolds cites the January & February 1909 issues of *The Bibelot* where Mosher first reprinted *A Vision of Love Revealed in Sleep* by Simeon Solomon, but mentions nothing about the same work appearing a few months later in the Miscellaneous Series in 1909. **See entry 429**.

Richards, Grant. *Author Hunting by an Old Literary Sportsman—Memories of Years Spent Mainly in Publishing 1897-1925*. New York: Coward-McCann, Inc., 1934, pp. 84, 88-90, 98. A large portion of the text is printed in "Memorial Tributes," Section V, page 394.

RLIN & OCLC (Research Libraries Information Network, and the On-Line Library Center). Mountain View, CA: The Research Libraries Group, Inc., 1996. The following additional manuscript holdings are reported on the RLIN & OCLC databases. Duplicate listings found in the *NUC of Manuscript Collections* are excluded.

RRAL93-A23	(two letters from Gilder to Mosher in Jeannette L. Gilder correspondence at Harvard University)
IAUG92-A497	(ALS, Francis Watts Lee to Mosher concerning *The Knight Errant* at University of Iowa)
PATV91-A34	(Gordon Bottomley correspondence at Temple University)
PATV92-A164	(Gertrude Traubel archives at Temple University)
NYCV91-A554	(Wilde Collection; twenty-eight letters from Mosher to W. R. Wilde, and six letters to Mary Hitchcock Wilde, plus other material, at Cornell University)
TXRC91-A21	(Houghton, Mifflin & Co. letter to Mosher about American editions of *The Rubáyát*, at the Harry Ransom Humanities Research Center, University of Texas at Houston)
OCLC 34986612	(W. Irving Way, book correspondence and notes, thirty-four items, includes three letters from Thomas B. Mosher, in Special Collections, Newberry Library in Chicago. There are two other letters relating to Mosher's *The Garland of Rachael* loosely inserted in a copy of this book [Wing ZP 983.M91127])
OCLC 29231575	(Four-page letter from "Michael Field" to Thomas Bird Mosher in The Adelman Collection at Bryn Mawr College Library)
OCLC 17020344	(Letter sheet to James E. Abbe, accompanied by a note from Mosher to Mr. Hammond at Yale University)
OCLC 34370340	(Letter from Henry Stephens Salt to Mosher. English Literary Authors Collection at the University of Michigan at Ann Arbor)

☞ Robinson, William A. *Thomas B. Reed—Parliamentarian*. New York: Dodd, Mead & Co., 1930, p. 406. **See entry 278**.

Rogers, W. G. *Wise Men Fish Here—The Story of Frances Steloff and the Gotham Book Mart*. New York: Harcourt, Brace & World, Inc., [1965], p. 52. In discussing Frances Steloff's early start in the book business, Rogers writes: "She decided to go to Maine... Her friends met her in Portland. On her return Brentano's at Twenty-seventh Street and Fifth Avenue hired her at twelve dollars a week, her former salary but now without any evening hours. She took charge of the 'little book table,' a jumble of booklets impossible to classify plus, as she remembers, some lovely Mosher editions—printed in Portland, Maine, on rag paper with deckle edge, gilt top, and handsomely designed pages. (Mosher editions of Michelangelo's sonnets, perhaps, or George Meredith's poems, gave Robert Frost his taste for fine printing.) For her own benefit she drew up a list of strange and difficult titles and wrote and rewrote them till she could spell them: the *Rubaiyat* of Omar Khayyam, *Quattrocentisteria* by Maurice Hewlett, and *Virginibus Puerisque* by Robert Louis Stevenson. People with a seventh-grade education would inevitably stumble over such puzzlers; so today would college graduates."

Rollins, Carl Purington. *Off the Dead Bank*. Typophiles Chap Book XIX. New York: The Typophiles, 1949, p. 117. This chap book reprints Rollins' essay on Maurice Hewlett's "Sandro and Simonetta" in the 1937 *Saturday Review of Literature*, in which he states that "I read it first in those days when the little books from Mosher's press, before we learned to attitudinize in our printing, lent to many a recovered treasure the charm of simplicity and decorum." For additional remarks by Rollins from another source, see "Modern Assessments" in Section V, page 411.

☞ Rossetti, William Michael. *Bibliography of the Works of Dante Gabriel Rossetti*. London: Ellis, 1905. **See entry 132**.

☞ ——. "Introduction" in *The Germ—Thoughts Towards Nature in Poetry, Literature and Art*. Being a Facsimile Reprint of the Literary Organ of the Pre-Raphaelite Brotherhood, Published in 1850. With an Introduction by William Michael Rossetti. London: Elliot Stock, 1901, pp. 27-28.

William E. Fredeman, reviewing R. S. Hosman's edition of *The Germ* in *Victorian Poetry* (10.1 [Spring 1972], pp. 87-94) demonstrated unequivocally that the Elliot Stock reprint is a typographic facsimile, a line-for-line (with two exceptions) reset of type in a slightly smaller typeface with minute variations (especially in the shape of the ?, !, and *) from the original. Only the wrappers are photo-facsimiles, but they are printed on a different paper. Stock corrected all but three of the typographic errors in the original, but introduced several new ones in the text, and transposed the wrappers of the second and third numbers, an alteration that immediately distinguishes the original edition from the reprint. Textual variations are summarized in a collation in Fredeman's review. Among many reprints of *The Germ*, the most recent is Andrea Rose's edition (first published by the Ashmolean Museum and the Birmingham Museums & Art Gallery in 1979, and subsequently twice reprinted [1984, 1992]), which summarizes Fredeman's findings in the preface, including his collation. In addition, Andrea Rose mentions Mosher on pp. *v*, and *xvii-xviii* of her preface.

Mosher acted as the American agent for 250 copies of this typographic "facsimile" of the original parts. In the separate introduction, William Michael Rossetti mentions that "before Mr. Stock's long-standing scheme [to re-publish *The Germ*] could be legally carried into effect, an American publisher, Mr. Mosher, towards the close of 1898, brought out a handsome reprint of 'The Germ' (not in any wise a facsimile), and a few of the copies were placed on sale in London [under the Guild of Women-Binders imprint]." Rossetti further notes "a very pleasant notice" of the Mosher reprint in the *Irish Figaro* for May 6, 1889. In the copies provided Mosher for his distribution in America, the following notice is printed opposite the title page of William Michael Rossetti's introduction: "Two hundred and fifty copies of the facsimile of THE GERM are printed for sale in the United States and have been acquired by Mr. Thomas B. Mosher. As the type has been distributed no more copies can be produced." The facsimile is housed in a quarter white paper over charcoal blue paper case which looks much like a Mosher book. The London edition of the 1901 Elliot Stock facsimile does not carry this notice, and is housed in a black folding case with gilt on the front cover and spine: **See entry 132**

THE
GERM
1850
o o
o

☞ Roth, William M. *A Catalogue of English and American First Editions of William Butler Yeats*. Prepared for an Exhibition of his Works held in the Yale University Library... New Haven, CT: Southworth-Anthoensen Press, 1939. **See entries 186, 188**.

☞ Russell, A. G. B. [Archibald George Blomefield]. *The Engravings of William Blake*. London and Boston: Houghton Mifflin Co., 1912. **See entry 347**.

☞ Sappe, D. C., ed. *HONEY JAR—A Receptacle for Literary Preserves*. Vol. III, No. 1. Columbus, Ohio: At the Champlin Press, At the Sign of the Green Wreath, November 1899. See Plate I, and discussion on p. 16. **See Appendix VII on Mosher's bookplate**.

Schauinger, Herman. *A Bibliography of Trovillion Private Press—Operated by Violet & Hal W. Trovillion At the Sign of the Silver Horse*. Herrin, IL: Privately Printed, Trovillion Private Press, 1943, pp. *v.* and 3. The opening lines of the Introduction mention that "Thomas Bird Mosher of Portland, Maine, set a high standard in the booklover's world for anyone who would seek to follow in his footsteps. Not only did he make a valuable contribution to his time by introducing classics of literature to many who would not have had them but for him, but he also, even after his time passed, is an inspiration and guide to many who seek to follow where he led." Later in describing the early influences on Hal Trovillion, Schauinger mentions how "William Marion Reedy, editor of the Reedy's Mirror, had aroused in him the love of books, and Thomas Bird Mosher of Maine had influenced him in the love of well printed, neatly designed, and beautiful books. Trovillion wished to follow the example of Mosher and produce beautiful books himself."—p.3

☞ Schreyer, Alice D. *The History of Books—A Guide to Selected Resources in the Library of Congress.* Washington, D.C.: The Center for the Book, Library of Congress, 1987, p. 54. "A long file of correspondence from Thomas B. Mosher concerns the publication of a Whitman anthology for which [Horace] Traubel wrote the preface. Mosher remarked that "personally, I don't quite like to see Whitman in Elbert Hubbard's typography." Mosher revealed that to him Whitman served as "a source of constant heartening up" and that he took great pains with the design and contents of *The Book of Heavenly Death*, published in 1905. **See entry 48.**

Seymour, Ralph Fletcher. *Some Went This Way—A Forty Year Pilgrimage Among Artists, Bookmen and Printers.* Chicago, IL: R. F. Seymour, 1945, pp. 107-08. Seymour's comments are quoted at length under "Memorial Tributes" in Section V, page 407.

Shanks, Ken [Kenneth H.]. "Thomas Bird Mosher" in the *Library Review 24.* Louisville, KY: The University of Louisville, November 1976, pp. 10-15. This paper, accompanied by three illustrations, largely draws upon Ray Nash's biography in Benton Hatch's *A Check List...* There are a few factual errors, e.g., indicating there are seventeen series of Mosher books (there were fourteen, plus the privately printed books), and stating the catalogues were entitled The Mosher Books as early as 1894 (this title only began in 1903). One of Shanks most delightful passages describes Mosher's prefaces: "In these sparkling paragraphs and in the other free flowing bits of writing in which he explained and promoted his publications, the man is seen at his rollicking best. In them is revealed the personality of a robust and ready man obviously capable of holding his own in any company." The author, Ken Shanks, was an electrical engineer and graduate of Purdue University. He assembled a large Mosher collection which formed the core of the collection now at the University of Louisville.

☞ Sharp, Elizabeth, compiler. *William Sharp (Fiona Macleod)—A Memoir.* New York: Duffield & Company, 1910, pp. 318, 322, 333-334, 345. **See entries 58, 121, 160, 164, 242, 352.**

Shay, Felix. *Elbert Hubbard of East Aurora.* New York: Wm. H. Wise & Co., 1926, p. 270. A delightfully humorous quip appears in his chapter on "Jokes and Hoaxes" (pp. 269-70) where Shay presents "among his [Hubbard] hoaxes some that deserve honorable mention were the folderol advertisements he printed in *The Philistine...*" including *"To Herbert S.:* Thanks for your well-meant letter, but the Roycroft holds no copyright on the Song of Solomon and can not therefore 'stop that man Mosher from pirating the stuff!' as you suggest. None of Solomon's stuff is covered by copyright."

☞ (Sheean Manuscript—A Mosher Book Collection). This is a seventy-two page manuscript on a large collection of Mosher's publications assembled by Oliver Sheean (ca. 1940). It gives details on many of the Mosher books, including Sheean's notes on particular titles, prices paid, source of purchase, and limitation. It's organized in chronological order within each series. The manuscript is located at Colby College. **See entry 309.**

☞ (Sheean Manuscript—Mosher's Library). Probably recorded ca. 1930, there are five, undated legal-sized ledger volumes in Oliver Sheean's hand (total of 132 pages, about forty-two book entries per page) with each set of books receiving only one line. This is the only surviving, nearly complete inventory of books in Mosher's personal home library (Bishop Collection). It does not include the books Mosher kept at his office on Exchange Street. No list has been uncovered which includes those volumes, many of which were lost in a fire at the business premises in 1915. **See entry 2.**

☞ (Sheean Typescript of The Mosher Books). This eighty-four page typescript, located at Colby College (and another copy, eighty-one pages, at Dartmouth College), is a list of the Mosher Books prepared by a Mosher Press assistant, Oliver C. Sheean, probably around 1931/32. The list was most likely prepared under Flora Lamb's guidance, and also most likely formed the basis of a bibliography Flora Lamb was hoping to produce for the Mosher Books clientele (an idea which she entertained as early as 1924), but the project never came to fruition. The list is often referred to by Benton Hatch who was able to trace the existence of some books only through this typescript. The typescript separately lists Van Gelder, Japan vellum, and pure vellum editions along with their limitations; however, the Japan vellum listings only record the issuance of each first edition, leaving second and subsequent Japan vellum editions unrecorded. The list also includes Mosher Press books published up to 1931. See also the Lamb Typescript of The Mosher Books. **The following mention Sheean somewhere in the annotations to the entries: 2, 40, 49.1, 55, 57, 82, 94, 124, 166, 167, 173, 216, 252, 284, 286, 292, 303, 342, 402, 408, 426.**

Sherbo, Arthur. "The Ethics of Reprinting: Thomas Mosher vs. Andrew Lang" in the *New England Quarterly—A Historical Review of New England Life and Letters*. Vol. 64, No. 1. Boston, MA, March 1991, pp. 100-112 (and also in *American Notes & Queries: A Quarterly Journal of Short Articles, Notes, and Reviews*. Vol. 3, No.4 [New Series]. October 1990). This article consists mostly of reprints of the exchanges over the piracy issue between Mosher, Lang and the editors which appeared in the New York-based periodical, *The Critic, an Illustrated Monthly Review of Literature, Art, and Life,* from December 1895-November 1896.

Shorter, Clement. "Beneficent 'Piracy' " in the *Literary Digest*. Vol. 48. No. 19. New York: Funk and Wagnalls, May 9, 1914, pp. 1113-1114. According to the introduction, Shorter's remarks were taken from the London *Sphere*. Shorter defends Mosher against the charge of piracy by James Blackwood, president of the British Publishers' Association, and R. B. Marston of *The Publisher's Circular*. He also points out the number of books Mosher published that were either out of copyright (*Dreamthorp*) or simply in the general public domain (*The Sermon on the Mount*). He also mentions that many British publishers, just a generation ago, freely stole the writings of Emerson, Holmes, Longfellow, and Cooper from America. A quote from this source is printed in "Memorial Tributes" in Section V, page 406.

Smith, Professor A. J. [Albert James], ed. *John Donne: The Critical Heritage*. Volume II. Completed with introductory and editorial material by Catherine Phillips. London and New York: Routledge, 1996, p. 102. There is a total of 139 entries which range from 1873-1923. The Mosher entry indicates that "The American publisher T. B. Mosher (1852-1923) gave eighteen of Donne's love-lyrics and 'A Hymn to God the Father' in the literary journal he edited. He introduced the poems with some appreciative passages from recent studies by Goose and Saintsbury, and added a warm commendation of his own (*Bibelot*, 3 (1897), 106)." Following this comment is an excerpt from Mosher's introduction to the selections in *The Bibelot* cited above.

Sowerby, E. Millicent. *Rare People & Rare Books*. Williamsburg, VA: The Bookpress, 1987, p.70. Mentions the attitude of the British auction houses toward the Mosher books. See quote from this selection under "Modern Assessments" in Section V, page 420.

Spencer, Geoffrey. "Limited Editions, Peoples's Prices: Mosher's Half Million" in *Amphora II*. Vancouver, Canada: The Alcuin Society, Spring 1968, pp. 14-23 (also reprinted in: *In Praise of the Book...* Vancouver, Canada: The Alcuin Society, 1992, pp. 2-8). A humorous account of an impecunious collector who had collected the Mosher books for some thirty years, first when living in England, then after emigrating to Canada. In building his modest collection he notes, "but the fun is in the chase. I'd give my eye-teeth, for example, for a copy of the 1925 [sic-1905] edition in Royal Quarto of the 14-point 'Kasidah'. If the devil happens to be among our members, he can have what's left of my soul in part payment." —p. 18

Steinhardt, Maxwell. "An Appreciation of Mosher" in the *Quarto Club Papers—1926-1927...* Limited to 195 copies. [New York: Pynson Printers, June 1927], pp. 43-54. This paper was read before the members of the Quarto Club on July 13, 1926. Steinhardt gives basic biographic details and repeats often stated quotes from the *Amphora*, and from Christopher Morley and Richard Le Gallienne with regard to the charge of piracy. Selections from this paper are given under "Memorial Tributes" in Section V, page 396.

Stern, Madeline B. *Imprints on History—Book Publishers and American Frontiers*. Bloomington: Indiana University Press, 1956, p. 366. This single entry indicates that following the death of Mosher, the press was supervised by Flora Lamb, and in 1942 was bought from Mrs. Mosher by J. G. Williams of Williams Book Store in Boston, and is now (i.e., as of 1956) continued by Harriet E. Williams, his daughter, with a specialty in "literary and scholarly works."

Stevens, Edward F. "The Kelmscott Influence in Maine" in the *Colby Library Quarterly*. Series I, No. 6. [March 1944], pp. 92-95. This brief collection of observations by Stevens (collected by Carl Weber) includes a selection of his remarks in Mathews' *Thomas Bird Mosher of Portland, Maine*. The balance of the article is on Bruce Rogers, mentioning his early design work for Mosher, and Rogers' influence on Fred Anthoensen. Stevens comments there were seven Kelmscott Press books in Mosher's library. The Sheean Manuscript of Mosher's Library reveals there were at least fourteen Kelmscott books in Mosher's library.

Strouse, Norman H. *A Collector's Decabiblon*. San Francisco: The Gleeson Library Associates, 1972, pp. 3-6 and 21. The first part of this printed address deals with Strouse's collecting The Mosher Books, and how the 1948 sale of Mosher's library provided the occasion for his first of "ten most exciting experiences as a collector," thus the title, a collector's ten top book experiences: *A Collector's Decabiblon*.

—. *How to Build a Poor Man's Morgan Library*. [Limited Edition]. Syracuse, New York: Syracuse University Library Associates, Christmas 1966, pp. 6-8. This address was delivered at the luncheon of the Syracuse University Library Associates on May 20, 1966 after the dedication of The Mayfield Library. It is based on a talk given before the Book Club of Detroit seven years earlier. Strouse mentions how the various facets of his book collecting were grounded in his introduction to fine printing through The Mosher Books.

—. "Thomas Bird Mosher—The Passionate Pirate. An Address by Norman H. Strouse." Unpublished address. November 25, 1960. This thirty-one page address, divided into ten parts, was delivered at The Rowfant Club in Cleveland, OH. The address formed the core ideas for Strouse's book-length treatment of Mosher in *The Passionate Pirate*.

☞ —. *The Passionate Pirate*. North Hills, PA: Bird & Bull Press, 1964. A Checklist (by series) appears at the end of this book. This list, though in need of revision, provided the model for the "Overview" in Section I of the present new bibliography. See "Modern Assessments" in Section V, pages 412-13 for an extensive quote from this work. The contents of this first and only full length biography of Mosher in book form includes the following chapters: Seafarer, Pirate, Publisher, Anthologist, Bibliophile, and Aldus of the XIX Century. For a review of this biography, see James Moran's review in *The Black Art*. Vol. 3, No. 3. London: Published by James Moran (Printed by Thomas Rae Ltd-Scotland), 1964/65, front cover and pp. 81-83. This book was also displayed at the Conference on Bibliography held at Penn State, November 1964 at which many of the Bird & Bull Press books were exhibited. **See entries 10, 139, 192, 239.**

Strouse, Norman H. See also (Free Library) and (Grolier) entries.

☞ Sturm, Rudolf, Herausgegeben. *François Villon—Bibliographie und Materialien 1489-1988*. Volume I & II. München, London, New York, Paris: K. G. Saur, 1990. Though this is a two volume set, all the bibliographical entries are in the first volume. This bibliography is not only thorough, but it is also delightfully illustrated throughout, sometimes in color. **See entries 17, 118, 302.**

☞ Sypher, Francis Jacques, editor. *A Year's Letters by Algernon Charles Swinburne*. New York: New York University Press, 1974. Sypher's introduction (pp. *xi-xxxviii*) is an informative publishing history *A Year's Letters*, including a bibliography of the work's appearance. It is interesting to note that Swinburne himself edited Mosher's edition to first provide a text for his regular publishers, Chatto and Windus. An extensive quote from Sypher appears in the entry for *A Year's Letters* (442). **See entry 442.**

Tanselle, G. Thomas. *Guide to the Study of United States Imprints*. Vol. 2. Cambridge, MA: The Belknap Press for Harvard University Press, 1971, pp. 619-20. This is a list of twenty-four books and articles relating to Thomas Bird Mosher (entries GM 8000.04-.41).

☞ Taylor, John Russell. *The Art Nouveau Book in Britain*. Edinburgh: Paul Harris Publishing, 1980. **See entries 30.01, 216.**

Tebbel, John. *A History of Book Publishing in the United States*. Vols. III & IV. New York: R. R. Bowker Company, 1981, pp. 436 & 662, and 427-28 respectively. There are some interesting notes in these references to Mosher, but there is also a good deal of inaccurate information, especially with regard to the Williams Book Store taking over the Mosher Press. The two most noticeable problems are the year assigned to the takeover (should be 1941, not 1942) and the almost complete gloss over the years Flora Lamb ran the Mosher Press. To follow the write-up in

Tebbel, one is told "The house [Mosher Press] had virtually ceased publishing before Mosher's death" and leaves one with the distinct impression that nothing happened between 1923 and 1941 which, of course, is not the case. In an interesting note, mention is made that "Ben Huebsch, of Viking, whose career in publishing had extended as long as Mosher's, and who thought him something of a pirate, although brilliant at the trade. Frederic Melcher, of *PW* [*Publisher's Weekly*], held a similar view." Mention is also made to Pearl Strachan's article, "Maine's Noted Press Finds a New Home in Boston" which appeared in *The Christian Science Monitor* for Feb. 21, 1942.

☞ Thompson, Susan Otis. *American Book Design and William Morris*. Foreword by Jean-François Vilain. London: The British Library, and New Castle, DE: Oak Knoll Press, 1996 (reprint of the original R.R. Bowker Company edition of 1977). *The* standard discussion on printing around the time Mosher published, with an excellent chapter entitled "Thomas Bird Mosher: The Aesthetic Pirate," pp. 190-197. The foreword mentions or discusses Mosher on pp. *xix, xx, xxv-xxvi*. Mosher is also mentioned as one of three influences on Will Ransom (p. 135). There are a few corrections to Thompson's original section on Mosher. On page 194 she mentions "the Hatch bibliography reveals nineteen titles by Morris..." This is a little misleading. There were fifteen titles published, but when factoring in the duplication between series, one comes up with a total of nineteen books. On p. 195, line 9, one should read "eighth" rather than "seventh." Also on page 194 she mentions there were "seven Kelmscott Press books in Mosher's personal library." Subsequent research reveals there were at least fourteen Kelmscotts on his shelves. Lastly, Thompson notes on p. 195 that Mosher used Jenson type as a text face at least once, on *George Meredith: a Tribute by J. M. Barrie*. In actuality Mosher used it as a text face on at least three other occasions: *Hand and Soul*, *Empedocles on Etna*, and on *In Praise of Omar*. Together these are rather small corrections compared to the overall strength of the original chapter nestled within a "classic" on American book design. **See entries 61, 88, 103, 106, 129, 139, 152, 397.**

—-. " 'Reform in Craftsmanship'—Books" in Wendy Kaplan's *"The Art that is Life": The Arts & Crafts Movement in America, 1875-1920*. Boston: Little, Brown and Company (Boston Museum of Fine Arts), 1987, pp. 294-295. Entry 156, highlighting Mosher's *Empedocles on Etna*, provides a brief summary of Mosher's publishing career and life. Thompson notes that the combination of his love of literature and love for fine printing "makes him an enduring figure in the history of American bookmaking." She also notes the influence of both the Kelmscott and Vale Press on Mosher's books.

Thomajan, P. K. *America's Oldest Private Press*. Herrin, IL: Trovillion Private Press, 1952. "Hal W. Trovillion got started in the private press venture in a novel manner... Back in 1908, inspired by the holiday keepsakes issued by that well-known New York importer of fine handmade papers, Thomas N. Fairbanks, Hal decided to issue some Christmas items... Along about this time Hal came under the influence of Thomas Bird Mosher, was greatly impressed by his literary taste and typographical manners, and as a direct result he aspired to producing his first complete book in 1913, under title of 'Neapolitan Vignettes'... The Trovillions take pride in carrying on the Mosher tradition—publishing rare gems of literature, old and new, with impeccable taste. In these editions, text, paper, design, decor, printing and binding are molded into one homogeneous whole."—pp. [3-5]. The text for this book was reprinted from the July 1952 issue of *The Inland Printer*, and also appeared in the newsletter, "At the Sign of the Silver Horse," Vol. XIII, No. 1. Herrin, IL: Trovillion Private Press, August, 1953.

Tinker, Edward Larocque. "New Editions, Fine and Otherwise" in *The New York Times Book Review*, October 5, 1941, p. 28. The text of this review is printed in "Memorial Tributes" in Section V, page 395.

(Tinker, Edward Laroque). *Trade Prices Current—Press Books—1937-1938*. New York, R. R. Bowker Co., 1938, pp. 67-79. These pages give author (in alpha order), title, date and price information on each book. Granted, this list is for 1938, but it helps to give some idea of the retail book prices of Mosher books in comparison to other private press books, as garnered from the American rare book trade.

☞ (Trovillion) *The Private Press—An Exhibition in Honor of the Fiftieth Anniversary of The Trovillion Private Press 1908-1958*. Foreword by Frank Luther Mott. [Lmtd to 100 copies]. Carbondale, IL: The Hornstone Press for the Southern Illinois University Library, May 1959. The Mosher productions of Matthew Arnold's *Empedocles on Etna* (1900) and Alexander Smith's *Dreamthorp* (1913) were both included in this exhibition along with the note that Mosher "was an early influence on the Trovillions." **See entries 95, 103.**

Turner, David. "Thomas Bird Mosher—A Reappraisal." Four-page typed address. Portland, ME, Nov./Dec. 1981. Turner addressed The Baxter Society on at least two occasions, the last one of which was on October 19, 1988, during which time he presented a slide show on Mosher. Along with Norma Carlson, David Turner operated Carlson & Turner Books in Portland, ME, which was sold in 1996. Both typescripts are in the Bishop Collection.

☞ Van Trump, James D. and Arthur P. Ziegler, Jr. "Thomas Bird Mosher: Publisher and Pirate" in *The Book Collector*. Vol. II, No. 3. London: The Shenval Press, Ltd., Autumn 1962, pp. 295-312. Though some facts on Mosher and his productions were not available to the authors in 1962 (Strouse's *Passionate Pirate* with his checklist only came out in 1964, and the Hatch bibliography in 1966), and there are a few errors on facts pertaining to the different series, this illustrated article ranks as one of the better, with a concise and superb section on the controversy over the Mosher piracies. Some of the errors appear on p. 300 which includes several inaccuracies: the *Songs of Adieu* is incorrectly assigned to the English Reprint Series, the titles in Bibelot Series books were said to be reprinted ten times in impressions of 1000 each, and the authors said the first three books printed were in the English Reprint Series. On p. 303 *Nature Thoughts* is identified as a series which, of course, could have been avoided at the time by consulting Mosher's catalogues. See lengthy quote from this work under "Modern Assessments" in Section V, page 412. **See entry 10.**

☞ Verster, Evelyn, comp. *Olive Emilie Albertina Schreiner (1855-1920); A Bibliography*. [Cape Town]: University of Cape Town Libraries, 1972. "Presented in partial fulfillment of the requirements for the Higher Certificate in Librarianship, 1947." There are earlier copies of this brief bibliography dated 1946. The Mosher edition of *Dreams* is listed as entry 11, but the entry doesn't list the date of the Mosher edition. **See entry 94.**

☞ Via, Marie, and Marjorie B. Searl, editors. *Head, Heart and Hand: Elbert Hubbard and the Roycrofters*. Rochester, New York: University of Rochester Press, 1994, p. 38. This work is, of course, overwhelmingly devoted to the Roycrofters, but includes a color photograph (plate 38) neatly contrasting an issue of Mosher's *The Bibelot* with Hubbard's *The Philistine*, in the section entitled "The Roycroft Printing Shop: Books, Magazines and Ephemera" authored by Jean-François Vilain. Both magazines are examples of "The Little Magazines" of the period. "Most of these 'dinky' magazines (so named because of their small size and lack of pretensions) lasted only a few issues, while some, like the *Philosopher*, the *Phoenix*, and the *Whim*, endured a few years. Only two, Thomas Bird Mosher's *Bibelot* and Hubbard's *Philistine*, lasted twenty years. Of the two, Hubbard's 'periodical of protest' (as he liked to call it) was by far the more successful, boasting in 1911 a subscription list of two hundred thousand." The number of subscribers to *The Bibelot* peaked to around four thousand from 1907-09. **See entry 18.**

Vilain, Jean François. "The Literary Pirate: the Covers of the Mosher Books" in *Craftsman Homeowner*. Vol. IV, No. 1. Spring 1993, p. 3. The contents are basically the article by Vilain and Bishop which first appeared in the *Trade Bindings Research Newsletter* listed below.

—. "The Passionate Promoter (Thomas Bird Mosher)" in *Arts and Crafts Quarterly Magazine*. Part II. Vol. V, No. 1. Trenton, NJ: Arts & Crafts Quarterly, [Spring 1992], pp. 28-31. The magazine's editor mixed up the title of this two-part article. The author intended the article's title to read: "The Passionate Pirate and the Passionate Promoter: Thomas Bird Mosher and Elbert Hubbard." Part I of this article dealt with Elbert Hubbard as The Passionate Promoter. Part II should have been The Passionate Pirate. The article covers basic biographical and publishing facts, discusses Mosher's literary piracy, and contrasts Mosher's publishing program with that of the Roycrofters under Elbert Hubbard. It is supplemented with three photographs of books and Mosher's portrait.

—. "Printing and American Arts and Crafts 1890-1910" in *Arts and Crafts Quarterly Magazine*. Vol. III, No. 3. Trenton, NJ: Arts & Crafts Quarterly, [Summer 1990], pp. 26-31. Mosher is discussed (primarily pp. 26-27) along with Elbert Hubbard of the Roycrofters, and the private presses and designers of the period found in Chicago, Boston, New York, and elsewhere. A photograph of the title page of Mosher's *Fancy's Following* (1900) heads the article.

Vilain, Jean François, and Philip R. Bishop. "The Covers of the Mosher Books" in *Trade Bindings Research Newsletter*. No.5. Edited by Linda Herman and Cynthia Bruns. Fullerton, CA: CSUF Library, June 1992, pp. 16-20. This article summarized the cover design research findings of Bishop and Vilain in preparation for the Temple Exhibit listed below. The article briefly mentions the examples of British designers whose work appears on the Mosher books. It also touches upon the American designers like Bruce Rogers, Frederic Goudy, Earl Stetson Crawford, and Thomas Maitland Cleland.

☞ —. *Thomas Bird Mosher and the Art of the Book*. Philadelphia: F. A. Davis Company, 1992. This 112-page catalogue commemorated the 100th anniversary of the books published by Thomas Bird Mosher, and reassesses his place in publishing history as a more central figure in the American revival of the printing arts. Widely known as a literary pirate, the study also shows him to be a "graphics pirate," borrowing much from British artists. It offers new research on Mosher's designs, methods and sources. The catalogue accompanied an exhibition at Temple University (summer 1992), and contains seventy-one black and white photographs in addition to detailed entries for books and materials exhibited. The work also contains an extensive index. Additions to Hatch were included in the 'Addenda & Corrigenda' section. A quote from this book is given under "Modern Assessments" in Section V, page 414. For a critical review of this book see: *PBSA*, Vol. 87, No. 4. December 1993, pp. 530-31. **See entries 1, 11, 29, 31, 40, 47, 50, 60, 62.11, 64, 66, 67, 67.2, 68, 71, 72, 73, 82, 86, 98, 100, 103, 106, 110, 111, 116, 117, 118.1, 121.4, 122, 122.1, 123, 130, 131, 132, 139, 141.1, 152, 154, 154.3, 154.4, 154.5, 171, 176, 177, 181.12, 182, 183, 186, 192, 192.1, 195.1, 199, 200, 207, 214, 216, 217.2, 219, 228, 231, 234, 235, 239, 242, 244, 246.1, 248, 250, 253, 256, 270.2, 274, 276, 280, 282, 287, 295, 296, 297, 298, 302, 309, 311, 315.4, 321, 331, 334, 334.7, 334.10, 335, 339, 341, 345, 347, 354, 355.2, 355.3, 356, 358, 364, 365, 366, 374, 374.4, 380, 387, 389, 405, 411, 424, 431, 436.3, 437, 439, 440.**

☞ Wade, Allan. *A Bibliography of the Writings of W. B. Yeats*. London: Rupert Hart-Davis, 1958. **See entries 186, 187, 188, 417**.

☞ Walsdorf, John J. *William Morris in Private Press and Limited Editions: A Descriptive Bibliography of Books by and about William Morris*. Foreword by Sir Basil Blackwell. Phoenix, AZ: The Oryx Press, 1983. The Mosher Press is one of the major presses included in this extensive bibliography. **See entries 61, 70, 84, 92, 133, 134, 135, 136, 148, 149, 150, 290, 359, 384, 389, 390, 396, 397, 419, 435.**

☞ Warde, Frederic. *Bruce Rogers—Designer of Books...* and Irvin Haas. *Bruce Rogers: A Bibliography*. New York, Port Washington: Kennikat Press, 1968. A composite reprint of the 1925 and 1936 editions respectively. The first contains a list of books printed under Bruce Roger's supervision, and the second work contains unrecorded work by Rogers from 1889-1925 missed in Warde. **See entry 152**.

☞ Warren, Arthur. *The Charles Whittinghams, Printers*. New York: The Grolier Club (Printed by DeVinne), 1896. A rich source book for Chiswick Press designs used by Mosher for many of his books, including some of his more substantial productions: *The Germ, Child Christopher and Goldilind the Fair, The Story of David Gray*, and head- and tail-pieces for many, many others in Mosher's different series. Apparently Mosher was an original subscriber to the book, and a copy was recorded in his library (see the Mosher library sales catalogue, Part I, #362). It presents an extensive overview of the Chiswick Press and the many initials, head-pieces, and border designs of Charlotte Whittingham and her sister, Elizabeth Eleanor, mostly all engraved by Mary Byfield. Reproductions of the border designs used on the covers of *Our Lady's Tumbler* (479), *The Silence of Amor* (618), and *The House of Usna* (290) can be seen in Warren's sections on "The Borders" and "The Woodcuts"; pp. 251-258 (borders copied by Mary Byfield from a 1525 Book of Hours printed by Geoffrey Tory of Bruges and reused in a prayerbook published by Longmans), and pp. 267-275 (border designs for Keble's *Christian Year*). See individual listings in the present Mosher bibliography for specific pages. Mosher or his printer may have photo-mechanically reproduced these designs, or a type supply house may have offered them. That he may have photo-mechanically done so seems to be supported by his manipulation of the designs in some instances, including switching design elements (see entries 290, 479 and 618), or enlargements and reductions in some instances. **See entries 48, 61, 132, 160, 164, 223, 258, 279, 281, 284, 306, 349, 352, 386.**

☞ Wheeler, Charles V [Van Cise]."The Important Private Library of Charles V. Wheeler of Washington, D.C. Part II (No. 126). English Literature. Early Printing, Colored Plate Books, First Editions, Association Items and The Edward FitzGerald Collection—The most complete ever offered." New York: The Walpole Galleries, July 29 & 30, 1919. Many of the *Rubáiyát* items in this catalogue were once in the collection of Thomas Bird Mosher, however, only select items are identified as once belonging to Mosher. **See entries 332, 336.**

Wheeler, Charles Van Cise. "A Bibliography of Edward FitzGerald, Composed of largely items in the collection of C.V.C. Wheeler including the collection formed by T. B. Mosher..." Unpublished typescript (carbon copy). 3 vols. Washington, D. C.: Prepared... for proposed very limited edition for private circulation only, 1919. Wheeler purchased Mosher's *Rubáiyát* collection and had intended to have Mosher publish a bibliography of FitzGerald's version of the *Rubáiyát*. This never came to pass, and Wheeler deposited his three-volume typescript in The Library of Congress in March 1920 (Call No. Z8301 .W56 [Office]). The carbon copy volumes were given by Wheeler to The Newberry Library in Chicago in May 1928 (Special Collections, Case Y 12 F585). The first volume includes British and American editions; the second foreign editions, parodies, etc.; and the third contains unique items, among other things. Page 118 of Volume I indicates that each Old World Edition (except for the 9th edition) included 100 numbered copies printed on Japan vellum. We have not been able to confirm this for entries

334.4 through 334.6 of the Mosher bibliography. Items which were once in the Mosher collection are so identified throughout the typescript. Volume I, p. 117 of the Wheeler bibliography records the FitzGerald *Rubáiyát* in The Bibelot Series; pp. 118-128 record the Old World Series *Rubáiyáts*, pp. 178-186 are reserved for the Vest Pocket Series editions; p. 176 lists the 1899 privately printed edition as the "Grigsby Edition;" and pp. 215-16 contain information on the 1902 facsimile edition.

☞ Wheeler, Henry O. "The Mosher Books." Unpublished address. Forty-eight page typewritten paper read before the Zamorano Club. Los Angeles, CA, September 30, 1936. A copy of this address is in The Donohue Rare Book Room, The Gleeson Library, University of San Francisco. Wheeler's talk covers, among other things, the close relationship between Mosher and W. Irving Way. Way was once part of the Chicago publishing firm, Way & Williams, and later moved to Los Angeles where he became a book distributor to California dealers. He was also curator of the Zamorano Club. Wheeler discusses the many Mosher books he acquired from Way's collection through Jake Zeitlin, including those with lengthy inscriptions and letters (quoted throughout the address). Through the same dealer he also acquired several books bearing the bookplates of Mosher, Henry W. Poor, and Herman M. Schroeter. Obviously, Wheeler was not only a Mosher enthusiast, but likewise had great respect for his former colleague, W. Irving Way. **See entries 2, 49, 286.**

☞ Wheelock, John Hall. *A Bibliography of Theodore Roosevelt*. New York: Charles Scribner's Sons, 1920. **See entry 407.**

White, William. "Thomas Bird Mosher and *A Shropshire Lad*" in *Serif* 5, No. 2. Kent, OH, [1968], pp. 30-33.

Who's Who. 4th ed. 1906-07. The Mosher entry varies slightly from edition to edition of *Who's Who*. The text of this edition is printed in "Contemporaneous Accounts" in Section V, page 389.

☞ Wick, Peter A., ed. *The Turn of a Century   1885-1910: Art Nouveau-Jugenstil Books*. Cambridge, MA: Department of Printing and Graphic Arts, The Houghton Library, Harvard University, 1970, pp. 13-14 (entry #8, John Gray's *Silverpoints*). **See entry 250.**

☞ (Widener, Harry Elkins) [Rosenbach, A. S. W., compiler]. *A Catalogue of the Books and Manuscripts of Robert Louis Stevenson in the Library of the Late Harry Elkins Widener*. With a Memoir by A.S.W. Rosenbach. Philadelphia: Privately Printed, 1913, pp. 157-158. Entry 116 describes a vellum copy of R.L.S.'s *Father Damien* printed by Mosher in 1905. Widener lost his life with his father in the sinking of the *Titanic* on April 15, 1912. Rosenbach noted, "he was the youngest collector who ever formed a noteworthy collection; his years were but twenty-seven. In the history of collecting, among the glittering names in the chronicle of books, there is not one that combined with youth the knowledge, the enthusiasm, the fine discrimination that he possessed... He was not merely a gatherer of rare and precious volumes, but a deep scholar, and an original and zealous investigator of the science of books." That an imprint from T. B. Mosher would have been selected by Widener is evidence of the value Mosher's imprint had to this connoisseur of books. The Widener literature collection was eventually transferred to Harvard where it finally resides in the rare book collection of the new library building built and dedicated by the Widener family in 1905 in honor of their son. **See entry 108.**

☞ Williamson, Dr. G. C. *Behind My Library Door—Some Chapters on Authors, Books and Miniatures*. With Illustrations. New York: E. P. Dutton & Company, 1921. Williamson recounts an episode when he gave Mosher's *Félise* to A. C. Swinburne, via Swinburne's mother, for signing. She viewed the book as a compliment to her son, and Swinburne himself replied that he considered the selection from his poems, "a judicious one." See Section II, entry 110, for the complete quote. **See entry 110 (see also 330).**

☞ Wirth, Alexander C. *Complete Bibliography of Lizette Woodworth Reese*. Baltimore: The Proof Press, 1937. This early bibliography lists fourteen first editions of Lizette Woodworth Reese's books including *A Branch of May* first published by Baltimore: Cushing & Baily, 1887 (Mosher in 1909), *A Handful of Lavender* first published Boston & New York: Houghton, Mifflin, 1891 (Mosher in 1915), and *A Quiet Road* in Boston & New York, 1896 (Mosher in 1916). The only book Mosher published first was *A Wayside Lute* in 1909. See also the *Lizette Woodworth Reese Collection*. University of Virginia Library, 1971. **See entry 434.**

☞ Wise, Thomas J. *A Bibliography of The Writings in Prose and Verse of Algernon Charles Swinburne*. 2 vols. London: Printed for Private Circulation, 1919 (reprinted London: Dawsons of Pall Mall, 1966). **See entries 147, 190, 297, 423.**

Witemeyer, Hugh, ed. *Selected Letters of Ezra Pound and William Carlos Willliams*. New York: New Directions Publishing Corp., 1996, pp. 8 and 12. An October 21, 1908 letter (ALS 22) from Pound to Williams mentions that Mosher is going to reprint Yeats. The note on p. 12 identifies Thomas Bird Mosher as the leading American publisher of fin-de-siècle poetry who declined to print Pound's *A Lume Spento*.

☞ Wolf, Thomas. "Thomas Bird Mosher: Historical Aspects of his Life and Work." Unpublished summer research grant paper. Swarthmore, PA: Swarthmore College, 1967. This 136 page research paper included original research done at the Huntington, Columbia, and Houghton libraries, and includes sections entitled "The Mosher Legacy," "Operating a Private Press (Mosher-style)," and "Cultural Custodian as Anthologist." The appendices include the text of the T. B. Mosher-Andrew Lang controversy as it appeared in *The Critic,* and an unpublished defense of Mosher's piracy written by Mosher himself. According to a note under the dedication, "this paper represents the first half of a full-scale biography of Thomas Mosher." So far as is known, no further work was completed. The paper is especially helpful in placing Mosher and his publishing activities within that small group of individuals around the turn-of-the-century who were concerned with spreading literature among the middle-class, and with protecting and helping to restore Anglo-Saxon culture in the midst of the transformations of modern industrial society. **See entry 302.**

☞ Wright, Samuel. *A Bibliography of the Writings of Walter H. Pater*. New York & London: Garland Publishing, Inc., 1975. Contains a biography of Mosher ("Thomas Bird Mosher: Man of Letters," pp. 157-59) and references on books and articles about Mosher (pp. 159-60). Wright also provides an account of "Walter Pater in Mosher's *The Bibelot* (pp. 161-62) and Pater's books reprinted in Mosher's various series (pp. 162-63). **See entries 62, 63, 89, 96, 102, 104, 127, 231, 312, 321, 322, 344, 359, 385, 421.**

Writers' Program (Maine). *Portland City Guide*. Compiled by workers of the Writers' Program of the Work Projects Administrations in the State of Maine... Sponsored by the City of Portland. American Guide Series. [Portland, ME]: The Forrest City Printing Company, 1940, pp. 166-167, 258. Though it is good to see that Portland formally paid homage to Mosher in its 1940 city guide, the information on Mosher and The Mosher Press contains several errors. Page 166 indicates "in 1895 Mosher started under his own name the Bibelot series of reprints..." It becomes clearer as one reads on that the "series" being discussed is, in fact, not a series at all, but rather the periodical, *The Bibelot.* This muddled description only perpetuates the confusion between *The Bibelot* itself, "The Bibelot Series," and the "Reprints from 'the Bibelot' Series." Additionally, the write-up often refers to a series as an "edition," e.g., the "Brocade edition." Another error is the 1859 date assigned to the original edition of Whitman's *Leaves of Grass.* It was the 1855 edition which Mosher used as the basis for his type facsimile. The write-up also indicates that "the Mosher Press was the first in America to adopt the dolphin and anchor device..." This is not the case, for Mosher was preceded by at least two Boston publishers who used an anchor and dolphin device decades before him: Hilliard, Gray, and Company, and Roberts Brothers. Furthermore, the writers indicate that the anchor and dolphin device was first introduced in the "Venetian Series." This is also incorrect in that the "Venetian Series," started in 1910, only uses an anchor device. Combined anchor and dolphin devices began as early as 1902 in the "Reprints of Privately Printed Books," the "Quarto Series," and in the privately printed books. On p. 258 the write-up indicates Mosher's office was at 45 Exchange Street since "that company came into existence in 1895." Mosher only moved to that location in 1896, prior to which his office was at 37 Exchange Street. Otherwise, the Mosher entry is roughly accurate, including its final statement that Mosher "was better known as a publisher in London than in Portland."

Wroth, Lawrence C. "Printing in the Mauve Decade" ("Notes for Bibliophiles" column) in the *New York Herald*, February 8, 1942, p. 18. For a major portion of the text pertaining to Mosher, see "Modern Assessments" in Section V, page 421.

Yorke, Dane. "That Man Mosher." Unpublished typescript. Biddeford, ME, ca. 1947. Consists of fifty-eight pages of typewritten material forming a chapter on the early formative years of Mosher's life up to 1891. The account presents information which is sometimes contrary to, or new to, the established folklore and myth repeated over and over in various tributes and memorial essays. The typescript, Yorke's notes, and supporting documentary material (manuscripts, diaries, programs, booklets, and correspondence) are in the Bishop Collection.

Addendum: *Edward Fitzgerald 1809-1909—Centenary Celebrations Souvenir.* [Ipswich, England: The East Anglian Daily Times], 1909, pp. 5, 7, 50-51. Mosher is listed as a patron, the lender of the plates used to illustrate the souvenir (taken from his own publication of *Edward FitzGerald: An Aftermath*), and is given a two page write-up entitled "An American Tribute" in which Mosher boasts of owning FitzGerald's commonplace book, and his annotated copies of 'Lucretius' and 'Shiller's Wallenstein.'

Appendices

1.0=227	27.0=299	62.13=452	102.1=176	135.0=152	167.0=742	192.1=684	233.0=116	279.0=140
1.1=280	28.0=332	63.0=470	103.0=143	136.0=218	168.0=210	193.0=323	233.1=179	279.1=167
1.2=424	29.0=366	64.0=150	104.0= 49	136.1=378	169.0=754	194.0=255	233.2=276	279.2=305
2.0=560	30.0=401	64.1=242	104.1=102	137.0= 5	170.0=562	194.1=633	233.3=415	279.3=306
2.1=600	31.0=444	64.2=526	105.0=252	138.0=587	171.0= 67	195.0=326	233.4=576	280.0=364
2.2=617	32.0=479	65.0=327	106.0=154	139.0=109	171.1= 88	195.1=581A	234.0=542	280.1=554
2.3=673	33.0=518	65.1=423	107.0= 43	139.1=166	171.2= 89	196.0=139	235.0=717	281.0=745
2.4=698	34.0=544	66.0=701	107.1= 56	140.0=362	171.3= 90	196.1=337	236.0=743	282.0= 25
3.0=590	35.0=566	67.0=104	107.2= 87	141.0=626	171.4=131	197.0=430	237.0=251	282.1= 34
4.0=440	36.0=594	67.1=236	107.3=130	141.1=675	171.5=165	198.0= 4A	238.0=287	282.2= 58
5.0=329	37.0=612	67.2=405A	107.4=203	142.0=289	171.6=339	199.0= 8	239.0=559	282.3= 93
5.1=458	38.0=367	68.0=740	107.5=271	142.1=381	171.7=600A	200.0= 16	240.0=359	282.4=133
5.2=646	39.0=628	69.0=534	107.6=338	142.2=495	172.0=683	201.0= 28	240.1=584	282.5=170
6.0=352	40.0=712	70.0=193	107.7=411	142.3=580	173.0=703	202.0= 51	241.0= 9	282.6=204
6.1=571	41.0=720	71.0=354	107.8=489	143.0=388	174.0=286	203.0= 80	242.0=186	282.7=239
7.0=317	42.0=607	72.0= 2	107.9=549	143.1=548	175.0=443	204.0=124	243.0=468	282.8=307
8.0=635	43.0=608	73.0=247	107.10=641	144.0=748	176.0=191	205.0=160	244.0= 1	282.9=524
9.0= 40	44.0=325	73.1=487	108.0=320	145.0=759	176.1=377	206.0=199	245.0= 64	283.0=328
9.1=235	44.1=422	73.2=694	108.1=523	146.0= 39	177.0=315	207.0=232	245.1=302	283.1=500
9.2=405	45.0=147	74.0=704	109.0= 47	146.1=269	177.1=488	208.0=476	245.2=521	284.0=505
9.3=569	45.1=207	75.0=709	110.0= 7	146.2=520	178.0= 37	209.0=357	246.0=105	285.0=539
10.0= 12	45.2=416	76.0=395	111.0=464	147.0= 77	179.0=516	209.1=582	246.1=447A	286.0=713
10.1= 30	46.0= 10	77.0=755	112.0=324	148.0=112	180.0=610	210.0=257	247.0=264	287.0=432
10.2= 53	47.0=184	78.0=397	112.1=421	148.1=175	181.0= 23	210.1=313	248.0=300	288.0=558
10.3= 83	47.1=237	78.1=634	112.2=581	148.2=493	181.1= 85	210.2=425	249.0=333	289.0=592
10.4=126	47.2=340	78.2=650	113.0=561	149.0= 48	181.2=163	211.0=436	250.0=368	290.0=195
10.5=200	48.0=318	79.0=517	114.0=627	150.0=148	181.3=234	212.0=356	251.0=402	291.0=211
10.6=266	48.1=412	80.0=256	115.0=664	150.1=277	181.4=267	213.0=398	252.0=445	291.1=449
10.7=404	49.0=609	80.1=618	116.0=224	150.2=454	181.5=369	213.1=651	253.0=480	292.0=507
10.8=596	49.1=699	81.0=194	117.0=722A	151.0=738	181.6=446	214.0=330	254.0=519	293.0=741
10.9=693	50.0=472	82.0=727	118.0=190	152.0= 13	181.7=482	214.1=429	255.0=545	294.0=229
11.0=258	51.0=680	83.0= 75	118.1=215A	153.0=285	181.8=547	214.2=606	256.0=567	295.0=532
11.1=346	52.0=654	84.0= 20	118.2=376	154.0=442	181.9=597	214.3=649	257.0=595	295.1=616
11.2=499	53.0=221	85.0=392	118.3=551	154.1=462	181.10=659	215.0=331	258.0=613	296.0=294
12.0=750	53.1=311	86.0=509	119.0=700	154.2=503	181.11=682	215.1=349	259.0=629	297.0=228
13.0=296	53.2=418	87.0=355	120.0=733	154.3=555	181.12=702A	215.2=461	260.0=640	298.0=361
13.1=348	54.0=677	88.0=246	121.0=182	154.4=620A	182.0=321	215.3=619	261.0=658	299.0=475
13.2=427	55.0=749	88.1=486	121.1=304	154.5=661	183.0=624	216.0=711	262.0=666	300.0=181
13.3=553	56.0=707	89.0= 70	121.2=406	155.0=433	184.0=735	217.0=146	263.0=670	300.1=370
13.4=674	57.0=757	89.1= 97	121.3=522	156.0=391	185.0=192	217.1=240	264.0=681	301.0=213
14.0=390	58.0=708	90.0=399	121.4=659A	157.0=114	185.1=602	217.2=341A	265.0=689	302.0=153
15.0= 22	59.0= 46	91.0=245	122.0= 42	157.1=177	186.0=260	217.3=453	266.0=692	302.1=345
15.1= 55	59.1= 62	91.1=408	122.1=129A	157.2=274	186.1=281	217.4=577	267.0=702	302.2=501
15.2= 84	59.2=273	91.2=630	123.0=591	157.3=524A	186.2=314	217.5=643	268.0=136	303.0=644
15.3=233	60.0=188	92.0=212	124.0=721	158.0= 63	186.3=347	218.0=510	269.0=220	304.0=248
15.4=481	60.1=375	92.1=450	125.0=225	158.1=270	186.4=386	219.0= 36	269.1=417	304.1=341
16.0=259	61.0=142	93.0=400	126.0=655	158.2=447	186.5=387	220.0=471	270.0= 21	305.0=435
17.0=298	62.0= 14	94.0=653	127.0=389	159.0=350	186.6=459	221.0=513	270.1= 54	306.0=185
17.1=428	62.1= 18	95.0=588	128.0=531	159.1=451	186.7=502	222.0=282	270.2=126A	307.0=244
17.2=605	62.2= 31	96.0= 72	128.1=574	159.2=598	186.8=529	223.0=668	270.3=162	308.0=189
17.3=648	62.3= 32	96.1= 99	128.2=615	160.0=250	186.9=583	224.0=508	270.4=334	308.1=310
18.0= 15	62.4= 33	97.0=533	129.0=672	161.0=365	186.10=604	225.0=564	270.5=568	308.2=456
19.0= 27	62.5= 57	98.0=394	130.0=107	162.0=216	186.11=647	226.0=512	271.0=716	309.0=746
20.0= 50	62.6= 91	99.0=438	130.1=371	162.1=342	187.0=466	227.0=262	272.0=478	310.0=665
21.0= 79	62.7= 92	99.1=652	131.0=108	163.0=578	188.0=710	227.1=426	273.0=728	311.0=141
22.0=123	62.8=168	100.0= 68	131.1=372	164.0=393	189.0=611	228.0=714	274.0=691	312.0= 69
23.0=159	62.9=169	100.1=132	132.0= 78	165.0=261	190.0=122	229.0=656	275.0= 4	312.1= 96
24.0=198	62.10=238	100.2=572	133.0=117	165.1=460	191.0=156	230.0=636	276.0=729	312.2=374
25.0=231	62.11=271A	101.0=214	134.0=217	165.2=690	191.1=498	231.0=157	277.0=719	313.0=688
26.0=263	62.12=373	102.0=113	134.1=343	166.0=706	192.0=667	232.0=158	278.0=715	314.0=474

315.0= 74	329.1=662	337.0=705	355.1=241	374.5=484	385.1= 60	396.2=575	416.0=295	435.0=223
315.1=101	329.2=687	338.0=760	355.2=376A	375.0=155	385.2= 95	397.0= 73	417.0=439	436.0=115
315.2=173	330.0=353	339.0=621	355.3=577A	375.1=209	385.3=171	397.1=100	418.0=761	436.1=178
315.3=205	331.0=556	340.0=187	356.0=623	375.2=279	385.4=272	397.2=309	419.0=118	436.2=275
315.4=452A	332.0= 6	340.1=278	357.0=536	375.3=384	385.5=492	397.3=632	420.0=291	436.3=309A
315.5=601	333.0= 19	340.2=455	358.0=540	375.4=527	386.0=144	398.0=288	420.1=420	436.4=414
316.0=293	334.0= 11	341.0=530	359.0=253	376.0= 38	387.0=103	398.1=419	421.0=249	436.5=525
316.1=457	334.1= 17	342.0=753	359.1=344	376.1=128	387.1=303	398.2=552	422.0=506	437.0=535
317.0=638	334.2= 29	343.0=322	359.2=579	376.2=201	388.0= 65	399.0=723	422.1=550	438.0=739
318.0=145	334.3= 52	343.1=671	360.0=297	376.3=268	388.1=164	400.0= 76	422.2=614	439.0=119
318.1=206	334.4= 81	344.0= 71	361.0=151	376.4=483	388.2=335	401.0=358	423.0=120	440.0=663
318.2=494	334.5= 82	344.1= 98	362.0=732	377.0=431	388.3=485	402.0=751	424.0= 66	441.0=722
319.0=477	334.6=125	345.0=586	363.0=718	378.0=319	389.0=222	403.0=639	425.0=137	442.0=196
319.1=686	334.7=161	346.0=138	364.0=197	378.1=413	390.0=219	403.1=660	425.1=448	443.0=290
320.0=726	334.8=265	346.1=336	365.0=593	378.2=490	390.1=379	404.0=679	426.0=756	443.1=382
321.0=230	334.9=403	347.0=110	366.0= 3	378.3=631	391.0= 45	405.0=589	427.0=292	443.2=496
322.0=557	334.10=546	348.0=183	367.0=585	379.0=744	391.1= 61	406.0=737	427.1=385	443.3=603
323.0=473	335.0=121	348.1=407	368.0=284	380.0=543	391.2=172	407.0=669	427.2=528	444.0=758
324.0=511	335.1=135	349.0=467	369.0=538	381.0=731	391.3=308	407.1=685	428.0=504	445.0=746A
325.0=678	335.2=135A	349.1=573	370.0=730	382.0=565	392.0=622	408.0=734	429.0=465	
326.0=316	335.3=180	350.0=351	371.0=752	383.0=396	393.0=360	409.0=254	430.0=736	
326.1=410	335.4=208	350.1=599	372.0=747	384.0= 26	393.1=620	409.1=380	431.0=657	
326.2=570	335.5=243	350.2=696	373.0=537	384.1= 35	394.0= 24	410.0=441	431.1=676	
327.0=283	335.6=312	351.0=515	374.0= 41	384.2= 59	394.1=127	411.0=541	432.0=724	
327.1=409	335.7=383	352.0=215	374.1= 86	384.3= 94	394.2=301	412.0=514	433.0=363	
327.2=695	335.8=497	353.0=563	374.2=129	384.4=134	395.0=106	413.0=434	434.0=469	
328.0=725	335.9=645	354.0=463	374.3=202	384.5=491	396.0=111	414.0=637	434.1=642	
329.0=625	336.0=226	355.0=149	374.4=301A	385.0= 44	396.1=174	415.0=437	434.2=697	

APPENDIX I-B

CONVERSION FROM HATCH TO THIS BIBLIOGRAPHY

1=244.0	61=391.1	122=190.0	180=335.3	240=217.1	300=248.0	358=401.0	417=269.1	476=208.0
2= 72.0	62= 59.1	123= 22.0	181=300.0	241=355.1	301=394.2	359=240.0	418= 53.2	477=319.0
3=366.0	63=158.0	124=204.0	182=121.0	242= 64.1	301A=374.4	360=393.0	419=398.1	478=272.0
4=275.0	64=245.0	125=334.6	183=348.0	243=335.5	302=245.1	361=298.0	420=420.1	479= 32.0
4A=198.0	65=388.0	126= 10.4	184= 47.0	244=307.0	303=387.1	362=140.0	421=112.1	480=253.0
5=137.0	66=424.0	126A=270.2	185=306.0	245= 91.0	304=121.1	363=433.0	422= 44.1	481= 15.4
6=332.0	67=171.0	127=394.1	186=242.0	246= 88.0	305=279.2	364=280.0	423= 65.1	482=181.7
7=110.0	68=100.0	128=376.1	187=340.0	247= 73.0	306=279.3	365=161.0	424= 1.2	483=376.4
8=199.0	69=312.0	129=374.2	188= 60.0	248=304.0	307=282.8	366= 29.0	425=210.2	484=374.5
9=241.0	70= 89.0	129A=122.1	189=308.0	249=421.0	308=391.3	367= 38.0	426=227.1	485=388.3
10= 46.0	71=344.0	130=107.3	190=118.0	250=160.0	309=397.2	368=250.0	427= 13.2	486= 88.1
11=334.0	72= 96.0	131=171.4	191=176.0	251=237.0	309A=436.3	369=181.5	428= 17.1	487= 73.1
12= 10.0	73=397.0	132=100.1	192=185.0	252=105.0	310=308.1	370=300.1	429=214.1	488=177.1
13=152.0	74=315.0	133=282.4	193= 70.0	253=359.0	311= 53.1	371=130.1	430=197.0	489=107.8
14= 62.0	75= 83.0	134=384.4	194= 81.0	254=409.0	312=335.6	372=131.1	431=377.0	490=378.2
15= 18.0	76=400.0	135=335.1	195=290.0	255=194.0	313=210.1	373=62.12	432=287.0	491=384.5
16=200.0	77=147.0	135A=335.2	196=442.0	256= 80.0	314=186.2	374=312.2	433=155.0	492=385.5
17=334.1	78=132.0	136=268.0	197=364.0	257=210.0	315=177.0	375= 60.1	434=413.0	493=148.2
18= 62.1	79= 21.0	137=425.0	198= 24.0	258= 11.0	316=326.0	376=118.2	435=305.0	494=318.2
19=333.0	80=203.0	138=346.0	199=206.0	259= 16.0	317= 7.0	376A=355.2	436=211.0	495=142.2
20= 84.0	81=334.4	139=196.0	200= 10.5	260=186.0	318= 48.0	377=176.1	437=415.0	496=443.2
21=270.0	82=334.5	140=279.0	201=376.2	261=165.0	319=378.0	378=136.1	438= 99.0	497=335.8
22= 15.0	83= 10.3	141=311.0	202=374.3	262=227.0	320=108.0	379=390.1	439=417.0	498=191.1
23=181.0	84= 15.2	142= 61.0	203=107.4	263= 26.0	321=182.0	380=409.1	440= 4.0	499= 11.2
24=394.0	85=181.1	143=103.0	204=282.6	264=247.0	322=343.0	381=142.1	441=410.0	500=283.1
25=282.0	86=374.1	144=386.0	205=315.3	265=334.8	323=193.0	382=443.1	442=154.0	501=302.2
26=384.0	87=107.2	145=318.0	206=318.1	266= 10.6	324=112.0	383=335.7	443=175.0	502=186.7
27= 19.0	88=171.1	146=217.0	207= 45.1	267=181.4	325= 44.0	384=375.3	444= 31.0	503=154.2
28=201.0	89=171.2	147= 45.0	208=335.4	268=376.3	326=195.0	385=427.1	445=252.0	504=428.0
29=334.2	90=171.3	148=150.0	209=375.1	269=146.1	327= 65.0	386=186.4	446=181.6	505=284.0
30= 10.1	91= 62.6	149=355.0	210=168.0	270=158.1	328=283.0	387=186.5	447=158.2	506=422.0
31= 62.2	92= 62.7	150= 64.0	211=291.0	271=107.5	329= 5.0	388=143.0	447A=246.1	507=292.0
32= 62.3	93=282.3	151=361.0	212= 92.0	271A=61.11	330=214.0	389=127.0	448=425.1	508=224.0
33= 62.4	94=384.3	152=135.0	213=301.0	272=385.4	331=215.0	390= 14.0	449=291.1	509= 86.0
34=282.1	95=385.2	153=302.0	214=101.0	273= 59.2	332= 28.0	391=156.0	450= 92.1	510=218.0
35=384.1	96=312.1	154=106.0	215=352.0	274=157.2	333=249.0	392= 85.0	451=159.1	511=324.0
36=219.0	97= 89.1	155=375.0	215A=118.1	275=436.2	334=270.4	393=164.0	452= 62.13	512=226.0
37=178.0	98=344.1	156=191.0	216=162.0	276=233.2	335=388.2	394= 98.0	452A=315.4	513=221.0
38=376.0	99= 96.1	157=231.0	217=134.0	277=150.1	336=346.1	395= 76.0	453=217.3	514=412.0
39=146.0	100=397.1	158=232.0	218=136.0	278=340.1	337=196.1	396=383.0	454=150.2	515=351.0
40= 9.0	101=315.1	159= 23.0	219=390.0	279=375.2	338=107.6	397= 78.0	455=340.2	516=179.0
41=374.0	102=104.1	160=205.0	220=269.0	280= 1.1	339=171.6	398=213.0	456=308.2	517= 79.0
42=122.0	103=387.0	161=334.7	221= 53.0	281=186.1	340= 47.2	399= 90.0	457=316.1	518= 33.0
43=107.0	104= 67.0	162=270.3	222=389.0	282=222.0	341=304.1	400= 93.0	458= 5.1	519=254.0
44=385.0	105=246.0	163=181.2	223=435.0	283=327.0	341A=217.2	401= 30.0	459=186.6	520=146.2
45=391.0	106=395.0	164=388.1	224=116.0	284=368.0	342=162.1	402=251.0	460=165.1	521=245.2
46= 59.0	107=130.0	165=171.5	225=125.0	285=153.0	343=134.1	403=334.9	461=215.2	522=121.3
47=109.0	108=131.0	166=139.1	226=336.0	286=174.0	344=359.1	404= 10.7	462=154.1	523=108.1
48=149.0	109=139.0	167=279.1	227= 1.0	287=238.0	345=302.1	405= 9.2	463=354.0	524=282.9
49=104.0	110=347.0	168= 62.8	228=297.0	288=398.0	346= 11.1	405A=67.2	464=111.0	524A=157.3
50= 20.0	111=396.0	169= 62.9	229=294.0	289=142.0	347=186.3	406=121.2	465=429.0	525=436.5
51=202.0	112=148.0	170=282.5	230=321.0	290=443.0	348= 13.1	407=348.1	466=187.0	526= 64.2
52=334.3	113=102.0	171=385.3	231= 25.0	291=420.0	349=215.1	408= 91.1	467=349.0	527=375.4
53= 10.2	114=157.0	172=391.2	232=207.0	292=427.0	350=159.0	409=327.1	468=243.0	528=427.2
54=270.1	115=436.0	173=315.2	233= 15.3	293=316.0	351=350.0	410=326.1	469=434.0	529=186.8
55= 15.1	116=233.0	174=396.1	234=181.3	294=296.0	352= 6.0	411=107.7	470= 63.0	530=341.0
56=107.1	117=133.0	175=148.1	235= 9.1	295=416.0	353=330.0	412= 48.1	471=220.0	531=128.0
57= 62.5	118=419.0	176=102.1	236= 67.1	296= 13.0	354= 71.0	413=378.1	472= 50.0	532=295.0
58=282.2	119=439.0	177=157.1	237= 47.1	297=360.0	355= 87.0	414=436.4	473=323.0	533= 97.0
59=384.2	120=423.0	178=436.1	238= 62.10	298= 17.0	356=212.0	415=233.3	474=314.0	534= 69.0
60=385.1	121=335.0	179=233.1	239=282.7	299= 27.0	357=209.0	416= 45.2	475=299.0	535=437.0

536=357.0	563=353.0	5588=95.0	614=422.2	640=260.0	666=262.0	693= 10.9	719=277.0	745=281.0
537=373.0	564=225.0	589=405.0	615=128.2	641=107.10	667=192.0	694= 73.2	720= 41.0	746=309.0
538=369.0	565=382.0	590= 3.0	616=295.1	642=434.1	668=223.0	695=327.2	721=124.0	746A=445
539=285.0	566= 35.0	591=123.0	617= 2.2	643=217.5	669=407.0	696=350.2	722=441.0	747=372.0
540=358.0	567=256.0	592=289.0	618= 80.1	644=303.0	670=263.0	697=434.2	722A=117.0	748=144.0
541=411.0	568=270.5	593=365.0	619=215.3	645=335.9	671=343.1	698= 2.4	723=399.0	749= 55.0
542=234.0	569= 9.3	594= 36.0	620=393.1	646= 5.2	672=129.0	699= 49.1	724=432.0	750= 12.0
543=380.0	570=326.2	595=257.0	620A=154.4	647=186.11	673= 2.3	700=119.0	725=328.0	751=402.0
544= 34.0	571= 6.1	596= 10.8	621=339.0	648= 17.3	674= 13.4	701= 66.0	726=320.0	752=371.0
545=255.0	572=100.2	597=181.9	622=392.0	649=214.3	675=141.1	702=267.0	727= 82.0	753=342.0
546=334.10	573=349.1	598=159.2	623=356.0	650= 78.2	676=431.1	702A=181.12	728=273.0	754=169.0
547=181.8	574=128.1	599=350.1	624=183.0	651=213.1	677= 54.0	703=173.0	729=276.0	755= 77.0
548=143.1	575=396.2	600= 2.1	625=329.0	652= 99.1	678=325.0	704= 74.0	730=370.0	756=426.0
549=107.9	576=233.4	600A=171.7	626=141.0	653= 94.0	679=404.0	705=337.0	731=381.0	757= 57.0
550=422.1	577=217.4	601=315.5	627=114.0	654= 52.0	680= 51.0	706=166.0	732=362.0	758=444.0
551=118.3	577A=355.3	602=185.1	628= 39.0	655=126.0	681=264.0	707= 56.0	733=120.0	759=145.0
552=398.2	578=163.0	603=443.3	629=259.0	656=229.0	682=181.11	708= 58.0	734=408.0	760=338.0
553= 13.3	579=359.2	604=186.10	630= 91.2	657=431.0	683=172.0	709= 75.0	735=184.0	761=418.0
554=280.1	580=142.3	605= 17.2	631=378.3	658=261.0	684=192.1	710=188.0	736=430.0	
555=154.3	581=112.2	606=214.2	632=397.3	659=181.10	685=407.1	711=216.0	737=406.0	
556=331.0	581A=195.1	607= 42.0	633=194.1	659A=121.4	686=319.1	712= 40.0	738=151.0	
557=322.0	582=209.1	608= 43.0	634= 78.1	660=403.1	687=329.2	713=286.0	739=438.0	
558=288.0	583=186.9	609= 49.0	635= 8.0	661=154.5	688=313.0	714=228.0	740= 68.0	
559=239.0	584=240.1	610=180.0	636=230.0	662=329.1	689=265.0	715=278.0	741=293.0	
560= 2.0	85=367.0	611=189.0	637=414.0	663=440.0	690=165.2	716=271.0	742=167.0	
561=113.0	586=345.0	612= 37.0	638=317.0	664=115.0	691=274.0	717=235.0	743=236.0	
562=170.0	587=138.0	613=258.0	639=403.0	665=310.0	692=266.0	718=363.0	744=379.0	

APPENDIX II
LIST OF ROYALTIES AND OTHER PAYMENTS MADE TO AUTHORS

Thomas B. Mosher was known as a literary pirate, and it is indeed true that he pirated many an English author's works, as did other American publishers of the day. Mosher's point was that he had a perfect legal right to texts which were not protected under the International Copyright Law and not registered in Washington. He felt especially justified if the British author and/or publisher either neglected the text or printed it in such a limited number that made it practically unavailable to a wider public. He called such texts, those "introuvables." It should be noted, however, that even if he had clear legal right to publish without an author's consent, he often at least asked for permission in exchange for a token payment, but sometimes just sent the Mosher version of the author's book along with his payment. Mosher sent Andrew Lang such an honorarium for his translation of *Aucassin & Nicolete* which sparked a vitriolic refusal from Lang.

There has never been any account of which authors received payments from Mosher, and which did not. Many writers on Mosher have assumed that he pirated just about everything, and only occasionally made some sort of payment. Some researchers (Van Trump & Ziegler, and Huntress) tried, in vain, to examine the account books said to be in the possession of The Williams Book Store of Boston, MA. They apparently did not realize that the account books were, in fact, never transferred to The Williams Book Store. According to a letter from Flora Lamb (now in the Bishop Collection), the account books were sent to Mrs. Mosher's home, and the remaining Mosher book stock was transferred to Boston. So the reason why many past researchers were unsuccessful in their exhortations was because the account books were never in Boston in the first place. Only one person, professor Nicholas A. Salerno of Arizona State University, reported to me that he had at least seen them once, but he apparently has no information from them, and their current whereabouts is unknown.

To help compensate for the lack of direct examination of the account books, a recently uncovered letter from Flora MacDonald Lamb to Biddeford, Maine historian, Dane Yorke (Bishop Collection), discloses some of this valuable information. Yorke was writing a biography of T. B. Mosher in the 1940's (unpublished), and he worked closely with Flora Lamb, Mosher's long-time assistant, who supplied him with first-hand information including the exact payments made to some authors. In a two-page letter dated Nov. 17, 1941 (on Thomas B. Mosher stationary), Flora Lamb reveals:

Nov. 17, 1941

Dear Mr. Yorke:

I have the books before me and can now give you the exact figures:

$67.50

Homeward: Songs	Royalty on 450 copies. Sale price $1.50 at 10% royalty
	No royalty was paid on the 25 Vellum copies.

Fiona Macleod. Paid outright for use of

By Sundown Shores ———————————	$32.00
Silence of Amor (1st Edn.)	48.00
Divine Adventure ————————— -	100.00
Deirdre and the Sons of Usna	100.00
Isle of Dreams ——————————-	49.26
The Hour of Beauty ————————	50.00
The House of Usna ————————	50.00
The Immortal Hour ————————	50.00
Nature Thoughts (Mrs. Sharp) ————————	50.00
From the Hills of Dream Paid for copyright	123.00
in this	

Garnett, Richard. De Flagello Myrteo

Paid Elkins Matthews for use	50.00

Bottomley, Gordon.	A Vision of Giorgione	24.65
" "	Riding to Lithend	25.00

---

continued on next page

McCurdy, Edward   Roses of Paestum   50.00

Hort, Gertrude   To-Morrow's Road   25.00

Russell, Bertrand   A Free Man's Worship
          Preface and right to reprint   24.26

Henry Copley Green.   The Children's Crusade.
          Paid for the translation   15.94

Lyttelton, Lucy.   Lyrical Poems   25.00

Hard, William   Paid for the right to
      reprint the Tribute to T. Roosevelt   25.00

Cheney, John Vance.   The Time of Roses
      Paid 10% royalty on the sale price of 75¢

Reese, Lizette Woodworth.   Paid her 10% royalty
      on all her books

Allen, James Lane.   The Last Christmas Tree   10% royalty.

Jones, Thomas S.   Paid him 10% on the following books
    at the sale price.   All royalties were paid that way.
        The Rose-Jar
        The Voice in the Silence
        The Sonnets of the Saints
        The Sonnets of the Cross
        Akhnaton
        Sonnets and Quatrains
The other books by Mr. Jones we bought of him what we sold.

Thomas, Edith. The Flower from the Ashes. Paid her 10% royalty.

Bradley, William Aspinwall. Garlands and Wayfarings. Paid him 10% royalty.

Scollard, Clinton.   Paid him 10% royalty.   Lyrics from a Library.

Upson, Arthur.   Paid Ruth Phelps $25.00 for the right to
          reprint his Sonnets.

    I note that he paid Miss Lenalie $90.00 to make the translation of "Mimes" and $50.00 for the translation of "R.L.S."

    When I come to go over my cost books I found that there were quite a lot which he paid outright for the use of and then some on which royalty was paid. Not too bad for a man who was called a "pirate."

    I won't try to write any more as I still have a lot to do. Rather funny how much accumulates in a few days. Just had an order from a lawyer down in Bay City, Texas. In fact he has been a good customer for many years. I think he buys a lot also to give away, as he buys a number of copies of the same book.

                Yours very truly,

                [*signature*]

APPENDIX III
MOSHER'S DUPLICATION OF BOOKS

The following book titles have appeared in more than one of Mosher's fourteen series, and further include overlapping appearances in either Privately Printed Books or in *The Bibelot*. Bibliographers and biographers have often mentioned how Mosher frequently re-published a title in a different series. The following alphabetical list gives a complete account of all instances where Mosher employed more than one series for the same title, however, a few qualifying remarks appear below.

Even though a given title is the same or nearly the same, there may be some differences in the book's contents. The book dimensions of different series necessitated different textual treatment, and sometimes textual material was added or dropped depending on size requirements. So though there are certainly variations to the complete text block, what is being shown below is a kind of "general public recognition" of a title as being in two or more series. The fastidious collector, the exacting bibliographer, or the literary purist could justifiably argue that the *Rubáiyát* in the Vest Pocket Series is not the same book—cover to cover—as the *Rubáiyát* in the Miscellaneous Series. Mosher did often switch the core text to another series, probably as yet another sales ploy, or simply because he loved the book. This general duplication is all that is being shown below.

Selections taken from a book and appearing in *The Bibelot* (e.g., several verses selected from *Leaves of Grass*, or from Macleod's *From the Hills of Dream*, or Lionel Johnson's *Poems*) are not enough reason to include that title in the chart below. These partial transferals are noted in the chart entitled "Portions of Works Appearing in *The Bibelot*." Also not included are books Mosher reassigned to another series. For example, the same quarto sized *Laus Veneris* (1899) was switched from the "Reprints of Privately Printed Books" to the "Quarto Series" when that series was newly christened in 1902. Mosher retroactively assigned similar volumes to the new series.

Note: Arabic numbers within parentheses refer to substantially different printings, i.e., different formats within a given series.

"SAME TITLE—DIFFERENT SERIES" CHART

BOOK TITLE	BETWEEN 14 SERIES		OUTSIDE 14 SERIES	
1. *Aes Triplex*	Vest Pocket		*The Bibelot*: VII, 10	
2. *Ann: A Memory*	Ideal Series		*The Bibelot*: IX, 11	
3. *Ariadne in Mantua*	Old World		*The Bibelot*: XII, 1&2	
4. *Astrophel and Stella*	Old World		*The Bibelot*: II, 6	
5. *Aucassin & Nicolete*	Old World	Vest Pocket		
6. *Billy*	Miscellaneous			Privately Printed
7. *The Blessed Damozel*	Bibelot Series	Miscellaneous		
8. *A Branch of May*	Lyric Garland	Lyra Americana		
9. *Celtic*			*The Bibelot*: VII, 11	Privately Printed
10. *The Child in the House*	Brocade	Vest Pocket		
11. *The Children's Crusade*	Brocade	Miscellaneous		
12. *Chrysanthema*	Miscellaneous		*The Bibelot*: IX, 1&2	
13. *Churches of North France*	Reprint Bibelot	Brocade	*The Bibelot*: VII, 3	
14. *The City of Dreadful Night*	English Reprint	Old World		
15. *Dead Love*	Reprint Bibelot		*The Bibelot*: VII, 6	
16. *The Death of Marlowe*	Reprint Bibelot		*The Bibelot*: III, 12	
17. *A Defence of Poetry*	Miscellaneous	Vest Pocket	*The Bibelot*: XIII, 1&2	
18. *The Distant Country*	Ideal Series		*The Bibelot*: XII, 12	
19. *Dream of Provence*	Ideal Series		*The Bibelot*: V, 4	
20. *Father Damien*	Reprint Bibelot	Miscellaneous(2)	*The Bibelot*: III, 6	
21. *Félise*	Bibelot Series	Old World		
22. *The Flight of the Princess*	Vest Pocket		*The Bibelot*: IV, 6	
23. *For Those Who Love Music*	Miscellaneous		*The Bibelot*: XI, 3& XVI, 3	
24. *From the Upanishads*	Miscellaneous	Vest Pocket		

continued on next page

BOOK TITLE	BETWEEN 14 SERIES		OUTSIDE 14 SERIES	
25. *George Meredith-A Tribute*	Miscellaneous (2)			
26. *Gertha's Lovers*	Reprint Bibelot	Brocade	*The Bibelot:* V, 1&2	
27. *Golden Wings-Svend...*	Reprint Bibelot	Brocade	*The Bibelot:* VI, 4&9	
28. *Growth of Love*	English Reprint	Miscellaneous		
29. *Hand and Soul*	Miscellaneous	Ideal Series	*The Bibelot:* I, 9	
30. *Happy Prince*	Brocade	Old World		Privately Printed
31. *Hollow Land*	Reprint Bibelot	Brocade	*The Bibelot:* III, 7&8	
32. *Homeward Songs*	Miscellaneous(2)			
33. *Hound of Heaven*	Golden Text	Miscellaneous	*The Bibelot:* XIV, 3	
34. *Idyl of First Love*	Ideal Series		*The Bibelot:* II, 8	
35. *In Hospital*	Lyric Garland		*The Bibelot:* VII, 1	
36. *In Memoriam*	Old World			Privately Printed
37. *In Praise of Omar*	Miscellaneous(2)			
38. *Italian Garden*	Bibelot Series	Venetian Series	*The Bibelot:* XIV, 8	
39. *The Kasîdah*	Old World	Miscellaneous(2)		
40. *Land of Heart's Desire*	Lyric Garland	Miscellaneous	*The Bibelot:* IX, 6	Privately Printed
41. *Laus Veneris*	Quarto	Vest Pocket		
42. *Lecture on Eng. Renaissance**	Miscellaneous		*The Bibelot:* XI, 7	
43. *Little Book for John O'Mahony's Friends*	Ideal Series		*The Bibelot:* XIII, 6	
44. *Little Garland of Celtic Verse*	Lyric Garland		*The Bibelot:* VI, 8 & IX, 5	
45. *Lodging for the Night*	Brocade		*The Bibelot:* I, 11	
46. *London Voluntaries*	Lyric Garland		*The Bibelot:* VIII, 1	
47. *Lucretius*	Miscellaneous		*The Bibelot:* XVII, 1&2	
48. *Lyrics* by Arthur Symons	Lyric Garland		*The Bibelot:* IX, 4	
49. *Lyrics & Sonnets* by A. Upson	Lyric Garland		*The Bibelot:* XV, 3	Privately Printed
50. *Magic in Kensington Gardens*	Miscellaneous		*The Bibelot:* XVIII, 11	
51. *A Masque Dead Florentines*	Venetian		*The Bibelot:* X, 1&2	
52. *Memories of President Lincoln*	Miscellaneous(2)	Lyric Garland	*The Bibelot:* X, 8	
53. *Mimma Bella*	Miscellaneous		*The Bibelot:* XIV, 6	
54. *Modern Love*	English Reprint	Old World		
55. *Our Lady's Tumbler*	Miscellaneous	Ideal Series	*The Bibelot:* V, 11	Privately Printed
56. *The Pageant of Summer*	Brocade	Vest Pocket		
57. *Passages from Song Celestial*	Lyric Garland		*The Bibelot:* XVI, 12	
58. *The Pearl*	Old World		*The Bibelot:* XIV, 7	Privately Printed
59. *Il Pesceballo*	Miscellaneous		*The Bibelot:* XVII, 11	
60. *Poems in Prose* by Wilde	Ideal Series		*The Bibelot:* X, 6	
61. *Poems in Prose from Baudelaire*	Ideal Series		*The Bibelot:* XV, 4	
62. *The Present Crisis*	Miscellaneous			Privately Printed
63. *Proverbs in Porcelain*	Lyric Garland		*The Bibelot:* VII, 9	
64. *Quattrocentisteria*	Brocade	Vest Pocket	*The Bibelot:* II, 5	
65. *The Renaissance Studies in...*	Quarto	Miscellaneous		
66. *Rhymes and Rhythms*	Lyric Garland		*The Bibelot:* VIII, 1	
67. *Riding to Lithend*	Lyric Garland		*The Bibelot:* XVI, 1&2	
68. *The Rose-Jar*	Lyra Americana			Privately Printed
69. *Roses of Paestum*	Miscellaneous		*The Bibelot:* X, 7	
70. *The Rubáiyát of Omar Khayyám*	Old World / Vest Pocket	Bibelot Series(2) / Reprint Privately Printed Books		Privately Printed (2)

*The sub-title to Wilde's *Lecture on the English Renaissance* is "Rose Leaf and Apple Leaf: L'Envoi." This is not a reprint of Rennell Rod's *Rose Leaf and Apple Leaf,* but only a reprint of Wilde's introduction, "L'Envoi."

continued on next page

BOOK TITLE	BETWEEN 14 SERIES		OUTSIDE 14 SERIES	
71. *Saint Guido*	Brocade		*The Bibelot:* IV, 7	
72. *XVII Designs by William Blake*	Miscellaneous		*The Bibelot:* XX, 12	
73. *The Silence of Amor*	Miscellaneous	Lyric Garland		
74. *The Sire de Malétroits Door*	Brocade		*The Bibelot:* II, 7	
75. *Sister Benvenuta*	Vest Pocket		*The Bibelot:* XIII, 12	
76. *A Song to David*	Reprint Bibelot		*The Bibelot:* VI, 5	
77. *Songs of Adieu*	Bibelot Series	Miscellaneous		
78. *Sonnets of Wingless Hours*	Old World		*The Bibelot:* VIII, 6	
79. *Sonnets from Portuguese*	Old World	Vest Pocket		
80. *The Sonnets Michael Angelo*	Old World	Bibelot Series		
81. *The Story of Unknown Church*	Reprint Bibelot	Brocade	*The Bibelot:* VIII, 3	
82. *The Sweet Miracle*	Ideal Series		*The Bibelot:* XI, 12	
83. *Tares*	Reprint Bibelot	Lyric Garland	*The Bibelot:* IV, 5	
84. *T B Moshe-An Appreciation*			*The Bibelot:* Index	Privately Printed
85. *Ten O'Clock*	Miscellaneous(2)			
86. *Thyrsis*	Golden Text		*The Bibelot:* III, 10	
87. *The Two Sides of the River*	Reprint Bibelot		*The Bibelot:* V, 9	
88. *Under a Fool's Cap*	Miscellaneous		*The Bibelot:* XVI, 5	
89. *A Vision of Love Revealed*	Miscellaneous		*The Bibelot:* XV, 1&2	
90. *Voice in the Silence*	Lyra Americana			Privately Printed
91. *William Morris-An Address*	Reprint Bibelot		*The Bibelot:* VIII, 9	
92. *Will o' the Mill*	Brocade	Vest Pocket		Privately Printed
93. *Wine Women Song*	Miscellaneous	Reprint Privately Printed Books		
94. *The Works of Arthur Symons*			*The Bibelot:* XVIII, 2	Privately Printed

Portions of Works Appearing in *The Bibelot*

(Note: Not included in the following "Numeric Breakdown of Title Appearances")

BOOK TITLE	SERIES	*THE BIBELOT, VOLUME, NUMBER*
1. *At the Sign of the Lion*	Miscellaneous	XX, 11
2. *Ballads Done Into English*	Lyric Garland	V, 7
3. *The City of Dreadful Night*	Old World	I, 8
4. *Dreams*	Miscellaneous	XVII, 10
5. *Dreamthorp*	Miscellaneous	XIX, 6
6. *Earthwork Out of Tuscany*	Miscellaneous	V, 8
7. *Echoes of Life & Death*	Lyric Garland	IX, 10
8. *Edward FitzGerlad—An Aftermath*	Miscellaneous	X, 11
9. *The Growth of Love*	English Reprint	II, 9
10. *From The Hills of Dream*	Old World	VI, 12
11. *The Hound of Heaven*	Golden Text and Miscellaneous	XIV, 3
12. *In Praise of Old Italian Gardens*	Vest Pocket	VI, 11
13. *Leaves of Grass*	Miscellaneous	XVIII, 5
14. *Little Garland of Christmas Verse*	Lyric Garland	IX, 12
15. *Marius the Epicurean*	Quarto	I, 4 & XVIII, 10
16. *Odes Sonnets of John Keats*	Miscellaneous	XIII, 3
17. *Poems & Ballads-2ⁿᵈ and 3ʳᵈ Series*	Quarto	IV, 12
18. *Poems of Ernest Dowson*	Miscellaneous	VI, 10 & XVIII, 3
19. *Poems by Francis Thompson*	Miscellaneous	XIV, 3
20. *Poems of Master François Villon*	Reprints Privately Printed Books	I, 2
21. *Songs Before Sunrise*	Quarto	XX, 6
22. *Songs of Innocence*	Old World	I, 1
23. *The Story of My Heart*	Old World	II, 3
24. *Story Without An End*	Brocade	XVII, 5
25. *Studies in Sentiment*	Miscellaneous	XVIII, 9
26. *The Renaissance Studies in Art...*	Quarto, and Miscellaneous	II, 10
(Several issues of *The Bibelot* included portions of this book)		III, 9
		IV, 4 & 9
		VI, 2
27. *Tristram of Lyonesse*	Quarto	XX, 6
28. *Twenty-One Poems*	Lyric Garland	X, 3
29. *Wine Women and Song*	Reprints Privately Printed Books	I, 3

Numeric Breakdown of Title Appearances

A. Titles appearing in 2 series: 19

B. Titles in 1 series and repeated in *The Bibelot*   43

C. Titles repeated in 2 series and *The Bibelot* :   13

D. Titles repeated in 1 series and repeated in Privately Printed books: 6

E. Titles repeated in 2 series, and repeated in Privately Printed books: 2

F. Titles repeated in 4 series, and repeated in Privately Printed books: 1

G. Titles repeated in 1 series, *The Bibelot*, and Privately Printed books: 2

H. Titles repeated in 2 series, *The Bibelot*, and Privately Printed books: 2

I. Titles both in *The Bibelot* and Privately Printed books: 2

J. Number of titles repeated **only within** one series: 4
    Homeward Songs, In Praise of Omar, George Meredith, and *Ten O'Clock*

    (Four other titles were changed within a series, but also appeared under other series
    Father Damien, The Kasîdah, Memories of President Lincoln, and the *Rubáiyát*)   _____

                                                                                    TOTAL: 94

K. FIRST MOSHER BOOK EDITIONS PUBLISHED IN THE 14 SERIES: 331

L. REPEATED TITLES "BETWEEN 14 SERIES" ONLY (A+C+E+F+H):   36

M. TITLES ALSO IN *THE BIBELOT* (B+C+G+H+I):   62

N. ADDITIONAL TITLES APPEARING, IN PART, IN *THE BIBELOT*   29

O. TOTAL TITLES APPEARING, WHOLE OR IN PART, IN *THE BIBELOT*   91

APPENDIX IV
FREQUENCY OF AUTHORS PUBLISHED
AND THEIR BOOKS

(3 or more appearances)
In descending order by frequency of appearance in Mosher's book publications,
with identification (in bold) of titles printed in more than one series.
An * indicates also printed in *The Bibelot*.

WILLIAM MORRIS

1. *Child Christopher* (Miscellaneous) 1900
2. **The Churches of North France** (Reprints from the Bibelot) 1901*
3. **Some Great Churches in France** (Brocade) 1903
   (same essay as #2 above, shared with two of Pater's essays)
4. *The Defence of Guenevere* (Bibelot Series) 1896
5. *A Dream of John Ball* (Old World) 1902
6. **Gertha's Lovers** (Reprints from Bibelot) 1899*
7. **Gertha's Lovers** (Brocade) 1902
8. **Golden Wings-Svend** (Reprint from Bibelot)1900*
9. **Golden Wings-Svend** (Brocade) 1902
10. *The History of Over Sea* (Brocade), translator, 1899
11. **The Hollow Land** (Reprints from Bibelot) 1897*
12. **The Hollow Land** (Brocade) 1900
13. *The Pilgrims of Hope* (Reprints Privately Print) 1901
14. *The Story of Amis & Amile* (Brocade), translator, 1896
15. **The Story of the Unknown Church** (Reprints from Bibelot) 1902*
16. **The Story of the Unknown Church** (Brocade) 1902
17. *The Tale of King Coustans* (Brocade), translator, 1899
18. *The Tale of King Florus* (Brocade), translator, 1898
19. *The Two Sides of the River* (Reprint from Bibelot) 1899*

OSCAR WILDE

1. *The Ballad of Reading Gaol* (Lyric Garland) 1904
2. *The Birthday of the Infanta* (Brocade) 1905
3. *The Fisherman and His Soul* (Brocade) 1905
4. **The Happy Prince** (Brocade) 1904
5. **The Happy Prince** (Old World) 1907
6. **The Happy Prince** (Privately Printed) 1919
7. *A House of Pomegranates* (Old World) 1906
8. *Intentions* (Miscellaneous) 1904
9. *Lecture on English Renaissance* (Miscellaneous) 1905*
10. *Poems in Prose* (Ideal Series) 1906*
11. *Poems of Oscar Wilde* (Miscellaneous) 1903
12. *Poetical Works of Oscar Wilde* (Miscellaneous) 1908
13. *The Portrait of Mr. W. H.* (Brocade) 1901
14. *Salomé* (Miscellaneous) 1911
15. *The Soul of Man Under Socialism* (Misc.) 1905
16. *The Sphinx* (Venetian) 1911
17. **The Young King** (Brocade) 1904
18. **The Young King** (Privately Printed) 1922

FIONA MACLEOD

1. *By Sundown Shores:* **Studies in Spiritual History** (Brocade) 1902
2. *Celtic:* **A Study in Spiritual History** (Privately Printed) 1901*
3. *Deirdrê and the Sons of Usna* (Old World) 1903
4. *The Distant Country* (Ideal) 1907
5. *The Divine Adventure* (Old World) 1903
6. *From the Hills of Dream* (Old World) 1901*
7. *The Hour of Beauty* (Old World) 1907
8. *The House of Usna-A Drama* (Miscellaneous) 1903
9. *The Immortal Hour* (Miscellaneous) 1907
10. *The Isle of Dreams* (Old World) 1905
11. *A Little Book of Nature Thoughts* (Vest Pocket) 1908
12. *Runes of Woman* (Miscellaneous) 1915
13. **The Silence of Amor** (Miscellaneous) 1902
14. **The Silence of Amor** (Lyric Garland) 1912
15. *The Tale of the Four White Swans* (Brocade) 1904
16. *Three Legends of the Christ Child* (Ideal) 1908
17. *Ulad of the Dreams* (Brocade) 1904
18. *The Wayfarer* (Ideal) 1906

ROBERT LOUIS STEVENSON

1. *Aes Triplex* (Vest Pocket) 1902*
2. *An Apology for Idlers* (Vest Pocket) 1905
3. *A Child's Garden of Verses* (Old World) 1899
4. *Crabbed Age & Youth* (Vest Pocket) 1907
5. **Father Damien** (Miscellaneous) 1897
6. **Father Damien** (Misc.—larger edition) 1905
7. **Father Damien** (Reprints from Bibelot) 1897*
8. *The Flight of the Princess* (Vest Pocket) 1912*
9. *François Villon, Student...* (Brocade) 1901
10. *A Lodging for the Night* (Brocade) 1900*
11. *The Sire De Malétroits Door* (Brocade) 1900*
12. *Thrawn Janet : Markheim* (Brocade) 1903
13. *Underwoods* (Old World) 1900
14. *Virginibus Puerisque* (Vest Pocket) 1904
15. **Will O' The Mill** (Brocade) 1899
16. **Will O' The Mill** (Vest Pocket) 1911
17. **Will O' The Mill** (Privately Printed) 1915

ALGERNON CHARLES SWINBURNE

1. *Atlanta in Calydon* (Old World) 1897
2. *Dead Love* (Reprints from Bibelot) 1901*
3. **Félise** (Bibelot Series) 1894
4. **Félise** (Old World) 1909
5. *Heptalogia* (Reprints Privately Printed) 1898
6. **Laus Veneris** (Quarto) 1899
7. **Laus Veneris** (Vest Pocket) 1900
8. *Poems & Ballads*-1st Series (Quarto) 1904
   (Reprint of **Laus Veneris**, but renamed)
9. *Poems & Ballads*-2nd & 3rd (Quarto) 1902
10. *Siena* (Venetian) 1910
11. *A Song of Italy* (Lyric Garland) 1904
12. *Songs before Sunrise* (Quarto) 1901
13. *Tristram of Lyonesse* (Quarto) 1904
14. *Under the Microscope* (Rprts Privately Printed) 1899
15. *A Year's Letters* (Reprints Privately Printed) 1901

WALTER PATER

1. **The Child in the House** (Brocade) 1895
2. **The Child in the House** (Vest Pocket) 1909
3. *Denys L'Auxerrois* (Brocade) 1898
4. *Duke Carl of Rosenmold* (Brocade) 1898
5. *Emerald Uthwart* (Brocade) 1899
6. *Essays from the "Guardian"* (Reprints Privately Printed) 1897
7. *Gaston de Latour* (Old World) 1907
8. *Marius the Epicurean*, I & II (Quarto) 1900
9. *A Prince of Court Painters* (Brocade) 1899
10. **The Renaissance** (Quarto) 1902
11. **The Renaissance** (Miscellaneous) 1912
12. *Sebastian Van Storck* (Brocade) 1898
13. *Some Great Churches in France* (Brocade) 1903
    (two essays along with a Morris essay)
14. *The Story of Cupid and Psyche* (Brocade), translator, 1897
15. *Uncollected Essays* (Miscellaneous) 1903

DANTE GABRIEL ROSSETTI

1. *Ballads & Sonnets* (Quarto) 1903
2. **The Blessed Damozel** (Bibelot Series) 1895
3. **The Blessed Damozel** (Miscellaneous) 1901
4. *Dante at Verona* (Venetian) 1910
5. **Hand and Soul** (Miscellaneous) 1899*
6. **Hand and Soul** (Ideal) 1906
7. *The House of Life* (Old World) 1898
8. *The New Life of Dante Alighieri* (Old World), translator, 1896
9. *Poems* (Quarto) 1902

RICHARD JEFFERIES

1. *Bits of Oak Bark* (Brocade) 1900
2. *Hours of Spring* (Brocade) 1899
3. *A Little Book of Nature Thoughts* ((Vest Pocket) 1903
4. *Nature and Eternity* (Brocade) 1902
5. **The Pageant of Summer** (Brocade) 1896
6. **The Pageant of Summer** (Vest Pocket) 1905
7. *Saint Guido* (Brocade) 1901*
8. *The Story of My Heart* (Old World) 1898

VERNON LEE

1. *Ariadne in Mantua* (Old World) 1906*
2. *Chapelmeister Kreisler* (Brocade) 1901
3. *The Child in the Vatican* (Brocade) 1900
4. *In Praise of Old Gardens* (Vest Pocket) 1912
5. *In Umbria* (Brocade) 1901
6. *The Legend of Madame Krasinska* (Brocade) 1903
7. *Sister Benvenuta & Christ Child* (Vest Pocket) 1911*

EDWARD FITZGERALD

1. *Polonius* (Miscellaneous) 1901
2. **Rubáiyát** (Bibelot series) 1894
3. **Rubáiyát** (Old World) 1895
4. **Rubáiyát** (Vest Pocket) 1899
5. **Rubáiyát** (Reprints of Privately Printed) 1902
6. **Rubáiyát** (Privately Printed) 1899
7. **Rubáiyát** (Privately Printed) 1923

WALT WHITMAN

1. *The Book of Heavenly Death* (Miscellaneous) 1905
2. *Leaves of Grass* (Miscellaneous) 1919
3. *A Little Book of Nature Thoughts* (Vest Pocket) 1906
4. **Memories of President Lincoln** (Miscellaneous) 1904*
5. **Memories of President Lincoln** (Miscellaneous) 1912
6. **Memories of President Lincoln** (Lyric Garland) 1906

ANDREW LANG

1. **Aucassin & Nicolete** (Old World), translator, 1895
2. **Aucassin & Nicolete** (Vest Pocket) 1903
3. **Ballades in Blue China** (Old World) 1907
4. *Ballads & Lyrics of Old France* (Old World), translator, 1896
5. *The Dead Leman* (Brocade), translator, 1903
6. *Helen of Troy* (Old World), translator, 1897

GEORGE MEREDITH

1. *An Idyl of First Love* (Ideal) 1906*
2. *Love in the Valley* (Golden Text) 1910
3. *Modern Love* (English Reprint) 1891
4. *Modern Love* (Old World) 1898
5. *The Tale of Chloe* (Old World) 1899

JOHN ADDINGTON SYMONDS

1. *Fragilia Labilia* (Reprints Privately Print) 1902
2. *Michael Angelo Buonarroti-Sonnets* (Bibelot Series) 1895
3. *Sonnets of Michael Angelo Buonarroti* (Old World) 1897
4. *Wine Women and Song* (Reprint Privately Print) 1899
5. *Wine Women and Song* (Miscellaneous) 1918

ROBERT BROWNING

1. *Italy My Italy* (Venetian) 1910*
2. *Lyric Love* (Vest Pocket) 1910
3. *Pippa Passes* (Old World) 1902
4. *Pompilia* (Old World) 1903
5. *Rabbi Ben Ezra* (Golden Text) 1909

MATTHEW ARNOLD

1. *Empedocles on Etna* (Miscellaneous) 1900
2. *Eugénie de Guérin* (Brocade) 1903
3. *Maurice de Guérin* (Brocade) 1903
4. *Thyrsis* (Golden Text) 1910*

MAURICE HEWLETT

1. *Earthwork Out of Tuscany* (Miscellaneous) 1911
2. *A Masque of Dead Florentines* (Venetian) 1911*
3. *Quattrocentisteria* (Brocade) 1898*
4. *Quattrocentisteria* (Vest Pocket) 1904

FRANCIS THOMPSON

1. *The Hound of Heaven* (Golden Text) 1908*
2. *The Hound of Heaven* (Miscellaneous) 1908
3. *Poems* (Miscellaneous) 1911
4. *Shelley-An Essay* (Miscellaneous) 1909

MARCEL SCHWOB

1. *The Children's Crusade* (Brocade) 1905
2. *The Children's Crusade* (Miscellaneous) 1923
3. *Mimes* (Miscellaneous) 1901
4. *"R.L.S."-An Essay* (Miscellaneous) 1920

J. W. MACKAIL

1. *The Eclogues* (Miscellaneous), translator, 1898
2. *The Georgics* (Miscellaneous, 2 vols.), translator, 1899
3. *The Sayings of the Lord Jesus Christ* (Miscellaneous) 1905
4. *William Morris-An Address* (Reprints from The Bibelot) 1902*

ERNEST DOWSON

1. *Cynara* (Lyric Garland) 1907*
2. *The Pierrot of the Minute* (Lyric Garland) 1913
3. *The Poems of Ernest Dowson* (Miscellaneous) 1902
4. *Studies in Sentiment* (Miscellaneous) 1915

JOHN RUSKIN

1. *The King of the Golden River* (Privately Printed) 1914
2. *Sesame and Lilies* (Old World) 1900
3. *The Story of Ida* [ed by Ruskin] (Old World) 1899

GEORGE GISSING

1. *Books and the Quiet Life* (Miscellaneous) 1914
2. *By the Ionian Sea* (Miscellaneous) 1920
3. *The Private Papers of Henry Ryecroft* (Miscellaneous) 1921

WILLIAM BUTLER YEATS

1. *The Land of Heart's Desire* (Lyric Garland) 1903
2. *The Land of Heart's Desire* (Miscellaneous) 1909
3. *The Land of Heart's Desire* (Private Print) 1903

RICHARD BURTON

1. *The Kasîdah* (Old World) 1896
2. *The Kasîdah* (Miscellaneous) 1905
3. *The Kasîdah* (Miscellaneous) 1915

Appendix V
Institutional Holdings

Major Research Collections

Arizona State University-Tempe, Special Collections, University Libraries (Hayden Library). Arizona State houses one of the most extensive collections of Mosher imprints and related material. The nearly complete collection of books in first and later editions and variants, covers 69.5 linear feet, including books from Mosher's library. Dr. Nicholas Salerno, in tandem with the Head of Special Collections, Marilyn Wurzburger, were the vigilant assemblers of the collection. In nine boxes there are also housed publishing materials, book lists, catalogue order forms, reviews, correspondence, financial records, estate and legal papers, personal items, photographs, and other memorabilia covering the period 1893-1929 (a list of this material is available). The manuscript material is the result of a gift from Thomas Bird Mosher, Jr. in 1970, and the purchase of a collection assembled by Oliver Sheean augmented the collection in 1985. The collection also has a number of Mosher books in fine bindings.

Harvard University, The Houghton Library. In 1948 Oliver C. Sheean gave The Houghton Library 1,654 manuscript items from The Mosher Press. This vast collection includes material relating to the mock Italian operetta, *Il Pesceballo*, by Francis James Child and James Russell Lowell, material relating to the controversy over charges of publishing piracy, and material on Mosher's literary magazine, *The Bibelot*. Correspondents represented by 15 or more items include James Lane Allen, George F. R. Anderson, Lucie Elizabeth (Page) Borden, Gordon Bottomley, William Aspenwall Bradley, William Stanley Braithwaite, Mrs. M. N. Dana ("Paul Allan"), Ernestine Louise Foster, Katherine (Tynan) Hinkson, Richard Charles Jackson, Mitchell Kennerley, Walter E. Ledger, Richard Le Gallienne, John Loder, Edward McCurdy, Christopher S. Millard (Stuart Mason), Louise (Chandler) Moulton, Grace Fallow Norton, William Marion Reedy, Lizette Woodworth Reese, George William Russell, Elizabeth Amelia Sharp, Clement King Shorter, Edith Matilda Thomas, and Anne Montgomerie Traubel. The Houghton and other university libraries at Harvard collectively house at least 585 of the Mosher books (492 from 1891-1923 and 93 post-1923).

University of San Francisco, Donohue Rare Book Room at The Richard A. Gleeson Library. The rare book room houses the vast majority of the Norman A. Strouse Collection. Strouse assembled one of the finest Mosher collections, and purchased the personal papers and manuscripts kept by Harrison Hume Mosher (Mosher's oldest son). Included with these papers are many photographs, correspondence, copyright receipts and assignments, Mosher's own poetry and essays (written under the pseudonym Richard Charles Merrill) showing his intense literary and intellectual activity from 1865-1871, legal documents, and typescripts. The manuscript portion of the collection is particularly rich in material written prior to 1875. The Mosher books cover 48 linear feet, and include many of the Japan vellum and vellum copies. The collection also has a number of Mosher books in fine bindings.

Significant Collections

Bowdoin College, Special Collections at the Bowdoin College Library. The Mosher Press publications, organized in order by Hatch number, take up 34 linear feet of over 600 books. There are also two folders of ephemera related to Thomas Bird Mosher, including two of his extensive law books catalogues which show Mosher's early ability to produce book catalogues.

Colby College, Special Collections at the Merton Leland Miller Library. There are 40 linear feet of books and other material from the Mosher Press, including books from Mosher's library. Some of the select items include fifteen pieces of correspondence to and from Mosher, a 30-page notebook recording some of the books in Mosher's home library, various checklists of the Mosher books including the Sheean Typescript (often referred to by Hatch and Bishop), a catalogue of a collection of Mosher books assembled by Oliver Sheean, newspaper clippings, a journal of Mosher's Old World Series tracing the books behind the Mosher reprints, and numerous pieces of memorabilia related to Mosher (including illustrations, specimen book covers, and photographs).

Dartmouth College, Baker Special Collections at the Dartmouth College Library. In addition to a modest selection of over 200 Mosher imprints, the special collections contain a manuscript box of holograph and typed material, including letters from Mosher to his wife, correspondence relating to the settlement of his estate, a manuscript catalogue of his library (the first page of which is pictured on p. [19] of the Hatch *Check List...*), the preliminary designs for Mosher's edition of William Blake's *XVII Designs to Thornton's Virgil* (pictured on p. [30] of the Hatch *Check List...*), two typescript lists of his publications, legal and business papers, and photographs. There are also letters from poet Robert Frost to Mosher, purchased from the 1948 sale of Mosher's library. Volumes I & V (1886 & 1890) of Mosher's copy of *The Century Guild Hobby Horse* are also located at Dartmouth.

Kalamazoo College, Special Collections at the Upjohn Library. There are about 550 volumes in the collection which was assembled by Robert Athol Huston, labor attorney, poet and bibliophile. To highlight this collection, the library sponsored a Mosher books exhibition called "A Modern Love of Literature" from June 7-August 30, 1991.

Maine State Library, Special Collections Department. The 36 linear feet of books includes the 14 series in both Van Gelder and Japan vellum states, in their original boxes.

Portland Public Library, Special Collections in the Portland Room. The library has a collection of about 40 linear feet. Mosher's assistant, Flora Lamb, provided many of these books to the library.

University of Louisville, Rare Book Department at the University of Louisville Library. This is the Kenneth H. Shanks Collection (Shanks was the author of the 1976 article on Mosher in the University of Louisville's *Library Review*). There are over 1,100 volumes covering 50 linear feet, and the collection includes some very rare items, e.g., one of three copies of *Verses and a Dream*. There are also a few notes and letters to or from Mosher.

University of South Florida, Special Collections at the Library of the University of South Florida. The library has over 615 of the Mosher books. The basic core of the collection was privately formed by Thomas Dreier.

Yale University. The primary Mosher collection is part of the Zeta Collection of the Yale University Library System. There are also various individual items at the Beinecke, Mudd and Sterling libraries. The collection takes about 21 linear feet, and most of the books in this collection carry the bookplate of Andrew Squire of Cleveland, OH, and are marked as the Gift of Edward B. Greene Yale 1900. Others were the gift of Miss Marie Louise Royael and Mrs. Julia Royael McCay, 1912.

OTHER NOTABLE COLLECTIONS

The British Library. An on-line search of the OPAC, pre-1976 Reference Collections located 126 Mosher books, and an additional 7 post-1923 Mosher books, 32 separately listed titles from *The Bibelot*, a set of *The Bibelot*, and 3 books related to Mosher. An additional 4 Mosher publications are listed in the British Library Catalogue.

Newberry Library, Special Collections. There are about 170 Mosher books in the collection including some significant items in the Wing Collection (a copy of *The Garland of Rachael* with related manuscript material loosely inserted, Emilie B. Grigsby's copy of *Mimes* on vellum, and a copy of Charles Van Cise Wheeler's unpublished bibliography of Edward Fitzgerald's translation of the *Rubáiyát* (Wheeler bought Mosher's personal *Rubáiyát* collection).

New York Public Library. There are 214 Mosher entries in *The New York Public Library Catalogue of Special & Private Presses in the Rare Book Division*. Vol. II. (Boston, MA: G. K. Hall & Co., 1978). The library also has a folder of ephemera.

Temple University. Special Collections Department of the Samuel Paley Library. Temple University hosted the "Thomas Bird Mosher and the Art of the Book" Exhibit in 1992. In addition to around 100 Mosher books and catalogues found in the Richard W. Ellis Collection, there are numerous letters in the Gertrude Traubel (daughter of Horace Traubel) Collection which chronicle some of the relationships of the family with Mosher. Mosher is also one of the prominently mentioned individuals in the Gordon Bottomley/Constable & Co. papers.

University of British Columbia, Special Collections (The Norman Colbeck Collection). The number of Mosher's books in this collection is well below the other institutions listed, but 26 Mosher books from collection are cited in the present bibliography. As a whole, the collection represents one of the finest assemblages of nineteenth-century publications, Edwardian poetry, and *belles lettres* which formed the literary and publishing backdrop for Mosher's tastes and publishing efforts.

University of California-Berkeley, The Bancroft Library. In addition to some of the books from the Mosher Press, there are seven of Mosher's books on vellum (five of which are bound by the Club Bindery) and two other Mosher books in outstanding bindings. These books were given to The Bancroft Library by Norman A. Strouse.

University of Texas at Austin, Harry Ransom Humanities Research Center Library. There are at least 290 Mosher books and related materials at the HRC, including 25 volumes from Mosher's library. Some of the holdings are located in the Christopher Morley Collection, and some are in the Edward L. Tinker Collection.

University of Virginia, The Clifton Waller Barrett Collection includes run of original letters and inscribed copies from Robert Frost to Mosher from the original sale of Mosher's library in 1948. Several of these letters appear in Lawrance Thompson's *Selected Letters of Robert Frost* (New York, 1964). Also, the papers of William Braithwaite include Mosher correspondence.

OTHER MANUSCRIPT HOLDINGS

In addition to the institutional collections listed above, there are manuscript holdings at the Huntington Library, UCLA's Clark Memorial Library, Haverford College, Columbia University, the University of Virginia, the University of Iowa, Cornell University, the University of Texas at Houston, Bryn Mawr College, University of Michigan-Ann Arbor, and at The Library of Congress (see the entries on the *National Union Catalogue on Manuscript Collections* and on RLIN & OCLC (Research Libraries Information Network & the On-Line Computer Libraries Center) in the "Bibliography of Thomas Bird Mosher."

APPENDIX VI
THE PERSONAL LIBRARY OF THOMAS BIRD MOSHER
- A Few Notes -

In the title of her *Lewiston Journal* article of July 7, 1928, Alice Frost Lord refers to the "two shrines" of Thomas Bird Mosher, the publisher's Exchange Street office in Portland, Maine and his personal library at his home in the Woodfords area—also called Longfellow Heights—just outside of the city. Upon entering the "cathedral dimness" of his home library, Lords' first impression was that of a "sea of books" packed ten shelves high and covering all four walls of a large room with fireplace and comfortable seating. A repository of nineteenth century literature, this was the enclave where Mosher tracked down the many texts which filled the pages of his own publications.

Mosher's library was dispersed in two 1948 Parke-Bernet sales, and their printed catalogues remain important sources for determining the contents of Mosher's personal library (including many entries detailing inscriptions, signed copies, and manuscript material), but there are other sources as well. One is Mosher's own 1889 inventory now in the Special Collections at Dartmouth College. Beyond being a mere list of books, this record is of added importance because it shows Mosher's reading background just prior to publishing his first book in 1891. For sheer comprehensiveness, however, another important source—now in the Bishop Collection—is the five legal-sized ledger books totaling 132 pages in which Oliver Sheean inventoried (ca. 1930) over 5,500 books, with many a single entry covering just one multi-volume set. When tallied with these and other recorded books known to be in personal collections and institutions, I have been able to record over 5,700 entries (again with each book set comprising only a single entry). All totaled, the home library must have held around 7,000 or more volumes. In addition, more books were located at the second "shrine," Mosher's Exchange Street office, but no inventory has been uncovered. There were also hundreds of books lost in the 1915 fire at the business premises; regrettably, no recorded details of this loss seem to have survived. Unfortunately, hundreds of periodical volumes were also never tallied.

Mosher formed several large collections of his favorite authors in addition to many books-on-books, bibliographies and other references, biographies, classical works, French authors in English translation, and to one of the larger *Rubáiyát* collections of the time (about 150 volumes plus related FitzGerald material). His very respectable Oscar Wilde collection of around 140 separate editions, Wilde's 1908 *Works* published by Methuen, and at least 34 related volumes, was his largest and included many first editions. Although not as extensive numerically (110, plus the *Complete Writings* of 1902), Mosher's collection of Walt Whitman included most of the editions of *Leaves of Grass*, including the first edition, third issue of the 1855 text, and several Whitman manuscripts procured through Mosher's connections with Horace Traubel. There were also substantial collections by, or on, A. C. Swinburne (64 vols.), Andrew Lang (57), Robert Louis Stevenson (56), Robert Burns (56), Arthur Symons (55, plus a collection of 18 ALS), Dante Gabriel Rossetti (43), John Addington Symonds (43), Vernon Lee (42), William Blake (41, all secondary material and facsimiles), William Morris (38), Richard Le Gallienne (33), John Keats (33), George Gissing (32), William Butler Yeats (31), Walter Pater (26), Richard Jefferies (25), James S. McNeill Whistler (24), and Hilaire Belloc (24). An enormous number of other authors fill in the spaces between these twenty-one primary authors.

Several other collections within the library are of special interest. One was a collection of letters from Robert Frost (1912-1914), including a few of his books and several typewritten, signed copies of his poems. Another notable collection was that of William Sharp and his feminine alias, Fiona Macleod. There were a total of 26 volumes by Sharp and 31 by Macleod, but the collection is most noteworthy for its 61 letters from Sharp (or Macleod) and 24 letters from Sharp's wife, Elizabeth. The library also contained numerous inscribed volumes to Mosher, a plentiful number of which were sent in hopes that Mosher would consider publishing them. In one from a young friend of Oscar Wilde's, J. M. Stuart-Young, who, in a loosely laid-in letter accompanying his *Osrac, the Self-Sufficient* (London, 1905), praises Mosher on his "sumptuous editions" of Wilde and asks if he would want to print *Osrac* in America. Mosher never did. A few other such books came to Mosher in this fashion, including from two young American authors, Robert Frost and Ezra Pound. To my chagrin, their books never appeared in a Mosher series either.

I would be remiss if I didn't say anything about the books from private or fine presses appearing in Mosher's library. The record of the English private presses helps to show the extent to which Mosher was aware of what his British brethren were printing, and how they were doing it. There were no fewer than 36 titles from Ricketts' Vale Press, 28 titles from the Daniel Press, 14 titles from Morris' Kelmscott Press, 17 from Ashbee's Essex House Press, 12 from the Eragny Press of Lucian Pissarro, 9 from Yeats' Dun Emer Press and 5 from the Cuala Press, 8 from Guthrie's Pear Tree Press, 8 from the Samurai Press, 4 from the Cobden-Sanderson's Doves Press (including the 5-vol., *The English Bible*), and 4 early productions from Hornby's Ashendene Press. Though not a private press, there were also no fewer than 55 of the Bodley Head's finely printed publications in Mosher's collections. Although Mosher's emphasis was on the English publications, he didn't totally neglect his American brethren, though these are decidedly fewer in number. There were 10 titles from the Roycroft Press, and 7 titles from the Elston Press. There were also titles from the Way & Williams and the Copeland & Day publications, from Seymour's Alderbrink Press, and several others, but in all fairness to the American side, these publications are still being separated from the bulk of entries in Mosher's library which I am preparing for later publication. Lastly, another collection of note on the American side was that of the books designed by Bruce Rogers. Mosher commissioned Roger's designs for some of his early publications, and Rogers continued throughout the years to keep in touch with the publisher. Of the 36 books in Mosher's library which were designed by Rogers, several were inscribed to Mosher, including Wordsworth's *IV Sonnets* (Cambridge, 1909) in which Roger's inscribed the front fly-leaf: "To the Aldus of the XIX Century from an amateur printer" (now located at the University of San Francisco).

A view of Mosher's home library in Portland, Maine

APPENDIX VII
A FEW NOTES ON THE MOSHER BOOKPLATE

The bookplate Mosher used in books from his personal library was designed in 1897 by Frank R. Rathbun of Auburn, New York, with the designer's monogram of an "F" with two "R's" mirror imaged on either side. The bookplate was part of an exhibit (entry 1371) of bookplates from the Club of Odd Volumes held at the Museum of Fine Arts in Boston in 1898. Mosher's bookplate is described as "emblematical pictorial" in the Burnham collection. The original plate was photo-mechanically printed on Japan vellum paper from Rathbun's original drawing, but the later scarcity and high price of Japan vellum may have necessitated Mosher's printing of the plate on Van Gelder paper. It has been said that when Parke-Bernet auctioned the Mosher library in 1948, any of Mosher's books that didn't have the bookplate were given one. These plates may have been from a reserve stock Mosher had prior to his death.

Another bookplate was designed for Mosher by Earl Stetson Crawford in 1922, but seems to never have been produced for inclusion in Mosher's books, at least no book has been located with this bookplate in it. The illustration is of Mosher's home library. The artist's final rendering, in the Bishop Collection, is reproduced on the next page. Earlier artist drawings of this bookplate also appear in the Special Collections of Arizona State University-Tempe.

According to the *Honey Jar*, a small 1890's Columbus, Ohio magazine which often focused on bookplates:

> First we have the plate of Thomas B. Mosher (of *Bibelot* fame). Concerning its origin the owner says it is drawn from the Old German.
>
> On a shield the base, sinister and dexter points of which round off into scrolls, an open book supported by two dolphins, tails entwined. Two demi-griffins of heroic size act as semi-supporters. On a ribbon beneath the shield and between a number of conventionalized flowers "Ex Libris Mdcccxcvij." Below is "Thomas B. Mosher." All within a serrated border.

—Sappe, D. C., ed. *HONEY JAR—A Receptacle for Literary Preserves.* Vol. III, No. 1. (Columbus, OH: Champlin Press at the Sign of the Green Wreath, November 1899), p. 16.

The bookplate to the right is rarely seen, but does appear in a few of his books and is loosely inserted in some copies of *The Bibelot*. The design is signed "e.a.c." (possibly Elizabeth Alden Curtis), an artist who provided the full title-page illustration for Mosher's 1912 catalogue (appearing in reduced form in the 1914 catalogue). The writing is reproduced from Mosher's own. The use and history of this bookplate is unknown. Mrs. Mosher had a similar plate of her own, but designed by a different artist. It could be that she had this plate produced to use after Mosher's death. Nevertheless we show this unusual bookplate because it does exist and is therefore part of the Mosher story (the original printer's block is at Arizona State University). Yet another bookplate designed by "e.a.c." is photo-reduced from the original used to make the title page of the 1912 catalogue. This

bookplate, printed in blue, is found in a blank book the size of the Miscellaneous Series' *The Blessed Damozel*, with blue paper boards and glassine wrapper, with various bookplates inserted, including this one (Arizona State University). The plate is 11 x 6.3 cm. with "Ex Libris" above the scene, and "Thomas B. Mosher" at the bottom flanked by two flowers. So far as is known, the plate was not used.

Unused bookplate designed by Earl Stetson Crawford.

LIST OF ILLUSTRATIONS

(The illustrations in this list do not include
the captioned photographs in the color section)

Frontispiece:
Thomas Bird Mosher at age 49, taken from the frontispiece
to the hard bound copy of *The Mosher Books* catalogue for 1909.

ILLUSTRATIONS TO THE PRIMARY BIBLIOGRAPHY
(BY ENTRY NUMBER)

INDEX

INDEX PRINCIPLES

Entry numbers in Sections II & III are indexed using one of three prefix letters: "B" (Bishop) for entries & annotations in the principal bibliography (Section II); "FL" (Flora Lamb) for entries & references in the first checklist of Section III; and "WB" (Williams Bookshop) for entries & references in the second checklist of Section III. Some entries in Section IV are indexed using "R" for relieure (French for bookbinder). All other citations are to section (Roman numerals) with corresponding page numbers (Arabic numerals); p. & pp. are employed to avoid ambiguity, that is, when page numbers might be confused with the aforementioned letter-prefix numbers. Titles, which are already listed alphabetically in Section II and therefore are not duplicated here, are listed under the name of the author; and unless otherwise indicated, titles refer to books issued by Mosher, Lamb or Williams. Titles are sometimes truncated without ellipses to save space.

Reference citations in the annotations throughout Section II are not included in this index (unless they appear elsewhere within the entries), because they are already alphabetically indexed in the second part of Section V (pp. 423-461). Likewise, the names of most binders or binderies are not herein indexed because they already appear in alphabetical order in Section IV (pp. 346-367). The names of individual graphic designers, however, are included in this index and are grouped under the main entry "Designers, engravers, artists."

LIST OF ABBREVIATIONS

The following abbreviations are employed in the index:

append = appendix or appendices	intro = introduction	ref = reference
bibliog = bibliography	ms = manuscript	rpt, rptd = reprint, reprinted
cat, cats = catalogue(s)	port = portrait	Sect = section
contrib = contributor	pseud = pseudonym	sel = selection
ded = dedicated to	ptg = printing	TBM= Thomas Bird Mosher
ed, eds = edition(s)	pub = published in or by	tp = title page
frontis = frontispiece	qtd = quoted	trans = translation, translator

---

A

Abbe, Dr. Robert, anonymous written memorial, *In Memory of Dr. Robert Abbe*, FL3

Abercrombie, Lascelles, review of Bottomley's "The Riding to Lithend" in *The Bibelot*, B33

Academy, The, text source: for "Symonds' 'Renaissance in Italy' " in Pater's *Uncollected Essays*, B421; for Hewlett's sonnets for figures of Sandro Botticelli in *Earthwork Out of Tuscany*, B97; for preface to *Primavera*, B311; for review of Solomon's *A Vision of Love Revealed in Sleep*, B429; for "Materlinck and His Art" in cat, B254

A. D., signed sel qtd in *The Poetical Works of Oscar Wilde*, B305

Adams, Arthur H., "London Streets" in *The Bibelot*, B33

A. E. (pseud), see George Russell

Agrippa, Cornelius, sel from *Occult Philosophy* qtd in Whittier's *Snow-Bound*, B358

Alcoforado, Marianne, *The Letters of a Portuguese Nun* (Old World, 1900), B196-196.1

Aldrich, Thomas Bailey, sel from qtd in Hay's *In Praise of Omar*, B171

Aldus, printing on blue paper, B335; source for format of Bibelot Series, B366; printer's devices, Sect I, p. 71; Mosher referred to as Aldus of the nineteenth century, pp. 70, 383

Books:
- *Italy My Italy* (Venetian, 1910), B179
- *Lyric Love* (Vest Pocket, 1910), B224
- *Pippa Passes* (Old World, 1902), B291-291.1
- *Pompilia* (Old World, 1903), B307
- *Rabbi Ben Ezra* (Golden Text, 1909), B319-319.1

Reprints in *The Bibelot*:
- "Toccata of Galuppi's," B19
- "Essay on Shelley," B25

Other appearances:
- "Memorabilia" in Shelley's *A Defence of Poetry*, B86
- Sel from qtd in Stevenson's *Father Damien*, B107, 108, 109; in Burton's *The Kasîdah*, B181-183; in Smart's *A Song to David*, B361

Brunner, H. C., "The Way to Arcady" and "Strong as Death" in cat, B255

Bryant, Hubbard Winslow, quote from & pub of Villon's "Omitted Lines," B302

Buchanan, Robert, *The Story of David Gray* (Miscellaneous, 1900), B386; *The Fleshy School of Poetry and Other Phenomena of the Day*, B423 (see also B158); other works cited in 3 append to rpt of *Under the Microscope*: full text of "The Session of the Poets" in 1st append; full text of "The Monkey and the Microscope" in 2nd appendix; and 2-stanzas "To An Old Enemy" from *God and the Man—A Romance* along with 2 further stanzas "To Dante Gabriel Rossetti" qtd together with "Buchanan's Apologia" and letter to T. Hall Caine, B423

Bucke, Richard M., sel from qtd in *Amphora*, B2

Buckeridge, E. G., "The Song of the Road" in cat, B257

Buckle, Henry Thomas, "Letter to a Gentleman Respecting Pooley's Case" in *The Bibelot*, B28

Buckton, Alice, "Vanishings," "The Song Celestial," "An Altered Chart," "Then and Now" in cat, B266

Buffalo Enquirer, The, Section V, p. 381

Bullen, A. H., sel from qtd in *The Death of Marlowe*, B83

Burana, Carmina, translation used in Symonds' *Wine Women And Song*, B439, 440

Burne-Jones, Sir Edward, "Essay on the Newcomes" in *The Bibelot,* B21

Burns, Robert, *The Jolly Beggars* (Miscellaneous, 1914), B180; *Tam O'Shanter* (Privately Printed, 1913), B399; frontis of Nasmyth portrait, B180; design source for rpt cover label: *Poems Ascribed to Robert Burns* (1801), B180; 'The Centenary Burns' (1896) text source for rpt, B399

Burroughs, John, sel from qtd in: *Amphora*, B2; in *Autumn Leaves from Maple Cottage*, B12; in Whitman's *Memories of President Lincoln*, B238-240; in cat, B207

Burton, Sir Richard Francis, *The Kasîdah* (Old World, 1896), B181-181.12; same (Miscellaneous, 1905), B182-182.01; same (Miscellaneous, 1915), B183; Cook edition (1900) pirates Mosher, B181; first appearance of port in Old World Series, B181.8; *The Kasîdah* (1905) privately printed for England, B182.01; sel from *The Kasîdah* in cat, B265

Bury, Richard de, sel from qtd in: *Amphora*, B2; in cat, B201

Bush, Dr. Frederic, *Songs of the Susquehanna* (Privately Printed, 1914 & 1920), B370, 371, FL13

Butler, Alfred J., sel from qtd in *Amphora*, B2; in cat, B250

Byron, George Gordon, sel from qtd in *By Bendemeer's Stream*, B52

C

C——, I, sel from qtd in *Amphora*, B2

C——, L. A., sel from qtd in *Amphora*, B2

Cade & White, photographers, port photo of FitzGerald, B334.8

Caffin, Charles H., qtd at length from review in *The Artist*, Sect V, p. 382

Caine, T. Hall, *Recollections of Dante Gabriel Rossetti* qtd, B423

Calcutta Review, The, memorial on Mosher printed in full, Sect V, pp. 407-10

Calmann-Lévy, pub, text source: B268

Calvert, Edward, *Ten Spiritual Designs* (Miscellaneous, 1913), B405; notice of death, and sketch of his life by Richmond in *The Athenæum*, B405

D

E

Foote, C. B., review from "Opinions of Bibliophiles" qtd in Sect V, p. 379

Forman, Henry Buxton, compiler, *The Prose Works of Percy Bysshe Shelley*, source text for rpt, B85, 86; forgeries, mentioned in B290, 419; sel from qtd in: *The Hollow Land*, B149; *The Pilgrims of Hope A Poems in XIII Books*, B290; *The Story of Amis & Amile*, B384

Fort, Adèle Brooks, *Splendor in the Night* (1933, 1934), FL27, 28

Fort, Paul, sel from qtd in cat, B263

Fortnightly Review, The

    Lee-Hamilton, Eugene, "Mimma Bella," text source for rpt, B243

    Macleod, Fiona, "The Divine Adventure" first appearance, B91; "The Immortal Hour" first appearance, B164

    Noyes, Alfred, poem "Fiona Macleod" used as preface in Macleod's *The Wayfarer*, B433

    Swinburne, A. C., essay on Rossetti's *Poems* (1870), first appearance of, B294; "Disgust: a Dramatic Monologue," source for rpt in *The Heptalogia*, B147; "Mr. Whistler's Lecture on Art," B403, 404

    Symons, Arthur, essay on Dowson used in *The Poems of Ernest Dowson*, B301

    Wilde, Oscar, "The Soul of Man Under Socialism" source for rpt, B378; six poems by rpt in *Poems in Prose*, B298

Fosdick, Harry E., sel from qtd in *Autumn Leaves from Maple Cottage*, B12

Foster, John, intro Dickens' *A Christmas Carol* and *Life of Charles Dickens*, B68

Fredeman, William E., qtd on: *The Germ*, B132; on Field's *Underneath the Bough*, B424; Intro, pp. 5-33

French, Elizabeth Short, *Once Upon a Time* (1932), FL29

Frontispieces, only two printed in color, B378, 394

Frost, Robert, "Reluctance" in cat, B257; sel from "Reluctance" in Index to *The Bibelot*, B39; intro in *The Arts Anthology, Dartmouth Verse 1925*, FL30; see Frost entries, pp. 433-35

Froude, J. A., note on Tennyson's "The Revenge" in *The Bibelot*, B35

Fryer, Eugénic Mary, *Unending Quest* (1932), FL31

Fugliesi, Giacomino, sel from translated by D. G. Rossetti in *Quattrocentisteria*, B315

G

Gaget, Maistre Antoine, Latin quote from, in Swinburne's *Poems & Ballads*, B296

Garnett, Richard, *De Flagello Myrteo* (Miscellaneous, 1906), B87; revised third edition source for, B87; "Three Fragment on Beauty" rpt from text source *Relics of Shelley*, B86

Gatigny, Francesca d'Aulby de, possible copyright holder for *Circum Præcordia*, B71

Gautier, Théophile, *The Dead Leman* (Brocade, 1903) trans by Lang & Sylvester, B80-80.1; sel from in: *Old World Lyrics*, B275; in *Amphora*, B2; in cat, B205

Gazette des Beaux-Arts, design source for Vittoria Colonna's portrait by Michelangelo, B241

Geddes, Patrick & Colleagues, pub, text source: B90, 121 (revised), 352 (revised); design source: B160, 352

Germ, The, Mosher's rpt (Reprints of Privately Printed Books, 1898), B132; original ed as text source: "The Blessed Damozel," B46, 47; "Hand and Soul," B139, 140; distributes Elliot Stock ed in America, B132; see also William Michael Rossetti entry on p. 453

Ghose, Manmohan, one of four authors in *Primavera*, B311

Gibson, Elizabeth, "All Things and Roses" in cat, B254; sel from qtd in *Amphora*, B2

Gibson, Wilfrid Wilson, "Song" in cat, B254; sel from qtd in *Amphora*, B2

Gilchrist, Alexander, sel from qtd in *XVII Designs to Thornton's Virgil*, B347

Giorgione, "For a Venetian Pastoral" qtd in *The Blessed Damozel*, B46

Gissing, George, *Books and the Quiet Life* (Miscellaneous, 1914), B49-49.1; *By the Ionian Sea* (Miscellaneous, 1920), B54; *The Private papers of Henry Ryecroft* (Miscellaneous, 1921), B313, FL32; sel from qtd in: B2, 264

Glaister, Geoffrey Ashall, entry qtd in *Glaister's Glossary of the Book*, Sect V, p. 418

Glanvill, Joseph, sel from *Vanity of Dogmatizing* qtd in *Thyrsis*, B412

Glines, Ellen, *Garden Untended* (1933), FL33

Goliardic literature, books on, see *Wine Women And Song*, B439

Gollancz, Israel, ed of *Pearl* (1891) consulted for S. Weir Mitchell trans, B286; Tennyson's poem used from 1891 ed, B287

Gomme, Lawrence J., reflections on Mosher from *The Colophon*, Sect V, pp. 400-01

Goose Quill, The, announcing Vest Pocket sales, B335.3

H

I

J

M

N

O

P

S

U

V

W

Y